PROFILE OF A RELIGIOUS MAN

BOOKS BY EDWIN ZACKRISON

Melvin Campbell and Edwin Zackrison. *Interactive Readings for Christian Worship.* (Lincoln, NE.: iUniverse, Inc., 2003).

———. *Readers Theatre for Christian Worship; Biblical Stories of Courage and Faith.* (Lincoln, NE.: iUniverse, Inc., 2003).

Edwin Zackrison. *In the Loins of Adam; A Historical Study of Original Sin in Adventist Theology.* (Lincoln, NE.: iUniverse, Inc., 2004).

———. *The First Temptation; Seventh-day Adventists and Original Sin.* (Bloomington, IN: iUniverse, Inc., 2015).

———. *About Tomorrow, Let God Worry; The Place of Time.* (Bloomington, IN: iUniverse, Inc., 2019).

———. *God's Camelot; The Security of the Kingdom.* (Bloomington, IN: iUniverse, Inc., 2019).

———. *Christians Are Recovering Human Beings; Returning to God's Reality.* (Bloomington, IN: iUniverse, Inc., 2019).

———. *People Under Construction; Life is a Journey.* (Pittsburgh, PA: Dorrance Publishing Co., 2020).

PROFILE OF A RELIGIOUS MAN

Confessions of a Religion Addict

By Edwin Zackrison

Foreword by Jerry A. Gladson

RESOURCE *Publications* · Eugene, Oregon

PROFILE OF A RELIGIOUS MAN
Confessions of a Religion Addict

Copyright © 2020 Edwin Zackrison. All rights reserved. Except for brief quotations in critical publications or reviews, no part of this book may be reproduced in any manner without prior written permission from the publisher. Write: Permissions, Wipf and Stock Publishers, 199 W. 8th Ave., Suite 3, Eugene, OR 97401.

Resource Publications
An Imprint of Wipf and Stock Publishers
199 W. 8th Ave., Suite 3
Eugene, OR 97401

www.wipfandstock.com

PAPERBACK ISBN: 978-1-5326-9904-7
HARDCOVER ISBN: 978-1-5326-9905-4
EBOOK ISBN: 978-1-5326-9906-1

NOVEMBER 2, 2020

All Biblical quotations, unless otherwise indicated, are from the Revised Standard Version of the Bible. Copyright 1946, 1952, 1971, 1973 by the Division of Christian Education of the National Council of the Churches of Christ in the United States of America.

Quotations appearing at the beginning of each chapter are taken from Ted Goodman (ed), The Forbes Book of Business Quotations (New York: Black Dog and Leventhal Publishers, 1997; and Laurence J. Peter, Peter's Quotations: Ideas for our Time (New York: Bantam Books, 1980.

Dedication

To MELVIN CAMPBELL, PhD
Educator and Friend

*To one who has inspired my life and encouraged me
during some of the most difficult times.
Deeply committed to representing what the church stands for,
he demonstrates the faith, courage, creativity and authentication
of the meaning of the gospel in the Christian walk.*

"Education makes a people easy to lead, but difficult to drive;
easy to govern, but impossible to enslave."

—Henry Peter, Lord Brougham

Confession

When you get to Heaven don't turn and stare
Others might wonder that you're there.
So, in your struggles when you think you win,
It could be wise to let the sinners in.

—Walter T. Rea

Contents

In Memoriam | xi
Acknowledgements | xiii
Foreword by Jerry A. Gladson | xv
Preface | xvii

CHAPTER ONE: **Religious Heritage** | 1
CHAPTER TWO: **Life in an Adventist Home** | 9
CHAPTER THREE: **In the Protective Custody of the Church** | 22
CHAPTER FOUR: **The Culture of Adventism** | 31
CHAPTER FIVE: **Identity Formation and Dad's Compassion** | 42
CHAPTER SIX: **Major Life Decisions** | 50
CHAPTER SEVEN: **College Years Set Life's Agenda** | 68
CHAPTER EIGHT: **Searching for Salvation** | 77
CHAPTER NINE: **Managing Change** | 90
CHAPTER TEN: **Reframing Life** | 100
CHAPTER ELEVEN: **Necessary Professional Developments** | 105
CHAPTER TWELVE: **Moon River** | 120
CHAPTER THIRTEEN: **Polishing the Dream** | 133
CHAPTER FOURTEEN: **Seminary Days** | 147
CHAPTER FIFTEEN: **Theological Excitement** | 160
CHAPTER SIXTEEN: **The Controversy Widens** | 181
CHAPTER SEVENTEEN: **Encounter with Life** | 203
CHAPTER EIGHTEEN: **Elder Walter T. Rea (1922–2014)** | 212
CHAPTER NINETEEN: **A Bump in The Road** | 225
CHAPTER TWENTY: **Life in the Parish** | 241

CHAPTER TWENTY-ONE: **Understanding Organized Religion** | 256

CHAPTER TWENTY-TWO: **A Search for Meaningful Ministry** | 271

CHAPTER TWENTY-THREE: **A New Direction** | 288

CHAPTER TWENTY-FOUR: **A Step into A New Direction** | 308

CHAPTER TWENTY-FIVE: **Entering Educational Ministry** | 321

CHAPTER TWENTY-SIX: **Mining the Depths of Knowledge** | 345

CHAPTER TWENTY-SEVEN: **A Tapestry of Subtle Shifts** | 359

CHAPTER TWENTY-EIGHT: **We've Got Problems** | 380

CHAPTER TWENTY-NINE: **We've Become the Problem** | 405

CHAPTER THIRTY: **An Anatomy of Betrayal** | 419

CHAPTER THIRTY-ONE: **Background of the Collegedale Purge** | 433

CHAPTER THIRTY-TWO: **The Collegedale Purge Begins** | 449

CHAPTER THIRTY-THREE: **Crisis at the College** | 465

CHAPTER THIRTY-FOUR: **The Wind Down** | 484

CHAPTER THIRTY-FIVE: **Resolution** | 502

CHAPTER THIRTY-SIX: **The Final Pleas for Support** | 516

CHAPTER THIRTY-SEVEN: **Settlement** | 521

CHAPTER THIRTY-EIGHT: **Closure** | 531

APPENDIXES | 541

   APPENDIX 1: The Educational Philosophy Behind the Methods Used in This Course | 543

   APPENDIX 2: The Collegedale Story | 546
        By Dr. Frank Knittel

   APPENDIX 3: Some Historical Observations on the Present Theology "Crisis" | 555
        By Dr. Ronald M. Springett

   APPENDIX 4: Remarks at the SMC Faculty Colloquium | 568
        By Dr. Frank Knittel

   APPENDIX 5: The Atlanta Affirmation | 586

   APPENDIX 6: A Response to the Atlanta Affirmation | 589
        By Elder Neal Wilson

   APPENDIX 7: Edward Heppenstall Support Letter | 591
        By Dr. Edward Heppenstall

APPENDIX 8: Remarks Before the Southern College Board of Trustees | 593
    By Dr. Edwin Zackrison

APPENDIX 9: The Image Problem | 602
    By Dr. Edwin Zackrison

Bibliography | 611

In Memoriam

FRANK A. KNITTEL, PhD

1927–2015

Educator, Administrator and Friend

*In memory of one who was so easy to respect and appreciate
as he demonstrated his ability to care and lead.
There are few people in my life who will always be remembered for their
support, concern, commitment and transparent, unselfish Christian love.
Dr. Knittel is at the top of that list.*

"The aim of a college education is to teach you
to know a good man when you see one."

—WILLIAM JAMES

Dear Ed—

Just a note to let you know how much I thrill with the successful ending to your degree chase. It has been arduous and sometimes threatening, but you have survived. It's great, and I'm so terribly glad for you.

    Ed, if I tried to say this personally, I would blubber and stammer, and all that. So, with an impersonal typewriter I say that you are ever a part of my life that a few fumbling words cannot adequately express. My admiration for you goes beyond being simply good friends—you are a special kind of friend who is good for the soul. Your pain has been great—mine has been wrenching as I have seen you hurt. There is no greater affliction than to see the people you love with an infinite feeling get hurt by the slings and arrows of outrageous fortune and by the gibes of hideous people.

    Just always know, Ed, that wherever you are, I am there too. Whenever you are in pain, I share that passion. For, you see, you are a great, wonderful, giant of a guy who took me into your heart. I cannot be more complimented. I can only look up to where you are on the pedestal on which I have placed you.

Frank A. Knittel
Loma Linda University
April 1984

Acknowledgements

Producing an exhaustive list of people who have influenced one's life is impossible. The following represents a "short list" of people who have strongly influenced my life. My apologies to those I missed.

*Dr. George Akers	*Dr. J. Cecil Haussler	*Elder Walter T. Rea
*Dr. Wilber Alexander	*Dr. Edward Heppenstall	*Professor Aage Rendalen
Ms. Connie Anderson	Dr. Earle Hilgert	Dr. Richard Rice
Mr. Joseph Anderson	*Elder Richard Hodnett	Father Richard Romero
Rev. Jeff Beasley	Dr. Dolcelyn Imperio	Ms. Leanna Rose
*Dr. Kenneth Blanton	*Mr. Edward Jasper	*Professor Royal Sage
*Elder Lowell Bock	Ms. Lorena Jeske	*Elder Cree Sandefur
Mr. Eugene Borg	*Dr. Carsten Johnsen	*Elder Bill Shelly
Elder Lyle Botimer	Dr. Robert M. Johnston	Dr. Darold Simms
*Mr. John Brodersen	*Dr. Frank Knittel	Professor Carol J. (Fawcett) Smith
Dr. Melvin Campbell	Mr. Wayne Knoefler	*Dr. Walter F. Specht
Elder John Champlin	*Dr. Hans K. LaRondelle	Dr. Ronald M. Springett
*Dr. Frank Chung	*Mr. Robert Lee Law	Mr. Jim Stagg
Ms. Helen Chung	Professor Edward Ley	Ms. Vivienne Tjan
Dr. Thomas Cory	*Dr. Roland Loasby	Dr. Larry Thomas
*Dr. Raymond Cottrell	Dr. Jeanne Lunsford	*Dr. Merlin Thomas
Mr. Roger Cox	Professor Rosalie Lynn	Dr. Nelson Thomas
Ms. Betty Cox	Dr. Michael McPherson	Dr. Wendel Tucker
Ms. Jane Crevasse	Dr. Leslie Mathewson	*Elder Stuart Tyner
Dr. Steve Daily	*Dr. Laurence Mobley	Ms. Margie Littell Ulrich
*Mr. Charles Davis	Rev. Robert Mountain	Dr. Smuts van Rooyen
*Dr. Raoul Dederen	*Dr. Ruth Murdoch	Dr. John Wagner
Mr. W. Michael Duewel	*Dr. W. G. C. Murdoch	*Ms. Laurie Warner

Acknowledgements

Dr. John Duge	Ms. Charleen Nugent	Professor Madelyn Warner
*Dr. Desmond Ford	*Dr. L. Calvin Osborn	*Professor Robert Warner
Ms. Sheila Elwin	*Ms. Jeannie Osborn	Ms. Sandie White
Dr. Jill Genobaga	Dr. Helmut Ott	Mr. Gary Wicklund
*Dr. Orlo Gilbert	Dr. Gary Patterson	Mr. Bruce Weaver
Dr. Jerry A. Gladson	Elder Fred Paulson	*Dr. Jerry Wiley
Dr. Laura Hayes Gladson	*Dr. Norval F. Pease	Dr. Steve Wyre
*Dr. Lorenzo Grant	Mr. Lonnie Pendleton	Dr. Florence Young
Dr. Fritz Guy	Dr. Norm Perry	Dr. John Youngberg
*Dr. Madelynn Haldeman	*Dr. Robert Pooley	Dr. James W. Zackrison

Deceased

Foreword

NOT LONG AGO AT the local library I picked up a new book. On the dust cover the words jumped out at me: *"This is a book to start on a Friday night."* If so, the line implied, make sure you have a long enough weekend to read through it because you can't lay it down once you start!

You are about to read such a book in Edwin Zackrison's *Profile of a Religious Man*. While he was writing it, Zackrison asked me to read excerpts of this book. However, when I started reading consecutively from beginning to end, I had a hard time putting it down. Zackrison's narrative is gripping, suspenseful, extremely personal, and filled with passionate, honest self-disclosure. In line after line it is obvious this book comes out of Zackrison's own personal, agonizing struggle to make sense of his inevitably disillusioning religious tradition.

Zackrison takes the reader on what can only be described as a dramatic personal journey from his earliest childhood, adolescence, college and graduate school experience, marriage, and finally into his ill-fated professional life as clergy and college professor in the Seventh-day Adventist denomination.

Born into a typical Adventist American home in Chicago, the child of second-generation Scandinavian parents, but reared in Southern California, where his father and mother had relocated for vocational reasons, Zackrison early commits to a religious life within the Adventist community. Through adolescence and early adulthood, he earnestly tries to comply with the strict institutional and religious rules of Adventism. With a fresh graduate degree from the denomination's main seminary in hand, he founds a new, flourishing congregation, and is soon invited to teach at the denomination's Southern Adventist University in Tennessee.

The fateful decision to join the faculty at this university, however, becomes the tragic turning point in his life, and plunges Zackrison into a theological maelstrom that eventually brings out a personal crisis of faith and, later, the loss of his marriage and home.

This book provides a rare glimpse into the very heart of the closed, insular Seventh-day Adventist world. He characterizes Adventism as a kind of intellectual prison for those who swallow it whole, shielding them from the larger world. The denomination's written and unwritten code "poisons the thinking."

Foreword

One empathically struggles with Zackrison as he seeks to make sense of his paradoxical faith community and how to live out its principles. He finally becomes a "religion addict"—the willing, passive victim of insidious religious abuse and exploitation. Throughout his Adventist experience a palpable, unnamed fear that casts its shadow over the entire denomination motivates him, symbolized in this book by the recurrent motif of the "black cloud." (See Chapter 2).

The black cloud is an image of the second advent of Christ that has its origin in an early visionary experience of Sister Ellen White, the denomination's prophet. Along the way he meets positive mentors, such as Wilber Alexander and Edward Heppenstall, whose lives seem larger than the religious tradition they represent. Casting a dark shadow over his experience, however, are many unscrupulous and dishonest Church administrators who belie the very faith they profess.

Zackrison grew up, he confesses, inside a religious system created out of an illusion. It was founded out of the failed prediction of Elder William Miller that the end of the world would come in 1844. Instead of acknowledging this failed prediction, early Adventists doubled down and managed to reinterpret the prediction to apply to a heavenly rather than earthly judgment. This reinterpretation now shapes a doctrine, known as the Investigative Judgment, which heavily emphasizes human effort toward salvation. Consequently, in the Adventist parochial educational system Zackrison hears much about messianism, apocalypticism, perfectionism, and legalism, but little of God's generous grace. Once in the ministry, where he thought he would be able to make a difference in peoples' lives, Zackrison experiences emotional and religious abuse, betrayal, and duplicity.

His narrative is meticulously documented, especially from contemporary, original sources, and contains nine appendices from other writers who with Zackrison lived through the Adventist religious crisis and whose lives were permanently scarred by it.

I was one of these persons. When I learned that Zackrison planned to publish his experience, I joined others in urging him to do so. This is a personal story that needs to be heard. It is a cautionary tale about the risks of involvement in religious systems that promote uncritical, world-denying, absolutist viewpoints. Unless narrated in such personal terms, the lessons of Zackrison's experience—and that of hundreds of other Adventists who suffered the same, damaging fate—will disappear unnoticed into the mists of time. Their stories will be lost.

Zackrison's redemption at the end of the book is finally found in his freedom from a tightly structured, toxic religious system. He recalls a friend's advice: "When you have security, you don't really live." By that standard, he says, "I have lived a very full life!"

Jerry A. Gladson, PhD
Richmond Graduate University
Atlanta, Georgia

Preface

> "Walk a mile in my shoes, just a mile in my shoes.
> Before you abuse, criticize, and accuse, walk a mile in my shoes."
> —Elvis Presley

When I was ten years old Dad brought home a five-inch television set. Don't conclude that the quality of the screen compares with my six-inch iPhone screen. But we were so impressed that we could see what was happening covered over the lack of clarity.

On that little screen I saw for the first time a talent show that featured *old* people. Every performer competing for cash prizes, was at least forty years old. In 1953, Dad took me to Hollywood, and we were in the live audience of that weekly talent show. I marveled that anyone could suggest that life could *begin* at forty. In my young mind that was when life was ending! Jack Benny would disguise his actual age by telling us that he was only thirty-nine. As a kid I failed to catch that joke. I could not come to understand how thirty-nine was young!

Today I am retired. Thirty-nine and forty appear to be far in the past. When ticket takers ask if I am a senior I am elated. You mean they couldn't tell?! Or were they just flirting with me?

This book covers incidents from the first forty years of my life. It is a journey book, which means this is the story of my journey through life for the first forty years.

Why? Who cares about my life? I have asked myself that question every day of the past thirty years that I have worked on this book. It covers some of only a little of my life. Who cares? Why write a book about any of my life? Nobody knows me. I'm not even sure my own children will read this book. Perhaps in some future moment of reminiscence, they might. I have received a few phone calls and emails from friends asking when my book will be out. But turning a question into a sale?—two different operations!

Preface

In my book, *The First Temptation*, I traced the treatment by theologians through the ages with respect to the original nature of the first biblical man and woman. Some believe they were created by God with original righteousness. Others hold that this is impossible because righteousness is the result of one's response to experience. This book is my response to experience.

Mine was a well-planned life. My formal planning had started when I was sixteen years old and I made my personal decision to become a gospel minister. What I write in this book is not based on perfect memory. I do not believe that the human mind works like a tape recorder reproducing every fact correctly. For the past thirty years I have attempted many times to put my fingers to the keyboard and tell my story, but I have never gotten far. Yet others have called and written and urged that I tell it.

There is a principle in nature that some things need to mellow, calm down, soak in, and the like. The refusal of winemakers to take a wine before its time is a notion I am coming to understand. It works with writers as well. Like a fetus signaling its mother that it is time to head for the hospital, a literary work stays in the mind until its time.

Throughout my professional life I have kept copious notes and preserved many records. But the last thirty years especially have taken so many twists and turns that I have increased my notetaking. To my knowledge I have thrown out few letters or cards that I have received or written since I graduated from college. I have kept notes on phone conversations and since email became so widespread and prevalent, I have had instant documentation. I have organized these notes now to where I have a remarkably verifiable set of events as they affected my life and career and I am ready to tell some of my story because I believe it is not just my story but the story of many religion addicts.

I hope this book will be of encouragement to some. I do not write it to seek sympathy with my journey. My trip is rather placid in the light of the great pilgrimage books that have been written over the centuries. But this story will tell of my effort to overcome biases and false assumptions—it will tell of my struggle for love and understanding and the place where I thought I was assured some degree of fairness and compassion.

My story will tell of my love of truth and justice. It will tell of religious people who have overstepped their bounds in cruel and mischievous ways, including myself. Not the least of my purposes, this story should be an encouragement to other Church workers who may be facing the same struggles I have.

One of the great tasks of every adult on this planet is to make sense of life. I inherited, through my family and my education, one way to look at life. That was the Seventh-day Adventist view. I bought it totally. I fashioned every decision around that view. I committed myself totally and completely to the carrying out of the Adventist mission: *to finish the work of God on earth*. And while that sounds a bit arrogant to me now, it was presented as the only way to view my mission.

Preface

In short, I became as messianic as Adventism taught me to be. A significant element in religious addiction is messianism—that God has appointed you in a way that he has not appointed anyone else to do a job.

Some readers will call me naïve. They will say, nothing here is new, it is the framework of any organization, we all knew that. But that surely wasn't true for me. Publicly, at least, this wasn't true for any of the other leaders. I was to believe that this was God's Church and when an important Church convocation decided, it was God's choice. I was told this over and over.

A prominent Church leader once told me that I could expect at least four raw deals in the Church if I remained in its employment. I viewed the statement as theoretical until I discovered that he had come to make sure several of us on his faculty got one of those raw deals.

I believed only the best in the Church. I trusted and supported the brethren to do what was right. And I refused to listen to those who tried to warn me of corruption in leadership. I still have little time for such perceptions since my addiction is not completely de-programmed.

In my education I had read of the battles of great Church leaders who were eventually thrown out of their churches. In my denominational education, I was largely led to see them as heretics, rebels, eccentrics, revolutionaries, apostates and as generally representing a lower form of spirituality. Herein lays my greatest disappointment with Church education. It basically asked me to surrender my previous biases in favor of accepting a new set of biases and assumptions, i.e., the denominational ones.

Edwin Zackrison, PhD
University of Phoenix, Retired
Chattanooga, Tennessee

CHAPTER ONE

Religious Heritage

"Religion is a disease, but it is a noble disease."
—Heraclitus

HINSDALE, ILLINOIS, OCTOBER 1941

In 1941, Hinsdale, Illinois, was a small western suburb of Chicago, on the direct rail line to the Loop. At its center was Hinsdale Sanitarium, founded in 1899 by Dr. David Paulson (1868–1916), an Adventist physician from Michigan, on the old estate of Chicago businessman, C. B. Kimball.[1]

Hinsdale was one of several of the Church's institutions in the Chicago vicinity, which also included Broadview College in La Grange and Pacific Press in Brookfield. The Sanitarium had survived the Depression and in the 1940s enjoyed rebuilding and refurbishing until it became the first-class medical center that it is today.

Shortly before the refurbishing, and a month and a half before the Pearl Harbor "day of infamy," I was born on my mother's thirty-ninth birthday, in Hinsdale Sanitarium, to an Adventist family of Church workers—printers, artists, musicians, educators, editors, and writers.

We lived in Brookfield because my grandfather was an editor at Pacific Press Publishing Association and my father worked at a large printing plant in Chicago.

---

1. Neufeld, *SDA Encyclopedia*, 586.

CHRISTIAN AND THE BOOK

On July 3, 1887, Christian A. Thorpe arrived in Chicago from Norway in the company of a family friend from Kristiansund, who had been in America for some time. On the journey, Christian's friend gave him a book that would change his life and bequeath a new religious heritage to his family. The book carried an intriguing title: *Thoughts on Daniel and the Revelation,* by Uriah Smith (1832–1903), an editor/author and college professor in Michigan.

While Christian did not know it at the time, Battle Creek housed the world headquarters of the Seventh-day Adventist Church, and was home to the famous Battle Creek Sanitarium, superintended by Dr. John Harvey Kellogg (1852–1943), famous for his break-through medical research and educational pursuits. He was also the inventor of breakfast foods such as wheat and corn flakes, as well as the developer of peanut butter.

C. A. Thorpe was born near Farsund, in the southern part of Norway. Raised on a small farm near the North Sea, he assisted his father in farming and fishing when he was young. When it came time to learn a trade, he moved into the city and learned cabinetmaking.

In America, he found a job working in a furniture factory in Chicago. While he had never heard of Adventists, he was fascinated by the contents of this book and its claim to unlock the secrets of the past, present and future. The more he read the more energized he became.

Step by step the book took him through the ancient biblical prophecies and their alleged historical fulfillments. He was snagged. Unable to get past the religious issues the book brought up, C. A. contacted the book's publishers. In the process, he was invited to attend a religious camp meeting in Bloomington, Illinois, where he heard a speaker at the convocation, Elder O. A. Olsen (1845–1915), a fellow Norwegian and the president of the Adventist Church organization. He found the same emphasis in Elder Olsen's sermons that he had read in author Smith's book.

Elder Olsen encouraged him to visit the campus of Battle Creek College. Still a young man, C. A. ended up moving to Battle Creek where to his delight he met Elder Smith, the author who had changed the direction of much of his thinking.

Christian had met Mary Andreasen in Chicago, and Elder Smith performed their wedding on March 20, 1891. America had provided a new life for them and the Thorpes believed that God had directed it all. These two Norwegians were convinced that God wanted them to be active in the religious work of their newfound faith.

The most logical calling seemed to be the Church's publishing enterprise. It was fully modern with new technology—power presses, the linotype (1884), paper cutters, book binders—that pointed to a great future for this work. Papers, periodicals and books could be distributed and dropped like "the leaves of autumn" wherever one traveled. Others would be attracted to "the message," just as C. A. and Mary had been.

From his own experience, C. A. believed that a book could yield souls for the kingdom. So, he learned the printing trade and eventually became a highly valued multi-lingual editor in the expanding Scandinavian publishing work of the Church.[2]

In 1874, the Adventist Church founder James White (1821–1881) had established the Pacific Seventh-day Adventist Publishing Association in Oakland, California, to evangelize the American west coast. In 1888, this printing plant became the Pacific Press and was later moved to Mountain View (in 1904) just before the devastating San Francisco earthquake, which destroyed its offices. The publishing house was soon rebuilt and the work in Mountain View continued for decades.

Branches were established in London, New York, Kansas City, Portland, and Regina, Saskatchewan. While they were all eventually closed, these printing plants established the mission of the Pacific Press as the center of the international publishing work.

Eventually the international headquarters came to be in College View, Nebraska, which seemed a reasonable location being near Union College, an Adventist school. This became the Thorpe home base for a time. In 1916, the Nebraska plant burned down. After the fire, the branch was moved again, this time to Brookfield, Illinois.

By then the Thorpes had four children, the youngest, Esther Virginia (1902–1992), would become my mother twenty-six years later.

OTTO AND THE BOOK

Back in Scandinavia another series of events was developing. In 1920, Otto Zackrisson, a local Stockholm businessman, was introduced to a curious publication, a Swedish version of *Bible Readings for the Home Circle*. The book changed the course of Otto's life.

Bible Readings was delivered by a strange salesman; a town drifter eager to get money for wine had discovered it with its covers torn off in a garbage can around the corner from Otto's bicycle shop. Otto gave the man twenty-five Swedish Ore (about five cents at the time).

The book was a virtual encyclopedia of biblical teachings arranged in a familiar catechistic form: question-answer-question-answer. No one knows what eventually became of the book, but had it still been around, it would have merited being showcased in a family museum given the impact it had on the Zackrisson family.

As Otto read the book, he found some of its teachings puzzling. Especially dissonant to him was the answer given to the question: What happens to people when they die? He had the answer to that—they go to heaven. But the book took issue with that and gave scriptural references to counter that view. Another question was: Which day is the biblical Sabbath? To Otto's amazement the answer to that question did not square with his tradition either. The book identified the dead as being in an

---

2. Christian, *Sons of the North*, 164.

unconscious sleep and argued that the biblical Sabbath was Saturday. Who had written this book? No author was listed, only a publishing company in Oslo, Norway.

About that time, Otto came across a flier advertising a series of religious lectures soon to be held in Stockholm. Curious for a discussion on these questions, he attended the meetings. Full of inquiries, inspired by the book, he wanted answers to both questions. When the speaker opened to questions from the floor he was ready. But he got no answers. The lecturer just said he would be covering both those topics later in the series.

The interchange led Otto to attend all the meetings. When the lecturer finally answered Otto's questions, he was astonished to hear agreement with what he had read in the book. Who was this lecturer? Who had published this book that had been retrieved from the trash, which agreed with this lecturer?

In those days, the religious affiliation of non-Lutheran Bible lecturers was often hidden until the time was "right" for disclosure—when attendance had substantially leveled out, so the speaker knew he was communicating with an agreeable segment of listeners. With the curiosity seekers gone by this time, only potential believers would be left, so the theory went.

Hooking people on a message before prejudice and bias could influence the outcome was the philosophy of the Adventist lecturer. Religious bigotry was a powerful force, and it could easily scare some people from even hearing "the Truth." Furthermore, revealing that you were an Adventist could result in persecution, vandalism, even physical harm.[3] Tents could be ripped and burned.

Stories were told of evangelists who had been thought to be revolutionaries, heretics, cult leaders or fanatics. It was little wonder that Otto had a hard time finding out who these people were. Along with his oldest son, Harry, Otto attended the meetings, and they discovered that *Bible Readings* was an Adventist book.

In 1921, after the meetings, Otto joined the Adventist Church along with Harry and other members of the family.

Harry had been studying electrical engineering since 1919 at Stockholm Technical School. He was a mathematician, an artist and a musician. At the age of thirteen he had played violin for the King of Sweden. He also played trumpet in the King's army band. He had the sensitivity and passion of an artist along with the logic and planning instinct of an engineer—an impressive combination.

Denominational officials labored with Harry to reconsider his engineering pursuits. The prophecies indicated that the Lord could return long before he could ever finish his extended engineering course, they argued. And how could an engineer really be of much use in the spread of the Adventist *Truth*? The end of time was imminent, and he needed to help prepare the world for it. This denomination would primarily have need of four kinds of professionals: medical workers (doctors, nurses), ministers

---

3. James White, the founder of the Adventist Church had had a big nail thrown at him. Spalding, *Origin and History of Seventh-day Adventists,* 1:49–50.

(evangelists, pastors, administrators), teachers (all levels) and publishers (writers, artists, editors, printers, pressmen, bindery workers).

Other than preachers and educators, the Adventist strategy for evangelistic success included two crucial prongs, or "arms," to "finish the work" so Christ could return. The medical work (or the health message) was the "right arm" of the Adventist message. This work would manifest the spirit of Christ and his compassion to the world and it carried soul-winning potential. Many people would listen to their physician before they would listen to an unknown lecturer preaching on a religious topic that sought to sway their minds away from their cherished beliefs.

Through the medical work, i.e., hospitals, sanitariums, orphanages, and doctor's offices, the world would encounter Adventists, learn their dietary habits and doctrinal truths, associate with their nurses, doctors, receptionists, janitors and anyone else who worked there. The medical work would improve the health habits of the world and encourage a balanced mind required to accept Adventist teachings. When people were in good health, they could read the Adventist publications with a pure mind and be convinced of "the Truth."

It was an enticing argument and Harry accepted it, dropped out of engineering school and moved to Denmark where he enrolled in the nurses' training program at the Adventist Skodsborg Sanitarium near Copenhagen.

Here were the roots of my religious existence. Harry Albin Zackrisson (1901–1975) would become my father two decades later.

WHEN HARRY MET ESTHER

In 1898, Dr. Carl Ottosen (1864–1942) had established Skodsborg Sanitarium on an old residence of the Danish King in a suburb of Copenhagen.[4] Many years later, around our family dinner table, Dad would tell his experiences during his student days in Denmark. My favorite story was the one about the student who filled up sugar dispensers in the cafeteria with salt. When a resident glutton opened the dispenser and dramatically poured all of what he thought was sugar on his pudding, took his first bite of what was salt covering his pudding, I would laugh until the tears came. Dad would enhance the story making it funnier every time he told it. I would ask him to tell that story over and I never tired of it.

During Harry's nurses' training, publishing officials from the Adventist headquarters in America visited the campus and they had another tale to relate. They convinced him that the best way he could hasten the Lord's return would be to devote his career to publishing work. They explained that when all the Adventist efforts were finally terminated, the books and periodicals could continue to win souls to the

---

4. Neufeld, *SDA Encyclopedia*, 1354.

Adventist warning message. More people would be in the kingdom because of the publishing work than any other Adventist work.

So that was where he should be—producing books—editing, drawing, printing, writing, selling "Truth-filled literature." With his natural aptitudes and interest in art and foreign languages he would find this work a good fit. Wishing to do God's will, Harry dropped his nurses' training and moved to Oslo, Norway, the center for the Adventist publishing work in Scandinavia, and began employment as a proofreader of Swedish Adventist literature. There he met Esther, the youngest Thorpe daughter whose father (C. A.) was now on a four-year assignment in Norway to edit and translate Adventist books into the Norwegian language.

Harry and Esther shared one serious "flaw." Her mother was not sure that her daughter ought to be "seeing" a Swede. Nor would Harry's friends overlook the "dangers" of his dating a Norwegian. It was not as controversial as an inter-racial marriage in America in the 1950s, but mildly scandalous, nevertheless. Harry ignored the cautions and went with his heart.

When the Thorpes returned to America, Harry accompanied them to finish his college education at Broadview College, the denominational center for Scandinavian Adventists in America, and near the Thorpes. While Harry was excited about going to America, he had planned to return to Norway after he finished school to help supervise the Adventist publishing work. But an administrative change intervened, and he ended up staying in America.

When I visited Stockholm in 1990, our guide at the Nobel Prize center in the Town Hall told us that during the 1920s, about a third of the Swedish population was in process of immigrating to America. There were Swedish Adventist enclaves in Illinois and Minnesota and Harry was the first in his immediate family to cross the Atlantic. A couple decades later two of his sisters would settle in St. Paul, Minnesota. Harry would find it impossible to return to Sweden until 1973 on vacation and several years after he had retired. He would never see his parents or some of his siblings again.

Now living in the Chicago area, Harry asked Esther to marry him. She accepted his proposal and they were married on November 14, 1926, in Brookfield. Harry's surname was inadvertently changed from Zackrisson to Zackrison, a spelling error made by immigration officers when he became a U. S. citizen.

Without a job and without any certainty about denominational employment, Harry, always an industrious person and comfortable with change, enrolled at Mergenthaler Institute (inventors and manufacturers of the Linotype type-setting machine) in Chicago and became a journeyman linotype operator. For the next eighteen years, he worked for the Forslund Printing Company in Chicago. He had abandoned two careers to become a printer of Adventist literature but to his dismay, he ended up working outside the denomination.

My brother, James Willard, was born in May 1932. I followed in October 1941.

Religious Heritage

FROM ILLINOIS TO CALIFORNIA

In 1944, Grandpa Thorpe retired from his editorial work in Brookfield. His second son, Dr. Louis P. Thorpe, a psychologist in private practice in Glendale and Professor of Psychology at University of Southern California in Los Angeles, encouraged Grandpa and Grandma to spend their retirement in Southern California, where the weather was delightful. Coincidentally, an invitation came from Glendale Academy, fifteen miles north of Los Angeles, for Dad to join the Academy Press to teach printing and serve as foreman in the composing room.

The pain of disappointment from his denominational work experience in Scandinavia had softened and Dad, whose confidence in the Adventist faith was strong, decided to take the offer. We all moved to Glendale. Jim, nine and half years my senior, was enrolled at Glendale Academy. Now both of us could get an Adventist education and be fitted for some slot in the Adventist enterprise if we chose.

A year later, Dad received an invitation from La Sierra College (now La Sierra University) in Arlington (now Riverside), sixty miles east of Glendale, to join the College Press. This seemed even better for now we could be educated in Adventist schools all the way through college, if time should last.

For the next several months, Dad slept on an army cot in the College Press. During the day, he worked in the composing room as foreman and taught college students the craft of printing. During lunch breaks and in the long summer evenings, he worked on building a two-car garage on the third-acre of land on Knoefler Drive that he had purchased half a mile from the college. On weekends, he drove home to us in Glendale in his black, four-door 1934 Plymouth.

When Dad finished the garage in 1945, he brought us to La Sierra to inspect what now would be our temporary home. He had built the structure all alone. He had mixed and poured the concrete floor, framed and stuccoed the walls and roofed the building.

Dad drove us up Knoefler Drive, little more than a cow path, to the spectacular and exciting unveiling of our new temporary home. This garage would be our home until a new house could be built just a few feet away on the front of the property. For the time being this arrangement would suffice. This was adventure for me. The war had left many in America poor. But we were together, and we were living life in the rugged west, committed to the Adventist message.

In the shadow of Sunshine Mountain to the south, Rattlesnake Hill directly behind us to the west and Two-Bit Mountain on the north, Dad had carved out a shelter for us. There were just a few square feet for each of us, but we cherished our real estate. And Dad would often remind us, "It may not be fancy but it is all paid for!"

So, we moved from Glendale to La Sierra: Grandpa, Grandma, Mom, Dad, Jim and me. We were in the country. We could have animals: dogs, cats, birds, goats, chickens, and ducks. And we eventually had all of those. For a four-year-old boy this was high adventure. I collected the eggs.

Grandma and Grandpa Thorpe had a little room added to the back of the garage. Jim and I were in one corner of the garage. Mom and Dad in another and a third corner served as the kitchen and dining area. I don't remember where the bathroom was but after a few months Dad bought a tin shower from Sears and attached it to the side of the garage. Until then I took my baths in a galvanized tub brought in and placed next to the kitchen stove.

The arrangement was tight and cozy. Mom did her best to keep us comfortable as we gathered around the wood-burning stove at night in the middle of the room and listened to the radio, our entertainment. I never reflected on the fact that we lived like poor people. When you are happy, you don't worry about such things.

Over the years, our garage would evolve into a storehouse, a workshop, and a temporary apartment. Once it even stood empty for the summer while we all lived in an army surplus supply tent out back. I never understood why—I just remember it was fun. In the eighteen years we lived in La Sierra, Dad never completed the garage door with hinges or springs and he never parked a car in it.

CHAPTER TWO

Life in an Adventist Home

*"Life comes before literature, as the material always comes before the work.
The hills are full of marble before the world blooms with statues."*
—Phillips Brooks

CITIES OF REFUGE

Jim was enrolled in La Sierra College Preparatory (High) School *and two years later I was enrolled in* La Sierra College Demonstration (Elementary) School. We were in the protective custody of the Adventist Church, as safe as one could be from the evils of a cruel, wayward world. Dad figured we were largely protected now from the onslaughts of public education that could introduce us to false teachings and bad influences. While I never heard him say it, I came to believe that he thought we could now be destined to choose Adventist approved careers and marry Adventist girls, if time should last.

A Christian education might have dangers of its own, but at least we were in an environment where everyone at school—administrators, teachers, and students—was a Church member. Classmates were the same people we worked and went to Church with. The simplicity of the situation represented Adventist thinking: The Old Testament cities of refuge mindset.[1] I was out of childhood before I learned that most Christians went to church on Sunday instead of Saturday. By then I knew that was wrong.

Our home was a library. When we moved into our new house most rooms had bookcases filled with all kinds of books. Dad regularly remodeled his study to accommodate his growing collection. Everywhere he went he carried a book and he taught

---

1. Num 35, Josh 20–21, 1 Chr 6.

me that books were my friends. His treatment of books bordered on reverence. He would have been excited at having a Kindle with 250 books in it. My brother and I each inherited this respect for books. I do not find it easy to part with a book even in its obsolescence. An out-of-print book can enter my realm of the classics.

My home today is full of books. I recently called a bookseller and when he took several boxes of these "friends" that he thought would turnover quickly in his little bookstore I suffered withdrawal pains. My oldest books are enshrined in bookcases with glass doors.

As a journeyman printer and craftsman, Dad had perfectionistic skills. He could tell by simply looking if a line was one point off in its spacing. The professional members of the printing trade richly valued his work. As a linotype operator he could work nights at the local newspaper, for five times the hourly wages he was making at Academy Press.

When we moved to La Sierra, Dad made such meager wages at the College Press that he found it necessary to work nights in Riverside at various print shops. I remember him being in such demand that he would be gone sometimes every night of the week (except Friday) earning the necessary funds to support us. Jim's work on the college grounds crew also helped with our tuition. One print shop owner even offered to give Dad his shop when he retired. Dad turned it down because he believed he was involved in hastening the Lord's coming by working for the Church.

Mom also went to work at the College Press as a proofreader and bindery worker. Not being the head of the household, she was paid about half of what Dad was making. This was denominational policy. This was a woman's sacrifice for the work of God and her recognized place in God's order. This would eventually be challenged in a lawsuit, which the denomination lost.[2] But that was a long way off from where we were in the 1940s.

With both my parents working I became Grandma's boy until I went to school. For the first ten years of my life I spent as much or more time with Grandma as with Dad and Mom. I awoke each morning to Grandma singing at the foot of my bed, "O, lazy Eddie won't you get up, won't you get up, won't you get up?" She would greet me with a smile, something you would be hard put to find in photographs of her. Her generation apparently rarely smiled in pictures. But when they sang to their little grandsons they had cordial smiles.

Each day Grandma walked with me to the bottom of Knoefler Drive to meet Mom and Dad as they drove home for lunch. She told me stories as we walked along. On one of these little walks, when we got to the bottom of the street, she taught me how to tie my shoes.

In this immediate post-wartime, housing was hard to find, especially on my parent's income. But I never heard discussions about our being needy. My parents worked for God and God would always provide because "the cattle on a thousand

---

2. McLeod, *Betrayal*, (1985).

hills" belonged to him. (Ps 50:10). His eye was on the sparrow and weren't we of more worth than sparrows? (Matt 10:31). "The lilies of the valley" neither toil nor spin. (Matt 6:28). We believed these word pictures. They were etched in my mind as a child. Ours was a religious home.

Dad paid cash for everything from his used cars to his building supplies. He shunned debt like the plague. Since credit cards were not a part of his culture shunning debt may have been easier than it is today, but I am not aware that he ever took a loan for anything. He would often say, "My little shack may not be fancy, but it is mine—I don't owe anything on it." And there was a sense of pride and accomplishment on his face when he said that.

THE BLACK CLOUD

Our home and our school worked together to create, mold, and give pattern to my life as a religious person. These institutions combined to compose me a religious man. What I learned at home was idealized at Church and supported at school. So, if I took it all seriously I was destined to become religious, inheriting from my environment an Adventist mentality that was typically characterized by four major elements: messianism, apocalypticism, perfectionism, and legalism.

Glaringly absent from this list of religious outlooks was *grace*. I learned little of grace as a child in the Adventist Church. While I heard the term used occasionally, definitions were so qualified by the emphasis on the laws of God (primarily the Ten Commandments) that I failed to grasp what was involved in God's grace as how he treated the undeserving. Grace was something I was to earn—the very opposite of the biblical meaning. Since we were treated that way and we treated others that way it stood to reason that God also was conditional in his bestowal of love—if I was faithful I might eventually receive the rewards of salvation.

Here was an insidious collection of Christian traditions—both Catholic and Protestant. In theological terms these would be called semi-Pelagian, Arminian, Judaism, and Puritanism. However, for a five-year-old theology as an abstract discipline was not something I could understand. Mine was a folk religion—inherited from my environment.

Our Adventist prophet, Sister Ellen Gould Harmon White (1827–1915), who we were taught shared the same gift of inspiration as the biblical writers, wrote words that were burned into my mind as parents, teachers, family members, ministers, and friends read them to us.

> Soon our eyes were drawn to the east, *for a small black cloud had appeared,* about half as large as a man's hand, which we all knew was the sign of the Son of man. We all in solemn silence gazed on the cloud as it drew nearer and became lighter, glorious, and still more glorious, till it was a great white cloud. The bottom appeared like fire; a rainbow was over the cloud, while around it

were ten thousand angels, singing a most lovely song; and upon it sat the Son of man. His hair was white and curly and lay on His shoulders; and upon His head were many crowns.[3]

Perhaps no other idea affected me more than this one paragraph from the hand of our infallible prophet. The thoughts in these few words formed my first notions of religion. I wanted to be in that number who would see Jesus' return and be caught up to heaven where we would fly like the angels and have pet lions and tigers that would lie down with lambs. It was a five-year-old's concrete vision of glory and eternal bliss. It was utopian.

More than anything else in the world I wanted to be ready when Jesus came back. I learned where the eastern sky began—looking directly out the kitchen window in our garage, right between San Gorgonio and San Jacinto peaks—that's where I believed the Black Cloud would appear. As a super-conscientious five-year-old I did not really understand what "being ready" meant, but I figured it had something to do with Church and going to Church usually involved wearing a suit. I kept my suit close to me and slipping into it when I saw the Black Cloud could mean I was ready. I was serious. The event could happen any day and any thought of finishing elementary school, high school, college or getting married, etc., was a waste of anticipation and emotional energy. None of this was going to happen.

THE ADVENTIST CULTURE

Seventh-day Adventism was born in the revivalist fervor of what is known in American Church history as the "Second Great Awakening" in New England during the early nineteenth century.

> The Methodist circuit riders and local Baptist preachers made enormous gains; to a lesser extent the Presbyterians gained members, particularly with the Cumberland Presbyterian Church in sparsely settled areas. As a result, the numerical strength of the Baptists and Methodists rose relative to that of the denominations dominant in the colonial period—the Anglicans, Presbyterians, Congregationalists. Among the new denominations that grew from the religious ferment of the Second Great Awakening are the Churches of Christ, Christian Church (Disciples of Christ), the Seventh-day Adventist Church, and the Evangelical Christian Church in Canada. The converts during the Second Great Awakening were predominantly female. A 1932 source estimated at least three female converts to every two male converts between 1798 and 1826. Young people (those under 25) also converted in greater numbers, and were the first to convert.[4]

---

3. White, *Early Writings*, 15, 16. Emphasis supplied.
4. "Second Great Awakening." *Wikipedia, the Free Encyclopedia.*

In the 1830s Elder William Miller (1782–1849), a Baptist lay preacher, had calculated, based on accepted principles of Protestant prophetic hermeneutics (interpretation theory) at the time, that Christ would return to earth in the fall of 1843. When the event did not occur, he discovered a flaw in his time schedule and readjusted the date to 1844. His linear time charts were based on his interpretation of the predictions of the Old Testament prophet Daniel to which he applied the day-year principle of interpreting prophecy, a common practice in his day. Basically, this method dictated that whenever prophecies involving time are given in the context of prediction, a day symbolized a year.

No one ever explained to us kids that these charts were based on a lot of controversial assumptions that prophetic interpreters of Miller's day had battled over for years. There was no consensus among biblical scholars as to how to understand time prophecies in any absolute sense. We were not told anything about that. This was dogmatically presented to us as settled.

These interpreters commonly played with the prophecies of Daniel looking for events that verified their viewpoints. To us the Adventist view was depicted as the undeniable truth. These teachings of our Adventist elders were confirmed by our Adventist prophet, Ellen White and were considered absolute—final and unchangeable. She was known affectionately to her followers as *Sister White,* and she was the last word on our understanding of prophecy, for God spoke to and through her. If the elders came up with a doctrine and she verified it by vision, that absolutized the Truth for us.

Often an Adventist might say, "I know 'The Truth' even though I'm not practicing it right now." "The Truth" was not to be questioned, though its livability and applicability might fall short. This was rooted in the idea that Adventists were right (biblical), which suggested (meant) that anyone who differed from this view was wrong (unbiblical). Its adherents called Adventism "The Truth."

Coming into The Truth meant becoming an Adventist. And it was always The Truth, not Truth, or a Truth. Adventists didn't have truth—they had *The* Truth. There was no other real religious Truth. If you found Adventism you found the genuine article. So deep was this notion that, as we were told, those who left Adventism usually became infidels, or atheists, and lost all interest in religion. Having once known The Truth [Adventism] they had nowhere else to go, our elders often reminded us. This was very powerful enculturation.

When Christ failed to return as predicted by Elder Miller, his followers scattered. Out of this "Great Disappointment," as we learned to call it, came new sects, one of which was the Seventh-day Adventist denomination, and it would become known among other Christians as a movement (or cult) born in the error of prophetic dogmatism.

Aside from probably Adventists and historians of American Church studies, few members of other churches knew, or cared, about the origins of Adventism. But the growing movement quickly developed a reputation for "sheep-stealing" (proselytizing), though we called it evangelism. Most new converts were from other Christian denominations seeking additional Truth to what they already had. Adventist evangelists would anonymously move into towns with their tents and wagons and quickly establish themselves as members of the last true Church, or remnant Church, proclaiming the three angels' messages as prophesied in Revelation 14.

At an expedient point in a series of meetings, or in a private conversation with those who had expressed an interest in accepting The Truth, the evangelists would eventually inform their interests that they were Adventists. This was exactly the method used in evangelizing all my grandparents.

The strategy was to hook people on the message before the prejudice against Adventism could create a barrier. Such marketing technique was not unique to Adventists. It is commonly used today especially with organizations that have an image problem. When was the last time you opened an email that offered you a free sweepstakes to realize that the prize you thought you would get was conditional on purchasing or committing yourself to something else?

After the Great Disappointment of 1844 several leaders of the movement spent serious time studying, trying to figure out what had gone wrong. Unable to rectify these things Elder Miller finally repudiated the whole movement as an error and it occurred to many others in the original movement that date setting was a mistake. But some persistent Adventists were convinced that their calculations of time were correct, based on the day-year principle. As a result, they shifted their focus to the *event* rather than the *time* of the event. So, they remained firm in their belief that the date of October 22, 1844, was not a mistake.

After some study time together (in Adventist history called the Sabbath Conferences of 1848) this little group concluded that the event was not the second coming of Christ but rather something that had occurred in heaven.

While Miller had predicted the second coming for October 22, 1843, and later 1844, he had interpreted "then shall the sanctuary be cleansed" (KJV) of Daniel 8:14 to mean "then shall the earth be cleansed." This was not a crystal-clear biblical teaching—it was built on several quantum leaps and assumptions. And most everything depended on the validity of the contemporaneous understanding of the day-year principle.

Elder Miller assumed that the long-standing view of other interpreters (that the Sanctuary referred to the earth) was correct. This had supplied him with the secret of the time of the second Advent (the *Parousia*). But here was not the only assumption he inherited from the winds of New England interpretation. The whole concept of time prophecy had been a Protestant interest dating back to Martin Luther (1483-1546) and before. The principle had served the Protestants well in their attack on the claimed authority of the Roman Catholic Church during the Reformation.[5]

---

5. The most extensive treatment of this subject can be found in Froom, *The Prophetic Faith of Our Fathers*, 2:184-202, 266-282, 464-505; 3:327-345.

The fact that Jesus had warned against trying to know the time of his return was surprisingly overlooked, reinterpreted, or met with outright avoidance. Jesus had taught:

> ³⁶ "But of that day and hour no one knows, not even the angels of heaven, nor the Son, but the Father only." (Matt 24:36)

Miller's insistence that the end had come short-circuited such teaching and his interpretation eliminated that passage from serious attention. How did this happen? Elder Miller and the early Adventists reasoned that the book of Daniel was a closed prophecy in Jesus' day. It was saved for opening until "the time of the end." And the understanding the time prophecies, as interpreted by those in the Millerite movement, began in 1798. Hence Jesus could not have known the time—but we can know it because the book of Daniel is now a prophecy opened to our understanding. And that included knowing the time of the *Parousia*.

The English KJV showed that Daniel's prophecy read, 14 "And he said unto me, Unto two thousand and three hundred days; then shall the sanctuary be cleansed." (Dan 8:14, KJV). Elder Miller thought that if he could just figure out when the 2300 days (which he interpreted as years) of Daniel 8:14 ended, he could know the date for the cleansing (KJV) of the earth at the second coming of Christ. To a biblical scholar Miller's view was a stretch, but his following became a populist movement and before long thousands of people were whipping up their fervor with him. William Miller's preaching needed the King James Version for its interpretation.

By December of 1844, it was apparent that something was wrong. That the date may simply be based on traditional Protestant principles of interpretation was not part of the concerns of those early Adventists. And so, they pursued a new interpretation of the *event* while leaving the time factor alone. This new notion would later be hailed (by Adventist writers) as the unique contribution of Adventism to Christian theology.[6] Other Christians generally saw it as a cover-up and a stubborn refusal to admit that they had been mistaken. Adventists were accused of inventing a face-saving device, a fantastic notion.[7]

---

6. In his book, *A History of the Origin and Progress of Seventh-day Adventists*, 2d ed., 181, M. Ellsworth Olsen (1873–1952) wrote: "About this time these Adventists also saw their mistake in supposing, as they had done in the period of darkness and uncertainty immediately following the disappointment that probationary time had ended. With the entrance of light on the subject of the heavenly sanctuary, it was seen that the advent message had a breadth of meaning which had not been divined before, and to receive the new light was but a preparation for giving it to the world." Adventist theologian Richard Rice wrote, "Seventh-day Adventists often described the doctrine of the heavenly sanctuary as their distinctive contribution to Christian theology." "The Relevance of the Investigative Judgment," *Spectrum*, 214:1, 32.

7. W. E. Read (1883–1976), "The Investigative, or Pre-Advent, Judgment: Does This Teaching Have Any Biblical Basis?" in *Doctrinal Discussions: A Compilation of Articles Originally Appearing in* The Ministry, *June 1960-July 1961, in Answer to Walter R. Martin's Book* The Truth About Seventh-day Adventism, 43.

Evangelical scholar Walter Martin (1928–1989) would write in his attempt to understand objectively the beginnings of Adventism.

> So far as this writer is concerned, [this Adventist view was] an attempt to escape the terrible calamity which befell the Millerite movement, and the disappointment and embarrassment that must have followed the failure of the Millerite prophecies and their interpretations of the Book of Daniel.[8]

The theological interpretation given to the year 1844 and the inability of Adventists to give up the date, due to the prophet's endorsement, became the occasion for the development of a new doctrine that, in the minds of many students of Adventism, would eventually rival the significance of the cross of Christ and engender serious heterodox ideas about the end of time as well as the significance of the Church itself. However, all theological aberration aside, it was this focus on the time of the end and the imminence of Christ's coming that added an exciting passion to my developing faith. Statements from the prophet's book, *Early Writings,* were read to us children at home, at school and in Sabbath School. These statements ironically brought fear to my heart. And the desire to live forever was kindled in my heart to the point that heaven-lost was everything-lost! Amid these experiential roots I was set to become a religious man.

A RELIGION ROOTED IN TIME

The zeal of Adventism was alive and well in my home. One never talked about the future without adding the words, "If time should last" . . . "if time should last and you graduate from grade school," . . . or "if time should last and you get married" . . . Everything in my religion was connected to time. The movement had been born in time—the movement was fueled by the idea of time. One endured everything in life because Christ could return any day and things would change. The Black Cloud could appear at any time. The Church needs your tithe and offerings now. Set up your wills and legacies with the Church remembered.

Of course, there was a series of events that needed to occur before the Black Cloud could appear—the seven last plagues, the administering of the mark of the beast to all who kept Sunday, the sealing of God's people who kept the Sabbath, the universal Sunday law. But the final events would move quickly in time as our prophet had written.

> The agencies of evil are combining their forces and consolidating. They are strengthening for the last great crisis. Great changes are soon to take place in our world, and *the final movements will be rapid ones.*[9]

---

8. Martin, *The Truth About Seventh-day Adventism,* 175.
9. White, *Testimonies for the Church,* 9:11. Emphasis supplied.

I cannot fully explain what this apocalyptic agenda did to my psyche and worldview as a little boy. It seriously affected all my planning for life and my general outlook on the world. It created places in my mind where I looked for the Black Cloud in time. It created a paradox in my life that I had to learn to live with—I took it all seriously.

I didn't realize that paradoxes are often the same as double binds—impossible possibilities. If time should last and I should enter a life's profession I would be very limited in what I could choose to do. Nothing that entailed violence or the breaking of the Sabbath or that enhanced or fed one's ego (like show business, professional sports, law enforcement, or even firefighting) was legitimate. In the Adventist academy we received a short list of careers we might pursue.

Adventism elevated uncertainty to the level of dogma in my young mind. Along with other questions in the faith (like 'am I ready for Jesus to come?' And 'does God love me in my sin?') I experienced a certain placidness and escapism. I became super-conscientious—with a total psyche committed and involved—never achieving but always trying. I had to learn how to prepare while expecting. I was not given checkpoints for my situation.

I accepted everything taught to me at face value and learned to tolerate the indefiniteness of each day of life. And I finally channeled all my legitimate planning into working for the Church as my parents had done. Nothing else made sense. In fact, there was an overarching notion that anything else seemed like a denial of faith.

Grandpa and Grandma Thorpe were our connection to the Victorian age. If we turned on the radio Grandma would leave the room because a preacher at camp meeting had declared that the radio was the voice of Satan. Grandma wanted nothing to do with the devil. For Victorians everything had its place and was meaningful as it stayed in that place.

My cousin, who I met decades after his Dad had left the Church, remarked that all he remembered about Grandma's house was that from Friday sundown to Saturday sundown you sat on a stool, and no one could drink Coca Cola!

CAMP MEETING

The Truth was emphasized at camp meeting. Classes were offered, and Truth-filled literature was available to help all become more fully entrenched ("grounded") in The Truth.

Our camp meeting was held ten days each year on the campus of La Sierra College. Since we lived only half a mile from the school all these benefits were readily available to us. Each summer the lawns of La Sierra College would be dotted with Army surplus tents where families from around Southeastern California moved in to eat Loma Linda vege-burgers (and buy cases of vegetarian foods), purchase Adventist literature and listen to sermons delivered by guest ministers, Church administrators, and missionaries from around the world. The meetings went from 6:00 am to 10:00 pm daily.

The sociological value of these camp meetings was significant in strengthening the forces that kept the hope of Christ's soon coming alive. These convocations created and maintained a culture that was familial and nurturing. I never missed a children's meeting during those ten days each year—Grandma and Grandpa helped see to that. These were religious feasts for all—young and old alike. And I was heart-broken when the camp meetings were discontinued at La Sierra for a variety of reasons, not the least of which, I was told, that the tents virtually destroyed the college lawns every summer.

THE DEATH OF MY PIONEER

In 1947, when I was five years old, Grandpa Thorpe died. I remember him as a tall, straight man who loved to walk and occasionally laughed. Of course, he wasn't tall but when you are five years old everyone is tall. He was respected as a scholar, writer, editor, teacher and minister. I seldom saw him out of his black suit and tie. But to me he was Grandpa who took me on walks and paid attention to me. To this day I treasure the two artifacts that I eventually inherited from him: his reading (magnifying) glass and his letter opener with the Norwegian flag sculpted into its thin steel handle.

His library disappeared during my childhood. Ministerial students from the college got wind of his book collection and visited Grandma regularly to obtain his books one by one. She was generous with the young men who were planning a life in the ministry. By the time my brother and I had become theology students all his books were gone.

In Glendale, Grandpa and I had walked along Chevy Chase Drive and watched a triplex being built. Several times a week we walked around the corner from McHenry Road to California Street and on to Chevy Chase Drive. The structure still stands today, more than seventy years later. Yet in the deep recesses of my memory I can still see it being built.

When we moved to La Sierra, Grandpa and I would walk to the college and watch the big Adventist Church being constructed. It would seat more than 2000 people—an enormous structure to me, with three balconies and two transepts. On the way to the Church we would stop at various places to rest, for Grandpa was in his late seventies. Those places became shrines for me—stops where we ate lemon drops from his bottomless, cavernous suit pocket. I still like lemon drops. I was his little boy and when he died I cried. I did not understand. I thought he was going to live to see the Black Cloud coming in the east.

I happened to be with Grandpa when he took his last breath. No one planned it that way; I just happened to walk into the room. It was my first and only experience of watching someone die. For a five-year-old such an experience was unforgettable. When the hearse came and took his remains to Redlands for the funeral, tears filled my eyes. Grandpa was gone—my special friend would walk and talk with me no more. No more Grandpa to hold my hand and talk to me as we walked. I would miss him immensely. Something about life was not right. His death was to move me to many ponderous moments.

Much later I would learn that Grandpa Thorpe was a real Adventist pioneer, serving the Church as an editor longer than his own mentor Uriah Smith, the well-known Adventist founder. But at five years of age my devastation stemmed simply from my personal loss. And then I became convinced that the wait would be short for I would see him again soon, probably in just a few days. He was sleeping in the ground and when the Black Cloud appeared he would be called back to life, raised out of the ground to meet Jesus in the air. Then we would walk and talk again, this time around heaven together and forever, probably sucking on lemon drops!

I had some sweet thoughts at Grandpa Thorpe's funeral. As we rode through the long, wide, straight streets of Redlands to his burial plot in Memorial Park, all the family was there—Mom and Dad, Jim, Grandma, the cousins from Sunland, the aunts and my uncle from Glendale. There was something nice about being together as a family. In future years I would attend most of their funerals as well. As a pastor I would even officiate at funerals at that same cemetery in Redlands. And each time I would visit my grandparents' graves.

DEVOTION

My views of Adventism were tempered by the devotion of my family. They were Christians. I came to see that they were Christians in faith and Adventists in practice, or, as one of my colleagues would say, "in sociology." Adventism was their affiliation. Christianity was their religion. And while I would go through a period in my development where I didn't recognize this dichotomy, somehow that distinction helped me as well as others I knew who occasionally struggled with the inconsistencies apparent in any organized religion.

Mom and Dad were people who prayed, studied their Bible and practiced their faith. Dad taught Sabbath School, gave mission talks, played piano and organ for Church, was deeply engaged in the publishing work and never wavered in his faith. Mom took care of all of us. She made sure we had regular worship at home. She read stories at bedtime, played piano in Sabbath School and Church and practiced with Jim and me with our clarinets. She also had the full responsibility of her parents living with us.

Some people told me, "Your parents were the nicest people we ever met." This blessing encouraged me to be a religious person. In this sheltered life I was nurtured. While the Adventist faith gave me little assurance of personal salvation, it at least told me that salvation was obtainable. Never knowing for sure that God loved me or would save me, at least I had this possibility held ever before me. It gave me something to work toward. Unfortunately for me fear was a stronger motivator than assurance or love.

When I would finally discover the assurance of the gospel I would become zealous in trying to emphasize to Adventist young people the importance of realizing that God loves you no matter what you do—for out of that realization grows one's desire and motivation to respond to him. Only in knowing God loves us can we have incentive to respond. The Church I grew up in always made it clear that it was my shortcomings, not the Church's, that were delaying the *Parousia*. Furthermore, ever to suggest that I was saved (in either past or present tense) would engender a kind of personal arrogance that only apostate Christians expressed.

Our prophet had forcefully instructed us.

> Those who accept the Saviour, however sincere their conversion, should never be taught to say or to feel that they are saved. This is misleading. . . . Only he who endures the trial will receive the crown of life. . . . Those who accept Christ, and in their first confidence say, I am saved, are in danger of trusting to themselves.[10]

Any Church has an obligation to tell the Truth, but when it is confused on such basic matters as what constitutes the gospel the result is often exploitation. I learned the gospel was all about me and that was not true. So, I was a willing and vulnerable target. I was being formed into the image of all the religious people around me who talked about the meaninglessness of *this* world in contrast to the significance of the next. But we all seemed devoid of assurance. Christianity was not so much a celebration as it was a quest.

Most of what I remember from our days in Brookfield was recorded in my father's 8mm home movies. There he recorded stuff that would become part of my cranial archives—automobiles I never saw, houses I have since visited, people arriving to reminisce—were all on the films. My first bath, my first attempt at solid food—Dad seemed to have missed nothing. Christmas with Grandma and Grandpa Thorpe, uncles and aunts, cousins and friends of the family, some I never knew dropping by, a brand-new car—other than in these films I remember only old, used cars. Dad recorded much of my history on silent 8mm film.

The war took its toll on the American economy and Dad had to change his approach to buying cars. When the war was over Dad was back on denominational staff wages, which precluded anything in the way of new houses or cars—just pre-owned cars now. He had a contact in Riverside who would call him about every four years—Bill Green at Glenwood Motors Chrysler-Plymouth.

"Have I got a honey for you, Harry!" Bill would say, and we knew we were going down to see the honey. So, we slipped in and out of used cars, only coveting new cars in magazine ads. What would it be like to go downtown and come home in a brand-new Plymouth—even if it were the Plaza model rather than the Belvedere? The question played and replayed in my mind. But it was futile—it was not going to happen. So, our

---

10. White, *Christ's Object Lessons*, 155.

1934 Plymouth was replaced by a 1941, then a 1947, then a 1951, and finally a 1955 two-tone turquoise and white Belvedere during my high school and college years.

After leaving Chicago, Dad never again owned a new car. He was serving and working for God.

PROLOGUE TO ADDICTION

I don't remember anything about the Swedish Church my family attended in Chicago. I was barely three when we moved to California. My brother has told me much of what I know of that period of my life. Dad and Mom played the organ and piano there. I attended the Sabbath School every week. Jim and I later visited the Church building in the 1960s. By then it had become a Pentecostal Church. Apparently Scandinavian Adventist Churches were no more.

I do remember our last trip to Minnesota before moving west. I traveled out of Chicago on the Burlington Zephyr with Mom and Jim. Dad drove up later. Mom had prepared hard-boiled eggs and we began eating them as we waited for the conductor to get the train going. They tried to teach me to drink from a straw, but I didn't catch the concept and was blowing instead of sucking. My brother told me that.

Whatever else happened on that trip is lost in time. At Uncle John's farm in Minnesota I played in the snow as men milked the cows. Unaware of my immediate location I was suddenly covered with a fresh cow pie from head to toe! The look on Uncle John's face is engraved in my mind to this day as he spotted me under the cow, covered. With the speed of a cheetah he ran, grabbed me, and threw me into the closest water trough. My fondness for the smell of dairies may have begun at that moment. Cleaned up and finally thrown into a warm tub in the house my mental videotape runs out.

In December 1944, two months after my third birthday, we arrived in Glendale, California, on Christmas Eve. Dad drove a bus out from the east for Glendale Academy. With newspapers and quilts wrapped around us in the heater-less bus, we headed out in the dead of winter for California. Students lined street corners in some of the small towns we passed through thinking their school bus had arrived. Dad would wave them away as they lined up expecting to board the bus.

As we entered the greater Los Angeles area I fell asleep and dreamed about Captain Midnight. When I awoke, at midnight, the bus rounded the corner of California Street and McHenry Road. There were Grandma and Grandpa Thorpe, Auntie Ruth, Uncle Louis and Aunt Alice, and all the Babcock cousins to greet us.

We were in California. Chicago was a part of my past and would only be revived later in life when I felt the tug to cheer for the White Sox. My commencement as a religious man was set.

CHAPTER THREE

In the Protective Custody of the Church

"We have no choice but to be guilty. God is unthinkable if we are innocent."
—Archibald MacLeish

SCHOOL DAYS START LATE

La Sierra, California, in the 1940s, was little more than a small Church college town with a dairy and farm of rolling fields of crops. La Sierra College had been established as a Church-owned and Church-operated boarding academy in 1922. It had developed to Southern California Junior College by 1927, and in 1946 had achieved full four-year college status. The campus was built on an old Mexican land grant called Rancho La Sierra.

La Sierra Heights was an unincorporated town in Riverside County with a branch U. S. Post Office on the college campus. A small collection of buildings—drugstore, dime store, appliance store, three markets and two gas stations—clustered at the intersection of five country roads known as five points—made up the village a mile from the college.

The primary school was a single building on the college campus. The secondary school met in the basements of Hole Memorial Auditorium and La Sierra Hall, also on the campus. The whole educational enterprise was part of La Sierra College and bore the name of the college in each entity: La Sierra College Demonstration School and La Sierra College Preparatory School. In 1962 these two divisions were separated from the college as La Sierra Elementary School and La Sierra Academy.

A year or so before I was to start first grade Mom woke us up before dawn and summoned us to the kitchen. There through the large window over the sink we saw a stunning sight. The entire sky was bright red in flames. The college appeared to be burning. Dad, Mom, Jim and I jumped in the car and headed for the college a mile away. What we found was unbelievable. I was only four years old, but my memory of the event is vivid.

The college wasn't ablaze—the elementary school was. The Riverside Fire Department was there. The LSC Fire Department from just up the street was there. Fire hoses were strewn everywhere. School officials discovered later it was arson. The building was a total loss. Parents and children alike were crying and wailing. "Someone has burned our school," I remember one little voice crying out.

Months later we heard that the school had been torched by someone who didn't want his boy to go there. Finally, word was out that he had been arrested. Not until over sixty years later did I hear a name—and I was shocked. His son was a friend of mine—in fact, he lived near us. The boy had taught me to play *Monopoly*, a game my father would later refuse to buy for me because it was played with dice. The boy also taught me to say, "Good Grief!" a practice that made Mom uncomfortable because, she said, it bordered on profanity. Sure, I remembered that guy. His parents were divorced so I never knew his father.

"Looters" were allowed essentially free reign. We were told to help ourselves to what was left. We got doors and windows that became part of our new home. Some of the charred lumber was useable and helped to cut costs for Dad. Some of the doors remained long after we occupied the house. "For the time being these will do," Dad said.

Just down the street from the College Press, the burned-out school became a place to walk and sit on the vacant cement floors and ponder great thoughts. Kids would talk and make friends. I wondered what God thought about all this. When the land was finally cleared, Palmer Hall, the college science center, was built on the plot. My brother helped wire the new center and years later I would take biology classes there. Quickly, ground was broken for the new elementary school down Pierce Street next to the Loma Linda Foods Factory.

La Sierra Demonstration School was modern and became equipped with adequate educational materials. The new school opened its doors to the community in October 1947. That was behind schedule. I was five years old. But my birthday was two weeks after the late start and so the administration made an exception; since the school was opening almost on my birthday, I could start as a five-year-old.

This school would be my educational home, in the protective custody of the church, for the next eight years. During that time additions were added to the school and adjacent acreage became the site for a new academy. Graduating from eighth grade my class would next become the first freshman class to occupy the new academy building on Ringe Road (now Golden Avenue). It was like God's hand was just one wave ahead of us moving us into modern facilities on cue.

Dad filmed my first day of school with his 8mm camera, recording my getting out of the old Plymouth, walking across the dirt field that would one day be a lawn, and entering the first-grade room where I met Mrs. Mary Groome, my teacher who would teach me to read and add. Sitting in front of me was Marilyn Anderson (the only person in the room I knew), daughter of the LSC president, a long-time Scandinavian friend of my family. Sitting behind me was Wayne Knoefler, who would become my first close friend. I discovered that Wayne lived just down the road from me and our friendship that continues to this day began then.

One morning as we met to walk to school, Wayne and I made a pact to live in such a way that we would meet each other in heaven. Of course, we both thought that would be maybe just days away, but if not, we had made plans. It was something religious boys did. Sometimes they even cited geography, like, "When we get to heaven, let's meet at the west end of the sea of glass!"

ADVENTIST EDUCATION: PREPARING FOR ETERNITY

The Adventist school system is an impressive educational plan that includes the requirement, among others, that all teachers and administrators be Adventists. In support of my home training I learned how to keep the Sabbath, what was expected of me as an Adventist Christian and what it meant to be "in the world but not of the world." (John 15:19, 17:14–19; 1 John 2:15–17). I learned all this, not only from ministers but from teachers as well. Those who spent as much time with us each day as our parents, modeled the religion to us as well as giving substance to all the subjects we studied.

Adventist education included home, school, and Church working together to present a holistic view of life. The requirements in our religious culture were usually stated in terms of abstinence and negatives: no meat, or at least no *unclean* meats,[1] no smoking, no alcoholic beverages, no coffee, no drugs, no Coca-Cola or any other caffeinated drinks, no chess playing, no checkers, no card playing, no dancing, no extra- or pre-marital sex, no solo sex, no movies, no jewelry, no Sabbath breaking, which meant working or seeking selfish pleasures from Friday sundown to Saturday sundown.

"Religious experience" was something I didn't understand, but I knew it was something I was supposed to have. Ministers and teachers were noticeably happy if we said we had a "good" religious experience. In our school God was the superintendent of history. He was the great mathematician and the source of all true science. And he directed us to choose the right marriage partner. God helped us to choose our professions—those where we could serve others and practice our faith. Police work was needed in a sinful community but was not a legitimate pursuit for Adventists. Police work would require bearing arms and working on Sabbath—not appropriate for those going to heaven.

The law profession was also questionable. As time went on and Adventists began to understand that lawyers would be needed for religious liberty work and to hold off the Sunday laws that were coming, law became more acceptable. We had

---

1. Lev 11.

discussions about what we could be when we grew up, and our textbooks and teachers gave us direction.

Culturally, ethnically, our school in the 1940s and 1950s in La Sierra was almost totally populated by white students and faculty. I was not aware of any written rule that our school was segregated on a racial basis. But other than Mr. Fredricks,[2] a maintenance man at the college—the man who drove around with a ladder sticking out of his broken, back window—I knew no black people. No one referred to Negroes as "blacks" (that would be offensive). They were "Colored" or "Negroes"—those were the *polite* terms.

Most of my classmates went to the same Church, attended the same functions—Sabbath School, Friday night young people's MV (Missionary Volunteer) Society meeting. Later a JMV (Junior Missionary Volunteer) Pathfinder Club was formed. This club was the Adventist parallel of the Scouts. In our system we had several "parallels" to societal institutions. Those parallels made for ease at keeping the Sabbath, ignoring heavy competition and the like—deepening the chance to maintain our standards. In short, our culture was Adventist.

In La Sierra Heights we had our own food factory, grocery store, dime store, post office, gas station, and medical offices. Our elders wanted us to have a secure Adventist environment in which we could form successful relationships, free from culture clashes. In that setting we could avoid mixed marriage—with a person of another faith.[3] "Can two walk together, except they be agreed?" (Amos 3:3, KJV). Among other examples that meant an Adventist would not only avoid marrying a Buddhist or a Muslim, but one would not even marry a Baptist. These were all "unbelievers."

NEW CONSIDERATIONS FOR ENCULTURATION

When two black families moved from Watts into houses on Knoefler Drive I experienced new enculturation. My life changed forever. I didn't understand why neither family attended our Church even though they said they were Adventists. Then I was told they had their own Church- a Colored Church—in Riverside. With the arrival of these families our school became integrated. Yet these new families endured racial prejudice that I did not know about. They dealt with these issues every day.

The families moved onto Knoefler Drive when I was about eight years old and I vaguely remember a stir at home. Dad was angry about something. I didn't understand what was going on. Getting angry was not Dad's style. I heard Jim explain to Mom, "That's the first time I thought Dad was going to slug someone!" What was that all about? I learned a lot of sociology in a very short time.

In talking to one of the neighbors, Dad had discovered that before we moved to La Sierra, the few old-timers living on Knoefler Drive had agreed among themselves

---

2. Name supplied.

never to sell their property to a Negro family. Now they were upset because one of group had broken the pact and two black families were moving onto Knoefler Drive. When Dad heard this, he was blistering. He stormed through the house and up the street for a confrontation.

"Why would you agree to such a thing?" he yelled as he chased the money-changers out of the temple. "These families have just as much right to live on this street as the rest of us. Not only are they Christians who love the Lord, they are even members of our own denomination!" Considering his own words, he stopped short of hitting anyone. Dad didn't hit people—logic was enough. He had made his point.

I was too young to understand. When I asked Mom, what was happening she said many people in America believed in the "Curse of Ham" doctrine. Today she would just have sent me to the internet:

> *The Curse of Ham* (also called the curse of Canaan) refers to the curse that Ham's father, Noah, placed upon Ham's youngest son, Canaan, after Ham "saw his father's nakedness" because of drunkenness in Noah's tent. It is related in the Book of Genesis 9:20–27.... The "curse of Ham" had been used by some members of Abrahamic religions to justify racism and the enslavement of people of African ancestry, who were believed to be descendants of Ham. They were often called *Hamites* and were believed to have descended through Canaan or his older brothers. This racist theory was widely held during the eighteenth to twentieth centuries, but it has been largely abandoned since the mid-twentieth century by even the most conservative theologians.[3]

> The story's original objective was to justify the subjection of the Canaanites to the Israelites, but in later centuries, the narrative was interpreted by some Jews, Christians, and Muslims as an explanation for black skin, as well as slavery. Nevertheless, most Christian denominations and all Jewish denominations strongly disagree with such interpretations due to the fact that in the biblical text, *Ham himself is not cursed and race or skin color is never mentioned.*[4]

So, the theory had landed on Knoefler Drive and I would hear the theory propounded for years to come. Dr. Martin Luther King, Jr. (1929–1968) would meet the doctrine but that was years away. The doctrine was far more widespread in La Sierra than I would have believed. My parents' behavior never showed any connection to these traditions. The economic implications of the Knoefler Drive agreement were pragmatic: the perception read that property value would decrease if a Colored family moved into a white neighborhood. The pact was to preserve value. That was the argument.

This was the 1950s and it would take another decade to begin resolution of the race issues. But the matter had been raised in our little world and the presence of black Adventists on Knoefler Drive would set in motion a development of thinking

---

3. "The Curse of Ham." *The New World Encyclopedia*, online encyclopedia. Emphasis supplied.
4. "The Curse of Ham." *Wikipedia*, the free encyclopedia. Emphasis supplied.

that eventually would ease some tensions. When these new families moved into the neighborhood I got a whole new set of friends. My new Colored friends remarked that my parents showed them "sweet acceptance." I don't remember any discussion about race from that time. What the old-timer neighbors had tried to do never landed with us kids.

One son was my age and became my best friend on Knoefler Drive. He later commented that my Dad was always one of his favorite people. He remembered a gentle, soft-spoken man who always had a roguish twinkle in his eye. He may have first seen that roguish twinkle the day he lost his balance and slammed his bicycle into our porch, flying off the seat through our open living room door and landing on the rug in front of my family sitting around reading and talking. He was unhurt, but we waited to confirm that before we all broke into laughter—so unexpected, it became his comical entrance that no one ever forgot.

The patriarch in his family was an accomplished artist who made his living painting commercial signs. In a short time, his signature signs appeared all around the Riverside area. He had a style that made his signs immediately recognizable. Soon his little red Ford pickup with complete painting supplies could be seen all over two or three counties. Since he had been a semi-professional baseball player in New York he was also an instant hit with the kids in the neighborhood. He taught us how to throw a baseball correctly among other aspects of successful ball-playing.

When another of the family's friends moved from Los Angeles to Riverside three more black students enrolled in our Church school. They also attended a different SDA Church, the same one as the families on our street. Unlike our friends who had moved into the center of a white neighborhood, this family lived on the very edge of La Sierra, separated from the overwhelmingly white community. From there they ran several different businesses over the years including a successful plant nursery.

As time passed the middle son, a member of my class at school, also became a close friend. In my 1956 high school yearbook, *Memory Trails,* his was the only black face. But the elementary school was another story—there were thirteen black students there. Eventually both of us would become Adventist ministers.

Those of us who lived on Knoefler Drive spent a lot of time together. We hiked, played ball, went camping, played cops and robbers, cowboys and Indians. Our summers were spent building forts on Sunshine Mountain, pitching tents, searching the trash dump in the Corona hills for wheels and axles to build hot rods. We rode home-made cars down the big hill up Knoefler Drive sometimes risking our lives. Our model was set largely by "The Little Rascals" of the "Our Gang" short movies that we watched each school day afternoon on the *Captain Jet Show* on Channel 2 from Los Angeles. They were forever building stuff and always with materials from the dump. The Corona trash dump was a daily destination for us in the summer.

The passion for baseball slowly invaded our interests. We built a backstop on the lot between our houses and when we were not camping out we were playing baseball.

One summer we set up a pitcher's mound and a home plate and pitched to each other, through the better part of a World Series. As a direct result, I eventually became a pitcher in high school and college, and my best friend became a catcher.

SEPARATE BUT EQUAL

This was white-dominated 1950s in a largely segregated Southern California. I can only conclude that we were living in a blind out of which we could not see, and our religion did little to protect us from it. In fact, it encouraged some dark behaviors and attitudes that were rooted in the widely believed Curse-of-Ham idea and shored up by segregation, which had been the law of the land since the Plessy v. Ferguson landmark decision of the U. S. Supreme Court in 1896. In this decision racial segregation was held to be constitutional and the term "separate but equal" was introduced. Segregation was ruled non-discriminatory.[5]

While the law spoke of separate but equal, sociological forces put the emphasis on separate. By more mature standards these concepts were very thinly disguised ways of accepting all out bigotry and prejudice as God-given expectations.

In maturity my friend and I would reminisce about these experiences on an adult level. By then both of us had finished doctorates, he in psychological statistics, and me in theological studies and developmental psychology. We were both working in the same city at the time. We reunited on the steps of the Church I was pastoring on the corner.

He just happened to be driving by the Church when he saw me talking to some elders on the street corner after a board meeting. We had a glorious reunion. We had both lost track of each other. He shared candidly stories of the pain he and his family suffered because of the attitudes in our community. These were subjects we had never pursued in our growing up days. Our neighborhood became integrated—but I hadn't felt his pain growing up.

PASTOR L. CALVIN OSBORN, LA SIERRA SEVENTH-DAY ADVENTIST CHURCH

The stories my friend shared seem sordid in a post-civil-rights-movement America. Our conversation began that morning in 1999, when he asked me if Elder Osborn was still alive. The story unfolded. At around the same time as these families were moving to La Sierra, we got a new pastor at the La Sierra Adventist Church. Elder L. Calvin Osborn (1914–2008) came to us from a San Diego pastorate.

A graduate of Washington Missionary College in Washington, D.C., Elder Osborn had grown up in the American Midwest. One of his first pastorates was Louisville,

---

5. These were known as Jim Crow laws. See the Smithsonian National Museum of American History internet site.

Kentucky, where he was popular with his congregation, especially for his *pathos*. He was the most likeable pastor I had met by my age of twelve. He showed interest in us kids. He filled his sermons with stories and exhibits that kept our interest as well as that of the adults. And he always ended his sermons on time! We were out of Church by noon—this was always high on young people's ratings lists.

His first major crisis in the La Sierra Church began when he was met by a small group of members concerned by the sudden influx of "Colored people" in the Church's elementary school. La Sierra was the largest congregation in the consortium of congregations that ran the elementary school, and so Elder Osborn seemed the obvious person with whom to voice their anxiety. They met with him in a clandestine, unofficial gathering of Church members, many of them office holders in the congregation.

They were distressed about what to do with "these people." Elder Osborn listened to their concerns. Knowing the American South from having worked there, he realized that these were sparks that could set off a powder keg. The people out west were probably as prejudiced as southerners were reputed to be, although there were no posted signs of "Colored Only" on restrooms, drinking fountains or in sections of restaurants. The west hid its prejudice behind a front of denial, that is, if you were white. The story from black people was another matter. But now a crisis was developing in some white minds. True feelings were surfacing.

In this revealing meeting the group of Church leaders told Elder Osborn that he needed to take a stand on this gathering storm. He listened intently without making a commitment. He just listened. Finally, in his wisdom, he asked the group to give him a week to think it over. Perhaps today the concerns would have sparked an immediate response, but he knew that he could be dealing with deep feelings and cultural tradition—and to some large extent unspoken ones. People fear what they don't understand.

A week later the group met again, and Elder Osborn clarified his position. Paraphrasing what my friend told me, and what Elder Osborn later confirmed in my conversation with him, he basically told the group that he was their pastor and as a Christian he had given careful thought to their concerns. He clarified that the Negro families were eligible to attend the Church's schools. My friend testified that whenever he came on to the academy campus Elder Osborn would intentionally seek him out to ask him how things were going. He testified that this pastor was functioning as his "guardian angel."

Elder Osborn's stand became a clarion call to support black families that had moved to La Sierra and had children in the elementary and high school by the time I reached academy. By today's standards his position looks normal and routine. By the standards of the 1950s it was heroic. This position did not erase what many white families struggle with, and did not eradicate expressions of overt, and in some cases unintended or unrecognized prejudice. But white Adventists were placed on the road to understanding their own fears.

Most of the whites in our community seemed to follow in the footsteps of Elder Osborn. Courage begets growth. Without any knowledge of this meeting I sensed community support and I realize that it influenced my own growth.

CHAPTER FOUR

The Culture of Adventism

"Intolerance is the Do Not Touch sign on something that cannot bear touching. We do not mind having our hair ruffled, but we will not tolerate any familiarity with the toupee that covers our baldness."

—Eric Hoffer

HOME, SCHOOL, CHURCH WORKING TOGETHER

My friend and I played clarinet in the La Sierra Academy band and in the early Sabbath afternoons, after we had all come home from our worship services and had lunch, I would go up Knoefler Drive to his house and we would play our instruments. Later in the afternoon his parents would take the kids to their Church and occasionally they invited me to go along with them to the young people's meeting. There we would sometimes play what we had been practicing earlier. Only later would I begin to understand the separate Church thing.

Other than this encounter with race relations, moving from our living room to the Adventist classroom was a move in remarkable consistency. Home and school worked together to make Adventists. Wherever we went we were with the same children. Five days a week we studied together, on Sabbath we worshiped together.

On Sabbath afternoons we walked around our La Sierra village and there we saw many of the same people we had been with in school all week or in worship earlier in the day. When we climbed Sunshine Mountain or Two-Bit Mountain on Sabbath afternoon we would meet more of our friends out on their Sabbath nature walks. Sunday we all went to work. Monday we were back together in school.

Our community was not a commune, but it had some communal traits. I knew no one who wasn't Adventist except my Uncle Louis who had left the Church after some academic shakeup years before at an Adventist college in the Pacific Northwest where he had been a professor. There was talk that he may have committed the unpardonable sin—having passed the point of no return. Only eternal damnation awaited those who had known Adventism and turned their back on it—that was my religious mindset. When we visited him and his family in Los Angeles I spotted some of them drinking beer. I feared for their souls.

THE SABBATH

For Adventists Friday was "preparation day." Most Church workers went home at noon to get ready for the Sabbath. That meant cleaning their homes and finishing the cooking before sundown when the Sabbath began. Shopping for groceries was part of the Friday afternoon ritual, although some finished their shopping by Thursday night.

We took our baths, polished our shoes, readied our clothes for Church the next day, cleaned the toilets, washed the car, scrubbed the floors, vacuumed and dusted the house—all before sundown on Friday. We learned how to make the Sabbath a day of abstinence from unnecessary work, personal amusement, and selfish activity.

What we were not to do on the Sabbath was determined by four biblical instructions—no work, no selfish pleasure, no idle talk, and no selfish pursuits[1] and in greater detail by our prophet. Sister White had left explicit directions. We were not to do any schoolwork on the Sabbath. Doing that would be making our studies "paramount to the expressed command of the Most High."[2]

She had written to a *Brother K* in 1876: "You have desecrated the Sabbath by bringing your studies into that holy time which was not yours to occupy for your own purposes. God has said, 'In it thou shalt not do any work.'"[3] According to Sister White doing assignments as well as reading secular literature would be a direct violation of the fourth commandment—it came under the general heading of "work." The instruction was clear.

> A partial observance of the Sabbath law is not accepted by the Lord and has a worse effect upon the minds of sinners than if you made no profession of being a Sabbathkeeper. They perceive that your life contradicts your belief, and lose faith in Christianity.[4]

Our conversation was to be *guarded* on the Sabbath: "Talking about anything or everything which may come into the mind is speaking our own words."[5] "Every deviation

---

1. Ex 20:8–11, Isa 58:13–14.
2. White, *Testimonies for the Church*, 4:115.
3. Ibid., 114.
4. Ibid., 248.
5. White, *Testimonies for the Church*, 2:703.

from right brings us into bondage and condemnation."[6] Talking about cattle, crops, losses, gains, were all "Sabbath breaking."[7] Talk was to be restricted to religious themes, "to present truth, present duty, the Christian's hopes and fears, trials, conflicts, and afflictions; to overcoming at last, and the reward to be received."[8]

The Sabbath time was not to be wasted in bed either. Those who sleep on the Sabbath dishonor God in so doing, "and, by their example, say that the six days are too precious for them to spend in resting."[9] And at the bottom line of truth was the overriding fact that the Pope had changed the Sabbath to "exalt himself above God."[10] Sister White wrote a lot about keeping the Sabbath, but perhaps her most complete set of instructions was quoted to us from her *Testimonies* in a chapter entitled, "The Observance of the Sabbath."[11] These were her explanations of biblical principles she claimed she got from God in vision.

My family followed these instructions as closely as possible. We were to anticipate the Sabbath throughout the week so as not to "break" the Sabbath when it arrived. The instructions included guarding the edges of the Sabbath, which meant being ready with house cleaned, food cooked, baths taken, shoes polished, and the like, well before sundown (at least half an hour) on Friday evening. It also meant that we were not to rush too quickly into our Saturday night activities, which would tempt us to make our plans on the Sabbath.

Quoting liberally from the Old Testament our teachers made some aspects of ancient Israel out to be the model for modern "Israel," i.e., the Seventh-day Adventist Church—the true Church that was to restore the Sabbath to its rightful place in contrast to Sunday, the apostate counterfeit introduced by false religions.

What did we do on the Sabbath? The day was to be a day of vigorous spiritual activity such as talking about and studying the truths of scripture and going on walks to see the beauties of "God's second book"—nature; and then to reflect on that experience. All this was required not just of the Jews but of Christians as well. The New Testament was seldom quoted except for prophetic materials from the Apocalypse.

We visited Christian friends and talked about religious blessings like the work of the Church through *The Voice of Prophecy*, the radio arm of the Church, and other missionary activities. We avoided any people who did not believe like we did or who might tempt us to desecrate the day in some way. While we didn't keep the postman from delivering letters to our mailboxes we usually waited until sundown to open them. We had other Adventists over for lunch and talked about the work of the Church. This was a day to remind us that we were Adventist Christians, being obedient to God.

6. Ibid.
7. Ibid.
8. Ibid., 704.
9. Ibid.
10. White, *Early Writings*, 65.
11. White, *Testimonies for the Church,* 6:349–368.

Radios, television sets and record players were all idle on the Sabbath. Those were amusements to be avoided. For us that also included swimming. When we went to the beach we went to enjoy a nature walk, not to swim. Certainly, we were not going to go surfing or water skiing. We might wade but that was only with our pant legs rolled up. We would never go in our swimming suits. And those few Adventists we knew who had swimming pools or power boats were expected to act accordingly. Ironically, perhaps calmly rowing a canoe would be acceptable.

The only radio program I ever remember my family listening to on Sabbath was *The Voice of Prophecy*. Religious recordings of VOP celebrities such as the King's Heralds gospel quartet and Del Delker (1924–2018), female soloist, eventually came on the market. They were acceptable. But Tennessee Ernie Ford and Elvis Presley, who also recorded hymns, were usually referred to as Saturday night music and frowned on as Sabbath violations.

Dad came into my room one Friday night alarmed that I was listening to the radio. When he saw that I was listening to some religious music on my phonograph he just asked me to turn the volume down in case the neighbors should hear and misunderstand (and think I had the radio on). We learned not only to avoid evil but also to avoid the appearance of evil. It was important to be thorough as Adventists. Deeper than that was the notion that a true Christian cares enough to avoid being a stumbling block to others.[12]

STRUGGLING WITH THE WORLD

We were taught to avoid worldliness. This was largely connected to dress, diet, vocation, associations and appearance. We grew up with the saying: "You can pick out an Adventist in an airport." That especially referred to the way a person dressed, for that could demonstrate a truly worldly person trying to attract attention to self.

Plainness was the key. No Adventist would be wearing lipstick, jewelry (certainly not pierced ears), immodest clothes (low necklines or high hemlines), bracelets, necklaces, rings or even a wedding ring. Many of these standards seemed aimed at women. How could men be worldly? Nevertheless, the notion also included reading matter, going to shows, music listening habits, and general decorum.

Show business was taboo. Dancing,[13] makeup, boisterousness were all involved as well. One Adventist leader explained to me that the theatre was all lies, and we should avoid lying. I asked him what that meant, and he said, people appearing on stage all have characters they are playing—those are lies; they are not those characters, so they are lying to the audience. That argument was designed to stop discussion—we weren't to question our elders.

---

12. Rom 14:13–23.

13. White, *Messages to Young People,* 392: "There are amusements, such as dancing, card-playing, chess, checkers, etc., which we cannot approve, because Heaven condemns them."

Attending movies, pool halls, bowling saloons, dances, horse races,[14] Broadway shows, live theatre,[15] nightclubs and other questionable places of amusement was to be avoided.[16] Bars and restaurants where alcoholic beverages were served were off limits. We weren't to bowl, gamble, play chess or checkers.[17] And one would never plan to make a living writing fiction or appearing in movies or plays.

These were all activities that our prophet had pointed out specifically as wicked, worldly entertainments. Participating in these would be cumulative evidence that one was not interested in seeing the Lord return. The fact that this instruction came from the prophet had the effect of elevating it to the level of principle. "If the Lord returned today would you want to be found in [you supply the place]?"[18]

Television was held with suspicion when it appeared on the market. Dad made it clear that we would probably never own a television set. Even radio and television as evangelistic methods for the Church were questionable to many members. As a young man I was told by one minister that as a rule Adventists could not participate in any amusements that took place inside of buildings. He proclaimed that we should only indulge in recreational activities that took place in the fresh air. I considered his instructions with interest. Yet even some outdoor things were considered bad. I learned that golf was a sport of the idle rich and a waste of precious time. Horse racing involved gambling even though it was done outside.

Competitive sports like football, baseball, hockey and tennis were not something Adventists should participate in professionally. We could dabble in them to the extent that we got physical exercise, but competition encouraged rivalry and Christians preparing for the Lord's return should not subject themselves to the kind of competition engendered there.

How could an Adventist high school student play any of these sports when they were largely offered on Sabbath, viz., Friday night? A case in point was the story of a young Adventist attending public high school who had joined the football team and

---

14. White, *Fundamentals of Christian Education*, 320: "While we shun the false and artificial, discarding horse racing, card playing, lotteries, prize fights, liquor drinking, and tobacco using, we must supply sources of pleasure that are pure and noble and elevating." Cf. White, *Sons and Daughters of God*, 280.

15. White, *Messages to Young people*, 380: "Among the most dangerous resorts for pleasure is the theater. Instead of being a school for morality and virtue, as is so often claimed, it is the very hotbed of immorality.... There is no influence in our land more powerful to poison the imagination, to destroy religious impressions, and to blunt the relish for tranquil pleasures and sober realities of life, than theatrical amusements." Cf. White, 406, 516.

16. Ibid., 398: "The true Christian will not desire to enter any place of amusement or engage in any diversion upon which he cannot ask the blessing of God. He will not be found at *the theater, the billiard hall,* or *the bowling saloon*. He will not unite with the gay waltzers, or indulge in any other bewitching pleasure that will banish Christ from the mind." (Emphasis supplied).

17. Ibid., 392.

18. Ibid., 398: "No Christian would wish to meet death in such a place. No one would wish to be found there when Christ shall come."

was accidently killed on the field during a game on Friday night. We heard the suggestion that it may have been God's judgment that he died for "breaking" the Sabbath.

Other stories circulated to help us deal with moral dilemmas connected with the Sabbath. A lady living in New England expressed concern that her husband was watching football on TV on Saturday night, which was permissible. But then she brought up that he should not be watching the game because of the three-hour time differential. Even though her husband was watching the game on Saturday night, the game was being played in the west on Sabbath. How did one solve that moral dilemma?

For as long as I could remember Dad was fascinated with ham radio. That led him to associates who broadened his horizons. One of Dad's ham radio friends introduced him to television and the possibility of repairing radio and television sets as a hobby. So, one day Dad came home with a five-inch Motorola television that his friend had loaned him. That day my value system began to widen. I learned, as a religious person, that if I indulged in moderation I was not necessarily being worldly. Later Dad came home with a twelve-inch set to repair. When he got it working, it stayed in the living room for some time. Finally, he bought a brand new seventeen-inch Motorola TV set and it became a member of our family for the next ten years.

The principle of moderation now became an integral part of my religious life. We attempted to watch *Faith for Today*, the Church's TV show, and *The Voice of Prophecy*, which for a short time was televised. Both shows started out as radio programs with a picture tube. They each had a male quartet and a speaker. They were filmed in a studio with a pulpit at the center. Still by some they were considered pushing the envelope, playing with sinful media. Both approaches were pursued by visionary pastors who thought only of reaching masses of people with the gospel. Not until years later would the Church accept and finally sponsor these efforts.

When I say we attempted to watch these shows I mean we were living behind Rattlesnake Hill and we found our signal from Mt. Wilson in Los Angeles blocked. These programs were on channels we could not pull in from Los Angeles. We got Channels 2, 4, 5. Channels 7, 9, 11 and 13 were all blocked by the mountain.

As television was integrated into our family culture, I became so enamored with it that the summer after my sixth grade I turned my room into a television studio. I built mock TV cameras and set up lights from Dad's dark room to put together TV programming. I took phonograph records and played them on Dad's 78 rpm record player like a disc jockey. I became a broadcaster, a news anchor, a variety show host and a newspaper editor. Neighborhood friends came in and ran the cameras and the boom microphones. I started a neighborhood newspaper and typed out editorials on Dad's portable Smith-Corona typewriter.

I learned the hunt and peck method of typing that summer. A classmate who lived on Raley Drive, the next street over from Knoefler Drive, and I worked together to turn my room into a "center of telecommunications." Obviously, there was no real broadcasting of anything, and my papers had no circulation but both of us got a lot of experience in media that summer.

Most of my friends and I could watch some television although our parents were strict—at first; mainly programs that had converted over from radio programs that we had been listening to—*The Cisco Kid*, *Red Ryder*, *The Lone Ranger*, *Flash Gordon*, *Roy Rogers* and *Gene Autry*. Just up the street at my friend's house, I would watch old English movies and gangster movies on Sunday mornings while Mom and Dad were at work. TV broadened my outlook on culture. Since we could only bring in those three TV stations even with our 25-foot rooftop antenna, we could only watch the CBS and NBC networks. I never saw *Superman* or *Disneyland*—they were on ABC, Channel 7. But we got *The Great Gildersleeve*, *Father Knows Best* and *You Bet Your Life* with Groucho Marx.

Captain Jet was our afternoon visitor from 5:00 to 6:00 p.m. and he showed cartoons, *Laurel and Hardy, The Little Rascals (Our Gang), Charlie Chase* and other Hal Roach short features. Dad's friends labored with him questioning his judgment in letting us watch *Laurel and Hardy*. But by this time Dad had learned to enjoy these programs with us. Mom never watched movies, but she liked quiz programs. She ironed and sewed to *I've Got a Secret, What's My Line? People are Funny* and *To Tell the Truth*.

That same summer I borrowed some of Dad's photographic equipment, wrote a screenplay, and cast a movie with some of my friends in it. It was patterned after a Hal Roach comedy short. My cast met several times for rehearsals but just as we were ready to start shooting, Dad had second thoughts and decided that was going too far. What could the future hold for an Adventist film director and producer?

He confiscated our equipment, including our undeveloped film and ended the project. The screenplay was scrapped, the cast was dispersed, and the film was never finished—not one frame was ever shot. But in my mind the work was still running around. I determined that I would do something someday that had to do with performing arts. I was disappointed, but the unfinished project had fed into defining a religious man. Dad was worried about what people would think. The next summer I attempted to revive some of my fervor for show business, but my friends' parents had other plans for their kids. Without their support my creativity in the arts soon withered.

Much later I would start and run a drama company in an Adventist school for ten years, several years after Dad had died. Mom, who was retired by then would say to me, "I wonder what your Dad would say if he saw you directing Broadway musicals!" I thought I already knew the answer to that question. I remembered when, as a college student, I had bought a score of Rodgers and Hammerstein's *Oklahoma,* and was playing the piano music one day when Dad walked into the living room. He became very serious and remarked that he didn't think I should be playing that "dirty show music." His timing was bad—he had walked in just as I was playing "I'm Just a Girl

Who Cain't Say 'No!'"¹⁹ Dad didn't like the title of that song. Such was just one factor in our struggle with the world and its culture.

OUR ANSWER TO THE WORLD: JUST SAY "NO" TO CULTURE

While attending movies was never a part of our home, even on television, the day would come when videos presented a new challenge to the Adventist value system. Later I would watch Adventists struggle with this new invasion of their Victorian world. If only Christ had returned in 1844 this entire struggle could have been avoided.

As an Adventist college professor, rearing children in The Truth, I would stand in line at the video rental store on Saturday night with various levels of clergy and other Adventists assembling our stack of videos for our Saturday evening entertainment. It was a rule of courtesy not to look at the titles on the videos any of us were renting for the weekend. These were movies we had never seen and would never go to a cinema to watch. One consequence of that stance was that few if any of us, were successful in selling this double standard to our children.

One of my Seminary professors would later comment: "Television gave Adventists a chance to pull the shades and make up for lost time!" Movies we never got to see in the cinema seemed safe viewing on a small black and white TV screen in the basement family room when no one else was around. And cable presented another invasion of our values. Reframing was required.

Several years later I would read Richard Niebuhr's (1894–1962), *Christ and Culture,* and become aware that Adventists weren't the only Christians who struggled with these value crises.[20] Niebuhr pointed out five approaches Christians have taken to this struggle, the first of which was to look at Christ as being against culture. In this approach Christians chose to rule out culture as a legitimate part of their lives. God could not bless worldly culture, they would contend, which was essentially a product of the evil age.

Niebuhr listed the alternatives:

1. Christ against culture.[21]

2. Christ of culture.[22]

3. Christ above culture.[23]

4. Christ and culture in paradox.[24]

---

19. Rodgers and Hammerstein, "I Cain't Say No," *Oklahoma* (1943). See Roden, Wright and Simms, *Anthology for Music in Western Civilization*, 1714.

20. Niebuhr, *Christ and Culture*, 1951.

21. Ibid., 45–82.

22. Ibid., 83–115.

23. Ibid., 83–115.

24. Ibid., 83–115.

5. Christ the transformer of culture.[25]

This black/white, either/or approach (Christ against culture) described my culture. And yet Adventists were essentially eclectic—choosing to follow their folk ways, which were seldom consistent. Dad had told me that when he first became an Adventist he would cross the street if he heard worldly music coming out of a bar or nightclub on the city street. This was a statement of faith for him against worldliness. He had softened in the ensuing years. Activities largely defined an Adventist and for me that was part of being a religious person. But I had to admit that watching TV gave us a chance to attend worldly activities on the screen that we would never have attended in person.

THE LIBERALIZING OF ADVENTISM

Many years before I began my formal education, Adventists sought accreditation for their schools. There were enough variables in accreditation requirements that a school could remain unique to its own convictions and Adventists played all the variables to their advantage. A striking example was the biological approach to natural science. We studied creationism and only heard of evolutionism through defensive critiques. The plan was that Adventist young people would be protected from the impact of evolutionistic doctrine by providing them with an educational system that would eventually include doctoral degree programs.

Ironically, Adventist education was one place where a degree of liberalizing was being made in the Church, Some Adventists would come to fear this because education and information are roads to freedom in all human societies. And thinking has often been a dangerous threat to creedal religion.

Academic freedom was not something Adventists would gracefully embrace; in fact, they have not yet accepted this as a *modus operandi* in some disciplines of learning. Limitations were required for carrying out the vision that certain Adventist theological aspects required. For traditional Adventism the ultimate purpose of education was to produce "the last generation." This theological element included achieving the ability to live without a mediator on earth, i.e., sinless.[26]

All Adventist education operated in this box. But this notion would especially characterize much of the crisis that would develop in several North American colleges in the 1980s. When Adventist schools began awarding advanced degrees, accrediting bodies demanded that the faculty possess degrees still not offered by the Adventist school system. This was a requirement that some in the Church complied with reluctantly.

As the system grew, it was with some reticence that academics would go away to worldly schools for a master or a doctoral degree. But that was the price of

---

25. Ibid., 83–115.
26. Andreasen, *The Sanctuary Service,* Chapter 21.

accreditation. Most would pay their own expenses to get this education. The thought was that once these outside doctoral degrees were earned by Adventist scholars, they would add credibility to the system having teachers with accredited doctorates in their respective fields.

Some critics saw this as a sell out to the world. Yet the unspoken wish of many was that when scholars returned from such training they would be the same Adventists they were before they left; only now they would have those academic letters behind their names. That assumption would eventually strike fear in the hearts of some parents who had counted on Adventist professors supporting whatever folk religion they had tried to instill in their children. Especially with the influx of young teachers with doctorates would this fear be intensified.

Folk religion would now sometimes clash with professional scholarship. Since from the beginning of all my education every person I encountered, students and faculty alike, was Adventist, I thought little about what I would do in life when I grew up. But I never questioned that my choice would bend to my Adventist convictions.

MY BAPTISM AND THOUGHTS ON POPULARITY

I was baptized in the La Sierra Seventh-day Adventist Church by Pastor Forrest Abbott on May 16, 1953, the day after my brother's twenty-first birthday. I was in sixth grade. The baptism was in the same building Grandpa and I had watched workmen build several years before. I was eleven years old. I remember feeling the cleanest I had ever felt when I came out of the baptismal fount. It was like the water was laced with strong Amway cleansing agents.

I had attended the baptismal class with my classmates. Adventists sometime testify later that these classes are a "cattle call" where people in the sixth grade are all baptized as a matter of routine. I have had conscientious college students visit me who wanted to be re-baptized because they felt they had not been responsible when they were baptized—too young, too pressured. But that was never my experience. Nobody pressured me. I knew what I was doing, and I wanted to do it.

I had pondered baptism for at least two years before taking the step. I would have gone to the water even if I were the only person in my class. This step was serious for me. I decided on my own, with no input or pressure from my parents, teachers or peers. In fact, other than placing me in a Church school my parents did not pressure me to take this step. They were surprised when I later announced that I had decided to become a gospel minister. They had never suggested that either, in fact Dad was astonished because I was so bashful. He said he could not picture me preaching a sermon!

Preparing for baptism I remember my shock at talking with one of my classmates and asking him if he was going to be baptized. He said he was getting out of the Adventist "stuff" as soon as he left home. He said he went to shows so he could sit in the balcony and smoke cigarettes. I was startled. This student's father was also an

Adventist institutional worker, sacrificing to keep several children in Church school, and I was not prepared for my friend's revelation. His family moved away after seventh grade, so I lost track of his quest to lead a worldly, non-Adventist life.

I was always the youngest kid in my elementary school classroom and the smallest, and I guess I was generally perceived to be the shy boy in the class. If I had any self-esteem in comparison to my classmates I was not aware of it. But at home I was free and happy. While school was routine and generally enjoyable, I was not a leader. But there were cliques in our class. There were those who thought of themselves as better than others and I was not part of that.

One day during recess two boys in our class got into a fight that turned into a shouting match and was brought into the classroom. When our teacher asked what was going on, the first boy blurted out shamelessly, "I used to be the most popular boy in this class. Now everybody thinks this new guy is the most popular." Here was a stunning exhibition of honesty. I considered both these guys my friends. Why would anyone care who was most popular? I had already observed that being "popular" had consequences and unhappy implications. It was all just a perception anyway.

In our eighth-grade year I developed more separation anxiety. Our class was too large for a single classroom, so the administration split us into two groups. Ten of us who had been together since first grade were put in a divided room with the sixth grade while the rest of our class was put in the regular eighth grade room.

To my initial delight two of my closest friends were in my room. But the outcome for me was a feeling of separation from the rest of my class. I never really got to know the new members of our class since they were in another building. I also began to realize the effect of my stature and my developing ganglisness on my involvement in sports.

Soccer became an important athletic event at La Sierra Elementary School. Mr. Olson, the main eighth grade teacher, had spent time in Cuba and was a top-flight soccer athlete. I tried out but never learned to enjoy the sport—neither to watch, nor to play. I watched classmates bouncing the ball off their heads and tried it a couple of times—it hurt too much. Softball was good but even in that sport I was the last kid chosen. That took an emotional toll.

We didn't play tackle football. It was too brutal for our elders. Instead we played touch football and flag ball. Again, I was last man standing in the choose-up line. When I was finally chosen I was put in the center position where I could do little harm—that was as humiliating as being put in right field in softball.

My big chance to star came one day when the ball took a bad bounce and landed in my arms during recess. I was so stunned that I just started running. To my surprise and glee, minutes later I had scored a touchdown! When I planted the ball in the end zone I discovered that I had scored for the other team. Trauma trickled through my weakening body as I began to realize that this was why only my teammates had been chasing me. Such experiences hardly enhanced my reputation as an athlete. I had serious work to do.

CHAPTER FIVE

Identity Formation and Dad's Compassion

"To procure life, to obtain a mate and to rear offspring: such is the real business of life."
—W. Winwood Reade

MIDDLE SCHOOL EXPERIENCE

During the upper grades in elementary school I was short and pudgy. If I played softball it was in right field, which in the big leagues was a good thing, but in grade school it meant last chosen. For some reason we never played hardball—softball was another Adventist substitution—another example of moderation. Softball provided faster movement, more exercise, and less competitive spirit, we were told. Hardball (baseball) encouraged rivalry.

My reversal in sports began in a curious manner. As a sixth grader I had my favorite radio heroes. They included *Mark Trail, The Lone Ranger, Clyde Beatty* and *Brer Rabbit.* Every week I especially looked forward to hearing the latest adventures of Clyde Beatty. He was a wild animal trainer who had his own circus. Listening to the radio was a theatre in the mind. I had ideas of what Clyde Beatty looked like and I would dress in white clothes, grab a whip and chair and teach the wild animals in my mind to do major acts for the circus. In the backyard I had staked out an area that I called my "Big Top."

When the *Riverside Daily Press* arrived one evening there was an announcement that Clyde Beatty and his circus would be performing in Riverside! I could hardly believe it! Talk about a dream come true—Clyde Beatty in my own town! I went to Dad and showed him the wonderful news. To my surprise he was ambivalent.

I discovered that for Dad circuses were on the grey list—he was not sure this was appropriate entertainment for an Adventist. In a family council I set forth the proposition that this would be an important addition to our growth and after some discussion Dad acquiesced. It was, after all, not much different than going to the zoo. But we would not attend any of the sideshows—they were frivolous and dehumanizing. Plus, what if someone should see us there?

Finally, he decided that we could go to the Tuesday night performance of Clyde Beatty's circus in Riverside.

I was floating. I could not remember when I had been so excited. I could hardly wait to tell a close friend at school the next day. When I shared the great news, he looked disappointed. He said he wished he could go. I just said, "I can solve that! Come with us!" His whole demeanor changed for he too was a Clyde Beatty fan. When I got home I learned that what I had done was a serious breach of family ethics.

When Dad got home from work that evening my friend's mother was on the phone. "I understand you and your family are going to the circus and you have invited my son to go with you. Is that true?" She was asking. She wasn't angry—just checking the veracity of his story.

Dad was on the spot, and he never liked being put on any spot—especially in these questionable moral dilemmas. He blanched and stuttered—saying something like, "We were just talking. We may not be going," were the words I heard coming out of his mouth. I collapsed. I had overstepped my boundaries. It was not my place to invite anyone to go with us to this controversial amusement. That was Dad's decision to make. Furthermore, all his worry about what people would think kicked into high gear.

I read his mind—now the whole school would know that we went to circuses. I was dead! When he hung up I wanted to hide. His teeth were crossed and that only meant one thing, he was not happy. He then announced to the family that the issue was closed: "Don't even think about going to the circus!" He was embarrassed and now he was forced to take a public stand.

I was devastated. In my excitement I had blown it. I begged, and pleaded, and promised and bargained. Nothing worked. I was wishing for something that rivaled the Daisy Red Ryder BB gun in *A Christmas Story*—always just out of reach. I finally threw myself on the bed and cried harder than I could remember ever crying before. That probably wasn't a good method either. Through my sobs I could hear Mom and Jim trying to reason with Dad in the next room. But nothing would change his mind. Dad could not believe that I had betrayed the family in my obsession with Clyde Beatty and his circus. I cried myself to sleep that night and suffered through the next day at school trying to cover for him. This was a deep wound.

On Friday, Dad and Jim picked me up when school was out. They said they were taking me to Riverside to buy me a present at Sears because they felt sorry for me in my disappointment. We went to the sports section in the basement of Sears, Roebuck and Company on Main Street, and Dad bought me a new softball and bat. Jim promised that he would teach me to play with this equipment because I was old enough now to begin practicing for the ball team at school. If they thought this was a good substitute for Clyde Beatty they were wrong.

Finally, I was smiling but still hurting. I could not shake the belief that I would never actually see my radio hero in action. The pain was bad, and I wasn't much comforted by their wish to relieve it. A bat and a ball couldn't take the place of Clyde Beatty.

We got back in the car and headed home. I didn't notice that the car was not going the usual route home—down Magnolia Avenue to La Sierra. Instead we were going home through Rubidoux, an alternate route through Pedley. I was trying to appreciate my new bat when I realized that we had turned into a large dusty vacant lot near Fontana. And there before me was a tent bigger than the one at camp meeting with flying banners and flags. There before my wondering eyes the big sign said, "The Clyde Beatty Circus!"

That afternoon was a highlight in my young life. My hero was in the ring with his lions and tigers, with his chair in hand, his whip snapping, and his pistol filled with blanks, ready to divert any frisky animal. I could hardly speak. Dad and Jim had talked over my disappointment. Dad had calmed down and finally reconsidered in favor of my feelings. To me this was significant and registered big.

I have often thought about that day. There are days that remain in the heart of an adult's memory of his childhood, and that was a high day in my life. I also learned something about Dad that day. He was a man of religious conviction, but he was a man of reasonable moderation. He became as much my hero as that man in the ring. We never discussed that day. It was simply sealed in my heart as an indication of my father's love. Years later I reminded my brother of this story. He had forgotten it. I hadn't.

COMPETITION AND RIVALRY

Our prophet made a distinction between the simple exercise of playing ball and those highly competitive games that engendered rivalry. Rivalry crowded out the missionary spirit,[1] it was selfish and had no place in God's plan,[2] it was cruel[3] and if indulged between schools it would "banish the angels" from those institutions.[4]

So, we never played other schools in any sporting events. Our intramurals did include a team on the college campus, but that was the closest we came to playing other schools. Since that was in-house apparently that was alright. I really didn't think that with my sports record I would face any challenge on this matter. How does one go about correcting a miserable reputation? My reputation: "last chosen."

---

1. White, *Testimonies for the Church,* Vol. 7, p. 173.
2. White, *Education,* 226.
3. White, *Testimonies for the Church,* Vol. 4, p. 222.
4. Ibid., 7:173–174.

About the time of graduation from elementary school, my close friend got interested in following major league baseball. Even though the Cleveland Indians were swept by the New York Giants in the 1954 World Series, he became an Indians fan anyway. His interest sparked a corresponding chord in me to pick a team. It seemed natural to pick the Chicago White Sox since I had been born in a Chicago suburb.

We both chose our favorite players. Mine was Nellie Fox, the all-star Sox second baseman destined for the baseball Hall of Fame. I saved my money and bought a Wilson Nelson Fox Personal Model baseball glove. It cost a whopping $35.00—a small fortune for a struggling kid like me in 1955. But that glove would last me through graduate school.

His hero was Herb Score, a young pitching sensation for the Indians. As a result, my friend began pitching in his backyard to his brother. He bought current issues of *Sport* magazine and cut out the full-page color pictures of major league baseball players and mounted them on his bedroom wall. I did the same. I picked southpaw Billy Pierce of the White Sox as my pitching model.

We both began pitching even though we didn't have any team to play for since our school only played softball. The new baseball season of 1956 opened with our knowing the backgrounds and current stats of all the significant players on our respective teams. Dad bought me an electric baseball game from the Sears, Roebuck catalogue, and my friend and I began a season of games between the Indians and the White Sox. It was our last hurrah before the total invasion of puberty. A year later we would have no more interest in the electric game. Summers had been filled with TV studios, making a movie (that never happened), and now obsession with baseball.

Somewhere during this time Elvis Presley became the rage of teenagers and rock and roll was born. All of this had little to do with religion and it was as though I had put religion on the shelf for a while. I was learning that we were to consider some things sacred and other things secular. Right now, the secular was taking priority.

This interest in baseball was bound to produce some positive results. Baseball had become my sport. I knew the players on my team. I could talk baseball better than do schoolwork. But I still had work to do to learn to play it well.

After an unpleasant argument with Dad I convinced him to buy me a pair of baseball shoes ("cleats" we called them). Ever-cautious Dad was dubious. He warned me that I could break my leg if I didn't learn how to run and slide carefully. He was against the idea. I assured him that no injury would ever occur. I would learn to slide safely. I would be very careful and ultra-responsible. And he finally accepted my promise.

I spent the summer before academy playing ball with my neighbor and his brothers—fielding grounders, batting, pitching. By the spring of my freshman year I tried out for the softball team—for right field—and I made it. Coach Schneider called me aside and said, "Eddie, right field is not your position. You should be playing second base." I couldn't believe it. I had only dreamed I was Nellie Fox. Now coach was showing confidence in my growth—a confidence I did not have. Despite his encouragement the season opened with me in right field. But I knew Coach had greater plans for me and I wanted to impress him.

We were playing a college team when I took my first time at bat—base on balls—I was on. The next batter flied out. I was stuck on first base. We were playing on the college field that had no fences. But the outfield was defined by a high bank covered with ice plant. Once a ball got past a fielder it would careen its way to the base of the bank with fielders chasing it. This could give runners an advantage.

The next batter hit through the infield and the outfielder lost the ball momentarily in the ice plant in center field. Seeing my chance, I ran around second base traveling as fast as my stubby legs could take me—a race against time (and ice plant). If I had looked over my shoulder I could have seen that the fielder had found the ball, and his throw would beat me by at least five steps. My sense told me to slide. This was my first slide of the season, the first in such big competition and the first in my new cleats. I hit the ground, leg forward, aimed at the bag. The hand of the third baseman came down hard on my leg before I hit the bag. I was out. But making the out was incidental.

In my haste and inexperience, I had misjudged the location of third base. I was a step ahead of myself. My cleats caught in the bag and I lay in pain on the ground. I could not get up. When I was finally helped up by the coaches, I could not walk. Carried to the dugout I saw a most fearsome sight: my ankle was beginning to swell. My left leg was in serious trouble.

That was the end of my softball career for that school year—only one at-bat, but a walk—so I was zero for zero. My greater fear was what Dad's reaction would be. His warning words and fierce objections to those baseball shoes came back to me like a nightmare on Knoefler Drive. Coach called Dad. He came to the field. He took me to the doctor. My leg was in a cast for the next six weeks. Dad just smiled. There was nothing to say. He was right. And Dad was never a braggart. All that concerned him at this point was that I was cared for.

"Those things happen," he said finally. His behavior was my model. I saw the roguish twinkle in Dad's eye.

REBELLION

School was out. The leg was set with a walking cast. That summer was not lost. It became a very productive time. I didn't go out much, so Dad provided me with work in house and put me on a salary. I learned the type case and became a type setter in Dad's home print shop. To pass the time I listened to classical records Dad had bought at the grocery store—type case setting to the background of Bach, Beethoven, and Brahms. I fell in love with the classics.

Looking back, pre-adolescence was the age to rebel. So, I had become lippy in seventh grade. And, I could make people laugh. I could talk back and quick quip. Sarcasm became an easy art. For many adults, middle school kids are not their favorite members of the human race. But junior high teachers are educated to deal with those behaviors at this stage of our development, and we had a very understanding seventh-grade teacher. We nudged and shoved at the limitations placed on us by our smothering religious faculty.

My spectrum of rebellion was not very wide. One of my friends and I boarded a city bus one Monday night. We told our parents we were going shopping in Riverside. That was a half-truth. Monday was the night all the stores stayed open until 9:00 pm and this provided the perfect alibi. We planned to sneak off to a movie. Other than the newsreels Dad used to take us to in Los Angeles before TV took over the news, I had never set foot in a cinema.

Getting caught could result in expulsion from Church school. I didn't know what Dad would do if he ever found out. But we felt compelled to rebel and this was a simple form. I remember the name of the movie—"All That Heaven Allows," with Rock Hudson, but my conscience struck me so deeply that I cannot recall one scene or relate any of the plot line. I have since seen it on cable, without one frame of *déjà vu*. The exhilaration was in doing this evil act.

One morning, during my sophomore year, we came to school and the junior class had committed vandalism. Bales of hay were smoldering around the quad as though someone had been performing animal sacrifices. No one was hurt. Little damage was done. But the sophomores began plotting to outdo the juniors.

The next night several members of the class invaded the campus, hoisted the chairs lining the quad onto the roof over the walkways. When students arrived the next morning, there was no place to sit in the quad. Some of the chairs were put on the chapel roof with its four-foot ledge. Those chairs were never found as they were not visible from the ground.

Months later someone tipped off faculty that the chairs were on the roof of the chapel. The administration found them and had them tossed over the side—smashing them in the thirty-foot fall to the ground. They were never used again but were hauled off to the dump.

I had only watched. I had not participated. And I had an alibi. Although I had heard that something was up I had been at Mr. Parker's home that night getting help on my algebra assignment for the next day. This protracted incident put the class of 1959 in a collective bad light and the administration was laying for anyone implied in such activities. No one was charged. No one talked. But that placed the whole class under suspicion.

More class struggles began. Discipline broke down. The principal gave up trying to have spiritually charged chapels three times a week and instead dismissed us to run around the campus during that time. Finally, he resigned. Students became more daring. And by the end of the year the school was in chaos.

A CHANGE OF SCENERY

My brother Jim, who had recently returned from military service, was now a senior ministerial student at the college and sensed that I was in with the wrong crowd and things could get progressively worse for me. By today's standards this wrong crowd might seem innocent. There were no drugs. If there was sexual activity I was oblivious to it. I was barely aware of who smoked or drank. None of my friends did, that I knew of. Some students smuggled gum into class.

Jim was right and shown by the next school year when the class of 1959 was decimated. A new principal, with a reputation of running the office like a prison warden, went through the records. No one doubted that the school needed this. Only half the members of my class were readmitted to school the next year! But by then I had been whisked away to a boarding school in the state of Washington. My baseball friend had also been raptured, but to a boarding school in Oregon. Jim had convinced Dad to let me go with him for a year to attend Auburn Academy, near Seattle.

"Eddie needs a change of scenery," Jim told Dad. "He has been here too long. Things are not going well at La Sierra Academy." By the time Jim graduated from La Sierra College in 1957, with a Bachelor of Arts degree in theology, he was married with two children. And he received an invitation to teach at Tacoma Junior Academy (grades 7–10), in the city where he had lived for several months while serving in the U. S. Army at Ft. Lewis. He felt that I would get a new lease on life in my new temporary setting.

Auburn was a Church-operated, secondary, co-educational boarding high school, located halfway between Tacoma and Seattle. Here was an Adventist haven of religion, out in the forest, with buildings built in anticipation of the second coming, i.e., wood frame, constructed on a semi-permanent basis back in 1919. Stone, brick, and glass, indicating a major behavioral change in contemporary Adventist eschatological thinking as well as denominational lack of wealth, have since replaced the entire campus.

Jim thought he might have trouble talking me into going to a boarding school, but it turned out that it was Dad who opposed the plan. Dad had moved his whole family to La Sierra partly to ensure his supervision over our lives, and now if he approved Jim's plan both his sons would be leaving at the same time—and the youngest son was not satisfactorily educated yet, probably not thoroughly indoctrinated.

Jim prevailed. Dad gave in. The arguments were straight out of Jim's classes in college—convincing, verifiably reasoned, logical, with a dose of fear and guilt mixed in. But now Jim had to convince me. When he mentioned it, I froze. How do I meet new people? As a shy person I did not relish the thought of making new friends. Now I would be cast into a whole aquarium of new fish, none of whom I knew or understood.

I was terrified. But Jim wisely introduced me to a most persuasive thought: we would be together for a year. He knew how much I idolized him. In Tacoma he would be only twenty miles away. He and Lucille and the kids would visit me on the weekends. I could go to Tacoma during my weekend leaves and vacations. He had observed my tears when he left La Sierra to serve those two years in the army. He was aware of my attachment.

That argument clinched it. I was in. I was working at the honey company across the street from my home that summer. It was a motley group—most of the workers were my age. For the most part this group was foul-mouthed and fun loving. I learned vocabulary that would later make me blush. And we egged each other on. I was mostly a follower, and my only hope of escaping this kind of life would be college or the army.

Yet despite these associates (who were more liberating than bad) I really had no doubts that I would go to college. Here was the one major decision I had made, though I had no idea what career path I might focus on. I had no direction except that it would be within the territorial boundaries that Adventism had set. I never really doubted that I was a religious man who would be an Adventist all my life.

I was searching for recognition and establishing my identity. Following others and succumbing to peer pressure are both part of the developmental stage we call adolescence but much of my identity was already established in my religious heritage. The protective custody was paying off even as I floundered and cast about. Nevertheless, for now life was $.65 an hour hammering frames for beehives, moving apiaries from Fallbrook to Bakersfield, and extracting honey in the warehouse.

Jim recognized the quicksand effect that associates could have. He was committed to the belief that your friends can take you places you didn't plan to go. And while he was supportive of my friends and me, he thought I needed a change to a new environment. So, the next chapter in my life was set. In the dry heat of Southern California, in the middle of July 1957, we headed for Tacoma. Jim's 1950 green Hudson was packed to the roof with all our belongings, plus wife, 2-year-old daughter, 6-month-old son, and 15-year-old brother, pulling the longest tandem trailer that U-Haul rented.

The Adventist custody of my life had just won another round and I was in for some major decisions in a much safer place—a place where I could ponder my life and where it was going. Auburn would solve my developing waywardness, clean up my language, and validate my decision to be a religious man for life. They were counting on that. By the time I graduated from Auburn I should know who I was and where I was going in life.

CHAPTER SIX

Major Life Decisions

"Man ought to know that in the theater of human life,
it is only for Gods and angels to be spectators."
—Francis Bacon

AUBURN ACADEMY

As the thin-finger rays of a new day stretched over the unusually calm waters of Puget Sound, the Green Tornado, Jim's 1950 Hudson, pulled into Tacoma, Washington, a city oddly reminiscent of a small-scale version of San Francisco. The hilly terrain of Tacoma made beginning drivers nervous, especially if they were maneuvering with a manual shift. A left turn from the main drag could result in what appeared to be a street heading straight up in the air.

I immediately loved the little city. I had been there only once before when we visited Jim and his family during his army stay. Landmarks stood out in my mind—a circus toy store (where I had seen model airplanes and cars), the *Top of the Ocean* Restaurant (where we had had fresh salmon), the Narrows Bridge over the Puget Sound and Brown and Haley Candy Company (where they made *Almond Roca* and *Mountain Bar*). That company was the sponsor of the *Amos 'n Andy* TV show. Tacoma was a cool place.

We met the Zachrisons (name spelled with an "h")—no relation to us that we knew of, though Dad had traced our heritages back to Sweden. Jim and Lucille had lived next door to them during those army days. The Tacoma Central Seventh-day Adventist Church was built on a narrow triangular-shaped piece of ground on a plateau above the business district. In 1957 it was new, and it hardly looked like a traditional church. I thought it looked contemporary. Others suggested that it looked more like a bus station. That thought stayed with me. It had the steepest balcony I had ever sat in.

A few blocks away stood an old, two-story, three-bedroom house overlooking a main street leading downtown. This house recently purchased by the local Church for a community services center would serve as home for the new teacher and his family. In two months, my school would start, but until then I would be staying with Jim and his family in Tacoma about thirty miles from Auburn. My quarters were on the top floor adjacent to the attic. I discovered that I had not completely overcome my fear of the dark in this rickety old house with its darkness and creepy sounds. I toyed with the thought that ghosts lived in the adjoining attic.

The summer was not one of inactivity. We attended camp meeting at Auburn. I landed a short-term job at Sunset Lake, the new summer camp being developed by the Washington Conference. I lived in an army surplus tent there. Finally, I spent a week at Auburn when Jim served as the dean of boys in Manous Hall, the freshman boys' dorm, as teachers attended in-service meetings. During that time, I worked in the academy cannery. We were canning peaches. I had never itched so badly in my life—peach fuzz.

This last week of the summer in the dorm helped me overcome some of my shyness. I made friends easier than I thought I could. I learned that many students coming in the fall would experience the same strangeness I felt for they too would be new. Auburn commonly enrolled students entering their third year of high school since local churches in the Washington Conference operated several junior academies (K thru 10). The playing field would be more even than I had anticipated. So, I wouldn't be the only replant pulled up by my roots and thrust into a new garden. Misery loves company!

Even with new friends I felt the homesickness creeping in on me. A year is a decade when you haven't spent time away from home other than going to a ten-day summer camp. The whole enterprise was beginning to seem like a mistake. When people greeted me at camp meeting I told them I was just "checking things out." Then I would write Mom and Dad encouraging them to move to Tacoma. I was living loneliness.

GETTING ORIENTED

The new school year began with work assignments. Everyone on campus was required to hold an academy job. For one thing boarding school was expensive, but also the Adventist philosophy of education required manual labor—where some skilled training in a trade could be achieved. The juniors and freshmen worked mornings and attended classes in the afternoon; seniors' and sophomores' schedules were the reverse of that.

Since I was not yet sixteen, I could not work in the Academy Wood Products, the furniture factory run by academy personnel, where the wages were the highest of any jobs on campus and involved operating or working around machinery. The factory paid $1.00 an hour. So, I worked on the maintenance crew for $.42 an hour, a wage that was generously raised to $.45 an hour after several weeks of reliable service. Adventist schools commonly had industries—always a farm and often several unique trades. The farm tied us to our agrarian roots, even though very few students worked there.

In addition to the furniture factory, Auburn had its own cannery, boiler room, maintenance department and grounds crew. The dormitories provided clerical work and dean's assistantships (called "monitors"). Teachers and administrators also had students on their payrolls. But the highest paying jobs on campus were still in the Academy Wood Products with its five departments—the yard, the mill room, the assembly room, the finishing room and the shipping room. The largest division was the mill room where the rough lumber was ripped, planed, glued, and shaped into the various parts for natural wood furniture distributed to major retailers in the northwest.

The maintenance crew was not exciting. We kept the physical plant in working order from repairing doors and replacing windows to constructing a new sewage plant for the school.

IN LOCO PARENTIS **AND THE ATTACK ON MUSIC**

Auburn Academy was a self-contained unit. The sawdust from the factory was burned in the boiler room to heat the buildings on campus. I noticed immediately the efficiency and the talent of the faculty and staff. They seemed never to be off duty. I was impressed that theirs was a work of love.

Life in this Adventist commune was controlled and sedate. We arose at 5:30 a.m. to Sousa marches piped-in through loudspeakers in dormitory hallways. This helped us get in the mode to wake up, shower, and hustle to worship in the academy chapel. Then on to breakfast in the dining hall on the lower floor of South Hall, the girl's dormitory, directly across from Gibson Hall, the boy's residence hall housing mainly upper division students. And finally, to classes or work at 7:30 a.m.

Auburn Academy, along with other Adventist boarding schools, was home away from home—*in loco parentis* [a society in place of parents]. The *Academy Catalog* made the importance of order crystal clear.

> Experience has shown that the purposes for which Auburn Academy was founded are best attained when the students, whose parents do not reside in the neighborhood of the Academy, live in the dormitories. It is the aim of the faculty to provide a home where kindness and courtesy reign. These graces, together with regularity and punctuality in the home duties, are important factors in the student's education. Loud talking, running up and down stairs,

entering rooms without the consent of the occupant, scuffling in the building are out of order.[1]

In loco parentis involved supervision—dress standards, what to bring, what not to bring to school, what led to dismissal, what food was served in the dining hall or allowed in the dorm, mail regulations—where to pick it up, when it was delivered—all the regulations were listed.

Of interest to many of us were the restrictions on personal items and values, especially music. No radios, phonographs, television sets or cheap music were allowed at the school.[2] If any of these items were brought to dormitory rooms, and we were caught with them, we were subject to expulsion from school until the item was returned home.

By the 1978–79 academy student handbook these items had become subject to confiscation. They would become the property of the school and would not be returned.[3] Confiscation was the rule in 1957 as well, but not stated quite so clearly. The rationale was sensible: "A full program of work, study, recreation, and worship is planned for all students."[4]

Other forbidden items included motorcycles, automobiles, motorbikes, firearms, air guns, firecrackers, oil lamps, candles, comic books, unwholesome literature, appliances and inflammable chemicals. Most of this made sense; no one wanted the dorms to burn down. But many found the rule about music invasive and something to ignore or challenge. Music and teenagers was a common courtship. Who could survive adolescence without popular music?

Music has always been a major issue for religious people. In the 1960s and 1970s it was not uncommon for an Academy Week of Prayer to include a record burning session when students brought their rock records, stacked them in the middle of the campus and lit a bonfire to state their new resolve to get rid of the devil's music. This never occurred at Auburn while I was a student there but later for a time this was expected for a genuine spiritual revival.

Sister White had set forth warnings regarding the evil in worldly music as differentiated from good music: "Music was made to serve a holy purpose, to lift the thoughts to that which is pure, noble, elevating, and to awaken in the soul devotion and gratitude to God. . . . Music forms a part of God's worship in the courts above, and we should endeavor in our songs to praise, to approach as nearly as possible to the harmony of the heavenly choirs."[5]

---

1. Auburn Academy *Catalogue* 1958–1959, p. 11.
2. Ibid., p. 13.
3. AAA *Student Handbook* 78–79, p. 6.
4. Ibid.
5. White, *The Story of Patriarchs and Prophets*, 294.

> Angels are hovering around yonder dwelling. The young are there assembled; there is the sound of vocal and instrumental music. Christians are gathered there, but what is that you hear? It is a song, a frivolous ditty, fit for the dance hall. Behold, the pure angels gather their light closer around them, and darkness envelops those in that dwelling. The angels are moving from the scene. Sadness is upon their countenances. Behold, they are weeping. This I saw repeated a number of times all through the ranks of Sabbath keepers, and especially in ——. Music has occupied the hours which should have been devoted to prayer.
>
> Music is an idol which many professed Sabbath-keeping Christians worship. Satan has no objection to music, if he can make that a channel through which to gain access to the minds of the youth. Anything will suit his purpose that will divert the mind from God, and engage the time which should be devoted to His service.... When turned to good account, music is a blessing, but it is often made one of Satan's most attractive agencies to ensnare souls. When abused, it leads the unconsecrated to pride, vanity, and folly.[6]

At school popular music could divert young people from their purpose for being there. Radios could be disruptive—study time, devotional time, tight schedules, could all be subverted. But for our overseers it was more than that. It was a religious issue. We were taught that Satan knew what emotions to press with his music. Music sung or performed in night clubs and bars had no place in a true Christian's life. "Music should have beauty, pathos, and power."[7]

Most popular music was *dance* music. And dancing had no place in a Christian lifestyle. Dancing led to young boys performing physical examinations on young girls, according to our Bible teacher. Girls be warned about what the boys have in mind for you! He constantly gave a word to the wise. Our principal had given a careful justification in chapel for the music department's purchase of a Hammond organ—apparently an instrument more closely identified with jazz and dance music.

In 1957 Elvis Presley was the prevalent teen idol and was well on his way to becoming the "king of rock and roll." Some of us had fun impersonating him as we had seen him perform on *The Ed Sullivan Show*. Rather than fight my attraction to Elvis' music, Dad bought me a couple of Elvis' records. It was a phase I would travel through and mature out of but at the time it was hard to explain the effect this music had on me. I just knew that I felt good when I listened to it. At the honey company the radio had been going all day on KPOP, the pop station in Los Angeles. So, I had come to know all the "Top Ten." Auburn would be a famine.

When a pastor in the area told me, "Elvis is a drip," I was not impressed. I didn't challenge him. That would have been inappropriate. But he cut off his credibility with

---

6. White, *Testimonies for the Church*, 1:506.
7. Ibid., 4:7.

me. The ream of material on music put out by the Church was easy to evaluate. If it had rhythm, beat and was popular it was probably bad.

In 1959 the Adventist *Church Manual* listed the dangers of music such as jazz or swing and lyrics expressing foolish or trivial sentiments. These types of music would be shunned by persons of "true culture."[8] In 1972 the General Conference Fall Council voted that,

> The Christian will not sing songs that are incompatible with the ideals of truth, honesty and purity. He will avoid elements that give the appearance of making evil desirable or goodness appear trivial. He will try to avoid compositions containing trite phrasing, poor poetry, nonsense, sentimentality, or frivolity which lead away from the counsel and teachings found in scripture and in the Spirit of Prophecy [Sister White's writings].[9]

The Fall Council statement continued,

> He will consider music such as blues, jazz, the rock idiom, and similar forms as inimical to the development of Christian character, because it opens the mind to impure thoughts and leads to unholy behavior. Such music has a distinct relationship to the permissiveness of contemporary society. The distortion of rhythm, melody, and harmony as employed by these styles and their excessive amplification dulls the sensibilities and eventually destroys the appreciation for that which is good and holy.[10]

This statement added the words blues, rock idiom and similar forms to the previous position. In the *Church Manual* of 1990, the statement was reinforced.

> Any melody partaking of the nature of jazz, rock, or related hybrid forms, or any language expressing foolish or trivial sentiments, will be shunned by persons of true culture.[11]

The academy adhered closely to these standards spelled out in Adventist position statements. Yet despite this, radios were hidden in students' dorm rooms and they were sometimes found and confiscated. If you had smuggled in your radio you stood a good chance of never seeing it again.

Students had secretly wired dormitory rooms with switches and speaker wires under baseboard moldings. Some ingenious set ups had switches located in the back of the main drawers of the desk so that a student could be studying and at the first knock on the door simply shut the drawer and the power to the radio went off. One had to be alert because a monitor or dean could enter the room at any time without

---

8. General Conference of SDA, *Church Manual* (1959), 208.
9. General Conference of SDA, *Guidelines toward a Seventh-day Adventist Philosophy of Music*. 6.
10. Ibid.
11. *Church Manual* (1990), 146.

warning. Once rules were made some creative minds set about to get around them even if they had a "religious" base.

One guy I had just met had a little crystal set with an earphone. After trying to listen to anything on it I surmised that the torture of trying to hear something was motivated more by the thrill of breaking a rule. Hearing a popular song on a crystal set was a miraculous event but hardly worth the bother. Radios in those pre-transistor days, even portable ones, were so large that trying to hide them was hard. Despite that some tried, but periodic sweeps of the dormitory rooms during times when we were away at work or in class helped to discourage us from becoming too daring. Second- and third-time offenders could be sent home.

THE ART OF BOARDING

Prohibitions were all a part of in loco parentis *where deans and teachers were the protective adults in our boarding society.* Conformity to these rules was considered critical for our success. They differed only in content from any other boarding schools in that they reflected the standards of the Church and helped define a religious person. The goal of the school was to produce religious people—a group of people preparing for eternal life in an earth made new. The aim was to produce as perfect an environment as possible for Christian young people.

South Hall housed the dormitory girls in its spacious three stories. Manous Hall, the dormitory in poorest repair, was the freshman and sophomore boys' dorm. Gibson Hall housed the junior and senior class boys. There were exceptions to these boarding arrangements. New boys were often put in Manous Hall. Juniors got to pick rooms in Gibson for their senior year.

I ended up in Gibson by default. The dean thought that I was the brother of Leonard Zachrison, a senior in room 32. So, he put us together. And it was a choice room, right up in the middle front, on the second floor. A bonus was that in the winter, when the leaves had fallen off the trees, one could look directly across the campus at the girls' dorm.

The dean's mistake was natural. Leonard and I were both from Tacoma and how many people with this name could there be in the state of Washington? Our names were spelled differently, but who would pick that up? To distinguish us apart Len's friends began calling him *Zach Q* (pronounced *Zatch Que*) thus shedding the old name, Zach (pronounced *Zack*) that he'd had for years. In my 1958 yearbook he wrote, "I'll always remember you as the guy that changed my name from Zack to 'Zach.' If you hadn't come along with the 'k' in your last name, I'd still have the former handle."

I remember Zatch Q more for his science brain. Study halls (from 7:30–9:30 p.m.) when we were all confined to our rooms, were never quiet at Room 32. Zatch Q carried a round slide rule in his pocket. The guys in the dorm would sneak into our room for help in math, physics and chemistry assignments. Len also contributed to my religious character. He said that one of his pet peeves was people who didn't close their eyes during prayer. "Whether you care about God or not," he said, "you could at least show him that much respect."

At the edge of the campus, close to Muckleshoot Ridge and Inspiration Point, was the Administration (Ad) Building, built in 1919, where most of our classes were held. The library was housed in a wing attached to the back of the Ad Building. These main buildings with their bright white wood siding glowing in the sunlight, along with the maintenance building, music building, and torpedo shaped gymnasium made up the campus proper.

The Ad Building was especially interesting. Any tour of the building seemed to reveal new hallways, nooks and crannies that housed administration, classrooms, seminar rooms, bathrooms, ASB offices, the academy chapel, and some teachers' offices. None of this was the new day academy I was used to at La Sierra, but there was tradition connected to each building that soon made me feel proud of the thirty-eight-year history of this school.

I understood this campus to represent denominational thinking—eschatological at its core. We were continually told that this movement, as we liked to call ourselves, was born in prophecy. William Miller's prophecy of the end of the world was still the touchstone of reality for us. When the movement became a sect and later a denomination we would never lose this notion that we were a people of prophecy. It all made perfect sense to me.

This idea was our identity—the Bible had prophesied that

> [12] "Here is a call for the endurance of the saints, *those who keep the commandments of God and the faith of Jesus*." (Rev 14:12. Emphasis supplied)

These would be the final instruments God would use to preach the last warning message of Christ's soon coming. We had no difficulty identifying our group and thought no one else who cared should have any trouble either. The commandments were the Ten Commandments, and how many churches kept the fourth commandment—the seventh-day Sabbath? It was simple logic and we thought that all of this should be clear to those who were led by the Spirit in their search for The Truth.

This predictive message would contain a strong moral directive to return to God's law (every one of the ten). This directive would be a legally based, warning of the judgment that had begun in heaven in 1844. Angels bringing a threefold message that included warnings about apostasy and phony spiritual powers as well as instructions to preach the everlasting gospel (the Adventist message) would represent it. And the warning was that its apostasy was to be proclaimed throughout the land.

> [8] "Another angel, a second, followed, saying, 'Fallen, fallen is Babylon the great, she who made all nations drink the wine of her impure passion.'" (Rev 14:8)

So, we pored over the prophecies to be aware of the work of Babylon, which we were taught was the Roman Catholic Church.

THE NATURE OF ADVENTIST SPIRITUALITY

Weekends on campus were devoted to worship appointments. Friday night started with Seminar, a voluntary devotional meeting where students led out and presented short religious talks. No attendance record was kept but we were strongly encouraged to attend and participate. After Seminar came Vespers, a required meeting planned by the faculty. Following Vespers we attended prayer bands that were planned by the individual class pastors. Prayer bands were voluntary. On Sabbath morning we were required to attend Sabbath School and Church Worship. In the afternoon we had the young people's meeting that usually ended around sundown, the close of the Sabbath. Our attendance at that meeting was also required.

One Friday night Vespers was especially memorable. All started out normally—song service, prayers, scripture reading, special music, hymn. After the introductions of the evening's participants by the boys' dean and the faculty member in charge of the meeting, we were told that this evening's meeting would involve the playing of an audiotape recording. It was a controversial message that might be spurious. However, because it seemed to agree with many of the last-day ideas of our Church it was probably worth listening to. It could be true.

We were then warned that there had been quite a bit of agitation wherever the tape had been played. For a precaution the dean let us know that we would be safe—that the faculty had locked the doors to the chapel and had posted guards at each entrance to the building in case priests in the area decided to storm the meeting. This possibility of religious intervention added a sense of urgency and excitement to the meeting. By now we were all eyes and ears; the dean clearly had our attention. Coffee could not have been more stimulating than these exciting notifications.

The story on the tape unfolded dramatically as we sat glued to our chapel seats. The speaker was allegedly a former nun in France. She was telling her painful story of abuse and betrayal. She told of her life in closed monasteries and convents. She was trapped. She could never leave the confines of this convent for she had taken an oath to stay there for the rest of her life. She told of births and abortions and priestly sexual abuse of the nuns. The nuns were slaves of the priests, she said. Nuns who resisted were subject to abuse.

The recording went on for over an hour. It was a dreadful account of abuse and crime and we *knew* it had to be true. It validated what we believed that every Catholic Church in Europe (and probably in America as well), had a torture chamber in the basement preparing to persecute Sabbath-keepers during the "great time of Jacob's trouble" to come. Convents and monasteries had to be worse.

As we exited the chapel that night we looked for signs of papal presence, of crosses or some indications that priests had tried to break in and disrupt our meeting. But we had been protected from such interference. We would hear more warnings about the apostate priests and their activities, but nothing was ever so vivid as this night to remember.

Such warning message experiences revived and affirmed my apocalyptic mindset that the second coming was imminent. It was coming soon, and once probation for each human being on earth had closed, the final events would be rapid ones. We would need to run to the hills and hide in the caves as the Waldenses had done in the Alps during the Reformation. I didn't know of any caves around Auburn, but I knew of some tin mine shafts around Riverside and Corona in case time lasted and I got back home.

Regardless of where we lived, the apostate Protestant Sunday keepers would pursue us. But God would protect us. Their guns would fall apart when they attempted to shoot us, their swords would crack in half—providing we were in the elect. Sister White had related her vision that God's people (the Adventists) would be climbing up a high cliff, first as a large group, then smaller as the group fell apart. Many would take their eyes off their goal and little by little the group would be thinned out as adherents gave up their faith, lost their footing, and fell into oblivion, never making it to the promised land. It was all in *Early Writings*.[12]

I thought of the Black Cloud. What had happened to me? I had become jaded by time and eroded by sneaking off to see Rock Hudson and Jane Wyman and adopting the vulgar language of the honey company and listening to Elvis. I had slipped away, slowly but surely, from the purity of the goals my parents and the Church had set for me. But new fires were awakening in my heart to do better, to try harder to please God, to be ready for that persecution when God would protect his people. But the devil knew my weaknesses and propensities and he would inform my persecutors of them in that "great time of Jacob's trouble."

At the beginning of the movement the advent believers had taught that probation had already closed for anyone who had rejected the 1844 message and the only event left to occur was the *Parousia*. But as time dragged on, longer than anyone originally thought possible, the message opened to the world again and evangelism became a viable activity for the Church.

The Shut Door controversy had been an embarrassment for many years. Our enemies had insisted on reminding us of this theological mistake, which they interpreted as an example of our arrogance and error. Nonetheless, with this idea of a true Church prophesied in Daniel and Revelation, came a sense of specialness that exists to the present day. Adventists know their doctrines are right. They may fall away from the Church, but they still know that their doctrines are correct. This people of prophecy are the apple of God's eye.

---

12. White, *Early Writings*, 14.

Connected with the movement was our prophet who continually reminded us as last day disciples that time was short and that we had a task God was expecting us to accomplish. The simplest slogan of focus was "the Church is here to finish the work." Sister White wrote voluminously (estimated 25 million words) and the overtone of virtually everything she wrote was laced with eschatological ambiance. Even though she died in 1915, she was usually spoken of by believers in the present tense, as though she was still alive.

Here I was on an academy campus built in 1919 by people who were not sure they would even occupy the buildings as they were constructing them. Yet the campus had been occupied for thirty-eight years. This is eschatological behavior. Along with what I had learned at home, that we must never plan too far ahead without adding the words, *if time should last,* there was the confession in buildings that the second coming was near, and the campus was temporary. Contrast could be seen in European cathedrals that have a history of centuries, apparently built to last for eternity. Even architecture can preach theology.

CLASS ELECTIONS

Soon after school started we had class elections. Gary Wicklund and I worked on the maintenance crew. We had become friends by now. The meal practices had also helped to introduce some new people. We had to sit configured with three boys and three girls at the table for each meal. The boys were to seat the girls and act with culture as we ate together. There was no way to predict with whom we would sit because we came into the dining hall through segregated lines (male and female) at opposite sides of the large hall. Through this method each meal became an experience in meeting new people.

When elections were held all students were sent to classrooms where they nominated their officers. Gary and I were each nominated for president of our class. I had never held a leadership position in all my years at La Sierra, so this was a surprise, a shock and frightening. Being shy added to the ambivalence. When the vote was taken both Gary and I were eliminated. Another boy won the election.

The office of vice-president always went to a girl. Then the next office up for a boy was class pastor and again I was nominated. I could not believe my ears. I had given no indication that I had any religious stirrings. I attended required chapels and worships and church because I had no choice. But being pastor of the class was not something I wanted or hoped for. The vote was taken, and I won: I was the new junior class pastor.

When I found out what this job involved my heart ascended to my throat. Of all the offices this one was the most public. Every Friday night after Vespers the class pastor was to call his class together and lead out in a short devotional talk followed by Prayer Bands. Any spiritual or religious activities planned by or for the class were the responsibility of the class pastor.

I had immediate painful thoughts of being locked into a position I did not want for every Friday evening of the school year, and at this point in the school year that looked like a decade. Now every weekend would be ruined. Just the prospect of obsessing over this all week, every week, for the whole school year, was horrific. And yet the thrill of being elected to anything kept me from withdrawing my name. Upon reflection I have suspected it was the popularity factor that launched me into the chance to find this a positive experience. It held me in place for the immediate time.

A week later our class president-elect left school for reasons I never knew. The office of president was open again. In this religious school no one ran for office. There were school rules against politicking, and it was policy that running for office would create hard feelings and somehow stifle the will of God. Rivalry came in different forms. Only a person God chose, as indicated by the faculty, should hold any office in the Student Association. For the clubs and classes, the rules were relaxed in that nominations were allowed. So, when the class met again, and my name was entered once again, along with Gary's, I secretly hoped for a moment that I might be relieved of my weekly pastoral duties for the class.

But this time Gary won. And so, the year was set—Gary Wicklund, junior class president; Ed Zackrison, junior class pastor.

God's will? At the time I could see nothing but popularity involved. While I couldn't believe I was popular I was flattered at being chosen for anything and I set out to do my job for the year. It involved study, and this forced me to think seriously about what I might do with my life. I slowly came to believe that God may have been in this. Somehow, he may be nudging me to think about working more precisely for him.

I had never considered becoming a minister up to this point, but toward the end of that year at Auburn I began to think of this possibility more seriously. I would walk in the woods with friends and we would talk about where our lives would be in ten years, and we would sometimes even pray together. There was never talk of being anything but Adventist, but Christian experience gradually became an item for inquiry.

It was one thing to belong to a social group such as a denomination. It was something else to talk freely about personal spirituality and religious experience with your teenaged peers. I considered only certain individuals qualified to hear my feelings about some of these things. There were private thoughts that I had never expressed to anyone, but by the second month I began to ascertain who these safe people were.

There were some guys I observed as having the courage to demonstrate their comfort with expressing their religious feelings. I decided that these were the guys with whom I could safely seek peer discussions. First, there was a short, little guy with big glasses who walked with a gait that was identifiable in the moonlight. He spoke for Seminar and was not ashamed or embarrassed to volunteer his religious outlooks in class meetings and classes or in person. He was not afraid to let anyone know that he was a Christian. I thought him a little weird but never obnoxious and for me *weird* was a compliment. To me this really meant *courageous*.

When I wanted to talk about religion I always knew I could talk to him. We would walk in the woods and reach into the deep crevasses of our souls. It was invigorating. I had not had this kind of experience since my first-grade friend and I made our pact to meet in heaven.

Another safe student was a friend from Alaska. He was two classes behind me, but his spirituality was transparent. He was from Ketchikan, a place I had never heard of until I met him. He was a devotee of Alaska and loved to tell of its charm and beauty and to clear up any misunderstandings we had that people of Alaska all lived in igloos.

He loved dogs and was upset when the U.S.S.R. in its space program, sent up a canine cosmonaut to test out the environment of pre-manned space vehicles. He also worked with Gary and me on maintenance and became a lightning rod for me to freely shock with negative vitriol toward religion that I did not realize I had. In response he did not appear defensive but simply replied, "I don't see it quite like that." Both his expression and body language corroborated his faith. His demeanor was so disarming that I was led to think soberly about where I was going with my life. I doubt he knew that.

A third student who directed my thoughts was a girl. She was also a freshman and she became not only a spiritual influence in my life but my first romantic encounter. She was a village student and when we first started seeing each other we had some serious discussions.

"Seeing each other" was different than formal dating. Dating as such was not supposed to be a part of our life at Auburn but a couple of times a year we could invite a person to attend a banquet or special event. Those who were seeing each other sometimes ended up going together, even going steady.

If a steady couple got too public in their affectionate expression they were disciplined by being put "on social." If a couple was put on social, they were not allowed to talk to each other or be seen together for a period of time—usually a month. Hence the public contact between the sexes was restrained.

Those who crossed this line, in the opinion of the faculty and administration, could eventually be sent home. We crossed the line twice—were caught once holding hands and again sitting next to each other on the bus on a band trip. For the second infraction we landed 2000-word themes on Christian behavior based on the writings of Sister White. However, we were never caught doing anything so serious that we were put on social.

By the spring I had asked her to the spring banquet, and we began going steady. Wearing the Casa Loma (boy's club) pin told the public that you were going steady. I never really asked her. I was so bashful I just slipped her my pin during the movie at the banquet and my heart skipped when she came to school the next day wearing it. Girls were pinned. Boys weren't.

As a village student living at home with her parents, she was not held to as tight regimentation as a dormitory student. I was invited to her home by her parents one

Sabbath for lunch, and it was there that they challenged me, "Ed, you should be a minister." I looked at her. She nodded, "Yes, I agree."

These were passing comments by people who hardly knew me. They were in the same category as those who had elected me class pastor without the slightest knowledge of my history or past. Certainly, they weren't acquainted with my honey company vocabulary. But these incidents stuck in my mind as times when suggestion had power. The walks in the woods, the preparation for Friday night meetings, and now this suggestion all worked together to direct my thinking about the meaning of my life and the direction it should take.

TROUBLE IN PARADISE

My brother was a support to me, but I didn't discuss any of these deeper thoughts with him. I made no religious decisions my junior year, I just spent meaningful time in thought. I fulfilled my duties as the class pastor and prepared my little talks for Prayer Bands on Friday evenings. This was a year to work on other things like making new friends and improving my GPA. But that year at Auburn had given me a new frame of reference.

One Saturday night just as second semester was beginning my roommate and I drove the four miles into Auburn to a modern bowling alley. We parked and walked into the building. As we walked through the door, casing the place, two faculty members walked up behind us and said, "Let's go home, boys!"

Back on campus we attended the evening social event in the gym. We played games and participated in the grand march. The grand march was a modified Adventist version of a square dance, though it would never be called a "dance"—Adventists didn't dance. The rest of the evening was routine but when the word got out that we had been escorted back to the campus by faculty members, I felt a degree of notoriety.

By Monday morning the campus was dancing with the story of our celebrity status and we were invited to the green carpet of the principal's office. Our principal, a tall, thin man with rimless glasses and a full head of white hair, invited us to sit as he began his statement of concerns we had committed a very serious offense. I was beginning to sweat. I was so innocent. I had never so much as touched a bowling ball. Although I guess I had intended to.

The administrator explained that we were considered student leaders on our campus (I guessed that he knew I was the junior class pastor and my roommate was yearbook editor). But, he continued, this was our first offense, so he figured that the government committee would go easy on us. Yet we had to understand that our innocence had ended, and we must learn from this experience. He would put our punishment in writing as soon as the committee met. He then ushered us out. I went out shaken. I had only been on campus one semester and I was already in trouble. How would I tell Dad? What would I tell him?

When I got back to the dorm I began to compose my letter. I knew Dad would be contacted by the school and I hoped to get to him first. I wrote that I had gone to a bowling gymnasium in Auburn without knowing that it was contrary to the school rules (I thought "gymnasium" was a unique touch and had a less worldly ring to it). Somehow "bowling alley" sounded much more depraved, almost as bad as "bowling saloon!" I would also have to talk to Jim about all this. But I felt he might be more understanding than Dad.

The next day I got the letter from the administration, dated February 12, 1958. It reiterated that I was a young man of noble object in life and that what I had done was unexpected. I was to write a 2000-word theme on the subject of recreation, and it should be on the principal's desk by February 28, 1958. Because I had left the campus without permission I was also automatically campus bound for one month.

Whether I had even thought about rules being broken is problematic. Rules were rules and we were to abide by them. Although I had never seen "bowling" included in any school rules was immaterial. I didn't defend myself. We were, after all, responsible for knowing them. I was aware that Sister White had put "bowling saloons" on the naughty list.

I noted that the *Student Handbook* said nothing about bowling. But the next year's Academy Catalog specifically added bowling to the list of questionable amusements: "Attending theaters, dance halls, poolrooms, gambling places, bowling lanes, or any place of similar objectionable character" laid a person "open to dismissal" from school.[13] So now I had had an influence on the formulation of rules at Auburn Academy![14]

MAKING A MAJOR LIFE DECISION

When the 1957–58 school year came to an end I returned to La Sierra with a different outlook on life. It was clear when I went back to work at the honey company that I no longer felt at home there. I was thinking different thoughts.

My brother and his family left after that year. They went to the SDA Seminary in Washington, D.C., and I returned to Auburn for my senior year. Dad drove me to Union Station in Los Angeles, where I caught the train to Tacoma, Washington. Our trip into the big city was quiet. I remembered how we had taken this drive before when Dad had taken off a day of work to treat me in Hollywood to see some TV audience shows. That was a day to remember—equaling the afternoon at the Clyde Beatty Circus. I could remember everything we did that day.

---

13. *Auburn Academy Catalogue* (1958–1959), 7. Emphasis supplied.

14. Interestingly, twenty years later at the same school, the *Student Handbook* omitted mentioning bowling lanes as questionable, only "dancing, attending theaters, pool rooms, gambling places" were still on the list.

Dad was happy I was going back to Auburn although partings were difficult for him. He knew the positive effect this was having on me. But his tender heart was once again touched by the fact that we would be apart. Neither of us liked departures. As I settled down in my train seat, Dad stood outside on the station platform watching through my large train window. His eyes were misty; tears were forming as he thought of another year of separation. His face told the story. This picture was indelibly fixed in my mind as the train pulled out and I thought about it for most of my trip north.

Dad walked along the platform until it ran out and then he just kept his eyes fixed until I was out of sight. From my window I could see him waving, freely expressing his emotion. This was vintage Dad—when Jim left on his honeymoon or to graduate school or on vacation we usually drove behind him for several miles to bid one last good-bye.

Many years later I would be reminded of Dad's wave as I watched Mom wave from her hospital window just six hours before she died. Life includes those profound waves of love and our sympathetic memory preserves them. That year at Auburn would be one of outward commitments. I was elected Casa Loma (boys' club) president and ASB treasurer, and each of these positions strengthened my self-confidence. But it was that previous year as junior class pastor that had had the most effect on my considering certain directions for my life.

Each year the school administration set aside three weeks designated as *Weeks of Prayer*. During two of these weeks (fall and spring) visiting ministers would present a week of meetings each. The third week (winter) was the Student Week of Prayer when Seminar students were the speakers.

During the Fall Week of Prayer, I made my decision to become a minister. Those coming forward in an altar call had to tell of their commitment to God. It was called a "testimony." I had feared this day. I had never gone forward in one of those "calls," and my shyness precluded ever giving a testimony.

So that autumn night was my first. I cannot remember that it was a good feeling. I just remember that it was a relief. Finally, to speak in front of my peers about my personal religious experience was something new. One might think that after a year as junior class pastor this would be easy, but those were formal duties, this was a personal statement—to some degree viewed as a life-time commitment. And it was impromptu.

Following that meeting I went to the Seminar sponsor, the Sabbath School advisor and the Student Week of Prayer committee to talk. I volunteered that whenever they needed a speaker or in case someone unexpectedly dropped out they could call me to fill in. I went back to my room and shook with an astonishing realization. What had I done? Where had my shyness gone—was it really gone, or had it simply lapsed into temporary hibernation? By the time I got back to my room the shyness had returned and my soul was vibrating.

During the second semester of my senior year I was asked to speak for the Sabbath morning Worship Service of the Student Week of Prayer. I was exhilarated. The fear of getting up in front was dropping away. I was an Adventist Christian and I was okay with that. I was a product of the protective custody of the Church. I was being what the Church had hoped I would be. I was being molded into the Adventist image of the ideal young person—a religious man.

I didn't understand the technical meaning of the gospel, but I knew some of the prophecies and I knew we were the "people of prophecy"—the only ones, probably, who really counted on this earth. And I could recite 250 memory verses and key texts on my Bible exam.

I knew that before the great controversy between Christ and Satan was over all who would be translated (taken to heaven without seeing death) would be Adventists. It was a good feeling, this feeling of illusion. But for me it was not make-believe. It was directional and incisive. I was part of the remnant people and there was a chance now that I would be ready for Jesus when he returned for his saints.

Little did I realize at the time how wrong these very feelings were—the theology behind them was devastating and destructive, but I was oblivious. Yet I believed what I was being taught. This is the insidious nature of toxic faith. It first poisons the thinking. Especially in youth it can substitute a false vision. But theologically and emotionally it then injects the last noxious perspective—legalism. While my soul was yearning to be free, it was also being traumatized by the fear of hell. In all the Weeks of Prayer I had enjoyed, or tolerated, the same sinister viewpoint had permeated. Are you ready for Jesus to come? So, I knew that whatever happened I would be to blame.

The emphasis on my faithfulness to God was all I ever heard in those first seventeen years of my life. I had not absorbed any emphasis on God's faithfulness to me. And therein lay the insidiousness of legalistic, toxic religion. Years later when I would make a banner for my Sabbath School class at the university that read "If we are faithless, he will remain faithful," I would be approached by a university professor who would take me to task for that statement. I pointed out to him that it was a verse quoted verbatim from 2 Tim 2:13. He was silenced.

He said he did not even know that text was in the Bible. But neither did I until I stumbled over it in my personal Bible study one day. That was not an emphasis in either of our upbringings as Adventists. It even seemed heterodox to us. We had both been taught emphatically that God loves those who work hard to please him. Whether that was what our teachers had intended to teach us was immaterial. That is what we both thought we had learned.

Even in my gradual awakening to God I knew one thing: I was not ready for Jesus to come. The toxicity of this emphasis was to tell me that I was the master of my fate, and that translated into my working out my own salvation, which meant I had to please God for him to save me. And that meant keeping the Ten Commandments faithfully. Most of all this was unconscious but when it entered my consciousness, at each call made by a preacher at a Week of Prayer, it was painful. Rather than answering the sense of undoneness and guilt with the gospel, I was continually bombarded with the notion of renewing my commitment to do better. I needed to pray more, harder, that Jesus would help me to be a better person.

This missed the point of the gospel that we are unable to please God. And rather than accept the claims of the gospel based in what Jesus had done for us, I was confronted with the false dilemma: either mysticism or legalism. I really didn't know there was another alternative. But what makes the dilemma "false" is that it rules out any other alternative than the two it asserts.

The whole message of the gospel was that Another had performed that pleasing work. This was too simple, too complicated, bordering on apostate teaching. What about all those nominal Christians who claimed to love God but broke the Sabbath every week?

But God works with us where we are. As I have grown and matured I am still amazed at the lack of grace and gospel in so much of my experience with organized religion. At that point in my life however, I was not ready for this insight. I was apparently right where God wanted me or the only place he could get me.

At graduation I bade my friends at Auburn goodbye and except for two or three of these friends I did not see any of them again for twenty years. Others I never saw again. I returned home as a rehabilitated Adventist young man ready for college with a clear mandate to become a minister. It was the first of several rehabilitations I would experience in my life.

I hit the ground running—I bought a Greek textbook three weeks before the new school year started.

CHAPTER SEVEN

College Years Set Life's Agenda

"Life would be infinitely happier if we could only be born at the age of eighty and gradually approach eighteen."

—MARK TWAIN

LA SIERRA COLLEGE

In 1959, La Sierra College was a small school of about 800 students. All its departments were modest by comparison to state colleges or even other private institutions. I would have preferred to attend Walla Walla College in the state of Washington because most of my graduating class from Auburn would be there. But financial circumstances did not allow that. Mainly, at La Sierra I would be living at home saving money. At graduation, Dad said he would think about my attending Walla Walla, but it was a whim of the moment. By the time we arrived home, he had decided I should stay at La Sierra.

I worked the summer on the grounds crew running the sprinklers on campus. Southern California has such a low rainfall that all the spacious college lawns needed manual watering. I completed a round of the campus each hour moving rain bird sprinklers. Eight rounds a day, six days a week—all summer.

Coming back to La Sierra was like moving to Auburn. Only about three or four of my old classmates from elementary and academy days went on to college at La Sierra so things were relatively new. But I was more confident now. Holding student leadership positions had helped. Knowing where I was going also gave me direction. Adventism set the agenda. I trusted that when I finished I would be hired by a Conference and serve the denomination as a pastor.

My model was Elder L. Calvin Osborn, pastor of the LSC Church. He was the most personable, understanding, empathetic and friendly minister I had ever known.

As a speaker, he reached my heart with his warm delivery and he met my need for encouragement and support. Over the four years I was at La Sierra College, there were many times when I went to Church discouraged and left with new vigor.

When I returned from Auburn, Elder Osborn was still the pastor, and I would listen to his sermon at the early service on the college radio station at 8:30 am, and then sit in the east balcony for the second service at 11:00 where I could watch his every gesture as well as taking notes. He introduced me to the concept that God is faithful to us before we show any interest in him. Each sermon carried hope. His messages were simple. and gospel centered. I began to feel assurance as my faith became more informed.

SCHOLARLY RELIGION

I began my freshman year at La Sierra with enthusiasm. I would pursue what I had been called to do. I started a filing system outlined in a book Jim had brought me from the Seminary. In fact, he helped me set up the file during his two-week visit before leaving with his family for the Caribbean where he was going as a missionary pastor. Everything I thought was important I filed: notes from Church, chapel talks, magazine articles and other religious materials. Some went on 3x5 cards, other stuff in the regular files. I typed out class notes and put them in notebooks.

I knew only a few people at school. Some teachers remembered my brother and called me "Jim." But I was at school to become a new person. I seldom saw old friends at college, because I was the only theology major among them. Several of my friends from the honey company went into beekeeping. Some went to college briefly, but the immediate income available to beekeepers was more attractive.

On Monday at 8:00 am, my college routine began with New Testament Greek class. Elder Royal Sage (1924–1982), a delightful man with a rosy smile and the look of a classical saint was the professor. He also taught the Life and Teachings of Jesus class I took on Tuesdays and Thursdays. Elder Sage's gentle approach to religion led me to a tranquil view of Adventism. He introduced me to an assurance of God's favor that complemented Elder Osborn's approach. This professor was a man of impressive wisdom and patient courtesy. He personified compassion and was a genuine scholar. Like some of my other teachers he was working on a PhD and divided his time between teaching and studying. This was in keeping with the determined effort of the college to be more credible as an institution of higher learning.

I left Professor Sage's classes with a better understanding of the gospel. Up until this time, I had mainly studied under returned missionaries, recycled pastors, guest speakers and camp meeting evangelists. But here I was studying under a professionally trained theologian. His influence would leave an indelible mark on my developing approach to biblical studies and ministry. He represented an emphasis I was not used to. He exuded no legalism, generated no guilt and did not emphasize that we needed to please God. Christianity was a religion to provide personal understanding. Jesus had pleased God *for us*. And here was the gospel theme—that God is faithful to us even when we are not faithful to him. These were seeds for me that would grow into a mature view of God.

A few days before the school year opened, I met another newcomer to La Sierra College. He came to speak in our youth Sabbath School. It was a national election year and I did a double-take because I could have sworn our guest speaker was vice-president Richard M. Nixon. He clearly enjoyed the confusion he was generating.

Elder George Akers (1926–2017) had been the principal in Virginia at Shenandoah Valley Academy and had just become the new dean of students at La Sierra College. He was one of those people who immediately captured you with his friendliness, his acceptance, his understanding and his congeniality. I did not know it at the time, but we were destined to become friends for life.

A NEW LOVE

When school started I began a new job at the College Press. Dad had something to do with that. He had always said he wanted to teach printing to his sons. Now he got his chance. I now saw my father in action as a meticulous teacher and a perfectionistic craftsman. He showered me with biased compliments about my "natural artistic gifts."

Some students have trouble learning the aesthetics involved in printing. He told me that I had the gift—for printing is an art. Layout and composition required artistic talents, and he put me immediately on major jobs that involved relatively sensitive design. Dad seldom revised anything I created. He started me in the lead room but soon put me on the academy newspapers being published at the College Press. Unlike my work on the grounds crew, where the clock seemed to stop when I punched in, time flew by when I was at the print shop. In my spare time, I did *pro bono* work for my student programs.

At the print shop, I met Mike, the salesman for the College Press. He was also a theology major, and a leader in the student association religious activities. We quickly became friends. Coincidently he and his wife had moved into the same house on Watts Street where Jim and Lucille had lived when they were first married. As program chairman for the college MV Society, Mike had created program teams made up of students who would take an entire Friday night program to Southern California churches. He was a first-class promoter.

I joined his program team and we traveled from Blythe to Orange County. We always had printed programs because I ran them on the proof press. Before the year was out, we had formed an evangelistic team that he called *The Heralds of Hope*. We published a monthly newsletter on his spirit duplicator, produced live Church programs, and dreamed great dreams for the future evangelization of the world. In the flyleaf of a copy of *Bible Readings for the Home* that he gave me on December 25, 1959, he wrote, "To my dear personal friend Ed, at the beginning of what we pray will be more than a dream!"

My list of spiritual influences grew each day. God brought people into my life who helped define for me the mission of my life. These influences were often subtle—a slight suggestion, a thought or idea brought in the ambiance of the moment that would grow into a new and exciting perspective on life; someone to go with me for a walk in the forest, someone on the job, or in the quietness of a Sabbath afternoon with a new family, and now the direct, powerful witness of fellow workers. This was how God worked with religious men. I suspected that every man was a religious man deep down.

During my first semester at La Sierra, I met a real love of my life. Jennifer Rochelle Tucker[1] was a bright spot in my freshman experience. I first saw this pretty young coed in my English composition class and found her to be mysteriously attractive. We were seated alphabetically, and T is not far from Z. Struck immediately with her beauty, I had the premonition that someday we might be together.

By the end of the first semester, I invited her to a Wednesday date night program in Hole Memorial Auditorium. It was the beginning of something good. My attraction to her led to visits in the foyer of the girls' dorm after school. When Mom noticed that I was now coming home later than usual, she asked me if there was "a girl." And I told her who I was seeing.

When she met Mom and Dad, Jennifer became a regular and welcome visitor to our home. My parents fell in love with her. On Sabbath afternoons we would all take rides together and Jenn demonstrated mutual feelings of affection for them. On Saturday nights, we would go to whatever the program was at the college, come home and play table games, or put jigsaw puzzles together with Mom while Mitch Miller and the gang were singing on the record player in the background. Mom enjoyed jigsaw puzzles and Jennifer joined her. She often expressed her love for my parents and especially how much she liked Dad's sense of humor.

Mom and Dad would banter, much to Jenn's delight. Never having had a daughter Mom and Dad showered her with all the appreciation that parents would show a much-loved daughter. In her enjoyment and acceptance of them, I felt affirmed. By May 1960, our relationship had developed to where I asked Jennifer to go steady with me, and she began wearing my Mu Beta Kappa (college men's club) pin. We had seen each other every weekend from the first of the New Year, and I was amazed how comfortable I was to be with her.

When the school year ended, and she went home for the summer to Northern California, I suffered the most serious case of separation anxiety I had experienced since going away to boarding school. I knew that the summer without her was going to be a long, lonely one. We could not afford long distance phone calls, so daily letters

---

1. Name supplied.

became the way of coping. I even kept a personal journal for the first time. I had never confronted such feelings.

She was a new Church member, baptized shortly before coming to La Sierra. With each date, I felt closer to her. We had come from similar economic backgrounds. She expressed an earnest devotion to her new Church though most of her old friends were members of a non-denominational Church she had attended at home. Sensing my denominational biases, she often conveyed her hope that I would accept her friends even though they were not Adventists.

Her contact with our Church had begun with a local pastor giving her and her mother Bible studies. They had joined the Church; she had finished public high school, and now had decided to attend an Adventist college. Her father was supportive but being a smoker, he was not allowed to take that final step—one he did eventually take. Being true to my calling, I instantly saw her Dad as a prime evangelistic prospect even though I had never met him. I had learned that a religious man often objectifies people that way—as "prospects."

Jenn's Christianity had not begun with her conversion to this denomination. Had she not attended La Sierra College, she told me, she would have pursued her education at another Christian college up the California coast. I noticed that my religious expression was more exclusive (even snobbish) than hers, but her patience with my dogmatism was helpful. Our contrasting approaches to those on the outside led me to consider her more mature, and I grew spiritually.

By summer 1960 Dad was training me on the linotype (lino) and when he went to visit Jim, who was a missionary in Curaçao, I filled in for him at the Press on the lino. I have always enjoyed keyboards whether they were piano, organ, or typewriter. And the lino came to me as second nature.

HAPPINESS RETURNS

As I sat at the lino that summer, I would think of Jenn and it made the day sweeter. The first week apart was the hardest. Letters helped but they were not the same as being together. I went to my job at the Press with a heavy heart and flogged my way through the day. It was as though part of me was missing. Every day I went to the mailbox to get my letter from Jenn. I had found love. And without her around, I was dragging through each day. But I enjoyed those letters.

On May 20, 1960, we had gone to Austin photographic studios in Riverside and had portraits made. I carried her 8x10 picture with me all summer. I knew that was the closest I would get to her for three months. I learned two sayings that describe the effect of distance: "Absence makes the heart grow fonder," and "Out of sight, out of mind." I found the former to be true. During those first couple of weeks apart, I knew I had found a soulmate. I was in pain. By the third week, I was plotting how I could catch a bus north to visit her. But I was working two shifts to make up for Dad's absence. Would the summer ever end?

Then on a hot summer day in July, I made my daily pilgrimage to the mailbox on Knoefler Drive and opened my daily dispatch from Northern California. The letter told me that she was coming back. She had been unable to find a summer job at home and so she had written the LSC women's dormitory and had been hired as a desk clerk. She asked if I could pick her up at the bus terminal in Riverside on Tuesday!

I read the letter several times. My soul was rejoicing. I could not believe my good fortune. Happiness was returning! As quickly as my pain began, it had ended. I was ecstatic. The letter came two days before she arrived. I was an hour early at the Greyhound Depot at the corner of Market and Seventh Streets adjacent to the old Riverside Fox Theatre. It was across the street from the old bus station where I had said a tearful goodbye to Jim seven years before when he left for the army basic training at Ft. Sam Houston in San Antonio, Texas.

When Jenn stepped off the bus in her new navy-blue dress, I couldn't believe my eyes. She was more beautiful than I had even remembered. She had cut her hair. It was now shoulder length. She was one who needed no makeup to improve where God had lapsed. Her eyes squinted shut when she flashed a smile that covered her face. Heaven was descending!

Romantic love was a new experience for me. Here was a mutual love. We could talk and never get tired. Every waking moment, every dream, every thought somehow had her in it. I knew now what had inspired the great poets though I had no gift of verse. That four-week separation had convinced me that this was the right person and that the rest of the summer would fly by. We worshiped together, we ate lunch together, and in the evenings, we talked on the phone together or sat on a bench on campus.

About the only public amusement we could conscientiously participate in was miniature golf. As good Adventists, we would not attend a movie theater or anything equally worldly. But we would sit on campus benches and talk when we got off work. My parents were just as ecstatic. Jenn was the epitome of affection and friendliness. She was unspoiled and unaffected by status or position. We both had religious goals. I know my parents hoped that in her I had found a life partner.

Around the third week after her return, Jennifer was promoted to night desk monitor, and we saw less of each other. She slept during the day and monitored the phones all night. But love is flexible. True love finds ways to compensate for losses. We worked our schedules, so we could spend time together. Each meeting was an island of romance and a treasured spot in time.

AND THEN TRAGEDY STRUCK

It wasn't a life and death tragedy. But it was a catastrophe. One morning in late July I was cutting leads and slugs on the table saw at the College Press. In those days before offset printing, everything in the composing room was centered on the linotype and the manual type case.

As an apprentice, I started at the bottom—in the lead room. Lead was recycled into fresh ingots for the linotype and someone had to melt it and pour it. That job usually went to the last guy in. The work was hot and risky because the lead, heated to 621 degrees Fahrenheit tended to splash when it was being fluxed, and I was not always careful in the process. Molten lead hitting bare arms is not pleasant. But I was good at making ingots and didn't mind the basic nature of the job.

By this time, I had graduated to the floor, which included setting type for headlines (sometimes by hand, sometimes by Ludlow typograph machine), laying out pages, spacing, getting pages ready for proofreaders and final approval from the foreman before going to the press room. Part of that duty included cutting spacing leads.

On a Friday morning, I had installed a new saw blade with specially designed tips for cutting lead slugs. On the following Monday, I was going through the routine of getting leads and slugs ready for a big week of jobs. I was a fast worker but at nineteen I was more careless than Dad wished. In my haste to finish the job quickly, I left the guard up on the saw and was cutting a volume of leads beyond a safe level.

The calamity struck so fast that details escape me, but while I was holding the leads with my left hand, they buckled halfway through the cutting and my hand went into the saw blade. It really does not matter how sharp a blade is when your hand is in it. Instinctively I jerked my hand back but the volume of blood spurting from my hand told me I had done serious damage. The area looked like a homicide had just taken place. So massive was the bleeding I could not see the full extent of the damage I had inflicted on my hand.

While the cut was extreme, I felt nothing. I ran to the sink and grabbed paper towels to soak up the blood that was pulsating from my hand and called for someone to help me. I was growing faint when they finally got me to a car and rushed me to the nearest medical center five miles away—to Dr. Lansing, the same physician who had set my leg four years earlier.

Left behind in the print shop, Mom and Dad were not aware of what had happened. They came out of their offices when they heard the noise. They saw the blood. They saw I was gone, and they were left to draw their own conclusions of what had just happened.

When one of the proofreaders approached the blood-covered table saw she fainted. Mom did a fast once-over of the saw and pulled out the lead drawer underneath. There she discovered an inch of an index finger sitting as though someone had gently placed it there. She started at the sight and concluded, correctly, that the body part was mine. The proofreader was receiving smelling salts.

One of the men in the composing room wrapped my finger and rushed it to the doctor's Arlington office. Meanwhile the doctor was working on my hand. I was feeling light-headed by now from loss of blood, but I never lost consciousness. As he cleaned my cut finger, he discovered that a little less than half of my left index finger had been severed.

By then almost an hour had passed, and I needed to make a decision. He offered the alternatives. If he sewed the severed part back on, I may have trouble with it all my life. It may not even be usable. We had no assurance that it would take because it has been completely severed for an hour. If there had been any connecting tissue, he would have no qualms about sewing it back on. The other alternative was to clean it up and settle for a shortened finger. But that was my decision.

Of course, it was a meaningless issue at this point since we didn't have the severed part anyway! But as Dr. Lansing was examining things, the rest of my finger arrived. I didn't care to see it, and the doctor continued to work. It seemed clear that he was not encouraging me one way or the other. It was my decision. I had friends with half fingers. I never thought I would join their ranks, but it sounded like this was the best alternative, so I told him to go ahead and sew it up—I would just have one less fingernail to trim. He went to work—scraping, sanding, and shortening the bone, to accommodate the remaining skin.

First, he deadened the pain. My hand had now begun to throb. Up to this point, the shock had kept away the pain. But now the trauma was wearing off, and my hand was starting to feel again. Finally, the bone fragment was clean and manageable, and he sewed carefully along the sides of the finger, and at last attached the two flanges of skin. Over the tender end, he placed a piece of hard, U-shaped plastic to keep the finger from inadvertently hitting things as I used my hand. The slightest touch could send a tortuous pain up my arm that would linger for quite a while. When his work was done, he discharged me with a week's supply of pain pills.

I returned to the campus just in time for the noon hour and I had already arranged to meet Jenn for lunch. When she saw my bandaged hand, she looked troubled, and her face revealed that she expected something grave.

"What happened?" she asked.

"I cut off my finger," I blurted out, unceremoniously.

She hesitated, and tears slowly welled up in her brown eyes.

Unbelieving and speechless at first, she finally ventured, "I'm sorry."

We sat in stone silence for an indeterminable amount of time on the campus bench. It was dispiriting to lose a finger, but it was comforting to be cared for and thought about. Jenn was calming and kind. She knew how to be reassuring. We didn't know how to carry on a conversation under the circumstances.

Finally, she examined my hand and asked if she could take off the bandage. I don't think either of us was prepared for what we might see when she gently removed the binding. It was grotesque, with the black sutures exaggerating their importance, and it brought more tears to her eyes. Ironically, such experiences can bring two people closer together. Every life has magical moments where one feels loved and whole, and often these moments come in the wake of pain and grief.

After the accident I took a couple days off work, but because of rush jobs at the print shop I went back to work before the end of the week. I learned that there is therapy in working and by the end of the week I was off my pain pills and life was returning to normal.

Gradually, I began to think of the consequences of the accident. What had I lost through this? Would I ever type again? What about the lino? And I have probably played my last piece on the clarinet—I guess I won't be joining college band in the fall. How will I ever gesture with my left hand when I preach? The thoughts came rushing through my mind.

It's amazing how perception of pain differs among us. For some, it is the loss of a mother to cancer, for others, the drowning of an infant in the family pool. For me, it was just part of a finger, minor next to those other examples. I guessed God had been merciful and that I should be thankful that it wasn't worse. Workman's Compensation paid for my sophomore year of college. Later someone would wryly quip, you have nine fingers left—that should see you through your PhD! Grim humor.

The immediate result was self-consciousness. I would spend the next year hiding my left hand out of embarrassment and the realization that people were staring. To this day, people still stare, but remarkably most people never let on that I have a stump. A few people will occasionally ask, what happened? At times Dad would take my hand and look at my short index finger, and I would see the tears in his eyes as his tender heart was touched by this untimely episode. This seemed more consequential to him than my broken leg. Was I accident prone?

CHAPTER EIGHT

Searching for Salvation

"In actual life, every great enterprise begins with and takes its first forward step in faith."
—August Wilhelm von Schlegel

MY SEARCH FOR SOME UNDERSTANDING OF SALVATION

My quest for the understanding of salvation continued throughout the summer though I never shared it with anyone. The College Press gave workers a ten-minute break in the morning, and another one in the afternoon. During these breaks I would lie on the lawn in front of the Press and read *Planet in Rebellion* by Elder George Vandeman (1916–2000).

Adventists published a *missionary book* each year for us to buy at a reasonable price and hand out to our friends. These books were supposed to be spread "like the leaves of autumn" and so they were available for the nominal cost of one dollar each. At that rate, most people could purchase a lot of leaves. *Planet in Rebellion* was the missionary book for 1960.

I had been intrigued with Elder Vandeman's creative *It Is Written* television program, founded in 1956, and so I had anxiously awaited the publishing of his new book. This popular book was destined to open new areas of understanding for me. I was particularly interested in chapter 13 entitled, "The Story of My Conversion." He explained some things more clearly than I had understood.

> "Verily, verily, I say unto thee, Except a man be born again, he cannot see the kingdom of God." Strong words, these. And Nicodemus did not quite understand. For he questioned the possibility of rebirth. But Jesus pressed home His point in yet clearer language: "Except a man be born of water and of the Spirit, he cannot enter into the kingdom of God." My wonder deepened at

these words of Jesus. Evidently such a transformation is possible. But how could it be brought about? I found my answer in John 1:13: "Which were born, not of blood, nor of the will of the flesh, nor of the will of man, but of God." The new birth was not something that could come about through *the will of man!* No wonder I had failed![1]

I remember feeling relieved after reading that chapter, as a weight lifted. I read the chapter a couple of times. I got another reminder that God's faithfulness to us was the key to grasping the meaning of the gospel. That meant that my faithfulness to him was always secondary. His faithfulness to me was primary. And then he finished the chapter with more meaningful words.

> For no man or woman is ever the same after he has heard the claims of Christ upon his soul. I knew then, as I know much better now, that it is possible for men with eternal destinies at stake to accept a theory of truth and yet be lost. For without the transforming process that comes alone through divine power, the original tendencies to sin are left in the heart in all their strength, there to forge new chains and impose a slavery that the power of man can never break.[2]

Whatever was expected from me was *response,* not *cause.* Any faithfulness I might have to God carried no merit so far as my salvation was concerned. My *trying hard to do right* or to please God was in no way the *basis* of my salvation. The gospel involved God's care for the world, of which I was a part, in sending Christ as a substitute to cover all my sin, not just the ones I had been able to remember and ask forgiveness for. He covered all. I covered nothing.

My experience in Weeks of Prayer had left me with an experimental folk religion that promised me I could eventually live a sinless life. And I had concluded that this was what God wanted from me. Elder Vandeman's book helped remove that responsibility and relieved a great deal of dissonance. I never measured up to the expected standard of holiness, nor had I ever known anyone who did. The story of his conversion was exactly what I needed at that very point in time as I sought to understand my position before God.

I had sung about being ready from the dawn of my reason. At nearly every camp meeting and worship service, and Week of Prayer I had sung the favorite chorus:

> Are you ready for Jesus to come?
> Are you faithful in all that you do?
> Have you fought a good fight?
> Have you stood for the right?
> Have others seen Jesus in you?[3]

---

1. Vandeman, *Planet in Rebellion,* 160.
2. Ibid., p. 162.
3. Pendleton, "Are You Ready for Jesus to Come?" *Advent Youth Sing,* No. 6.

I thought I understood the question. Christians have always been concerned with their standing before God. But have all Christians grasped the meaning of what theologians called *ordo salutis*, i.e., *Latin* for the sequential order of steps in salvation, which began and ended with God's work for us? Reversing the order and putting the emphasis on personal holiness not only resulted in confusion but produced unwarranted arrogance and legalism.

In answer to the question the chorus was asking, I honestly had to reply, "No." I was not qualified for eternal life, i.e., "ready for Jesus to come." For me that deep concern had never been translated into assurance of salvation. My understanding was relieved, but it would still take time for it to seep into my practical life. I would see later in my life that here was a flaw in my theology.

THE STRUGGLE FOR ASSURANCE

My sophomore year in college was both a success and a disaster. My schedule included work at the College Press and a full assortment of general education classes that hardly caught my fancy. By the end of the school year, I was looking at the worst academic record I had ever racked up. That much of it had to do with the time I was spending with Jennifer was self-evident, but I had been taught that true love should contribute to one's getting good grades. This perplexed me because my relationship with her was so significant. I pulled the two lowest grades I would ever earn in college.

I attributed my poor record to boredom with the non-religion classes I had to take. I did not see the relevance of what I was learning to life in general. I wanted to get into "the good stuff"—theology and ministry. General Psychology class was thoroughly bewildering to me, and the fact that the professor had announced that he was experimenting with our class, only gave me more excuse to justify my confusion.

Another part of my problem was that I spent most of my study time on the one class I saw as challenging and relevant: Introduction to Theology. I was consistently at the top of that class, pulling a straight A on every assignment and examination. My Greek also improved, moving me from a C average to a B by the close of the school year.

Some of the problems I experienced in my non-religion classes were centered in my own spiritual journey. My struggle for assurance of salvation became an increasing concern. As a religious man studying to prepare myself for a spiritual mission, I felt that I could share only what I had experienced. The standards had been set so high for me spiritually that I continually failed to meet them. But spirituality and religion were synonyms for me. I made no distinction. I was a religious man; hence I was a spiritual man. Life included two clear categories, secular and sacred, and I continually saw them as unconnected.

PROFILE OF A RELIGIOUS MAN
MY INTRODUCTION TO THEOLOGY

During this sophomore year, a new influence entered my life, Professor Wilber Alexander (1921–2016). He would introduce me to the connection of intellect to religion, and that would make a major change in my philosophical development. Jim had told me that Elder A (as his students called him) would be returning to the faculty after his doctoral leave, and that I should take every class he taught. It was good advice, and I entered his class anticipating a fountain of wisdom. When I was in elementary school I had been acquainted with Elder Alexander. He was a college student then. His daughter and I attended the same school and his wife worked with Mom in the bindery. But then I was just a kid. Now he was my professor.

Elder A was a tall, thin, handsome, balding man with what had been a shock of black hair now slightly graying. He was warm with an engaging charisma—hugely popular with students of all disciplines. He was a master preacher, and a man of a few well-chosen words who used the Socratic method of teaching. He was the first professor to confront me with the penetrating question. I had never had a teacher who could see straight through all issues to their natural implications. He could reduce any question to its basic core—to the issue. He was a master teacher. And he would have a profound impact on how I thought about a meaningful life. Religion would never be simplistic again.

Introduction to Theology was the first class required for theology majors alone. The class was small—eight students. We sat around a large table in the office of Dr. Walter Specht, the Religion Department chair. Elder A required that we develop seven Christian doctrines from personal biblical research and to present each of them in written and oral form to the class. Each module was to include questions we would ask when approaching the doctrine, our class notes, a research outline and a usable Bible study on the doctrine. Here was my introduction to a philosophical approach to religion.

This was not pure philosophy for there was a practical component to everything he did in class. He taught me to appreciate theology. Until then I had not studied religion systematically. Having studied Bible in every class from first grade to college I now came to see the order in salvation from an issue-oriented approach. For the first four weeks I didn't grasp what we were doing, but as the semester progressed, the class came together, and I realized I was thinking through my religion instead of just repeating other people's thoughts.

Our textbooks were the Bible, *Seventh-day Adventists Answer Questions on Doctrine,*[4] and Strong's *Systematic Theology,*[5] a three-volume set that had been bound in one volume by reducing some whole sections of the material to very small type.

---

4. SDA Leaders, Bible Teachers, and Editors, *Seventh-day Adventists Answer Questions on Doctrine,* (1957).

5. Strong, *Systematic Theology,* (1958).

Our class met two hours a week and we were to read two hours a week outside of class as widely as the time frame allowed.

Questions on Doctrine was a new kind of book of theology put out by the Church. It was written by a representative group of Adventist Bible scholars in response to questions formulated and presented by Dr. Donald Barnhouse (1895–1960) and Rev. Walter Martin (1928–1989). These were well-known critics of sects and were interested in setting the record straight about where Adventism stood on some of the great pillars of the Christian faith. Their critique at the end of the process was only that Adventism had changed nothing in their theology. They had only learned to explain it more clearly in language non-Adventists could understand.

My mind was being shaped for philosophy and theology, and I felt pleasingly challenged by this approach. To approach religion from a more scientific method was exciting. My faith up until then, I began to realize, had been infantile, and basically apologetic (in defense of the faith) and catechistic (questions and answers). I saw that both approaches could be simplistic. Theology had many shades of meaning that I had not realized before taking this class.

Aside from the efforts by Elder Osborn and Elder Sage to open some windows for me, my faith was largely rooted in memory verses and Bible stories. These were important basic data, but they did not force me to think much about the larger theological issues of life. If I had a proof text to answer the question, I was satisfied. Now I began to perceive that my college professors were trying to challenge our minds to go beyond mere memory work.

Elder A would often suggest that he was not interested in our regurgitating his thoughts on a sectional exam. He wanted us to build intellectual arguments for our faith. This new enterprise was called thinking! Theology is not something a person feels. It is not a set of good works. It is not synonymous with faith, nor is it necessary for salvation per se. It is a cognitive activity in which "one thinks as carefully and comprehensively as possible about the content, basis, and significance of one's religious faith."[6] Theology is something you do.

Real theology was a new adventure. All of us in the class were excited at what we were finding, and we shared freely and discussed together this systematic approach in class. The examinations were "bears." All essay, these exams typically led us to fill two "blue books" (16-page examination booklets). One fact that became clear to me was that though I was converted and thoroughly Adventist, my growing up in the Church, going to all the Church run schools, attending Sabbath School and camp meeting, had not prepared me to express persuasively the simple roots of the gospel. I had never seen my faith as something beyond a Bible study with a collection of proof texts lined up together. I knew little or nothing about the background of the books of the Bible

---

6. This definition was given by Dr. Fritz Guy, Professor of Theology at Andrews University SDA Theological Seminary.

and I surely had never systematized its teachings. But in Elder A's theology class I was allowed no excuse.

While these were elemental exercises, I saw them as great strides in my development. I realized then that many of us never get it. Too many of us seldom think about our faith to any degree of depth. Small minds talk about people, Elder A would say. Medium-sized minds talk about things, big minds talk about ideas, he would finish his comparison. This was enough to begin forming a refreshing philosophy for me. I could see that most people I knew fit into the first and second levels, and now in this class I was being introduced to the third level.

A CASE IN POINT: THE NATURE OF CHRIST

We hurried into class one day faced with the assignment to explain the moral nature of Christ. By now, we were in our second semester of theological study and most of us were beginning to feel more confident.

My confidence grew from the fact that I didn't have to study to answer this question about Christ's nature. I already knew the answer. If there was one truth I had learned from first grade on it was that Jesus was just like us and because of that he could understand us. In fact, he had a sinful nature like we have. Had he not had our nature, he could never be our example showing us how to overcome it. I had a pat answer—the traditional Adventist viewpoint, I thought. The gospel implications of such a view—not carefully thought out.

Settling into our seats, we got our notes ready for the questions. I had all my bases covered. I hoped he would call on me. He didn't disappoint. He asked me right off to explain my understanding of the moral nature of Christ and I was elated. I set forth what I thought were the orthodox Adventist arguments.

I explained that Jesus was like us in every way except that he didn't sin. And because of that he could understand us and be our example. And just like that it was over. I had scored. I was prepared, and I had to have impressed everyone with my orthodoxy. I didn't realize that I had not only jeopardized the biblical meaning of the gospel, but I had also redefined the nature of sin. But ignorance is bliss.

Now it was Elder A's turn. He asked me why I thought Jesus had to have the same nature we had. My answer was clear: because he could not qualify as our savior and example if he didn't. He had to overcome temptation just like we do. To do that he had to have the same moral nature we have. He asked me if I believed that I needed a savior when I was born. Again, I was confident—of course! And he drove it in—before I had committed any sins had I needed a savior? My answer, yes, of course. I was sure of that answer.

He was drawing out the issue now. Did I say that Jesus was like me in every way? I made sure he understood what I had said—in every way except that he didn't sin. If he had sinned he couldn't have been our example. I was still quite proud of my answers until he brought the discussion to a close. I had insisted that Christ had to be like us in every way except he didn't sin but then he underscored everything I had said and asserted, "you were born sinful and therefore you were born in need of a Savior." So, in conclusion, "you are saying that Christ was just like you when he was born, so then he was born in need of a Savior just like you were."

He paused to let it sink in. I really hadn't thought of that before. So, he asked, who was Christ's savior? He had my attention, as well as the attention of everyone else in the class. The room was so quiet I could hear the sweat breaking on my brow. The paint was cracking on the walls. I knew enough about the plan of salvation to understand that the answer couldn't be God, for if that were the case, what had Christ come to earth to do on our behalf? My mind was racing to grasp the deeper implications.

Things were clearing up. The issue in sin deals with loyalty to God. When Adam sinned, he declared that God was too strict, that his requirements (instructions, laws) couldn't be kept because he didn't have the ability. But that would make God responsible for human sin so that couldn't be true. When Jesus became a man, he came to prove that Adam had the power to obey God and therefore God was just in creating Adam the way he had. That meant that Jesus had to start from the same legal vantage point as Adam or he would have needed a Savior as we do.

Suddenly I realized that I had thought that we don't start from the point that Adam started because we have inherited thousands of years of sin. What did that mean? The sweat was no longer developing—it was dripping off my face.

Now I was stuck. And in that ditch into which my own logic had pushed me, I learned a point of theology I had never faced before. It was as if the heavens opened and God took my hand. Elder A had joined Elder Vandeman in taking off another burden. Theology was integrative. Academia met my spiritual needs.

> [13] "If we are faithless, he remains faithful—for he cannot deny himself." (2 Tim 2:13)

The fact is that we are always unfaithful. And without a second Adam, one who had the same moral nature as Adam, our salvation couldn't be accomplished. Adam was tempted and fell. The second Adam was tempted and did not fall. But I was in the first Adam until, through a new birth, I became in Christ, the second Adam. *The issue was not example. The issue was salvation!* Christ was still my example but not in the sense I had suggested. He was first my savior, and without that salvation first, I could only hope to be a moralist at best.

Dr. Alexander had not scored a victory of changing my truth. His victory was in changing my approach to discovering truth. And that single class period caused me to begin reframing my whole approach to thinking and life. My religion was making sense.

Only later would I discover what earlier Adventists had written—something obviously missed by my previous instructors.

Paul clearly teaches that we are constituted sinners by the disobedience of Adam. Rom. 5:12. Here is *the first imputation,* that of Adam's sin to the whole race, who sinned in him and died in him. Now follow the parallel in Christ. He bore "our sins in His own body on the tree." "He hath made Him to be sin for us, who knew no sin." This is *the second act of imputation.* Then follows *the third act of imputation,* in that Christ was made "our righteousness," so that "we might be made the righteousness of God in Him." See 2 Cor. 5:12; 1 Pet 2:24.[7]

Seventh-day Adventists believe that the human race died "in Adam." When Adam sinned, the human race was "in Adam." In his loins then were all who have ever lived or ever will live on this planet. His fall was the fall of the race that was "in Adam." The sentence of death pronounced upon him fell also upon the race, for the race was "in Adam." His guilt became their guilt. His punishment was their punishment. The change of nature that he experienced they also experienced. When Adam became a sinner the race "in Adam" became sinful, as they were born they could be born only in sin, with a fallen nature, under the sentence of death, doomed to perish. Man has a fallen, a depraved, and a corrupt nature out of which his own individual sins grow. He cannot restrain them nor check them, because he cannot change his heart, his nature.[8]

TALK OF MARRIAGE

Near the end of my sophomore year I was more convinced than ever that in theology I had found the right pursuit in life. Second semester had gone better. Jenn and I were seeing more of each other, and my grades were improving. Somewhere during this time, Dean Akers entered our lives. I received a note that he wanted to see us in his office in the administration building. I wondered what that was about. He said that he had been watching the two of us and considered us both to be potential leaders on campus.

What was coming next? I sensed a "but" coming. And I was not let down. *But* he had some counsel for us. My stomach tightened in anticipation of what was coming next. And his lecture began. We were too intimate in public. He had received concerns about us from faculty members. He was concerned as well. So, he cautioned us about things like holding hands on campus and sitting too closely to each other on benches. He encouraged us that he respected us and hoped this would be our only visit in his office.

The visit was never repeated. Nevertheless, a chill went up my spine as I tried to come to grips with the official wall of nameless, faceless masses. In the future, I would learn that this was standard procedure in a religious society. How people think and

---

7. "Life in Christ," *International Sabbath School Quarterly,* Second Quarter, (1896), 15.
8. Haynes, *Our Times and Their Meaning,* 364.

what people gossip about affects the whole system. Hadn't Dad tried to teach me that? What will people think? he had said.

Furthermore, in religious settings sources do not have to be disclosed, and while this faceless mass may only include two people, one has no way of knowing when told that several people have been talking. The impression may be left that there were hundreds of people reporting. This is power in the hands of an administrator. I would learn that the conversation should not continue until I was told who these people were.

Here was a fact of life that had hardly touched me up till now. But I was training to become a public figure and I had been given a foretaste of what I would face many years later. I felt defensive and wishing to face my accusers, but I was dealing with my elders and I had learned well that this would be out of place.

Then Dean Akers unexpectedly eased our anxiety. He named the three teachers who had issued the observation. That's all—the nameless, faceless masses were three people. I appreciated him for being up front with us. No one likes accusation, no matter how insignificant it may seem to onlookers. As a ministerial student, I could see my credibility at stake, and we were to do our best not to offend anybody. It was the dean's only visit with us, and there was no 2000–5000-word research paper from Sister White's writings this time. We were in college.

Dean Akers had been respectful but firm. And we were never talked to about this subject again. We were not rebels. We were in love. The residual effect was wider. The fact was, contrary to the dean's estimation that we had probably talked of getting married, we had never talked of marriage up to that point. I thought that we were too young, and that we had a lot of school to finish before such topics could be seriously addressed. Nonetheless, because of this visit with the dean, our next conversation together was about marriage. Dean Akers had opened the door, and we were now talking about going through it. Our relationship changed after that visit.

Shortly after this, Jenn shared with me her decision to switch to a nursing major. Her freshman year had been filled with general education classes, but she felt it was time to declare a major. And so, she became a pre-nursing student. Logistically speaking, this would involve two years away from La Sierra to take the nursing program, which was not offered on campus. We talked of possibly becoming missionaries, and this would fit into our plans as we began discussing marriage.

The discussions moved toward planning to become engaged at the right time. This was not the right time. We were both nineteen, and I didn't want to make "the mistake" Dad said my brother had made when he had gotten married after his sophomore year in college, dropped out of school, gone into the army and come back to school with a family. Dad mentioned that too often, I thought—though he never mentioned that because of Jim's "mistake," his college bill was paid for by the G. I. Bill. But this was the lesson I had learned.

So, we put marriage things on hold. Even so, none of this kept me from going into Riverside to a jewelry store to price an engagement watch. We were serious. We talked seriously about both of us finishing college at the same time, and then getting married. And so, we became engaged to become engaged. At the right time I would present her with the watch for her to wear on her right wrist. This was the way Adventists announced engagement, we wore no rings. But until the real engagement happened no one was to know of our arrangement. At the right time we would let people in on our plans. When would that time come?

A NEW DIRECTION

The summer of 1961 was set for more full-time work at the College Press. But then I made an arguably colossal mistake in my so far carefully planned life. Dad was the first to point it out, but I was not of a mind to listen. My religion taught me that there would be wolves appearing in our lives dressed in sheep's clothing and who knew if Dad might be one of those wolves? It was my decision to become a minister, not his. My teachers and mentors were now first on my advising list. And so, I insisted that my new decision must override his advice. I decided to spend the summer selling Adventist books. We called it colporteuring.

In the 1960s the student colporteur movement was active and strong. As in Dad's early conversion days, Adventists still believed that the publishing work would someday be the main channel of communication left to spread the unique Adventist message. And it was the colporteurs—the traveling religious book salesmen—who would finish the work. All through my academy days, I had listened to student colporteurs coming back from their thrilling summers, telling of their stimulating experiences of witnessing through the books they sold.

A colporteur sold Truth-filled literature to the public. Going house to house, the colporteur was on a messianic mission of sharing the Adventist good news through the brightly colored, beautifully illustrated books put out by the Church's publishing houses. Many felt they were overpriced. A set of ten volumes of books averaging about two hundred pages each sold for almost twenty dollars a book when Golden Books were selling for a quarter. But there was no question about the quality of the publishing—it was outstanding and impressive.

The content of the books was not unique, except that it emphasized the Sabbath and the judgment. But for the most part these books were paraphrased Bible stories with color pictures on every page. Because they were our books, we believed that God would use these books in a special way. Much of the markup would go toward our college tuition in the form of a scholarship.

We were instructed that when a Conference president interviewed a prospective theology graduate hoping for a Conference internship, he might ask several questions. The two that carried special weight were: Have you colporteured? And, are you married? These were significant prerequisites for obtaining successful ministerial placement. Apparently, colporteuring would give a foretaste of the ministry in training a young man to knock on doors and expound on the scriptures.

When the full-time Conference colporteurs arrived on the La Sierra College campus, my classmate and a fellow theology major approached me proposing that we spend the summer together getting this requirement out of the way. At first, I froze. The very thought of going up to a strange door was not something I relished. I had shied away from Ingathering, the annual Adventist drive to raise money in support of missions and the Adventist educational system. But Ingathering only required knocking on a door and asking for a donation from a stranger. Engaging people in conversation and trying to sell them a two hundred dollar set of books was not something I was so sure I could do successfully.

This was the big leagues. But I knew this would be a requirement some time. By now I had come to see it as part of the ministerial preparation territory. So, I agreed to listen to the pitch given by the Church's publishing representatives. We attended the promotional meeting and enjoyed the free lunch, and I was swept up in the excitement. There were representatives from Arizona, Utah, Hawaii, Nevada and California.

As professional salesmen in religious garb, these men presented colporteuring as the crowning achievement of our ministerial training, and I bit into the bait with the intensity of a blood-sucking vampire. These men were professionals in the art of persuasion. They made us feel that we could probably finish the work that summer. Christ might come before autumn and we might never go back to school again. Wouldn't we like to be part of such a catastrophic event in the life of planet earth? Their appeal had a cosmic sweep. They included every sales pitch one could invent and then cloaked it in religious raiment that made me *know* that turning down this opportunity was the same as denying my very call to the ministry. This was a test of authenticity.

I left that meeting a changed young man. I was going to be a colporteur. I would go with my colleague to Central California and we would transform the city of Merced. We both signed on the dotted line. We were in for the adventure of our lives. We were going to finish the work in Merced, a little town on the famed Highway 99 just north of Fresno in the heart of the fertile San Joachin Valley of Central California.

I breezed into the print shop for work that afternoon as though I had been packing for heaven. When Dad asked me why I was so happy, I announced that I had signed up to spend the summer as a colporteur. He looked at me like I had just been touring other planets on a UFO during the noon hour. "You have a job lined up right here in the College Press for the summer," he responded, "I have trained you for this job. What if I must replace you and train someone else? You may not get this job back in the fall when school starts again!"

Nothing he said grew roots. It was done. I was going no matter what anyone said. And surely, a simple appeal to the practical reality of paying a school bill was not going to stop me. God would bless me. This was something ministers-in-training did. This was part of finishing the work.

While Dad never said it, I wondered if he was carried back to the days when he had been recruited by the same "Irrational Conscientious"[9] appeals in Europe. I must believe he thought of what he had given up becoming a publisher in the denomination and how many heartaches that had brought him. He had counted on the words of the publishing people, but when he began his training in America, he lost his sponsorship and employment. He didn't bring up any of this, however. He just showed his disappointment by quietly encouraging me to stay at the Press. I really didn't know what I was in for, he said. His *déjà vu*? This was my speculation.

My mind was set, and when school was out, after spending an invigorating week with Jenn and her family camping at Yosemite National Park, I reported for work in Merced. I was equipped with a set of the books, several possible promotional blurbs and a briefcase. My partner had started the week before I arrived. We were camping in the Merced Adventist Church school on cots in classrooms. We bathed in the bathroom, cooked in the school kitchen and roughed it.

A couple of Conference publishing representatives had been dispatched to help us get started. The first day we went from door to door without any sales. By the end of the day, it was clear that if we were going to finish the work, we would have to have a little more divine cooperation. After two days of beating on doors, the Conference representatives went back to their headquarters in San Jose, and we were left to apply what we had seen them do at the doors.

My rep was aggressive, so I imitated him. This was against my nature and my discomfort was evidently apparent. The days passed without any sales. By the end of the second week with not one sale to my name, I was ready to call it quits. I had never embarked on such a difficult task.

Each morning we started the day with worship, then we folded brochures, and finally we got up the courage to go into the territory, but with little success. It was only the first of July. I could return to La Sierra and work in the College Press without having lost much and having gained something—a little understanding of one thing in life I would not want to do. By the second Friday, with no sales or interests in my order book, I started packing.

My colleague was beside himself. He finally convinced me to go with him to San Jose to talk to the publishing director for the Conference, and I reluctantly agreed. We spent two hours in the director's office while he recited all the joys of colporteuring. Nothing he said had any effect. I was broken. Finally, he asked me to sleep on it over the

---

9. "Irrational Conscientious" is not a negative evaluation. It is Stage Four in the values development research of psychologists Peck and Havighurst in their behavioral findings published in their book *The Psychology of Character Development*, 7–8. In this stage "An act is 'good' or 'bad' to him because he defines it as such, not necessarily because it has positive or negative effects on others.... It is characteristic of children who have accepted and internalized the parental rules, but who have not attained awareness that the rules are man-made and intended to serve a human, functional purpose. Consequently, they may be so rigidly 'moral' that they sometimes act to the detriment of others."

weekend. I agreed but knew I didn't have to. Nothing was going to change my mind. This decision was based on two-weeks of solid failure. We headed back to Merced.

Bright and early Sunday morning, I called Dad and told him I would be returning on the bus that night. I had not anticipated his response: "You will not come back," he said, "I have replaced you at the Press, so you have no job here. You will stay in Merced for the remainder of the summer." Seldom had I heard him being quite so definite.

I was devastated. I was going to be held responsible for my decision. But I could not stand to think of another day in Merced. On the other hand, if I returned to the college, I would probably be back on the grounds crew and maybe even have no place to live. I was almost willing to consider that when it hit me that I was going to have to stick this one out.

The summer was a disaster in my eyes. At the College Press we had printed a lot of the publishing department promotional materials—I had set the type and made up the pages. And the general tenor of the message had to do with the need for a colporteur to have a positive attitude. I had to confess that I had only a negative attitude by now. To make matters more intolerable, I had no chance to see Jenn for the whole summer.

Every day was the same—hot and dry. The motivation to get into a house with air conditioning gradually grew greater than selling the books. My timidity had little chance to show itself, and I learned a few things about talking to strangers. So far as sales went, I certainly set no records. But by the end of the summer I had sold a few books. To encourage me, Dad also bought copies of most of what I had to sell.

Finally, the slowest summer of my life came to a merciful end, and I returned to college in the fall a much humbler religious man. I had fulfilled an assignment for future employment, and now I could answer the administrator's first question in the affirmative—no need to give a lot of details.

My junior year was facing me. I put the summer behind me, and I dug in for upper division class work. I was hardly aware that this year would result in another of what I have come to believe was a colossal mistake. This mistake would be far more serious than the last one. And it would involve Jennifer.

CHAPTER NINE

Managing Change

"If you want to make enemies, try to change something."
—Woodrow Wilson

A BUNDLE OF BIASES

The last two years in a college program can be intense. If you have planned well, your general education is out of the way and now you are finally compelled to grasp once and for all why you chose to go to college in the first place. My classes were all upper division now and mostly in my major field. During my sophomore year I had finished the sciences designed for the theology major—not very challenging. Instead of taking technical courses, we were given general courses in physical and biological sciences—each of which qualified us at a bonehead level. I had not taken a science or math class since I did poorly in high school algebra.

I did not know at the time that someday I would be a college professor myself, sitting on general education committees that put together curricula for all disciplines. There I would find myself insisting that all college students should have real math and science classes in their general education instead of watered-down courses formed specifically for religion students.

Curriculum is not the entire answer—I simply fulfilled some requirements as I suspect other students did, but I often failed to learn materials that could have broadened my education. Requirements were tightened as time passed, and when I became a religion professor and academic advisor, later in life, I had to face some theology majors howling that these classes in mathematics and science were too hard and too competitive, and how are these relevant to education for the ministry anyway?

My junior year was a revision in time. Jenn was now in nursing school some sixty miles away. I was concentrating on my major and found some of my perspectives changing. Socially my circle was small. I was not dating, and my group of friends consisted mostly of theology and religion majors.

I perceived a clear separation between those who took theology and those who took pre-medical education. Adventism presents the minister-doctor team as a powerful evangelistic combination. The health message is lauded as the "right arm" of the Adventist gospel. Yet in college my experience was that the future ministers and future doctors largely avoided each other. I viewed the pre-meds as materialistic and worldly. They often came from doctors' homes, drove sports cars and wore name brand clothes while I rode an old bicycle and wore shirts my mother hand-made for me out of flour and chicken feed sacks. I did not understand their society and especially couldn't see how this was connected to finishing the work. I was judgmental and arrogant, but I was religious. I was a microcosm of the remnant mentality. That someday we would be a team for winning souls was a reality that seemed remote.

Theology majors were special. We were in tune with the realities of imminence. We were the concerned group on campus who were into a grown-up version of the Black Cloud mindset. Christ was coming soon. This was no time to be dawdling with the world, buying things, driving expensive cars, being preoccupied with items of this world. There probably was no time to take medicine, that long drawn out course of study that seemed reserved for a few guys who lived a fast, jet-set life. When all was said and done, what was life anyway? Big houses? Swimming pools? Cadillacs? Motorboats?

Medicine produced a certain kind of Adventist that was not in the plan—as outlined and encouraged by our prophet. How could people who indulged in such things influence the hastening of the second coming? This kind of Adventist seemed only cultural to me. And cultural was not a complimentary term in my vocabulary, especially when applied to religion.

My views were infantile. In my state of idealism and immediate social setting, I had little grasp of a bigger picture—that professional people were largely the financial backbone of the Adventist Church. I saw only the present and the past. The place of money in the Church was a thought so far removed from me that it was not a consideration at all. I was studying theology, the queen of the sciences, which included important subjects like exegesis, biblical languages, hermeneutics, homiletics and great philosophical insights.

I was a religious man being educated for a religious mission not of this world. I was God's foot soldier, being educated for God's special corps. And all that involved a total commitment to the cause. Life had a hierarchical structure. Some things were more important than others. Time was not going to last long enough to chase unimportant pursuits. I realize now that my view of Christ's imminent coming influenced the decisions I made. Without that hope I may have thought more carefully about those decisions.

As I worked around campus I learned I was not the only one who thought that way. One staff person working with us on a project on the grounds crew was commenting about a Cadillac print ad in *Life* magazine, which had a caption that read "The Standard of the World." "There you have it!" he said. "Those people in the Church who claim to be Christians, but drive Cadillacs are showing people that they are controlled by 'The Standard of the World.'" He was precise in his condemnation of those who could not get their priorities straight in a fallen and falling world. I did not disagree with his perception.

He quoted teachers at the college who had said as much. He cited pastors who had helped him form these perceptions. I knew he was right. I prayed that I would never fall into that trap of getting. It was the nature of those who were falling off that cliff in Sister White's vision. How could a rich man get into heaven? It would be easier for a camel to go through the eye of a needle than for a doctor to get to heaven, I paraphrased Jesus' teaching. [23] "And Jesus said to his disciples, 'Truly, I say to you, it will be hard for a rich man to enter the kingdom of heaven. [24] Again I tell you, it is easier for a camel to go through the eye of a needle than for a rich man to enter the kingdom of God.'" (Matt 19:23–24). I was oblivious to the toxicity of my messianic mission as well as the extent of my bundle of biases.

LIFE WITHOUT JENNIFER ON CAMPUS

My junior year in college was a year without Jennifer since she was away in nurses' training. In a world of cars and cell phones, distance and contact seem irrelevant. Today a man can call his friends ten times a day on his iPhone, and they may be only four miles away at their office. But then things were different. Long distance calls were expensive, and I couldn't ride my bicycle to Glendale. Neither of us had a car so if we saw each other, either I had to borrow Dad's car to drive the two hours to Glendale (no freeway to Glendale in 1961) or she had to take a bus to La Sierra. So, we were back to writing daily letters.

When I finished my ordeal as a colporteur, Mom and Dad drove to Merced to pack me up and bring me home. Jenn came with them. Before school started, I had a chance to see her several times. Once school started we both got busy with academia. My job at the College Press was over—I had been replaced, so there was no opening. As much as I had enjoyed it, I really didn't miss it. I was a serious theology student now, so I would be spending my time with other pursuits. I got a job as a reading assistant in the LSC Religion Department.

Managing Change

DR. J. CECIL HAUSSLER

My new boss was Dr. J. Cecil Haussler (1899-1986). Professor of Biblical Studies. Dr. Haussler was a short, thin, grey-haired man with a keen sense of humor. He had a Doctor of Philosophy degree from the University of Southern California, where Uncle Louis taught, and he could quote Sister White proficiently. He seldom made religious or theological assertions without quoting her as his authority—and always from memory. His life demonstrated his devotion.

Dr. Haussler was a humble man who drove basic Fords and lived on a small two-acre ranch on La Sierra Avenue where he grew produce that he marketed. He sent the proceeds to missionaries whose needs of which he was aware. Over the years he had sent thousands of dollars' worth of tractors, trucks and other equipment overseas. Here was an example I cherished—a saintly individual who was clearly committed to the cause. No pool, no big car, no palatial mansion. His "middle name" was total commitment. He was also the brother-in-law of the General Conference president, Elder R. R. Figuhr.

To work for Dr. Haussler, I had to sit in every class he taught—Daniel and Revelation, Prophetic Interpretation (a class for non-theology majors on the life and ministry of Sister White), Church History, Eschatology, and Spirit of Prophecy, a more intensive class on the life and ministry of Sister White, for theology majors.

He paid me to sit in on his Eschatology class on Monday nights and keep track of every student who contributed to the discussion. Whenever a student read a quotation or spoke up with a suggestion or substantive insight, I would write it down in the grade book and his/her participation grade would be affected. Active participation was a requirement for passing the course.

Dr. Haussler had taught at Southern Missionary College in Tennessee and had experienced a rough time there. I got the impression that he had been run out by some unknown powers that be. His wife wrote me many years later and shared that their years in Tennessee had been especially hard times. His wife was not a complainer. Despite his bad experience, he had picked up the spirit of the Adventist South. He had been influenced by the "Sutherland mentality."

After moving Battle Creek College to Berrien Springs, Michigan, and renaming it Emmanuel Missionary College, Edward Alexander Sutherland, M.D. (1865-1955) had moved South in 1904, armed with Sister White's counsels about how to do medical missionary work.[1] He had joined P. T. Magan, M.D. (1867-1947), and founded Madison College in Nashville, where he served as its president until 1946. During that time, Madison College became the mother of the Adventist self-supporting institutions in the Southeastern United States.[2]

---

1. "Edward Alexander Sutherland," *SDA Encyclopedia,* 1442.
2. "Madison Academy," Ibid., p. 827.

The mission of Madison College was to work for the people of the Southern mountains. The strategy was to set up small self-supporting sanitariums and schools all around the South. Graduates of Madison started about forty such institutions. Over the years the self-supporting workers developed into something of a fraternity of people who considered that they were following *the blueprint,* a favorite term of Adventists to express the principles of education outlined and taught by Sister White.

These institutions were miniature plantations where those who lived in semi-communal settings, raised their own food, built their own buildings, educated their young, and operated industries that paid the major bills. That training included the mission of educating people to live eventually "without a mediator" in the eschatological future. In addition to this the members of the self-supporting work among Adventists contributed liberally of their funds to make sure that this unique work survived.

In this setting a subtle suspicion of the official Church hierarchy and its tithe-supported denominational leadership slowly developed. While there were some exceptions, many of these self-supporters became critical, judgmental, and even cynical in their outlook on the denominational leadership. They largely viewed the Church leadership the way I had viewed doctors—as necessary but not very religious, in fact even worldly, and quite overrated. These self-appointed reformers often seemed ready to go on the offensive with their criticism of the denomination. The shutting down of Madison College presented a prime example of what they felt justified in criticizing. When the college was about to go under financially in the 1960s, the Conference, as an angel of mercy, took it over, presumably to maintain it or turn it into a college-level trade school.

Elder Horace Beckner (1911–2000), pastor of the Southern Missionary College Church for over a decade, became the first denominationally appointed president of Madison College. Reminiscing later about what happened at Madison, he claimed that when he went there he had no inkling that the Southern Union Conference was planning to strip Madison of its academic status as a college and turn it into an Adventist academy. He said that he believed the school was to become the first Adventist trade school—something many devoted Church members thought was long overdue.

Especially with the advent of accreditation and influx of the intellectual religion represented by the book *Seventh-day Adventists Answer Questions on Doctrine,* some felt the need to go back to Sister White's blueprint. There was an element in Adventism that believed that denominational schools were becoming too worldly. Nonetheless, rather than flourishing with this new-found mission, in 1964 the Madison doors closed. Elder Beckner was out and the institution was reorganized as Madison Academy and Hospital.

Madison's immediate competitor was Southern Missionary College, just 130 miles to the Southeast. Madison alumni, who were viciously loyal to the sixty-year enterprise, felt betrayed. They looked around for a successor to Madison, one that would decidedly not be Southern Missionary College. Eventually Wildwood Institute in Wildwood, Georgia, would be thought by many to be that center, though not all institutions ended up recognizing its leadership.

Dr. Haussler worked in the Adventist South long before all these holy wars erupted. It was a South of placid but serious loyalty to Sister White and her views of medical missionary work, and the fact that she had hand-picked the location of Madison College was stressed. Wherever you went in the Adventist South, you were not far from a little sanitarium or school founded and operated by Madison alumni. Usually the school and the sanitarium were together.

When he moved west, Dr. Haussler bought two acres of land in La Sierra just below the Hole family mansion and immediately set about creating a small ranch. On this little farm he provided a retreat from whatever tension the encroaching town might be creating as well as amazing crops from fruit orchards to vegetable fields, which he harvested each year and turned into equipment and funds for the mission field. When my brother Jim later became president of the Honduras mission, Dr. Haussler sent him money to help purchase vehicles for the mission office.

Dr. Haussler was a farmer *par excellence*. His slight frame usually carried a farmer's tan, and any visitor to the little ranch on La Sierra Avenue was bound to find him riding his tractor, fertilizing, harvesting or weeding his fields. Here was a deeply spiritual leader on the La Sierra faculty. For as long as I was in college, he led out in a Sabbath morning Bible study and prayer group at his house. We would walk from the campus to his house, leaving early enough to arrive at the 6:00 am meeting. Each semester he would cover a different religious topic and each weekly session we would form prayer bands and then make the four-mile trek back to the college for the weekend services.

I thought if I ever became a college Bible teacher, I would like to have such meetings at my house in the early Sabbath hours. I had a dream that I would someday own a house designed with an outside entrance and a study large enough to accommodate a couple dozen students meeting at dawn on Sabbath to discuss spiritual topics and pray together.

Working for Dr. Haussler was an enriching experience for me although he had been one of those professors who had complained to Dean Akers about Jennifer and me and our PDA. I never forgot his references to his work in the South and the clippings and pictures he showed me from the local newspapers there degrading him as "the boy preacher." But I did not find myself relating personally to any of his troubles, and I never got the facts straight about what had happened. Whatever he shared sounded unbelievable.

How could anyone who was so deeply committed to the Lord and the Adventist Church be run out of anywhere? I finally concluded that whatever happened to Dr. Haussler had to be connected to non-Adventist elements, not to the Adventist community of faith. Surely nobody in the Church would treat a minister of such deep piety that cruelly.

That I might someday relive to any degree what Dr. Haussler had gone through in that same community I could never have foreseen. At that point in my education I had no intention of becoming a teacher. I had no desire to move from California (unless it was to a missionary appointment with Jenn), nor did I believe that time would last long enough for me to face any such crisis. I could not wrap my head around any idea that fellow Adventists would treat any minister that way. Furthermore, no one could claim a purer Adventist pedigree than I was building.

My future looked bright though I thought little about it—I was simply in the hands of God. I had even endured a summer of colporteuring and however disastrous I thought it had been, it was now in my resume and it was something I would never have to repeat.

MAKING ANOTHER SERIOUS MISTAKE?

To hear me talk no one would have guessed that my summer of selling books had been a fiasco. I was elected vice-president of the Colporteur Club. My colleague was elected president. Building on our MV format of program teams, we formed teams that could bring programs into churches on Friday nights with the colporteur theme.

Several of us in the club gave talks regularly at churches in the area about the joys of colporteuring and its value for finishing the work. We reflected on our summer as though it had been a smashing success. Even though I knew that my feelings at the end of the summer had been feelings of relief rather than accomplishment, I refused to believe that I was typical. I lived in this world of illusion in which everyone else had an exhilarating experience and that it would be such for anyone who decided to go. I viewed all through the Adventist notion, that the publishing work would be a deciding factor to influence serious people to become Adventists.

The year started with stacks of papers to grade and a host of exciting classes in my field. My goal was still clear: to finish my theological studies, get a call, and become an Adventist pastor. With Jennifer gone, I had more time to concentrate on my studies. But I also found myself wondering if I had had enough social experience to decide whether Jenn was really the one. My mind began to wander. I began to think and wonder. Perhaps I had fallen too quickly in love. Maybe I had fallen too hard too soon and had not given life enough of a chance. What did I know of love? How many dates had I had in my timid and bashful youth? The first girl I ever kissed had made the first move. Who was I to judge the nature of romantic love anyway? I was overthinking.

I didn't realize how destructive such mental meanderings might be at my age. I was too young and sheltered to be facing the kind of decisions I had to make. And I found my mind shifting between absence makes the heart grow fonder and out of sight, out of mind. I tried to stop but the thought of two more years without Jennifer began to sink in. Christ would probably return before we could finish school. I would not have another girlfriend because heaven would intervene.

We were only two years away from the long awaited "siege" of La Sierra College by Catholics. Mike had suggested to me that if I ever graduated, it would be in the basement of Hole Memorial Auditorium by candlelight with the dreaded Catholics besieging the building. We believed we were that close to the end of time.

How had I painted myself into this corner? With Jennifer gone, perhaps I was thinking clearly. I was getting back my old religious fervor and focus, recalling the reality of the Black Cloud. I couldn't believe how distracted I had become. I began to understand St. Paul's counsel that it may be better for a minister not to be married.

> [1] Now concerning the matters about which you wrote. It is well for a man not to touch a woman. [2] But because of the temptation to immorality, each man should have his own wife and each woman her own husband. [3] The husband should give to his wife her conjugal rights, and likewise the wife to her husband. [4] For the wife does not rule over her own body, but the husband does; likewise the husband does not rule over his own body, but the wife does.
>
> [5] Do not refuse one another except perhaps by agreement for a season, that you may devote yourselves to prayer; but then come together again, lest Satan tempt you through lack of self-control. [6] I say this by way of concession, not of command. [7] I wish that all were as I myself am. But each has his own special gift from God, one of one kind and one of another. (1 Co 7:1–7)

A fleeting thought: maybe I should remain single all my life. Christ was coming soon. But didn't I love her? I thought so. But how mature was I after all? At nineteen years of age, what could I really know? When she came to spend a weekend with us in La Sierra shortly before the new school year began, I was shocked that my infatuation was fading. I realized for the first time that this kind of thinking was affecting our relationship. Or was it God's will that we end it. I was living a religious life alone. It seemed more genuine in many ways. I thought I felt controlled.

Maybe this was a good time to test our love for each other and separate for a while. Maybe I needed to date for a while—experience a little liberty. What if we had just become blind—and in that blindness we had made plans that would not end well? Surely if it was real, a separation wouldn't change anything.

Maybe my judgment was warped. Think, think, think. Where was I going? And was I overthinking? How would she help to fulfill my mission in life? But then, didn't I need more of a social life—my whole ministry would be one of social contact. I had an appetite for what grading papers and taking upper division work could not fulfill. This ambivalence was not healthy. If anything happened to our relationship through these two years of being apart, my parents would be devastated. But they were not the ones planning marriage—this was my life. And so, the mental boxing match continued.

By the fall SA retreat, I was almost persuaded that our relationship needed revision or serious examination. She took a leave from her school on the weekend of the

SA retreat held at Cedar Falls, the junior camp in the San Bernardino mountains. By the end of the retreat I was more troubled than ever. But I couldn't understand why.

Disillusionment with our relationship was turning into flights of fantasy and thoughts of freedom. There were girls at the retreat I would never be able to date because I was essentially committed—trapped—stuck. And the one to whom I was stuck didn't even go to school here. These were destructive thoughts and they were affecting my equilibrium.

Were my thoughts becoming adventurous? They certainly distracted me. I was here to study God's plan, and my social life had been part of that plan. We had it laid out. We would both finish at the same time and go together to Seminary as a married couple. It was very simple. We had made the plans together. What was I thinking? How could I allow these questions to unravel those plans?

When we got home from the retreat, I was to drive Jenn to Ontario where she would catch her Sunday afternoon bus back to Los Angeles. But I wanted to talk to her first. The weekend had not been good. Something was just not the same. My mind was too active. I borrowed Dad's car and we drove to a remote part of La Sierra where there were hundreds of acres of orange groves. This was where the high school kids parked late into the night. It was known in La Sierra as *Lover's Lane.* Today the whole area is gone—replaced by many square miles of houses, as far as the eye can see. I had never taken a girl to *Lover's Lane* though I had chauffeured (as bodyguard) some friends there once.

As we talked, she asked a lethal question, undoubtedly hoping to bring me back to my previous excitement in her presence. She had never detected such ambivalence from me. She looked at me squarely and asked, "Do you think we should break up?"

I sat in silence. Where did that come from? I had not faced this reality. Suddenly I was confronting a major decision. I did not know the consequences of my action at this crossroads. Stupid thoughts of being hog-tied, controlled and hen-pecked floated through my mind. It was an irrational reaction that only made things worse. This was not good. But all my blabbering merited it. Our plans hung in mid-air. We had a two-year history of talking together. But this was a different direction. What our relationship might become if I said yes was shrouded in mental fog. I was unhinged now.

I thought, in a bout of delusion, that couples who break up can remain friends. But that thought was irrelevant. We had once talked of the possibility of such a thing happening. But I don't think that either of us believed we would ever break up, so we had never spent serious time with that discussion.

Probably neither of us was prepared for my response as I took a plunge. I heard my answer in the affirmative. It was as though I were outside my head listening to this conversation. Her reaction was quick. She didn't push me. She had always taken me seriously. I have rethought that moment many times over the following years. Almost sixty years have passed, and I have not figured out why I responded as I did.

Slowly tears welled in her eyes.

"Honey, I'm sorry," I ventured feebly, attempting to continue the discussion. I knew these were just words. What to say?

Then she told me, "Don't call me 'honey.' If you don't mean it then dispense with the language." Instantly she became a different person—it was as if I suddenly didn't know her. I was no longer in our groove, and that if we weren't together, I would not be privileged to use the language of the groove.

We sat there for a short time—I have no idea how long. She asked for no explanation. I guess we were both in shock. After a few minutes I started the car and headed for Ontario. I do not remember that we shared any more conversation on the trip. The twenty miles seemed like a hundred. She got out of the car at the bus depot, took her bag and purse and walked out of my life.

CHAPTER TEN

Reframing Life

"Plan ahead: It wasn't raining when Noah built the ark."
—RICHARD CUSHING

LIFE WITHOUT

We wrote two or three letters after that day, but we never saw each other again. In time I came to view this as a mistake with far greater consequences than my anguished summer of colporteuring. I never got over that day. There is no way to estimate the pain that decision caused me, and I was daring enough to think that she might feel the same way. I would never be the same again. Two days later I was ready to call and admit my mistake, but my classmate who was a sophomore at the time, visited me and offered counsel. He had just broken up with his high school sweetheart and he suggested that I do nothing for two weeks. If I could make it two weeks I would be alright.

I had chomped on a bitter pill. I thought the whole thing was irrational and stupid. But the thought of something better kept crossing my mind. I had come to doubt our relationship through no fault of hers. I questioned our plans. I had only irreligious thoughts. Jennifer remained good friends with my parents until the day they died. I later heard that she had married. I saw pictures of her children since she made sure my parents were kept up to date. Photographs appeared around the house and I still run across them in Mom's scrapbooks.

Dad was devastated by my decision but tried not to show it. Finally, he tried to talk to me about it, but I told him to mind his own business. Mom couldn't figure out what was wrong with me. Here was a girl they had adopted and deeply loved. She had enriched my life and clearly hoped to become a minister's wife. We had even talked about being missionaries. The minister and the nurse—the marriage of the two messages—gospel and health. And now it was gone. Yes, it was a bitter pill. The full impact, however, would only be felt in the years to come. The immediate effect was pseudo-exhilaration.

Stubbornly and irrationally, I planted my feet in the ground and lost myself in my studies. I was a jerk, but I had to get on with God's work. That was what Adventism had taught me to do. Eliminate anything that causes you to be diverted from your calling. In my rationalizing, I saw Jennifer as one of those obstacles and so I got on with my life, or so I thought. The whole thing was wrong. Now I had to live with it.

LIFE ON THE REBOUND

Some major aspects of life were developing in my psyche. I had been taught that there were three major decisions I was responsible for: Would I accept and serve God? What would I decide to do for a life work? And who would I choose for a wife? I thought all three had been covered until now. But the third question was now in conflict.

My GPA improved, clear evidence, I rationalized, that I had made the right decision. I spoke in churches on the weekends. Everything now was geared to doing God's work. I even had a few dates. Since I couldn't play in the band anymore, I joined the college choir and sat with girls on the bus as we traveled for concerts. But nothing turned out to be serious. I was experiencing social life but not enjoying it. Nothing I experienced could compete with my friendship with Jenn. I was floundering, flopping around like a fish on a pier.

Toward the end of the school year, I asked out Annie,[1] a freshman, who had come to La Sierra to study mathematics. All I had heard about her was that her father was a physician somewhere in the Los Angeles area. My feelings about pre-meds and worldly physicians resurfaced, and I was conflicted. When I asked her out she reciprocated by inviting me to Sabbath lunch at her house. With a couple of my friends I attended her home Church and then was taxied over to her house. This trip proved to be the beginning of a new friendship, though I did not allow myself to think of anything beyond acquaintance at the time. I was on the rebound and I wasn't going to get serious.

My Sabbath at this home was enjoyable. I discovered that her grandfather had been one of my mother's teachers at Broadview College in Chicago. Her family was Scandinavian, the mix was mine—her father: Swedish; her mother: Swedish-Norwegian.

We compared notes and found several Church connections. Here was a delightfully hospitable family that made me feel accepted. I sensed that this could develop into something more than just an occasional date. But I was not ready for any intensive relationship. I was gun-shy. It was time to concentrate on my preparation for God's work.

---

1. Name supplied.

Mike reminded me of his prediction that time would probably never last long enough for me to graduate from college. That imminence of the end of time was continually racing in my mind. The Black Cloud was nearer than ever now. I had no doubt that time was short and probably there would be no time for any serious relationships. Christ was on his way. Was I ready? No, I wasn't. Any day now the end could come and so I hit the books harder. I reminded myself that I was a religious man and I must remain focused.

All these thoughts of what is reality and what is important ruled me. It was an Adventist thing. I knew now I was a religious man. Religious men make a practice of denying themselves things of pleasure. "If time should last" was my mantra in a way it hadn't been before. It was an escape, but it gave me meaning. I told myself I had been diverted by my relationship and I must not allow that to happen again.

I studied the Old Testament major and minor prophets and the prophecies of Daniel and Revelation. I took the hardest course I knew. Instead of the regular New Testament epistles class I took Pauline epistles in Greek. Bring it on, I was ready. I ran for no SA positions. There was no time. "If time should last"—I had to be ready to take a church, to be the best minister I could be. I was obsessed. My grades continued to improve.

What I was still struggling with was what it meant to be a Christian. I had had some snapshots, but nothing streaming. I wanted to be faithful because that was what was important in life. Now I had broken someone's heart, I dared to think. But my own heart was also suffering. I didn't realize how compulsive this kind of behavior was. I didn't think of my life psychologically, I thought in religious terms. I didn't realize the toxicity of my faith—I didn't even know the term.

Despite knowing better, I once again began seeking to gain God's approval, and with new intensity. My denominationalism fed this notion. It is an obsessive phenomenon that is common to religious fundamentalism. My dogma was all I knew, and there were no safeguards to protect me from this compulsiveness.

The more obsessive I became, the more laud and praise I got. In my Church I believed the harder you worked, the better you were. But the logical outcome of this kind of religious obsession is either pride or discouragement. I learned that they go hand in hand. Surprisingly they complemented each other. The better you are, the stronger the perception becomes that you aren't really very good. And so, you vacillate between delusion and depression as you are animated by perfectionistic notions.

The Apostle Paul's experience became mine in a new way.

> [14] We know that the law is spiritual; but I am carnal, sold under sin. [15] I do not understand my own actions. For I do not do what I want, but I do the very thing I hate. [16] Now if I do what I do not want, I agree that the law is good. [17] So then it is no longer I that do it, but sin which dwells within me. [18] For I know that nothing good dwells within me, that is, in my flesh. I can will what is right, but I cannot do it. [19] For I do not do the good I want, but the evil I do

> not want is what I do. [20] Now if I do what I do not want, it is no longer I that do it, but sin which dwells within me.
>
> [21] So I find it to be a law that when I want to do right, evil lies close at hand. [22] For I delight in the law of God, in my inmost self, [23] but I see in my members another law at war with the law of my mind and making me captive to the law of sin which dwells in my members. [24] Wretched man that I am! Who will deliver me from this body of death? [25] Thanks be to God through Jesus Christ our Lord! So then, I of myself serve the law of God with my mind, but with my flesh I serve the law of sin. (Rom 7:14–25)

But it was all hidden both from the public and from me and I took refuge in the good works I was producing. Better grades, better words, nicer things to do for others, praying for forgiveness, reciting my sins, flogging myself for my mistakes, and finally a flurry of activities to mask my inner emptiness. It all went together—the ambivalence, the legalism, and the compulsiveness. Often one learns things that he isn't taught and my junior year in college was so filled with this dissonance that I could not unpack it fully. People get hurt because they misunderstand our intentions. But at the same time, you hurt yourself because the emptiness eats at you and you mask it in "good."

Desperately in need of an authentic relationship with God I plodded through that year of unsettledness in a very confused state of mind. Annie appeared in my life off and on. When she invited me to go with her family to go water-skiing on the Colorado River I agreed to go, but then in my on-again-off-again behavior we didn't see each other for several weeks.

A NEW RELATIONSHIP BEGINS

One day as I was grading papers at my desk in La Sierra Hall, I sensed that someone was standing next to me. It was her. Annie said, "I came to see if you are still planning to go with us to the river." It had been so long since we had seen each other that I was sure that date was off. But she had the courage to approach me and I said complacently, "I guess." It was a half-hearted committal. But early the next Sunday morning I had my bag packed to go to the river.

We had fun. Her parents taught me to water-ski. The Cadillac and the boat fit my perception of the worldly Southern California Adventist physician. It was no surprise to me. The surprise was how nice these people were. They didn't seem pretentious, just comfortable. They didn't appear to be worldly. They seemed to have the same notion of imminence that I had. They just enjoyed a different level of living than I had ever been accustomed to.

Theirs was a rarified life of manners and etiquette, which set you apart. They knew how to cut one's bread in half before buttering it, how to scoop one's soup away from instead of toward your mouth, how to wait for the hostess to give the signal when to start eating, how to wait for the hostess before taking the first bite of dessert.

Their table was set with fine china and sterling silver, and we drank from crystal goblets. Their napkins were made of fine linen and were encircled in sterling silver rings. These were all crucial trappings that implied order, style and planning. This was a new plateau in living. By contrast, I had grown up with jam jar drinking glasses, and Betty Crocker tableware Mom had obtained by saving box tops from Wheaties. I hadn't noticed that the food tasted much different.

God had blessed them, they told me. They cared about others and participated in all sorts of Church activities. They filled major, powerful Church lay positions on the local school board, at their local Church and at the Conference level, and rewarded those on these boards who agreed with their perspectives of how the work should be conducted. They did nice things for others with their money and while they insisted they were not rich, they wanted for nothing. Their house and luxury cars were paid for. Their children were in Church school. They were influential in all levels of Church activity.

Unlike these people, my parents both worked full time, in fact, Dad worked two and three jobs at a time. While my parents attended my school performances, they seldom had time to go on school outings or spend days shopping for bargains.

Frankly, none of those things had seemed important to me. I had wished we could have more people over on Sabbath for lunch, but I never connected that to how tired my parents may have been at the end of their heavy work week. Somehow the idea of having a college teacher and his family to our house for Sabbath dinner may have been overwhelming to them.

Watching these new friends entertain created some dissonance for me. I immediately saw the difference between this outlook on life and the one in which I had grown up. Cadillacs were on my black list but they were nice to ride in. I was reframing and rethinking my own views of where material things fit into my religion. How, indeed, did material blessings fit into my religion? I didn't grasp it yet, but I was observing a new world order of existence.

CHAPTER ELEVEN

Necessary Professional Developments

"Presumption is our natural and original malady. When I play with my cat,
who knows if I am not a pastime to her more than she is to me."
—Michel de Montaigne

A VISIT FROM THE CHURCH

When the phone rang in the dorm I was startled because I seldom got phone calls there. It was the secretary in the College Religion Department alerting me that I was scheduled for an interview at 8:00 the next morning with Elder Cree Sandefur (1914–1994), president of the Southern California Conference.

I was a college senior. My Selective Service status had been changed by the dean's office from I-A (regular army) to I-A-O (conscientious objector) to 4-D (ministerial student). I was nearing the end of my education that had been uninterrupted since I was five years old. I had held several part-time jobs—jobs designed to help me make necessary funds to pay for school. But this was serious. This was my first career interview. At 8:00 am, I was in the Religion office in La Sierra Hall, dressed in my new black mohair suit with black tie and crisp white shirt. I had polished my shoes for the occasion, and I was slightly nervous.

I had met Elder Sandefur before. He had been our speaker at a Religion Department retreat at Idyllwild, the Conference junior camp in the San Jacinto mountains. I had seen him leading out in Conference convocations and most recently at an evangelistic campaign at the Los Angeles Sports arena with the *It is Written* team. Here was an influential Adventist leader, a person I considered to be devout, creative, open-minded, intelligent, exciting, and generous. His Conference was one of those progressive centers of Adventism, and he was known as open to real innovation. There was a saying among theology majors—"A call to Southern California Conference is a call from the Lord!" Now I had been scheduled to interview, at his request.

As I walked in, Elder Sandefur stood up from behind the desk, a smile covering his face. He too was dressed all in black. He reached out to shake my hand. He called me "brother" and invited me to have a seat. I smiled politely and sat down. He revealed that he had his eyes on me for some time.

I sat up stiffly in my chair. I was not a climber. I had never visited, called or written a Conference president asking for a job or even an interview. I didn't think I had to. If God wanted me, he would make it known. I had always taken it for granted that God would provide my future. It was part of the committed life. He had called me. He would lead me. Now here was a man who I greatly admired telling me he had been watching me for some time. He had some questions for me to address. I thought I knew what they would be, and he didn't disappoint me.

Have you colporteured and are you married? Those were the questions. And even though he knew the answer he followed the script. I explained that I had done a summer of colporteuring in Merced and served as vice-president of the Colporteur Club on campus the following year. He liked that. He admitted that he knew I was not married but wondered if I had any prospects that might materialize by the time I graduated? I admitted that I was not married but that I had a prospect. So, in ten seconds it seemed, the past few months flew through my mind like a historical panorama.

THE SUMMER OF 1962

I knew that during my senior year I would have some important decisions to make. All my preparation for the ministry was now on the line. But an important qualification was marriage. I was pretty sure I had to be married to get a call. For one thing, I knew my life would change that year because I would be living in the dorm. The College Press had closed it's doors in the summer of 1962, and for most of that spring my parents had devoted their spare time to finding new jobs, not necessarily an easy adjustment when they were entering their sixth decade of life.

Dad had planned to retire in his little shack (as he called the house he had built). Several of the Press employees had applied to the Loma Linda University Press but the jobs available there were limited in number and soon filled. For some reason Dad never applied there. That meant that my parents would move, and I would live in a college dormitory.

Dad had been offered a print shop in Riverside by an older couple who had hired him many times to work part-time in the evenings. As I understood Dad's story, the owners had no children and they were very fond of Dad and his professionalism. He could not only manage the shop, he could own it, they told him. I never knew any other terms of the deal.

Dad respectfully turned down the offer because he wanted to stay in denominational work. He was especially concerned because according to Church policy at the time, he told me, if he were out of denominational work for five consecutive years he would lose all his pension benefits. Furthermore, he needed to work a few extra years to get the maximum retirement benefits because he had been out of the Adventist work force for so long in Chicago. For Dad decisions like these always favored the work of the Church, to which he was totally committed.

By the end of the 1962 academic year, my parents were both hired by Pacific Press Publishing Association in Mountain View, 400 miles north of Riverside. Dad would be in the language department. Mom would work in the bindery. They would be moving. Dad would get the house ready to sell in June.

Meanwhile I had my own agenda. The La Sierra College Choir, of which I was a member, would be performing at the General Conference quadrennial session in San Francisco during the summer vacation. Singing to thousands of Church members would be an adventure. To add to the excitement, we would be recorded and featured on a special commemorative album on the Chapel Records label. The college had chartered a bus for the trip, and we were scheduled to sing the second weekend of the convocation.

At the age of eight I had attended my first General Conference meetings with my family. I remembered meeting two of my aunts visiting there from Sweden. For me it was a huge camp meeting. I recalled my shock when we all went out to a restaurant to eat lunch after the Sabbath morning worship service—something I could not remember ever doing before—paying for a meal on Sabbath? All the world leaders were there so it must be okay. But the fact that I retained that troubled memory meant that down deep I was not at peace with it. We hardly ever ate out at all, but certainly never on Sabbath where money was exchanged, and people were made to work.

In Sabbath School at the session I had heard electrifying storytellers from faraway places—people who had written books that Mom had read to me at bedtime. Elder Eric B. Hare (1893–1982), the most breath-taking storyteller I had ever heard, was there in person! He had been a missionary to the Karen tribe in Burma and had written *Clever Queen; a Tale of the Jungle and Devil Worshipers,* and *Treasure from the Haunted Pagoda.* My mother and my teachers had read these books to me, keeping me spellbound.

Elder Hare was a master of the "cliffhanger" and I couldn't get enough of his stories. He was there in 1950 to tell his stories. I thought he was a better storyteller in person than he was a writer. He was an actor, and his stories came alive as he told them. He had recorded these stories. They were for sale at camp meeting on little 45 rpm vinyl disks. Eric B. Hare—Adventist star, personality, celebrity—superb theatre!

"Uncle Arthur" S. Maxwell (1896–1970) was there. He wrote *The Bedtime Stories, The Children's Hour,* and *The Bible Story,* the ten-volume set that retold the great narratives of the Bible. My favorite book was his modern good-deeds mystery, *The Secret of the Cave*. Our elementary school teacher had read a chapter a day after noon recess, keeping us in suspense until the final chapter.

Uncle Arthur was a native of England and still had enough of the British brogue to make the whole set of stories he told deliciously enjoyable. He was another Church celebrity and he was there when I was eight years old. That was twelve years ago, but it had left a permanent impression in my mind. General Conference had been exciting for a child. This giant camp meeting would surely be just as exciting now.

The quadrennial meetings were not always held in San Francisco, but they were in 1962, and I had just completed my junior year of ministerial education. I would be there. Things were different now. I would not be going there for stories. I would be there as part of a performance and to meet people who might influence my life professionally. Now I would go to the adult meetings and surely they would prove to be as thrilling and electrifying as the stories had been.

Adventist celebrities would also dominate the presentations at the adult meetings. These included Dr. H. M. S. Richards (1894–1985), Sr., speaker of *The Voice of Prophecy* radio program, and Elder George Vandeman (1916–2000), speaker and producer of the television program, *It Is Written*. Wayne Hooper (1920–2007), a longtime member of *The King's Heralds* quartet, would be directing the music and introducing us to the new theme song he had written for the occasion, "We Have This Hope."

Now I took a new view of these servants of God. I was in training and these inspiring speakers would feed my soul as well as give me models to emulate in my ministry. These men would talk about the *Parousia* and the place of Adventism in sacred history. They would assure us once again that we were a people of prophecy and most of us would live to see that day when Christ would return to earth. This would probably be the last General Conference convocation held on this earth. The Black Cloud was closer than it had ever been before. The time of earth's history was ratcheting up (or winding down) to five minutes before midnight!

There was a bonus this year. Annie's family decided they would be there too. I would go up on the chartered bus, but I would come home in a metallic royal blue 1960 Cadillac. After the trip to the Colorado River, I had been invited to join them for their vacation at Clear Lake, north of Sacramento, after the San Francisco convocation. When I got off the bus I was spirited away into their custody and put on display for their friends, mostly medical people and clergy.

I was authorized to drive their car, and we went sightseeing when I was not rehearsing. We ate pizza with classmates and members of the choir, at Fisherman's Wharf. We drove around Golden Gate Park and parked by the docks. We rode the cable cars up and down the hills for mere pennies. We ate in China Town. We were tourists and we ran around with our friends until the night was late. I was amazed how many friends I suddenly had when I was driving a Cadillac (probably just my imagination). We were only in San Francisco for a weekend, but it seemed longer as we crammed so much into those few days. Then we were off to Clear Lake—camping and water skiing.

INSENSITIVITY TRAINING

I gave no thought to Dad back in La Sierra finishing up the house and packing to move. He was also preparing for the sale of the house. When he commented later how much he had missed me those two weeks I hardly registered the thought that he meant he missed my being there to help him. He said it several times for emphasis. Only later did I unpack his meaning more correctly.

On June 20, 1962, dad turned sixty-one and the work of finishing the house must have been taxing although he had always been a workaholic. My being gone at that critical time showed my insensitivity, but I was young and selfish, and I probably would not have changed my plans even if he had asked me outright to stay and help him pack up and move. Religious men sometimes have bigger fish to fry.

By the time I returned from San Francisco and Clear Lake, Mom and Dad had moved—the house was empty. In Mountain View, they had found and rented a small, one-bedroom duplex about six blocks from the Pacific Press. Because the place was so small they had gotten rid of many of their belongings. Since I was not there I lost the chance to claim any of Dad's books, which I would have liked to have had. He gave away most of his library. The twenty-volume set of The Book of Knowledge went with them. I still miss it.

In the house on Knoefler Drive everything was gone except Grandpa's desk and a few of my possessions that I had put aside, like my small library of books, a bookcase, and my file cabinet, all of which I took to my college dorm room. The place exuded quietness as I stood alone and thought of many happy times I had experienced there. Now only friendly ghosts of the past occupied the place.

Here were the rooms where Grandma had once lived. Jim had lived and moved out of this house and Grandma had become mortally injured here, after which I had had half the house to myself. Dad had converted Grandma's old kitchen into a darkroom for his photography. I had moved back and forth from Jim's old room to Grandma's old bedroom and finally come to rest in her room at the front eastern corner of the house.

Jim's former bedroom had been my TV studio for a summer, and we had moved the piano, the phonograph, and the records in there. It had an outside door and I had slept many summer nights on the porch adjacent to that entrance, along with Sparky, my pet toy terrier, pretending to be camping.

After coming back from my junior year at Auburn I had painted the room in a two-tone pastel resembling my room in Gibson Hall. Dad had rebuilt whole sections of the east end of the house because the original blueprints included no closets. When Dad wasn't working overtime, he was at home building hallways, closets, and bathrooms. Because of this the house never got finished. He figured he would complete it when he retired, but now those plans had changed.

When the college administration announced that they would be building a state-of-the-art printing plant for the College Press on Raley Drive, just a block from our house, we had rejoiced. But their plans changed. Behind these changes of plans were La Sierra's aspirations to become a university and the intense flirting going on between La Sierra College and Loma Linda University. La Sierra wanted to be a university and Loma Linda needed an undergraduate college. To the administration the marriage seemed right. The two campuses were only twenty miles apart. But this put several of the present programs at La Sierra in flux. Suddenly the plans for the new printing plant, once considered essential for the school, were scrapped and many of the staff members were left looking for work. The Board decided the combined university didn't need two print shops.

Rather than being able to finish his house in the next five or ten years, Dad was now faced with finishing it in two weeks—the two weeks I was gone doing Church work and qualifying to work for the Lord. All these thoughts crossed my mind as I walked through the home of my childhood and youth. Suddenly I felt strangely alone. Stunningly, the house was finished—from beginning to end—by Dad's hands. Ironically, just as no car ever spent the night in Dad's garage, so our family never spent a night together under the roof of our completed house.

PONDERING DAD'S CREATION

As I stood in the living room I pondered Dad's creative work. It hit me as never before what I owed my parents. I was awed by the solitude as I stood alone in the living room where we had listened to the radio programs and watched the TV shows. We had played games, put jigsaw puzzles together, listened to Mitch Miller and the gang and viewed Dad's home movies. Jenn had been there many times. I wondered how nurses training was going for her.

Dad had added a little print shop of his own behind the living room where he had produced the celluloid prints for Hansen's Global Church Films—used in making slides for evangelists in their Adventist meetings throughout North America and the English-speaking world. My mind was going a mile a minute—flashing back to so many experiences here in no order or sequence.

Since the house had not been sold Dad had appointed me its caretaker. I re-roofed the whole place—the only big job Dad had left for me. I mowed the lawn and kept the house locked up. Now I had some time to reflect. I would work all day and then come over to the house in the late afternoon and work until dark.

This was still my home. It was as if a part of me could not let it go. Somehow, the dorm, with all the excitement of living life as an adult, lacked the quality of life I had enjoyed here. I had a hard time comprehending that others would eventually take it over and that I would no longer be free to enter at will. Here was the house, *my* house, I had lived here since I was four years old. I had watched it rise from a vacant lot to a three-bedroom home. As a developing religious man, I thought of the Bible promise that someday we will have homes that we would build and no one else would own or live in.

> [21] They shall build houses and inhabit them;
>   they shall plant vineyards and eat their fruit.
> [22] *They shall not build and another inhabit;*
>   *they shall not plant and another eat;*
> for like the days of a tree shall the days of my people be,
>   and *my chosen shall long enjoy the work of their hands.*
> (Isa 65:21–22. Emphases supplied)

I had celebrated sixteen birthdays here. I looked at the door where Grandma had wandered in the wee hours of the morning around Christmas time in the early 1950s. She had become confused in the dark, stumbled over the Christmas tree in the corner of the room, fallen and broken her hip. It was Mom's self-fulfilling prophecy—realizing the fear that Grandma might fall and break her hip. Mom had done her best to guard against that. As it turned out this accident was the beginning of Grandma's end. She never fully recovered from that fall. Mom hired a private nurse, but she knew that time was running out. My loving Grandma, who sang to me and taught me mundane realities, was soon buried next to Grandpa in Redlands Memorial Park.

All this hit me as I stood in the old living room—the corner where the desk once stood, where Dad wrote his weekly letter to his father on Friday night, with a special fountain pen that he used for nothing else. I recalled that fateful Christmas eve telegram Dad had received from Sweden that his Dad, Grandpa Zackrisson had died. I thought about how hard Dad had tried in vain to keep the news from spoiling our Christmas.

I looked over toward the dinette where Mom had served tuna casseroles and Swedish rice on Friday nights for as long as I could remember. And even though Mom and Dad were still alive, I was face to face once more with the promise of the reunion that would come in the wake of the Black Cloud. I knew it would be soon. But in the meantime, I had to pursue my calling to help finish the work.

As night fell, I climbed into the long, royal blue Cadillac, which I had brought home from Clear Lake for Annie's parents and drove slowly back to the dorm.

MY SENIOR YEAR IN COLLEGE

During the summer of 1962, I was back to work on the college grounds crew. I had lined up a job much to my liking—running the college garbage truck all morning, dumping the contents in the Corona landfill, breaking for lunch, and then riding a lawn mower all afternoon. These jobs were fun, and they would give me a chance to get a good tan. I also took a summer school class—*Twentieth Century Literature*—from esteemed professor, Dr. Lawrence Mobley.

I didn't know that the summer was planned for me already. When I accepted the invitation to vacation at Clear Lake, I discovered that I had set myself up. This I had not expected because at the end of the previous school year I had decided that I would not be dating for a while. As a parting gesture of appreciation for the river trip I had invited Annie to go flying. A long-time friend of mine who was a very careful pilot, had given me a standing invitation to fly with him.

We took off from the Rubidoux Municipal Airport and cruised around Southern California. It was my first time up in any plane and while I had no desire to become a pilot it was an exciting experience. Annie reciprocated with the Clear Lake invitation. One thing had led to another and we were seeing each other every weekend.

I was living in Calkins Hall, the upper-division men's dormitory at the college. My roommate in the fall would be a theology major who lived in Hawaii. We had met during our freshman year and become friends. We were both village students then. His father was a Church official and was now in another Conference. He wouldn't be in town until the fall, so I had the room all to myself until then.

The summer was busy. Between work, study and relaxing in the evening I enjoyed the summer. Student workers would congregate around the dorm to eat pizza, tell jokes or just enjoy talking. Some had cars, so we would go into Riverside or Arlington and walk around stores that were open in the evening. There were some theology majors in residence that summer. Two of them had cars. If we lined them up for a weekend date in Los Angeles, they would take me to Annie's house. Annie's parents were hospitable. Her mother, arguably the best cook I had ever known, would always feed us.

Annie and I began writing to each other, despite my resolution not to date, and her letters came with more invitations for visits to her home. I would go into the city on Friday night, sleep in a room in the basement, and go with them to Church on Sabbath and outings in the afternoon. Saturday night we would play ping pong, cards, and table games, or we would attend functions at the Church or go to Pacific Ocean Park, a big attraction on the Santa Monica pier in 1962. And there was pizza ordered in from the pizzeria around the corner from their house.

This new life was smooth and free from stress. Worries about expenses and money were never entertained. Whatever we needed was provided. My attempts to help with expenses were always rebuffed. I was a guest in this hospitable Scandinavian-American home. With my parents gone from La Sierra and most of my friends away for the summer I soon found my trips to the city an island of refuge in a busy week, and I came to look forward to them. These were generous and creative people, who shared a similar heritage with my family.

Being around them lent a flavor to my life on a scale I had never experienced before. I had not thought of myself as a member of a special cultural group, even though my home was filled with Scandinavian paraphernalia. This family with the similar artifacts and books all around their house reminded me of my roots. I didn't grasp that I was being courted by this Viking clan. I took everything at face value, not realizing that I may have become a chosen one.

I thought of their hospitality as good. I was a religious man responding to the blessings of God. And I was inexperienced and naïve. But I was completely drawn in. Each weekend got me in deeper until by the end of the summer our relationship had become a romance and the thought of ending this friendship had vaporized.

I thought I was being cautious. Jenn and I had no contact, but she was not out of my mind. Part of my apprehension stemmed from the fact that I did not experience the level of infatuation with Annie that I had with Jenn. I was older now—more mature? More serious? Good questions. Maybe that explained the lack of infatuation? I was reminded that our prophet and our teachers had warned us against infatuation—it was false love, "puppy love," nothing important to a genuine relationship—a danger if one was contemplating marriage. It was not something on which to build a marriage.

I was vulnerable—in transition, on the final leg of my initial education for ministry, and by now a true believer in the messianic role the Church had presented to me. I was expecting God's blessings and Annie was becoming one of them. In Rodgers' and Hammerstein's Broadway musical, "The Sound of Music," as Max walks around Captain von Trapp's estate in Salzburg, Austria, he remarks, "I like rich people. I like the way they live. I like the way I live when I am with them!"[1]

I had not yet heard those lines and I could never have conscientiously verbalized those thoughts. Even if they were true they would never be spoken in my perception as a religious man. People take advantage of a truly religious man—never the reverse. I was putty in their hands. All our plans were their plans. They always had money for anything we wanted to do, and they made many suggestions as to what we wanted to do. As a starving college student, I had nothing. All the money I made during the summer went to pay my school costs. So, the fit was nice. What seemed vast to me seemed frugal to them.

Being from a family of fixers I was impressed that when a major appliance broke, they often just bought a new one—a refrigerator, a dish washer, a color television, a new Cadillac. They patched some but new was better. No doors from burned elementary schools graced their home. Everything was state of the art. And yet I detected nothing ostentatious, flashy, or show off. Rather there was a contented reserve about the family.

That summer was a tempest of activity—amusement parks, Ringling Bros. Circus, table games—Mahjong, Risk, Sorry, Monopoly, Wall Street—and card games, lots of card games. Good Adventists never played with regular playing cards. The cards

---

1. Rodgers and Hammerstein, *The Sound of Music*, Act 1, Scene 9.

of the world were sacrilegious cards—we had learned that from our Week of Prayer speakers in academy. Each of those symbols on cards represented something bad—the Joker, for example, represented Jesus the offspring of an illegitimate affair between the Queen and the Jack, our speaker had told us; so, all card games were played with *Rook* cards, which duplicated popular card games of the day but dispensed with the evil symbols.

Annie's mother introduced us to several new card games that summer. And there was always the enjoyable food and stimulating company. By the end of the summer, I felt like I had a new family. With no real reason to stay at La Sierra on the weekends I had accepted all their invitations. When school started in the fall we found it natural to think of ourselves as a couple even though we had dispensed with such traditions as going steady. By now that was something high school kids did—not a mature symbol necessary to our more serious stations in life.

At the beginning of my senior year my old friend from the College Press entered again. He was divorced now and had switched majors from theology to religion, so he could finish college with his class. He was working as an insurance investigator at a large, reputable firm in downtown Los Angeles and needed a place to live nearer his job.

When I introduced him to the family he considered their home to be a perfect location and he proceeded to charm them into renting him that room in the basement where I used to stay the previous summer. Annie's mother did his laundry and treated him like one of the family. When he returned to the city after school he would take my laundry to her as well. I was living a privileged life without comprehending it.

THE GROOMING PROCESS

I didn't know what "grooming" meant or even that it was happening. I was sufficiently grounded and self-confident not to be flattered by their attention, and hence I did not pick up on it.

Annie's father was the son of a prominent physician, Grandpa Doc, who owned a clinic in an upscale mid-western suburb. I was told that some church administrators considered him "the terror" of the Conference. It was a tongue-in-cheek description of a strongly opinionated physician who was a big supporter of the Church program. But big supporters often attach strings to their support. Church leaders found that it was a smart move to meet with him soon after (or before) taking office. He was a Viking!

Grandpa Doc had been a Bible teacher in the Swedish/Danish/Norwegian Adventist institutions of mid-America before returning to medical school. With this background he was a close friend of Scandinavian teachers and administrators who were members of one of the larger cultures in that part of the country. He had also been a close friend of another Viking, Elder M. L. Andreasen (1876–1962), a professor at Union College, in Lincoln, Nebraska, and later administrator at the General

Conference and professor at the SDA Theological Seminary in Washington, D.C. My mother had been in Grandpa Doc's classes, so our families were already connected.

When I met the grandparents in their home I felt like I was being ushered into a throne room. It was not a bad feeling. They were beaming at the thought that not only was their granddaughter dating a ministerial student, but a purebred Scandinavian—a Viking. I felt appreciated. Grandpa Doc immediately began giving me theological and historical books. He loved to show me his library and his latest finds. And many of them were priceless.

One of his hobbies was reading religious history. He loved to surf the used bookstores for discoveries of old conservative Christian materials. When he came to California we searched Hollywood together exploring used bookstores. His library was impressive. He especially liked sources that Sister White had quoted in her popular book, *The Great Controversy*.

As time went by, I was introduced to other significant Church members of Scandinavian extraction and felt drawn in by them. The family was proud that Annie had been the private secretary for Elder Andreasen when he produced his *Letters to the Churches*, a series of pamphlets he wrote criticizing the book *Seventh-day Adventists Answer Questions on Doctrine*, which eventually had led to his defrocking by Church leaders.

The family felt that a close friend had been dealt a grave injustice by Church leadership. "Prez" they called him. His defrocking would have far-reaching results throughout the denomination and eventually touch my life in a painful and most unexpected way.

This was the first time I had been a Scandinavian on my own. Other than my blond hair, blue eyes, and red cheeks, who would have thought anything about my nationality? I had no accent, no national costume, certainly no second language—nothing to betray that I was anything but a normal red-blooded American. Most of these people were like me—no one was talking Norwegian or Swedish. This was a party of second and third generation Scandinavian Church members.

As nice as they were, I sensed that dynamic leadership was a very important element in their lives. They boasted of their involvement in Church politics. They clearly believed that their own judgment was as good as or better than their pastors and Church administrators. For me it was the old theology-premed conflict again, only this time played out on an adult, professional scale.

They were generous, fun, and opinionated, but I had a hunch that it would not be wise to cross them. They knew what they wanted, and they usually got it. As a kid looking in, I only vaguely grasped the politics they spoke of. This was new territory for me. And I supposed that somewhere in the mix, money was a significant element.

I felt that they had put me on a pedestal with all of them—the whole clan. Though I was not a member of this family, they made me feel special because of my nationality and professional pursuit. I felt showcased and paraded. If a trophy had feelings, I imagined, this must be how it felt. It was not an unpleasant feeling, but I wanted distance. This was a family of physicians and that was a special class who knew it. Yet they seemed excited at the possibility that they might have a minister joining the family. I was in a new playing field as a religious man. How did I feel? Ambivalent came to mind.

I surmised that Annie's father had learned a lot about Adventist politics from Grandpa Doc. He had held all the important leadership positions available to a layman during his years at his big Church in Los Angeles. The White Memorial Church (built in honor of Sister White) was the Church serving the city campus of Loma Linda University in the 1950s and 1960s. It was connected to the White Memorial Medical Center, which had been established around the turn of the twentieth century. "The White," as it was called, was a training ground for Sister White's much vaunted minister-physician teams.

The new domed sanctuary was constructed in the mid-1950s and had a seating capacity of 2300. It was the talk of the Adventist nation. Rightly or wrongly The White quickly gained the reputation of being the center of Adventist liberalism. The reasons seemed flimsy. Punch was served after Church in a patio built between the main circular sanctuary and the modernistic Olivet Chapel with its penetrating red, white, and blue stained-glass windows. Some outspoken Adventists perceived this to be a subtle form of the Protestant coffee hour.

In the 1950s a lot of Adventists still saw other Protestants as nominal Christians, the spiritual children of the *harlot* of the book of Revelation.

> [1] Then one of the seven angels who had the seven bowls came and said to me, "Come, I will show you the judgment of the great harlot who is seated upon many waters, [2] with whom the kings of the earth have committed fornication, and with the wine of whose fornication the dwellers on earth have become drunk."
>
> [3] And he carried me away in the Spirit into a wilderness, and I saw a woman sitting on a scarlet beast which was full of blasphemous names, and it had seven heads and ten horns. [4] The woman was arrayed in purple and scarlet, and bedecked with gold and jewels and pearls, holding in her hand a golden cup full of abominations and the impurities of her fornication; [5] and on her forehead was written a name of mystery: "Babylon the great, mother of harlots and of earth's abominations." [6] And I saw the woman, drunk with the blood of the saints and the blood of the martyrs of Jesus.
>
> When I saw her I marveled greatly. [7] But the angel said to me, "Why marvel? I will tell you the mystery of the woman, and of the beast with seven heads and ten horns that carries her. [8] The beast that you saw was, and is not, and is to ascend from the bottomless pit and go to perdition; and the dwellers on earth whose names have not been written in the book of life from the

foundation of the world, will marvel to behold the beast, because it was and is not and is to come.

⁹ This calls for a mind with wisdom: the seven heads are seven mountains on which the woman is seated; ¹⁰ they are also seven kings, five of whom have fallen, one is, the other has not yet come, and when he comes he must remain only a little while. ¹¹ As for the beast that was and is not, it is an eighth but it belongs to the seven, and it goes to perdition. ¹² And the ten horns that you saw are ten kings who have not yet received royal power, but they are to receive authority as kings for one hour, together with the beast. ¹³ These are of one mind and give over their power and authority to the beast; ¹⁴ they will make war on the Lamb, and the Lamb will conquer them, for he is Lord of lords and King of kings, and those with him are called and chosen and faithful."

¹⁵ And he said to me, "The waters that you saw, where the harlot is seated, are peoples and multitudes and nations and tongues. ¹⁶ And the ten horns that you saw, they and the beast will hate the harlot; they will make her desolate and naked, and devour her flesh and burn her up with fire, ¹⁷ for God has put it into their hearts to carry out his purpose by being of one mind and giving over their royal power to the beast, until the words of God shall be fulfilled. ¹⁸ And the woman that you saw is the great city which has dominion over the kings of the earth." (Re 17:1–18)

Critics charged that in time The White would probably be serving real coffee between or after services. How much of the Revelation 17 prophecy of Protestantism applied to The White was debatable? The tall, dark, artistic windows in the sanctuary, depicting apostles, were well done from an artistic point of view, but the characters were arguably grotesque-looking. Little metal plaques on the windowsills beneath the windows displayed the name of the wealthy doctor's wife or family who had donated the window, again like in those nominal non-Adventist Churches.

To top things off, the Church featured something unheard of in Adventist Churches: a split chancel—two pulpits on the platform with a communion table between them. The divided chancel invited controversy and criticism. Adventists traditionally arranged their Churches with the pulpit in the middle of the platform to demonstrate that they were a Word-centered denomination. Preaching was center. Only table-centered Churches had divided chancels to demonstrate that their worship was centered in the communion service, or the eucharist, too Catholic for Adventist tradition.

There was also a disguised cross atop the tower on the front of the Church. Another connection to Romanism, some people said. The organ at The White came at the price of some entire Adventist Church plants, and the organist and choir director were professional showmen in their own right. These were some of the opinions that were bandied about by those in the pews when I enrolled at La Sierra College. By the time I moved to Michigan for Seminary, the tone had become even more critical.

Under the leadership of a psychologist-pastor, The White was perceived to be the wealthiest congregation in the Southern California Conference, if not the whole North American division. A Church full of medical doctors and professionals generated a lot of money. The sanctuary was so full every week that Annie's Dad had printed up Reserved signs, which he placed on seats to assure that his family and friends would always have places to sit.

My first visit to The White was with my parents and my girlfriend from Auburn, who was visiting me during the summer of 1958 following my junior year. We went to worship at The White in the morning, picnicked in Griffith Park in Glendale in the afternoon, and later visited Forest Lawn attractions and the Planetarium. I remembered The White simply as a huge Church, something I had been taught that Adventists had mixed feelings about, because of history in Battle Creek. During my visits in 1962, virtually every Sabbath during the summer, I came to appreciate what The White was doing—making formal worship meaningful and beautiful.

Since the autumn of 1961, a new pastor now filled the pulpit. Dr. Wilber Alexander, my mentor from my early college days at La Sierra was now the senior minister. When he got up to preach his first sermon at The White, he looked down from the pulpit and saw a row of his students sitting there and later testified that tears nearly welled in his eyes. We had all protested when he left La Sierra and pleaded with him not to go. Fortunately for us he came back to teach Homiletics (the art of preaching) my senior year.

For many years, The White was the most politically important Church in the Southern California Conference. Money talks, and often wants to be represented with extra votes and support for special projects. Regardless of where Annie's father learned his politics he was a master of manipulation. His political acumen and money, coupled with his wife's celebrated hospitality, presented a formidable challenge to any pastor who came to The White.

He had graduated from the College of Medical Evangelists (CME), now Loma Linda University, in the 1940s. Rather than return to join the family practice in the Midwest he chose to join the faculty of CME on the Los Angeles campus where he taught for a short time. Later he joined the staff of a local hospital, where he was when I met him.

A MARRIAGE PROSPECT

As I sat across from Elder Sandefur, I was a political neophyte. With the insight that I have today of how the Church's political system works, I recognize all kinds of monsters of political operation that appeared to my youthful self as very noble Church people. But they were closeted gargoyles. I couldn't have been more innocent than I was when I sat before Elder Sandefur that day.

I was a senior in college, looking for a future working for the Lord. I did not think politically. I thought religiously. I was truly a *tabula rasa* waiting to be written on. I was a religious ideologue, collecting my file material for my future sermons, honing my typing skills, hitting the books and getting involved in extra-curricular religious activities to gain experience and understanding of people. Theology and Church were my aim in life. The thought that the Church was anything but God-led, headed by prayerful and devoted men of God, had not yet occurred to me. I had grown up to believe in the movement.

I had been reared in a family that sacrificed dearly for the cause, and who did not enlighten me as to the politics involved. I was not street-smart about how the denomination functioned other than what I had learned in my college Church Administration class—and that was for the most part dealing with hypothetical scenarios.

When people later attempted to teach me how to use the system to my advantage I judged this to be mangling and therefore questionable. These were things Adventists had always condemned in other denominations, especially in the Catholic Church. How could God's work be advanced through politics? God guided his work not politicians. Time and observation would eventually change my perspective on all this. That's the value of experience. As the Chinese proverb of Chuang-Tzu goes, "You cannot speak of ocean to a well-frog, the creature of a narrower sphere. You cannot speak of ice to a summer insect, the creation of a season."[2]

I saw everything concerning the Church in religious terms. Following my early education, I believed that God was leading his Church and that its leadership had been placed there by God himself. I saw Elder Sandefur as God's appointed leader at a critical time in the life of the Church, namely, the last days. I was humbled in his presence. I had expected neither his request nor his invitation. The thought that there may have been political aspects to his singling me out for a job with Southern California Conference never entered my mind, though it has since.

Whether Annie's father, as the very important layman that he was, or perhaps Dr. A had talked to Elder Sandefur, I would never know. To me, it was merely God recognizing me as one he had been grooming for a place in the work.

My marriage prospect was eighteen years of age. I was twenty. By later standards that would have been considered young. But by the standards of the day it was typical marriageable age. Many young women got married right after high school graduation. Even though the socio-economic state of our homes was different, she came from a home with similar religious values as mine.

One of these values we shared was the view that getting a college education was a small investment in one's future, and in these days almost a requirement for success, but in addition Annie, like many young women, saw college as a place to go prospecting for a husband. She had just begun her sophomore year in college when I sat for my interview with Elder Sandefur.

2. Goodman (ed.). *The Forbes Book of Business Quotations*, 263.

CHAPTER TWELVE

Moon River

"Take away love and our earth is a tomb."
—Robert Browning

NEW AREAS OF DISCUSSION

My plans for the following year would involve going to the Adventist Seminary in Berrien Springs, Michigan. The pressure was on to get married, but again her parents made it clear that she was not to consider marrying anyone until she finished college. That piece of information just slipped out somewhere—it was not a part of any marriage discussions we had ever had.

With Jenn I had already tried waiting and failed. But I had not seriously contemplated marriage when Elder Sandefur questioned me about it. Like Dean Akers before him Elder Sandefur got me thinking about it. It was not an entirely new thought. The subject had once come up briefly.

On a Sabbath afternoon, a week before school began, we rode with my program-team friend and his new girlfriend to Huntington Beach to sit by the ocean at sunset and talk. We wouldn't swim—we were Adventists. Good Adventists didn't swim on the Sabbath. Swimming or rambunctious playing in the surf (or surfing) would be personal pleasure-seeking thus Sabbath breaking. We might wade. We relaxed on blankets and talked. And then the moment happened.

With no lead up she introduced a completely new topic of discussion. She reminded me that she wasn't to think of marrying anyone until she finished college. We had never discussed marriage. We had only dated weekends through the summer.

So, wondering where this was coming from and where it was going I said nothing. And then she brought it to particulars. It was enough to lead me to speculate and my mind was shifted into some details. Believing where this was heading I dropped into range. Did I love her? I didn't *not* love her. But was I *in love* with her?

I didn't think I had the feelings for her that I had had for Jenn. But was that a reliable objective norm? I analyzed myself and examined my feelings. I really wasn't ready for this discussion. Two months before I had vowed to break off this relationship before school started. Was this to be a test of my seriousness?

She was talking again. She revealed that her parents had brought up the subject and had affirmed how much they liked me. My response was that I liked them too, and I remarked how much I had appreciated the good summer they had provided.

Now she stammered a bit. She shared that they had told her that they knew I would be leaving for graduate school after this school year. I was impressed that this was not so easy for her now. But it was well-planned. She said they reminded her that I would be making major decisions this year and one of them might have to do with getting married, since that was a requirement for my professional career. Now they told her why they had brought up the subject. Basically, they said, while they wanted her to finish college before she got married, they would hate to lose me. So, if it came out that way—she could be sure that we had their approval, provided I would agree that she would finish college at Andrews and allow them to pay her tuition.

And so, she had said it. It was hardly a masked marriage proposal. I was stunned. I didn't dislike it. I didn't dislike anything in our conversation. I was flattered and elated. This was not the road I had planned. It was a proposal! I had no intention of discussing marriage at this time. Yet I was in deep. I had accepted the hospitality of a very tight family system for the past three months. I had skied behind their boat. I had eaten their food. I had slept in their house. I had learned proper etiquette at their table. I had gone to amusement parks, parties, and the circus, all at their expense. I had driven their cars. They had become my family for the summer. We were all Vikings!

Was I now being called to pay back what they had invested? I didn't dare think that. Becoming a member of this family was not a bad thought. But it was my nature to overthink everything and there were pressures here that I had not anticipated. I thought of her little brother. He was the youngest in the family. He was about eight years old that summer. We had instantly hit it off together. I had determined to win him over early, so I brought something to give him each time I visited—a piece of candy, a toy—something to surprise him. I had always wanted a little brother and this guy came close to filling that role. Was that reason to get married?

He was brilliant; with opportunities I'd never had. All his wants and needs were catered to. His Dad's hobbies became his pursuits. His father was preparing for the day when socialized medicine would take over his profession, and he had studied electronics and television repair as a possible second profession. Little brother was surrounded with electronic paraphernalia and hobbies. A standard joke in the family was that "he had been born with an oscilloscope in his hand!"

Annie continued, "My parents told me that if we were to get married next summer, you would have to agree to let them pay my tuition for the last two years of my college education."

I never felt that I was being manipulated. Everything was so smooth. I had always thought it was the guy's place to bring up such a subject. But she had opened the discussion shamelessly. I wasn't ready for this talk, but I didn't avoid it. Planning my future was exciting, planning it with someone could be thrilling. Jenn and I had had many of these planning sessions. But in the end, those had led nowhere. I wasn't over that. And probably this was just talk. Young people talk.

As we sat on the beach talking about the future, I was not thinking about my upcoming job interview at all. But now I was sitting with Elder Sandefur and certain roads were open. I could have "a call"—I had colporteured and I could have a prospect for marriage—and after Annie's proposal at the beach, she had revealed herself as more than a mere prospect.

"I do have a prospect," I said. Elder Sandefur stood and extended his hand. He would get back to me over the next week or so. In the meantime, he would present this to the Conference committee. They made all the decisions while seriously considering his recommendations. If anything transpired in the meantime that was relevant to my decision. I was to let him know.

I got his message. He gave me his card and saw me to the door. I don't remember walking or running. I just floated away. I had never been invited to meet with a Church leader as an award for being a good student. I imagined the day would come and now that it had, I was not fully prepared for it. I hadn't known how it felt to be wanted. I still knew little of denominational politics or personal power. I was swept away by this fast-moving tide of events.

On my way out of the office, I asked the secretary to cancel other upcoming interviews. Of course, I would accept this call if it came. A call from Southern California was spoken of as the plum among theology students, allegedly the richest Conference in the world, allegedly the most progressive. Few people get this break so early in life. I was apparently at the top of my game.

Annie's father was either on the Conference committee or was close friends with some members on it. He had promised his daughter his support if I asked for her hand. A job waited for me when (or if) I got engaged. None of these factors had compromised my innocence. But life was closing in. The pressure was on.

THE BIG DECISION

I was sitting on the hallway floor Friday night outside Calkins Hall room 32 chatting with my College Press friend. We were discussing the latest developments in our lives. I had been silently engaged once. I still didn't really know if I was over Jenn. But I believed that our relationship was over, even though I still carried a torch which no one knew about. I was sure she didn't. Since no one could read my emotions or my mind this was a non-argument. I shared it with no one. I was ambivalent—unsettled, yet ecstatic. Things were going well in most areas of my life, but some seemed a little fast. Winding up college carried its own pressures. It is sometimes hard to enjoy fast. My wish to experience a wider social life had not really been fulfilled. This was what we were talking about.

I shared the conversation at the beach. He knew the family and liked them. What was there not to like? He had been entertained at their house along with me. He made a few pertinent remarks and then asked me a very personal question. Did I love her? My own hesitation in answering troubled me. I told him I *thought* so. And he drove it home. He asked me what I was waiting for? It was like a bolt of lightning had gone through me. God must be behind this. Religious men look for signs. All the signs appeared positive. How could I not see that? I would make the move.

SORRENTO'S ITALIAN RESTAURANT

It was October 1962. I took a bus for downtown Riverside to a jewelry store on Main Street and looked at watches. Our culture required that a faithful member of the Church present a special watch as the token of engagement for the female rather than a ring. Until the wedding it was to be worn on the right wrist.

Engagement rings, even marriage rings, were considered jewelry and thus were not considered acceptable behavior.

> Americans can make their position understood by plainly stating that the custom [of wearing a ring] is not regarded as obligatory in our country. We need not wear the sign, for we are not untrue to our marriage vow, and the wearing of the ring would be no evidence that we were true. I feel deeply over this leavening process which seems to be going on among us, in the conformity to custom and fashion. Not one penny should be spent for a circlet of gold to testify that we are married.[1]

Sister White had written to her contemporaneous members in the Church. There was a qualification connected to this instruction- if a country of origin considered the wearing of a wedding band to be necessary for a married couple, one should have no objection to the wearing of the ring.[2] But in mid-twentieth century America the

---

1. White, *Testimonies to Ministers and Gospel Workers,* 180–181.

2. Ibid., 181. "In countries where the custom is imperative, we have no burden to condemn those who have their marriage ring; let them wear it if they can do so conscientiously; but let not our missionaries feel that the wearing of the ring will increase their influence one jot or tittle. If they are Christians, it will be manifest in their Christlikeness of character, in their words, in their works, in the home, in association with others; it will be evinced by their patience and long-suffering and kindliness. They will manifest the spirit of the Master, they will possess His beauty of character, His loveliness of disposition, His sympathetic heart."

taboo on wedding rings in the Church was pretty much absolute. I was determined to respect such admonitions as faithfully as though they had been written that day. I picked out a Longines ladies' watch that was in my budget, put a down payment on it, and decided to pay the rest on time. Dad had bought Mom a Longines watch as an anniversary gift, so I figured it must carry the epitome of value. I had a small savings in the bank and knew I could pay for it.

Annie's parents had left a car for her use that week at school when I phoned and invited her to go for a ride. The night was illuminated by an unusually bright full moon when I whisked her from the dorm. I had hidden the little box under the driver's seat. We drove her mother's red and white Oldsmobile station wagon to Lake Matthews, a traditionally romantic spot about five miles from the college. There we parked briefly. I did not plan to stay long in this place—stories had circulated for years about couples being attacked and Lake Matthews was set in a wilderness too secluded to take the chance of tempting psychopaths who might be on the prowl.

With the engine running we looked at the moon's image shimmering on the dark lake. I reached surreptitiously under the car seat where I had hidden the little box that held the engagement gift. Then I made it official. What had begun with a chat at the beach now developed into a full-grown marriage proposal. I started, "I have given this a lot of thought and prayer, and I believe that God has great plans for both of us."

This was how religious men talked. And though God-talk may not appeal to the uninitiated, such talk was virtually required. This shows that he is in touch with his faith, that he is humble, that he has given divine guidance consideration and it's due.

I opened the little box and the precious item inside, slowly, to encourage some suspense. Coming directly to the point, I uttered the words: "Will you marry me?" And I displayed the watch in my hand. Way prepared. Desire expressed. Question posed. She answered yes.

We embraced and kissed. It was done. We would spend our lives together in ministry. We would rear children in the fear of God (which meant in Adventism). We had not discussed much of this, but I now knew her parents would support our decision and I considered that important. Her reverence for her parents was serious. Anything they approved was enough for her. And she had already confessed that they approved of me. At the time I saw that as a positive factor in our future.

We drove down the hill and through the orange groves to Sorrento's Italian Restaurant on Magnolia Avenue in Arlington and ordered root beer and a large cheese pizza. *Moon River* was playing on the jukebox. It became our song.

THREE MAJOR LIFE DECISIONS: "IN THE CAN"

I was amazed at how fast the major decisions of my life had fallen into place just during this month. Those major decisions were "in the can," as they would say in movie making.

There are three great decisions a religious man makes in life: God, career, wife. These decisions were all ratified in the month of October 1962—the month I turned 21.

I called Elder Sandefur with the news the next morning. Before the week was out, I was officially invited to join the ministry team of Southern California Conference. My immediate thoughts on the matter? God was incredibly good!

PONDERING BACHELORHOOD

On June 9, 1963, I received my Bachelor of Arts degree in theology with a minor in biblical languages. I had not excelled in Greek, but I had progressed from a C my freshman year to an A my junior and senior years. I took every Greek class the college offered so I would be ready for Seminary. I had been elected pastor of my graduating class—the class of 1963. Two days later, Annie and I were married in the Alhambra SDA Church on Chapel Street before 250 relatives, friends and acquaintances. My theological mentor and now Annie's pastor at The White, Dr. Wilber Alexander, officiated.

Dr. Walter F. Specht, my major college professor, found great humor in repeating his homegrown joke over and over—"Ed became a bachelor on Sunday and lost his bachelorhood on Tuesday!" And then he would laugh. His laugh was contagious.

Having a wedding and a graduation so close together is probably something like having a birthday a week before Christmas. Which carries more meaning?—which takes priority?—marriage or career? I had learned that God comes first, family comes next, and career comes last. But how does one separate God and ministry? God was my career. I would never solve this dilemma.

From the beginning of my marriage I felt that pressure. Everything in my well-planned life from my education to my Church expectations kept the career first in my life. I had always talked of marriage, but now it became apparent that I had not planned for it in the same way. I seriously believed Christ would have returned before this.

I couldn't imagine that anyone marries planning to fail. Certainly not a religious man. Nevertheless, I have talked to people who *left the door open*—"if things go bad I will bail out," they would tell me. For me that was never an option—once married, always married. Marriage was for life. I taught it, believed it, preached it, lived it—never doubted it. A religious man could work through any problem, any frustration, any difficulty—he had God and the song says it:

> He is able more than able
> To accomplish what concerns me today
> He is able more than able
> To make me what He wants me to be.[3]

---

3. Noland and Ferguson. "He is Able," (1989).

And he could do it without anyone outside the marriage knowing there was any kind of frustration at all. The decision to marry was as crucial as conversion, or a call to the ministry. I knew that here was a perception I would never change. Divorce was not an option for solving problems in a marriage, not even for solving a problem marriage.

In our Church the breakup of a home was the cause for "acceptable murder"—not the physical taking of a life, just destroying the future for the now second-class citizen. Rumors are the avenue through which some in cults express their toxicity of religion. Truth suddenly becomes the least of the concern of those who see human carrion to scrape off the pew. That is part of the toxicity. Happiness is not a justifiable aim in a cult. In organized religion heretics are worthy of character assassination and divorced people were often treated like the worst of heretics.

TELEGRAMS DURING THE CUBAN MISSILE CRISIS

We had announced our engagement to the student body at an Associated Students of La Sierra College (ASLSC) evening program. Because of our big smiles our picture appeared as a joke in the student newspaper as an advertisement for a toothpaste. "Our group had 25% fewer cavities!" the caption read.

I had been elected ASLSC Religious Activities Director and president of the Collegiate Christian League (the new name for the LSC Missionary Volunteer Society) for my senior year. I was to manage the student-sponsored religious program of the year from student vespers to retreats to devotionals to creative and inspirational ideas such as student evangelistic meetings, program teams, and writing "Religiously Thinking," the religion column in the *Criterion,* the college newspaper. Annie had joined me in that venture. She was a capable writer and I asked her to function as the public relations chief for religious activities.

On the weekend of the Cuban missile crisis, we sent telegrams to our parents telling of our marriage plans. Since we assumed they were all expecting an announcement from us, we decided that sending telegrams would be a creative way to give them the news.

While we were dictating the telegrams the Western Union operator expressed her surprise that we would be announcing our engagement on the weekend that the world was about to blow up. She was not joking. The cold war was at its peak. President Kennedy had notified the Russians that he would allow no Soviet missile build-up in the western hemisphere and that the U. S. would blockade the island of Cuba. The world was in turmoil. The air was electric with fear. But this escaped us. God would work it all out. This was not how the world was to end. We were going to get married first. And no Sunday law had been passed yet.

CHOPPED LIVER IN PARADISE

During Christmas vacation the family rented a cabin at Lake Arrowhead for a family weekend retreat. Mike was there, and he and I were invited to teach the lesson for Sabbath School at the cabin. The subject of the lesson was *witnessing*.[4] I never caught what we had said that put her in tears for the next three days until finally on Tuesday I got a frantic phone call from Annie's dad that I needed to come into the city and talk to her mother. I had been served notice regarding the discord I had caused in the family. I was astonished. We had been engaged for two months.

With some confusion and a lot of fear I borrowed a friend's car and made the pilgrimage, fifty miles west of La Sierra College. When I got there, I was ushered into the dining room where a red-eyed, drawn-faced, normally-in-control woman sat sobbing. Our conversation was set to be awkward. She started—we had harassed her and her husband. She had never known a finer Christian than her husband, and we had mocked him in our Sabbath School lesson presentation, making him out to be otherwise.

What had we said? We had covered the material in the lesson pamphlet that Christian witnesses talked to people about their faith and probably gave Bible studies rather than making the pastor do all the work. She presented this as evidence that we had singled out her husband because he never did any of this. He gave loads of money to the Church and that was all he had to do to be a good Christian witness. She felt that our suggestion was criticism directed squarely at him. And it was unfair. Furthermore, what kind of people were we that we would attack him when he had made all these arrangements for us to have such a nice weekend together?

I was blown away. I couldn't figure out where Mike was in all of this. Since I was the one sitting at the table I surmised that I was the guilty one. We had taught the lesson together—we hadn't written the lesson. My friend was not the one marrying into this family so somehow the blame came down squarely on my head.

I had not been reared in a confrontational home and I was not comfortable with this. I was at a loss how to evaluate this moment. I was not even plugging into the charges. Clearly, whatever we had said was perceived to be very offensive. I listened. I was chagrined. I was too unsophisticated, too naïve. I had been carrying out a family request to help teach the lesson, and somehow while fulfilling that assignment I had hit a vein without knowing.

My parents always taught me to respect my elders and I had learned that lesson well. I bought into the notion that whatever had happened was my fault. I apologized (for what I wasn't sure). But the vision of challenge had sowed the first serious seeds of doubt, seeds that would not sprout immediately. At that moment I didn't see this incident as dysfunction, I simply blamed myself for doing something very bad. That

---

4. *Sabbath School Lesson Quarterly*, "Dynamics of Christian Witnessing," First Quarter, (1963). The lesson for January 5, 1963 was entitled, "All Christians to Be Witnesses."

was what a religious man did—he owned up to his faults and repented of them. Those who have gone before were supposed always to be right.

As I returned to the campus I was chopped liver. I had earned it. I had deserved it. My religion told me that. I had not modified what I found taught in the Sabbath School lesson to meet the level of people I was teaching. But in my heart of hearts I dared to be offended. I didn't really believe I deserved what had just happened.

When I visited Mom and Dad in Mountain View during spring break two months later, I didn't relate this experience. But I was struggling with questions about taking this marriage step. By now we had been engaged for four months; and I was troubled. I was intimidated, but I swept it under my work at finishing up college. Again, I could mediate anything.

My calling was to *be* a mediator. That meant accepting my responsibility for causing such a problem for these fine people. Yet I didn't understand people who gave a lot of money, or some felt that once they gave the money they were entitled to controlling how and where it was spent. This was foreign territory to me. Over the years that Tuesday night experience would become clearer. I would learn what vein I had tapped into.

EVALUATING THE EVALUATION

Something was wrong. Religion addicts can throw away their better judgment in favor of what they perceive to be following God. Our plans were not feeling right. There was mismatch. Something was wrong. I began noticing family traditions that hadn't bothered me before. This family had worship meetings every morning and evening, reading the *Morning Watch* book and having prayer. It seemed unnatural to me and somehow the readings had no translation into life.

I came from a home where we worshiped together—we didn't have worship. The distinction seemed semantical but to me there was a difference. It was the lack of spontaneity. Except for sundown worship on Sabbath, which was our one planned time during the week in my home, we worshiped whenever we felt like it. I don't recall it ever being scheduled.

That wasn't a major problem. How could I criticize people seeking the Lord in any way they chose? Just because certain traditions vary should not make a difference. Adjust. The problem was that now I was getting picky. Why? We were getting married. The two of us had some similarities in our backgrounds, but there were enough differences that I began entertaining the thought that this may not work. A fearsome thought. Or maybe I didn't want it to work—a more fearsome thought. Perhaps I missed Jenn and thought about that future being over. I knew that door was closed forever, but the thoughts invaded me.

While Jennifer and I had come from different Church heritage we had clearly shared a common commitment. Nothing we did had been for traditional reasons. We had similar socio-economic backgrounds. Her Dad was a city utility worker, my

Dad was a printer. They both worked with their hands, they faced the hardship of balancing a tight budget every month. Neither of us ever cared much about material things or having money in the bank—it would probably be nice, but love was more important. And why were these thoughts emerging now?

My mind went back to earlier conversations. Annie had sat at the college library table when I studied there. Freshmen did not have evening library privileges, but she worked there so her case was different. She struck up conversations with me. Her sister had told her I was married. I made it clear that the notification of my alleged marriage reported in the *Criterion* was a mistake. In fact, Dad had written a letter to the editor to clear up that incorrect announcement. She seemed relieved and more interested.

I thought of the pursuit. The river, the summer of activity, the water skiing, Clear Lake, the proposal at the beach. Then my head shifted gears—to my unfortunate break-up with Jenn on Lover's Lane—the very fact that I thought it was unfortunate was a subtle bombshell to me. My mind was reeling—it had all been so fast; the pressure to marry, the call to the ministry, the need to be married to fulfill that calling.

Ambivalence was setting in on me, big time. But that Tuesday night visit was a coffin nail. It raised my suspicions about the reality of the minister-doctor team. It had indeed been a power struggle. And when her mother had seen us being "too cozy" for her liking as we watched television with the family, she had talked to her about such things—I had put my arm around her on the couch. According to her, our behavior was not appropriate. For a moment I was back in Dean Akers' office.

When she said she didn't want to be an invasive mother-in-law I wondered what she was really telling me. I guessed she was just being a mother. But we were engaged. I could hardly organize my thoughts into a cohesive whole.

Were previously focused goals becoming unraveled? My mind was free-associating. Had I made a mistake in getting engaged? Was this a rebound? Had I tried to prove something I didn't have to prove? Was I moving too fast? Was it too late to back up and think again? Was I in too deep? Was I being over-reactive? Was I just getting married to fasten down that call? Today I understand overthinking like I didn't then!

A TROUBLED TRIP FROM SAN FRANCISCO

As I boarded the plane on Sunday morning in San Francisco to return to college, I thought I was deciding—should I really go through with these marriage plans? Should I call the whole thing off? Vacillating thoughts and feelings danced in my mind during the flight back to Los Angeles on Pacific Southwest Airlines. Questions flowed through my head. I had to face some very serious personal issues—from a new concern.

How could I do this? Suddenly I was not marrying a person, I was marrying a family, an invasive, enmeshed family. But I was in deep. I was starting to ask—a dysfunctional family?—aren't all families dysfunctional? This one thinks it's not—don't all dysfunctional families think that? These people were taking over my life. Had I made a mistake? But they were such nice people—such good people. They were Vikings. And in my way of thinking, they were rich people. They were perceived as influential people—Church leaders, in the very denomination where I would be working. Did I love them or her? Where was the infatuation? I knew that there was a difference between infatuation and love, but I believed they should accompany each other. What fun is love without infatuation? My immaturity was glaring at me.

Did other religious men ask these questions? Or was I being overly ponderous? And suddenly the fifty-minute flight ended seemingly before it began. I was on the ground, on the tarmac at LAX. And there were people there to meet me. The family was at the airport to pick me up.

Her mother was especially manic. I didn't know why. She blurted out excitedly that I was in for a jolt when I saw what she had at home! My mind was only partially present. I was preoccupied with my new task. I was doubled over with doubts. And so, I exhibited a contemplative quietness. How was this going to work? Suddenly things were not as easy as they had seemed on the plane. The trip from LAX seemed shorter than usual as the new long sleek white Cadillac pulled into the driveway. We entered the garage and started climbing the series of stairs through the basement and up the long steep staircase to the main floor of the small mansion.

She hurried us down the hallway. I followed through the short hall to the room that had been the girls' bedroom when they were growing up. Now it served as a guest room when neither of the daughters was home from school. I arrived at the door that had been thrown open for my wondering eyes and what I was to behold would complicate things further.

THE ALHAMBRA PYRAMID

There, along the far side of the room, a small pyramid was growing: gifts—wedding gifts! They were from Robinson's, The Broadway, Bullocks, The May Company—all the finer stores of Southern California. I did not presume to think that any of these gifts had come from my family or their friends. We mostly shopped at Woolworth and Sears. At her family's direction we had registered at all these fine stores for silver (sterling) and china (Lenox), goblets (lead crystal) and appliances (Kitchen Aide, etc.). These were mostly from stores I had never been in.

I was, what's the word? Awestruck? Stunned? Bewildered? Perplexed? Baffled? Puzzled? Confounded? Confused! This added to whatever had already been building all day. The thoughts on the early morning plane had not envisioned this scene. It was clear that people of culture and wealth were taking us seriously and responding accordingly.

Now I realized I was in something far over my head. The romantic visit to Lake Matthews did not involve us alone. A whole invisible society was materializing. We had not made plans that touched only us. This touched people I had never met. The commitment represented by our engagement reined in doctors and doctors' wives, and proud parents of classmates. This was big time!

We had made a serious move by announcing our engagement. We were now owned by the public—largely a public I was unfamiliar with. The chase was over. To change things now seemed impossible—thoughtless, insensitive, inconsiderate, discourteous. If I carried through on my plans to break this off, what would we do with these gifts? We couldn't keep them.

What about all these people who took us at our word? How could I be responsible for disappointing them? How could I overrule such a majority opinion? I guessed I needed to re-think what I had been pondering. I was the one who had posed the official marriage question.

So, I retreated to a pre-flight mentality. What would people think?—Dad's mantra kicked in—in a whole different setting. We were a long way from our simple celebration at Sorrento's. Would a later possible divorce be less embarrassing for a wealthy family than a cancelled engagement? I had nowhere to turn. I had no model to follow. So, when a religious man has nowhere to turn where does he go?

I turned to the back of my mind where I had stored all the escapes the Church had supplied me with: None of this really mattered because Christ was coming back soon. Time would probably not even permit us to get married. The Black Cloud was nearer than any of us realized. And this would be our deliverance.

How lucky was I that I had not exposed myself to the family with what I had been thinking—even planning? The words of the popular song played in my mind, "Oh you can't go to jail for what you're thinking . . ." *Context* different, *thought* valid. I guessed my episode had been a fleeting one—cold feet.

Time to adjust again: I would hang a scrim in front of all that stuff I had been thinking about on the plane. I was getting married. That I didn't belong here was a haunting thought.

THE PAULINE MARRIAGE COMPLEX

I should naturally expect that I would be nervous about the step of getting married. I had had better moments than the ones on the plane—times when my mind was clearer and my decisions more accurate. I would go with those.

One of my friends who had scheduled his wedding two days before ours, also a theology student, had developed a Pauline marriage complex. Suddenly, in the middle of his engagement, he acquired the conviction that St. Paul's teachings applied to him. What was that complex? Paul had written,

> [6] "I say this by way of concession, not of command. [7] *I wish that all were as I myself am. But each has his own special gift from God, one of one kind and one of another.*" (1 Cor 7:6–7. Emphasis supplied)

> [26] I think that in view of the impending distress *it is well for a person to remain as he is.* [27] Are you bound to a wife? Do not seek to be free. Are you free from a wife? *Do not seek marriage.* [28] But if you marry, you do not sin, and if a girl marries she does not sin. Yet *those who marry will have worldly troubles,* and I would spare you that. . . .
>
> [32] *I want you to be free from anxieties. The unmarried man is anxious about the affairs of the Lord,* how to please the Lord; [33] but *the married man is anxious about worldly affairs, how to please his wife,* and his interests are divided. (1 Cor 7:26–28, 32–33. Emphases supplied)

My friend caught an emphasis in the Apostle's teaching that he had not seen and suddenly he came to new senses that a wife and family would just be in the way of his ministry. But in the last minute he changed his mind and went through with the wedding.

I guessed this was now my Pauline moment. The stack of gifts shook me to a reality I had overlooked, we were getting married—let's look at this as a cup half-full instead of a glass half-empty. God was blessing us. I hid the questions behind me. If I was not fully in love I could (and would) learn to be. If I did not fit in this family I would learn how. Probably I was the dysfunctional one.

Even if I was not clear on how to carry out ministry with a person who maybe did not share my commitment, God would make a way. Remember, some decisions we made now were not that crucial because Jesus was coming soon. That is our task, after all, to preach and teach. God will guide and make up for whatever we lack. No one is perfect. There was no time to have children. Who could tell if time would even last until June 11, 1963?

But what if it did?

CHAPTER THIRTEEN

Polishing the Dream

"We do not really feel grateful toward those who make our dreams come true; they ruin our dreams."

—Eric Hoffer

THE COURAGE TO CARE

Time did last. The consecration speaker on graduation weekend, Friday night, June 7, 1963, was Elder Cree Sandefur, my new boss from the Southern California Conference.

As the pastor of my senior class, I was responsible for giving a short response to Elder Sandefur's talk. I felt good about this. I felt like I was part of a new team. I had made good decisions: to colporteur, to graduate, to marry, all part of the overall decision to work for God. Somehow, they were all related. And I was finally marching in step. As the Swiss philosopher Henri Frédéric Amiel wrote, "The man who insists upon seeing with perfect clearness before he decides, never decides. Accept life, and you cannot accept regret."[1] I could go with that.

My pastor's response to Elder Sandefur's talk, "The Courage to Care," reflected the thoughts of a religious man in the making with an unrecognized prophecy of his own life.

> As each senior class graduates from this college, the members cannot help but wonder if they might be the last senior class to march down the aisle of this church in caps and gowns, for they realize the nearness of the end of time as

---

1. Goodman (ed.), *The Forbes Book of Business Quotations*, 191.

they face the complacency of the world and the seeming impossibility of God's continuing to allow sin and degradation.

But this evening we congregate as a class to examine the very purpose for which we have pursued a Christian education. Not only have we attended here that we might prepare ourselves to face the future financial responsibility of making a living, though this is important. Not only have we spent four years at La Sierra College, so we could attain scholastic excellence. We have come tonight to a point of basic preparation to face the opportunities and disappointments of this life because we care about this world. By that we mean we care about the people who live in this world.

We plan to be physicians so that we might bring to a dying physical society the healing effects of modern science in conjunction with the comfort of the gospel. We train to be teachers that we might stimulate a career in the hearts of young people as our teachers have produced an attitude of concern in our hearts. We look forward to being journalists that we might communicate an essay of hope to the unheralded thousands who wait behind curtains of darkness.

The world sarcastically grunts, "Who cares?" as an abandoned child scoops an apple peeling off the street—his only nourishment. The world utters, "Who cares?" as a man dies from an incurable disease because he trusted in the deceptions of his fellow man and because he did not know the truth. The world challenges, "Who cares?" as a once happy couple terminates their joyful marriage in a divorce of lifelong heartache and bitterness.

As consecrated future social workers, pastors, counselors, evangelists, and all inclusively—as Christians—we optimistically face this world's condition of frustration, believing that God will protect us from the fallout of complacency that could cause us to lose courage as well as eternity.

Tonight, as a class, we consecrate ourselves in dedication to the service of our Lord that He might sustain and strengthen in us a courage to care.[2]

THE HONEYMOON

We left on our honeymoon on Wednesday morning. We had spent our first night together at the Statler Hilton in Los Angeles where my best man had arranged a room for us. Now we were off to the cabin at Lake Arrowhead for a few days before leaving for the university in Michigan. We were honeymooning in the same cabin where we had given that infamous lesson study on witnessing. I hoped the cabin wasn't cursed in some way. That last experience hadn't been the greatest. Putting that thought aside, I anticipated that this was to be a week of uninterrupted affectionate expression—alone at last. Lovers in love.

---

2. Zackrison, "Class Pastor's Response to 'The Courage to Care,'" June 7, 1963.

One can only begin to understand the anticipation that a young religious man could feel at that point in life as one grasps the context of the early 1960s and our religious agenda. That we ever reached this chronological point was a miracle. The true believers certainly had never thought time would last long enough even to graduate from college much less enter marriage.

We were now 119 years removed from when our pioneers believed the second coming of Christ would occur. But hope was still alive. Some were even predicting that Christ would return in 1964—exactly 120 years from the Great Disappointment of 1844. That predication was based on an interpretation from Jesus' Olivet discourse (Matthew 24) where he spoke of the end being as in the days of Noah.

Rather than exegete the passage, those who pushed this view overlooked the context of the chapter and focused only on the time factor—claiming that Noah preached for 120 years and then the flood came.

> [3] "Then the Lord said, 'My spirit shall not abide in man for ever, for he is flesh, but his days shall be a hundred and twenty years.'" (Gen 6:3)

> [37] As were the days of Noah, so will be the coming of the Son of man. [38] For as in those days before the flood they were eating and drinking, marrying and giving in marriage, until the day when Noah entered the ark, [39] and they did not know until the flood came and swept them all away, so will be the coming of the Son of man. [40] Then two men will be in the field; one is taken and one is left. [41] Two women will be grinding at the mill; one is taken and one is left. [42] Watch therefore, for you do not know on what day your Lord is coming. [43] But know this, that if the householder had known in what part of the night the thief was coming, he would have watched and would not have let his house be broken into. [44] Therefore you also must be ready; for the Son of man is coming at an hour you do not expect. (Matt 24:37–44)

It was an attempt to keep apocalypticism alive, and the excitement it generated demonstrated that the believers were still anticipating with baited breath the Black Cloud that would introduce the end of this world and the beginning of a new one. But so far, time had lasted. The Black Cloud was still a future event. And we were on our honeymoon. Dr. Laurence J. Peter would write, "A husband may forget where he went on his honeymoon, but he never forgets why."[3] And some husbands are religious men.

For a religious man, especially one of legalistic persuasion, sexual intercourse outside of marriage was fornication, the unmarried version of adultery—something condemned by the Ten Commandments, written with God's own finger on tablets of stone.

> [14] "You shall not commit adultery." (Exod 20:14)

---

3. Peter, *Peter's Quotations: Ideas for Our Time*, 324.

> [16] "And the tables were the work of God, and the writing was the writing of God, graven upon the tables." (Exod 32:16)
>
> [13] "And he declared to you his covenant, which he commanded you to perform, that is, the ten commandments; and he wrote them upon two tables of stone." (Deut 4:13)
>
> [4] "And he wrote on the tables, as at the first writing, the ten commandments which the Lord had spoken to you on the mountain out of the midst of the fire on the day of the assembly; and the Lord gave them to me." (Deut 10:4)

Both official religion and personal convictions forbade fornication. And so, this honeymoon week would be a rite of passage into the affectionate and intimate aspects of married life. I had no doubt that in his grace God had extended time, so we could participate in this together. Many young Adventists in my generation, when questioned about the time of the *Parousia*, would say that they hoped Christ would not return before they could get married. What many meant was they hoped Christ would not return until that could have sex and for them that involved marriage.

Of course, some did not wait for marriage, but the ultimate embarrassment to any religious family was the gradual appearance of a swelling female abdomen out of wedlock. More than one co-ed had suffered this embarrassment and disappeared from our college scene.

This was basically pre-pill, pre-Roe v. Wade America, and the odds of hiding one's sins were not what they would soon be. But a religious man did not consider hiding anything. His life was to be transparent, as our prophet had written,

> Everything that Christians do should be as transparent as the sunlight. Truth is of God; deception, in every one of its myriad forms, is of Satan, and whoever in any way departs from the straight line of truth is betraying himself into the power of the wicked one.[4]

Despite this, a religious man was not yet sinless, so he might participate in those acceptable sins that brought no offense or embarrassment to God, family or himself. But certainly, going "all the way" was out of the question. We read articles about this in *The Youth's Instructor,* the Church's young people's weekly periodical that threw great fear in young hearts in anticipation of their trip to maturity. Ironically, some sins were even expected. For a naïve boy who never went below the neck this could be a painful diagnosis—being accused by his girlfriend or her friends of being a person of questionable hormonal development, even if said with tongue-in-cheek. The social stress was strong, and the natural propensities were naturally inviting.

Intimacy meant three things: necking, petting, and sex; and they were progressive. Even though an artificial distinction, this was part of our religious culture. The first restricted to the neck and up, was expected in a romantic relationship. The second,

---

4. White, *Thoughts from the Mount of Blessing*, 68.

including everything but penetration, was frowned upon and warned against, because of where it could lead, but also to some extent a gauge of virility. Girls were expected to hold the reins, or put on the brakes, when the boys tried to go too far. Since the girl had the most to lose, she was expected to decide how far was too far.

The third was taboo—a religious man would simply not consider it appropriate to venture into this area until the wedding night. It was a matter of respect for the trusting woman. And it was called going "all the way." The common definition in our society was that "sex" referred to penetration and this activity would end one's virginity. Those girls who allowed the boy to go "all the way" were usually considered loose, even sluttish. Some guys bragged of their conquests but none I knew wanted to marry "a slut."

I heard about a guy who confided that he wanted to marry his girlfriend. But she had attended public high school and he was worried that she might not be a virgin. He doggedly questioned her about her past to decide whether she should be his bride someday and whether she would make a good wife.

When their relationship had finally developed to the point of talking marriage, she finally felt she could trust him, and so she told him she was not a virgin, a fact she deeply regretted. He was so devastated by her admission that he determined that he could not marry her. And what might have been a vibrant marriage ended. Her conversion and convictions, her loyalty to him, the trust in him that had led her to share this painful truth, made no difference. He apparently now thought of her as a slut and not worthy to be by his side.

Sexual intercourse before marriage between two loving people would make them both fornicators. Our academy Bible teachers and Week of Prayer speakers told us that for boys this would be the an almost irresistible temptation, and if we succumbed or caved in under such pressure, we would regret it for the rest of our lives. Such views resonated with a religious man. Abstinence was the only life accepted by God. But petting was often viewed as a grey area. We were taught these things from birth to protect us from irreparable harm.

All our speakers for the annual Weeks of Prayer would hit the subject somewhere during the week. Sometimes they would have a meeting for the girls with no boys present, and then a meeting for the boys with no girls present. Our Bible teacher continually warned the girls in his classes that some (probably most—possibly all) guys wanted to take a girl out to give her a physical examination. He told us that even in marriage we would be tainted for life if we participated in such depraved activity.

In short, this level of sexual expression was not permissible behavior outside of marriage, if one was a Christian. Obviously, he did not believe that petting was a grey area. As I drove to the honeymoon cabin at Arrowhead, I knew I had made it—I had succeeded in making it all the way to marriage—a virgin by Adventist definitions. And now I would be free to express my affection for my wife.

Profile of a Religious Man

DEALING WITH DISILLUSIONMENT

As things turned out, our week of intimacy and bliss ended almost before it began. We headed back the next day and spent the rest of the week and the weekend at my in-law's home and on Sabbath, we attended Church services at The White. We still had the consolation of knowing that the Black Cloud would soon restore our happiness. I knew that, and I dismissed from my mind the disappointing beginning of our marriage. I couldn't have thought of everything. Who can evaluate one's marriage in the first two days?

I had one advantage: my religion had given me a gift. Toxic religion helped me perceive denial as part of the normal Christian life. Because of this gift, I was able to polish my dream. I could carry on my life without considering that anything was wrong with my marriage. Whenever something became an issue, I could use God to cover it up.

I surely would not go to a marriage counselor or a psychotherapist, as separation or divorce was as serious as suicide. If word got out that we had seen a therapist, we would be perceived as weak, inadequate, lacking in maturity or in the worst scenario, dancing with the devil—not a good position to be in when starting out a life of gospel ministry.

God was stronger than any human counselor—with him we should overcome any frustrations in our marriage. As religious youngsters, we had been taught that psychology was a pseudoscience no more credible than phrenology and mesmerism.[5] About these so-called sciences of the mind, our prophet had written:

> The advantage he [the devil] takes of the sciences, sciences which pertain to the human mind, is tremendous. Here, serpentlike, he imperceptibly creeps in to corrupt the work of God.
>
> This entering in of Satan through the sciences is well devised. Through the channel of phrenology, psychology, and mesmerism, he comes more directly to the people of this generation, and works with that power which is to characterize his efforts near the close of probation. The minds of thousands have thus been poisoned, and led into infidelity. While it is believed that one human mind so wonderfully affects another, Satan, who is ready to press every advantage, insinuates himself and works on the right hand and on the left. And while those who are devoted to these sciences laud them to the heavens because of the great and good works which they affirm are wrought by them, they little know what a power for evil they are cherishing; but it is a power which will yet work with all signs and lying wonders—with all deceivableness of unrighteousness. Mark the influence of these sciences, dear reader, for the conflict between Christ and Satan is not yet ended.[6]

---

5. White, *Messages to Young People*, 57. This material originally appeared in an article in the *Review and Herald*, (1862).

6. White, *Selected Messages,* 2:351–352. This article originally appeared in an article in *The Signs*

Sister White made a direct correlation between the sciences of the mind and the coming of the lawless one of 2 Thessalonians 2.[7] Whoever the lawless one was, he was in cahoots with Satan. Relying on another to carry you through difficulties was a sure channel through which the devil would gain access to one's mind and turn one into an infidel.[8]

These counsels on psychology had been published by Sister White in 1862 but those who had codified her writings had presented them as absolute and warned against overlooking them and compromising with modern society. With the establishment of institutions of higher learning, psychology eventually became an acceptable academic discipline, and both psychologist and psychiatrist were listed in our academy youth problems textbook as legitimate pursuits for youth who chose not to fill a position in the Church.[9]

This created another double bind. Adventist colleges began teaching psychology and setting up psychology departments, though they first included them in the college Education Departments. Still psychology continued to have a stigma attached to it. And going for counseling, even to a pastor, was often questionable for a religious man preparing for the ministry. Furthermore, I knew the dangers of psychology because my uncle had become a psychologist and left the Church. There was no question in my mind that this was more than correlation—I saw this as cause and effect.

UNDERSTANDING RELATIONSHIP

We had only been married a week, but there was already an emotional distance between us. The distance had to do with our reticence to acknowledge that we were emotional beings not just rational, religious, or theological entities. We had feelings and those feelings were legitimate. Time would surely sort out some of this but for the moment it was a minor crisis. To paraphrase, one week does not a marriage make.

Then too, Mike had been wrong. No Catholics had held siege at my graduation. The ceremonies had not been in Lower Hole Memorial Auditorium by candlelight. And now I was married as well. But we were still on the edge of time—the world could still end any day. And any frustration with my new situation as a "bachelorless bachelor," as Dr. Specht had put it, was relieved by my religious view of time. This was a very convenient and durable defense mechanism.

The word sex had entered our lives. But how do two people know if they are sexually compatible if they have grown up in a culture that does not allow one to explore that question? Relationships involve individual needs. Physical needs are not

---

of the Times, (1884).

7. White, *Testimonies for the Church,* 1:290. This was first published in her seventh testimony (1862).

8. White, *Selected Messages,* 2:351.

9. Jemison, *Facing Life: Guidance for Christian Youth,* 371.

hard to define, and they are listed as basic in Abraham Maslow's hierarchy of needs.[10] But we had to work through these frustrations on our own. We felt fortunate that we had a prophet who spoke to virtually every topic we needed help with. Since Sister White's death, many compilations from her writings had been put together including *The Adventist Home, Child Guidance,* and *Messages to Young People,* all dealing with these issues.

Even talking about feelings, according to Sister White, was risky for a religious man. It was unwise to study our emotions. It could result in the *enemy* "presenting difficulties and temptations that weaken faith and destroy courage. Closely to study our emotions and give way to our feelings is to entertain doubt and entangle ourselves in perplexity. We are to look away from self to Jesus."[11]

One's needs are often confused with one's wants. For us the wants/needs were supposed to be discernible. I had grown up in a very warm and expressive home and now I noticed that the family I just married seldom touched each other. I had a limited experience with romantic intimacy, but I knew I needed warmth and touching. I never knew what hers was.

Some questions you politely stayed away from. No one would ever ask you, have you ever masturbated? In our generation this was not even a subject that anyone mentioned in polite company much less discussed. We just knew that our prophet had condemned such selfish intimacy with threats that anyone engaging in what she called secret vice would have serious physical and mental difficulties in life.

The only time I ever heard anyone address the subject in public was when a Seminary teacher asked his Youth Ministry class to find a biblical reference that focused on the subject. Undoubtedly, he hoped to bring the topic into the open for these aspiring youth pastors. The class had difficulty finding anything at all. Then a wisecracking student announced that he had found a verse. 10 "Whatever your hand finds to do, do it with your might; for there is no work or thought or knowledge or wisdom in Sheol, to which you are going." (Ecclesiastes 9:10). I was told that the class exploded in laughter. The professor was not amused. The class, however, could hardly regain composure for the rest of the class period.

A denominational administrator told me once that all boys masturbated and anyone who says different is lying. I didn't know what survey or study had led him to that conclusion, but it was a striking assertion. These incidents underscored the rarity of any discussion on the topic.[12]

The social and religious pressures brought to bear on clergy often conspired with Puritan attitudes toward female sexuality to turn ministers into what a colleague once

---

10. Maslow, "A Theory of Human Motivation," *Psychological Review*, (1943).

11. White, *The Ministry of Healing*, 249.

12. J. White (ed.), *A Solemn Appeal Relative to Solitary Vice, and the Abuses and Excesses of the Marriage Relation* (1870). This book contains virtually everything Sister White ever wrote about sex and masturbation. Also, of interest is Numbers, *Prophetess of Health: A Study of Ellen White,* (1976).

called a third gender, a fraternity of emasculated and frustrated men forced to live in denial of their sexual needs. It was not surprising that some ministers buckled under the pressure. My future mentor would impress upon me that there were two ways to get kicked out of the ministry. He put it a different way: "Don't get caught with your hand in the till or on the women!"

In our religion I was learning that sex was not something you talked about like in the movies, or you might end up like the student whose marriage plans had gone awry when he discovered on her own testimony that she was not a virgin. I don't remember hearing the word "pregnant" used in polite speech until I was in high school. I grew up in a sexually silent world. What I knew about sex was mainly gained when I climbed trees in the neighborhood with my young acquaintances and we talked about it on the highest tree limbs. But this was considered dirty talk. And we laughed a lot. It was non-religious banter.

During my junior year in high school, my brother gave me a book on the facts of life.[13] He got permission from Dad to give me the book. Mom later apologized to me about silence on the subject and told me she had always thought it was Dad's place to talk to me about such things. I don't recall that he ever did (except for approving this book).

I read my brother's book through, especially the sections on girls. I already knew most of these things from what I had picked up in the trees. I had pieced the facts of life together on my own. The book corrected or explained a few misunderstandings but mostly it confirmed in rather sterile and clinical language what I already knew, or thought I knew. It helped clarify some things.

I thought this would be a natural topic of discussion in marriage but to my chagrin, I discovered that I was now married to someone who balked at talking about such things. We had both been brought up in silence. I forced myself to believe this was something we would have to grow into with time.

PREACHING IN THE BEDROOM

An important aspect of any successful ministry is the happy home life of the minister and his wife. Feeling used can be a serious issue in a marriage from both viewpoints. I do not know exactly when I became aware that we each defined intimacy differently, but I remember that by the end of our first month of marriage I was invoking the writings of the Apostle Paul in the hope that she might take heed. Not helpful! The bedroom is not a place for a sermon.

> ² But because of the temptation to immorality, each man should have his own wife and each woman her own husband. ³ *The husband should give to his wife her conjugal rights, and likewise the wife to her husband.* ⁴ For the wife does

---

13. Duvall, *Facts of Life and Love for Teen-Agers*, (1956).

> not rule over her own body, but the husband does; likewise the husband does not rule over his own body, but the wife does. ⁵ Do not refuse one another except perhaps by agreement for a season, that you may devote yourselves to prayer; but then come together again, lest Satan tempt you through lack of self-control. (1 Cor 7:2–5. Emphasis supplied)

I was preaching that the duty of a married couple was to submit to each other's intimacy needs—that this was part of the wedding vows to love one another in marriage. In fact, to disobey this command was not only infidelity but grounds for separation—though I never thought I would consider taking such a drastic step myself. It was a ploy to shake some reality into our relationship, but it was a very poor way to communicate. Giving vent to my frustration and disappointment led nowhere and we became more polarized in our stubbornness.

My approach was driven by desperation but not informed by wisdom. Not surprisingly, it didn't work. I learned that preaching in the bedroom is counterproductive. Every impromptu sermon made the situation worse. Our needs may have been different, but I thought we could find common ground through scriptural instruction. Furthermore, why had she not told me about her view of intimacy during our courtship?

I was feeling wounded by what I interpreted as rejection. While she was not moved by my attempts to make her feel guilty, I was especially susceptible to guilt myself. At first, I tried the storming-out-of-the-house routine, hoping to be stopped and intimately caressed by a repentant and guilt-ridden lover. But that never happened.

I would get in my car and drive around Southwestern Michigan for an hour or two to cool my disillusionment only to return, not to a dejected or worried wife, but one who was so relieved by my absence that she had gone to sleep. I was looking emotionally unstable even in my own eyes. I was surely building a case for seeking help from a clinical psychologist somewhere, someday. But violating religious principle was not permissible.

Each new encounter turned my anger into hidden rage. And to deal with that, I turned unconsciously to denial. We had been taught that indulging anger, resentment, and all kinds of unkind tempers would lead to gratifying our lustful desires. Our prophet had given clear instruction.

> Above all, let there be no shadow of hate or ill will, no bitterness or sourness of expression. Nothing but kindness and gentleness can flow from a heart of love.[14]

> The servants of Christ are not to act out the dictates of the natural heart.... This is what Satan wants them to do; for these are his methods. It is the dragon that is wroth; it is the spirit of Satan that is revealed in anger and accusing.[15]

---

14. White, *Testimonies for the Church*, 2:52.
15. White, *The Desire of Ages*, 353.

I felt my anger deepening—and with it, my guilt. So, my driving increased until I had toured most of lower Michigan and parts of Northern Indiana and Eastern Illinois. It was a miserable existence but never something to which I would admit, and over time it would take its toll. A religious man was not to be an angry person and apparently, he was not to be horny either. When these barriers were erected, two things happened, anger was internalized, and the psyche gradually attempted to drop intimacy from the marriage.

In our case, intimacy was not an answer to estrangement nor was it a way of making up after an argument. Rather, it was an occasional reward for not having an argument. By insisting on or expecting an intimate married life, I had brought dysfunction and perversity to our marriage, she said. But denying my needs was impossible and unwise.

One day when the topic turned to our increasingly chilly relationship, she announced that we were not libidinously matched. I was the one who was frustrated, not her, but she wanted to help me with it. She simply didn't need the same intimacy that I did. She would let me have a probationary period of one week. If, during that week, I could treat her as well as she deserved, I could have one short intimate encounter.

This solution had come from an article in a popular magazine where the author proposed that wives who were frustrated by their husband's uninvited intimate advances, should solve such frustration by setting up a date night. It had proved to be a workable solution in the life of the author, and it should prove victory for any woman whose husband fulfilled the conditions she laid down.

I saw this as denying the clear instructions of the Apostle Paul on the authority of some unknown journalist of forbidden psychological background. Then I was warned that unwanted intimate advances, even in marriage, were now being tried in courts of law as rape cases. It was the beginning of a stress that dragged on for decades. What to do? A religious man does not act precipitously. Besides, Jesus could return at any time. That was now my only hope.

LIVING IN DENIAL IS A SELF-DEFEAT

Sometime later, I was enrolled in a Seminary class in Pastoral Psychology taught by Dr. Charles Wittschiebe (1908–1991), Professor of Applied Theology. Ten years later, he authored the first Adventist book to speak openly on the subject.[16] While I longed to seek counsel from him, I knew how other seminarians talked about people who were seen entering his office—they were thought to be people with deep psychological problems.

The word could get back to their Conference president and question their own suitability for the ministry. So, I listened attentively to what he had to say about marital intimacy in class. He was the first Adventist professor who had addressed these

---

16. Wittschiebe, *God Invented Sex,* (1974).

issues openly and sensibly from a professional viewpoint. I hoped someone would ask my questions. I was not courageous enough to ask them myself. So, I waited and listened carefully.

Finally, a student told me that Dr. Wittschiebe had addressed these questions in another section of the class. A student had asked him what he thought of being married to a woman who only allowed her husband to make love to her once a month? The class had erupted in laughter. At that, I was glad I hadn't asked any such question myself. Dr. Wittschiebe had paused, thinking about the question, before venturing. He then remarked that if the guy was talking about himself, he didn't seem to be too depressed about it. More laughter.

The student never missed a beat and announced transparently to the class—tonight was the night! The class of sixty seminarians howled with laughter for the next fifteen minutes, and I did not discover what Dr. Wittschiebe finally answered. I had received no help in bringing relief to my growing desire for what I considered a normal married life.

By the end of the summer, I was beginning to suspect that our relationship was not going to change and that I was going to have to get with the program or find another profession. I fretted and fumed but ended up channeling my frustrations into my faith and its eternal hope. I felt trapped and deceived. I had no inkling before our wedding that it would come to this.

As a Christian husband I determined to make the best of my situation, capitalize on all the good points of our marriage and accept the fact that intimacy frustration did not nullify the commitment I had made in my marriage vows. An unhappy marriage was a trap no religious man could free himself from. There was no way out—marriage was final. Marriage was to be an experience of equality and support, spontaneous expression of affection and empathy. I suppressed my self-pity and determined to make things work.

I knew cognitively that when only one person in a relationship gives and gives, the other can become a tyrant, but I rationalized that Christ was coming soon, that we were living on borrowed time, and that was the real issue. Of course, that was not the real issue but with no qualified third party to help and having religious convictions that basically forbade getting help from a third party, I continued in my state of denial. I was not looking for a solution—I was looking for an escape. Denial as an answer to any problem is a mistake.

A QUICK TRIP WEST

When school was out that first summer, we decided to make an unscheduled, unannounced, speedy, surprise trip to California during our six-week break before the fall semester. We invited two of our friends who were also from Southern California and they were game. So, we jumped into our Chevy II Nova SS and set out for Clear Lake where the family was vacationing.

We would surprise them. We did. Then we called Mom and Dad and they drove over from Mountain View. We had all the family together for a weekend of water skiing, talking, and playing games. It was delightful. I felt that my resolution had been vindicated. And I began to believe that all my doubts had finally been put behind. I was learning.

On Friday we drove over to Mountain View to spend the weekend with Mom and Dad before driving down the coast and then back to Michigan.

MORE TROUBLE IN PARADISE

We arrived in Mountain View, a small city in the heart of what would become Silicon Valley a decade later. The city was located sixty miles south of San Francisco on Highway 101. The Pacific Press Publishing Association had been in Mountain View since shortly after the turn of the twentieth century. Dad and Mom had moved there the year before but could not afford a house, so they had rented a small duplex that was not very accommodating to visitors. Most of the time, they were alone, so space was not so much a consideration. They had gotten rid of most of their belongings and found the smaller space more fitting to their lifestyle—less housework, less upkeep.

As we entered the small apartment, my wife's entire countenance changed. I had looked forward to this being a cordial weekend together but when she saw a picture of Jennifer on Dad's desk, she became livid. I did not understand. Surely Dad was free to have pictures of anyone he wanted in his own home. In private I got an earful. She held that this was unacceptable and inappropriate—he thought nothing of her feelings and had no right to mock her like that. Again, I was caught off guard. I simply couldn't see the issue. I wrote it off to another marital adjustment.

I thought I better try to correct it. Early on Sunday morning, I heard Dad in the back of the house carrying out trash, so I thought I would talk to him in private. Instead of letting the two of them work it out, I went to bat for my wife. I inadvertently broke an important principle of problem-solving and barged into the mine field. I started by suggesting that I wanted to talk to him about something kind of sensitive. I continued that she felt unaccepted because of Jenn's picture on his desk.

It was a bad beginning. Probably too direct. Using the second person singular came across as an attack. One of the first rules of communication said that we should not use the second person, especially with children. But apparently that went for parents too. Then, rather than stopping, thinking and rewording, I kept going, digging the hole deeper. I revealed that I felt she was not considered a part of our family and I hoped he could help me. Perhaps he could show her more attention or come up with some way to demonstrate that he accepted her.

I had said it. And I thought initially that it had gone rather well. I knew almost nothing about the mediation process. I would learn later that all I had really done was contribute to further polarization. After a few minutes Dad stared at me with a hurt look. His backlash defense was that he was an old man and she was a young woman. How could I expect that he could give her more attention? It wouldn't look right. He didn't understand why a picture on his desk was any of her business. Jennifer had always been like a daughter to them—she wrote them, she visited them, she called them. She always kept in contact with them. He and Mom fell in love with her when we were dating and that had never changed. Nor did he think anything should change.

He was probably right. I was sweating. I had presumed to educate Dad, something that had never worked well in the past. Why did I think it would work now? And what exactly did I expect him to do—take her to the Ringling Brothers Circus? Hold hands with her? Hug her? She was not an easy hug.

It struck me that now I had made two people mad. And it was becoming clear that their resentment was being directed at me. I had only intended to bring them together—but I had accomplished the exact opposite.

Dad finished his reaction by telling me that if she had a beef with him she should let him know and maybe talk to him about it. Then he finished with another stinger— Did I realize the I had never even introduced her to them? The nerve I touched was deep. I had never sold this relationship in any way that he could accept it. And he demonstrated in this retort that I had not married her because they loved her.

But the conversation was over. I had blown it. I wanted to ask if he wanted me to introduce him. But that wouldn't have been simple sarcasm. It would have been total stupidity. Apparently, this had been hanging around his neck for some time.

The two never made up. They tolerated each other stiffly, and it was a bit easier when the kids came along, but I never got any indication that they ever liked each other. They were civil. But I was caught in the middle with my hopes for peace and tranquility, and unable ever to realize either. She would eventually reveal to me her true feelings when she warned me that if I every became like him she would divorce me. It was rough sledding. And we were only three months into this marriage.

After returning to Michigan, I would sit in the University Press composing room setting type on the same model type setting machine Dad had spent so much time teaching me to operate, feeling the tears of futility burning my eyes as I wondered how to resolve this estrangement. Occasionally I would see a tear fall to my lap before I could brush it aside to avoid embarrassment. I had never felt so helpless or so desirous of drawing two people I loved together.

Life was not going as I had planned. What was happening to my religion? It all seemed irreparable to me. I turned out to be right. It was never repaired. I had been introduced to a notion of alienation. I found it to be a horribly painful reality, and it would come to dominate my life.

CHAPTER FOURTEEN

Seminary Days

"A thought once awakened does not again slumber."
—Thomas Carlyle

BERRIEN SPRINGS, MICHIGAN

Berrien Springs is a small village located on U. S. Highway 31 between Niles and Benton Harbor in the Southwestern corner of the "hand" of lower Michigan. The decision of the Adventist denomination in 1959 to move one of its two universities to this little country town was a curious one. The SDA Theological Seminary was now to be located out in the farmlands and fruit belt of Michigan far from the libraries, airports, culturally rich centers, world-class museums and political excitement of Washington, D.C. It would also be far from the denominational headquarters, in whose backyard it had been since its founding.

Berrien Springs was the seat of Berrien County, home of the Berrien County Youth Fair and the historic courthouse that housed the Village Seventh-day Adventist Church. The little settlement was dotted with a few quaint Victorian style homes and several simple farmhouses along with a drug store, a market, a sporting goods store, a couple of gas stations, an automobile dealership, a hardware store and a news stand. Berrien Springs was the home of the small Adventist Emmanuel Missionary College. Nothing indicated that it was about to become an academic center that would draw students from all over the world.

The area also had the dubious distinction of enjoying four extreme weather seasons. As a General Conference institution, the new university would enroll students from around the world, many from earth's equatorial belt. These students would be faced immediately with the need to purchase a new wardrobe—topcoats, parkas, snow boots, scarves, gloves and long Johns. Those of us from such places as Southern California could find the winters especially hostile. Few places in America could boast of a greater annual snowfall than Berrien County.

Because of the perceived lack of rationale for such a strange move, rumors began to spread about why Berrien Springs had been chosen. The most prevalent rumor, one that spread all the way to the west coast, suggested that this decision was more the vision of Adventist landowners in the area seeking to increase their property value than the careful planning of true academicians. It was said that some professors simply retired rather than move to Michigan while others moved with a great deal of reluctance. I heard sarcastic remarks about the move from professors. But Adventists predictably take such actions because they believe they are being led prophetically.

BACKGROUNDS OF HISTORY IN MICHIGAN

While the re-location of Potomac University from Washington, D. C., to Berrien Springs, Michigan, was controversial, it was not out of line with the type of moves Adventist administrators made. As one of our Seminary professors told us in class, speaking of another administrative decision to move the Los Angeles campus of the School of Medicine to Loma Linda, "The sides line up their quotes from Sister White and the side that can produce the tallest stack of quotes wins."

Michigan held nostalgia for Adventists. Though the movement was born in Maine in the mid-nineteenth century, the center of operations was moved to Battle Creek, Michigan, early enough in its adolescence to gain the reputation of being a mid-western Church. Church leaders found Battle Creek to be a superlative springboard for the world-wide dissemination of its health message, and it was there that it had established the Battle Creek Sanitarium made famous by John Harvey Kellogg, M.D. Battle Creek was also the site of the first Adventist college, Battle Creek College, where young people could study in a private, denominational setting.

Books such as *The Cornflake Crusade*, by Gerald Carson (1957),[1] *The Nuts Among the Berries*, by Ronald Deutsch (1967),[2] and *The Road to Wellville*, by novelist T. C. Boyle (1993)[3] have given some satirical versions of Battle Creek as the center of America's health reform movement. In fact, Boyle's novel was turned into a cinematic comedy (1994) starring such well-known actors as Anthony Hopkins, Bridget Fonda, Matthew Broderick, John Cusack and Dana Carvey, and it made savage fun of Kellogg and his competitors in Battle Creek history.[4]

By contrast, Adventists see their stay in Battle Creek and their move into the health food and health care industry, publishing and education, as divinely led

1. Carson, *Cornflake Crusade: from The Pulpit to The Breakfast Table*, (1957).
2. Deutsch, *The Nuts Among the Berries*, (1967).
3. Boyle, *The Road to Wellville*, (1993).
4. Parker (Director, Screenwriter), "The Road to Wellville," (1994).

ventures. They also have produced books chronicling their history in Michigan. Understandably, these accounts give a substantially different picture of the Adventist place in Battle Creek history.

Dr. John Harvey Kellogg[5] was at the center of the Adventist health movement along with Sister White and her husband James. Seeing potential in the young John Harvey, brother of the future cornflake king, W. K. Kellogg (1860–1951), the Whites sponsored him to study medicine at University of Michigan and Bellevue Hospital Medical School in New York.

Kellogg's training in medical school as well as his natural leadership ability would ultimately make him qualified to operate the Sanitarium. Even with his medical training, Kellogg's first love was health education and his efforts at the Sanitarium were as educational as they were medical. He taught classes constantly during his long tenure at the Sanitarium and Battle Creek College, where he was later president as well as a professor. In addition to his teaching and practicing medicine he wrote fifty books.

Nevertheless, as time passed, Kellogg fell out of favor with some top Church administrators and a political conspiracy was created to bring him down.[6] In spite of the fact that Kellogg denied all charges brought against him, his membership in the SDA Church was finally withdrawn in 1907.[7] The charges against him changed from the original judgments of heresy, insubordination and dishonesty to simply Church non-attendance, non-tithing and antagonism toward the spiritual gifts in the Church (Sister White).

The theological issue that had precipitated a lot of the controversy (the charge that Kellogg was a pantheist) was not introduced as a reason for his being disfellowshipped, although this is a major reason he is demonized in Adventist classrooms and popular history. Adventist histories draw a consistently negative picture of Kellogg despite his many contributions to the Adventist health care industry (which continue to this day) and his almost single-handed formulation of what became known as the health message. In these histories he is described as headstrong, ambitious, stubborn, domineering, jealous, a one-man show, critical of anyone with less education,

---

5. A chief historian of the work of John Harvey Kellogg was Richard W. Schwarz, (1925–2013), Professor of History at Andrews University. While he wrote several papers on Kellogg his major contributions were *John Harvey Kellogg, Father of the Health Food Industry,* (1970), and *John Harvey Kellogg, M.D.*, (1970).

6. "Elder A. C. Bourdeau, and Dr. John Harvey Kellogg: Interview at Dr. J. H. Kellogg's House, Battle Creek, Michigan," (1907) [Hereinafter referred to as *The Kellogg Interview*]. This interview gives a different picture than that portrayed in denominational literature and is not referenced in Richard W. Schwarz, *Light Bearers to the Remnant: Denominational History Textbook for Seventh-day Adventist College Classes,* (1979), which textbook was used in Adventist colleges since 1980. Schwarz quotes only denominational sources for his portrayal of Kellogg in the first edition of his book. This book has since been revised and updated as Richard W. Schwarz and Floyd Greenleaf, *Light Bearers: A History of the Seventh-day Adventist Church,* (2000). No reference to the *Kellogg Interview* is included in the revised textbook either.

7. Schwarz. *Light Bearers to the Remnant*, 296.

suspicious of associates, resentful and disparaging of those he worked with, independent, strongly reactionary toward Sister White's counsels, and especially critical and judgmental of the General Conference administration.[8]

What could have been viewed as strengths in most other bureaucratic organizations, have consistently been used against him. Some of these qualities have been applied by critics to Sister White, but when the Church leaders chose between Dr. Kellogg and Sister White they came down on the side of the prophet.

The struggle to get rid of Kellogg is known in Adventist history as the "Kellogg Crisis." This manifested itself in several ways but usually refers to theological and financial aspects of the controversy. Kellogg did not contest the decision to disfellowship him.[9] While this could be his desire to be thrown out of the Church, he claimed it was just the opposite, but denominational historians often take his words out of context. Kellogg became perceived as the bad guy.

By his own testimony Kellogg claimed that he had never forsaken any of the Adventist doctrines, he had never been a pantheist nor believed in pantheism, had remained open to counsel, especially from Sister White, and continually asked for guidance in the management of the Battle Creek Sanitarium. He claimed that because of the rumors being spread about him by A. G. Daniells (1850–1935), president of the General Conference, and W. W. Prescott (1855–1944), a prominent Adventist Bible teacher, he had come to accept the fact that he would probably be dropped from Church membership someday. He called Prescott a liar and carefully explained why. He called this plotting to undo him, Prescott's trick.

In Kellogg's words, "Elder Evans came to my house when he got back and said, 'Prof. Prescott, W. C. White and Elder Daniells have bound themselves together in a conspiracy to ruin you and I have letters which I think will prove it.'"[10]

> It is a wicked and unchristian and unbiblical method of procedure. I have never been asked to appear before the church to answer to any charges at all. Yet I am condemned everywhere. Certainly, I ought to be turned out of the church if I have committed robberies, if I am doing those things. But it should be pointed out wherein I have done these things, and I should be given opportunity to make restitution. I am ready to make restitution if the things are pointed out to me. I am ready to make restitution.[11]

---

8. These terms are a few of those chosen to describe Kellogg in Schwarz' textbook *Light Bearers to the Remnant*, chap. 18, entitled, "The Kellogg Crisis, 1901–1907," 282–298.

9. Ibid., 296.

10. *The Kellogg Interview*, 33. The paging of this interview will vary with whatever copy the reader should obtain. I have two copies, one a typescript and another I obtained from the internet. The internet copy is easiest to obtain so I am using its pagination. For website see the following: http://www.ex-sda.com/john.htm. Further research is easily obtained by simply guiding your search engine to "John Harvey Kellogg."

11. Ibid., p. 36.

> I expect to be turned out of this church, but I shall make no protest against it. I said, I will not on any account withdraw from the church, and I will not ask to have my name dropped; I will do nothing of the kind, because if I do, that will immediately be used as a pretense and published everywhere as proof that I have withdrawn from the church—withdrawn from the truth which I have believed in for all these years, which I have been raised in—that I have repudiated it. And it will be said everywhere that I have done it when I have not done it, and it is not the truth.... I believe just what I have believed for the last forty years, and I am standing by everything I have stood by. I have not changed.[12]

Despite his confession of loyalty to both the faith and the prophet, Kellogg was dropped from membership on November 10, 1907, and destined to carry the mantel of heretic, dissenter and apostate. The leaders did not take any of Kellogg's affirmations seriously and simply refused to talk to him anymore.[13] Saying it was useless to try to reason with him, or that somehow Kellogg was driving them to nervous exhaustion, seemed to justify the negative attitudes leadership had toward him. It is problematic to determine which side demonstrated more stubbornness or head strong attitudes, but there is no question which side held the final authority.

Kellogg's generous and dedicated work for the Adventist denomination clearly carried no importance once the politicians had acted and the prophet had spoken. There is a principle in business that says—if you have a serious argument with your CEO you need to start looking for another job because your days are numbered. The principle holds true even if you win the skirmish. You have a target on your back.

The same principle is true in Church bureaucracy. The difference in organized religion is that God is usually on the side of the highest echelons of Church clergy. Being authorized to lead often seems more important than being qualified to lead. But for the religious man such a principle is hard to grasp. In fact, one probably cannot grasp it until one becomes the focus of the political machinations. The first time I heard of a church administrator say, "God is not your boss, I am," I had serious thinking to do. I had not heard him say that in the pulpit or at a workers' meeting. This claim was reserved for the office, person to person.

Fires eventually destroyed nearly the entire Adventist establishment in Battle Creek including the Sanitarium, the Dime Tabernacle, and the Review and Herald publishing plant. Dr. Kellogg rebuilt his empire in Battle Creek but by then the Church leaders had moved headquarters out of Michigan to the nation's capital, and the

---

12. Ibid., p. 22.

13. Schwarz, *Light Bearers to the Remnant*, 296ff. Schwarz gives the denominational account of the Kellogg crisis and repeats several times that the leaders simply came to the place where they refused to meet with Kellogg. No one argues that Kellogg may not have been eccentric, but history demonstrates such superior abilities that it takes very little imagination to see the kind of threat he posed to the Church's leadership of that day. This overkill to discredit people who make creative suggestions or pose any kind of perceived threat to the leadership would become routine in denominational history.

denominational college to Berrien Springs in Southwest Michigan. The original Battle Creek College was now renamed Emmanuel Missionary College in its new location.

The whole controversy, or crisis, surrounding Kellogg was unknown to me when I enrolled at the Seminary except that in all my training I had learned that Kellogg was one of the bad guys. I sometimes pondered over this as I ate my Kellogg's Corn Flakes for breakfast—here was a cereal created by an Adventist. What had happened? The crisis would become much more relevant to me in the not-too-distant future. I would come to understand that these kinds of standoffs in Adventism were sometimes the rule rather than the exception and in roughly every generation another big one erupted.

This Kellogg phenomenon, which I would conclude much later in my thinking, was a major political power struggle. It had become known in Adventist history as "the alpha apostasy." The fact that the prophet predicted that there would be another one like it—"the omega apostasy"—set some Adventist eschatological minds in gear for the future.

THE DEVELOPMENT OF ADVANCED EDUCATION IN ADVENTISM

Adventists are strongly intimidated by the counsels of their prophet. And although she died in 1915, they usually quote her in the present tense as if she is still alive writing her counsels to the Church. From a political standpoint, this pressure still serves the purposes of whatever administrators happen to be in a position of power at the time.

Sister White was an agrarian. With her writings in hand one could virtually ignore the major transformative historical event of the Industrial Revolution. She wrote of the advantages of the farm and insisted that all Adventist institutions not only have a farm but be far enough from any city so as not to be polluted by its iniquity, instructions largely ignored by the organized Church today.

On the other hand, she counseled that Adventist institutions should be near enough to the cities that they could evangelize and work them. As a result, Adventists built many of their institutions in relative proximity to a major city, but in the years after the prophet's death, cities had generally sprawled into the backyards of many of these Adventist havens of refuge. This was especially true of the Washington area where Potomac University was being slowly strangled by the city.

Most of these institutions were educational enterprises that boarded young people and functioned as *in loco parentis*. As such, they were to provide a religious environment for the nurturing of young Adventists. In addition, they were to provide safety and remoteness from the crimes and worldly temptations of the city. Parents and students alike paid a small fortune to protect themselves in these Adventist villages.

The SDA Theological Seminary had been established in Takoma Park, Maryland, a suburb of Washington, D.C. The school had opened in 1934 as the Advanced Bible School on the campus of Pacific Union College in Northern California where it provided a series of summer seminars for Adventist ministers and teachers. Four years later the school was moved to Takoma Park, in the shadow of the Church's world headquarters, which had been moved from Battle Creek after the fires.

Most Adventist ministers and professors at that time would not risk their faith by attending a worldly or confessional graduate school. This home-grown addition to higher education was therefore welcomed by many who felt the need to satisfy their inquiring minds. Gradually the school became popular with North American Adventist ministers, and its location in Washington was considered ideal.

This Seminary was not only located at the hub of Adventism, but Washington, D.C. was a cultural nerve center in the United States. Anyone attending the Seminary had easy access to some of the finest libraries, museums, hospitals, universities and cultural heritage that America had to offer. And, of course, there was the Library of Congress, the ultimate center for research.

Staffing the school was an exercise in cognitive dissonance. To have a faculty with advanced training that carried credibility, the school needed professors with advanced degrees from accredited universities. So, at first the faculty was made up of some who had received master's degrees at their own expense, usually in safer disciplines such as speech, religious education, history, archaeology, or perhaps church history.

Textbooks consisted of conservative works like Augustus Strong's three volume set, *Systematic Theology*. Though Strong was a theistic evolutionist the bulk of what he wrote was evangelical in nature. Most of the uniquely Adventist sources consisted of sermons and reprinted periodical articles of Sister White and earlier pioneers that had been compiled into evangelistic and apologetic works.

Some teachers, like W. W. Prescott, Alonzo J. Wearner (1892–1964) and M. L. Andreasen (1876–1962), had written books on specific aspects of Adventism that would put the non-Adventist sources in correct ideological context and give the Seminary the special, confessional flavor expected from an Adventist institution of higher learning.

As the years went by, Adventists relaxed their grip on education, and one by one, the Seminary faculty became more highly qualified until by 1942 the school was offering the Master of Arts degree and meeting in winter, spring and summer sessions. Eventually the school would offer more advanced degrees—the Bachelor of Divinity (1945), and the Master of Theology (1959) degrees. None of these graduate degrees was accredited.

In connection with Washington Missionary College, the Seminary became a school within the new Potomac University in 1957, but the problem of campus space soon confronted the architects of the program. At that point serious consideration was given to relocating the institution for more breathing room. More centrally located Adventist campuses were available with land obtainable for growth, and many wondered why Michigan, with its difficult transportation connections and extreme weather, was the final choice.

By the time I arrived in Michigan, in 1963, the SDA Theological Seminary was a part of the new Adventist university consisting of undergraduate, graduate and seminary programs. It had recently been re-christened Andrews University (named in honor of Elder J. N. Andrews [1829–1883], an early Adventist missionary and scholar) and the building program was vigorously ambitious as the General Conference poured its money into making this a premier university.

Those who collected Sister White's statements about Adventist institutions being located out in the country had won this round. By the 1970s, some at Andrews would promote this institution as having the vision of becoming a "Harvard of the West," under the brief administration of President Grady Smoot.

The graduate theological program had collected perhaps the most impressive and qualified Adventist faculty available at the time. These were former administrators and department chairs from theology departments of Adventist colleges around the world. There was no professor under whom I would sit who did not push me to the limits in scholarship and exacting research. I was excited and anxious to move ahead with my education.

AN ESTEEMED THEOLOGICAL FACULTY

At Seminary I studied under such scholars as Dr. Siegfried Horn (1908–1993), a graduate of University of Chicago, world-renowned archaeologist, editor of the Seventh-day Adventist Bible Dictionary, and chair of the Old Testament Department. Other professors included Dr. Earle Hilgert, chair of the New Testament Department, who had recently returned from finishing his doctorate at the University of Basel under Karl Barth, arguably the most influential Protestant theologian of the twentieth century. Dr. Edward Heppenstall (1901–1994), a graduate of University of Southern California, and a deeply committed Adventist theologian, chair of the Theology and Christian Philosophy Department, had dedicated his life to producing qualified pastors.

These men had all contributed their scholarship to the production of the impressive seven-volume set of the *Seventh-day Adventist Bible Commentary* as well as the influential and credible theological work, *Seventh-day Adventists Answer Questions on Doctrine*. Other scholars such as Dr. Sakae Kubo (New Testament), Dr. Kenneth Strand (Church History), Dr. Daniel Walther (Church History), and Dr. Norval Pease (Church Ministry), rounded out a program of which the denomination could justly be proud.

The plan was that I would be sponsored by Southern California Conference for one year to receive a *Certificate of Internship*. After that, I would return to the Conference where I would work off this debt with five years of ministerial service. At that point I could accept any invitation to go elsewhere if I chose. As a married person, my stipend would be $218.00 a month. Out of this income I would pay apartment rent, school tuition, groceries, insurance, books, medical expenses and any other family expenses like car upkeep and gasoline, etc. This income was considered adequate for survival and a sponsored student was expected to take on no additional employment, although his wife could, and some Seminary wives did.

Our original plan was to spend the summer in Mountain View where we both had secured jobs at the Pacific Press Publishing Association, I as a copy editor, and she as a bindery worker. But upon the encouragement of Andrews' recruiters, we were enticed to go directly to the university where jobs in the University Press would be lined up for us. We were assured that we would be housed in Garland Apartments, the university apartments for married students, and both of us could start school in the fall. We figured one move was enough, so we cancelled our plans at the Press and moved directly to Berrien Springs.

We arrived in the middle of a summer heat spell and were introduced to humidity. There was no air conditioning in Garland Apartments but a colleague of mine from La Sierra College days, met us behind the apartments and handed us a five-inch electrical fan. When I saw him, whom I had hardly known in college, I recalled only the sad picture painted for me by one of the theology students at La Sierra. He had told me that in conversation with the department chair he had discovered that all theology majors had been placed in sponsorships for the following year except this student. No Conference president had called him, and the chair was disappointed. He liked the reputation of placing all "his boys," and this troubled him. Nevertheless, at the last-minute he was picked up by a Conference and had proved to be an able scholar at Andrews with a special aptitude for scholarly work under the tutelage of several scholars. He made it clear that his La Sierra people would be looked after. And he flashed an understanding and proud smile. He also asked me to be patient—he assured me that he would get us an air conditioner! It was my introduction to his politic—underdeveloped at that point but already pragmatic. I don't think I have ever spent a night in so hot an apartment. It was amazing how much relief that tiny fan brought.

Upon moving into B-17 in Garland Apartments we were unceremoniously informed that we would not be allowed to live there if I was not enrolled in summer classes. The assurance we had received in a letter from the administration suddenly meant nothing. I must either register for school or find a place off campus to live until the fall semester. This was a setback. We had planned to save three months of the money we would make since we had very little in our bank account to begin with. Now that seemed compromised.

I took what funds we had and deposited them in a new checking account at a bank in St. Joseph. I was starting to feel married, figuring out budgets and incomes and rental agreements. I hardly had time to resent this administrative decision. I enrolled in two Seminary classes. Each day I put in a few hours at the University Press on the linotype, while Annie worked full-time in the bindery. My classes every morning were New Testament Archaeology and Righteousness by Faith.

My professors were Dr. Hilgert and Dr. Heppenstall, the latter a friend of my family since 1945 when we moved to La Sierra. He had been chair of the LSC Religion Department as well as the pastor of the La Sierra Church, which met in Hole Memorial Auditorium on campus. While carrying out these responsibilities, he had also been teaching twenty-five semester hours a week plus working on his PhD at University of Southern California in Los Angeles. He was the pastor who had inspiring the building of that new church that Grandpa and I had watched being constructed on our walks together around La Sierra.

INTRODUCING ANDREWS UNIVERSITY

My official introduction to Andrews University came at registration for the fall semester. I was directed to the Department of Student Finance, and even though we had letters guaranteeing us university housing, the director had overruled them. Apparently, we were caught in a major misunderstanding. As I cleared my bill and financial affairs the director let me know that I needed to put down all the money for my tuition expenses for the fall semester of 1963–64 in advance.

As a sponsored student I was paid monthly. I did not have money to pay for an entire semester in advance. He paused, investigating my eyes. He took off his glasses and leaned across his desk. Other students said he told them if they couldn't pay ahead of time perhaps God was not planning for them to be at Seminary. He didn't say that to me. He just related the policy to me—I needed to present payment for the full semester if I planned to enroll. I paused, trying to process what I had just heard. Was he serious? Hadn't the Conference already decided what God's will was here? I repeated my words, "I'm a sponsored student, paid $218.00 a month. I can only pay monthly."

He leaned back in his chair and made it clear that my situation was impossible. I either paid my tuition for the fall in advance or I would not be enrolled. With that the interview was over and I could not register. I went back to the apartment in despair. I couldn't be angry because I had been taught that anger was a sin. So that night I sinned boldly—because I was very angry. I called Elder Sandefur.

In the meantime, my feelings about Andrews University were specifically focused on the finance director. Apparently, this full monthly stipend was a new policy recently passed by the General Conference to build up the Seminary enrollment as well as to strengthen the education of new ministers. When I called Elder Sandefur he told me not to worry, he would take care of it.

The next day I was miraculously registered—had my phone call solved the problem? Or was it a dozen other calls that the school must have gotten that night? I gradually discovered that my cynical attitude toward the finance department was unfortunately shared by several other Seminarians.

Seminary Days

OUR FIRST SEMESTER TOGETHER

The fall semester of 1963 began for me with a full slate of Seminary courses, and with every class period I became more excited and convinced that I had chosen the right profession. Annie was enrolled in her undergraduate program as an English major. We were starting to settle down and I was sure now that I was in love. All those frustrations I had dealt with were in check.

The greatest advantage of being a religious man was that you had resources in powers outside yourself. Though nothing had really changed in our relationship, my attitude was softer. I attributed it to the Spirit of God—a resource the religious man always draws on. Each morning I prayed that my attitude would be in God's hands and tempered by his love.

By Christmas I was a committed Seminarian studying night and day, writing papers, doing research on issues I took to be of eternal value and finally we had our first Christmas together in knee-deep snow. We were dirt poor, but our primary needs were covered. We soon discovered the Berrien County welfare office and each month I picked up our allotted supply of pinto beans, dried milk, cheese, butter, and flour. Since we were both vegetarians we passed on the lard and the canned meat.

We had no television or telephone, but I still had the transistor radio Dad had given me for my high school graduation. So, while we saw none of the John F. Kennedy assassination events of November 22, 1963, we were able to listen as each new shocking news bulletin that broke on WBBM news radio from Chicago.

I was headed for a St. Joseph barber shop for a Friday afternoon haircut, listening to speculation on the radio that Richard M. Nixon might consider running against John F. Kennedy again for president in 1964. When I came out of the barber shop and started up the car all the news was shifted to the catastrophic event that had occurred minutes before. The top news feature was, "President John F. Kennedy shot in Dallas!" By the time I got home, his death had been confirmed. But after the word "shot," the rest of the afternoon, evening and next day was a blur. I couldn't believe it. Whether Kennedy fans or not the assassination was America's loss of innocence.

In 1960 I was not old enough to vote but if I had been, my choice would have been the vice-president Richard Nixon, a Republican. Everyone I knew personally was a conservative, and to vote for a Catholic Democrat would have been to introduce the end of time. The presidential race of 1960 had been dirty. All the anti-Catholic religious whack-jobs had come out of their hiding places, and we were back in the America of the 1840s, described as "antiforeign, anti-Catholic, and antipapal all at the same time."[14] During this period, books against Catholics and papalism were produced freely.

---

14. Clark, *1844: Religious Movements*, 1:203.

Thanks largely, but not completely, to *The Great Controversy,* a book by Sister White, in the same genre, the anti-Catholic anxiety was still alive in the Adventist Church. While most anti-Catholic books played out their course and were no longer written on a large scale, Sister White's book was regarded by Adventists as inspired and therefore absolutized a form of anti-Catholicism in the Church.

Adventist evangelists always included at least one crusade message on the mark of the beast (Revelation 16:2), which identified the Catholic Church and the Pope as the "beast" of the Apocalypse.

> ¹And *I saw a beast rising out of the sea, with ten horns and seven heads,* with ten diadems upon its horns and a blasphemous name upon its heads. ² And the beast that I saw was like a leopard, its feet were like a bear's, and its mouth was like a lion's mouth. And to it the dragon gave his power and his throne and great authority. ³ One of its heads seemed to have *a mortal wound,* but *its mortal wound was healed,* and the *whole earth followed the beast with wonder.*
>
> ⁴ Men worshiped the dragon, for he had given his authority to the beast, and they worshiped the beast, saying, "Who is like the beast, and who can fight against it?"
>
> ⁵ And *the beast was given a mouth uttering haughty and blasphemous words,* and it was allowed to exercise authority for forty-two months; ⁶ it opened its mouth to utter blasphemies against God, blaspheming his name and his dwelling, that is, those who dwell in heaven. ⁷ Also *it was allowed to make war on the saints* and to conquer them. And authority was given it over every tribe and people and tongue and nation, ⁸ and all who dwell on earth will worship it, every one whose name has not been written before the foundation of the world in the book of life of the Lamb that was slain.
>
> ⁹ If any one has an ear, let him hear:
>
> ¹⁰ If any one is to be taken captive,
>   to captivity he goes;
> if any one slays with the sword,
>   with the sword must he be slain.
>
> Here is a call for the endurance and faith of the saints. (Rev 13:1–10. Emphasis supplied)

> ¹⁶ Also it causes all, both small and great, both rich and poor, both free and slave, to be marked on the right hand or the forehead, ¹⁷ so that no one can buy or sell unless he has the mark, that is, the name of the beast or the number of its name. ¹⁸ This calls for wisdom: let him who has understanding reckon the number of the beast, for it is a human number, its number is six hundred and sixty-six. (Rev 13:16–18. Emphasis supplied)

Crusade speakers generally prepared their audiences to some degree for this shocking revelation by preaching two or three sermons on the Adventist interpretation of certain prophecies of Daniel and Revelation. We who were in the Church, however, were regularly instructed by our ministers and teachers that we were not anti-Catholics but rather we were opposed to the Catholic *system*. Such a distinction may have been fragile at best, but we knew what it meant. We were certainly suspicious of any Roman Catholic who might run for political office, and God forbid, president of the United States. We all knew that the loyalty of a president to his Pope would be greater than to his country.

By November 1963, I had almost adjusted to having a Catholic Democrat in the Oval Office. Despite so many dire predictions generated by religious men, the Black Cloud had not appeared, no universal Sunday law had been decreed, and I had to admit, Kennedy was more charismatic than any president I had ever seen in action. But I suspected I was letting down my guard—principle, not personality, must rule!

The death of President Kennedy was not the only shock of 1963. During Christmas break we got word that our beloved La Sierra College president had been struck down by a heart attack. We had last seen him at graduation in May and since Dr. Fabian Meier was only in his forties the thought of never seeing him again was not something that had ever entered our minds. Such sadness coming in the wake of the president's assassination only helped us realize that age is not a factor in this world of sad transitions. We just hung on every piece of news with our hearts saddening in the process.

In our loneliness at Christmas we each took $10 from our little income and bought as many presents for each other as we could with the money. Paperbacks ran anywhere from twenty-five to fifty cents so my present from Annie was a small stack of books under the tree. While we would have liked to surprise the family with another unscheduled trip to California, we found it too costly, so we spent our first Christmas together in our apartment. Since most of our friends had gone somewhere for Christmas we were alone.

As my monthly checks had arrived, I had saved a little money out of each to apply toward the purchase of some green goblets that matched our everyday dishes. In addition to the $10 worth of gifts I was able to surprise Annie with a complete set of transparent green goblets and tumblers. That was a bonus to add to our wedding presents.

Our first married Christmas, the poorest we would ever experience, was also the only one we would ever spend alone. But we were on our own. We were getting help from nowhere except our earned income, and the spirit of ownership was fulfilling. I was planning great things working for God and I was glad I had changed my mind that morning in the guest room.

CHAPTER FIFTEEN

Theological Excitement

"The trouble with most people is that they think with their hopes or fears or wishes rather than with their minds."
—Will Durant

A NEW BOOK

In 1957 a new theological book appeared under the title Seventh-day Adventists Answer Questions on Doctrine. I was a junior at Auburn Academy when the book was published. At that time, I was unaware of any theological controversy in the Church. I grew up believing that wherever you attended anywhere in the world you would find unified belief, consistent values and generally harmonious agreement in all matters of faith and practice.

We always felt right at home visiting another Adventist Church whether we knew anyone there or not. Our denomination was a family, and as far as I knew we were a happy family. Whether we met together in Europe, South America, or Idaho, it made no difference in my mind. Family is family, and in my eyes, we were an innocent worldwide community.

Questions on Doctrine would eventually be used as a political football and would play a major role in ending this innocence for me. But things didn't start out that way. The book was written and published to clarify and explain Adventist beliefs in language that non-Adventists, perhaps the more scholarly types, could relate to.

The yearly missionary books that the Church produced had their place, but they didn't answer some of the questions that scholars would pose to inform Adventists about their faith. In fact, some scholars found popular Adventist presentations to be confusing and contradictory. There were almost no tools designed to attract or reach the educated, biblically-informed mind. And unfortunately, these professional students with inquiring minds would see Adventist missionary books as simply uncritical propaganda designed to proselyte.

I guess I didn't think other Christians really cared to dialogue with us, who they considered to be a hopeless, deceitful cult. And the way we typically portrayed other Christians as apostates, heretics, and nominals, led me to conclude that many of us wanted no dialogue with them either. We often heard talk about speaking with "our friends the Catholics," but I certainly wasn't aware of any Catholic I could honestly call a friend. As a youngster I remembered briefly making acquaintance with a kid next door who told me he was Catholic. I marveled at the fact that such a nice kid would someday grow up to persecute me and my family. All this business about Catholic friends I saw as mostly evangelistic rhetoric. Who would want a Catholic friend knowing what we knew? Unless, of course, we could make an Adventist out of him.

For the most part both sides considered approaching the other to be a hopeless venture. We shouldn't waste much time on people who refused to listen (or to change), and that included those scholars who should know better. If they were indeed true Bible scholars, then why didn't they keep the Sabbath?

When Dr. Donald G. Miller, a prominent evangelical preacher/theologian, and author of one of our Seminary homiletics textbooks, *The Way to Biblical Preaching*, addressed our Seminary Chapel, this was precisely the question one of the Adventist Seminarians stood up and asked him—in front of everyone gathered there. A legitimate question? Some thought so. The chatter in the Seminary halls was pro and con on why Dr. Miller was even invited to speak for Seminary Chapel. As a Sunday keeper what did he have to say to SDA Seminary students? Some students, especially those new to the Church, took it upon themselves to confront him.

Into this scenario of ambivalence—a concern to reach out on the one hand, and a conviction to remain special on the other—the book *Questions on Doctrine* was dropped. Attempting to fulfill a serious, constructive need, the authors had carefully written a book designed to open a dialogue with our friends the apostates, instead of attacking them. It was a novel gamble and a new approach to me. Apparently, no one anticipated what kind of firestorm this book would set off. Some believe this was Adventism's first big adventure into the land of theological renewal. For decades, we had been preaching to ourselves; now leaders were confident enough in our Christian identity to address issues that concerned other Christian scholars as well. This was no small challenge.

FUNDAMENTALISM VS. THE NEW THEOLOGY

In the American Christian world around the turn of the twentieth century the Fundamentalist movement was born and set out to counter the influence of theological Liberalism. In church history this Liberalism was known as "new theology" infiltrating mainline churches. Fundamentalism was confronting and renewing Christianity in its core beliefs.[1]

This new theology emphasized the rejection of the Bible as the sole and infallible authority of truth. It stressed the immanence of God—teaching that every human being had a spark of divinity within that needed developing. This theological element involved a repudiation of any form of the doctrine of original sin and put in its place the inherent goodness of human nature, which led to a human potential that redefined the primitive Christian view of sanctification.

In this new theology, Jesus became the first Christian rather than the savior of the world. As such, he became an example of what human beings could become if they believed in him, a form of utopianism. With this also came a replacement of the substitutionary atonement of Christ (an idea that liberal theologians viewed as barbaric) with a view that the cross primarily had a moral influence on humanity to encourage people to live good lives. The movement was skeptical of supernaturalism, as understood historically, and science gained an ever-greater role in redefining what was essentially a *poetic* creation account. (Gen 1–3).

To counter this movement, Fundamentalism set forth its basic tenets—not in formal creeds but in fundamental beliefs. Adventists were not a part of this movement but because of their stand on the literal days of creation, the young age of the earth, and a few of the other "fundamentals" such as the virgin birth of Jesus and the inspiration of the Bible, they were attracted to some of its goals and methods.

Fundamentalists viewed Adventism as a heterodox cult. Nevertheless, as movies and other entertainment avenues and lifestyles became popular in the first decades of the twentieth century, Adventists found themselves in essential agreement with some of the social and cultural values of Fundamentalism.

Fundamentalism was not technically a denominational affiliation but rather a set of beliefs that cut across and through confessional groups. Although Fundamentalists in general rejected Adventism as a deceptive, non-scriptural cult, many of them embraced the well-known Adventist amateur geologist George McCready Price (1870–1963)[2] the father of modern creationism. They accepted his views as scripturally defensible and helpful in their battles with evolutionism.

In 1925, the movement suffered a serious blow to its credibility with the notorious Scopes monkey trial held in Dayton, Tennessee, to challenge a new state law forbidding the teaching of Darwinism. The polarizing effect caused by the trial resulted in a mockery of Fundamentalist creationists even though they won the legal case with three-time U. S. presidential candidate William Jennings Bryan (1860–1925) as

---

1. For a credible and interesting account of these movements see Hordern, *A Layman's Guide to Protestant Theology,* Rev. Ed., (1968).

2. Schwarz, *Light Bearers,* 434–436.

prosecutor and spokesman. Bryan was strongly affected by the writings of Price and used his arguments in the trial.[3]

J. Gresham Machen (1881–1937), a noted conservative scholar and theology professor at Princeton Theological Seminary in the 1920s and 1930s, and a theological architect of the new, conservative Westminster Theological Seminary (1929) in Philadelphia, stated openly his discomfort with certain aspects of the Fundamentalist movement. He found it questionable because it lacked historical perspective, it did not appreciate scholarship, it substituted skeletal creeds for historical confessions, it lacked concern for precision in the formulation of Christian doctrine, it drifted into hang-ups with perfectionist obsessions (like bans on smoking, movies, jewelry, etc.), it showed little or no concern for transforming culture, but was satisfied primarily with being other worldly, and it had a penchant for pre-millennialism.[4]

By the 1940s, Fundamentalists were feeling the ridicule, and things were made worse by German scholarship, which had continued to invade American Protestantism. Furthermore, the extremism of many Fundamentalists was not helping the cause to gain credibility. At the same time, two world wars had done their part in shattering some of the new theology's major tenets, not the least of which was the notion that humankind was by nature good, and that society was continually improving.

Fundamentalists were not the only group to recognize problems associated with the liberal new theology. Another movement, generally known as Neo-Orthodoxy, arose to counteract theological Liberalism while retaining its scholarly achievements. Karl Barth, Rudolf Bultmann, Richard and Reinhold Niebuhr, Oscar Cullman, Emil Brunner, Dietrich Bonhoeffer were some leading this movement. These men had all been schooled in Liberal theological traditions, but they had come to believe that Liberalism distorted both historical Christianity and human nature. Neo-Orthodoxy purported to revert to some of the goals of the Reformers without denying the scientific breakthroughs of the previous century.

These changes motivated a new breed of Fundamentalists to re-examine some of their positions in favor of more moderate views. As a result, the 1940s saw the emergence of Neo-Evangelicalism, a movement that set about to correct these aberrations of Fundamentalism with a new return to historical Christianity.[5]

---

3. "George McCready Price," *Wikipedia, The Free Encyclopedia*: "Price's defense of creation science (and attacks on evolution) first achieved wide notability in 1925 when his theories and arguments were utilized heavily by William Jennings Bryan in the famous Scopes Trial. Bryan had appealed to Price for assistance, but Price was busy teaching in England. Price advised Bryan to avoid science during the trial if possible. During the trial, defense counsel Clarence Darrow, sneered 'You mentioned Price because he is the only human being in the world so far as you know that signs his name as a geologist that believes like you do . . . every scientist in this country knows [he] is a mountebank and a pretender and not a geologist at all.'" Cf. Numbers, *Spectrum* 9, 22 (January 1979).

4. See Stonehouse, *J. Gresham Machen: A Biographical Memoir*, (1987).

5. Hordern, *A Layman's Guide to Protestant Theology*, 54–65.

Major spokesmen and architects of the Neo-Evangelical movement included Edward Carnell, D. Elton Trueblood, Bernard Ramm, Billy Graham, Donald Barnhouse, Carl F. H. Henry, to name a few. They abandoned the old Fundamentalist approaches in favor of a conservative Christianity that was more credible, less harsh, more scholarly, less radical, more socially minded and more open to dialogue with other Christians.[6] At the same time, it preserved the orthodox view of scripture as the objective norm of religious truth. Members of the group attended Ivy League and European universities for their graduate work and began opening graduate schools like Fuller Theological Seminary on the west coast and Westminster in the east. The movement gained ground through the publication of Neo-Evangelical magazines such as *Eternity* and *Christianity Today*.

These were the type of scholars (not the old separatist Fundamentalists) who would dialogue with the Adventist leaders in the 1950s and who would be addressed in *Questions on Doctrine*. They sought to be fair and honest in their evaluation of Adventism and they were willing to correct hurtful errors of judgment made in the past. To those who researched the cults, wrote books about what they saw as sectarian movements, or influenced public opinion about the orthodoxy of religious movements, Adventists looked more like a cult than a Christian denomination.

The classic Fundamentalists, however, were not the only ones whose minds were closed. Too often, Adventists had appeared unwilling to dialogue with people they called apostate Protestants. This was an old attack introduced by early Adventists who expected the Lord to return any day and who were endeavoring to clean up the mistakes of the Protestant creed-makers. This made Adventists look arrogant and dogmatic with minds wide shut.

While Adventists had officially repudiated their early views of the Shut Door doctrine, which denied salvation to anyone who had not been part of the Millerite movement, in practice the notion lived on that only those who sided with Adventists would be saved at the end. Many Adventists never made the adjustment required by the twentieth century and they would periodically emerge in the shape of fringe groups, which caused friction in the Church by seeing themselves as the guardians of Adventist orthodoxy.

By the 1950s, the whole theological climate had changed. Now there were several Adventist scholars and Neo-Evangelicals at reputable universities who could understand professional jargon. *Questions on Doctrine* was the first publication of its kind designed to meet a new generation of educated Establishment Evangelicals. Despite later criticism, it is unfair to attribute a sinister motive to the authors of *Questions on Doctrine*. Neither Adventists nor Evangelicals would be clamoring for the other's

---

6. For an insightful description of the kinds of Evangelicals, namely the Schools of Orthodoxy, see Quebedeaux, *The Young Evangelicals: Revolution in Orthodoxy*, 18–40. Quebedeaux identifies: "Separatist Fundamentalism," "Open Fundamentalism," "Establishment Evangelicalism," and "New Evangelicalism." These categories clarify Fundamentalism in all ages.

approval. It was an honest effort to understand each other and see how many core beliefs both groups held in common.

One of the historical problems of Adventism was that no authoritative, scholarly presentation of Adventist doctrine had ever been published. Books published in the past by Adventist authors often held contradictory viewpoints. Likewise, statements from Sister White commonly used to establish various theological positions, were not always in agreement. This inconvenient fact gave rise to different interpretations of Adventist theology, and Adventist scholars realized that her writings were of such a nature that they could not always stand as the last word on doctrinal issues.

THE PURPOSE AND EFFECT OF *QUESTIONS ON DOCTRINE*

I never heard anything negative about Questions on Doctrine *when the book was first released.* It was part of the progress that came because of the Church's new commitment to higher education. The book was given away freely; in fact, as a high school student visiting various Adventist congregations, I was given three or four complimentary copies of the book.

Leaders and scholars alike hailed *Questions on Doctrine* as the most credible theological work ever produced by Adventists. We all knew it was not written primarily for an Adventist audience and consequently, its theological statements were framed in a language that other Christians could better appreciate.

My college theology faculty had thought it was a worthy project to speak in that language; in fact, they used *Questions on Doctrine* as a textbook in two of my college religion classes and taught us that part of our mission as ministers was to learn how to speak to scholars as well as the lay mind. There was no indication that they saw any major theological changes in the book. It met a crucial need of clarifying some of those hazy areas that had created problems for us. It also made our uniqueness more scripturally credible.

In college, I first came across the books that labeled the Adventist Church a cult. Books written by Christian apologists about cults or sects invariably lumped Adventists together with Mormons, Jehovah's Witnesses and Christian Science. Though they shared some of the traits of these other groups, Adventists themselves felt strongly that they had been wrongly labeled, since they saw themselves as Christ-centered, biblically based, and engaged in completing the task begun by the Protestant reformers.

Adventists, however, did not consider themselves just another denomination, but rather God's chosen Church, the steward of Present Truth, which they understood to be God's last message to the world before the *Parousia* of Christ. Clearly, if Luther were alive today, he would be an Adventist—so the thinking went. The movement had been commissioned to finish the Reformation, or in denominational language, "to finish the work," which creed-writers, traditionalists, and theological Liberals had seriously hampered.

Adventism was the one true Church on earth—the remnant group of apocalyptic fame.

⁵ "So too at the present time there is a remnant, chosen by grace." (Rom 11:5)

¹² "Here is a call for the endurance of the saints, those who keep the commandments of God and the faith of Jesus." (Rev 14:12)

In my undergraduate preparation for the ministry, I read books by ex-Adventists E. B. Jones, a twenty-year Adventist missionary and worker, and D. M. Canright (1840–1919), one of the brightest of the early Adventist pioneers and one-time architect of Adventist doctrine, who had left the movement and published a book in 1889, that remained in print to the present.[7] As a minister, I would need to know what our vulnerable points were and how to answer them. Elder Canright took Adventism apart one brick at a time. I wasn't impressed. As a college student, I read all these books to answer them, not to be indoctrinated by them. I surely knew what side I was on.

To balance off my research I also read *In Defense of the Faith: The Truth about Seventh-day Adventists: A Reply to Canright,* by William H. Branson (1887–1961),[8] a former president of the General Conference. The arguments against Adventism in Elder Canright's book were answered in Elder Branson's book.

I also read materials from the Defense Literature Committee of the General Conference, which usually began with the committee's perception of the dissenter's relationship to the Church—these men were portrayed as incorrigible, insincere, even delusional troublemakers—people like Ballenger, Kellogg, Fletcher, Houteff, and the Brinsmead brothers. After reading these official accounts, I had no question that all of them had deep personal psychological and relational problems that led to their attacks on the Church's leadership. Hence, they could have no theological credibility either.

According to the former-member genre of literature, Adventists were legalists who didn't know that the New Testament materials in Romans and Galatians had ever been written. These critics pointed out that Adventists had tried to cover up the Great Disappointment of 1844 by creating a theology that denigrated the cross of Christ by introducing a false atonement. They were wrong in many other areas as well: soul sleep (conditionalism), and the destruction of the wicked (annihilationism), for example, the books claimed.

Earlier Adventists had held an Arian position on the person of Christ presenting him as the first created being instead of verily God, the second person of the Godhead. Arguments between later Trinitarian Adventists and other Christians had largely missed their mark since neither side made much effort to understand the current views of the other. These misconceptions crept into the cult narrative of Evangelicals,

---

7. Canright. *Seventh-day Adventism Renounced*, (1948). Originally published in 1889.
8. Branson. *In Defense of the Faith; The Truth About Seventh-day Adventists,* (1933).

and with time, Adventists looked worse and worse. The negative implications of this for evangelism were staggering.

The most devastating of all the attacks on Adventism by other Christians was the claim that Adventists had no savior because they believed that Christ was a sinner, a position allegedly supported by some of Sister White's earlier writings. Critics would always anchor their attacks in the writings of Sister White since she was the one constant authoritative norm of Adventism.

Some Adventists did not help matters by constantly insisting that those who rejected their scriptural interpretations were candidates for "the mark of the beast" for they were riding the Papal monster, or they were drinking of the wine of the red woman's fornication. [2] "With whom the kings of the earth have committed fornication, and with the wine of whose fornication the dwellers on earth have become drunk." (Rev 17:2). The charges were all put in biblical jargon, but they came across as hostile accusations. Some Adventists seemed to show no desire to be understood and dismissed those who disagreed with them as apostates. They even seemed to be proud to be thought of as a cult. These were the ones some Adventist Church leaders in conversation with Dr. Barnhouse called the lunatic fringe of the Church.[9]

While our college professors did not dwell on these differences, they did teach us that we could and should answer and correct any misconceptions with clear biblical answers, that this was a part of the responsibility of being a minister. We were to work with everyone who God brought to us, and that included intelligent and learned people—ministers of other faiths especially. But the Adventist publishing houses were not being very supportive. Much of what they were turning out was considered by non-Adventist critics to be propaganda. Businessmen ran the publishing houses, and the bottom line demanded that they maximize sales.

While *Questions on Doctrine* was not an evangelistic tool in the traditional sense, the publication of this apologetic work suggested that evangelism was a gradual process. And it meant that other Christians might see Adventists as legitimate fellow travelers on the pathway to heaven instead of enemies to be denigrated and condemned. As a result, Adventism began to get more fair press in some of these Neo-Evangelical publications.

I cared very much that people had a correct view of us—it was the proper concern of a religious man. With the assurance of our most vocal critics that they had changed their mind about Adventists being a cult, untold thousands of people would eventually listen to the Adventist message, people who earlier would have dismissed it out of hand. We had all been taught that when people honestly listened, the Spirit could lead them to The Truth.

9. See Andreasen, "The Incarnation—Was Christ Exempt?" *Letters to the Churches*, 9–10. Cf. Barnhouse, "Are Seventh-day Adventists Christian? A New Look at Seventh-day Adventism." *Eternity*, Sept. 1956. Dr. Barnhouse quotes Adventist leaders: "They further explained to Mr. Martin that they had among their number certain members of their 'lunatic fringe' even as there are similar wild-eyed irresponsible in every field of fundamental Christianity."

Profile of a Religious Man
HOW *QUESTIONS ON DOCTRINE* CAME TO BE

The story behind Questions on Doctrine *is a positive one; one we would only find out many years later.* In the 1950s, Elder T. E. Unruh, president of one of the Pennsylvania Conferences, contacted Dr. Donald Barnhouse, editor of *Eternity* magazine. Elder Unruh had heard Dr. Barnhouse mention Adventists on the radio and he took issue with the notion expressed that Adventism was a cult. Elder Unruh was such a gentleman that Dr. Barnhouse was intrigued. A meeting was arranged so that the two could talk.[10]

Eventually additional meetings took place between representatives from the General Conference and Dr. Barnhouse, with some of his assistants, among whom was Rev. Walter Martin, then a doctoral student specializing in what he called non-Christian religions of American origin.

The meetings were initially confrontational[11]—both sides had *baggage*. But as they got to know one another, the atmosphere became cordial enough to allow for a full and fair examination of Adventism. Church administrators and theologians would answer honestly the questions posed by the Neo-Evangelical group. Dr. Barnhouse and his associate, Rev. Martin, would take a fair and honest look at Adventism to see what misperceptions and misunderstandings they might have.

Dr. Barnhouse and Rev. Martin carefully prepared a series of questions dealing with aspects of Adventist dogma that seemingly put the denomination in the category of *cult*. Two books then appeared—*Seventh-day Adventists Answer Questions on Doctrine* (1957) and Rev. Martin's book, *The Truth About Seventh-day Adventism* (1960).[12]

The two groups had originally agreed that both books would be sold through the regular distribution centers—the Adventist network of Book and Bible houses and the evangelical bookstores throughout North America. But when Rev. Martin's book came out, church leaders balked at his polemical denigration of sensitive Adventist peculiarities such as the Investigative Judgment, the Law and the Sabbath, and Sister White.

When the Adventist leadership reneged and refused to distribute Rev. Martin's book in Adventist bookstores, the book was distributed only through evangelical outlets. When I was a theology student in college, I purchased my copy as soon as it was released and read it through rapidly and with great interest. As usual, I read with a view to answering Rev. Martin's arguments.

A series of articles written by Adventist theologians and biblical scholars immediately appeared in *The Ministry* magazine challenging Rev. Martin. These were

---

10. Unruh, "The Seventh-day Adventist Evangelical Conferences of 1955–1956." *The Adventist Heritage*, 4:3, 1977, 35–36.

11. Ibid., 37.

12. *Seventh-day Adventists Answer Questions on Doctrine: An Explanation of Certain Major Aspects of Seventh-day Adventist Belief,* (1957). Cf. Martin, *The Truth About Seventh-day Adventism.*

later compiled and published in a second denominational book, *Doctrinal Discussions*.[13] Nonetheless, what had been hailed throughout my formative academy and college years as a great addition to Adventist scholarship would soon become the focus of controversy in some quarters of the Church. As with other publications of this nature, the book was issued without a byline. Instead, it said, "Prepared by a Representative Group of Seventh-day Adventist Leaders, Bible Teachers, and Editors." I later discovered that a few of my Seminary professors were part of that group that contributed to the book.

Trouble would begin when a retired Adventist minister, who had not been consulted in the preparation of the book, publicly objected to its publication. Elder Milian L. Andreasen, a former Church administrator and Seminary professor, had authored a book on the Adventist Sanctuary doctrine and a short popular commentary on the Epistle to the Hebrews. He was also on the contributor list of the *Seventh-day Adventist Bible Commentary*, the massive seven-volume series that came out in the 1950s. He was alleged to have written the section on Hebrews.

Upon reading *Questions on Doctrine*, he issued a series of pamphlets he called *Letters to the Churches*,[14] which appeared in the early 1960s. As these messages came out from his pen, the response to them varied. Some blamed his opposition to the book on senility; others suggested that he was reacting precisely because he had not been consulted. In the fundamentalist wing of the Church, however, many were ready to canonize him.

Clearly none of these evaluations was particularly flattering to a man who had been a loyal churchman for over sixty years. Fueled by Elder Andreasen's attacks on *Questions on Doctrine*, especially the conspiracy-minded elements in the Church went wild. The general interpretation I heard was that his unsolicited observations seemed unwarranted and unfair. Furthermore, critics said, he seemed to miss the point of the whole project, and that it was indefensible to be impugning the motives of the Church's highest leaders. Elder Andreasen's pointed attack on key leaders seemed unprecedented. I was frustrated that such behavior could be present among the remnant of God's Church on earth. Was a religious man supposed to act the way Elder Andreasen had?

THE ANDREASEN CONFLICT

Retired in Glendale, California, Elder Andreasen read the Adventist message in Questions on Doctrine *the way it had been translated into evangelicalese and claimed he could not recognize it as historic Adventism.* He then struck out on his own and announced

---

13. Ministerial Association of General Conference of SDA. *Doctrinal Discussions: A Compilation of Articles Originally Appearing in* The Ministry, *June 1960-July 1961, in Answer to Walter R. Martin's Book,* The Truth About Seventh-day Adventism, (1961).

14. Andreasen, *Letters to the Churches*.

to the public that the "Omega apostasy" had begun, and it was time for the faithful to rise and meet it head on.[15] His series of *Letters* were addressed to those Adventists interested in saving the Church from this last great apostasy allegedly predicted by Sister White. He asserted that the Church had to maintain its role as a messianic movement. Elder Andreasen especially took issue with the book's position on the nature of Christ, the nature of sin, and the nature of the atonement.

The suggestion that the atonement of Christ was in any way complete at the cross, he claimed, would be a repudiation of the Adventist Sanctuary doctrine. From there, his criticisms spilled into other areas of Adventist doctrine and polity. In each *Letter*, he added more complaints. Adventists had published thousands of pages of dogmatic theology through the years, some of which were contradictory and confusing. And true to their *modus operandi*, the writers had used a plethora of quotations from Sister White to arrive at their conclusions. Rev. Martin recognized this:

> For many years, Seventh-day Adventists have been handicapped by the lack of a comprehensive volume which adequately defines their doctrinal position. Many excellent publications clearly set forth certain aspects of Adventism, but for doctrinal information one has had to rely upon statements by Ellen G. White, Uriah Smith, J. N. Andrews, F. M. Wilcox, F. D. Nichol, W. H. Branson, Carlyle B. Haynes, L. E. Froom, and others. Except for the brief statement of fundamentals in the Seventh-day Adventist yearbook, the average Adventist has been somewhat handicapped because of conflicting theological opinions within the denomination, and even expressions in the writings of Ellen G. White were sometimes ambiguous. So Seventh-day Adventists have found considerable difficulty in presenting a definite, comprehensive explanation of their faith.[16]

Too often Adventist writers would quote the prophet's statements to prove their points instead of seeking biblical evidence, even though the denomination had always insisted that its only authoritative source of religious truth was the Bible. Often her statements were taken out of their context, but because they were words from "the pen of inspiration," a common Adventist phrase, they supposedly proved the veracity of the writer's position.

I was increasingly bothered by the fact that the prophet's statements were so often used to prove opposing viewpoints. But one thing was very clear: unofficially Adventists viewed Sister White's writings as an inspired commentary on the Bible. Therefore, to know what the Bible meant, you had to study her writings. This was implied in the common Adventist expression, "according to the Bible *and* the Spirit of Prophecy . . ." And yet the official creed of Adventism was not "this *and* that," but rather "the Bible and the Bible *only*." Although her writings were used as an inspired commentary the

---

15. Ibid., 63–64. Cf. p. 64: "All this was written to meet the apostasy in the alpha period. We are now in the omega period which Sr. White said would come, and which would be of a 'startling nature.'"

16. Martin, *The Truth About Seventh-day Adventism*, 47.

Church officially denied attributing this role to her. Yet this inconsistency in Adventist interpretation of scripture was not missed by the critics of Adventism and played into their hands to make Adventism appear to be a cult.

The denomination was now faced with a dilemma. To help the most ardent opponents of Adventists to see that it was not a cult, the writers couldn't use Sister White as a final court of appeals as they might have done in arguing with other Adventists. Since Adventism had always claimed that the Bible was its *only* rule of faith and practice, it was now given the chance to prove it. Adventist historians and leaders had to answer biblical questions without the use of denominational jargon, which had made it more difficult for non-Adventists to understand the organization's position.

When the members of the committee met to begin work on *Questions on Doctrine,* Elder Andreasen was not present. He had traditionally been on these types of committees. So, a member of the committee raised his hand and asked why he wasn't there. This innocent question was met with a kick under the table. During a break, the kicker talked to him and asked, "Haven't you heard about the feud between Andreasen and Froom?"[17] No, he hadn't.

From that point on, some have suggested that there might have been no *Letters to the Churches* if Elder Andreasen had been on the committee. This was the view of several who knew the situation and the personalities as well, but it was speculation. The error of the leaders was a political one, not a theological one, they claimed.

To understand the Andreasen conflict, three things are usually mentioned as necessary ingredients: (1) He was eighty years old (an insulting and probably unfair old-age perspective); (2) He had written books on the sensitive subjects dealt with in *Questions on Doctrine* and thus had established himself as an authority on these topics; and (3) He was not consulted in the book's production.

Looking only at theological considerations might be misleading. Some Adventist scholars have suggested that having Elder Andreasen on the committee might have helped him see the struggles the leaders and teachers were going through to answer the questions that had been posed to them. And he could contribute to how such a task could be handled. At least he could have been heard and would, presumably, have been on board to support the publication of the book.

A prominent Adventist minister once told me a truth I was not ready to accept but saw illustrated in much of these so-called theological (political) fights in the Church: It is a simple fact of life that we were men before we became theologians. This creates a great deal of difficulty where our positions and deeply held opinions are concerned. This was undoubtedly a factor in the Andreasen conflict. He reminded me once more of the human condition.

---

17. Froom (1890–1974) was Professor of Church History at Potomac University at the time. He was the Adventist historian who was instrumental in several major research projects for the Church. He was also foremost in the production of *Questions on Doctrine.* Interestingly, Dr. Froom was a member of the Danish Adventist elite as was Elder Andreasen. See *Sons of the North,* 196. Was this a skirmish between two Vikings?

I later listened as one of my college professors shared his observations of a Prayer Meeting he had attended where the speaker attacked a famous and well-respected mentor for his views on the doctrine of original sin. My former professor told me that the pastor had preached for an hour against original sin, all the time proving the authenticity of the doctrine by his behavior! Such confrontations are troublesome for a religious man. Even though he realizes he lives in the enemy's land, he may still entertain an idealism inherent in the teachings of the gospel; he still views the Church as a place of peace—certainly a place of honesty.

In his *Letters*, addressed to the Church in general, Elder Andreasen claimed that the leaders had needlessly sold out to the evangelicals. And he maintained that the use of non-traditional theological language in these areas would compromise the teachings of Adventism because it would lead to even greater confusion.

My professors, both at La Sierra and Andrews, argued just the opposite—it was time to speak in language that other scholars could understand to let them know that Adventists were Christians in the very core of their belief system and that they should not be lumped in with the traditional cults. This was the only sensible thing to do, according to them.

Furthermore, our prophet had given strong guidelines regarding our responsibility as ministers to speak to and convince non-Adventists (including ministers) of the truth of our message. Despite Elder Andreasen's objections it seemed to me that what the Church leaders carried out in publishing *Questions on Doctrine* was in harmony with the clear-cut instruction Sister White had given. She had written, "*Our ministers should seek to come near to the ministers of other denominations. Pray for and with these men, for whom God is interceding. A solemn responsibility is theirs. As Christ's messengers, we should manifest a deep, earnest interest in these shepherds of the flock.*"[18]

> Much has been lost by our people through following *such narrow plans that the most intelligent, better-educated classes are not reached.* Too often the work has been so conducted as to impress unbelievers that it is of very little consequence,—some stray off-shoot of religious enthusiasm, entirely beneath their notice. Much has been lost for want of wise methods of labor. *Every effort should be made to give character and dignity to the work.*
>
> It requires much wisdom to reach ministers and men of influence. But why should they be neglected as they have been by our people?[19]

As troubling as these disagreements may have been in some quarters of the Church they seemed to focus more on the language of theology than on the substance of Adventist beliefs. After reading all Elder Andreasen's critical materials, I still wasn't clear whether he was more concerned about the doctrines of *Questions on Doctrine* or

---

18. White, *Testimonies for the Church*, 6:78. Emphasis supplied.
19. White, *Evangelism*, 562–563. Emphasis supplied.

the politics of the Church leaders. Theology seemed to be merely the barrel through which he blasted the denomination's leadership.

As time progressed, adversarial movements within the Church would produce papers of a new order, papers attacking the leadership of the Church. These were little more than complaint rags, with whole sections devoted to nothing less than page after page of letters from critics ruthlessly attacking the organized Church and the brethren. This was a sociological phenomenon that I couldn't understand.

To me these Adventist leaders were men appointed by God to their posts, and now they were being maligned and slandered. Who were these self-appointed critics? I would learn later that much of this was not driven by religious concerns at all; some were nothing but merchants of discontent, i.e., people who made their living opposing Church leadership. It was a rude awakening for a religious man. Identifying the "Omega apostasy" was like the quests for Noah's Ark—they paid off big time for those leading the search but produced little results.

Some felt that the Adventist laity had had so few places where they could give feedback to the ordained leadership of the Church that these papers provided some release. But even that rationale could not justify this approach for a religious man. The *Layworker* and the *Sanctuary Fellowship Awakening Newsletter* were two papers that were little more than religious tabloids. These would spawn other such tabloids as time passed. In fact, one dissenter would later visit me and suggest that this was a better way to make a living than working for the Church. He had been chair of an Adventist college Religion Department when I knew him as a student at the Seminary.

As I occasionally read copies of these papers that dissenter groups sent or that came across my desk in the library, I was aghast at how incredibly judgmental much of the material was.

AN ENVIRONMENT OF CONTROVERSY IN THE CHURCH

The result of all this agitation was an environment of controversy in the Church—a wrangling that festers to this day. Having such a notable celebrity in Adventist circles as Elder Andreasen, as the standard bearer of the opposition to denominational leadership, caused first confusion and then polarization. But more significantly, it gave license to whole new groups of self-styled reformers to try to provoke the eschatological purge of Adventism known as the "shaking" of the Church.

Elder Andreasen's approach set a precedent that said it was legitimate to revolt against the leadership of the Church if you thought the leaders were wrong. This was something entirely new to me. Up to this point in Adventist history, it was the leadership that had identified apostasies and heresies. Now the tables were being turned. Elder Andreasen here followed the example of Dr. Kellogg, who had called specific leaders liars. But I was not aware that Dr. Kellogg had taken his criticisms to the Church public in the same way Elder Andreasen had.

The Adventist Church has been in a civil war ever since Elder Andreasen's letters came out. These tabloid-type attacks were rationalized as permissible because the prophet had urged Adventists to meet the iceberg of end-time apostasy head-on. The wise "virgins" in the Church had to guard Adventism against this apostasy.

> [1] "Then the kingdom of heaven shall be compared to ten maidens who took their lamps and went to meet the bridegroom. [2] Five of them were foolish, and five were wise. [3] For when the foolish took their lamps, they took no oil with them; [4] but the wise took flasks of oil with their lamps. [5] As the bridegroom was delayed, they all slumbered and slept. [6] But at midnight there was a cry, 'Behold, the bridegroom! Come out to meet him.'
>
> [7] Then all those maidens rose and trimmed their lamps. [8] And the foolish said to the wise, 'Give us some of your oil, for our lamps are going out.' [9] But the wise replied, 'Perhaps there will not be enough for us and for you; go rather to the dealers and buy for yourselves.' [10] And while they went to buy, the bridegroom came, and those who were ready went in with him to the marriage feast; and the door was shut.
>
> [11] Afterward the other maidens came also, saying, 'Lord, lord, open to us.' [12] But he replied, 'Truly, I say to you, I do not know you.' [13] Watch therefore, for you know neither the day nor the hour." (Matt 25:1–13)

For those who spent their time looking for the "Omega apostasy," this was more than a bump in the road. At last, the long expected eschatological apostasy was there for all to see in the publication of this much-trumpeted book. People of a certain mind-set found such simplistic thinking very inviting. I could see no similarity between Sister White's "Alpha and Omega apostasies" and Elder Andreasen's claim, but it was now to be that I would run into such wild speculations. *Questions on Doctrine* was destined to cause more trouble than Kellogg's alleged pantheistic book, *The Living Temple*. Elder Andreasen identified *Question on Doctrine* as "new theology," a term that would later dominate some Adventist discussions in the 1980s.[20]

Seeking to avoid a schism, leaders from the General Conference flew out to California to talk to Elder Andreasen and asked him to withdraw his criticisms for the sake of Church unity. They were not the first to plead with him. Professor George McCready Price (1870–1963), the well-known Adventist creationist, author of twenty-three books on various aspects of the faith, and retired in Loma Linda, wrote him at least two letters in 1959, as ten years Elder Andreasen's senior.

> I am afraid that the great law of heredity from your Viking ancestors has made you forgetful of the fact that the Master was kind and courteous even with Judas. Sr. White has told us to treat even our opponents as being honest. In contrast with this, how continuously have you been attributing the worst motives

---

20. See Andresen, *Letters to the Churches*, 44, 68.

> to what our leaders have been doing in Washington and charging them with dishonesty and double dealing.
>
> Even old men like us ought to be capable of discussing controversial topics in a calm, objective fashion with anyone who pointedly disagrees with us. I have talked with scores of educated unbelievers among the high-class scientists of America and Europe, and I think I could still do so without excitement or a show of ruffled feelings.[21]

The General Conference leaders explained that Elder Andreasen needed to recognize that the brethren were trying to give a correct view of Adventism in language that the inquiring evangelical leaders would understand. But he held his ground, accusing them of undermining Present Truth and maintaining that he would remain true to the faith. He had declared war and chosen a position on the battlefield from which he could not retreat.

The end of the matter seemed inevitable. Elder Andreasen was defrocked. In Adventism, this was the ultimate punishment—to have your ministerial credentials taken from you in battle. Nonetheless, this did not bring an end to the matter. Instead, it created a martyr for the cause, and gave the conspiracy buffs more grist for their mill. For these people, the "Omega apostasy" was an impending disaster, and now an esteemed theologian had identified it as a heresy slithering around at the very heart of the denomination. Heresy was in the air, and the heresy hunters in the Church followed his lead.

Elder Andreasen wrote regarding his rough handling by the Church administrators.

> And so the word has gone out, "Shoot the Watchdog." And it is being done. May God pity our leaders. They are fulfilling prophecy. I pray for them. I am not bitter. I am not vindictive. I am enjoying a sound Christian experience. And I pray for my beloved church. My head is bloody, but unbowed. *Paul went down to defeat, but he had the consolation that a crown awaited him.* As for me, "Here I stand. I can do no other. God helping me." The fight is not finished. It has just begun.[22]

Elder Andreasen had now implicitly identified himself with both St. Paul and Dr. Martin Luther. Following his lead, his disciples stood up all over the world rhetorically implying that Sister White was the basis of Adventist truth. This was apparent by their lack of appeal to scripture and their appeal to Sister White as an inspired, and therefore authoritative, commentary of the Bible. While they claimed to follow the *Fundamental Beliefs* that maintained the Bible as the basis of all Adventist doctrine, their writings demonstrated that their ultimate authority was the writings of Sister White since she was a modern prophet—the messenger to the Laodicean Church.

---

21. Price, "Letter to M. L. Andreasen," (September 13, 1959).
22. Andreasen, "Shooting the Watchdog," (January 19, 1962.) Emphases supplied.

Before he was done, Elder Andreasen had attacked nearly every avenue of Adventist communication from periodicals, to schools, to Sabbath School; from editors to administrators to teachers.[23] He liberally quoted sentences and parts of sentences from Sister White to justify his view that the Church was experiencing the great apostasy of the end time. The intense attacks that he and his followers launched against anyone who reprimanded them, forced the Church to choose between progress and tradition. Thanks to the challenge from Rev. Martin, Elder Andreasen claimed the Adventist leaders had excised all the unique viewpoints that Adventism had brought to the religious world.

Citing the *Sabbath School Quarterly* entitled "Christ Centered Doctrines," for the last quarter of 1960, he noted that the Sanctuary, the cleansing of the Sanctuary, Christ in the most holy place, the third angel's message, the remnant Church, the Spirit of Prophecy (Ellen White), the 2300 days of Daniel 8:14, the 70 weeks of Daniel 9, the middle of the week, the commandments of God and the faith of Jesus, the seal of God (Sabbath), the mark of the beast (Sunday-keeping), and health reform *had all been left out of that Quarterly.*

This allegedly demonstrated that the authors no longer considered any of these doctrines to be Christ-centered doctrines, he said. Coincidentally, he claimed, these were the same doctrines that Barnhouse and Martin had claimed were keeping Adventists from being appreciated as evangelical.[24] Thus to gain the approval of the evangelical world, the leadership had thrown the fundamentals of Adventism overboard.

Adventism has always been a denomination that pulled its members primarily from other Protestant groups. Adventists had long viewed the Reformation as incomplete. Instead of continuing the work of the great Reformers, Adventists claimed, their followers had set up creeds. They had therefore spoken out against the writing of creeds—the work of the Church was not to produce creeds carved into stone but rather to return to the faith of the original New Testament Church before it had become corrupted by Rome; a biblical Christianity.

In college, we were learning that Adventism could be defended from the Bible—indeed it must be so, because that had been its claim from the beginning. But Elder Andreasen, who so many loved and admired, was now essentially arguing that Sister White was the basis of Adventist teaching though he would not say it that way. Interestingly, one scarcely finds a reference to scripture among the myriad of Sister White quotes in his *Letters*. The same approach was even more forward in most of the writings of his followers.

So, the controversy steamed on. As a college student, I heard of the conflict but thought little of it. The general perception that I picked up, if anyone talked about it at all, was that the prophet had predicted just such a thing, that great lights would go

---

23. See Andreasen, "The Sabbath School."
24. Ibid.

out. We figured that Elder Andreasen was simply one of the greater lights. Sad, but she had told us to expect it.

Religious men have little time for such diversions. Sadness resided in the quarters where I circulated—surely a man who had given so much to the cause should not do this to hurt it. After the leadership had spoken I went on with my work. Regrettable, but no matter how brightly your light had shone, when it was out . . . it was out. And we all knew that probably even greater lights would go out before the Black Cloud of the *Parousia* appeared. In a strange way, that brought some consolation with it—the end was near.

For Elder Andreasen, this was a deeply emotional issue. He wrote:

> I am sorry that we as ministers have not done more thorough work. I am sorry that I as a teacher have not established my thousands of students more firmly in the faith once delivered to the saints. I suppose there are those now teaching others who once sat in my classroom and are now teaching what Peter calls "damnable heresies." 2 Peter 2:1. May God in His mercy forgive me.[25]

At this time in my education, I was oblivious to the political ramifications of what had happened in the Andreasen case. That would become apparent much later. For us as ministers in training, this was a theological issue. But Elder Andreasen had lashed out at the leadership and for that it was reasonable that he would pay with his credentials. To him, this was the "Omega apostasy."

Claiming that he had personally known many of those involved in the "Alpha apostasy" of the Kellogg era, he believed he was speaking out against the great apostasy that the prophet had predicted. In time, this line of thinking would infiltrate the schools and the editorial offices of the Church. In a speech he prepared in his own defense but never delivered because he claimed he was never given a chance to be heard, Elder Andreasen wrote:

> It is a fundamental principle recognized everywhere that when a man is under accusation, he has a *right to be heard*. Whether it is a Chessman or an Eichmann, whether it is a small matter of the theft of a pin or an apple, or if it is the murder of six million Jews, *the man has a right to be heard*. This is an accepted principle in all nations. And if the man cannot defend himself, the state will furnish the best legal talent. Luther was heard. So were all other heretics. Hitler was the only ruler in modern times who violated this rule. What about Adventist officials? What about Eld. Figuhr?[26]

So then, Elder Figuhr (1896–1983) was someone parallel to Hitler? Elder Andreasen detested the idea that he had been promised to have his credentials restored if he would

---

25. Ibid.

26. Andreasen, "Introductory Speech by M. L. Andreasen." Elder Figuhr was General Conference president at the time.

cease writing anymore inflammatory letters. But he maintained that he was led to stand up for The Truth, and in Sister White's words he was called up to "Meet it! Meet it!"

Speaking again of Elder Figuhr, he wrote,

> It is evident that a person, who has such dim perception of his responsibility and duty, is unfit for his post.... He has violated a fundamental principle, he has sinned *"with a high hand,"* and has committed one of the worst sins in the calendar. He has sinned grievously against man and God. He has insulted God and one of His ministers.[27]

By taking away his credentials, he argued, *leadership* had relegated him to the level of a dog that has no ability to speak. And yet he had devoted his entire life to the Church. It was a sin that was hardly forgivable. "May God save His church from rulers of this kind."[28]

I would learn later that this tactic of no trial was a pattern—as had been demonstrated in the cases of Elder Canright, Dr. Kellogg, Elder Fletcher, Elder Ballenger and other alleged heretics. In each case, Church leaders had felt that dialoguing with these people was hopeless because these men were clearly wrong and there was no reason to labor further with them. Once the leaders made their decision, there was no further need for discussion, and often, as in Elder Andreasen's case, the decisions were made behind closed doors without the accused being present. In some religious organizations this was called "shunning."

THE CONFLICT COMES CLOSE TO HOME

The Andreasen conflict had an interesting relevance to me because as a religious man I had married into a family that was very close to "Prez" as they called him. Elder Andreasen was a member of the Scandinavian Adventist elite, and we were Vikings who stuck together. Annie had been his private secretary when he dictated his *Letters.*

Grandpa Doc was a close friend of Elder Andreasen and occasionally complained to me about the sellout of Elder Figuhr and Dr. Froom. He maintained that the set of Bible commentaries put out by the Church was a mistake and should never be referred to as "the" *Seventh-day Adventist Bible Commentary.* He charged that they were heavily tainted by the same scholars and administrators who had written *Questions on Doctrine.*

I felt the pressure from the family's personality cult around Elder Andreasen. But the fact was that the publication of *Questions on Doctrine* had opened a window that let fresh air into the Church. As Thomas Carlyle had said, "A thought once awakened does not again slumber."[29]

---

27. Ibid.
28. Ibid.
29. Goodman (ed.), *The Forbes Book of Business Quotations,* 832.

In my Research and Bibliography class during my first semester in the fall of 1963 at Seminary, I chose as my term project, Elder Andreasen's view of the moral nature of Christ.[30] When I finished my project, I gave Annie's family a copy of my manuscript and their response was simply that they were sad I never got to meet Elder Andreasen—*"he was such a nice man."*

My research involved a study of the doctrine of original sin, which Elder Andreasen claimed Adventists did not hold and that they had never taught. I read everything Elder Andreasen had written including unpublished material from my father-in-law's files. So, intrigued and puzzled was I with this startling claim that twenty years later I would devote my doctoral dissertation to a history of the Adventist theological treatment of Adam's sin in relation to his posterity.[31]

Professor Price, a premier Adventist scholar, professor and author, in his poignant letters to Elder Andreasen questioned him on his approach.

> My dear Brother Andreasen: You correctly say that "Few, even of our ministers, know anything of what Sr. White calls the great law of heredity" (p. 13). But to the many Adventist ministers who do not know this law should now be added the name of M.L.A. For you are not only misinformed about this scientific law, but are now in a fair way to confuse still further the minds of others by attributing to Christ's human nature your own false ideas of this law. And this is a horrible thing. . . .
>
> I have read your No. 6,[32] but I do not find in it that anybody need answer at any time. It is just a tiresome rehash of your old complaint that the book *Questions on Doctrine* is not a good Adventist book. . . . No, your No. 6 is just a rehash of your old argument that the present generation of Adventists do [sic] not pronounce Shibboleth quite the same as you used to pronounce it two generations ago.
>
> Why should they? I thought this is a "movement," not a *status quo*. If we as a people can't learn anything or change for the better with the passing years and decades, I would feel uneasy. I have never thought that we had all truth, or were already perfected. This book[33] was advanced light. . . .
>
> And I thank God for the fifty pages of Appendixes,[34] with the careful compilation and classification of some of the more important statements of the Spirit of Prophecy regarding the nature of Christ and His work as Priest and Mediator. These fifty pages are alone worth the book's entire cost. They have cleared up many points for thousands of Adventists who never did have an adequate view of these topics. And if any intelligent Adventist will read just

---

30. Zackrison, "M. L. Andreasen's Position on the Moral Nature of Christ." Term paper, Research and Bibliography, Andrews University Seventh-day Adventist Theological Seminary, (January 1964).
31. Zackrison, *The First Temptation: Seventh-day Adventists and Original Sin*, (2015).
32. Referring to Elder Andreasen's *Letters*.
33. Referring to *Questions on Doctrine*.
34. In *Questions on Doctrine*, 641–692.

> pp. 650 to 654 I think he will be quite immune to your attempts to muddle him about Christ's having the passions and propensities of humanity.[35]

Professor Price explained the most significant issue. After caricaturing Elder Andreasen as one who, in the words of Sister White, would stubbornly set himself against the view presented, and would act out the natural feelings of the heart, he appealed:

> Why, even Dulles, or Nixon, or Herter, in their discussions with their most bitter opponents behind the Iron Curtain, never think of having their talks open to the public, and never ask for a tape recording of what goes on. At the close of their talks they agree with their opponents in framing a unified or mutual statement to be given to the public. That is all. Why can't a veteran Adventist minister be equally courteous and reasonable? I wonder why?[36]

Controversy would now find its way into Adventism on a regular basis and as a religious man I would have to deal with it. Ironically, for all the objecting from Elder Andreasen and his disciples, the evangelical leaders couldn't see that Adventists had made any changes in their theology.[37] I never was convinced that this whole conflict had much to do with theology. And history would repeat itself.

---

35. "Letter to M. L. Andreasen."
36. Ibid.
37. Martin, *The Truth About Seventh-day Adventism*, 7–14.

CHAPTER SIXTEEN

The Controversy Widens

"Everybody wants to be somebody; nobody wants to grow."
—Johann Wolfgang von Goethe

SEMINARY OPENS NEW ISSUES FOR DISCUSSION

As I sat in classes at Seminary, I felt ignorant facing issues of modern theology—but I had come to graduate school to have that ignorance dissipated. My professors addressed issues I had never heard of as though we should be familiar with them—we were, after all, college graduates.

Our curriculum included the studies of soteriology (the study of salvation), Christology, anthropology, inspiration and revelation, the law, the covenants, exegesis, eschatology, archaeology, Hebrew, Greek, science and religion, Old and New Testament history and backgrounds, church history and research methods. In addition, there was the practical segment of working in churches on the weekends, and classes in evangelism, preaching, pastoring, administration, psychology, sociology and pastoral counseling. All these areas of study were designed and organized to give us credible approaches to critical problems from a religious perspective. But despite my excellent La Sierra College education I sometimes felt like a novice.

The faculty was challenged by two distinct goals, theory and application. There were times when we were not clear whether we were expected to become theologians or ministers. To judge from our courses, the emphasis was on academics. The pure ministry classes were not generally considered very challenging or prestigious. Attempts by the ministry teachers to introduce more challenging topics were sometimes caricatured by the more academically inclined students as inane and shallow. I heard some students say these were men with degrees in speech—what did they know of theology? Knowledge puffs up (1 Cor 8:1), Paul said, and academic arrogance is a weed that thrives in institutions of higher learning, be they ever so religious.

Dr. Heppenstall was the most diligent in bringing these two goals of theology and ministry together, with his extensive experience as a pastor and his brilliance as a theologian. In addition, he was passionate about our Adventism. I soon saw that his great concern was to educate intelligent, thinking ministers who were both informed theologians as well as focused pastors.

He spoke of his own conversion as a young agnostic. He had witnessed the harassment of a Baptist co-worker at the workplace in his native England. After reaching out to him, this young man had brought him to Christ and awakened in him the desire to know more. His search had led him to Adventism, the pastoral ministry, and finally to youth work and education.

A fervent scholar, Dr. Heppenstall often used the Socratic method to help us think through our faith by asking leading questions—those we might expect in the field as well as questions we needed to ask ourselves to get to the bottom of a theological inquiry. His thoughtful desire to establish Adventism as a genuine biblical faith was constantly demonstrated in his life and classes. He was very much aware of what a delicate balance it was to combine our love of people with our love of knowledge and wisdom.

Often he would challenge us with the question, How much error can you believe and still be saved? Then he would remind us that we are saved by faith, not by knowledge, and we must always work to keep faith in the focus of our ministry. His lectures and discussions were informative and stimulating and he prayed at the beginning and end of each class period. I appreciated most of all that he was modeling ministry even in the way he conducted his classes. The content of his lectures kept our ministry in mind as well. Frequently he applied deep inquiry with practical application to the pastorate.

My Seminary experience was a matter of life and death to me. I totally bought into the need for balance of knowledge and nurture. I took every class period seriously. I didn't question why I was at Seminary. God had called me, and I would answer that call by focusing obsessively on his work. I learned to take notes like I'd never done before. After each lecture, I would retreat to the university library to type out what I had just heard. If I had classes back to back, I would spend the night at home typing out my notes on the blue portable manual Royal typewriter Dad and Mom had given me as a present when I started college. My file was growing, my collection of class notes was multiplying.

As important as the study of apologetics was, it was by no means the total focus of our studies. This was a time for informing, shaping, and framing and not the least—understanding who we were and why we were here. We were continually reminded of the "big picture" and where all the details and specifics fit into that painting. As a religious man, I thrived on what I was learning.

We learned the big names in theology and biblical studies—Brunner and Barth, Cullman and Berkouwer, Bultmann and Albright. We not only read them, we wrote reviews of their works—pro and con. Some of the work was overwhelming at first but I pressed on, determined to be the best I could be. We studied our enemies' arguments to understand them and see why they were formulated as they were. We tested them by the Bible. We learned the difference between the interpretation and the application of scripture.

We took preaching classes and stood before our classmates as they critiqued both our content and delivery. This process was at once a horrifying and exhilarating experience. We listened to sermons on every student's hobby—from the importance of the law to why we should not have white wall tires on our car. We wondered how these topics would affect future congregations.

We had classes that were distinctly Adventist, like Prophetic Guidance from Elder Arthur L. White, our prophet's grandson and head of the Ellen G. White Estate in Washington, where all the prophet's works were archived. He was dynamic, dramatic and fascinating in what he revealed and what we took to be the historical, literal truth. He was more than a dynamo—he was theatrical. He could hold a class spellbound for the two hours a day that we met with him. We learned about the human Sister White as well as her prophetic ministry—her soft sides as a family person, her hard work as a minister, and her interest in people. And we learned about how the prophetic gift worked.

Elder White emphasized that she never read from a literary source before she saw something in vision. Everything she wrote for the Church and the public was the result of direct special revelation from God and when she made statements like "I was shown," or "I saw," she was speaking of what she had seen in a vision from God. She would not breathe during visions that sometimes lasted for hours, he told us. She would demonstrate superhuman strength during some visions, and at other times she would have no strength at all, lying powerless on the floor.

All charges of plagiarism were simply the blatant lies of those who hated us. The sheer volume of her writings was all original with her, we were assured, and it should impress us beyond measure that she was a true prophet. God had chosen a broken, weakened vessel, with only a third-grade education to guide the Church in these last days. Her school days had come to an early end after a cruel attack in which a fellow student had thrown a rock that hit her in the nose. Little Ellen had hovered for weeks between life and death before God raised her from her sick bed and prepared her to become his messenger for the last days.

All her critics had been answered by Elder F. D. Nichol (1897–1966) in his book, *Ellen G. White and Her Critics*.[1] Most of the attacks had originated with Elder D. M. Canright but they had been expanded by other misguided souls. We were to remember that all God's prophets had had their critics and Sister White was no exception.

---

1. Nichol, *Ellen G. White and Her Critics*, (1951).

We were assured that there was little in her life or writings to criticize and that there was certainly no argument of substance to undermine her credibility. Any attempt to do so would be a fulfillment of two of her most well-known predictions:

> *The very last deception of Satan will be to make of none effect the testimony of the Spirit of God. . . .* Satan will work ingeniously, in different ways and through different agencies, to unsettle the confidence of God's remnant people in the true testimony.[2]

> *There will be a hatred kindled against the testimonies which is satanic.* The workings of Satan will be to unsettle the faith of the churches in them, for this reason: Satan cannot have so clear a track to bring in his deceptions and bind up souls in his delusions if the warnings and reproofs and counsels of the Spirit of God are heeded.[3]

THE IMPORTANCE OF THE PROPHET

We learned that any person claiming to be a true prophet of God had to pass four biblical tests. and Sister White had passed them all. (1) Their teachings had to agree with the Scriptures. (Isa 8:20). (2) They had to live what they preached. (Matt 7:20). (3) They had to teach clearly that Jesus was God in human flesh. (1 John 4:2). (4) Their predictions had to be fulfilled in history. (Jer 28:9).

Nothing new there. We had covered all this in college in a class called *Gift of Prophecy*, but now we were at the graduate level and doing further research into the history and claims of our prophet. And our professor had known Sister White, his grandmother. We felt with distinct uniqueness the clear assurance that what she pointed out in scripture was the Present Truth. We were assured that we could rely on her interpretation of the written word.

We sensed the certainty behind her pointed messages to specific Church workers. We learned to treat these messages as though they had been written directly to us. These writings were depicted as having been virtually dictated by the angel that accompanied her in vision. In fact, she claimed she was as dependent on the Spirit to write down her instructions to the Church as she was in receiving them in the first place.[4]

Nine volumes of her published counsels to the Church were called the *Testimonies for the Church*. Some of these were general instructions addressed to the Church. Others were written to specific organizations like schools, Conferences and local

---

2. White, *Letter 12, 1890*. Emphasis supplied.
3. White, *Letter 40, 1890*. Emphasis supplied.
4. White, "Questions and Answers," *Review and Herald* 30:17 (October 8, 1867), 260. Reprinted in *Selected Messages*, 1:37.

churches. Still others were directed to individual Adventists who needed spiritual work done in their lives. It was clear that she was the Church's pastor at large.

We read about her predictions and their fulfillments. We learned how her books were put together and what the White Estate did to protect them from attack as well as mismanagement (and misapplication). We read of miracles in her life and how God had led in her special prophetic ministry. All this added up to a distinct authority. It is no wonder that many concluded that if we didn't understand a text of scripture, we should go to Sister White for its meaning. I came to understand in a new way why so many articles I had read in Church publications were basically compilations from her writings. The Church was on a quest for pure Truth, and her works were the contemporary depository of The Truth.

A PLACE TO MEET LIFELONG FRIENDS AND FUTURE EMPLOYERS

Seminary was not only a place to study—it was a place for making new friends and connections—people who would become an integral part of the Adventist social network and administrative structure. Some would become our colleagues, others our bosses. Some would become Church politicians, others scholars, and some would support us, and some would betray us. Some would remain faithful, others would leave us.

We didn't dwell on who would fill what role, but all this was part of our Church theology. The threat of false teachers and false prophets was never far away from any discussion. Here was where we could retreat to explain the unexplainable or perhaps lick our own wounds when we were misinterpreted or treated badly. We didn't know the end from the beginning, and I was never one who wanted to, except for the assurance that we were all looking forward to the Black Cloud that drew nearer with every passing day.

One classmate I met early on was Keith Brown.[5] He and his wife were graduates of Southern Missionary College and they lived directly across the hall from us in the married housing quarters. We met one hot summer night just before school started while I was making grilled cheese sandwiches. I had left the door to our apartment open to get some cross ventilation. Keith was a gourmet cook and the inviting aroma coming from our kitchen made him tap on the open door and introduce himself. He was shocked to see us eating grilled cheese sandwiches with ketchup, but from then on, he later told me, he adopted the practice. And that was the beginning of a lifelong friendship.

Keith and I had almost all our classes together—we were both enrolled in the Master of Arts program so our curriculum was similar. We also shared comparable viewpoints on most everything in our faith. Where we differed, we found it easy to learn from each other. He was the only person I had ever met who had grown up in

---

5. Name supplied.

the South. Other than that, we had very similar backgrounds—both born and reared in the Church, attending Adventist schools. We had grown up in the custody of the Church and were true believers in the faith. He had been a little boy in the his southern Church when Elder L. Calvin Osborn became his pastor. And it was Elder Osborn who became my pastor in La Sierra when I was thirteen. We both shared a deep respect for this pastor and mutual friend.

The Browns shared interesting stories from SMC, a place I had barely heard of. My brother had talked of attending the school at one time but had never followed through. Dr. Haussler had taught there, and I knew it was a small Adventist college near Chattanooga, Tennessee, very conservative, in the buckle of the Bible belt. It was a campus of old red wooden buildings. But Keith showed us the architect's renderings of the "Ten-Year Plan"—a layout that resembled a southern plantation with colonial buildings, red brick with tall white columns. The drawing was awesome, and this new campus was to be completed by 1974.

Keith had worked his way through school at a large bakery near the college. He spoke of his job greasing the pans with animal fat, although the pastries themselves used only vegetable shortening in their list of ingredients. It was a technicality, he said. And he claimed that he had never had such soft hands as he did during those years! Keith was only at Seminary for a year and we graduated together with our Master of Arts degrees the following August 1964 before he went to his Conference assignment as an intern. We would stay in touch and meet again several years later under very different circumstances.

Back when school began, I experienced the beginnings of what would prove to be another important friendship in my life. Attending a student get-acquainted night in the dining hall at the university center I was with friends from La Sierra. As we chatted, the student leaders called for our attention to introduce a man who would deliver a speech about the new school year.

The speaker was probably in his early thirties—I figured he was probably a GI who had returned to college and most likely one of the S.A. officers. His black hair was cropped short and he danced when he talked in a staccato style. Every word that came out of his mouth was well-chosen, weighty and often humorous. His articulate use of the English language was impressive.

Before he was done everyone was chuckling. I sensed an ownership among the students—this was someone they liked. No wonder they had elected him to whatever office he held. Who was this guy? Not a student? Not an SA officer? I was amazed to discover that he was the Andrews University dean of students. So young. So with it. The word was "charismatic." He clearly had it. And he came across not only as magnetic but as knowledgeable.

I asked around and found that he had attended Adventist schools and graduated from Union College in Lincoln, Nebraska. He had been a boy's dean in an Adventist academy in Kansas where he had been a colleague of my music teacher at La

Sierra Academy. He had later gone on to finish his PhD in Colorado. This was typical in Adventist society—so many people you *didn't* know knew people you *did* know. From graduate school he had come to Andrews to teach English and serve as dean of students. He was riveting in every word he uttered. I was not surprised when I later learned he was also a member of the Mensa Society.

Dr. Frank Knittel (1927–2015) had entered my life, if only through an introductory speech. Our paths would cross in more professional ways in times to come though we would not meet formally for another half dozen years.

A PLACE OF VARYING THEOLOGIES

The hallways of Seminary Hall were alive with discussions and arguments. More controversy spewed there than in the classrooms—students in groups discussing theology, biblical studies, higher critical methodology, problems in science and religion, views on creation—what to do with the rocks that were dated at two million years and had fossils in them. Here was a workshop in dynamic motion.

The discussions were exciting and free. We were at liberty to listen, think, talk, even argue. Clearly, Adventism was vibrant and healthy—dynamic. In fact, Seminarians were expected to think and to question. This was the road to informed certitude. That commitment to thinking was vital. How else could religious men and *women* validate their faith? Yes, there were a few female students—usually from foreign countries. I was in exceptional company. We were all religious people. I had no reason to think anyone here was any less a believer than I was. We were all here for the same purpose—*to finish the work God had called us to do.*

We learned that crafting a good question often took more skill than spewing out a pat answer. We gained much by asking questions. And our teachers expected us to think. It was obviously a new exercise for some in the class, but I found it exhilarating. Some older ministers, too often used to offering up irrational and hortatory pronouncements from the pulpit, were often met by the professor with, "Elder, it's not true just because you say it!" We young guys found this to be great sport. Some older ministers seemed to be overly dogmatic, and they stepped into the foray at every turn.

"Come with me down the primrose path," our professor might say. And the older guys who ventured down it would soon find themselves entangled in thorny problems they could not easily extricate themselves from. We quickly learned to avoid making irrational and hortatory pronouncements that couldn't be substantiated by argument and good biblical evidence. Some of us had been down those paths and didn't want the embarrassment of mediocrity.

We listened to the arguments regarding the synoptic problem, form criticism, what biblical inspiration meant, the relation of philosophy to theology and the nature of divine revelation. I heard talk in the halls of Seminary that sometimes alarmed me and at other times warmed me. I recalled what Dr. A had said in college—small minds talk about people, medium-sized minds talk about things, great minds talk about ideas. Seminary was an idea center.

The Adventist Sanctuary Doctrine was a problem for both future college teachers and ministers. Dr. Heppenstall worked tirelessly to establish it from scripture. Most professors never mentioned it, others only did so in passing. All of them considered it an important part of our heritage, our history, our identity; but details were seldom forthcoming. We all assumed its truth and ascribed its problematic aspects to a lack of understanding on our part.

Some professors refused to make any theological judgments on anything, choosing rather to retreat to their own areas of discipline. One professor said it was puzzling that the one significant contribution of Adventism to the theological world (the Sanctuary Doctrine) was a doctrine that no non-Adventist scholar had ever accepted on either theological or biblical grounds. We would have to deal with this as pastors and teachers in the future.

The whole issue of 1844 was being discussed and questioned by students. I kept hearing from colleagues and professors that it was time for Adventism to "enter the twentieth century." The implication was that there were far more pertinent issues in the ministry than simply defending old Adventist positions. No one was dogmatic about these things.

Seminary was a place where ministers informed their faith. To doubt was not to destroy; to doubt was to clarify, to think through both sides of an issue so that our faith could stand the strongest scrutiny. Some truth resided in Descartes' method of doubt where if one could not doubt, one could not think. In fact, thinking, doubting, were evidence of one's own existence. We who were encouraged to internalize that truth need never be worried, scared or defensive. Any Truth can stand the heaviest attack, the strongest examination, the most intense scrutiny. If it couldn't, how could one know it was truth?

Our prophet had written a great deal on that very subject.[6]

> There is no excuse for anyone in taking the position that there is no more truth to be revealed, and that all our expositions of Scripture are without an error. The fact that certain doctrines have been held as truth for many years by our people is not a proof that our ideas are infallible. *Age will not make error into truth*, and truth can afford to be fair. *No true doctrine will lose anything by close investigation.* We are living in perilous times, and it does not become us to accept everything claimed to be truth without examining it thoroughly; neither can we afford to reject anything that bears the fruits of the Spirit of God; but we should be teachable, meek and lowly of heart. There are those who oppose everything that is not in accordance with their own ideas and by

---

6. White, *Counsels to Writers and Editors*, 33–42.

so doing they endanger their eternal interest as verily as did the Jewish nation in their rejection of Christ.[7]

The fact that there is no controversy or agitation among God's people, should not be regarded as conclusive evidence that they are holding fast to sound doctrine. There is reason to fear that they may not be clearly discriminating between truth and error. When no new questions are started by investigation of the Scriptures, when no difference of opinion arises which will set men to searching the Bible for themselves, to make sure that they have the truth, there will be many now, as in ancient times, who will hold to tradition, and worship they know not what.[8]

In class we had a chance to question our professors on these hallway discussions. Our professors were open to these discussions, and I don't recall one instance where a professor appeared threatened by any question we asked. It was exciting to be a student at a university that welcomed inquiry and debate. Professors spoke to issues that we brought up and went the extra mile to give us clear, biblical answers.

FACING SCHISM AT SEMINARY

By my second year in Seminary, I sensed a schism developing between the New Testament Department and the Theology Department. It was subtle at first but as time went on, it was clear that a polarization was under way. Some blamed Dr. Heppenstall, others blamed Dr. Hilgert. Some blamed no one; they just saw this as a dialogue between brilliant people. But gradually it came down to whether Adventism should remain evangelical or espouse Neo-Orthodox principles that would "bring it into the twentieth century."

The controversy was not related to the *Questions on Doctrine* discussions that Elder Andreasen had brought up. Those were considered a closed issue. Only the Australian movement known as Brinsmeadism was continuing that fight, and the Church had already eliminated it from consideration. If the fundamentalist end-time "Omega apostasy" was discussed at Seminary, I don't remember it. And yet, such discussions would have been especially appropriate there. The current controversy seemed, if at all, to have more in common with Kellogg's "Alpha apostasy" than the *Questions on Doctrine* conflict. No one I heard saw any connection between the Kellogg crisis and the Sanctuary Doctrine issue.

The conflict over Neo-Orthodoxy eventually was so serious that Church Conferences were told to be suspicious of New Testament majors who weren't already

---

7. White, "Christ Our Hope," *Review and Herald* 69:50 (December 20, 1892), 623. Emphasis supplied.

8. White, *Testimonies for the Church*, 5:707. Emphases supplied.

sponsored. Several of them didn't get hired the year I graduated. There was talk that whole classes of unsponsored New Testament majors might not be hirable.

Andrews University president Dr. Richard Hammill and Dr. Heppenstall had both been contributors to the *Questions on Doctrine* discussions and had authored articles in *Doctrinal Discussions*. Both were very involved in defending Adventism against Neo-Orthodoxy. But apparently others on the faculty were not as concerned about the literal nature of historic elements in the Bible as they were about making Adventism more contemporary. We soon learned that making Adventism contemporary represented far more of a threat to historic Adventism than *Questions on Doctrine* had ever been.

The issues that divided the Seminary concerned the nature of biblical authority and inspiration, not the questions Elder Andreasen had raised. What was at stake was how we were to look at Truth. And when Dr. Heppenstall routinely critiqued the existential elements in Neo-Orthodoxy, students were beginning to interpret his lectures as aimed at the New Testament Department.

Having grown up in the Adventist Church and having attended denominational schools, I was familiar with all the doctrines of the Church. But mine had been primarily uncritical study. I knew how to "prove" them from the Bible by means of proof-texting, but I had never had a chance to study them from the point of view of theology and biblical studies.

In college we were introduced to exegesis, a scholarly methodology to arrive at the original meaning of a biblical text. That meant setting aside the simple proof-text method I had learned in high school and by reading such Adventist books as *Bible Readings for the Home Circle*. From the first day of college, my professors stressed the notion that a text taken out of its context was a pretext. Applying this principle brought us to the discovery that the proof-text method, as practiced by many untrained and unskilled exegetes, often treated the context as superfluous.

I sat in classes on soteriology and Christology as Dr. Heppenstall and Dr. Thomas Blincoe brought out the issues raised by biblical scholars who had not accepted the Adventist conclusions with respect to the 1844 movement, the 2300 days, and the Adventist linking of Daniel 8:14 with Leviticus 16. It became increasingly clear that some of our traditional arguments needed stronger biblical foundations to meet formal criticism. It was time to delve shamelessly and unthreateningly into the scriptural text for our answers.

My New Testament classes with Dr. Hilgert and Dr. Kubo were based on a different approach—a modified historical-critical method. When we studied the Apostle Paul's letters to the Romans and the Galatians, we studied them verse by verse. This grammatical-textual method took us into the style of writing, the social and religious practices of the days when it was written, the culture and the thought at the time of the composition. We studied these books in the original language of *koine* Greek.

This method required an adjustment for me—treating the Bible as an ancient document. All my life the Bible had been treated as an Adventist sourcebook. I had read Adventist books and the writings of our prophet to find out what the Bible meant. Now I was learning to be a scholar, so I could have the tools to figure it out myself. My traditional method was being turned on its head. I came to appreciate why critics of the Church thought we were a cult—waiting to hear what the creed or the prophet told us and then searching for texts to prove those beliefs. I was learning Hebrew, so I could read the oldest manuscripts of the Hebrew scriptures. I was learning to do Greek exegesis to grasp the nuances inherent in the New Testament texts. Now I was forced to let the Bible inform my perception of truth instead of just traditional Adventist answers.

At times this was frustrating for I had to deal with elements of folk religion in my own thinking. And I began to realize how much of my Church's religion was informed by traditional folk religion. But the study was so rich I found myself increasingly excited by it all. Processing these conflicts in combination with what I was hearing in the hallways from New Testament and theology majors resulted in the most energetic dialogues. A professor's lecture is one thing, a student's interpretation and application may be quite another. New Testament scholars were being hailed as progressive and theology students were accused of being unduly attached to an allegedly indefensible nineteenth century Adventism. I was clearly in the big leagues now. It would take some time before I would grasp the full implications of the developing controversies.

DR. EDWARD HEPPENSTALL, PASTOR AND PROFESSOR OF THEOLOGY

Dr. Heppenstall struggled with the issues in Daniel 8 and the Adventist view of the investigative judgment. He arrived at an approach to these issues that he saw as truer to the context of scripture than that presented by early Adventists who had had no formal training and who relied on the proof-text method to arrive at their views. Furthermore, they had relied heavily on the Protestant eschatological uncritical interpretative methods of their day.

I followed his rationale throughout his classes in soteriology and eschatology. I realized more and more his uniqueness as a scholar in that he cared as much about our development as gospel ministers as interpreters with good skills. He put caring for people ahead of correct theology, a priority spelled out in scripture.

> [44] "Then they also will answer, 'Lord, when did we see thee hungry or thirsty or a stranger or naked or sick or in prison, and did not minister to thee?' [45] Then he will answer them, 'Truly, I say to you, as you did it not to one of the least of these, you did it not to me.' [46] And they will go away into eternal punishment, but the righteous into eternal life." (Matt 25:44–46)

Dr. Heppenstall spoke to our Christian mission, not just our denominational parochialism. I could see that his religion was Christianity and his sociology was Adventism. He did not bog us down in unimportant minutiae but rather helped us to spend time with the big issues of our faith—most of all those dealing with soteriology.

Twenty-five years later, in Anaheim, California, at a regular meeting of the Andrews Society of Religious Studies, I would be asked to make a presentation in which I was to reflect on Dr. Heppenstall's influence as a teacher.

> Thousands of ministers and former students could join me in exclaiming that the influence of Dr. Heppenstall as a teacher is incalculable. The clear and consistent witness of over sixty years of ministry has been a constant inspiration to us. His incisive thinking expressed in sermon, worship talk, seminary and college lecture, discussion group in the mountains or by the sea, or simply in a dormitory room has made us come to grips with the issues of life.
>
> His theological awareness and clear thinking have challenged us to value truth. His scriptural certainty has provided us with a surety that gives us direction in a world of ambivalence and ambiguity. His pastoral concern has made us realize that devotion to people may at times prove more important than theological correctness. His treatment of people has inspired us to realize that in this world people are all that really count. His worship of God has made us believe there is a God. His counsel has shown us his humanness. His pathos has brought us courage to care. His acceptance has made us feel our worth....
>
> Dr. Heppenstall taught us to think. He was never satisfied with simple regurgitation of material he had lectured to us in class. He was the only teacher I had at Seminary who allowed his opponents to take a class period occasionally to explain their opposition to his views. It was part of the educational process to let them have their say and then let the class have at them.[9]

There was no topic that Dr. Heppenstall would not take on—no question was beyond his competence. We were, after all, religious men training to be professionals and his help in dealing with a subject under discussion had its practical elements for ministry. But not all students saw things his way. And as the controversy grew among the faculty over the question of authority and the nature of revelation, we could see the sides lining up. The critical element in Neo-Orthodoxy was the philosophical existentialism of Søren Kierkegaard, the Danish philosopher. And this had become a controversial topic at the Seminary.

In Dr. Heppenstall's classes we were introduced to a modern version of Adventism while in our New Testament classes we were confronted with contemporary theology. Reality was a bit more complex, but it was enough to raise concern at the General Conference. Dr. Heppenstall critiqued Neo-Orthodoxy especially based on

---

9. Zackrison, "Edward Heppenstall: Influence as a Teacher." A paper presented at the ASRS, November 17, 1989, in Anaheim, California.

its existential interpretation of revelation. He strenuously objected to the principle that revelation can be true to faith but false to fact. In his class on *Revelation and Inspiration* he sketched out some of the implications of such an approach for the crucial Adventist understanding of scripture as both authoritative and normative.

We examined the views of Barth, Brunner, Bultmann and other Neo-Orthodox scholars—the pros and the cons. Dr. Heppenstall took a clear stand on the issues. His influence on the theological education of young ministers was so pervasive that the General Conference would eventually set up special study groups to deal with this issue.

In time, some professors at Seminary would move on to other universities and Dr. Heppenstall would get some of the blame for that. He was deeply affected by this. He considered these scholars his friends and we revered them all as our professors. But teachers usually have little control over harsh administrative decisions. As a thorough-going Adventist religious man, I realized the importance of keeping our institutions as ideologically pure as possible. Losing at least three contemporary-minded theologians was a price that had to be paid, I thought. After all, if you don't want to teach Adventists what they want to hear, or what is considered orthodox Adventism, why would you teach in an Adventist university? It was a pat argument—logical, final, and creedal. But it wasn't much of an argument when it came to settling serious academic issues. And it was divisive.

Dr. Heppenstall saw the importance of honest dialogue despite the threat that philosophical existentialism posed. But people in official positions often see things differently from professional scholars. The question of how to deal with perceived heterodoxy has ever been present in tight conservative confessional groups—and we were one of the tightest. Identifying the issues seldom appears to be a simple task, especially with those night/day thinkers who can't see that we frequently live in the dawn/dusk of our thinking.

Those who had seen M. L. Andreasen as their mentor in the heresy-hunting approach surrounding *Questions on Doctrine* seemed not to care or even be aware of the real battle brewing in the Church. In fact, there were those who were more moderate who would say, if you are trying to identify the "Omega apostasy" you need to recognize that our prophet had predicted it would be like the "Alpha apostasy." In what way? There had never been a consensus of agreement on answering that question. So, the attempts to stick people with heresy were scattered. For too many "Omega apostasy" became a label to put on people who didn't agree with whoever was using the label. To a scholar this was too convenient and took a person out of the realm of theology and into that of political science.

I was never an apostasy hunter, but it seemed to me that if you were going to argue that way, somewhere in the "Omega apostasy" there would be that pantheism that Dr. Kellogg had been accused of. And the existential softening of Adventist orthodoxy that came in the wake of the attempt to bring the Church into the twentieth century would certainly qualify as an "Omega" better than Elder Andreasen's claims that certain of his feuding brethren were repudiating significant beliefs. It seemed that the betrayal of faith would be subtler.

I remember the "Alpha" and the "Omega" apostasies being mentioned in SDA history class, but no significant lecture time was given to them. Graduate school was a place to inform your faith not a place to become preoccupied with a great deal of subjective prophetic speculation. Critiques presented in class by Seminary professors were always of the most professional nature not conspiracy theories.

Disagreements did not justify personal attacks. With some students the story was different and eventually the Church would feel it was time for another theological house-cleaning. The result would be a shift to a faculty with emphasis on Reformed theology rather than contemporary theology. But that was a transition that would take another ten years. It was not without its critics either.

A NEW PERSONAL DILEMMA

Meanwhile the year was coming to an end. Annie was finishing her junior year and I was about to graduate. Upon graduation I was to report for duty to Southern California in September. I had opted to get a master's degree rather than just a certificate of internship. This involved extra academic work; specifically, it required passing a Greek qualifying examination and writing a thesis or two major projects.

Enter a colleague from La Sierra, a student tutor for the Greek exam. He was a master teacher. A few sessions with him, and few students had any problem passing the test. He was a gifted teacher who had learned to teach Greek in English. Thanks largely to him I easily passed the qualifying test. In August 1964, I graduated with a Master of Arts degree in Theology and Christian Philosophy, with minors in Old and New Testament studies.

Now we faced a dilemma. My wife had another year to go for her undergraduate degree and I had finished my work. I called Elder Sandefur and asked if I could be assigned an internship close to La Sierra College, so she could commute there to finish her senior year. He said that didn't sound plausible but that I could make a request in writing and he would submit it to the Conference committee, the executive body that made those kinds of decisions.

Then the General Conference passed a new policy that the Bachelor of Divinity would now be the minimum educational requirement for an Adventist minister. The BD was a three-year degree past the bachelor's level. We talked it over and decided it would be best to stay at Andrews for another year. She could finish her BA and I could finish a BD.

When we wrote our letter to the committee we included the inquiry about possible sponsorship for another year since the new denominational policy had just been passed. By the end of the week we had the verdict. The committee would grant me a leave of absence without pay to finish the BD and I would still be obliged to serve in the Conference for five years upon completion of my work. But no sponsorship. I would have to pay my own way.

These are the kinds of decisions a religious man prays over, and so with the appropriate thought and prayer we decided to request the unpaid leave of absence. We would both get jobs. After all, how hard should it be to earn $218.00 a month, which would cover all our expenses? Annie got a job as a secretary in the college Religion Department working for Dr. Alexander, who was now the chair of the Religion Department in the College of Arts and Sciences. I went to St. Joseph and got a job at the *St. Joseph Herald Press*, the daily afternoon newspaper, as a linotype operator. I was able to work full time during the break between summer and fall sessions—I saw it all as providential.

To our surprise, two weeks later we got another call from Elder Sandefur. The committee had met again and reconsidered our request in the light of the new General Conference requirement and he was happy to tell me that they had voted to sponsor me through the BD program. But he reminded me again—I would still be obligated to work for the Conference for five years. We were elated. I quit my job at the newspaper, Annie kept her job. Now we had sponsorship plus her income. Life was improving all around. I had believed all this would work out. A religious man prays regularly and sets out to lead a life consistent with his principles. God was in charge, and we were his servants.

One evening as I walked up the steps of James White Library, two students stopped me. I assumed they were Seminarians, but I didn't know them. The first spoke, "We hear you are staying another two years for the BD degree." I was surprised. Who were these guys? The other spoke, "Don't you believe Christ is coming soon? You won't have time to finish and you will be wasting your time when you could be out there working in the field, saving souls." I was taken aback. I immediately flashed back to college when Mike had told me that if I ever graduated from college it would be in lower HMA by candlelight with the Catholics laying siege to the college.

I also was reminded of the time I was involved in the annual college speech production, *Our Town*, during my senior year, and as I walked to class one day a student had stopped me and asked, whether I believed in Sister White. When I asked what he meant, he reminded me that I was involved in a speech drama production and that Sister White condemned speech drama productions. These kinds of confrontations were not uncommon in Adventist society. People felt they were at liberty to invade your life and dictate your behavior. In no case had I offered any justification. I was in an Adventist school being educated for God's work. That was enough for me. If Christ came while I was in Seminary how could he condemn me? After all, the BD program was a Church policy. I dismissed such challenges as attempts to get my focus off what I was being educated to do in life.

HINSDALE, ILLINOIS

Another development reinforced the idea that we had made the right decision. Late that summer I was picking up my wife at her office in Griggs Hall and stuck my head into Dr. Alexander's office to say hello, when he gave me a new challenge. He reminded me that I had told him long ago I wasn't interested in college teaching but that he had an offer than might be of interest to me. He was looking for a teacher in the Andrews affiliate at Hinsdale School of Nursing and wondered if I might consider it. He would have me teach two classes each semester. I had a Master's degree in theology and would fit the bill perfectly. I would have to drive to Chicago every Friday and teach all day for the Religion Department and of course I would be paid.

I was speechless. Maybe I wouldn't mind doing some college teaching. I was becoming glutted with information, and this could be a good outlet. Plus, it would give us the extra income we needed. And it would give me a chance to see how much I might like college teaching. If there was one person who could charm me into such a challenge it was Dr. A, and I heard myself saying, "I'd love to!"

Two weeks later I was driving to the hospital where I was born twenty-two years before. I would teach religion classes to college nursing students. I was nervous. I had seldom seriously entertained the thought of being a college instructor and now in three weeks I had gone from sponsorship to no sponsorship, to newspaper typesetter, to renewed sponsorship, and now to university instructor.

We had never seen so much income as a married couple. Teacher stipend, secretary salary, and Conference sponsorship more than doubled our income from the previous year. I talked with Dr. Pease, director of the Seminary field work program, and he allowed the Hinsdale appointment to be my field work for the year, so we dropped the Bangor SDA Church assignment where I had been doing my field work for the past year. I knew that God was leading, and I was enjoying it.

Dealing with our early marital problems was on hold. I had accepted Annie's proposal for a date night once or twice a month and now I lived in denial concerning the need for intimacy in a marriage and I threw myself into the thrill of activity—endless activity—that left me deeply fatigued by the end of the day. Over the years to come, I would become a master of this kind of energy-driven life. My natural perfectionism fed it, and my denomination was thrilled with every hour they could get from me. I was there to serve God and God was my career. I was a religious man.

Fridays began around 3:00 am. Greater Chicago is two hours from Berrien Springs today, but in 1964 Interstate 94 had not yet been completed. I found the quickest connections across Indiana to Illinois and finally to the Illinois Tollway that deposited me about two miles from the hospital. Winter slowed things up. The winter weather in Illinois was as wicked as in Southwestern Michigan. And yet, the first semester went by without a hitch.

I was an obsessive teacher—I expected much from my students but gradually I had to adjust the workload as I heard the students' complaints. I had not carefully considered that I was in graduate school and these students were just out of high school.

One especially dreadful winter morning I climbed into my car with my notes in my briefcase and headed west to Hinsdale. The weather was very severe. Somewhere near Michigan City, on the divided highway, I came up behind an eighteen-wheeler hauling new Cadillacs. He was going slowly. It was sleeting. The visibility was bad. It was dangerous driving. As I ate the dirty snow and sleet thrown up on me by this truck I calculated my speed and his and decided I could pass him slowly. I eased around him on the left until I was about even with his cab. I was being pummeled with the snow his big wheels were tossing, but I knew if I passed slowly I could be in the clear.

Being new at snow driving I had not figured on ice below the surface of the thin layer of snow. I believe it is called "black ice." Slush is not too difficult to drive in, but unexpected hidden ice patches can be deadly. Whatever I hit below the surface seemed endless. My Chevy II Nova SS went into a broad slide at forty-five mph. It careened to a perfect sidewise position. Instantly I knew that the car we had gotten as a wedding present from Annie's parents was going to be my casket. Totally out of control, my car slid treacherously into the oncoming, early morning traffic of eighteen-wheelers. I was staring out my side window, looking directly into the headlights of one of the biggest trucks I had ever seen. I was helpless. Only one thought went through my mind—so this is what it's like to die.

No panoramic flashing of my life. No prayer on my lips. No feelings of remorse. I just sat there paralyzed—unable to do anything but grip the steering wheel. I knew it was over. I think I closed my eyes.

THE ADVENTIST UNDERSTANDING OF DEATH

Adventists don't believe people go directly to heaven at death. No one is consciously with God or now looking down or coming around to comfort those still alive on this earth. Adventists come from a long line of Christian tradition known as Conditionalism.[10] While they agree with the Apostle Paul who wrote, 8 "We are of good courage, and we would rather be away from the body and at home with the Lord" (2 Cor 5:8), they don't interpret this as rock solid anthropological detail about human death. In scripture heaven is not a natural inheritance—it is a promise to the believer in Christ.

Eternal life for them is dependent on the verdict of the "investigative" judgment, better described as the universal trial that precedes the *Parousia*, when people's records are thrown open so that every intelligent being in the universe has a chance to verify that God's judgments are fair. All this is to vindicate God against Satan's alleged

---

10. For a brief history of Adventist conditionalism see Zackrison, *The First Temptation*, 183–197.

accusation that he has no right to save sinners. And all of this must take place before anyone enters heaven.

However, one describes what happens to a person at death, the next thing one will be conscious of (if he makes it through the "pre-advent" trial successfully) is the smiling face of Jesus—whether one died in 1964 or in 42 A.D. Those who do not make it through the trial successfully, will see only the saddened face of Jesus indicating that they have missed the second coming and will now go directly to eternal annihilation where, according to Adventist theology, the time they will burn will be in proportion to the nature of their sins—the devil burning the longest. So however long it might be, the waiting period is from a person's death until Jesus returns in the Black Cloud. At that point rewards are given out.

Therefore, death can best be characterized as a sleep—a very sound sleep, with no grasp of the passing of time—no dreaming, just unconsciousness. The life lived is in storage—not unlike a computer where a document can be saved to a disk and brought up later. In this illustration the memory bank is God's mind and he is perfectly capable of restoring one's previous identity, but without any of the effects of sin (or desires to sin, known as propensities).

The concept is not so much different than that of some churches who expect heaven at death. For the person who is dead there is no sensation of time. Death and eternal life meld into one event, as far as time is concerned. So, to the dead it will seem that they went to heaven when they died. As one well-known non-Adventist minister told us in a Sabbath School discussion that Adventists looked at death from man's viewpoint whereas he saw death from God's viewpoint.

The only experience I had personally to compare to death was when the doctors took out my tonsils. One minute they were spraying ether in my face, the next moment the nurse was offering me a dish of sherbet. That's what it's like to die, they taught us. It was the same view as that held by Jehovah's Witnesses—both movements shared a Conditionalist tradition.

We were excited when, in 1958, Dr. Oscar Cullmann, the celebrated Protestant theologian and professor at University of Basel and the Sorbonne in Paris, published a little book entitled, *Immortality of the Soul or Resurrection of the Dead?*[11] setting forth a view of death very similar to the Adventist position. His volume was a study in New Testament Theology.

Dr. Cullmann held that the immortality of the soul was a Greek philosophical concept, whereas the New Testament view was resurrection of the dead. He approached the New Testament as basically building on Old Testament notions rather than Greek philosophy. Such words as "death," "soul," "spirit," should therefore not be given Socratic or Platonic definitions but should instead be read in the context of the

---

11. Cullmann. *Immortality of the Soul or Resurrection of the Dead? The Witness of the New Testament* (1958).

Jewish connection between sin and death. Greeks saw death as something willed by God. Jews took an opposite view.

We could be troubled by the fact that Cullmann was both a Neo-Orthodox theologian and a friend of the Popes, affirming that St. Peter was the rock to which Jesus addressed his famous statement.

> [16] Simon Peter replied, "You are the Christ, the Son of the living God." [17] And Jesus answered him, "Blessed are you, Simon Bar-Jona! For flesh and blood has not revealed this to you, but my Father who is in heaven. [18] And I tell you, *you are Peter, and on this rock I will build my church,* and the powers of death shall not prevail against it. [19] I will give you the keys of the kingdom of heaven, and whatever you bind on earth shall be bound in heaven, and whatever you loose on earth shall be loosed in heaven." [20] Then he strictly charged the disciples to tell no one that he was the Christ. (Matt 16:16–20. Emphasis supplied)

Many Protestant theologians ended up agreeing with him on this interpretation, abandoning the old Reformation argument, while his view on the nature of death hardly convinced anyone. Christian theologians refused to budge on that view and most of them condemned Cullmann's conclusions. The Protestant world's rejection reinforced the Adventist conviction that Satan would oppose our God-given truth for these end times. We were just glad to find a reputable New Testament exegete who agreed with us, or perhaps better, one we could agree with.[12]

---

12. Bultinck, "Dr. Oscar Cullman: conditional theologians." *Christian.bultinck@ skynet.be.* (2010). "Dr. Oscar Cullman was a famous 20th Century New Testament scholar who held a conditionalist view of the nature of man.

"Born in 1902 in Strasbourg, Dr. Cullmann was a Lutheran scholar in New Testament and Early Christianity at the University of Strasbourg (1930–1938) and Basel (1938–1972) and at the same time in Paris. . . . He debated with famous theologians like Albert Schweitzer, Rudolf Bultmann and Karl Barth. In *Christ et le Temps* (1947) he defended the position that the New Testament only refers to 'linear time' — yesterday, today and tomorrow; and that any Philosophy that tries to mix other Metaphysical concepts of time cannot be found in the New Testament. This position led him to write an article on 'Immortality of the Soul or Resurrection of the Dead?'

"This article defended the conditionalist position from an academic point of view. As a much respected scholar in Europe, Cullmann taught that the minority can be right on this issue.

"He asserted that 'This remarkable agreement (among his opponents) seems to me to show how widespread is the mistake of attributing to primitive Christianity the Greek belief in the immortality of the soul.'

"Cullmann's article presented death as the wages of sin, and the last enemy. It presented Christ as the First-Born from the dead, and it presented the dead as those who sleep. This article led to deep controversy in some protestant Reformed denominations (for example in the Netherlands). The article was an unexpected support from the academic world for those Christian denominations that hold the doctrine of conditional immortality. These include Seventh-Day Adventists, Advent Christians, and The Churches of Christ, Life and Advent. Oscar Cullmann became doctor Honoris causa at the Universities of Lausanne, Manchester, Edinburgh, Lund and Debrecen. In 1972 he was elected member of the Académie des Siences morales et politque. He died in 1999. We give tribute to an outstanding conditionalist theologian."

Profile of a Religious Man
EVENTS THAT CALLED FORTH MY BELIEF ABOUT DEATH

There was no crash. There was a sensation of spinning, but my car never rolled over—just around and around like the endless spinning tops we had pulled with a string on Knoefler Drive. Finally, the car came to a stop. I was dizzy. I saw no angels. Everything around me was brilliant white but there were no clouds of glory. The snow was coming down harder now.

Where was I? And what had happened? And more importantly, why had it happened? Opening my eyes slowly I discovered that my car was in the opposite lane facing backwards. I was shaking—but not from the cold. I saw no cars or trucks in any of the four lanes of the highway even though it was at the height of the busy traffic time. I was alone in a snowstorm. My car engine was still running. As I regained my bearings I instinctively realized that if I did not get off the road something worse could happen. I quickly maneuvered to the shoulder where I shook for more time. All my emotions were vividly awake now as I pondered how closely I had come to dying.

It was a miracle. It had to be a miracle—one moment looking into the lights of a Mack truck, the next minute sitting on the side of the highway having missed a certain encounter with death. Why was I spared? As a religious man I concluded that God was not done with me yet. He had plucked me from the very jowls of death. When a religious man can't understand an event or a phenomenon he has at least two options open to him: either it was God, or it was Satan. Ouija boards, magicians, mediums, spiritists, astrology, even acrobats and psychics were probably all the devil if one could not understand them or explain the feats they accomplished.

In fact, the reason the best psychics had only an eighty percent success record was very likely evidence of demons. God kept the devil from knowing everything. One could identify true prophets by their perfect record and the fact that they agreed with the Adventist understanding of the Bible—particularly the Sabbath.

There was one exception to this prediction thing—there was the notion of conditional prophecy. If the conditions of the prophecy changed, in terms of human response, then the prediction could not be fulfilled exactly as prophesied—like Jonah and the city of Nineveh. God had told Jonah:

> [2] "Arise, go to Nineveh, that great city, and cry against it; for their wickedness has come up before me." (Jon 1:2). [4] "Jonah began to go into the city, going a day's journey. And he cried, 'Yet forty days, and Nineveh shall be overthrown!' [5] And the people of Nineveh believed God; they proclaimed a fast, and put on sackcloth, from the greatest of them to the least of them." (Jon 3:2, 4–5)

That prophecy seemed to fail because "the people of Nineveh believed God." (Jon 3:5). So, there was no longer any reason to destroy Nineveh. That was a conditional prophecy. But that did not make Jonah a false prophet. This exception could be an out for a psychic, but we generally looked on psychics as lucky or demonic.

Little here made sense. I was still alive. That made the least sense. It could not happen. The trucks were aimed directly into my car. Yet they were gone, and I would be late for my appointment in Hinsdale now. I slowly turned my Chevy II Nova SS around and crept back onto the highway. The weather had not improved, nor did it throughout the remaining miles of my trip. I recounted repeatedly what had just happened and prayed with my eyes open all the way to the school.

What did God have in store for me that he had shown me such mercy? I did not know. I only knew that I was alive and could carry out my task for another day. Somehow, I appreciated life a little more after that. I was convinced that God had plans for me and I had only to continue in my education to be his representative. That is how a religious man thinks. God is always the focal point, but after such an epiphany another piece of life's puzzle falls into place.

I have had close friends go through comparable experiences, friends who did not survive. I have given up trying to understand why. I could not see that this had anything to do with who was more important to God. I surmised that the question of death would always be a puzzle to us. Some people talk as if they are experts on the subject, but let's get a grip on things; no one has been there and come back. It is all speculation or a function of the brain that none of us really understands. If you are religious, you interpret your holy books the way that makes most sense to you.

Growing up as a Conditionalist, I supposed I would remain in that belief for the rest of my life. No other view really seemed rational, biblical, or even historically verifiable. But then why was it important in the long run? Like other transformative events such as the Kennedy and King assassinations, or the explosion of the space shuttle, or the terrorist attacks on the World Trade Center, we cannot forget the initial thoughts that we had and the effect they have had and continued to have on our life.

HOMEWARD BOUND

The following year I did not teach at Hinsdale. I was winding up my education at Seminary. The theological controversies even paled a bit as I anticipated the moderating effect that work usually brings. There was labor out there, and I was about to join the force. The somewhat artificial life of school was coming to an end, and all that I learned was going to be tested by the real world out there. My wife had graduated with her Bachelor of Arts degree in English. I had finished my Bachelor of Divinity requirements by January 1966 and would graduate *in absentia* in June.

On a wintry Saturday night, we partied in Garland Apartments with colleagues and professors—playing Risk, Monopoly, eating pizza and drinking 7Up. The Heppenstalls and Vicks were there. Annie had spent the last year or so as their secretary at the Seminary. Dr. Alexander was on study leave in Edinburgh, Scotland. Other friends had already finished and returned to California. But some friends were there—we would relive this night for several Christmases to follow—after that night it became our tradition to have families gather for a Christmas party in Southern California.

Thirteen couples from Southern California had been sponsored during our three years at Andrews so we would be going back to do ministry alongside people we knew. Life was very much intact. The church was alive. The Conference was wealthy. The excitement of a dynamic work force committed to finishing the work of God was evident to all of us.

I was ready to be a professional gospel minister. My religion had been tried and graded. We were keeping too busy to think about our marriage problems. Nothing had really changed except my attitude. We still hadn't gotten any professional help, but there is something about taking on a job where you are expected always to be an example for others that makes it possible to imagine that all is well when serious problems are staring you in the face. Instead of dwelling on our incompatibilities, we looked forward to going back home. I had learned that in my life, at least, there was never going to be a dull moment.

CHAPTER SEVENTEEN

Encounter with Life

"You can observe a lot by just watching."
—Yogi Berra

INTERNSHIP

SEMINARY DAYS HAD COME to an end. It was now time to move into the reality of pastoral life. I received an update from Elder Sandefur that I would be assigned as an intern at a suburban Los Angeles Church. My mother-in-law, who lived in the area had picked out and secured an apartment for us a couple miles from the Church. This was a Church that had run into hard times. It was close enough to the Loma Linda University Medical Center, Los Angeles campus, that for years it had enjoyed the support of physicians and medical personnel who taught and practiced there. At one time, I was told, some forty physicians plus other professionals were listed in its active membership.

A moderate-sized church, it had thrived under exciting pastorates and built a beautiful new Church facility in the early 1960s. When we were married there in 1963 the Church was new and considered "a plum" in the Conference. Nonetheless, the university consolidating its campuses in Loma Linda had caused a serious problem for the congregation. Professionals, who had lived in the area, some for many years, had moved to the inland empire, sixty miles to the east, to work on the staff of the main university campus.

While commuting may have continued with some during the week, making that extra trip on weekends and remaining active in the Church's life did not prove practical for many of them. By 1966 the Church was deeply in debt and its attendance was plummeting. In addition, some relationship problems had adversely affected several families in the congregation. The Church was in difficulty.

The new pastor was a stately figure in his late fifties when he became the senior minister of the congregation. He had followed a diminutive, vivacious and personable charismatic whose passion was public evangelistic meetings. That pastor had worked effortlessly and baptized scores of people in his short two-year stint. By contrast the new pastor under whom I would work was tall, soft-spoken, and slow-moving. He looked Johnsonianly presidential next to his former Reaganesque dynamic.

Originally from South Africa, the new pastor had an engaging smile and enough of an accent that people liked to hear him speak. But when he came to Southern California public meetings were not going to be his focus. He was expected to use his fund-raising expertise to pull the Church out of debt and place it on a stable financial footing. He had served as a Conference stewardship director (professional fund-raiser) in the Adventist Southeast with a reputation of success. His ability to relate to retired people, encouraging them to bequeath their fortunes to the Church, was legendary.

He had been senior minister of a college Church in the South for many years. He had later accepted the presidency of a college in Nashville. He thought he had gone there to save the institution that was going under financially and had been taken over by the Southern Union Conference. The Union administration had other things in mind and two years later they reduced the college to a high school. He told me he knew nothing of these plans when he accepted the responsibility, and it had been painful to him. Here was a wound he would carry with him for a while. From that position he had gone to the Church headquarters in Atlanta where he spent the next couple years raising money for the Conference. It was while in Atlanta that he was invited to Southern California to get this troubled congregation out of debt, paid for and thriving once again.

Unfortunately, things were not going as planned. Southern California was not the South. First, the Church was composed largely of young, dynamic couples with children, not senior citizens. Things were changing rapidly and some of the old ways were threadbare. Professional people often like a subtler approach to fund-raising than he was used to taking. In addition to this he was carrying a lot of painful baggage.

MY FIRST MINISTERIAL JOB: WE'RE DEPENDING ON YOU

When I arrived in Southern California, Elder Sandefur met with me at Conference headquarters in Glendale. We exchanged pleasantries and renewed our growing friendship. I had always respected him and my three years at Seminary had deepened that admiration and appreciation for his leadership. I considered him not only my mentor up to that point, but a good friend. He had always faithfully visited us in Michigan and once even borrowed our car for a day. I figured only a trusting friend would willingly ask to borrow your car. I was pleased.

Now we would get down to the business at hand. He had a reputation for exuding confidence in his interns. I doubt that the Southern California Conference had ever had so many educated interns entering the field at the same time. There were several of us scheduled to enter the field over the course of the next two years. But now he had instructions for me.

He was quiet. He leaned forward on his desk in a confidential pose as he explained that he was assigning me to a troubled Church for my internship. But he admitted that he must be candid with me. He affirmed that the pastor was a "good man" who they had brought in to conquer the debt problem. But things were not going well. In fact, it was to the point that they would soon be making a change. He had a couple of men in mind, but he needed to take care of this pastor first.

Then he switched the focus to my work. He had confidence that I would encourage the people and bring a continuing spirit to the Church. Changes would be made, so just stay firm and connected. It seemed only fair to him to let me know that. It was a compassionate directive. It was also a startling announcement.

Elder Sandefur showed confidence in me and that felt good, but he was hardly treating me traditionally as an intern. I was just out of Seminary. I had virtually no field experience aside from the little I had acquired while in school. But he was assuming a maturity that I wasn't sure I had. To have this laid on me was gratifying but it placed me in an awkward position. Yet this was Elder Sandefur's *modus operandi*. He took risks, cleared up problems and depended on young men without much experience, to stretch their capabilities and bring freshness to a situation. This was like a rite of passage. How else could I learn this?

So, I appreciated his openness and his trust. I was clearly part of his team now. Here the old and the new were meeting. Despite his past successes and his alleged expertise at fund-raising my new pastoral mentor was perceived more as the old guard who did things in conventional ways. And this meant that he had his faithful supporters. Elder Sandefur represented a new ministry that was exciting and anxious to make changes necessary for progress to occur. He had a remarkable appreciation for Seminary education unlike some other executives I had been told about, who feared higher education and were freely talked about in the hallways of the Seminary.

When I reported for work the first week I found my new boss in the Church kitchen throwing pots. Pottery-making was one of his hobbies. It may have been therapeutic. I was not alone as an intern. Larry Downing was also there. Larry had graduated from Pacific Union College the same year I had finished La Sierra. He had married a medical student who had taken her medical education in Ann Arbor at University of Michigan, while Larry was at Andrews.

They had moved back to Southern California before Larry had finished his theological education. Juggling her education and his had led Larry to work out an arrangement with Fuller Theological Seminary in Pasadena to finish his work there. In the meantime, he was working at this Church and I had come to relieve him. With the delay in the beginning of his class work we ended up working together for about six weeks. We became lifelong friends.

Our mentor seemed at times to be overwhelmed with two interns and a Church in trouble. Sometimes he took us on his visits together, other times he let us go alone. We worked on a giant map of the greater Los Angeles area in the office, placing pins where each Church member lived. Larry oriented me to some of the Church situation.

I pondered Elder Sandefur's disclosures but kept them to myself. I figured this was a Conference challenge. I was looking forward to a well-planned internship and I was beginning to doubt that such was in the offing. Adventist ministerial education was supposed to come in three phases: undergraduate college (four years), graduate school (three years), and internship (three years). And then ordination, which brought full authorization to function in all lines of ministerial work: pastoring, counseling, weddings, baptisms, etc.

It was increasingly clear that our mentor was still suffering from the blows he had received even though he was trying to move on. He told and retold his story. But I had no words of comfort. The idea that the story could be true was not one I was anxious to hear. I was green. I was still in my ideological stage and believed the Church to be the apple of God's eye. This meant the leaders were led by God to make the decisions they made. This further implied that you could trust them to do what was right. Yet this was a reasonable man and he clearly harbored deep feelings about what had happened to him. He showed Larry and me pictures of the college parade in which he rode in a classic automobile that he and his son had restored together. I admired his talents and his care for his son.

Now I began to feel the awkwardness of my position. Increasingly Church members told me how weary they were becoming of the pastor's constant offering appeals and his many sermons on tithing and stewardship. I felt my own discomfort but supported his program faithfully. Nevertheless, the congregational giving had been drying down to a trickle. It appeared that we were barely keeping the doors open. The financial problems caused by the professional medical people moving away and the alienation people felt toward the sermons on money led to further membership flight.

LEARNING MINISTRY

At the Church I moved into the office provided for the associate pastor. I built new bookcases to house my ever-growing library. I covered all the walls with my books. I was in a dream—my own office, telephone, and desk. So far life was going as planned with hardly a glitch. At last I was a pastor. And yet there was a living paradox afloat. While I was secure I felt stifled by the news that the enterprise seemed crumbling. I really was at a loss to know how I could make a difference.

The pastor did his best to give Larry and me some internship training. He took both of us on as many visits as he could. We visited those whose names appeared with pins on the big map in the office. We made our calls by geographical strategy to save time and gas. Many of these people claimed they hadn't received a visit from a pastor for years. However, having three pastors troop into their home unexpectedly was overwhelming to some of them. When asked to pray some would refuse. Some were embarrassed.

We followed up names of people who had inquired about Bible studies through *It Is Written* and *The Voice of Prophecy*. Most had no interest. But these visits occupied much of our day. Other than my externship at Seminary and the evangelistic field school I had attended during the previous summer, this was my first real encounter with pastoral life. I was assigned to preach one sermon a month and I was required to make visits—sometimes together, sometimes alone. My mentor gave me some freedom to try things. Undoubtedly, he surmised that my being fresh out of school I must have a wealth of ideas I wanted to initiate. I started Bible studies. I started my own visitation program. But I was learning that authentic results can take a lot of time.

A watchword in the ministry was patience. I would get people almost ready for baptism and then they would move away. I found that frustrating because every month we had to fill out a Conference report listing all those we had baptized. I soon observed that in the pastorate I must take a day at a time despite the great plans I may have laid. But I was not so patient. I liked closure, and nothing seemed ever finished in this work. As one of my colleagues remarked, "When I get done with my sermon on Sabbath morning I go home and start wondering what I will preach on next week!"

Then there were the Church board meetings. Our Church had a board of close to fifty members—a small congregation in itself—but generally if 10–15 people showed up for the meeting, those present felt free to do business. I was not aware of any quorum required for business to be done.

The board met once a month and most of the business dealt with the financial crisis or what to do with people on the books who never attended or who never contributed. Board meetings became the monthly meeting to drop names from membership—sometimes several at a time. Many of the goals set by the Conference for the local church were based on the members listed on the books. One way to cut down financial obligations to the Conference was to cut the "dead wood" off the books. The pastoral staff pursued updating the books with a passion. This lowered all our subsidies, but things still did not improve. Some of those leaving were transferring to other congregations in the area.

Another unwieldy group was the school board. The size varied, but it was based on representative membership from a dozen churches in the valley. I had relatives on this board—one was chairman of the board and his brother-in-law was also a member of the board. Both had children at the academy and were big financial contributors to the school. It seemed that if there was a chance to argue these two would grab it. As a member of this board I soon discovered another aspect of awkwardness I suffered.

Complicating the issues further, our congregation had not paid its subsidy to the academy for several months either for capital improvements or for operations. A significant number of board members were becoming uptight over this and were speaking out. Other churches were beginning to claim poverty and threatening to withhold their subsidies in favor of paying their own bills. And they were using us as their example. Withholding of operating funds made the school situation especially tenuous.

Our helplessness to pay the monthly subsidy, due to our fiscal troubles led some to campaign with the Conference to have the pastor moved, replaced or fired. So now I was caught on the horns of a dilemma. As the momentum built to move him I was becoming a lightning rod. This situation had to produce a scapegoat and I figured I was a logical choice for that dubious honor.

I knew Elder Sandefur's plans and the mantle he had laid on me. I knew of my relatives' plans and heard their complaints about our congregation. I knew my plan simply to get an internship that matched my university education and would get me ready to pastor a Church of my own. But my role also involved loyalty to the pastor, my immediate superior and personal mentor. And I became aware that I was being viewed as a kingpin in a plot to unseat him, when I didn't think I had any control in the matter. I was feeling frustrated.

My mentor came to distrust me. Our relationship began to disintegrate. As an intern I found these political irritations unsettling, but I knew that interns were powerless in the organization. This was my first serious personal encounter with Church politics. As a religious man, however, I could resign all to God, pray and work harder at the Church, which I did.

In his supervision meetings with me my pastor never introduced the subject of our conflict, but I sensed his feelings and I heard things. Many years later, when he was retired in the South, his attitude would resurface as he testified to have me fired from the faculty of Southern Missionary College where I was a theology professor. He held that I had a history of disloyalty—harking back to my internship under him. That was painful.

Because nothing was ever out in the open we continued our strained relationship day after day, playing like all was fine. Some things you simply endured until the Black Cloud appeared and delivered you. I was more an observer of these phenomena than a player. I was trying to understand these workings of bureaucratic reality and how they related to doing the work of God.

In my slowly developing realism I pondered once again those initial instructions of Elder Sandefur to be patient as they solved the problem to everybody's satisfaction. So far as our work was concerned, days were largely routine except for one area—caring for the dead. During these eight long months that we worked together the pastor averaged a funeral a week. I took part in all of them. Many involved final visits from nursing homes to the burn center at the Los Angeles County Hospital. He had excellent bedside manner and his services were masterfully presented—well-organized, carefully planned thoughts, empathetic and comforting selections. One thing was clear: when I finished this internship, I would be prepared to conduct funerals!

YOUTH PASTORING

As I looked around the congregation for other work to do I was attracted by the possibility of working with the young people. The Conference was pioneering this area of youth pastoring and there were several new youth pastors around Southern California. Our Church had a new, functional youth chapel with classrooms waiting to be utilized. Young married couples in the Church were helping to lead but there were few organized activities coordinated from the Church office. By now Larry had gone and I was the sole intern.

As I pondered what might be done I visited with the pastor and asked him if he would see light in my serving as his youth pastor during my internship. He was delighted at the thought. We were in competition with the other SDA churches, located close to the academy and natural hangouts for the academy kids. My challenge was how to attract them, five miles west of the school. I formed a youth activities board with both adults and teenagers on it. We met once a month and laid out plans to reclaim our kids.

The new youth board organized a series of Friday night programs, outings, and a summer activities club for academy students. We soon had a group of about twenty-five kids attending regularly—several reclaimed from other congregations and others recruited. This developed into my personal pastoral challenge. It became clear to me that whatever congregation put on the best show on Friday nights got the kids! Other youth pastors had told me that, and they were right. The challenge was to be relevant and meaningful to them. Raw reality was setting in. We alternated programs: a talk, a quiz, a movie, a panel discussion; something different each week.

In the summer we took the kids hiking, camping, to Dodger and Angel baseball games, to the beach, on a San Pedro harbor cruise, to Disneyland. We even had a weekend where two of our students took over the Church pulpit and preached for the worship service on Sabbath morning. On the weekends we worshiped and had discussion groups. We organized Sabbath School with people who cared about and understood adolescents. When we threw parties, people showed up. Church members opened their houses, pools and pizza ovens to the kids.

I was immediately confronted with remembering names. I had a little book in my inside coat pocket where I wrote down the names immediately upon meeting the new kids. People love their names but for some of us the skill of transferring new names to our long-term memory is something we struggle with.

When one of our quick, smart fourteen-year-olds came to me later and volunteered, the first thing that impressed her about me, she said, was that I remembered her name. I didn't tell her my method. Then I perceived the value of my little book—that was my method—write down names as soon as I heard them. Her name was one of the easier to remember because her mother had been our wedding coordinator three years before. Nevertheless, I appreciated her compliment.

FURTHER COMPLICATIONS

As we were getting our program in full swing a new complication occurred. In the summer of 1966, at the General Conference session in Detroit, Elder Sandefur accepted a promotion to the presidency of the Columbia Union Conference in Washington, D.C. I supposed every Conference president secretly wanted to lead a Union, as administrator over a group of local Conferences. It was generally considered a step-up. The move was not unexpected. He had been president in Southern California for half a dozen years. But I felt orphaned. My chief pastoral mentor was leaving.

I tried to face the fact that his plans for our Church might go with him. While I was enjoying my work as youth pastor, I knew I was not functioning as an intern but more as an associate pastor. And in that capacity, I knew I was flying by the seat of my pants. I was reading the meager materials I could find at the local religious bookstore, available for youth pastors, and relying on my planning experience as an SA officer from college.

We had very little youth ministry training in Seminary. I couldn't find anything published by our denomination except some outdated books on dating and courtship and a series of pamphlets put out by the Conference youth department on the evils of the worldly life—drinking, smoking, dancing, movies, drugs, etc.

I kept Elder Sandefur's words about a replacement to myself. But with his leaving I felt like a ship without a rudder. I realized now how much I had relied on him for the past four years—ever since that interview in the Religion Department office at La Sierra College. But almost as soon as Elder Sandefur left, my pastoral mentor announced that he had accepted a call to another Conference in the Columbia Union. Elder Sandefur had followed through!

Now things were more complicated. I was ambivalent. I was enjoying my work but now I would be an interim pastor until a new minister was appointed. That would involve functioning essentially without any authority—no president and no pastor. But Southern California was a strong Conference and God would provide. That's how a religious man thinks and therefore functions. I pressed on with my plans for the fall—now preaching every week and running the youth program and I waited for further news. The movements came more rapidly than I had expected.

A NEW CONFERENCE PRESIDENT

"We have just elected a new president," my father-in-law announced as he breezed excitedly into the kitchen at his house. He had just returned from Conference committee meeting and was excited. I was anxious to hear the rest.

The new president would be Elder Helmuth C. Retzer (1916–2009), president of the Nevada-Utah Conference and former Sabbath School secretary of the Pacific Union Conference. He was the father of my college classmate, a member of the *Sanhedrin,* our college religious action group. I had visited their home back in college when they lived in Glendale. Now he would be my boss. My job was to help hold the congregation together until a new pastor was appointed. As it turned out this situation would hold for three months.

In our get-reacquainted visit in his office, Elder Retzer told me that he had someone in mind and wanted to run the name by me since I had been in that Church now for several months. He revealed that he wanted Elder Walter T. Rea to pastor the Church. Elder Rea had been at Pomona for nine years and was maybe ready for a move. That was all he told me. Whatever else went on in that conversation was lost as my mind reeled once again.

CHAPTER EIGHTEEN

Elder Walter T. Rea (1922–2014)

"It is well to think well; it is divine to act well."
—Horace Mann

CHANGES BEGIN

I didn't know Elder Rea personally, but I had two snippets of perception: one positive, one negative. I had seen his Ellen White compilations on sale at the Adventist Book Center. There were three in the series: *Old Testament Biographies, New Testament Biographies,* and *Daniel and the Revelation*. I had looked through them but had not purchased any of them. Nevertheless, I thought they looked good. My second snippet was more problematic. I had been told he was an ultra-conservative, bordering on the lunatic fringe. And as these kinds of perceptions typically are, this impression had been formed without any primary evidence—just hearsay—from a good friend—"someone in the know."

My mind rewound to an academy teacher who told me she had been confronted by Elder Rea about an assignment she had made for her students. The students were assigned to read and analyze a novel. Elder Rea had taken issue with this assignment and considered this a major violation of Sister White's prohibition on the reading of fiction. The confrontation had left the teacher feeling personally invaded and unprofessionally dealt with over the incident.

Acting on this perception I politely asked Elder Retzer to move me to another Church if Elder Rea was appointed. The wish was not granted. Interns have no say in such decisions and my naïveté was demonstrated in my even making such a request. By early fall Elder Rea had been appointed as the new pastor and I was still there—more evidence to me that interns had no voice.

Elder Walter T. Rea (1922-2014)

THE NEW PASTOR

The new pastor would begin at the first of the year, January 1967, but he would come by to meet me and look over the Church three months early. He instructed me that I should hold the Church together until he got there. His beginning did not attract me. He walked into my office, looked at my carefully handpicked library, chosen according to the pastoral bibliography lists I had followed in graduate school. It was the beginning of a masterfully chosen ministerial, theological library. He looked around and then with a sweep of his hand proclaimed, "Chaff! Why do you waste your time and money on these kinds of books?" I didn't know that he was quoting Sister White.

I cringed. Suddenly I was the teacher who was being verbally confronted about an assignment. My collection of books numbered in the high hundreds and I had been working diligently on my library since I was in academy. I was proud of my library. I had Bible commentaries and Bible word books, lexicons and notable theological works both historical and systematic from college. I had joined several religious book clubs and every time I enrolled one of my friends in the book club I got a free book. Recently I had concentrated on reference works.

My love of books was something with which Annie had never quite resonated. I saw books as the tools of my trade, but she saw them as an extra special expense. When I had taken a $20.00 a month book budget at Seminary she was upset. She was going without hair spray, she told me, and I was spending money on books. When Dad sent me money for books this became a serious bone of contention. The budget was soon suspended.

To me an attack on my library was an attack on me, my family, my religion—having a library of good books was a part of being religious. I had grown up in a home where libraries were important and impressive. My brother had books lining the halls of his home much like my father had. I had followed suit. Grandpa was an editor and Uncle Louis wrote scholarly works and college textbooks on child and developmental psychology. Dad produced books for his living. And when I had worked for Dad in the College Press I had printed up my own nameplates that now dignified the inside cover of every precious volume in my collection.

I hesitated and then timidly asked Elder Rea what he read. He was quick to respond. He was getting to me and he appeared to know it. He told me that he read only the Bible and the writings of Sister White. He had joined a non-fiction book club, *Mainstream Book Club,* for other material. He held that his combination of reading kept him in touch with the modern world as well as the assurance of reading pure Truth. Then he added that he did not even own a television set and asked how he could preach against the TV if he had one. He reminded me that television is just fiction acted out.

When he moved into his office sometime later he showed me what he meant. He had two or three shelves of non-fiction hardbacks, a Bible, and a complete set of the red books (Sister White's writings), along with the three-volume Ellen White *Index*. Bookstands were located on either side of his IBM electric typewriter so that the set of prophetic books were always within arm's length for doing his research.

He was investigating her writings all the time "mining out pure Truth." I later discovered that he had the same arrangement in his study at home. At either location he could do his compiling of her counsel on any subject. Two complete sets of her published writings! But with respect to my library I was offended by his remarks. I viewed his approach to reality with suspicion.

Seminary prepares you to be skeptical of extremism. This was hardly the voice of a scholar, I thought. Now I could certainly see how *Gone with the Wind* would never be a book on one of his shelves! It hurt me to be talked to like that. I didn't deserve it. All I knew about this man was in the form of rumor. I took it as an invasion of my sincerity, my very being—who I thought I was. I was dead serious about the ministry and my training had produced a personal awe for scholarship. I had received a slap in the face—a rap on my education—something I had invested in for years.

Then I noticed the diplomas on his wall. I studied them. Elder Rea had three bachelor's degrees—in theology, in speech and in business. He also had three master's degrees—in speech, in business and in American historical studies—all from California State University, Los Angeles. He told me he had done enough work at Andrews University SDA Theological Seminary extension classes to get a master's degree in religion as well. He never wanted to put in the last semester of residence in Berrien Springs to graduate. He was also working on a PhD in communication at University of Southern California in Los Angeles.

I was thinking I was prejudging him. I learned that many people had, probably because of his direct talk. This man was no mockery of education—no academic slouch. But he was a different kind of scholar than I had worked under anywhere and I would learn from him over the next eight months. My internship had begun and my encounter with life was about to take a turn that would affect the rest of my life as a religious man. Here was the first person I had ever met who really took Sister White that seriously and he was about to transform my own perception of her.

MY NEW TRADITION

Elder Rea stated clearly that he was my boss now. Sitting me down in his office he asked me point blank what I did around the Church. I told him I was the youth pastor. And he bluntly said that I would not be doing that anymore. I would now serve as his intern. His son would take over the youth program and I was officially relieved of those responsibilities. He explained that it was his job to train me to be a pastor and that he took that responsibility very earnestly. While he didn't know for how long I would be with him he knew it couldn't be very long.

He told me that some pastors give their intern the work they don't want to do. I had known of some who washed the pastor's car and ran errands to the post office. Elder Rea made it clear that he did not believe in that approach. He assured me that he would do nothing but require me to *watch him*. He told me that I was to watch him do everything involved in running a Church. I would be instructed to keep the Church books for a month, learn how to read a balance sheet and watch him visit Church members, interests and the like. I was to watch how he managed a Church. He was to show me how to reduce the administrative work of a pastor to a lower percent of my job.

He would give clear instruction geared to getting me ready to pastor a Church. He told me that he would call me every week when I got my own pastorate to follow up on my training. He then proceeded to make clear what my title would be under his leadership. I was not to be his assistant or his associate. I would be his intern. I would learn by watching him, not by doing my own thing. "When you leave me," he said, "you will be ready to pastor a Church." And then he made it clear that he may not be my perfect model but at least I would know one way to do things.

He added another requirement. After our time together, each day he said he would always ask me how I would have done things differently than he did, maybe even better. He would expect me to give him honest feedback on his work.

The long class lecture ended with clear direction: no regular preaching assignments, no Prayer Meetings on Wednesday evening. He needed the exposure, so he didn't want me taking much time in front of the congregation. I was not there to pastor. I was there to learn from him. However, he said, if I ever had a burden on my heart, I should let him know and he would give me the pulpit. I could also teach a Sabbath School class if I wanted to or give Bible studies. I had that freedom, but it was not part of my regular assignment.

Here was an honest and frank instructional session. I was being tempted to like some things about this guy despite the insults I felt I had endured. He surely made himself clear and I felt I was back in school—something I liked. He was very serious about all of this. I began to think I was going to get an internship after all! Then with a twinkle in his eye he closed his first class-period: "Associate, assistant, what's the difference? You abbreviate them both the same way!" And he chuckled.

I chuckled back though I was so academic at that point that I would have chosen to miss the humor to correct his grammar that the abbreviations were not the same. But I had gotten his point. I decided it was as close to a compliment as he could dish out at that point. He had made one fact very plain: I would not be his "ass"—his pack animal! I was far more important to the work than simply to be a worker bee, a non-thinking automaton, a cog in the gears of a giant machine. I was beginning to pick up on his vision. I was expected to make a difference, to think, to be independent.

As time went on Elder Rea chided me to begin disagreeing with him lest he be tempted to throw me out of his car! And I came to understand what he meant. He wanted feedback. The problem was, he was so quick and so far advanced of anything I knew about the pastorate that I could hardly keep up much less offer meaningful critiques. His parting shot that first day was his brutal challenge: "Someday I hope to meet the real Ed Zackrison!"

He apparently meant not the black-suited, politically correct speaking, tall and smiling ideologue who painted everything with his religious brush. He didn't add those last words, but I sensed that this was what he meant.

I went home late that first afternoon an emotional basket case. I felt he was being unprofessional. He had mocked my Seminary education. He had laughed at my library. I resented the meeting and wondered where I was going from here. He was harsh, brash, rude, discourteous and cruel. He was everything the English teacher had claimed. How did I get into this? What was happening to my pristine view of the ministry? How was I to be transformed into some advocate of truth—a side of which I had never seen before. I began to realize that I had already accepted a view of myself that was far off the mark of reality.

I shared my battered feelings with Annie. She went to bed. Sympathizing was not her strong suit. She just said something about his being a freak of nature so not to let it get me down. I turned on the television and watched it until midnight. It had not been a good day.

A NEW UNDERSTANDING

Within a few days I began to change my initial views of my new mentor. Elder Rea was direct, said what he meant, created instant admirers and haters, but I decided he was not discourteous or harsh. He was not abusive he was definite and truthful. He was an iconoclast—busting down the questionable images of the mind and the idols of lazy thinking to which religious people are so prone to resort. Behind that veranda beat a heart that was tender and concerned. Little by little I began to see this.

Here was a pastor who dealt daily with the real things of life. Nothing was covered in candy-coated theological language or political correctness. Little was camouflaged in euphemisms to protect simplistic approaches to serious issues. It was these qualities that would cause him to be loved or despised. I soon learned that some people, often in leadership positions, would find him to be irritating and obnoxious. He was sometimes called controversial, a term he claimed not to understand but privately may have found honorable.

One day, in the fall, shortly before he was to take up residence, Elder Rea was in his office going through the Church files when he called across the secretary's office that was located between us. He asked me to come into his office and close the door for he had found something that he wanted to share. As I entered his office I observed an ominous feeling reflected in his face. I shut the door and he invited me to sit down.

He laid a closed file folder before me on his desk. He was emotional. I was confused—there were tears welling in his eyes.

Quietly he let me know that in the folder he was holding was the resolution of the Church's financial crisis. This was the first I had heard from him about the debt. I realized that he had probably been brought with the understanding that he would create solvency—to succeed where other pastors had failed. I had heard that he was a financial genius.

My curiosity peaked. He slowly opened the folder, laboring to control his emotions. He obviously had something to reveal that was touching him deeply. The folder, which he had found in the office file cabinet, held a mysterious significance. For the next few minutes, he pulled items out of the folder and explained their significance. Here were financial statements and letters outlining negotiations and plans made by the Conference administration years before with a prominent Southern California bank. It was a virtual map that deciphered our congregation's present financial crisis.

As I understood what he was telling me, the materials revealed that the Church had worked out a deal years before through the bank and the Conference to finance a Church building program. Much of what he was revealing was puzzling to me and I began to realize his business ability. Probably if things had gone the way they were going when the deal was made, all would have been fine. But a lot changed. And when things did not work as planned the local congregation was left to solve its problem.

He explained the ins and outs of the arrangement that had gone sour through the problems in the Church, the Loma Linda move and the resulting dwindling attendance. He repeated it again for my slow grasp. When the Church was fiscally strong, the policies went well. But when the exodus began, and the pastoral problems arose, the congregation was left with the debt and the problems that were carrying them to financial oblivion.

The Conference had a new administration now and the chances were that they knew nothing of the details found in this folder. And with the new administration there was a good chance it didn't. When Elder Rea finished his presentation, he was in tears. He represented joy for the victory of this discovery, and disbelief that the congregation had been abandoned. This secret had been in the files all this time.

I asked him what this all meant. The answer was simple—the debt will soon be paid! He unfolded his plan to share this with the administration, a new group of leaders who were not around when the deals were made. His hope was, he told me, that they agree to help the Church out of this situation. We went into the sanctuary and prayed together about the issue.

My lack of business acumen kept me from clarifying anything. I simply asked for the bottom line, what would happen if the Conference didn't help? His answer burned into my heart when he said, "We'll declare bankruptcy!" I looked in disbelief, so he repeated—"We'll declare bankruptcy!" In confusion I asked another question—"How can we do that?" He paused and then had a question for me—"Who owns this building?"

Of course, I knew that in the Adventist system all properties were owned by the Association, which was the legal arm of the Conference. No local congregation owns its own property. The local church raises the bulk of the money for the Church property, but the Conference holds the title to it. Hence the Church was owned by the Conference even though the local congregation paid most of the bill. This was denominational policy met through years of planning.

Who would have suggested that? Who would have thought that? The congregation was suffering a lethal disease and yet it was expected to pay the debt. But it seemed irreverent to bring up this reality. It might even be interpreted as disloyal and arrogant. Even though the Conference had helped create this problem to point it out could seem like a form of blackmail. But it wasn't—it was business. Who would ever have the courage to point that out? Who would have the audacity to threaten to share this with the congregation?

Bankruptcy might have been his euphemism in emphasizing the double-bind the Conference was in. In other words, teamwork at this point was the most important tactic. And so, this would be our strategy to get an impossible situation resolved. He had not gotten the Church into this unenviable position. Nor had the new administration. But ultimately it could be a unique Conference problem. At the rate we were going it seemed clear that not only would we never be able to pay the debt without help but there may be no Church left in the not-too-distant future.

I remember vividly that trip to Conference headquarters in Glendale. I was not invited into the meeting, but when Elder Rea emerged from it I knew he had scored a victory. Again, he was emotional. He could hardly speak as he shared the outcome of the meeting: the administration would take care of the problem with conditions. And tears streamed down his cheeks.

The terms: we were to raise the money to pay off the entire school subsidy, something that was lagging way behind and hurting the operational and capital budgets of the academy. And we were to raise our Ingathering goal (the Adventist annual campaign for funds collected from the public), something the Church apparently hadn't done for a few years. Raising the Ingathering goal was the task given to me to accomplish.

Elder Rea immediately called a Church business meeting and those attending pledged all the needed school funds instantly. I organized the Church and we raised the Ingathering in three weeks. I was seeing unity like I had not yet seen in this congregation.

According to Adventist policy a Church building cannot be "dedicated" until it is debt free. Within about two years the Church was dedicated with a full retinue of Conference officials rejoicing that we had finally cleared its debt. Elder Rea had the congratulatory letter from the Conference administration perma-plaqued and mounted in a prominent place on a wall in the Church office. He had understood the political implications of what was in that folder and so had the Conference administration.

THE POWER OF CHURCH POLITICS

On the surface God seemed to have intervened and made possible the continued ministry of the Church. But behind the scene the maneuverings of political action had pulled this off. The reason our previous pastor couldn't accomplish this task was that he either had not done the research or he was unwilling to use it to the advantage of the local congregation. I got a glimpse that in Church organization you had to have the goods to pull off the miracles.

As a religious man, believing that everything was done in prayer sessions, I found these proceedings devastating to my naive view of Church. I had a chilling feeling when I realized how close this congregation had come to losing its identity, ministry, even its existence, because no one could reveal the facts as to why it was in such an economic black hole to begin with. Surely someone knew.

What Elder Rea discovered in that file, and then revealed to the administrators, is what changed the situation, not just prayers for more giving. But I took it all as an answer to prayer, unable to fully grasp the human implications. With this episode as an early backdrop in my internship, my mentor began to educate me, i.e., to inform my understanding of working in an organization.

I listened sometimes skeptically to instructions I had never encountered before. He often used Coca Cola as a representation of the business world. If I worked for Coca Cola, he would say, I wouldn't think so much about the decisions the company made. I would understand the policy and I would accept it or quit. But in the Church, I had learned that I was working for God and that made a difference in my thinking. The religious filters made that difference. God making the decisions of the Church through the Conference administration gave a certain superiority to the pronouncements. As a religious man how could I leave if I disagreed with a policy or procedure? God had guided the committees that made the decisions. To be against those policies was to be against God. This was a serious consideration—and one of the most somber double binds I would face.

A RENEWED INTERNSHIP

So, my internship had begun. Our first major task together was to visit every Church member listed in our Church directory. As we prepared to carry this out Elder Rea saw the large map in the office with all the pins. He declared that project a waste of time. Without waiting for a comment, he pulled the big map off the wall, broke it over his knee into several pieces, and tossed the pieces in the trash can. Our Church secretary applauded. I shuddered as I thought of the hours Larry and I had spent preparing that map. We had learned the importance of making such a map at Seminary.

Finally, I was able to speak, and I asked him that if the map was not helpful how did he make his visits? He told me he thought logically, which meant he just went through the membership book and visited members as they came up in the list—alphabetically. He was the boss. So, we began going through the book in alphabetical order because he insisted that this was more logical than going through the list geographically. He did make exceptions for those who lived in other counties.

As we traveled from home to home visiting members in the Church book, we talked. He began by telling his story as a new Adventist convert attending Pacific Union College, listening to speakers who came on campus to talk at Vespers or Chapel or Church Worship. Invariably they quoted the prophet and he would go up to them afterward to get their references for the quotations they had used. He collected every statement from Sister White that he could find to guide him. He put them all in notebooks for further reference.

As he compiled these statements, arranging them in a logical, instructional way, he noticed something that he found disconcerting. Between what she wrote and what the denominational leaders did there was often a serious disconnect. He made it a habit to ask the leaders why this was. He got a variety of answers, none of which really impressed him because most of them sounded like rationalization. As time went on, this practice brought him into frequent confrontations with administrative leaders and pastors.

He told me about denominational politics from his personal experience. Some of his instruction was so brutal that I discounted it because of his personality, or I treated it in isolation. Much of it seemed unbelievable. The "brethren," as administrators called themselves, surely couldn't be as misleading or downright crooked as he sometimes implied. He spoke of his own obsession with truth and I interpreted this as his "Elijah complex."[1] The data was often too extreme for me to process.

He told me he had sought a call out of the South because of the rigid politics there. I listened with simple concentration. How could I deal with this? On the other hand, none of it touched me. I was convinced that none of this existed where I was working. I had not the least concern about the surety of my employment.

Although I had already seen the pastoral condition and the congregational financial challenges, both of which had been highly political in nature, I did not connect the dots that this could ever happen to me. I could never picture myself in trouble. In the end the right would always win, and I had no intention of being on any side but the right side. In the subsequent weeks I noticed that other ministers in the Conference

---

1. The idea that "I" am the only faithful person left in the Church taken from Elijah's experience (1 Kgs 19:9–18) in the cave in Mt. Horeb (Sinai) when in his discouragement he cried to the Lord: [10] "I, even I only, am left; and they seek my life, to take it away." (vs. 10). God assured Elijah that [18] "I will leave seven thousand in Israel, all the knees that have not bowed to Baal, and every mouth that has not kissed him." (v. 18).

were talking in much the same way. The main difference was that they seemed better at avoiding confrontations. They were less public about their complaints. They evaluated in private and smiled in public.

LED BY THE PROPHET

Eight months with Elder Rea was a double-headed arrow. On the one hand, I learned that Adventism was a spiritual movement to save souls. On the other, I began to see that it was also a political machine—a religious corporation with all the bureaucratic realities of any other business firm—protective of those who were loyal to people in power and terrified of any public disclosure that could hurt the cash flow keeping the machine oiled and running. There was an in-group.

What I didn't fully comprehend was that I was inheriting a reputation by working day-by-day with Elder Rea even though this was an assignment I had not requested. So much was this the case that my ordination committee eventually would spend two hours interrogating me on political issues about my loyalty to the brethren and my perception of the work. Not one question would deal with doctrine or theology.

Elder Rea continually emphasized the importance of remaining loyal to the cause and respectful of the duly appointed leadership. Unfortunately, there were too many times when the cause and the leadership seemed to be on alarmingly different tracks. If push comes to shove the religious man must take the high road and remain true to his principles rather than the personalities involved. He reiterated that in any enterprise that is truly Godly, principles must take priority over personalities. My mentor's understanding of loyalty started with God. Here he emphasized the pure sources of Truth, which he believed to be the Bible and the prophet, whose authority was subject to establishment by scripture. He did not believe in verbal inspiration as some of his defensive critics would one day accuse him.

Elder Rea insisted that since Sister White's writings were the latter-day revelation to the Church, not only the laity but also the leadership should follow them. In all his instruction I found clarity of many of the principles I had learned in my Seminary education. I found a practical application of the theory. I believed this was what an internship was supposed to be. I was observing a veteran minister in action along with a running commentary on every aspect of pastoral work.

Elder Rea's preaching was forthright and clear. He spoke to current issues and seemed to have a clear understanding of the spiritual realities of his congregation. He did not beat around the bush. I came to see him as a model pastor. And the congregation began to grow. His sermons were devoted to explaining how Adventism was relevant to actual life. His sense of humor helped to fascinate his audiences until the attendance eventually grew to over 300 and then 400 and then 500. After I left to pastor my own Church, I received reports that the attendance had grown to where the sanctuary was essentially full every week.

I studied his preaching method and research strategy. I found myself trying his approach with an eye on the future when I would have to prepare a new sermon every week. I went on a new study program under his direction. I began getting up earlier in the morning and reading the writings of the prophet more diligently. I went to the EGW *Index*[2] and read all three volumes through, just to grapple with the breadth of the subjects on which she had written.

As I read I jotted down topics I would like to research. My initial list included close to five hundred subjects. I calculated that an extensive study of all those subjects in these volumes of "pure Truth" would surely keep me busy throughout my ministry.

I got rid of our television set, selling it through the classified pages of the newspaper for a fraction of its worth. When asked by the buyer why I was selling it so cheap I simply answered that I didn't have time for it anymore. Annie was worried. But she supported these changes. I'm not sure she ever really agreed about the television. Though she said she had always wanted to marry someone who shared her religious values, she probably felt that I was starting to push the envelope a bit too far. But she didn't openly object.

Delving into the writings of the prophet I found amazing materials of what I perceived to be of infinite worth. I had no question that Sister White had received all this material in vision because that's what I had been taught over the years and even at Seminary. Furthermore, that's what she had claimed, so I could relate to all these materials as having come straight from God. Now was my chance to test the teachings.

In my study I made compilations of her statements. While I was at Seminary I had received the works of the father of a schoolmate of mine from La Sierra Elementary School. I had read some of these compilations from the standpoint that this effort seemed fanatical. But now I viewed things differently. I began making my own set of compilations, something like his though with a greater appreciation for the context of the statements, based on my graduate school education.

Depending on the topic my study might take a week or two to complete at the rate of four hours a day. Some were longer because they were more involved. If the topic dealt with the last days I could plan to spend a month researching it. Devoting this large block of time each day to my new project I made significant headway. Even my typing speed increased since I was compulsive about producing notebooks of material that looked like a graduate student had been at work.

In my quest for Truth I ran across choice statements outside of the topic I was researching. These I typed on half pages and carried in a daybook, which included the gems of Truth found that day. Everywhere I went I carried that daybook and freely shared my findings when I was with my ministerial colleagues. Some of them became worried that I was becoming fanatical. However, these findings were eventually the topic of every conversation that I had with my friends and two or three of my

---

2. White Estate, *Comprehensive Index to the Writings of Ellen G. White,* 3 Vols. (1962).

peers began their own projects based on the inspiration they received by catching my enthusiasm.

One friend even got rid of his television set and quit eating meat! Another friend from college and a fellow intern, brought all his Sister White books to junior camp, where we were both fulfilling our annual week-long assignment supervising the kids and in our spare time we made compilations together and shared our findings.

I would follow this study method and continue these projects for the next ten years. Elder Rea had taught me how to do outlines of Sister White's books and these I used as the basis of my sermon preparation. Scripture was incidental as found in her chapters. The prophet became for me an inspired commentator of the Bible. I had learned this at Seminary, so it seemed natural. My addiction was deepening.

THE CEDAR FALLS CAMPFIRE BOWL

Before leaving my internship, I was called in for one last assignment. Elder Rea had been invited to give a short talk to the Conference workers' meeting at Cedar Falls, the Conference youth camp in the San Bernardino mountains. The presentation was to be on the topic, "What an Adventist minister does all day."

As part of my internship under Elder Rea, I had been instructed to keep track of every piece of correspondence that came from the Conference office and to post the events announced there on a large calendar. It became apparent after about five months of this project that Adventist ministers had conflicts between Conference events and local congregational responsibilities and were sometimes expected to be in four or five places on the same day at the same time. Clearly, we were facing a logistical crisis.

When he made his presentation, Elder Rea invited people from the administration to represent their area of work by holding one of my monthly calendars on the stage in front of the workers. They came forward as he called them and stood before the ministers. The president held January, the executive secretary held February, the treasurer held March, and so on. Once each officer was in place, Elder Rea proceeded to demonstrate the conflicts in loyalty that each pastor faced by showing the facts represented on the calendars.

The workers became increasingly humored as the realization sunk in. It was grim humor. But as the workers laughed and enjoyed the occasion more, the administrators felt compelled to mask their embarrassment with silly grins and forced smiles. They appeared only to be enduring this, no longer were they enjoying it. And the point was made. Revisions in Conference communicative policy and expectations needed to be instituted.

To finish off his lecture Elder Rea had me roll in, from the back of the Cedar Falls campfire bowl where we were meeting, all the letters that we had received from the Conference for one year, taped and stapled together end to end. The roll was two feet in diameter and more than covered the aisle way of the assembly bowl. The whole production was a living demonstration rather than a boring lecture.

Remarkably this one presentation resulted in a major overhaul of consolidating correspondence from the offices at the Conference. The fact was that we were sometimes receiving seven separate letters from Conference departments in one day—to the point that many ministers were not even opening the letters—just trashing them immediately.

In a last-ditch effort to get ministers to open their letters the Conference treasurer began putting our monthly paycheck in a letter from a department picked at random. When ministers complained that they had not received a check that month, they immediately revealed that they had simply thrown away their Conference mail unopened except for the letter from the treasury office. The number of embarrassed ministers was shocking.

As I look back on my internship I realize that those eighteen months under two such different ministers did as much to mold my role as a minister as the previous three years in Seminary had done. I found both pastoral mentors to be deeply committed and spiritual men. They both taught out of their experience that had involved deeply painful events in their past.

I could not have calculated that Adventist politics, like all politics, forgets nothing that has gone before. My future would be influenced and tainted by the association of these two men in very different ways. When I left to pastor the Camarillo Church in 1967, I was still very much an idealist and could not have known that my experience under both ministers would return to haunt me when I faced my own trials with Adventist politicians. In their zeal to serve the Lord, religious men often miss the political implications of organized religion.

CHAPTER NINETEEN

A Bump in The Road

> "The great secret of successful marriage is to treat all disasters as incidents and none of the incidents as disasters."
> —Harold Nicholson

TENSIONS IN PROFESSION AFFECT HOME LIFE

ABOUT A YEAR INTO *my internship tensions were beginning to take a toll.* Not the least of these was living in such proximity to family. My mother-in-law had announced to me before our marriage that she would never be the stereotypically invasive mother-in-law. She was just going to be supportive—she said.

Young couples need to have enough detachment from their roots to allow them to establish their own family. Without that, they simply become an extension of the old family. Those three years we had spent in Michigan were at the right distance from family. Now being so close was proving to be too convenient a way of escaping some of the crises we needed to face and solve on our own terms.

Celebration of all holidays at the house became an unspoken expectation. On the surface this seemed cozy, but I soon felt I was back in college. If we visited my parents in Mountain View it would be after the holidays, never on the holidays. Weekends, except when Church duties called, were becoming a repeat of our early courtship. Often, we went there for Sabbath lunch, which then was often extended into the evening.

When her father needed a bookkeeper, he hired Annie, to help our budget. The intention seemed good, but it added to my frustrations when frequently she would work late and sometimes even stay overnight at the house even though we lived only five miles away. I had a problem with that.

When I was a child, Dad, excited about being out in the country, ordered some baby chicks through a mail order catalog. In the normal course of time these chicks developed into full grown hens and roosters and began their own nesting activities. Fascinated by the thought of a new batch of chicks I could hardly wait for the big day when those eggs would hatch.

Finally, I spotted an egg with a little bill poking through and my heart was touched. I was troubled by the struggle the chick was putting forth to extricate itself from its little egg prison. So, I did what I thought was the compassionate thing to do—I helped it out of its prison. Cracking the shell, I pulled the tiny wet, furry creature out and laid it under the heat lamp. It died within the hour. As tears streamed down my cheeks, Dad explained what seemed so illogical to a little boy. Without that struggle, he explained, the chick would not develop the strength it needed to survive in life. I knew then that I was responsible for its premature death.

Now I was watching my in-laws fall into a comparable trap. With the best of intentions, the family was making it difficult for us to establish our identity. And we were playing right along with it. Nobody was at fault. Everyone was trying to help. But the principle of growth was being short circuited. Everything was good—the food, the conversation, the entertainment, the rest. What was missing was room for us to exercise our responsibility to entertain as the new family.

To complicate things further, the tensions at work were growing. Between being a member of the Conference committee and chair of the school board, as well as on the board of elders at a competitive Church in the constituency, my father-in-law seemed omnipresent in my professional as well as my personal life. Again no one was to blame—we were simply caught in an unfortunate placement situation.

When Elder Rea initially took the position that his Church could not pay off its subsidy debt to the school, he fell out of favor with the family, much as our previous pastor had. This time I determined not to go through that crisis again. I felt keenly the friction in being caught between family and career. But these were crises we needed to face ourselves without continual family intervention. Breaking that eggshell was our developmental task. No one could break it for us.

The situation at the school was getting worse. One night after a particularly embattled school board meeting lasting into the late hours of the night, Elder Rea, who found solace in writing verse, went home and penned a simple rhyme describing his version of what had happened that night. He was unwinding. While his allusions were mainly to Conference personnel who had been invited into the meeting to lean on the rest of us in favor of the largest Church represented on the board, my family was implicated. The piece was more than a simple poem. It described the political philosophy of those who would use religion to control the vote of the board.

No board member of a religious institution wants to be against God, but I was beginning to see that there are people on boards who identify their will with God's will and use that certainty to manipulate other board members. Elder Rea was not intimidated by such power plays and in his poem, with stinging humor, he exposed it for what it was. In the morning, he gave me a copy of his latest verse.

> I saw God come again last night; I wondered if He's real.
> The car He drove said Cadillac, but God was at the wheel.
> He talked of fear and dread and guilt if I should fail to heed;
> He did not hope to reach my soul; He did not fill my need.
>
> He called down fire from the clouds, invoked the wrath of men;
> The clergy sitting in the front all said a weak amen.
> And when He finished with His act, He left me with no turn.
>
> He did not try to win my mind nor set my soul at ease,
> He only sought by tragic means to all my actions freeze.
> To place my body on the rack and give it one more turn,
> To gain that one more ounce of flesh or of me He would spurn.[1]

The board meeting that had spawned this poem was a painful one. While I have forgotten the issues we discussed, I remember that administrative personnel from both the Conference and the Union Conference had been imported to dominate the dialogue with the "God's-will," and the "we-are-all-interested-in-God's-work" rhetoric. They implied that those who did not vote the way these brethren wanted were against the work and will of God. Coincidently the "will of God" seemed always to correspond to the will of The White, the largest (and wealthiest) Church in the constituency, which also had the most members on the school board.

As my appreciation for Elder Rea's leadership and direction grew, I felt the negative impact it had at home. For the family, this was an important battle for control. Family members had been on the school board for so many years that they displayed a generous degree of ownership. In their eyes, they had earned their influential position, and new pastors who resisted them were treated as uninformed or temporary. Yet the brunt of the financial responsibilities ultimately fell on the shoulders of these pastors.

Outspoken pastors like Elder Rea were clearly a threat to the traditional guard because they represented growth and new perspectives for dealing with the challenges facing the Church. The fact that they represented change, often for the better, was resented by those who had always done things a certain way. The pain of my position was fueled significantly by the fact that, whether imagined or real, I felt like I was expected to take the family's side. Annie had graduated from the school many years before and although she was not connected with it in any official capacity, she was a member of the family that had had a crucial role in building and maintaining the school over the years.

Furthermore, the comings and goings of the board, its decisions and its personalities, were freely discussed at the house whenever the family got together. The

---

1. Rea, "I Saw God Come Last Night." (1967).

discussions held nothing back and the sarcasm and veiled threats made me uncomfortable as my loyalty to Elder Rea grew. In public all were polite but knowing that it was not real, made me feel isolated. Out of respect for my elders and my position in the family, I did not challenge anyone. I took in what they were saying while biting my lip. But living with divided loyalties made me once more indulge in my old doubts about my marriage.

THE TRIP TO FRESNO

Out of frustration, I finally broached the subject with Elder Rea during a five-hour trip to Fresno where we were to attend a Pacific Union Conference constituency meeting in the spring of 1967. When I had spilled my guts, he responded frankly: if what I had said was true I hardly had a marriage and I was in for some rough sledding. I had said more than I had planned.

That night in the motel I listened and watched as he composed another verse just for me—hoping to encourage me but seeking to express my own sentiments in this personal crisis.

> If I could walk again this way, my choice would still be you.
> For I have watched the many go but all I want is two.
> No fancy frills you may possess, but still my heart you hold.
> I long to take you in my arms if I could be so bold.
>
> I dreamed so many days ago of just this spot in time.
> When we would share each secret hurt but still be yours and mine.
> If I could walk again this way my wish would simply be
> That you would love as I love you and always live with me.
>
> That like the snow on yonder hill that melts with coming spring
> The love we share would melt our fears and make our union sing.
> That as you bend your wayward will to match my skipping trends
> The love we share will straighten paths to where we both would end.
>
> If I could walk again this way my choice would still be you.
> If you're as sure of this one thing, I know we'll see it through.[2]

I read the poem several times. He had captured some of my deepest feelings. Being held at arm's length, constantly put in conflict with family, suffering the lack of intimacy because of my own professional conflicts, I was hurting. The poem became a prayer—*my* prayer.

After the meetings in Fresno, we drove to Yosemite to de-winterize the Rea cabin in the foothills of the Sierras. We went home through Mountain View to visit Mom and Dad. That evening Dad and I walked the streets of the city together as I sang to

---

2. Rea, "If I Could Walk Again This Way." (1967).

him my tale of woe. I hardly organized much of what I was saying—it just flowed out. I told him I was trying to make this marriage work, but I was becoming skeptical. Yet I was particularly concerned that my entire career was at stake. Everything I had planned for my life seemed in the balance. College, Seminary, all my education could go down the drain, not to mention my convictions and calling.

Dad's response I would never forget: "You must work in God's plans, not yours. This is a test of your faith." Not letting the thought register, I explained that the market for divorced ministers basically did not exist—not in our denomination. He and I both knew that nobody would ask why this happened—they would just defrock me in their mind. From the denomination's point of view any minister's marriage that split up meant another woman. If they didn't know of any, they would invent one. Facts were not important perceptions were the issue.

A minister whose marriage failed automatically became grist for the Church's gossip mill. The tabloids were not the only institutions that attracted bottom feeders. These people made it their business to purify the Church by means of prurience. Of course, they purported to be very sincere. They had little doubt that they were personally selected by God to do that kind of work.

The notion of the innocent and guilty parties helped to encourage such people. The fact that there are no innocent parties in a marital breakup was not part of the conceptual inventory. I knew of one case where a minister high up in the Church hierarchy had divorced his wife and married his secretary. He remained faithful to the Church for the next forty years but was never again allowed to preach, teach a Sabbath School lesson, hold an office or represent the Church in any official capacity. Had the Church relented, God would have held it accountable for his sins.

Sister White had made that clear:

> God holds his people, as a body, responsible for the sins existing in individuals among them. If the leaders of the church neglect to diligently search out the sins which bring the displeasure of God upon the body, they become responsible for these sins.[3]

So, although this former leader had nearly perfect attendance at Church every week, his ministry was over, and his Church profession was terminated. I never knew why his marriage had broken down. To the Church, only three facts mattered: alleged indiscretion, divorce, remarriage. Verdict: guilty party. And that disqualified him from any service in God's Church if he lived.

If you were the innocent party, you might, if you were ambitious, leverage your story for sympathy and a career within the field of education. You might serve in a school as a teacher, a dean or a provost, a principal or a president, if you had not

---

3. White, *Testimonies for the Church,* 7:269. Cf. Ibid., p. 265: "He [God] shows us that when his people are found in sin, they should at once take decided measures to put that sin from them, that his frown may not rest upon them all."

come up through the ranks of clergy or ministry, and if you were perceived to be the innocent party. You would not be shunned and with luck, you would be treated like the Church was instructed to treat everyone—with a degree of grace.

But the perceived guilty party was done for. The treatment for the guilty party was the cold shoulder of rejection. Formally, you were not shunned, but divorce was invariably followed by social alienation. If a minister couldn't make his marriage work, how could he possibly be trusted to function in the ministry? All that education, all that caring, all that shepherding, all that dreaming, all that planning—all gone. If this were Coca Cola you could go to Pepsi Cola and receive acceptance. But this was God and if you reject God there was no place to go legitimately.

Grace for the guilty was almost unheard of. The Church did not deal in nuance, whether in theology or ethics. One prominent SDA minister had explained it this way: There are three perspectives on a broken marriage: (1) his story, (2) her story, and (3) the truth.

As time passed I would learn of a few exceptions. One minister went on to pastor a large college Church. I never knew the circumstances except that it was said he had connections and had done something of a job to ruin his ex-wife's reputation thus establishing him, in the eyes of the important committees, "the innocent party." He went on to re-marry and have a family and pastor one of the largest Adventist Churches in North America. Much of this was as scripture said it should be, but this was a rare demonstration of grace in the Church. If there was a question about who was innocent and who was guilty, the one who married first after a marital break-up would usually end all doubt and then some action would be taken. But for all practical purposes a perceived happy marriage was an acid test of competency and commitment.

"You must work in God's plans, not yours. This is a test of your faith," Dad had said. That was perhaps the most serious father-son talk we had ever had. I shared with him, for the first time, doubts I had encountered before my wedding—the decision I had made to break it off, the house full of presents, my turn around, and these lingering feelings of failure.

I didn't share our intimacy problems. I suspected that being from two different worlds even our Scandinavian heritage was not going to contribute much of a resolution to our situation. Nor was this going to be resolved through religion. Yet religion was supposed to solve anything. As a religion addict I could not get past that thought.

When I had finished my long story, Dad surprised me again. Rather than lecturing me about the commitments I had made, like he had when I went to Merced six summers before, he assured me that if we split, I would be welcome to stay with them until I got my feet on the ground. He made it clear that this was a decision I needed to make once and for all (and probably soon) and that sometimes we must step back to catch perspective.

I found myself validated by his words. "You must work in God's plans, not yours. This is a test of your faith." Such counsel resonates with a religious man. This was the closest to Dad I could remember ever feeling. He had sensed my ambivalence but had not interfered. I had not asked for help, he had not offered any. Now things had changed. Some things were out in the open.

We left the next morning for Southern California. I related my conversation with Dad to Elder Rea. While I had been encouraged by Dad's counsel, Elder Rea suddenly took another turn, perhaps to make sure I had looked at the consequences. He told me not to let Dad influence my decision. In fact, he objected to Dad's offering to take me in because that would suggest that divorce was okay when it was not.

I was confused. I didn't know how this squared with his previous observations. I felt my marriage disintegrating and now I didn't know who to listen to about what to do. But I knew it was my problem. By the time we arrived home, I was determined to act. I didn't deserve this kind of treatment even if my career was in the balance. A marriage with no spontaneity and so little intimacy had disillusioned me. All the doubts rolled back on me.

Upon returning home I shared my misgivings and her response infuriated me: she wanted me to talk to her parents! Why? This was none of their business. This was our problem. They were not the managers or architects of our home. But in my extreme naïveté I hadn't accepted just to what degree we were caught in the web spun by our families and how deeply it was affecting our home.

Had we been able to move on from marriage to a separate family? Did we have a marriage that had produced a separate family? I was finally facing the reality: No, we had not. I began to despair, for the first time, at the influence of this family on my life. Breaking up was no longer an option—this wasn't a courtship anymore but a legal, contractual arrangement. Freedom, at this point, could only be bought at the price of flushing a career down the drain.

I was consumed with guilt as my thoughts strayed into forbidden territory. They had to be swept under the rug. They had to be put away. How else would I be able to stand upright before God when the Black Cloud appeared?

THE PAIN OF CONFRONTATION

I finally decided to meet with her parents. I was too shy to bring up anything about our intimate life. I dwelt simply on the issue of the family's assertive influence in our lives. I was reliving that previous visit back in college when I was called upon to placate them. But this was a far more complicated encounter. I had left that earlier meeting with a degree of relief but without any permanent resolution. That should have been a wakeup call, but I had chosen to ignore it. Ironically, this one would be little different. Once again, all negotiating would be done on their turf. I would only learn later how significant that was.

Baring my soul, I revealed that things were not working out. I did not share what I thought was none of their business. After all, I was not there to convince them of anything, merely to inform them of possible outcomes. I was not seeking counsel. I really didn't understand why the two of us couldn't solve this or at least with the help of an objective third party. When I finished, instead of suggesting either support or understanding, my father-in-law stared me down and with a stiff quivering lip declared that I had the most to lose.

Now I knew who was in charge. All bets were off. I understood that this was more than an observation—this was a threat. These words sent shivers down my back as I caught the message. I was shaking as he pontificated from his large padded executive chair, and I did my best to conceal my inner turmoil. I was struck with who I was dealing with. If I crossed them, I could be assured of losing everything I had ever hoped to do in life. I had stupidly placed all my eggs in one basket. I was sure that God had called me to this ministry, but I had no such certainty when it came to my marriage. Unfortunately, if I opted out of my marriage, it wouldn't matter what ministry God had in mind for me.

To lose my ministry now would be the end of all my great plans and delights in life. I had no backup plan. While I did not have the vocabulary to describe these feelings at the time, I came later to understand that they were characteristic of religion addicts: nothing can be allowed to stand in the way of the religious goal, not even one's happiness. My goal was to be God's minister. God would make it happen.

I left shaken and angry. I realized then that there was no way to get out of this marriage without sacrificing my career, my livelihood, my mission, and my faith; and that I was not willing to do. I would endure. I had that ability and God would help me. And Christ was coming soon to rescue me. Years later an influential, divorced relative would tell me, "Don't ever go into a divorce unless you are prepared to lose everything." He shared the experience of a man who had faced that counsel and gone back with his wife to preserve the things of worth to him in his life. After six months of trying again to make his marriage work, he had come back to announce, "Okay, I'm ready to lose everything!"

It was not counsel I would have heeded at the time. I would not have believed it. What I interpreted as being faithful to God at the time would have precluded such considerations. Yet I had no one to counsel with but the prophet of my church. I read everything in her writings that had to do with psychology and those who practiced it and I became even more suspicious of this pseudo-science than I had been previously. The professional help that we could have used at that point was once again sacrificed on the altar of nineteenth century fundamentalism.

Sister White's teachings were clear:

> The true principles of psychology are found in the Holy Scriptures. Man knows not his own value. He acts according to his unconverted temperament

of character, because he does not look unto Jesus, the Author and Finisher of his faith.[4]

She connected psychology directly with Satan:

> In these days when skepticism and infidelity so often appear in a scientific garb, we need to be guarded on every hand. Through this means our great adversary is deceiving thousands and leading them captive according to his will. *The advantage he takes of the sciences, sciences which pertain to the human mind, is tremendous. Here, serpent like, he imperceptibly creeps in to corrupt the work of God.*[5]

> The sciences of phrenology, psychology, and mesmerism are *the channel through which he* [Satan] *comes more directly to this generation* and works with that power which is to characterize his efforts near the close of probation.[6]

> The minds of thousands have thus been poisoned, and led into infidelity. While it is believed that one human mind so wonderfully affects another, Satan, who is ready to press every advantage, insinuates himself, and works on the right hand and on the left. And while those who are devoted to these sciences laud them to the heavens because of the great and good works which they affirm are wrought by them, *they little know what a power for evil they are cherishing;* but it is a power which will yet work with all signs and lying wonders—with all deceivableness of unrighteousness. Mark the influence of these sciences, dear reader, for *the conflict between Christ and Satan is not yet ended.*[7]

She continued with the place of Satan in all of this:

> He [Satan] is well pleased to have the knowledge of these sciences widespread. It is a plan which he himself has laid that he may gain access to minds and influence them as he pleases. . . . This entering in of Satan through the sciences is well devised by his satanic majesty, *and in the minds of thousands will eventually destroy true faith in Christ's being the Messiah, the Son of God.*[8]

> As we near the close of time, the human mind is more readily affected by Satan's devices. He leads deceived mortals to account for the works and miracles of Christ upon general principles. . . . Satan took advantage of the weak, suffering condition of Christ, who had taken upon Him our human nature.[9]

The real clincher for me came from a book I had read many times. Now it had new meaning as I sought to understand God's will for my life.

4. White, *My Life Today,* 176.
5. White, *Selected Messages,* 2:351. Emphasis supplied.
6. White, *Testimonies for the Church,* 1:290–291. Emphasis supplied.
7. Ibid., Emphases supplied.
8. Ibid., 290–291. Emphasis supplied.
9. Ibid., 293.

> It is not wise to look to ourselves and study our emotions. If we do this, *the enemy will present difficulties and temptations that weaken faith and destroy courage.* Closely to study our emotions and give way to our feelings is to entertain doubt and entangle ourselves in perplexity. We are to look away from self to Jesus.[10]

These counsels hit home. I was clearly in the wrong: I was doubting, I was clamoring for my own way; I was placing my ministry in jeopardy. The more I researched the subject, the more I decided that I had been deceived by my own religious education. If my professors knew that these counsels existed, they had either hidden them from me or somehow rationalized them away. So, I reformed—and as I plowed deeper into the inspired writings, I steeled myself against any kind of psychology or counselors. It was an extreme position, but it seemed to be the only safe course of action.

THE PERSPECTIVE OF FAITH

Religious people have often been torn between their faith and a reality that all too often undermines it. But the more conservative believers are, the more inclined they are to cover the troublesome landscape of life with the scripture map of faith. While some Christians can find a religious solution to these inherent conflicts with reality, others cannot, and the result is a behavioral form of cognitive dissonance that we often refer to as compartmentalization.

One of the tragic examples of this is a professor I was told of. His wife had reacted with such revulsion to his love making on their wedding night that she had informed him that that was it. She would not submit to that again. To save his marriage and his career, he agreed to live as brother and sister for the duration of their marriage, which lasted for many decades, childless, of course.

What very few people knew was that he lived a double life. Occasionally, he would heed the call of the wild when nature would overcome nurture. In class the slightest hint of inappropriate language would meet with his strong disapproval and warning that ministers don't use that kind of language or tell any shady type of stories. He was a model professor, learned and exemplary, but out among the trees on certain nights he would meet a young female student who offered some privileges his wife did not. He died a faithful minister in the eyes of all, with a deeply spiritual reputation.

Such an arrangement would be intolerable. It violated every value embraced in the New Testament teachings on marriage and relationship. My ministerial mentor's counsel helped to place such stories in perspective. He would tell me: Remember in all my thinking I was a man before I was a Christian. Religion will not override one's sexuality.

---

10. White, *The Ministry of Healing*, 249. Emphasis supplied.

A Bump in the Road

In a last-ditch attempt to save our marriage, we finally agreed to go together to a third, detached party for some spiritual counsel. He was reputed to be safe, but I still felt that for a religious man this was seriously pushing the envelope. I took comfort in the fact that he also believed in our prophet and would do nothing knowingly to violate her teachings. He was a minister, not a therapist. Southern California Conference had hundreds of Adventist ministers. Seeing him was also convenient. We could just make a social call. Another added benefit: he did not charge for any services. We first had individual sessions with him.

One day in my private session with him, he shocked me. He told me a story that he felt might carry some insight. He said he had been told by a young wife that the man she married had taken advantage of her before they were married and that she felt he had abused her, so she found it hard to relate to him intimately. What had made it worse was that he was a spiritual man who truly loved her.

In his questioning of the young man he asked what they had done, assuming that he had forced her to have sex with him. He denied that. Sex meant sexual intercourse and he had always believed that this kind of premarital intimacy was not a part of any life but marriage. Fear of pregnancy, he said, was never an issue. Doing what was right was his personal concern. For him it was a spiritual issue.

The minister wanted a clearer explanation from him. What exactly had he done that made her feel abused? When he told him in graphic detail what they had done the minister replied, "Well, that's nothing. All couples do that." The young man was now confused. Where was this going? Finally, the young man asked, "So you assumed that I made her have sex with me?" And the minister admitted that it was his assumption. She had not really said that. The young man was thoroughly humiliated and defensive. It was not enjoyable. But in the guise of religion it was somehow permissible to be probed like this.

The minister then said, "I tell you this story so you can know the power of words. And the tendency perhaps all of us have to exaggerate whatever we hear through assumptions. I learned much later that there was an ethical principle set forth by Dietrich Bonhoeffer that believers do not have an obligation to bare their souls to people who have no authority to ask invasive questions.[11] I didn't know why religious people thought they had the right to intrude on and dissect your soul with their prying questions, yet I accepted it as fair. Such acceptance made me more uncomfortable.

Why did I feel compelled to answer questions immediately or at all? It was part of the perfectionistic make-up of my religion. I had been taught: "Everything that Christians do should be as transparent as the sunlight."[12] Our prophet had written that, and I had concluded that anybody had a right to pry into my life. After all, there was nothing there that could be wrong or embarrassing anyway. I had not yet entertained the notion that innocuous things could be misunderstood or misinterpreted.

---

11. Bonhoeffer, *Ethics*, 266–269.
12. White, *Thoughts from The Mount of Blessing*, 68.

The prophetic words did not take into consideration the many judgmental neurotics in the congregation who needed something negative to feed on, however contrived, nor did they hedge against the inventions of toxic people out to hurt you. The theological adage, "a text without its context is a pretext," applied just as much to life itself as to the interpretation of the biblical words. Unfortunately, it was a principle that was sinned against in both settings.

"That's nothing, all couples do that!" He had exclaimed and he seemed to be almost more relieved at that conclusion than the young man was. He had feared that he had before him a fornicator—one who was unworthy to witness or be married. I asked him again if he could clarify what that young man had been accused of. He just told me that he had "taken advantage of her."

Staying with the story I asked him if he had assumed the rest from that unclear charge? He said, yes, he had. Then he said, "The young man asked me if she had told me what *she* had done? I told him she hadn't." And he said something astonishing: "Then I won't tell you what she did either." I guess he assumed that I could let my own imagination carry me from there. The story was not very clear and I wondered how it had anything to do with me. But I was informed. I figured that the issue was punishment.

In love we can be genuine but misunderstood. He added one last idea. Whatever this young man had done to violate her conscience, she admitted that she allowed because she didn't want to "lose him." I wasn't sure that the counseling had been very helpful. It depressed me to think that this guy would be doomed to live a life of coldness and emptiness instead of a life of intimate and romantic warmth. Was that what he was trying to emphasize? I turned inward to wonder. There had to be something deeper here that I just wasn't seeing.

Our therapy meetings ended after only a couple sessions. Being a religious man, it was my duty to absorb guilt and live in a kind of painful, life-long exile from my emotional needs—in Catholic terms: lifelong penance. I had to change my attitude to preserve not only my marriage but also my ministry. So, despite it all I was confronted with the issues plain and simple. Would I accept this way of life to keep my ministry and my marriage? The decision was made, I determined that I would. Both my ministry and my marriage meant too much to me to lose. God would give me the strength.

WHERE WAS GOD?

During this period in my life I was struggling with my view of God's involvement. Was it really God's will that I continue like this? Of course, it was. We weren't done yet. I had listened to my colleagues talk about being married to their best friend. I had watched the carefree intimacy that they displayed in talking and interacting together. What was wrong with me?

I explored my own attractiveness—maybe that was the deeper cause of our detachment. Intimacy had now become a prize to be sought or bought. No mere holiday would do the trick. I tried writing love notes and putting them under pillows. They became trash cluttering the bed. I bought flowers. I made breakfast and served it in bed. But all these things were interpreted as resorts of a desperate man.

Trying was part and parcel of my religion, and not just limited to my personal relationships. The fact is, love is not the product of trying—just the opposite. In trying we come across as wimps. When the ministerial counselor asked whether I was a man's man, there was an embarrassing silence. His next question was to her, Should intimacy be treated like giving a piece of candy? The silence in the room became more oppressive.

A religion of *trying* is debilitating. Trying and doing are separate. There is a stereotype that says that when men get married, they want their wives to stay the same, while women want their husbands to change. Like all stereotypes there is some truth here. But the fact is that marriage represents a social paradigm shift that requires both parties to change.

As I was struggling with this issue, I received a call from the Conference office.

THE LORD APPEARS

Now what? Elder Retzer was on the phone. He wanted me to come to his office for a little talk. Paranoia set in immediately. Who had gotten to him? What did he know of my very private and personal thoughts? No, he couldn't know. But what about the family council? Could that have gotten out? Had some family member had an audience with the Pope? Up to this point my thoughts had been hidden except for the family and a confidant; so, who had betrayed me? Assumptions were beginning.

As I drove to Glendale, I was adjusting to the possibility that I might be required to quit my ministry. I had no idea what I would do, but I was only twenty-five years old and maybe life held some alternatives. I did not like the direction in which my emotions were driving me. My religion had told me not to study my emotions, and I had done nothing but violate that injunction in the past few months.

As I entered the office, we exchanged pleasantries. I had always appreciated Elder Retzer as a friend, but the employer/employee relationship was new to me. Part of me waited for the stone to drop. So far as he knew, I had been an exemplary intern. I had helped in various Conference activities such as the Sabbath School department and the young people's department. I had spoken for youth rallies around the Conference, I had written Sabbath School lesson helps for Elder Hardin. I had held Weeks of Prayer in academies. I thought my youth program had gone well. Parents were sending me kind notes. Young people were calling to thank me for caring and the work I had done. What could this visit possibly mean?

Finally, Elder Retzer got to his point. He let me know that he had been watching me. And he got serious. I thought—here it comes!—someone else has been watching me! But continuing slowly, making sure I appreciated what he had to say he reminded me that I was a good friend of his family. His son had even been a groomsman in our wedding. He paused. Breaking the silence, he said he wanted to run some ideas by me. He was clearly satisfied with his disclosure. None of this conversation was matching my expectations, and he admitted that he was quite happy about the plans he had to share.

The stone was in the air. But I wasn't hearing any reprimand. He was upbeat. And then he laid it out: He had been working with a group of Church members in a little town of 10,000 population about sixty miles up Highway 101. They wanted to start a new congregation and had requested the services of a pastor.

My paranoia was beginning to diminish. The group, he revealed, was largely from Oxnard, Newbury Park, Ventura, Santa Paula and Ojai. A major trailblazer was a local physician, who had been pushing this project for several years. And it looked like the time had come to act on his wishes. Elder Retzer made it clear that in his opinion this was a strong group of believers. Then he made his point. He wanted to know if I would be interesting in organizing this group as a company and developing them into a full congregation. Far from expressing any lack of trust in my credibility or ability, Elder Retzer was extending to me a great responsibility.

THE CHALLENGE TO PLANT A CHURCH

Plant a church? I was ready! I had fallen on my sword prematurely. And he continued by suggesting that I drive to the town and look around. He told me it was a beautiful place to live. And he encouraged me to go home, talk it over and get back to him in a week or so with my decision and questions.

As I prepared to leave, I asked him a stupid question—How do you plant a Church? It seemed like a logical question at the time but not one to ask your boss who has just laid out the challenge. His answer was publishable. He made it clear that that's what they had hired me for! And then he added: "Be a friend of all and a pal of none!"

GOD HAD ANSWERED MY PRAYERS

I believed God had visited the office that day. My doubts dissipated like fog in the morning sunlight. Things could finally be okay. We could work out our differences. I could learn to be more attractive—a man's man? I would meet whatever standards were expected of me. I felt renewed. My ministry and mission had been validated. It was exciting to receive the call of God. I left the office, climbed into my car and headed north on the Ventura Freeway. God was at work! I wanted to see the place to which he was calling me.

My enthusiasm mellowed as I drove. I realized that I had to reframe everything in my mind—my marriage, my career, my calling to the ministry—in reverse order of importance. They were all up for re-evaluation. I was interested—please keep posted! The trip was exciting but also veered toward the frightening. Reality was taking a bite out of my exhilaration. Though thrilled at the prospect, I seriously knew almost nothing about how to plant a Church. But I knew that it would work out. I was ready. I hoped. For the next three months I waited for some firm news. No news.

I began to make plans for the summer youth program even though I didn't know how long I might be around. Life went on as usual except for the fact that I had a carrot of deliverance dangling before my face—the answer to the crisis I had been mired in for the past few weeks. The prospects of moving made me look more positively at my life. Realistically, whose marriage is perfect? We were young—we could work out our differences. We had a lot going for us. I swept my irritations under the rug once again and focused on what I had wanted to be since I was seventeen years old—a pastor.

Even though religious men frequently believe that time may end any day, they are compelled to live as though time will never end—the paradox of living in an evil age. They make plans, for that too is part of being religious—being responsible. This paradox was highlighted every four years as the General Conference met and the administrators announced that this would undoubtedly be the last convocation we would ever hold on this side of the New Jerusalem. The Black Cloud would appear before we could meet like this again. And then we would stand and sing together: "We have this hope . . . hope in the coming of the Lord!"

Yet despite these announcements, the leaders were already planning with some large city for the next quadrennial session—New Orleans, San Francisco, Utrecht, Toronto, St. Louis, Atlanta, San Antonio, Indianapolis. It was a paradox that religious men lived with. Planning, but harboring the thought of not having to carry out those plans. Where there is hope there is life.

Before we were officially notified about our move, we had a serious talk together. Like a traditional chauvinist, I presented my wife with some requirements. She was going to quit her job at her parents. She was never to spend another night in their home if we lived so close to theirs. She was to see her doctor about things. To my surprise she agreed to it all. It was not my finest hour and I discovered it was no more fun to issue orders than it was to endure hardship. I wanted our life to be spontaneous. I was frantic for our marriage to work but at the same time I was not willing to throw away my career if my efforts were unsuccessful. It put me in an impossible situation.

She would tell me later that she had attributed my crisis to my mental illness and since she also had been committed to our marriage, she had bided her time. That was her style as opposed to my ineffective way of preaching biblical sermons in the bedroom.

So, we would take it out on each other in different, more socially acceptable ways. We had already perfected the art of denial and hiding communicative flaws under the rug. But what happens in the corridor of a dysfunctional marriage is that all the doors of the hallway that in the beginning had been wide open, one by one are closed. The best answer would be to deal with those challenges immediately, but religion provides a convenient blanket under which to sweep all problems. Nor did it help that our traditional theology taught that while sins could be forgiven, they were not erased until the final judgment. For Adventists all forgiveness was provisional, just in case we would change our minds and turn our back on God.

Here was strong motivation to keep going, remain true, keep the faith, pay our tithe, keep the Sabbath, etc. In short: keep *trying*. This is the lethal experimental side of a legalistic religion. Putting sins in the depths of the sea was not an Adventist belief. Consequently, this was the formula for destroying any real understanding of assurance.

PULLING UP STAKES

I broke the news that we were moving—I didn't know when, but probably before the summer was over. Annie had been teaching at a local public high school, so this would require her to put in her notice and pull up stakes. She seemed as excited about it as I did, and that felt good. Probably we both knew instinctively we needed a change of scenery. Now we might think about buying our own home, and maybe I could appreciate her family better from a distance. Our lives might be our own; perhaps the intimacy would follow. I dared to dream. I had this hope.

I was rethinking our marital commitment in the light of this new mission. I caught a glimmer that we might be able to solve our incompatibilities or learn to live with them. I would come to appreciate the irreverent but profound principle: "Never try to teach a pig to sing—it frustrates you and it irritates the pig."

The official letter arrived in June 1967. We were to hold our first Church service on July 1. When the call came through, it took our minds off our troubles and funneled our energy into the excitement of packing and the prospects of shouldering a heavier and more meaningful responsibility. Jesus was coming soon—it was time to focus on that. That would be our grand escape.

By becoming a pastor, I would have achieved one of my first professional goals in life and I was very enthusiastic. We would have our own house. Maybe we could even think about having children. Surely things could turn around now. It was worth *trying* for.

CHAPTER TWENTY

Life in the Parish

"He who has burned his mouth blows his soup."
—GERMAN PROVERB

CAMARILLO, CALIFORNIA

IN 1967, "CAMARILLO, CALIFORNIA" *was synonymous with California's celebrated State Hospital.* If you said you were "going to Camarillo" people commonly assumed that you were either visiting an inmate or being inducted into the large mental hospital run by the state. One Church member asked me in all seriousness if the Church I was going to pastor was located directly on the hospital grounds. "Camarillo" was well-known in Southern California, even if misunderstood.

The town itself, with a population of less than 10,000, had a significant Catholic population and had been incorporated just three years before. Located on U. S. Highway 101, this small bedroom community was exactly halfway between Los Angeles and Santa Barbara.

On a hot spring afternoon, I drove into the City of Camarillo for the first time in my life. Exiting on Lewis Road I found myself hardly knowing where to go next. Finally, I was heading toward the State Hospital, which was hidden among trees planted at the foot of Conejo Mountain. Its Spanish-style buildings were spread out across the gently sloping meadow in the bottom of the Santa Monica Hills. Since I was going in that direction, I decided to look around a place I had only heard about, the hospital. The site was impressive.

The facility would be closed in the late 1990s and later redesigned as the newest of the twenty-three campus California State University (CSU Channel Islands). But in the 1960s it was operated as an institution where people with addictions and developmental and mental disabilities were committed. Some professionals look back on institutions like this one with a degree of horror. During Governor Ronald Reagan's terms of office responsibility for taking care of people with mental disabilities was shifted to county facilities.

After driving around the campus I circled back toward the City. I drove down Ventura Boulevard observing the little shops and business establishments. I saw a Baptist Church designed as a California mission and the large Catholic Church that stood on the west side of the freeway like a sentinel overlooking the whole City from a knoll on the old Camarillo Ranch.

When I turned up Las Posas Road and crossed the freeway again, I spotted an Episcopal Church, then a little yellow First Christian Church and finally a Presbyterian Church. I knew there must be more churches, but perhaps these were ones we would pick from in choosing to rent when we established our new congregation. I did not see the United Methodist Church on Anacapa Drive in Camarillo Heights since that area was not on my tour. Nor did I know that the group I would pastor had already negotiated a deal with the Methodists.

THE ORIGINAL GROUP

Our first meeting was held in the home of Camarillo dentist Dr. James McAninch on Mission Drive. The group was small but impressive, largely professional, and clearly excited about realizing a long-anticipated fulfillment of their dream. They were members of SDA churches in Oxnard, Newbury Park, Thousand Oaks, Santa Paula, Ojai and Ventura. The level of positive energy in the living room was invigorating.

I was presented immediately with reports of the wonderful attributes of Camarillo that were applauded by the prestigious and trustworthy *National Geographic Magazine* as one of the top ten most enjoyable places to live in America. I was advised that several airline pilots had chosen to live there, they said, because upon flying north they had noticed this jewel between the ridge and the beach. Settling in the hills surrounding the City, they did not consider the commute to LAX, fifty-five miles to the south, too big a sacrifice.

Dr. McAninch practiced in Port Hueneme ten miles to the west. He and his family were members of the Oxnard Church and seemed to be the main driving force in this effort to plant the new Church. Dr. Muff, a physician with a thriving practice in Camarillo, had also agitated for years to get people motivated to establish a Camarillo congregation and now he was finally going to see his wishes fulfilled.

Tee Gilbert, an employee of the local public-school system, and his family were well-known in the Conference for their young people's work with the Conference Pathfinder Club. (I knew where he would be assigned). And John Brodersen, a contractor in Ventura, and his wife Joyce, were also members of the Oxnard Church, and anxious to be involved in the new venture.

Dr. George Vannix had been an Adventist minister, had gone back to finish his medical education and was also practicing in Port Hueneme. Dr. Fred Delay, an optometrist, was active in local City politics on the board of parks and recreation. John Carpenter was a hospital administrator and had agreed to serve as Church treasurer.

Dr. Frank Chung had an OB/GYN practice with offices in Oxnard and Camarillo. His wife Helen had a master's degree in nutrition from Cornell University, and was well-known for her cooking schools. Most of these exciting members had young children. I was immediately enthusiastic that we would have active young people's activities—Sabbath School divisions and Junior Missionary Volunteers (Pathfinder Club).

They were all there that night. The principal adults in attendance ranged from 30–50 years of age and they would soon be joined by others, some senior citizens and others with young families. I could hardly believe that such an "instant congregation" existed anywhere. My work was already largely done.

I was naturally uneasy as I entered the meeting. Seminary had given no training in planting a Church. This was all new territory for me. But as I caught the spirit of these people the enthusiasm was contagious, and I could see that this was going to be an exciting and challenging venture. It is not an exaggeration to say, this congregation was already "planted." Only growth was the order of the day.

The traditional Adventist method of Church planting had been to start a "branch" Sabbath School designed to attract people interested in religious questions, sign them up for Bible studies and gradually build a "company of believers." After a "company" had been established and begun to thrive as a firm group, it could be formed into a "congregation" with full self-sustaining capacity—leadership and finances.

These methods were written up in little tracts from the Sabbath School department, but they were not part of our professional education. We were taught public evangelism and were required to attend an evangelism field school, which I had done in Southern California during the summer of 1965. But no classes in Church planting or even branch Sabbath School were held. I did have a year's experience working with Mike in the "The Heralds of Hope" where we started and maintained a branch Sabbath School in Home Gardens, a little unincorporated village between Riverside and Corona that had reportedly been a "Hooverville" during the Great Depression.

The professional education in Church growth that ministerial recruits receive in all Evangelical seminaries today was not common in those days. Personal evangelism was largely defined as giving Bible studies (or "Bible readings" as they were often called). Getting the doctrines straight was crucial for Adventists. We were there to teach people The Truth, which meant (though we never worded it this way) the SDA interpretation of the scriptures.

JULY 1, 1967

About half an hour with this Camarillo group was all I needed to realize that I had little to worry about. I was there mainly in an advisory role to these very capable, competent people. They presented me with a list of Church officers: elders, deacons, deaconesses, Church clerk, treasurer, organist, pianists, Sabbath School personnel, and a full page of all the offices in a typical Adventist Church down to the ushers. This Church planting was not a new thought for them—some of them had been hoping and planning this event for many years.

We met for worship for the first time as a formal company on Sabbath, July 1, 1967. Seventy-five curious people attended the first service. This was an electrifying day as everyone filed in, many functioning in their new posts. Children's divisions hummed with activity as ladies ministered to the young people of the flock. I preached the first of a series of three sermons I called "The Three Great Essentials of the Church." They were sermons I had prepared in Seminary and preached before on faith, hope, and love. (1 Cor 13:12–13).

So mature was this company that it was graduated to full congregational status in an unprecedented three weeks. On July 15, 1967, the Conference administrators drove up from Glendale for an afternoon meeting to organize the Church as an official congregation. Often such officialdom takes years, but this was clearly a strong company.

The afternoon meeting was invigorating. Elder Retzer spoke on the nearness of the Black Cloud—when the little boy thought he heard the clock strike thirteen, he exclaimed, "It is later than it has ever been before!" I had finished my series that morning. I knew my file of sermons was thin and that soon I would have to prepare a new message each week, but for these three busy weeks these were the best I could offer.

I hit the pavement running. Elder Rea had taught me that the best way to get going in a new situation like this was simply to go door-to-door searching for people who wished to study the Bible. Within two weeks I was holding Bible studies in twenty-five homes. One interest was such a heavy smoker that every Tuesday I studied with him and felt I was becoming addicted to nicotine.

I visited all the Church members during the first month. We organized young people's activities. The Church elected Tee Gilbert as our new Pathfinder director, and he started the Camarillo Pathfinder Club in my garage—an effort that would produce top trophies and honors in its class at all the Conference events over the next three years.

We began Prayer Meetings on Wednesday nights. I prepared and preached a brand-new sermon every week using my newly acquired methods learned from Elder Rea who called me faithfully every Monday morning to see how things were going. Elder Rea had shown me how he outlined chapters from Sister White's books, then filled in the blanks with personal experiences and finished the sermon off with a biblical setting. "You follow this method," he reminded me, "and you can know that you are always preaching pure Truth—and you will never run out of material." I followed this method faithfully and meticulously. My study program of four hours a day now had meaning. I had a place to share insights I was accumulating from my study.

On July 22, 1967, I began a new series on the parables of Christ in which I outlined my view of the ministry. It was based on my outlining activity in our prophet's book *Christ's Object Lessons*. At last I was clear on how to get substantial and strong material for sermons. I was at home. My most blissful religious hopes had been realized. I was a pastor. I failed to notice the gradual legalistic tone of my sermons nor would I have admitted that this tone was coming from my study sources.

THE CHARTER CHURCH, JULY 15, 1967

As a young pastor I faced some disadvantages in my first pastorate. The biggest hurdle was that I was not ordained. Our denomination did not follow the practice of ordaining its ministers straight out of Seminary like many denominations did. Instead there was a probationary period in which one proved himself worthy of the status and authority.

In the 1960s this process of ministerial education typically took ten years from the beginning of college to ordination—the final recognition of qualification. This involved four years of College, three years of Seminary, and three years of Internship and assistantship in the field. If a minister did not go to Seminary, he might not be ordained until he had been out of college for four years. But no set rule was followed consistently.

Some men were ordained sooner, others later. I had met ministers who were in the field ten years before being ordained and others who were ordained in three years with no theological degree. But Southern California was a progressive Conference that strongly supported the Seminary program and so I was not to the end of my probationary period when I became the pastor at Camarillo. Though I was a licensed minister I was not a credentialed minister. Credentials came only with the official rite of ordination. The practical outcome of my present position was restricted authority. I could not perform marriages or baptize new members.

My salary was substantially lower than that of an ordained minister. Yet as a pastor I received budgets from the Conference that were higher than what most Church employees earned. In fact, we were not called employees; we were called workers. And we could fill up our cars at the Conference fuel pump in Glendale at a reduced rate.

Elder Rea had let me baptize the people I had studied with and prepared for baptism, but he had to stand in the baptistery with me for he was ordained, and I was not. It was a matter of policy designed to keep tight control on those called to the professional ministry, but in my own pastorate this arrangement was inconvenient. I had to schedule an ordained minister to come to the congregation to provide these services.

Since the Methodist Church did not have a baptistery that would accommodate baptism by immersion we would meet at the Oxnard SDA Church, or at the home of a member who had a swimming pool. When we later rented a Baptist Church for a short time the facilities were more accommodating.

On July 15, 1967, exactly fifty people signed the Camarillo charter becoming the first members of the Camarillo SDA Church on a balmy Sabbath afternoon. Elder Retzer delivered the sermon extolling the fact that time was about to close, and we would soon be in the kingdom. But meanwhile we must work hard to finish the work. It was a common Adventist theme. And then the charter-signing took place.

One of these signers of the charter was a physician who sought me out and explained, "Pastor, you will not see me in Church very often. But don't worry about me. I teach a Bible class at my office on Sabbath mornings during the worship service at Church to familiarize people to coming out on the Sabbath. Then, when I think they are ready I bring them to Church."

I was suspicious of such narrative. This was probably an excuse for skipping Church. But when several weeks later he brought ten people to Church worship, ushered them onto an empty pew, and sat with them, I saw that he was serious. Eventually all ten were baptized and became active members of the congregation. During my five years in Camarillo I would baptize fifteen more from his class. I now had a positive cameo of the minister-physician team to help supplant some of my skeptical views from college of the "Theos" and the "Pre-meds."

INITIATION TO PASTORAL LIFE

Annie and I found a little bright yellow two-bedroom house to rent down the street from the United Methodist Church on Anacapa Drive. It had a two-car garage and a breezeway with a small backyard that included a little citrus grove. Although it was a rental this was our first real house. Alongside the house was a little 4 x 20-foot fenced yard and I immediately bought some chickens to raise there. I was back in the country and chickens somehow underscored that!

The front lawn was surrounded by a white picket fence. As you looked at the house, you fully expected to see Donna Reed open the door and come out to greet you. It was the kind of house that many young couples dreamed of in those days. We were disappointed that it was not for sale—only for rent.

The ministry was much as I thought it would be. An extended family room became my study and I partitioned it off with bookcases to house my ever-growing library. We had had many squabbles over my love of books. I viewed them as tools. She still saw them as luxuries and reminded me often that since she was going without hairspray to make ends meet, I could go without books. Now that I was on a predictable and more livable salary, the arguments were less frequent even though our income was only about $100 more a month than it had been in Seminary. My employer expected me to have a book budget.

On that Founders Day I arrived home around 5:00 pm and was straightening up my study when the phone rang. It was another of the charter members of the Church.

"I would like to meet with you and get some witnessing materials," he said. "This is a good time to start our lives anew and I have a number of people at work who keep asking me religious questions," he continued. He told me that he and his wife had been Adventists for six years. I gathered up some material for him and he picked it up the next day. He was in construction and worked in Oxnard. This was the beginning of a new friendship.

Nothing in life remains static, a fact that religious men can find hard to accept. Dr. Dietrich Bonhoeffer, a German theologian during WWII, spoke of our inability to cherish those moments when we enjoy the physical presence of the people of God. We pass like ships in the night, not knowing that soon we may have no contact at all. Life can suddenly sweep away these beautiful friendships. As a result, we look back and long for them, but they are gone.

> Between the death of Christ and the Last Day it is only by a gracious anticipation of the last things that Christians are privileged to live in visible fellowship with other Christians. It is by the grace of God that a congregation is permitted to gather visibly in this world to share God's Word and sacrament. . . . The physical presence of other Christians is a source of incomparable joy and strength to the believer.[1]

Jim and Nancy,[2] with their children, represented those very talented Church members whose contributions are often underrated. And within two years they were fulfilling a cross section of major congregational tasks. They became human fixtures in most aspects of Church life. Jim was soon elected an elder, lay activities leader and Sabbath School superintendent. Since all their children were in the Camarillo Pathfinder Club, they led out there too.

Meanwhile we were looking for a house. We had the money in the bank for a down payment that Annie had made while teaching high school. After a year of rented quarters, we were able to buy a model house in a new development on Rocklyn Street. We were excited. We put down the money we had saved, took out a second mortgage loan, and moved in to our roomy new four-bedroom house. We were buying our first home!

As a model home, the house came with landscaping and fences all artistically installed. This was a mansion to us, and it quickly became the Church's second home as well. Our use of the Methodist Church was limited and so our garage became the

---

1. Bonhoeffer, *Life Together*, 18–19.
2. Names supplied.

Pathfinder room, meetings of all kinds were held in our family room and bedrooms and members felt free to drop by uninvited. We loved it.

Mrs. Patricia Johnson was elected choir director and every Friday night the choir practiced in our family room. Many of my sermons received their final touches with the choir singing in the adjoining room. This saved the Church money and our new home became the hub for the members. This is how I had pictured the ministry. We were in a Donna Reed world!

And then we hit our first snag.

THE FIRST SNAG

Since I had been a colporteur in Merced during the summer of 1961, I thought it might be a good idea to invite a couple of student colporteurs to Camarillo for the summer of 1968. My unpleasant memories had faded, and I once again believed this would be a good way to get names of interested people in my City.

Annie was pregnant, but we talked over the suggestion and decided we could house a couple of college students for three months. I contacted members of my old youth group who had just graduated from high school and who I hoped to entice into ministerial education. One of them had been our speaker during Youth Day where I was youth pastor. Two young men were more than excited at the prospect of living with us for the summer.

When our two student colporteurs, Bruce and Doug, arrived in town and started to work, they were immediately arrested by the Camarillo Police Department. Now we discovered there was a City ordinance against door-to-door selling by any organization established in town for less than five years. I called the Conference office for help. We had assumed that even if there was such an ordinance we were a Church organization, and this would be a matter of religious liberty. We had not done our homework—we were essentially hiding behind our interpretation of the U.S. Constitution. I had forgotten that this same thing had happened to us in Merced seven years before.

Church representatives from the Conference Religious Liberty Department drove out from Glendale to represent us before the Camarillo City Council. The City took the position that any organization, even a Church, that was younger than five years, was not considered established in Camarillo and would not be given solicitation rights in the City. Since we were barely a year old, we would not qualify. Our Church officials pointed out that the City of Camarillo was only four years old itself, so was it not recognized as part of the community either? Furthermore, the Conference had owned land in Camarillo for more years than the City had been incorporated, in anticipation of someday building a local Church. This argument did little more than irritate. The City fathers asserted that the law held, and our colporteurs would have to cease and desist.

Now we were really convinced that this was an infringement of our religious liberty. The government was meddling in the work of the Lord. As Adventists we knew we would be persecuted for standing for right, so this really didn't surprise us at all. Fight we must.

We reviewed the First Amendment and underlined the part that seemed to apply to us:

> *Congress shall make no law respecting an establishment of religion or prohibiting the free exercise thereof;* or abridging the freedom of speech, or of the press; or the right of the people peaceably to assemble, and to petition the Government for a redress of grievances.[3]

After receiving this news, the Conference officials issued their statement to the City Council threatening a test case against the City of Camarillo on the grounds of the First Amendment of the U. S. Constitution. If necessary, their statement claimed, they were prepared to push this issue all the way to the U. S. Supreme Court. We all believed that dereliction on our part to fight each battle as we faced it would eventually lead to the national Sunday law.

Not wishing to face this kind of litigation, the City fathers took a deep breath and issued our young salesmen special exemption licenses to work for the three months in the summer of 1968. Winning battles is not the same as winning wars and we were in a religious liberty war. The local daily newspaper had few hot stories to compare to this one and suddenly the Adventist Church became the subject of controversy throughout the paper. The publicity let the public know we had arrived in Camarillo, but I had never counted on this kind of coverage. I was beginning to regret the whole situation when I woke up to the next set of headlines in the *Camarillo Daily News*.

Elijah Muhammad's Nation of Islam, better known as the Black Muslims, suddenly appeared in Camarillo to receive their religious rights in wake of the Adventist victory. One can hardly begin to grasp the terror of this development among the population of this little non-black community.

Virtually untouched by the developing social chaos of the 1960s, Camarillo was suddenly confronted with a perceived militant racist group. Here was an organization that lived and operated in the ghetto, not an upscale community like Camarillo. It thrived where people were black, impoverished and discriminated against. At least that was the general assessment in our community. Didn't "these people" burn down half of Los Angeles two years before, even invading the white communities in the foothills? And now the Adventists had invited them to invade Camarillo. And this was the fear we heard talked about. This was the press coverage we were getting. Perception is truth, they say.

People find life hard when their status quo is disrupted. "Why don't they all just go get a job?" The stereotypical echo of evasion. This was a historic period of social

---

3. *U. S. Constitution,* First Amendment. Emphasis supplied.

awakening in America, and racial unrest was a significant part of the reframing—or correcting of past wrongs. Our community was not exempt of race-based fear, but Camarillo could be called a white community even though it was an upscale balance of white, Hispanic, and Asian, many of whom were professional. I saw little evidence that the community had confronted these issues before.

I doubt that our little City saw the Adventists as having anything to do with the completion of the Protestant Reformation, though that's how we viewed ourselves. Some saw us as inviting racial unrest and uprooting their settled way of life. Weren't America's all-consuming events related? This would develop into the era of the Manson murders (1969) and the attempt to start all-out race wars in America.

A pattern was developing—President Kennedy assassinated (1963), U. S. involvement in a Viet Nam civil war (1965), Malcolm Little (aka Malcolm X) assassinated (1965), Watts riots (1965), Martin Luther King assassinated (1968), nationwide rioting in the wake of the King assassination (1968), Robert F. Kennedy assassinated (1968), and now the Black Muslims were invading Camarillo because of the Adventists (1968). We were right up there with the big guys! This chronology didn't even include the war protesters, Jane Fonda, the Jesus people, the hippies, the Chicago democrat convention, the smoldering feminist and gay/lesbian rights movements. This was 1968.

The 1960s became a synonym for almost every kind of social revision imaginable. But much of it flew past us like a frisbee at a Church picnic in our safe little community. As Adventists we were concerned with the Sunday law being passed and we knew all these other events were just deterrents to keep our minds off the real issue: that the Pope was working to nullify the U. S. Constitution.

The final sign of the *Parousia* would be passage of a law in America that said anyone who did not honor Sunday as God's holy day would be executed. So, we were directly involved in the fulfillment of prophecy. Sister White had foretold all of this.

> Those who honor the Bible Sabbath will be denounced as enemies of law and order, as breaking down the moral restraints of society, causing anarchy and corruption, and calling down the judgments of God upon the earth. Their conscientious scruples will be pronounced obstinacy, stubbornness, and contempt of authority. They will be accused of disaffection toward the government.[4]

> The dignitaries of church and state will unite to bribe, persuade, or compel all classes to honor the Sunday. The lack of divine authority will be supplied by oppressive enactments. Political corruption is destroying love of justice and regard for truth; and even in free America, rulers and legislators, in order to secure public favor, will yield to the popular demand for a law enforcing Sunday observance.[5]

---

4. White, *The Great Controversy Between Christ and Satan*, 592.
5. Ibid.

Religious movements are rarely able to avoid a confrontation with the cultural forces of their times. Somehow, time is a potent fuel for driving these movements and a powerful motivator for winning converts. Our religious movement was very much imbedded in time. As with other sects and cults, Adventism thrived on the stress that time and end-time delay created.

The Lord had delayed his coming because Adventists hadn't done their work. Christ could have come right after 1844 had there been less bickering and more faithful living. Sister White had mentioned several dates before when Christ could have come had the Church been more active and faithful. From the messianic point of view of the Church, it stood to reason that Adventists were responsible for the delay of the Advent.

By now, we could add two world wars, the Korean war, the Viet Nam war, and all the events of the 1960s. If it was our fault that Christ had not return, then it was our fault that these events had occurred. This was the *weltanschauung* of Adventism. And so powerful was this view that the Adventist Church of the 1970s would turn away from an emphasis on the gospel to a renewed emphasis on end-time and the prophetic uniqueness of the movement. But doomsday messages bring no comfort. On the contrary, they can cause intolerable fear. They have always remained popular, however, because they can be used as explanatory devices to make sense of social unrest and revolution.

Now we were perceived to be at the root of the public unrest in Camarillo—and the presence of the Black Muslims created a fair amount of insecurity. None of us was sure how this had much to do with our being persecuted for the Sabbath, except that we were Sabbath keepers and we were being persecuted. However, correlation does not prove cause and effect.

In a denomination that searches for events to fulfill its notion of prophecy little is beyond speculation. This crisis was a foretaste of things to come. The crunch did not help our young men in their efforts to sell religious books and sign up people to take Bible studies. They were followed all over the city by the Black Muslims selling their books much the same as our colporteurs. Both groups were considered public nuisances. Rather than labeling this race or religion, the community voiced their disapproval of our disrupting their routines.

What started out as a community that simply didn't like people knocking on their doors, tramping through their front yards or appearing uninvited on their front porches was now beginning to function with medieval-like suspicion. Some of the active members of our Church were employed at City Hall and they felt the pressure, avoidance, and suspicion from fellow workers more keenly than the rest of us. The questions they were asked at the water cooler were at first inquiring, and then sarcastic and finally cynical. The City offices were not a happy workplace for our members. For several weeks they faced the question: "Why are Adventists threatening the City with Supreme Court action?"

The demographics of Camarillo showed a low level of ethnic diversification. Most of the non-whites were agricultural workers or professional people. The standard of living in this community was comfortable. The persecution I had brought on our members was the first major crisis in the new Church. From that point on, I sensed that some of our members harbored hard feelings behind a mask of pasty politeness, and that endured for the five years of my tenure. People who had regularly spent time with us on Friday nights no longer dropped by. That hurt.

Even worse was the fact that no tangible results came from the colporteur experience other than their own personal experiences. I had thought it was my problem back in 1961 when I went through such disillusionment about this method of sharing the faith, but now I suspected that only a small group of people have the gift required to be effective in book ministry. I began replaying my own difficult days in Merced. Seeing our boys struggle was like looking into a mirror for me.

In 1968 our Church taught essentially nothing about spiritual gifts except that our prophet had been the recipient of one of them. Hers was the only gift that mattered. The gift of evangelism was apparently a construct of words alone. Everyone was supposed to have that gift if they were just committed enough. All the other gifts listed in scripture were really treated as just one that everyone was supposed to have: the gift of total personal commitment. If you were committed enough, you could do nearly anything effectively about winning souls. I began to ponder how the Church could grow if the book ministry was as ineffective as my own, and these two young men's experience led me to believe.

We made it through the summer, but I regretted putting the new congregation through such a trying time. In my own exuberance, I had not anticipated generating such negative publicity by engaging in activities that were not necessary to our work of sharing the gospel. And that still didn't consider the effect it had on our two colporteurs and their view of ministry.

At this period, I was entertaining the notion that maybe we weren't really called primarily to preach the gospel—we were rather called to make Adventists. I never reconciled how this helped our status in the community but as a religious man I wrote it off as the devil's work to stop our attempts, to share no matter how feeble our efforts.

THE EXPERIENCE OF BIRTH

A great event on August 20, 1968, overshadowed all the negative outcomes of the colporteur incident, at least for our family. Annie and I had been married for five years. I had agreed to a truce at home and given up the idea of spontaneous intimacy. It was part of the negotiations to prove that I was mature enough to be a father. After the upset when I had considered separation, Annie made it clear to me that bringing children into the world was too serious an undertaking so soon after my questionable behavior. I therefore tolerated this and tried to prove my commitment to her.

My feeling of never reaching these standards was growing. She didn't originate these standards—these were the product of my whole religious addiction. They were characteristic of my creed and my professional life. Growing up, I vaguely remembered my father jokingly using a phrase often that I found intimidating. "Normal people don't act that way," he would sometimes say when he wanted to adjust my behavior. For some reason that phrase resonated negatively with me. I found it daunting. Dad was a powerful influence in my life, and I wanted him to be able to approve of everything I did. As a result, I found myself very susceptible to the guilt. And I couldn't deal with this; I could only react to it.

Dad's suggestion of abnormalcy, which he probably did not mean to make, set up the troubling prospect in me that I was not normal. I wanted so much to be normal. By accepting normal as an infinite goal, I failed to see how I was surrendering personal power to him and later to virtually everyone else who used such intimidation. The phenomenon invaded my marriage as well. It was a form of Adventist perfectionism—just in different terms. If you weren't perfect, could you ever say honestly that you were normal?

This surrender was translated into an ideal of religious experience. Surrendering that old self-will, that selfishness, that self-centeredness, that egocentricity (there was no end of terms for it) was the key to genuine religious experience. I really thought that all who claimed or sought the surrender of their will to God were as honest and sincere as I was.

Ironically, this kind of surrender may not be genuine commitment at all, but it is set forth as such in the life of the religion addict. It becomes a powerful tool in the hands of control freaks whose passion is to maintain the unquestioned authority of the organization and its orthodox doctrines. It has always been a driving force in the history of cults.

I was beginning to pay serious dues to this unspoken perfectionism from my spiritual resources as well as my self-respect. If I did not demonstrate proper spiritual surrender, this so-called commitment, I would be considered unspiritual and irreligious, as well as a bad husband. These thoughts were terrifying for a religious man.

Hoping to be considered normal I came to accept my wife's coldness as my problem as I scurried around like a chameleon to please her. But hers was an affection that could never be earned. I could only be a father if I was normal. And if I was not perceived as such, I would continually be called emotionally unstable as well. Dad had laid the seeds and I was allowing them to sprout.

I thought I was succeeding. I just did not know that I was expected to mask any feelings of inadequacy to survive. And so, my greatest success was achieved in receiving her "permission" to become a father. The whole dynamic was a strange mixture of control and personal coercion; and more cruelly—it was fueled by the spiritual. To be religious I was ready to do most anything within the realm of my faith.

Profile of a Religious Man

The most glorious event of my life was the birth of my firstborn, early one morning. I had never experienced such ecstasy and scarcely dared to believe I was deserving of such a blessing. In those days we were given no advance information before the delivery whether we would be getting a boy or a girl. When people asked, "What do you want—a boy or a girl?"—one usually responded with that hackneyed line: "We don't care, so long as the baby is healthy!"

The thought that this very statement effectively conditioned our minds to relegate any baby who might be born with developmental disabilities to something less than human was never acknowledged. Heaven forbid that such a catastrophe could invade our Donna Reed world. Of course, there was always Camarillo State Hospital where such a parental embarrassment could be dumped and forgotten. Or if a friend had a child with developmental disabilities our response would be, "Oh, I'm so sorry,"—ironic, to say the least for a Christian who serves a God who loves and cares for the whole dysfunctional human race.

We did not have to face this. Our baby was born normal, smart and healthy. Any prejudice toward children with disabilities never had to surface. It was immediately clear that we would have a rocket scientist in our family (or anything else she wished to pursue in life). She was bright, advanced, and clearly superior. Anyone who disagreed was surely naive and mistaken. She would remove all doubt to the contrary by one day graduating from medical school.

For some reason we had picked out several girls' names but no boys' names. Perhaps it was telepathy. She had a shock of red hair and a couple of bumps on the back of her head, which we called "horns" but the doctor assured us those would go away.

Even as I look at her baby pictures today, I would say that she was the most beautiful baby girl I had ever seen. Because our doctor was also an elder in the Camarillo Church I could stand in the doorway of the delivery room and watch as she was delivered, made her first cries in the world, and hustled off to the nursery for clean-up. I was also allowed to take pictures of the new arrival. This was unprecedented in those days when expectant fathers were kept behind glass or herded off to the father's room awaiting news of their new offspring.

When Adam first laid eyes on Eve he uttered the first lines of poetry the world had ever heard.

> [23] Then the man said,
> > "This at last is bone of my bones
> > > and flesh of my flesh;
> > she shall be called Woman,
> > > because she was taken out of Man." (Gen 2:23)

And I became a poet that day. No prose could describe the feelings of a father who is a religious man.

I am involved in the miracle of birth.

> I have been given the privilege
> > of participating in creation.
> This is the purpose of life after all.
> I pledge to make no mistakes.
> Even though God's creation went awry
> > and his people turned against him,
> > this will not happen to me.
> I will win her affection forever.
> I will fulfill her every need.
> I will bond with her and serve her
> > as a father is supposed to serve.
> I am a religious man.

I thought of the future. There would be years of fascination as I watched and guided her. And then there would be grandchildren (maybe four) and the continuation of the legacy. She would respect me, and I would love her. What a mistake I would have made if we had separated. The Lord was coming, and we would greet him with a babe in arms—surely time would not last long enough for her to grow up even though the reflection was pleasant.

These thoughts raced in my mind as I moved through the day and finally arrived at the Church. When I walked into Prayer Meeting, I took a piece of chalk, and wrote in big block letters on the blackboard, "JILL ROCHELLE."

The little Prayer Meeting group stood and applauded—they understood. Here was a bonus from God—a God who had created us in his image. I got to feel a little bit like God that day. It was a good feeling.

CHAPTER TWENTY-ONE

Understanding Organized Religion

"I do not feel obliged to believe that that same God who endowed us with sense, reason, and intellect has intended us to forego their use."
— GALILEO GALILEI

TORN BETWEEN CONGREGATION AND DENOMINATION

Rules of thumb are sometimes helpful though not always accurate. Near the end of my second year at Camarillo, the Conference committee nominated me for ordination. By my third year the pain of our confrontation with the City had eased, but I never felt that I had fully regained the trust I had once enjoyed with the members connected with City Hall. It had been an unfortunate experience that had impacted my standing in the congregation.

Gospel ordination was a milestone for the professional religious man. This step indicated recognition by peers and superiors. It also granted one the full authority of the ministerial office. In the Church venue, ordination functioned much like a license for a physician. It was the capstone on a minister's professional preparation, a rite of passage through which he could now apply much of what he had learned in his college and graduate education, as well as his internship. Ordination meant that now I was not only *qualified* to be a minister but *authorized* as well, approved to carry on all the ministerial tasks as an official representative of the denomination. For me, a religious man, ordination was not only the Church's approval; it represented God's smile as well.

Such power is delegated. In Church ministry, authority ultimately comes from God. But what form does God take? A religious man believes that this authority comes through God's representatives on earth. And I accepted what I was taught. In a cult or sect as well as in a denomination or Church these representatives are the appointed and elected officials. This was certainly true of Adventism. Once the leaders were elected, or appointed, we believed that God worked through them.

An important part of any organized religion is the acknowledgement that these officials speak for God and are led by God. This idea was set forth at virtually all convocations of the Church. In Adventism, authority is officially asserted through committee action. These committees are often appointed, though some are elected through quasi-democratic procedures. To speak against the committee was perceived as speaking against God and could result in the charge of insubordination, as I would one day learn painfully.

The ultimate punishment was being defrocked or even unordained, something I had never heard of until well into my ministry. God no longer recognized an unordained person as called to the ministry. The move to *unordain* a minister was made by the "First Minister of the Church," a doctrine introduced by Elder Neal Wilson, president of the General Conference during most of my tenure as an Adventist minister. By "First Minister" he was referring to himself and it was justified because of the forensic setting of the situation. But to some this sounded Papal. So far as I knew the term had never been used before some legal proceedings that called for clarification. At the front end of the spectrum, any minister who did not recognize the guidance of God in the decisions of executive committees could not expect to be ordained.

Anyone who lost the sanction of the denomination faced the bitter reality of having to reframe his religious and professional life. Professional religious men are usually tied to some religious, *viz.*, social organization. When ministers were caught stealing from the Church coffers, committing adultery (which, for Adventists, included homosexuality), or falling out of the faith (serious theological aberrations that somehow were perceived as threatening the existence, rationale, or fundamental reason for the organization), discipline (punishment) usually followed. How could one who was committed to this sacred work ever fall away from the faith?

What was of greatest concern for me was the academic aspect of the faith. I had seen academic shakeups in the Church—people who had gone on for higher education outside of Adventist institutions and had lost their faith. As a result, they were usually relieved of their positions. Many left the Church completely. Others hunkered down and survived by aligning themselves with the political winds of the day sweeping through the Church. Some started anti-Adventist or ex-Adventist organizations or new sects. A few joined other Churches. Still others began independent ministries. This seemed to be more prevalent in North America where higher education was encouraged for teachers and pastors.

We had often been warned of the dangers of falsehood, so my line of defense was to be wary of advanced studies, especially in the field of theology. Yet despite this danger I never lost my interest in seeking the most advanced education that opportunity might offer. My faith was intact; falling away could never happen to me. Furthermore, I figured I was relatively safe in the Adventist graduate school system.

Nevertheless, I occasionally saw a colleague drop away. One classmate who lived with his family in our Garland Apartments complex and who was also sponsored by the Southern California Conference dropped out of the ministry during his internship. He claimed that he would seek other work because, he said, "Nobody cared." That was a conundrum to me. What could he mean? He obviously had lost his way. We had all thought he was called to the ministry—now this. So sad.

This promising young minister went back to law school seeking a different professional path in life. Since faithfulness was a function of commitment, I could only conclude that was where his problem lay. One could only stay committed through hard work and one's behavior, known as good works. I determined that I would work hard to stay committed.

If I ever had the opportunity to go to graduate school, I would not let it undermine or circumscribe my faith. I would never let my guard down. My convictions would remain strong. Nothing would be allowed to sidetrack me from my task. This determination was serious and strong. I was a religious man and I sought to live out my religion in all sincerity. Nonetheless, making no real distinction between my family and my profession was a mistake destined to affect both. Camarillo would be my real time, real life testing ground.

At the Camarillo Ministerial Association, I made friends with another Scandinavian, the pastor of another local Church in town. We had several talks about theology and Church politics. One day, after a conversation together, he uttered some troubling words. "Ed," he said, "you seem ripe for defection." His words sank in slowly. I tried not to show it, but I was shocked that anything I had said could have been interpreted that way. I was just being honest. But like Mary, the mother of Jesus, I pondered those words in my heart.

What had I said? I had just been talking shop. Yet such honest, open talk could backfire. Does a pastor not dare "talk shop?" Apparently, this could sound disloyal. I would learn this the hard way—that my understanding of loyalty was not the understanding that those in power shared.

In Adventism, working as a team meant obeying the leadership. This included abiding by a hierarchy principle that was both Catholic and Protestant: the distinction between leaders and workers was never to be violated. If a worker was elevated to a leadership position through some committee action I observed that he seldom acted like a worker again. Workers did not step over the line without eventually suffering consequences.

As a minister I never missed a workers' meeting usually held by the leadership every other month at Conference headquarters. These meetings were the equivalent of sales meetings for business firms. At these meetings leadership shared what was expected of the workers. Leaders and workers were all ministers. Teachers were never called workers unless they were ordained. These distinctions were reinforced whenever a leader gave a speech. The term leadership thus became a substantive for the collective authority of elected officials. Many an exhortation included the appeal to the wishes of leadership, as though leadership was a person.

THE EFFECT AND MEANING OF ORDINATION

I never anticipated the letdown my ordination would bring. Surprisingly, I found myself troubled by the whole process. Even the ordination sermon presented on that warm September Sabbath afternoon at the old Lynwood camp meeting auditorium gave me pause for reflection. The speaker, a director of the Ellen G. White Estate in Washington, D.C., asserted that when we were ordained, we became different. From the content of his message, I took him to mean superior. The expectations were higher. Our importance was elevated. This echoed the instructions of a member of my ordination committee, who had hugged me after our examination meeting to whisper in my ear, "You are a different man now." He meant, "You are now like us!"

As a leader was to a worker, so a clergyman was to a layman. We were to understand the importance of our position in the hierarchical structure of our organization. Yet I didn't feel any different. I tried to be puzzled as to what he meant though I feared I understood perfectly what he had implied. I was a young religious man who cared as much about my own spiritual welfare as I did about others. How did that make me different? But this concept would follow me throughout my ministry. Sometimes I would be treated differently than other men. I was seen to be privileged—speaking for God, exemplifying his way of life. I was also to be held to a "higher standard"—a different standard. I was no longer allowed to do some things a layman could do.

A spotlight was permanently trained on the ordained, religious man. And that would carry different expectations as well—the price of privilege. For example, I was always to act a certain way—as though everyone was watching. Judging from my ministerial models I concluded that showing too much humanity was to be avoided.

I was to be a role model. I found that to be an intolerable responsibility—a pressure I had a hard time dealing with. Because I never bought into it completely, I may therefore have failed some people who needed their pastor to be an icon. Most ministers seemed to love this notoriety. I was sure I hated it. I saw this as arrogance. Such status was a double-edged sword. Not only did we invite criticism if we were perceived to be too far out of the mainstream, but in some cases our endorsement also carried weight by giving people an excuse or permission—to eat, to attend, to wear, to speak, to think.

I recalled an experience my mother-in-law had shared with me about when she and her family had traveled with Elder Andreasen through the eastern United States some years before. When they came to New York City, Elder Andreasen said to the family, "You must see Radio City Music Hall."

He meant they should go to the show there. But this would be considered questionable amusement for an Adventist, especially if a movie was playing there. So, when it came to buying tickets, he declined to purchase one for himself. He was a minister and could not compromise his credibility by attending such a place. Someone might see him and misunderstand. But it would be okay for her family to attend because they were not in the ministry. So, while they enjoyed the show Elder Andreasen waited outside. For him as a minister it was a question of example.

For this family, attendance at Radio City was given a seal of approval, if you weren't a minister. When Annie and I visited New York several years later, Annie insisted that we attend a show at Radio City Music Hall though neither of us would ever have thought of attending a common cinema. Interestingly, at the time we visited New York, Radio City was showing a current Hollywood movie. But this place was okay because Elder Andreasen had approved it. Without that sanction, neither of us would have attended the show.

We saw *The Yellow Rolls Royce* starring Shirley MacLaine. The feeling of attending a movie at a movie theater with the approval of the SDA clergy was an incredible experience. No guilt. I didn't know if "the angels waited outside for us." For Adventists, Cinerama shared the same endorsement.

PROGRESSIVE BEHAVIOR

For nearly ten years I had looked forward to my ordination day. I had finished college, colporteured, gotten married, finished two master's degrees, completed a valuable internship under two ministers and was a senior minister of a Church. All of this was moving toward that supreme goal. Only a man could achieve gospel ordination in the Adventist Church. No woman would ever officially reach this elevated status. Every effort to open this avenue of power to women was stifled by leadership, time and again. It was a man's Church. God had said so, through leadership.

Without ordination no one moved up on the authority ladder. The Church was safe from any woman ever reaching such positions as Local, Union or General Conference president, all of which required ordination and all of which would give major decision-making authority to them. Even after a major lawsuit (which the denomination lost after ten years of court battles, and which had resulted in more equitable salaries for women), females would be denied these positions of authority on allegedly biblical grounds.

This issue would come to the forefront at the 1995 General Conference in Utrecht, Netherlands, and there it would be stopped once and for all, mainly through the influence of third world representatives whose culture kept women "in their place." The decision was made to continue the existing discrimination against women. This was God's will, the Church leadership said.

Women were not to hold the privileged position of authority that came from having access to what was called gospel ordination. One of the most common arguments was that of the slippery slope—the "what-next argument." Those using this tactic held up placards and passed out literature at the Utrecht meetings that read: "First Women, Next Homosexuals!" Signs and literature to this affect were plastered around the area where the convocation was being held. Booths set up on the grounds displayed literature arguing against women's ordained leadership in the Church.

Inside the hall God spoke from the floor in response to presentations given from the platform. Many complained that the argument for, presented to the delegates in session in the form of a tired, dull lecture by a retired Seminary professor, could not compete with the argument against, presented through a sophisticated and entertaining Power Point production, using snappy, high definition visuals in brilliant colors on the giant screen on the stage of the mammoth auditorium. Through this presentation God had spoken to Adventists and told them not to allow women into the sacred status of gospel ordination. The use of modern technology was a stroke of genius.

Before the next quinquennial session there would be such stiff resistance to the notion of women's ordination that the new world president would simply announce that the issue was dead and that it would not be allowed on any further agenda for discussion. And so, the voice of God had once more spoken, this time through the Norwegian GC president now at the ship's helm—through the First Minister of the Church. No further developments have occurred though the arguing goes on.[1]

In 1969, however, no one even intimated that women could be ordained, so this was no issue then. But I was a religious man. I had been handed this opportunity. I had been granted an anatomical structure that allowed me to be authorized. Yet much to my amazement, I found that I also had to deal with a political hurdle I could scarcely have foreseen.

For two hours my ordination committee quizzed me about my feelings, as an Adventist minister, about the Church as an organization. In everyday language, that meant Church politics. I was not asked to explain any theological position or whether I had any problems with Adventist orthodoxy. No one on the committee questioned my theology. Obviously, I was perceived to be sound on those matters. It was my politics they wanted to know about. As it was, I had no politics—I was a religious man.

> What happens when a pastor disagrees with the Conference president?
> What does it mean to be loyal to the brethren?
> What is your position on the authority of the Conference committee?

These were the unexpected types of questions they hurled at me. Annie grabbed my hand as she felt my body tensing. At the same time, she interrupted and asked for clarification on a question. She knew my frustration was showing and that discussion would buy time and calm me down. She knew that I believed in the importance of individual responsibility and loyalty to policies that were harmonious with the

---

1. For the present writer's position on this subject of women's ordination see the chapter, Zackrison, "Inclusive Redemption," in Habada and Brillhart (eds.), *The Welcome Table: Setting a Place for Ordained Women*, 155–178.

teachings of the gospel. But when the inquiries continued to follow a political line of questioning, I began to feel I was not among friends. The room suddenly had a strange eeriness to it.

The reason these handpicked men were following this line of inquiry seemed clear to me. I had interned under Elder Rea—an appointment, I reminded myself, made by the Conference committee. But I was also falsely perceived as having been part of the alleged coup that had attempted to unseat Elder Retzer at the last Conference constituency meeting. In addition, all the allegations of my original pastoral mentor that I had been disloyal to him were coming back, swarming around my head.

This additional element made things worse. Elder Rea was considered a gadfly—an unpredictable troublemaker. *Why?* As a member of the Conference committee he kept asking for rationale from the administration when they presented their positions. He was continually asking what Sister White wrote on logistical issues. And he often inquired why her instructions were not being followed. I had been his intern—it was guilt by association.

These sometimes-irreverent questions were posed by a worker to leaders. Elder Rea was a worker not a leader. Questioning policy could be evidence of disloyalty. However, he believed loyalty meant a mutual acceptance of the faith, and that Sister White was the faith. Elder Rea always did his homework and quoted the prophet, asking why decisions made by the Committee too often failed to take her counsels seriously. This irritated leadership, and now my examiners would try to discover whether I was loyal to them by their definition or possessed the same perceived rebellious streak as my mentor. What affect had Elder Rea had on me?

This would all play out in many challenging ways in the future and I would learn that being a religious man was never enough for leadership. I had to be a loyal man, a company man, a team member and a man who demonstrated his love of God by supporting whatever came out of the committees of the organization. These were God's decisions not the directives of a group of ordinary men. Organized religion had many secrets that I knew little about. I had no real appreciation at that time of the depth of my religious addiction or how hard it would be to break free of it.

THE SOUTHERN CALIFORNIA CONSTITUENCY MEETING

While my internship under Elder Rea was probably the reason for most of this interrogation, I knew that another factor also may have contributed to it. The Southern California Conference constituency meeting of 1969 was held in the Vallejo Drive SDA Church in Glendale, three months before my ordination examination.

The Camarillo Church, now almost two years old, was to be officially voted into the sisterhood of Churches at that meeting. I would make the speech to the gathering that would place Camarillo in nomination. In addition to this, we hoped to get new representation for the Churches in Ventura County on the Conference committee.

These were my foremost concerns as I readied myself and our Camarillo delegates to attend—oblivious to what that day was to hold.

I met with our three delegates to explain how the procedure worked. "Never in all my years as a Church member," one of our representatives told me, "has a pastor ever sat us down and explained these procedures. I always thought that God was simply leading out as we prayed." I didn't share with him that up until the weekend before our meeting, I had little idea myself about how the elections worked. Until then, these things were shrouded in obscure policies.

I had gone to my father-in-law for help. "Was there some way to get new representation on the Conference committee?" He was happy to let me know what The White had been doing for years to get their representatives into important positions. It simply involved a series of political moves that could be implemented by those who knew what they were doing whether they were praying about it or not. For me, what he shared was a behind-the-scenes look at what was happening on stage once the curtain opened. He told me that all one hundred congregations of the Southern California Conference would have representatives present at the constituency meeting proportionate to the size of their congregations.

In separate conversations, both he and Elder Rea gave me the same instructions: First, send your most able communicator to the "big committee." That committee would be composed of one representative from each of the one hundred congregations. Then, when the big committee breaks up into groups (from districts or counties) to caucus, your communicator has the task of persuading his caucus to put your choice on the nominating committee. If he is truly a great communicator he should have no problem doing this.

Finally, the question arose as to who the best person on the nominating committee would be. Elder Rea explained that they might ask whether at the last constituency meeting a minister or a layman represented our group. If it had been a minister then they would probably ask for a layman this time, or vice versa. So, we should be ready for that possibility.

We sent our professional politician active in City politics in Camarillo and a smooth, polished persuader with a charismatic persona. When the counties caucused, our representatives were told that a layman had been on the nominating committee previously, so they suggested a minister be put on the committee this time. Both my advisors had been spot-on as to what would take place.

Our representative put my name into nomination, campaigned briefly and won. Hence, I was appointed to this temporary but important committee. Now my task would be to nominate Dr. Frank Chung to the Conference committee when the nominations opened. That was the only task I had to carry out that day on the nominating committee.

Process usually functions well if you know what the policies and procedures are. This was my first experience in watching God work in the Adventist process. But because of my religious background I was surprised and feeling a bit guilty. This was just a simple procedure in Church politics that I had hitherto left up to God, not realizing that not all agreed on how God worked. Although there were no campaign speeches, at least not from the pulpit or the floor, this was really a political convention with one major exception: the outcome was to be considered the result of God's direct intervention. This was the Adventist approach to authority. The meeting was a worship session, which included prayer and the singing of a hymn.

The Adventist administrative system claimed to be a modified congregational form of Church government. The congregational aspect consisted mostly in generating a revenue stream for the Church hierarchy. Ultimately, all power was placed in a central Church system where most major decisions, even those concerning the local congregation, were made by a majority of clergy salaried by the organization.

Some criticized this approach as involving conflict of interest. We who identified with the Church dismissed these critics as uncommitted or ignorant of how God worked through his people. Many of us never saw those who were turning the wheels and gears of power behind the curtains of our ecclesiastical Oz. Those who questioned the policy decisions of the clerical hierarchy could expect to be accused of disloyalty.

In the early 1960s, lay representation at the various administrative levels was sparse. Adventism had established a hierarchical form of government, with some similarities to that of the Catholic Church, a fact that was shrouded using different terminology. The clergy had most of the votes, and a few laypersons (who were approved by the clergy in power) largely token representatives.

Administrators disputed this analysis because they held that God was guiding all their decisions. Their description of God's regard for the Adventist Church bordered on viewing the church as a theocracy, though again this term would never be used to describe their thoughts. But an examination of how the denomination was run could lead one to that conclusion. And for many this was clearly one mindset.

The Adventist view that God worked through his Church, rather than individuals, was set forth by our prophet in a statement that was widely quoted. She had written:

> I have been shown that no man's judgment should be surrendered to the judgment of any one man. But when the judgment of the General Conference, which is *the highest authority that God has upon the earth,* is exercised, private independence and private judgment must not be maintained, but be surrendered.... If you should let the power in the church, the voice and judgment of the General Conference, stand in the place you have given my husband, there could then be no fault found with your position. But you greatly err in giving to one man's mind and judgment that authority and influence which *God has invested in His church in the judgment and voice of the General Conference.*[2]

---

2. White, *Testimonies for the Church*, 3:492–493. Emphases supplied.

While this statement referred to the General Conference in session, the thought gradually gained momentum that this might also refer to Local and Union Conference decisions as well. Some ministers gave lip service to individual creativity, but when it came to face the bureaucracy they usually gave in to committee actions or left the denomination. And there was usually that overriding concept of God's leadership mediated through the organization. Furthermore, an aura slowly gathered around the statement turning it into almost an Adventist version of the ex-cathedra (infallibility) doctrine in Roman Catholicism.

Now I was learning the way God worked in this denomination. Perhaps God had inspired the policies. At any rate, anyone could follow those policies and get some things changed. Knowing the policies was the key. But I had never seen a working policy for the Church and was not sure it was even available for study. My advisors had taught me how to use the policies, something that had escaped me through my whole theological education; and we were on our way to changing the personnel on the Conference committee. To me it all seemed like plotting.

My father-in-law had asked rhetorically, "Do you think it just happens that The White usually has a member on the Conference committee?" Initially this question troubled me. I saw this as political manipulation, something that was not supposed to happen in the Church, according to my theological perception. I had never looked at the Church as anything but God's instrument on earth, and the thought that politics could determine policy decisions was new and probably objectionable to me. A cynic would have called me brainwashed or under a form of mind control. But there was no room for cynicism in my psyche—just innocence or naïveté.

A religious man relied on the intervention of God. He did not confuse divine intervention with human manipulation. There simply was no room for politics in a religious organization. Consequently, when we accomplished our goal so easily, we could only conclude it was God's will and not politics. All the rules I had learned relative to competition and rivalry also applied to politics. There had to be a different word for it all—providence came to mind.

The nominating committee was secluded for its work immediately after lunch. Elder Neal Wilson, president of the North American Division, gave us instructions. He reiterated that God was leading and that there was no place for politics in the Church. I thought deeply about what he was saying because I was there to politic for change by suggesting a new Church representative on the Conference committee. Yet I surmised that this could not be politics because I had been duly appointed to carry out the task.

POLITICS IN ACTION

I had not thought much about anything except getting a new representative. It struck me now that we were there to nominate the whole slate of officers as well—executives, departmental people, as well as Conference committee members. I had been focused on the primary task that this had slipped from my thinking. When directions were finished, we looked at the slate of officers we were to fill with nominees to be presented to the corporate body in session. But before we could even get started, we faced an unexpected twist. People began lining up outside the room insisting on being heard before any nomination decisions were made.

Speech after speech followed, all on the same subject: The current Conference president should not be re-nominated to his position. For the next couple of hours, we sat listening to people from all over the Conference making speeches supporting this main argument. I was caught off guard. Our job was bigger than I had thought. Was this a conspiracy?

I was impatient. I knew nothing about any alleged incompetence of the president. I dismissed the speeches one by one. But as the minutes ticked by it became clear that people from diverse groups in the Southern California Conference area were passionate about the problems they perceived to be Conference-wide. This was all new to me.

All I could hear was their insistence on their right to express their concerns. I could discern no central conspiracy. These people didn't even seem to know each other. I was not the only unordained minister on this nominating committee. Larry, my former colleague from internship, was also there, sitting on the other side of the room. He was now pastor of his own congregation. I wondered how he got on this committee. Perhaps he knew how the system worked too. If so, where had he learned it? Or maybe God put him on the committee.

Throughout the proceedings we occasionally exchanged glances as we began to see the political stuff developing. I didn't immediately grasp the unenviable predicament he and I were in as unordained pastors. Was this a professional suicide trip?

Buying into Elder Wilson's assurance that no politics were involved here I was still thinking this was God at work. But I also experienced a sense of exhilaration growing out of the realization that we were being taken seriously in our comments on this committee. There was urgency here. This was real time. What we said was perhaps going to be influential. This was God's work, and we were his decision-making instruments. Perhaps we were speaking for him. I listened intently to the evidence being presented. If this was a conspiracy, it clearly involved all ethnic groups, all geographical areas of the Conference, and both genders.

When the chair finally took a straw vote, it was clear that if the vote were taken at that point, the committee would not re-nominate this sitting president. The chair left the room to talk with the president. When he returned, he shared the news with us that the president would prefer to face a floor fight rather than accept the results of this nominating committee. He asserted that this committee was made up of his enemies. But all we had done was to listen to the long line of people seeking to be heard.

I began to realize the gravity of the situation. I knew I wasn't his enemy. I knew I was there representing my constituent Churches. I only knew a couple of people on the committee and I had never seen them as enemies of the president. The stubbornness of the sitting president extended our deliberation by more time. The delay spread suspicion among the delegates on the floor that the members of the nominating committee were trying to undermine the executive leadership of the Conference. Word filtered back into the committee. I couldn't believe what I was hearing. Nothing could have been further from the truth. We were just fulfilling our task of listening to laity.

Word reached us that pity for the president was spreading across the floor as delegates waited impatiently. The tension grew heavy. Things became emotional. Yet our committee continued to listen to testimony, and to cast preliminary ballots. As the complaints continued with increasing credibility the committee became closer to making a decision. Rather than accept any of the straw votes, the chair just kept taking more votes. But every vote seemed to get more embarrassing. It seemed logical that he would be there to support the president of the Conference.

Then in an instant the chair switched his tactic. He encouraged the committee to stand its ground and maintain its decision not to re-nominate this president. "If this is your decision," he said, "then in the interest of God's work you should stay with that decision." I didn't realize until a long time later that I had just witnessed the supreme political behavior of Elder Wilson. But at the time I was confused. He knew that the time was ripe for the committee to be rejected and the floor to speak. Masterfully done some would say.

Now my confusion was complete. I had never seen anything like this in the Church—here was another rite of passage, a loss of innocence for me, a shattering of my view of the Church as a China doll. I don't know what I had expected—a bolt of lightning, a quiet voice from heaven, a blazing finger writing on the wall, a confound conviction? The first three phenomena were absent but the fourth one was certainly playing out. I was intrigued by what was happening, but my theological education was not helping me much.

After several secret ballots, more speeches, and more minutes of testimony and discussion the committee cast a final majority vote. And it sent to the floor the name of a current president from another Conference as its choice. The battle now shifted to the representatives at large. Loud voices for the president began speaking up from various quarters of the auditorium. The whole meeting turned into a political convention. Some of the loudest speakers and most passionate supporters of the president surprised me—they were people who had not appeared particularly supportive of him in the private groups that clustered around at Minister's Chorus rehearsals and workers' meetings. Had they changed their minds? Or could they see that their support of the president was germane to their careers?

As the battle heated up on the floor, the president sat on the platform listening to it all. He looked like a ghost—I tried to imagine what was going through his mind. I could not understand why he wanted to hear all this. On the other hand, perhaps he was having as much trouble believing what was happening as I was. The longer the protests continued, the more out of hand the meeting got until finally one minister got up and made a tear-filled speech that God had not guided this nominating committee, and that it was now up to the large body of representatives to overrule this nomination. He asserted that it was time to reelect this president by acclamation for that was God's will.

With shouts of "Amen," "Hallelujah" and catcalls decrying the evil nature of the nominating committee members, emotion swept through the crowd and the delegates proclaimed the president by sweeping acclamation for another two years. This was apparently what Elder Wilson, the master politician, knew was coming. But my head was swirling. I was suffering from severe culture shock.

I never again saw organized religion in the same light after that day. I had been elected to the nominating committee without harboring any negative bias toward the president—in fact, our personal history went back several years, and it had been a good history. Now I had watched influential ministers make emotional speeches for all to hear in his presence. I had watched as due process was overthrown. It was like watching the backroom dealings of a Tammany Hall political machine. Only the cigars and Jack Daniels were missing. That day I lost my innocence as far as the Church organization was concerned.

Peers and colleagues, fellow workers, have told me I was simply green and naïve; that this was common and politics reigns in all organized religion. But when I heard them get up in front of Church gatherings talking about tithing and Church support I heard the same beliefs that I held—that the Church was guided by God and there were no politics. Did they believe that laymen couldn't handle the truth they shared with me? I fought more than ever the temptation to view all of this as a deception. It was emotionally upsetting. And then it hit me: What would this do to my ordination chances? I was a member of a committee perceived to have conspired to bring down a sitting Conference president. And he had won a battle I didn't even know would be fought.

The dissonance was painful: ordination was good, politics were evil. Was I wrong on both counts? Certainly, I was wrong in thinking that the Church as an organization was sincere in its condemnation of political intrigue. If it was carried out by elected officials, leaders did not have an issue with it. But this was an insight that only gradually dawned on me as I gained more experience.

THE RELIGIOUS IDEOLOGUE CHALLENGED

I hardly slept that night. So much of my conservative religious mindset had been shaken. I was not the only one who had been shaken by what had happened, but mostly others dealt with these unpleasant insights in ways that differed from mine. Some would tell me again that I was naïve—that they knew all along that denominations were a political entity at the organizational level.

Monday morning quarterbacking was easy. Doing your duty in the heat of the battle was something else. Yet these same worldly-wise people would use the line over and over that there must be no politics in this organization—that God was leading his Church and he hated politics. I was beginning to reframe what God's leading meant. God apparently led some more than others and those happened to be the ones in power now.

When the committee finally reconvened after the floor fight was over it moved swiftly through the rest of the slate of personnel. The president was not invited in to chair the rest of the committee's business, which I was told would have been done ordinarily. As a result, he had no voice in choosing any members of the Conference committee that he would have to work with over the next two years. Whether this was his choice, or the decision of Elder Wilson was never made clear. At first, I thought this curious but then I realized the implications of the previous several hours of deliberation. Whoever made the decision, the president did not have a voice in choosing a cabinet.

Within minutes we got to the formulation of the Conference committee. This was my moment—why I had been appointed to this committee in the first place. The chair asked simply, "Who does the Ventura County district want to represent it on the committee?" I answered, "Dr. Frank Chung." It was seconded and voted unanimously without discussion. As far as I knew I was the only person on the committee who even knew Dr. Chung. By this time, the issue I had come to speak to seemed so immeasurably small that it got virtually no attention at all.

My mind was reeling, trying to adjust my religious outlook. Why did I live in an ethereal, almost make-believe world? What had my Seminary education done to prepare me for any of this? Why had I been so intent on discarding the instructions regarding church politics when Elder Rea had tried to explain them to me from his experience?

I remembered the admonitions of Seminary professors who had told us to be honest on our Conference reports and to be cautious, for we would meet small men who had climbed into high places. Now, like time bombs, these thoughts were going off in my head. But it still took some adjustment to deal with it. From now on, this was something I had to keep in mind. *Authorization* vs. *qualification*: How did all this relate to the mission I had bought into back there in that fall Week of Prayer at Auburn Academy in 1958?

When I got home that night the phone was ringing. The voice on the line was a member of the new Conference committee we had just elected. He spoke empathetically: "I'm sure you may be worried about your ordination. Don't be! Any attempt to hold up your ordination will be seen by the Conference committee as unwarranted revenge. The president does not have a particularly friendly committee to work with." The voice hung up. The conversation did not help me sleep that night. I had been traumatized by organized religion.

CRITICAL THINKING IS SOMETIMES PAINFUL

Some facts are painful to the religious ideologue. To move out of the groove that has been conscientiously chiseled for years is not easy. Probably it takes a crisis, or crises, to shake one out of an established mind-set and adopt a more accurate viewpoint of reality. Thoughts that have formed through many years of family associations and close-knit Church experiences are not easily reframed. These are thoughts that have been shaped within the protective custody of the Church and have created one's dominant outlook on life. In some respects, new converts may have an advantage here.

I had never questioned seriously the notion of the imminence of the Black Cloud. I believed it would be soon. Nor did I question it after this experience. My mission was to bring the message of imminence to an unsuspecting world. Though these political aspects were new elements to reckon with, they did not interfere with my belief structure since I did not allow these new facts on hold to encroach on my theological certainties.

Within the week, I heard the rumors that two unordained men on the committee had been either part of a coup or behind it. The word reached me that the president was hurt that I had turned against him. He had just taken me to lunch the week before the meeting. His son called me and expressed surprise that I would stab his father in the back. The trauma was just beginning. I went into a state of denial. I refused to believe that anyone could accept such foolish talk.

CHAPTER TWENTY-TWO

A Search for Meaningful Ministry

"How can I possibly serve another person in unfeigned humility if I seriously regard his sinfulness as worse than my own?"

—Dietrich Bonhoeffer

FEELING THE NEED FOR A CLEARER PURPOSE

THERE WAS PLENTY OF work to be done in Camarillo. I turned my attention from the confusing politics of organized religion to the personal aspects of calling. Once more I focused seriously on the need to formulate, for myself, a carefully thought through, workable philosophy of ministry of my own.

I had thought about this a lot. But up until now I'd mainly imitated approaches I had learned from those I admired—favorite teachers and trusted pastors. They had been my role models, though mostly from a distance. Like a singing artist who performs a song from the 1950s, getting people to take him seriously requires him to bring something special to his performance, namely, giving the song his own original flare.

Now I needed to concentrate on why I was here and what I was supposed to do about it. I had been taught to think. Now was my chance to do it. Do what? Think! I didn't perceive at the time how risky thinking could be. Thinking people evaluate things. Evaluation raises questions and small people (the term our professors had used to describe people with questionable qualifications who sometimes worked themselves into authoritative positions) do not generally like questions they have not formulated—questions that probe, questions that they interpret as threatening their judgment or power (authority).

Even though all of us were warned about such people I still had a hard time believing there were these kinds in Church leadership.

THE BASIS OF PASTORAL SUCCESS

A young minister can train and study in college and Seminary but much of what he learns is seldom organized into a cohesive, practical base from which to launch meaningful ministry. His education may have little to do with the reality of the context in which he is working. He has the option of being creative or running programs that are given to him at the workers' meetings held regularly by the Conference administration. He can become program-oriented; indeed, he can become programmed.

My pastoral mentor had emphasized repeatedly that so far as the Conference leaders were concerned the areas they considered crucial were the tithe, the ingathering, and the baptisms, in that order. This conclusion had come from his years of observation while serving on executive committees and as a pastor. He claimed that when a pastor's success was discussed on those committees it was around tithe, ingathering, and baptism. This made sense to me—these were realms directly affecting the local organization financially and represented success to leadership—thus their intense focus on money first.

I was to keep my totals up in those three areas, which would determine if I was being a success in organized religion. If my congregation's tithe dropped I would stand a good chance of being transferred or demoted. If my Ingathering goal was not reached, I was in trouble for Ingathering was a considerable amount used for the financing of the Church's educational and missionary work. Baptisms represented new members and indicated that I was working.

He emphasized that I should not argue about policies. In my position I could not change policies. And nobody told me I had to *like* every policy. I must *follow* policies. And he drilled into my brain the thought that there are three areas in business and politics, perhaps in all of life: principles, policies and values.

As pastors most of our discussions were centered in values—"I think this . . ." "I think that . . ."—these were tip-off preludes that a value assertion was forthcoming. "I like classical music . . ." "I hate rock music." All value statements. In the pastorate, we would face value statements constantly. People had their own opinions about what reality was, and most of these, especially coming from people not used to critical thinking, were largely statements of opinion, i.e., values.

Policies, on the other hand, were formal ways in which organized businesses (or Church entities) did things. These were rules and laws made by people in positions of authority: Congress, courts, boards, executive committees. A smart man would accept that this meant simply—here are policies and you are not going to change these—certainly not at the level of an intern.

You may not like Ingathering, don't gripe or complain about it—you don't have to *like* it—just *get* it! This is not to say that policies can never be changed, but the change will have to come from people authorized by the organization to make those changes.

Finally, principles were the eternal laws of the moral universe. For the religious man these principles were from God, and there were some things one did simply because it was right to do them.

There may even be times when policies conflicted with principles. An example of this was Martin Luther King, Jr. who conscientiously broke laws (policies) that conflicted with eternal laws or higher principles—hence his justification of civil disobedience under some circumstances. I began to see how similar organized religion and the business world were with respect to the importance of the bottom line. The major portion of the Conference budget came from the tithe funds (all of which were collected in the local congregations but remitted exclusively to the Conference). In most congregations the tithe was the lion's share of the offerings collected each week.

Church policy was that once the congregation had given its tithe, it must then concentrate on paying its own bills. One thing was clear—the tithe was the obligation of all Church members, local expense offerings were free-will, though strongly encouraged. The tithe went to the Conference, which paid the ministerial personnel—the local Church did not pay their pastor directly.

The money raised through Ingathering (the yearly world-wide denominational charity drive) was also sent to the Conference. If a local congregation raised more than its goal (set by the Conference), a small percentage was rebated to it. We generally understood that allegedly one-third of the annual world budget was taken from the Ingathering funds. Meeting this goal was a significant factor in any minister's success. In most North American Conferences, the Ingathering goal was set at twenty-five dollars per member per year, which in 1966 appeared steep. This money was raised largely from the public through business solicitation and door-to-door visitation.

Only one congregation in our local Conference had openly challenged the method of raising the Ingathering funds from the public, claiming that most of the money raised in their city for the missions did not go to missions (a term that implied "foreign"). Rather it stayed in California to finance Adventist parochial schools, which did not suggest anything foreign.

It was standard among denominational ministers to complain or joke about Ingathering. One prominent minister had told us in workers' meeting that when he gets to heaven he will look up Jasper Wayne (1850–1920) and punch him in the nose![1] This was just shop talk, not something to be repeated to the laity. Furthermore, such jocular comments were only meant to ease some of the pressure ministers felt to raise this money each year. Ministers in general did not like raising money. They wanted to spend their time preaching the gospel.[2]

---

1. Jasper Wayne was the early Adventist who put together the "harvest ingathering program" in the Church in 1903. Schwarz, *Light Bearers to the Remnant*, 346ff.

2. When the leaders of this questioning congregation called for open discussion about fund-raising from the public, they became tagged as a rogue group. In the denomination such a reputation is virtually impossible to erase. Eventually these same congregational leaders examined the tithe structure as well, suggesting that the denominational approach to the tithe may not be as scriptural as leadership

These probing questions grew and eventually spread to other aspects of Church government until the Conference committee, whose task it was to weed out dissenters, dissolved and reorganized the congregation with only those deemed faithful.[3]

EXAMINING THE REALITIES OF THE PROFESSIONAL MINISTRY

My mentor had been right. The Ingathering was important. Questioning it not only hit at the heart of the denomination's authority structure, it implied that the very methodology used by leadership should be open to examination by the laity, i.e., the shareholders. But the reality was that any examination or criticism was perceived as a threat by the administration since the money constituted a major source of yearly income.

Church members were encouraged to raise the money, for religious reasons—biblical admonitions, love for God. God, gold, or glory—those are the basic motivations for any personal action in this world, my mentor had instructed. And it is true in the Church as well. My suspicions grew that those three Gs were not as clearly separated as I had always assumed. I realized that this must be factored into my understanding of meaningful ministry.

The tithe was defined in various ways, as one-tenth of a member's possessions,[4] one-tenth of a believer's income,[5] or one-tenth of a person's increase.[6] The tithe was to be calculated on the basis of the amount received or earned.[7] Once it was marked as such on the offering envelope and put into the Sabbath morning collection plate, or sent in to the local Church office, it was not to be used for any local Church needs. Instead it went to pay the ministers and Conference office workers and general expenses at any level above the local congregation. Whatever a congregation raised for its own needs (like for buildings, upkeep, additions, outreach, personnel reimbursements, stipends or wages) was outside the sacred tithe.

Members were required to pay, or rather, to return, the tithe to God for all they owned: wealth, goods, property and the like—these were only a loan from God to begin with.[8] Being accepted into Church membership carried this personal pledge to return the tithe to God. This was not a free-will offering. It was the payment of a debt

---

had asserted.

3. The case was a situation that developed over the better part of a decade and was far more involved than simply a case of challenging the tithe and Ingathering practices. But from its beginning, this situation was seen by leadership as a threat to Church authority and a clear disruption in the status quo that ultimately reflected negatively on the inspired instructions of our prophet. An interesting commentary is an article by Charles Randall entitled, "The Burbank Case: Do Seventh-day Adventists really have a Representative Church Government?" *Adventist Perspective*, (December 2000).

4. White, *Messages to Young People,* 308.

5. White, *Gospel Workers,* 222.

6. White, *Testimonies for the Church,* 3:394–395, 510, 546. See also ibid., 5:150.

7. Ibid., 4:467.

8. Ibid., 5:267–268.

to God[9] and the failure to pay it honestly was to defraud[10] and rob God;[11] indeed, it was embezzlement of God's property.[12]

One might say that the tithe was a lease on life or rent, although these business-type terms were never used. Covetousness leads a person to rob God[13] and those who succumbed to this sin would suffer God's curse in this life.[14] Such a sin was to be confessed to God and the Church.[15] Even the plea of poverty was no excuse.[16] Sister White had detailed this concept for us:

> The tithe is God's *portion, not at all the property of man,* and the scripture declares that he who withholds it is *guilty of robbery.* Who, then will stand with clean hands before the Lord?[17]

Where was this God to whom we were to hand over all this money—where was this tithe to be deposited? It was to go into God's treasury.[18] And we all knew that treasury to be the Church in its infrastructure—the clergy at the Conference level—those committees led by prayer and fasting. Put another way, when one ruled out the individual's judgment as to where the tithe should go, and one dispensed with the local congregation's opinions of how to spend the tithe, one must logically conclude that the term "God," in this context, meant the Church hierarchy. Of course, to put it that blatantly would sound blasphemous therefore nobody dared say so openly, even if they thought so. This was not something for us to question if we wanted to succeed in the work. Nor did we. This did not mean that the tithe was a simple matter.

Since the New Testament provides scant information relative to a tithing system for Christians, Sister White, God's latter-day spokesperson, was our guide. She asserted that the amount one owes God was to be computed freely by the individual Church member.[19] And it was always to be voluntary.[20] Thus the believer's conscience and benevolence were to be the guide.[21] This sounded explicit to most of us.

My conscience was clear as I paid a tithe on my gross income, even though as a minister my salary was composed of tithe funds already gathered from Church

9. Ibid., 149.
10. Ibid., 3:394.
11. Ibid., 409.
12. Ibid., 394.
13. Ibid., 6:387.
14. Ibid., 5:275.
15. White, *Counsels on Health,* 374.
16. White, *Testimonies for the Church,* Vol. 2:59.
17. White, "A Test of Gratitude and Loyalty," *Review and Herald,* 73:45 (November 10, 1896), 709. Emphases supplied.
18. White, *Testimonies for the Church,* 4:474. See also White, *Acts of the Apostles,* 338.
19. Ibid., 5:149.
20. Ibid., 3:393.
21. Ibid., 394.

members. Ministers were expected to tithe the tithe from which they were paid. But when questioned about the finality of one-tenth, we could not be dogmatic. In my thinking, one could not go wrong by giving God the benefit of the doubt and simply paying on one's gross income. For several years I even paid a double-tithe—twenty percent of my gross income. So, what was income? Or increase? Before, or after taxes? The arguments were endless for and against. I let the personal arguments fly. But I was concerned about the implications of these questions for ministry.

It seemed that the religious character of a member must be considered. If a member did not pay tithe or did not pay an honest tithe, should he/she be eligible to hold a Church office? Or even be a member? Could a person be an elder or deacon or some other leader who did not pay an honest tithe? And how was honest determined? Wasn't the seriousness of this issue underlined by the fact that dishonesty in tithe-paying was recorded as robbery in the books of heaven[22] and that God's curse rested on those who practiced such dishonesty and sin?[23]

Our prophet told of farmers whose crops were destroyed when they didn't pay an honest tithe.[24] Once more we had decisive instructions that seemed clear on the surface:

> Let none feel at liberty to retain their tithe, to use according to their own judgment. *They are not to use it for themselves in an emergency, nor to apply it as they see fit*, even in what they may regard as the Lord's work.[25]

> Some have been dissatisfied, and have said, "I will no longer pay my tithe, for I have no confidence in the way things are managed at the heart of the work." But will you *rob God* because you think the management of the work is not right? Make your complaint, plainly and openly, in the right spirit, to the proper ones. Send in your petitions for things to be adjusted and set in order; but *do not withdraw from the work of God, and prove unfaithful*, because others are not doing right.[26]

Occasionally, when the tithe income of a local Church was dropping, a pastor might panic and begin threatening his congregation that he was going to check the books before the nominating committee met to suggest officers for the next year. This ticklish situation had the potential of backfiring for it could (and did) create the perception that the worship leader was now functioning as an auditor to survive in his profession. And it confused the motivational factors of the member's religious life in that this leader had now moved from religious mentor to business administrator—a scenario

---

22. White, *Counsels on Stewardship*, 77.
23. White, *Testimonies for the Church*, 5:275.
24. Ibid., 6:390.
25. Ibid., 9:247. Emphasis supplied.
26. Ibid., 249. Emphases supplied.

that continually invited the criticism of members and non-members alike. How many times had we heard that the Church was only interested in money?

Becoming a watchdog or detective was not something our Seminary education had emphasized. Our prophet made it clear that if we knew of sins in the Church (and surely robbing God had to be one of the more heinous ones) we were responsible for those sins if we did not fix the situation.

> One sinner may diffuse darkness that will exclude the light of God from the entire congregation. When the people realize that darkness is settling upon them . . . they should seek God earnestly, in great humility and self-abasement, until the wrongs which grieve his Spirit are searched out and put away.[27]

> If the leaders of the church neglect to diligently search out the sins which bring the displeasure of God upon the body, *they become responsible for those sins.*[28]

> If wrongs are apparent among his people, and if the servants of God pass on indifferent to them, they virtually sustain and justify the sinner, and are alike guilty and will just as surely receive the displeasure of God; for *they will be made responsible for the sins of the guilty.*[29]

> He [God] would teach His people that disobedience and sin . . . are not to be lightly regarded. . . . When His people are found in sin *they should at once take decided measures to put that sin from them . . . but if the sins of the people are passed over by those in responsible positions, his frown will be upon them, and the people of God, as a body, will be held responsible for those sins.*[30]

> In vision I have been pointed to many instances where *the displeasure of God* has been incurred by *neglect on the part of His servants to deal with the wrongs and sins* existing among them.[31]

THE CRITICAL NEED FOR AN INTELLIGENT MINISTRY

During my internship, my pastoral mentor had demonstrated the importance of intelligent ministry. But without our daily dialogues I was now facing the challenge of synthesizing my own materials. I kept in contact with him, and he was an able consultant, but now I was on my own—responsible for the outcomes on my own turf. I never forgot my mentor's simple formula for success considering Conference concerns: tithe, Ingathering, and baptisms, in that order.

27. Ibid., 3:265–266.
28. Ibid., 269. Emphasis supplied.
29. Ibid., 266. Emphasis supplied.
30. Ibid., 265. Emphases supplied.
31. Ibid., 266. Emphases supplied.

I refused to check the books to see what people were giving. I believed that was invasive, intimidating and frankly, none of my business (nor had my mentor ever suggested that I should). He would agree with me completely. But was this in violation of those pointed instructions from the prophet? As a religious man I had an innate confidence that if I was careful to preach the truth, the tithe would naturally follow. Doing the right thing was an ambiguous notion, and it was not a rare occurrence for ministers I had listened to, to take their congregations on guilt-trips from the pulpit by embedding hard-hitting tithing statements in their sermons.

For whatever the reasons, the tithe base of our congregation never waned in the five years of my tenure. Nor did any of the world, Conference or local offerings. And we always reached our ingathering goal. The baptisms averaged ten a year, which for a small Church of fifty charter members was considered significant. In fact, my Conference president had suggested that two baptisms a year in a Church our size was enough to demonstrate that I was a successful minister.

THE PLACE OF PROGRAMS IN MINISTRY

That Adventists loved programs soon became apparent. When a pastor is up against a tight time schedule and the pressures of his day-to-day ministry, the appetite for new programs can seem insatiable. Programs were presented to us at workers' meetings in such a tempting way that each seemed to be the answer to the ever-present task of finishing the work. We were practically guaranteed that each program suggested there would be successful if we did it right.

Unfortunately, the ultimate effect of some programs was short-lived. I found myself in bookstores searching for avenues of success. Against my better judgment I caught myself looking for those books our professors had warned us against—sermon illustration books, sermon outline books, sermon collection books, interlinear Bibles, analytical Greek and Hebrew lexicons. These were crutches, they had taught us—they stifled a minister's growth and creativity. Canned illustrations, as they were called, were not as enlivening or meaningful as personal experiences and most of those book stories were probably not true anyway, no matter how sensational, effective and tantalizing they sounded.

Knowing the original languages for ourselves was more important than leaning on some crutch produced by linguistic scholars. But how does one keep these ancient languages alive? One of my colleagues said he did so by reading one page of the Greek New Testament and one page of the Hebrew scriptures each day without the aid of a crutch. But then he had solid motivation—he wanted to be an ancient languages professor and he eventually became one. I didn't consider that to be a typical solution, nor was it an ambition of mine.

The no-crutch hypothesis was good in theory, but it was so set in an academic idealism that it could hardly be applied to the field and a profession filled with daily trivia. I was sure that programs had to fall under the same warning for they too could become crutches. Yet I was ready for a set of crutches that could give me a routine and create an equilibrium that the ministry did not inherently offer.

Other than the workers' meeting, continuing education for Adventist ministers in 1967 did not exist. Our education at Seminary was considered all that was necessary for our beginning needs. Even when I requested permission to take some extra school work at Fuller Theological Seminary, our Conference executive secretary called to tell me that after I had been ordained, and had worked for several years successfully, and showed some possibility of promise, the Conference committee might allow me to take a class.

I didn't find much encouragement in that—we were probably looking at another eight to ten years for all that to occur. And so, I concluded that my formal education was substantially over. Why this should have surprised me, demonstrated some of my own religious addiction. I had heard my own mentor's tales about how he was caught attending a speech class at USC and forced by leadership to drop the class and abandon his program because it violated Conference policy.

Many institutional approaches in the Church had started out as programs. For example, the Sabbath School was originally a program that was transformed into an institution with regular publications designed to create a sense of worldwide community. While it had been adapted from the Sunday School movement of mainline Protestantism, it had proved an effective way to indoctrinate the young and stabilize the older members of the congregation as well as the larger denomination in general. It was considered the study center of the Church.

The unity provided by the Sabbath School also accounted for the awareness of (and partial funding for) foreign missions. The weekly hour and a half spent in Sabbath School on Saturday mornings provided a reminder of the missions that the denomination was sponsoring as well as studying the same Bible lessons that every other Adventist congregation in the country was studying. A member in Peoria could discuss the lesson with someone in Miami or Seattle as they had all studied the same passages last Sabbath. And they were all planning for the thirteenth Sabbath mission offering that would be taken up at the end of the quarter for some part of the world field that had been selected by Church leadership.

Other programs were applied universally as well, such as the educational system, the Conference departments, and the mass media evangelism of *The Voice of Prophecy* (radio), *It Is Written* (television), *Breath of Life* (television) and *Faith for Today* (television). These outreach approaches had been innovative programs started independently of the Church bureaucracy by highly creative and visionary pastors and evangelists who believed in the potential effectiveness of the developing mass media.

Creative pastors saw a future through radio and television but had to fight the camp meeting speakers who had convinced Grandma that radio was the voice of the devil and other such perceptions. Forward-looking ministers, such as Elder H. M.

S. Richards (1894–1985), Elder George Vandeman (1916–2000), and Elder William Fagal (1919–1989) realized that these channels could be significant avenues to evangelize the masses. In time, the leadership reined them in as major denominational outreach vehicles. Through institutional control they were monitored to make sure their broadcast ministers conformed to official denominational perspectives.

The downside of being dependent on the Church structure was that too much creativity could arouse suspicion among leadership. Especially was this true of *Faith for Today*, the Church's first major success to enter the television field. Originally, *Faith for Today* was a local program in New York and followed a simple Church worship service format. People could sit in their front rooms and enjoy Church on television complete with a pastor and a male gospel quartet. Then the attached commercial on the backside of the program could offer books (usually copies of the sermon just presented) and Bible lessons for viewers who might be interested in a free home Bible correspondence course.

The pastors in the areas where these seekers lived would then personally visit the graduates of the free course and invite them to attend their Church or offer to answer questions they might have with a view to persuading them. The aim was to provide a Bible study series that would lead them to baptism and Church membership.

When *Faith for Today* later introduced *Westbrook Hospital*, a drama-based series where people's immediate needs were met by Christian doctors and nurses (and the fictional chaplain, Elder Fagal) in a primary care hospital with regular characters appearing each week, the critics were once again on hand to attack these new attempts at reaching a modern audience.

Applying accepted principles of marketing strategy, the producers had in mind a target group. They focused more on reaching people who didn't find Church services attractive or people who were concerned with more practical aspects of their lives than doctrinal or creedal religious statements. The writers recognized that their target group included mainly people who simply did not attend Church.

These practical areas included marriage, family, disappointment, illness and various crises that often occur in human society. The dramatic approach of *Westbrook Hospital* was like *This is the Life*, the show produced by the Lutheran Laymen's League. Rather than preaching, the program was a masterfully written and directed situational drama modeling behavior. Theological ideology came later in the free Bible correspondence course, but the hooks were in the drama.

In my conversation with the director of the program I learned that even though this show presented "the right arm" of the Church's message in action, there was some criticism of *Westbrook Hospital*. It ranged from, Why are Adventists into theatre? to What's wrong with the good old message? Dealing with everyday realities was not to the liking of some members who thought the public needed to hear more about the antichrist and the seven last plagues. On another front was the old opposition to the fiction of drama.

Eventually *Westbrook Hospital* ran its course. When Pastor and Mrs. Fagal, originators of *Faith for Today,* turned the reins over to Dan Matthews and others, still more contemporary approaches were used. *Lifestyle Magazine,* a show resembling Phil Donahue and Oprah Winfrey and the early TV news magazines became popular with some, but again it was criticized because some members couldn't see where this was making Adventists.

Nevertheless, being under the control of central leadership, these novel approaches were more vulnerable to the disapproval of critics who were substantial financial donors to the Church. Why should we put money into ventures that did not yield results? And "results" meant making Adventists—baptisms. The closest most pastors came to be a part of the established denominational media programs was following up the leads generated by them. Their names were regularly sent to the local ministers.

My first encounter with these leads was as a graduate student in the Seminary-directed evangelistic field school in Southern California during the summer of 1965. The result of these encounters was so disappointing that I come to dread them. Many of the people I visited were not aware that they would be personally visited, and they resented the intrusion. Yet there was that illusion that such leads were probably better than the alternative—cold turkey visits door to door. It brought back memories of my summer in Merced.

Programs, particularly those that did not develop into institutions, generally originated in the creativity of an intuitive pastor whose unique approach had been useful to him and had shown a degree of success in meeting its goals. As such these programs were typically short on field-testing and usually connected to the personality of the pastor who created them. Program promotion is always accompanied by testimonials that include lines like, "If I can do it . . . anyone can do it!" I learned the hard way: that was not true.

On non-religious television infomercials, such testimonials frequently carried a disclaimer along the bottom of the screen that read "These Results are not Typical," even as the testimonials were being delivered. Church programs, however, never included this reality check reminder. The religious people I knew traditionally implied that if this program wasn't succeeding, it was because someone wasn't working hard enough—and that someone was you. You are probably not committed, or your own religious life must be lacking. It was like we were reading the book of Job. But because of its success elsewhere, a program could be packaged up for other pastors to use—usually with very high recommendations. At this point slogans were formulated and employed, and the program was off and running.

TESTING THE PROGRAMS AS MEANINGFUL MINISTRY PHILOSOPHY

As a parish pastor I was now dealing more directly with the various departments in the Conference office. These departments were the primary program-producing agencies of the denomination. Departmental directors (or "secretaries" as they were called) were under subtle but strong pressure to justify their positions (salaries and budgets) by providing programs for pastors to meet their evangelistic needs. We were all team players. So, at every new workers' meeting we were presented with another program, together with the delicate implication that this could be a panacea for the professional ministry.

These programs were in addition to the institutional expectations a pastor was already to support. We were not usually required to implement every new program that was presented, but each one was presented attractively, and some of us were serious and desperate for ideas and ready to try anything that came with a formal endorsement. The first few months of my pastorate were bound up with these programs. I was expected to be a company man, a team player and a loyal person—all of which I was. As a religious man I saw these goals as paramount.

In the fall of 1967, I launched my first major effort at teaching my congregation soul-winning techniques. It was called the SAVES (an acronym for Southeastern [California Conference] Audio-Visual Evangelistic Society) program, an all Church member involvement approach we had used in college for an evangelistic series in Rubidoux and Perris.

As the name implies the program was not original with us—we had applied it as formulated by the Southeastern California Conference lay activities office. We had been seven dedicated theological students in college (who called ourselves "the Sanhedrin"). Someone in our group got hold of the SAVES training manual and introduced it to us as something we could do to show that we were proactive in our faith—a grass roots movement.

So, we struck off on our own to hold four weeks of meetings in Rubidoux and later in Perris during my junior and senior years. The SAVES program had prepared for our public meetings. We hadn't baptized anyone through this program, but we figured that was only because we were students and who takes students seriously? We had failed, not the program. That was our opinion. We thought it had been a good experience, and we were convinced the program was sound and could yield good results. Now was my chance to prove it.

I determined to succeed with this program. The program started by holding strategy meetings with the congregation in my garage every Sabbath afternoon. For several weeks we worked on the map of the city, listing addresses of every house within the city limits. Next, we produced logbooks, folders containing twenty addresses arranged geographically around city blocks. Going two by two, according to biblical admonition, Church members would take a logbook and knock on the door of each of the twenty homes listed there for the next five weeks—same couple, same homes, each week. They would jot notes of response in the logbook.

The visits would start out with general Christian literature but get progressively more denominational as the weeks went by. We had a stack of attractively printed leaflets asking provocative questions like "Where Will You Spend Eternity?" "Is Satan in Charge of Hell? Can He Be Trusted?" and "Holy Wedlock or Unholy Deadlock?"

By the fifth visit, so the plan went, these people would have become our friends and would be ripe for an invitation to take a series of Bible studies or even attend Church. At the close of the Bible studies these new converts would find it natural to request baptism in the Church. Soul-winning couldn't have sounded easier or more logical. But theory can be more optimistic than successful practice. Instead of finding a lot of new friends, our crusaders, as visitors were called, discovered that this is seldom how friendships are formed. With rare exception, friends were made in contexts where there was some mutual purpose or shared interest.

In our case, I found a timid reluctance even on the part of our crusaders to fulfill this task. One member asked me to let him examine the list of people in his logbook before launching out on his visits. He explained that he did not want to meet any of his clients who might wonder why he was standing on their front porch, knocking on their door—professional ethics, image, exploitation, taking advantage, personal intrusion. That was okay. I was just glad he was involved.

Preparing for the campaign was a big undertaking. This entailed some serious lay training, from how to react to people when you knock on their door to how to give a Bible study. Most of the Church members turned out for the mapping and logbook production. Fewer turned out for the door-to-door visitation. Just a few showed up to learn to give Bible studies.

Later I would read *The Gospel Blimp*. It was as though the author had been observing our efforts. The progression through the fictional story followed faithfully every step in our progress. In the end the moral was drawn concerning how friends are made, and converts are attracted.[32] Here I learned a valuable lesson, that the physician in my Church who was ministering to people and then bringing them to the class in his office had the right stuff.

Despite this diminishing participation I refused to see this as a reflection of the spirituality of the congregation. The program was daunting, but it gave many a chance to do something they had never known how to do. It was an organizing of religion. We were selling Adventism. We assumed that somewhere in the process the dissemination

---

32. Bayly, *The Gospel Blimp*, (1960). In his interpretation of the story, Rev. Bayly explains, (p. 77): "And the blimp? Why the wonderful Gospel Blimp is every impersonal, external means by which we try to fulfil our responsibility to witness to our neighbors. Gospel programs over the radio, messages on billboards or in tracts: these are some of our blimps. They either supplement our own personal witness or else they're substitutes for involvement with our neighbors—the sort of involvement that George and Ethel discovered toward the end of the story."

of the gospel would occur. We were a new congregation and I believed we could grow by using this program.

By most benchmarks used to evaluate success in business, our results were dismal. Nevertheless, the residual effects were glorious—people working together in an evangelistic process—at least at first. We had never laid out a clear vision or mission statement with this approach. We simply assumed we all knew why we were doing these things. A tangible result for any of us involved in the effort would have been new converts to Adventism. That meant conversion and commitment to Christ. We were finishing the work.

We completed the first round of mapping and visitation in ten weeks, with a significant turnout from the congregation—fully sixty percent of the membership was involved in some way or other. But then most of the visitation teams had been rejected in their original twenty visits—either the people told them not to come back or were conveniently out of town on Sabbath afternoons. This created a depression in my original group of excited parishioners who had trusted my claims that this would be a way to fill the Church on Sabbath mornings. I was not aware that one person any of us had visited ever attended a worship service.

So, the initial enthusiasm waned. My pep talks carried less clout as time went on. By the second round of the program, we were down to about ten percent of our original participants. Previously involved members were polite as they discontinued their participation—they needed to spend more time with their families—they had other engagements on Sabbath afternoon—they couldn't be tied down to a five-week commitment that might be followed up with a year of Bible studies. But I sensed that too many were simply discouraged with the whole program. A small number even told me so.

In the end, no new names were ever added to the books of the congregation through this program, though we ran it for nearly a year. It was time to find something else that perhaps worked better, or at all. I became painfully aware of how easy it was to resort to guilt trips with members. Lack of support could so quickly and conveniently be dumped back on Church members who had initially showed such excitement.

Even more painful was having to admit that perhaps programs like this simply didn't always work the way we thought they should. They looked good on paper but applying them was another story. What had I done wrong? A truly religious man often finds himself glomming on to the responsibility for the bad results.

I set a new goal for myself—I would visit twenty homes each day by myself, invite people to study the Bible with me and look for the results that we had hoped for when we worked together. Two weeks of that yielded an impressive number of people to study with, but in the end the results were the same. The only people I ended up baptizing were already in the class being held at the doctor's office. I felt that my visits seemed superfluous to them.

MORE MODEL EXAMPLES OF FAILURE

Sharing my experience about all the programs I tried is not necessary here. This program was the model example of failure. Eventually I became skeptical of any program that involved too many people who might not follow through.

When a pastor presented another new program, "Dial Your Family Bible," at another workers' meeting, I really hoped that I had finally found the workable program I had been searching for. I could run this program from my study and follow through alone by visiting the people who left their names. I would have to rely on no one in the congregation. I would now assume the position of professional pastor. Instead of functioning as coach of the team, I now became the team.

To set up *The Magic of Telephone Evangelism*,[33] the title of the training manual, one needed a telephone answering machine, a second phone line, a set of Bible study lessons, and a two-line classified ad in the local newspaper. This was like a miniature *It Is Written* program on the phone. I could do this. Perhaps I had found my pearl of great price!

I had an old tape recorder my father-in-law had lent me. I set up a recording studio in the closet of my study. Each morning I took the two-minute message from the book and transcribed it onto tape, making sure there were no errors in my presentation. Then I transcribed my recording to the answering machine. I placed an ad in the local newspaper with the number to call and I sat back and waited for the converts to file into my Church.

I set up the *School of Bible Prophecy* to handle the correspondence. I was the speaker, the professor, the principal of the school, the receptionist, the technical director and the secretary. I would grade all the papers, make all the visits, and do all the work. I didn't need to rely on anyone for the third area of my success as a minister—baptisms. I also didn't need to listen to the excuses for not participating.

After a year of "Dial Your Family Bible" I still had no significant results. I had regular callers—"The Frito Bandito" called at least once a week to leave an amateur radio program for my entertainment. I listened each day as other people put together satirical sketches (they only had thirty seconds to perform). I concluded that these people were not laughing *with* me.

Then after a few months, my answering machine started to act up. This was in the days before sophisticated, reliable electronic devices—certainly no digital stuff. The Church had voted to buy an answering machine that cost nearly $1000—a lot of money in 1969. This machine was the one recommended by leadership in workers' meeting. But the machine developed serious idiosyncrasies. Sometimes it would not trip its switches correctly and messages would be garbled. I might have attracted ten messages in one day, but they had been reduced to a single second of playback and all I would hear would be a "Brrrrrrrrrrr-rrrrrrrrrrrrrrriack... Beep!" Or some brain

---

33. Metcalf, *The Magic of Telephone Evangelism*, (1967).

splitting, spine-shattering sounds like that. If the "Frito Bandito" happened to leave his weekly message that day, I was never to find out.

When our machine finally gave up the ghost I took it back to the address printed on the manufacturer's sticker placed conspicuously on the top of the unit—somewhere in Van Nuys. The company had moved, closed, left no forwarding address—the office and the whole building were vacant. I reluctantly turned off the machine and closed my studio. No more would a caller hear my cheerful voice, "Greetings—this is Dial Your Family Bible! . . ."

Another year had passed, and we were no closer to finishing the work than we had been three years before. Ministry was still undefined. It was clearly not a hard science. But whatever, it was a hard activity. And it had to be my fault. I was missing something. I guessed I had been educated to be a theologian, rather than a minister. And I began to make that distinction. I took the failure very hard. As a religious man I needed to check my personal commitment—what was I doing to impede the work of God? This is how religious men think.

Flitting from program to program had diverted me from forming a workable philosophy of ministry. After several miserable attempts at success by way of programs, I became skeptical that any of them would be helpful. My first reaction was to abandon all of them. On the recommendation of other ministerial colleagues, I took my *Time* magazine to workers' meeting, so I wouldn't be attracted by another set of promises that would fail. I was becoming cynical. And it was in my cynicism, with no one to help me that I began to think seriously about leaving the ministry.

DISILLUSIONMENT SETS IN—BIG TIME

Leaving the ministry? The very thought had to be suppressed. I had lived, breathed, and slept the ministry since I was seventeen years old. But I was clearly failing and that meant to a religious man misplacement. Pastoring a Church, preaching and teaching, holding meetings, giving Bible studies, visiting the sick, visiting the newborns, marrying and burying—no question these were ministry. I was doing all these. But I was refereed by baptisms and those were not happening.

So why was I feeling unfulfilled? What was lacking? I was insisting that religious experience had to be deeper. My personal spiritual life was intense. Every morning I was praying and reading, every day I was working to make sure I was worthy of the tithe-sourced salary I was being paid. Night after night I was out in meetings, holding classes, giving Bible studies, pushing Adventism. But the results? Lacking.

I buried the cynical ideas. Jesus was coming soon. The Black Cloud would soon deliver us all and the perfect utopia would occur. But despite this there was a void. The work was never done. It was somewhere around this time that Annie assigned to me a new theme song: "Somewhere Over the Rainbow!" And whenever I would begin to express disappointment with my work, she would start singing the song, and I would retreat again. Obviously, she was frustrated with my flailing around in my search for a successful approach to ministry. And she had that right.

One afternoon I was making visits in Ventura when I drove past Ventura Community College. The college was registering students. I pulled my car over and walked into the registration line. On a spontaneous lark I filled out all the forms. I would pursue a dental career and leave my frustrations behind once and for all. I was still young enough to seek a new direction.

I would become a dentist!

CHAPTER TWENTY-THREE

A New Direction

"A philosopher is a person who never feels badly after he has made an ass of himself."
—Laurence J. Peter

THE NERVOUS RESTLESSNESS OF THE SUPER-CONSCIENTIOUS

Why was I so restless? I tried not to think about how laughable it looked for me to be signing up for undergraduate classes. I was an ordained minister with a bachelor's degree and two master's degrees and now I was going back to a junior college? I ignored the reality that this might be a passing thing—that tomorrow I might feel differently about scrapping my ten-year educational investment in life.

My flirtation with dentistry proved to be an "Over the Rainbow," out-of-body experience. I had no interest whatever in dentistry. But as I registered for my classes I was more conflicted about the Conference policy—perhaps since I wasn't taking any theology class this was not in violation of that policy. But in my frustration, I feigned not to care. For some reason I was disillusioned with the whole ministerial enterprise. Nothing was like I had expected it to be.

At the end of the registration line my counselor asked me to produce my transcripts from high school. I didn't carry them around with me, and this visit was a spur of the moment thing. So, she asked me to bring them back in the morning since it was so late in the day. I could finish my registration then. Of course, she was right, the day was too far gone for me to go home, find the transcripts and return. Home was twenty miles away. I agreed to be back in the morning.

By the next morning the lark had flown. I never completed the pre-dentistry route—I never even started it. I wrote out a list of questions that helped me talk myself out of that new direction. It didn't take much. My decision had not been well-crafted.

When I gave it serious thought I could not want to be confined to a small room, the size of a death-row cell, drilling teeth for the rest of my life. Even my own view of dentistry hardly helped qualify me to pursue it!

MY RENEWED SEARCH

With each passing week I was fighting the temptation to see my ministerial education as being of little pragmatic value. But I could think of no alternatives at that point. I returned to the notion that God had called me to be a minister. Did anything make sense? Did that make sense? What to do? I would hit the red books harder than ever. I would do exhaustive studies on what our prophet had to say about this calling.

The *Testimonies* held the key. I believed it—I knew it. But rather than solving my inquiries I found more frustration. The state of my life, the state of the Church, my perceived state of the ministry; my mind reeled. The more I read and studied the more judgmental and perfectionistic I became. And so, I looked at the immediate task before me: studying, visiting, preaching, teaching and planning a new Church building. It was time to reframe.

I started with a review. I had begun my tenure at Camarillo with a series of weekly business meetings with all the members of the congregation invited. And so, I would go back to that beginning and see where I had gotten off track.

In these meetings I had explained my understanding of the responsibilities each of us had. I had explained that as a new congregation we might follow a more democratic approach than they might be used to. I wanted each member to have a voice in the direction the new Church should take. Decisions should be made by the group and I would expect anyone who objected or had alternatives to reveal them, to speak up courageously and be heard by all members present. Most of the members thought they would like this approach. Was this not effective ministry? The notes I saved from the first meeting read,

> We have three meetings together each week—Sabbath School, Sabbath Worship, and Prayer Meeting. If you do not attend all three you only get part of the menu. We will call board meetings when they are needed but for now we will have monthly business meetings. All of you are busy people and you probably don't feel the need of yet another meeting, so this should come as good news.
>
> According to the *SDA Church Manual,* our working policy, the congregation in session must do the major work of the Church. Mostly the Church board is only allowed to make recommendations to the congregation, so we will open our discussions with the whole Church and all of you can be a part. What you vote in these meetings will become policies and rules for this Church to follow.

As I studied what I had said I realized that here was a major element of my philosophy of ministry: serious member voice and participation that counted. Following my mentor's lead, I would start with the Church policy book: The *Church Manual*.[1] This source revealed that the Church board was to be called by the pastor when needed. But the congregation in business session was *the* only official body authorized to make the directional decisions of the congregation. The initial elements in this philosophy of ministry had a goal: unity of membership toward a specified purpose.

I began talking to some of my college classmates now at work in churches, and I found a variety of mixed motivations for their ministry. Some were using the pastorate to get into college teaching—they believed this was their only avenue to that goal and they reluctantly admitted it. Others wanted to be Conference administrators. But they were careful where they let that be known. They did not want to be classified as selfishly ambitious.

The man who shared with the wrong people that he wanted to be a Conference president could almost count on never reaching that post. If asked about such a position he invariably needed to say demurely, "May the Lord's will be done." But as the saying went among pastors, when a minister got a call to pastor a bigger Church or to be president of a Conference, his wife was home packing while he was praying publicly for guidance. It was satirical humor, but we suspected it carried a suitcase of truth—after all, couldn't one do ministry outside the pastorate?

I had entertained none of these ambitions. I viewed all of them with a degree of suspicion—religious disdain—righteous indignation, for they all seemed to compromise one's purpose for being in the pastorate. God's man was led by God, not by glory. I cared nothing about a larger Church, a college position, or an administrative post—of that I was sure. In fact, as calls came to larger churches and college positions I found myself conflicted and I turned them down—twelve invitations in all, over a three-year period. I could not accept a call until I had resolved some of these basic elements in my ministerial philosophy. I determined not to use moving as an "escape."

I had to know what I was about—how God could use a religious man who was totally committed to him. Staying at one place for a reasonable period was a sign of religious valor and respectability. I believed that a pastor who had been in one place for five years was farther advanced than the pastor who had been in five places in five years. It seemed evident that moving five times only yielded one year of experience. Dr. Haussler had called this staying power "total commitment." And it made sense—I bought it completely.

In my new attack into the red books, I started by reading *Gospel Workers* one hour a day, studying the place and function of pastors. This book was a compilation of statements drawn from Sister White's writings; it was not her original production. Articles and letters perused by trustees of her estate were gathered together to give us insight.

---

1. *Church Manual*, (1959).

These trustees were the guardians of the inspired corpus of Adventist materials. Who would disagree that all the words were inspired? Some of the instructions may have been taken out of their original context but they were still written by "the pen of inspiration" as Sister White was called in Adventist tradition.

At first my Prayer Meetings resembled watered down Seminary classes as I largely parroted and paraphrased material from the lectures I had come to love in graduate school. My sermons were either talks I had prepared for my preaching classes or revisions of notes I had taken in Seminary classes from professors I respected as great religious men and women. All this began to change with the new influx of Sister White from my intensive study.

I sometimes strained to make practical applications because I was still a young pastor and not a *time-seasoned worker* yet. As I prepared my sermons I became frighteningly aware of the sheltered life I had lived. The youth pastors I knew were often new converts and could share experiences from their previous lives of sin—they had been into drugs, sex, bad music, drinking, smoking, even criminal activities. God had delivered them from these dark sides of life.

Often their talks were long descriptions of the sinful lives they had led with a short conclusion praising God for deliverance. I wondered if I should regret having had no such disclosures to make. Instead I drew from my simple childhood or my college experience. As my old sermons ran out I employed the new approach my mentor had taught me.

While my professors had largely formed my ideas of ministry, as a new pastor I now found that I was required to meet the expectations of my Conference president, my senior pastor, the people in the congregation, and not the least of all, my wife, her family and finally myself. Working in these multiple theatres was at first overwhelming because a young minister can feel very aware of what people think of him and mistakenly think he can satisfy all of them. Add to that the fact that my professors were global, giving approaches that may have worked for them in a variety of what seemed irrelevant and disconnected settings—foreign lands, missionary enterprises, administrative positions.

Then there were the articles I read monthly in *Ministry* magazine and other Adventist periodicals. I felt my confusion being fueled for I was by nature a sponge for ideas that sounded reasonable.

Another frustration staring me in the face was figuring out what to do with *the day*. I knew there was time for study, but that was not all a minister was supposed to do. As ministers in preparation we had all been instructed that time management would be a challenge. I had no idea how raw that warning was until I faced it. No boss or professor sat there and dictated your assignments. There was no clock to punch, no bells rang between activities. Every night we were required to chronicle what we had done on our Conference report, which we mailed in at the close of each month.

Filling out that report each night left me alone with my conscience. Some had told me that a minister's integrity was on the line, others said the report was meaningless because nobody at the Conference office ever looked at it. But on that report was room for visits made, Bible studies given, and baptisms. No line there for *studying*. Not even for *meetings held*. If you taught a class in Bible doctrines did you count the twenty people who attended as Bible studies: twenty? Or Bible study: one?—since it was only one hour in length.

The first few weeks were no problem. I knew what I had to do. I had fifty members to visit. But then what? And there was the occasional forgetful Church member who called the Conference to report that no pastor had been to visit in over two years. When called on the carpet for this very infraction of ministerial responsibility I shared the record I had kept of all my visits. This record showed that here was the only person in the Church who had received weekly visits from me for two years. Given the many assignments that flowed from headquarters I soon began to wonder how I could serve two masters: the Conference and the congregation.

I never had any complaint about my salary and benefits. I was always told and believed that Adventists took good care of their ministers. We had book allowances, rent allowances, travel allowances, all in addition to our salary. Extra travel was reimbursable along with *per diem* and we got a cost of living increase each year. We even got discounted gasoline at the Conference pump whenever we came into the office in Glendale. The health benefits were good with eighty percent coverage in basically all the areas our family might need—medical, dental and optical.

An added benefit I had known nothing about was the unending number of medical personnel in the Church who insisted on receiving no remuneration for treating the pastor and his family. Ironically, I found this intimidating rather than a blessing. I was a religious man, not a monk who expected a free ride. It was a part of an ideology I did not understand. I had no grasp of being a gracious receiver. And I found *receiving* uncomfortable. I finally recognized this was a part of the minister-physician team we had learned about in school. Refusing this benefit was considered rude.

Finally, my Adventist education was not turning out to be as monolithic as I had thought growing up in my little La Sierra community of Southern California. I now had to struggle with those Seminary and field terms that were so slippery to define—terms like *conservative, liberal, neo-orthodox, right wing* and *left wing*. Adventism had traditionally attempted to be different from all other churches. Not until the *Questions on Doctrine* controversy did there seem to be an attempt to be conciliatory with those who our prophet had generally declared to be *apostates*.

PROFESSIONAL EXPECTATIONS

I attended the Camarillo Ministerial Association for fellowship with ministers of other persuasions. When I ordered a baked potato at the first luncheon, one of the ministers asked me the question of the day: "When will your Church lift its ban on meat-eating?" This was another new experience and I guessed I wasn't comfortable with that perception. I explained that was a personal preference not a denominational requirement.

There were no federal regulations for preachers in America. Some principles of privacy and confidentiality were mandated, but formal licensing based on one's education and experience was left up to individual Church organizations. No professional accreditation procedure was in place for Adventist ministers other than the required academic degrees and recommendations of professors and other qualified friends. We received our ministerial license when we began our work either in the field or at Seminary. Ordination came later as did a more adequate salary. In fact, ordination was the closest we came to any equivalent board examination in other professions.

Each university professor had his own burden to share regarding ministerial philosophy but few shared comparable backgrounds. And I doubted that some of them had much pastoral experience at all. Being a school that educated the world, Andrews University had professors from all over the globe. Most were excellent scholars, but some had little to say about the nuts and bolts of pastoral ministry. On my brother's recommendation I had listened most carefully to Dr. Alexander and Dr. Heppenstall for my practical ideas. Both had been successful parish ministers. But even so I graduated with a very academic view of ministry.

Working at internship for a year and half had helped. But the two pastors I worked under couldn't have held much different philosophies of ministry from each other. Elder Rea had insisted that I critique him continuously—something I found intimidating. But now, as the pastor of my own small Church, I set out conscientiously to synthesize all that I had learned.

I increased giving Bible studies. I beefed up my classes at Church—pastor's class on Sabbath morning, mid-week Prayer Meeting became a class in studying the books of the Bible, the time of the end and the health message. Gradually I turned all my work with the congregation into educational ministry—giving Bible studies, working with young people, understanding the Bible, winning souls.

I began to speak at youth rallies and Weeks of Prayer in Church academies and grade schools. I packed my banjo and traveled to San Gabriel, San Fernando, Portland, and Seattle. My time in the administration of the Church was minimal now, as I had been taught how to do that. The leaders in the Church had freedom to develop their domains. I was starting really to enjoy pastoring. My one-day flirtation with dentistry had vanished.

The 1960s were a period of great upheaval in North America. Young people were expressing themselves in new ways. Events had changed the society I grew up in. I had not witnessed the societal effects of assassinations, but now young leaders had been gunned down. The Vietnam war was perceived by young America as the most immoral war in American history. No one I knew bragged about being a Vietnam veteran.

Daily protests spilled over into all facets of American life, especially on college and university campuses. Pictures appeared weekly of college administrative offices taken over by cigar and pot-smoking college students. High-profile murders hit the headlines at a record pace. War protest marches, civil rights demonstrations, campus revolts—we were in a rapidly changing world.

In 1969 I received an invitation to become the first campus chaplain on the Riverside Campus of Loma Linda University. By then things were going so well at the Church that I was conflicted. I had enjoyed youth pastoring and I knew I would enjoy that new position. But my views of the pastorate had leveled, and I wasn't sure I wanted to trade a Church for a campus; not just yet, anyway. This would be the first position of its kind in a pro-activated Adventist college system where students were making new demands on administration. Furthermore, I wasn't sure how society on an Adventist campus had changed.

I visited the La Sierra campus, went to the dorms, met in rooms and lobbies to see where students were on the idea of a campus chaplain. I met with the pastoral staff and the Religion Department and many faculty members to understand their take. I met with the Conference administrators who would be writing my check. And I finally turned down the offer. I just wasn't passionate about it.

My trip to Auburn, Washington, in 1970, to hold a Week of Prayer at my academy *alma mater* was especially rewarding. I ran across an architect in the city who was designing and building churches. When I walked into his office in the City of Auburn, I saw a set of plans laying on his desk for an SDA Church he had designed for McKinleyville, California. It was very attractive and unique.

Later I found the same design in Glendale, Arizona, being built by my Seminary friend Keith Brown and designed by the same architect. I stared in amazement at the beauty of his design. I had just laid eyes on what would someday become the Camarillo Church. When I arrived home, I had a whole set of plans in my attaché case for the building committee to study.

For membership input we posted pictures, in the foyer of the Church, of fifteen different designs the congregation might choose from. After several weeks we took a congregational vote. The McKinleyville Church was the one chosen by the congregation. As a result, our building committee sent representatives to Northern California to photograph and observe the new Church, which was in its final building stages.

With an actual plan before us, we were on the move. Suddenly I had a lot to do. I started systematically driving around the City looking at possible building sites. The Conference had bought land in the town several years before, but it had not turned out to be an attractive site to our needs since it was located next to a proposed public park. We ended up selling it to the City. This caused another spate of articles in the *Camarillo Daily News*, filled with letters to the editor written by people who thought we should have *donated* the land to the City.

Site after site fell by the wayside for various reasons—too small, too big, too remote, zoning issues, drainage problems and tight City regulations. I became a professional land hunter spending as much time at the Ventura County offices as needed. Our congregation moved from renting the United Methodist Church on Anacapa Drive to meeting at the First Baptist Church on Temple Street for worship and limited activities, on the possibility that we would buy a piece of land adjacent to their building.

After a year or so we finally got the drainage studies on the Baptist land and found the costs of land preparation prohibitive. When we informed the owners that we could not afford to buy their property because of the developmental costs we found our stay to be less comfortable and we ended up returning to the Methodist Church.

Over and over our search ran up against closed doors. Camarillo was still a new City. It was a carefully planned community and we had to fit into that plan. But all during this time we were putting money in the bank. At this point things began to change.

SEARCHING FOR A CENTRAL THEOLOGICAL PRINCIPLE

Every philosophy of ministry is rooted in some central theological principle. Discovering that principle involves identifying and comparing numerous traditions represented in North American Christianity. In general, we all agreed that we were Christians although surprisingly, Christianity was not clearly defined in our thinking.

Christianity did not come to us in the twentieth century through an unbroken line of agreement from the time of Jesus Christ. Historically, it had split into two major divisions long ago: eastern and western. Adventists were clearly in the western division. Growing up Adventist I had the unrealistic notion that our Church was unique in its beliefs, conduct, tradition and especially its Truth. As I matured and pursued my education it became very clear that Adventism was a child of its times—conditioned by many facets of the American religious experience. Yet dividing Christianity into western and eastern was not enough. Western Christianity developed in the Roman Catholic tradition and then in time split into Catholic and Protestant. With our attitudes toward and warnings against Catholicism we could conclude that we were Protestants.

We were proud of our Protestant roots. In fact, we pictured ourselves as called by God to finish the work of the Reformation. That meant we were not to follow Luther or Calvin where they were when they died. We were to continue doing the kind of work they had been doing in layering back the great falsehoods that had evolved over centuries and had become the great apostasy, namely the development of the Roman Papacy, which was destined to bring all the prophesies of Revelation and its symbolic beasts and scarlet women to fruition in a last attempt to usurp the prerogatives of God on earth.

As important as these ideas were, we were not simply Protestants. We were reformative Protestants carrying on the duties of recovering the Present Truth for this time.

Protestantism itself was divided into three historical, theological traditions: Lutheran, Calvinist, and Radical Reformation. Here our identity was not so clearly defined. I had never really understood these divisions as plainly as I did when I got through graduate school where we studied theological development and historical Christianity.

My college education had been more concerned with piecing together parts of all three of these traditions without scrutinizing their sources other than the Bible. But at Seminary we studied the Protestant heritage as progressive rather than categorical. I cannot remember that any professor identified Adventism as being legitimately or exclusively placed in any one of these categories. Sister White was our catalyst and she grew up in the Methodist tradition.

Our sectarian movement identified itself as being prophetically assigned the place of the remnant Church at the end of time. As such it was eclectic regarding the Protestant Reformation. Though they were probably to be regarded as great men of God, no reformer was completely correct for us in his views or actions. Each was uncovering some important Truth lost in the middle ages. But neither was any reformer completely wrong. Our job as the prophetic fulfillment of the remnant notions of the apocalypse was to connect all the dots that would finally present the Truth, and for this we had been given a prophetic voice. Only Sister White was presented to us as infallible.

This feeling of being the only ones who had rightly integrated the elements of Truth uncovered by the reformers gave us our historical and prophetic identity. We had The Truth. We were the remnant people. We were the people who would go through to the kingdom of glory except, of course, for those many who would leave us. Not everyone who claimed to have the "Present Truth" would endure to the end. Only a small group would finally make it up to the summit of that long hill our prophet had seen in her early vision. The Black Cloud was now more imminent than ever.

Those who would benefit eternally would be small due to apostasies in our own ranks. The power of evil was strong, and many would be led astray by the world. That worldly straying could include anything from wearing a wedding ring, to eating meat, to enjoying ballroom dancing, to using a drum set and guitars in the worship services of a congregation.

When it came to a central or cohesive theology or behavior we had elements across the board. We rejected the theological core of the Catholic Mass (transubstantiation) and the Lutheran Eucharist (consubstantiation) in favor of the symbolism of the Lord's Supper trumpeted by the Radical Reformation. Historically we identified more with Zwingli and Wesley than Luther, Calvin, or the Pope. As it turned out we were much like the Methodists who celebrated the communion service once a quarter. That made sense—Sister White had come from the Methodist tradition.

We were told the quarterly procedure was a tradition, only if we asked. But we didn't ask. Quarterly was not a biblical mandate. The Christian Church (Disciples of Christ) tradition of celebrating the Lord's Supper weekly was probably closer to the biblical teaching that said, [26] "For as often as you eat this bread and drink the cup, you proclaim the Lord's death until he comes." (1 Cor 11:26).

Christians in all traditions claimed their views to be scriptural and yet they did not all agree on specific points. So, God had to ordain one denomination to set the benchmark of Truth. And that was us. We were the remnant Church.

> [12] "Here is a call for the endurance of the saints, *those who keep the commandments of God and the faith of Jesus*." (Rev 14:12. Emphasis supplied)

> [17] "Then the dragon was angry with the woman, and went off to make war on the rest of her offspring, on *those who keep the commandments of God and bear testimony to Jesus*. And he stood on the sand of the sea." (Rev 12:17. Emphasis supplied)

We were not a table Church (those who made communion the center of worship). We were a Church that preached the Bible. The word of God was central to our worship. Hence our pulpits were in the middle of the chancel, not split like the Catholics or others who came to worship by breaking bread.

These differences could be dismissed for two reasons. I was in an Adventist graduate education program learning how Adventists did things, and if I had any question about what the Bible really taught I could always study the writings of our prophet. She had given us the last word. In the end it was the remnant Church that counted—the leftovers from apostate religion were gathered together as God's true Church. And I was part of that true Church.

So, while we represented a cross section of western Protestant thought and Radical Protestant practice, our real concern was this prophetic distinction. I was a minister in the true Church. And in practice that meant that we had the last word on these things as we tied theology to our everyday lives. Yet even though we could refer to ourselves as the "remnant Church" we were never to consider ourselves "the remnant." Not yet.

In the early days the advent group held that they were "the remnant." But this was finally rejected because it was based on the notion that the door to salvation was shut in 1844 and after that date no one would be saved but those in the "movement." So "the remnant" were those in the original Millerite movement. Sister White had had a vision to that effect.[2] As new converts asked to become part of the Church the

---

2. This is a disputed position. The Ellen G. White Estate, keeper of the archive of Sister White contends that she never held this closed-door theory. D. M. Canright, early SDA pioneer and friend of Sister White held that she did. The argument is basically that she held the doctrine of the Shut Door from 1844–1851. She says she received a vision in 1849, which gave her a "new view" of the "open and shut door." (*Early Writings*, 86). Elder Canright wrote, "All the early Adventists, with Miller at their head, explained the parable [of the ten virgins] in that way [that those without 'oil' were shut out, lost, probation ended]. And they were correct. When their set time passed they were dazed. They still insisted that their message had been right; probation had ended. They still hoped the Lord would come, and expected him any day. They ceased exhorting sinners, ceased praying for them, and said, 'The door is shut.' This is the origin of the 'shut door' theory. . . . It was not until five years later (1849)

leadership worked things around to make that possible and the doctrine was dropped once and for all.

The distinction between "remnant" and "remnant Church" made room for two ideas—many would yet come into true belief and many would yet fall away to false teaching. In salvation nothing was really finished yet—the ministration in the heavenly Sanctuary was still making its decisions as to who was who in the grand scheme of present salvation. It was a distinction that would yet be debated by Adventists of all stripes. And it was a distinction that brought great criticism from non-Adventist apologists.

THE SDA CENTRAL CORE OF WORLD VIEW

The central core of our world view was the "great controversy" theme made popular among us by Sister White. Authors before her had used it. John Milton (1608–1674) had written an extensive poem long before.[3] And in more modern times C. S. Lewis used the same theme very effectively.[4] It basically told the story of humankind from creation to re-creation—from Eden lost to Eden restored. So, my philosophy of ministry would be couched in this theme.[5]

Our job as ministers was to function in the role of people involved in the restoration process—theologically this would include a correct understanding of justification and sanctification. And because God was active in judgment we were to fulfill our role of purifying the Church on earth as it prepared for an eternity with God. Educating for eternity was our role—and as in any good educational system this included grading, testing, and evaluating. Our denomination decried the fact that the "nominal" churches had largely abandoned the process of discipline. But that was to be expected when the same churches had essentially played down or completely dropped the doctrine of the judgment.

Many evangelicals saw the judgment as having occurred at the death of Christ on the cross. They saw Jesus' intercessory work in heaven beginning at the ascension when Christ sat down at the right hand of the Father. (Heb 1:3). That was part and parcel of the gospel taught in the New Testament.

Adventists, on the other hand, had a much more complicated scheme of salvation. They saw the intercessory work of Christ in two parts—from the ascension to 1844 and from 1844 to the *Parousia*. The cross set up the potential, the Sanctuary

---

that Seventh-day Adventists invented the theory of an 'open door' from Rev. 3:7, 8." Canright, *Life of Mrs. E. G. White,* 104–105.

3. Milton, *Paradise Lost,* (1667), and *Paradise Regained,* (1671).

4. C. S. Lewis' books play on this theme, especially in his *Perelandra, Screwtape Letters, Chronicles of Narnia,* and *Mere Christianity.*

5. Jehovah's Witnesses emphasized the same schema. Jehovah's Witnesses, *From Paradise Lost to Paradise Regained,* (1958).

carried it to fruition. This was a doctrine born in the 1844 movement. Ushering in the end (in 1844) Christ moved from the intercessory work in the first apartment of the heavenly Sanctuary to the judgment work in the most holy place.

Such theology gave permission to the Church, indeed obligation, to practice a similar kind of judgment on earth, cleaning out the overt sins of the Church was one of the prophet's major tasks. Her many *Testimonies* were primarily focused on these judgmental actions. And we were told the stories of ministers who were living secret immoral lives, who, when speaking at camp meetings, etc., were *outed* in public by Sister White.

The *Testimonies* were replete with letters she had written to workers and teachers, even relatives, who were cherishing such sins as meat eating, not paying tithe, ignoring clear principles of health reform, breaking Sabbath rules, and practicing poor parental habits or immorality. These stories coupled as they were with the need for the Church to continually purify itself in the face of the judgment process, which could begin at any time for anyone, created a mentality in the super-conscientious that too often led to fanaticism.

These stories were not lost on me. Morning after morning, long before the sun had appeared in the eastern sky, I was reading these chapters, excerpting thoughts in my daybooks and buying into this as the work of the pastor. My ears became tuned to almost anything a Church member said to me about the questionable actions of other Church members. This deacon was seen smoking; this woman was washing dishes in the kitchen at the State Hospital on Sabbath; this young member was going to work half an hour before sundown on Friday and getting off work several hours after the sun had gone down. I was soon at the point where I dreaded to answer the phone for fear that another religious tattletale was on the line.

Was this the job of a pastor—to follow up all the leads on the religious scandalous in our midst? I had threats from well-meaning people that I would be held accountable if I didn't clean up these lives. And I did not get this only from Church members. I supplied my own list based on my research each morning. These instructions trickled ("flowed?") into my sermons.

In addition to comments about reading novels, playing meaningless games, wearing jewelry—especially the wedding ring—attending the theatre, or movies, getting angry, and one of the worst sins of the age—owning and watching a television, I attempted to preach the gospel. I could not overcome the impression I was leaving that the gospel was to be understood as overcoming these propensities.

As I look at the sermons I preached during this period I shudder at their overarching tone. My concept of justification and salvation was compromised by my emphasis on these externals. "Majoring on minors" some would call it. But to me it was the sand in the oyster—irritating the shell fish; it was the thorn in the side, the worm in the apple, and so I spent much time thinking and preaching about these things— thinking I was preaching about the apple, the thorn, and the pearl irritation produced.

The immoral sinners in the Church needed cleansing. How were they cleansed? By quitting their sin, of course—stop watching TV, guard the edges of the Sabbath, take off that wedding ring, and quit eating meat. There were positive sides to this too, but they were so shrouded in religious jargon that I could scarcely have told what they meant.

One night, while still an intern in the city, I had listened to my mentor, the most avid devotee of Sister White's writings I had ever known. Here was a man who not only read the *Testimonies*, he lived them. This Wednesday night included a scheduled disfellowshipping period to follow the regular Prayer Meeting talk of the evening. He talked about psychology and sociology and how these disciplines had misled our culture and presented a substitute for the genuine article of Christian life. His sources were exclusively Sister White's writings. Upon conclusion of his talk we all prayed together and then sat back for discipline to be administered.

Most of those who had been earmarked for disfellowship were not present. Either they didn't care to be publicly embarrassed or they were simply so far gone that they didn't care about anything religious—certainly not about being Adventists anymore.

One young couple, however, was there to be dropped from membership and they wanted to speak to the congregation. They were there to defend themselves, or to speak to the motion to drop them. They were guilty of divorcing their spouses and marrying each other, and now they were to pay for it with the public shame of excommunication. The husband asked to speak. He was a clinical psychologist and he first addressed some of the ideas the pastor had covered in his talk that evening.

The young man essentially said that as he had sat there and heard his profession trashed before the group, he thought it was okay. He mentioned that not everyone understood what psychologists do to help people face life and put their lives back together. He thought it was not clear if his profession had anything to do with the plan to excommunicate him and his wife from fellowship. But he wanted the congregation to know that it had not really helped to put their lives together after the pain they had been through. This was a heart-touching speech. He didn't ask for any special consideration and the vote was taken, and the couple was unanimously thrown out.

I never forgot that evening. It has been over fifty years and the event is still etched in my mind. What troubled me more than anything was the self-justification and pride I felt as we voted to cut away this wart on the face of our congregation. This not only provided an example of public agitation by two young people clearly deluded in the direction of life they had chosen to take, it in some way demonstrated what the pastor had just talked about—psychology leads to self-justification or rationalization and excusing of personal sin.

Here was a major element that had to be injected into my philosophy of ministry—true ministry had to include these elements of judgment and cleansing. How else could a congregation demonstrate the righteousness of Christ? Somehow this fit the great controversy that we were all engaged in—what could be called the battle motif of scripture—Christ fighting the armies of Satan for the capture of human souls.

As I pondered this major element years later at Camarillo I thought, at the age of twenty-eight, I now had the subject matter of my philosophy of ministry. And I went to work—preaching, visiting, threatening, wooing and proceeding in my cleanup. It was time to bring the work to an end—to finish the work in Camarillo.

THE BATTLE MOTIF IN MINISTERIAL PHILOSOPHY

After several personal encounters of calling people to account for their personal behavior I began to struggle with my own intuitive conscience. This procedure was taking a serious toll on my spiritual life. How was this different from the battles Christ led against the Pharisees? Where did this leave the struggling soul? Yet who was I to sit in judgment on them? I was not Christ—nothing new there!

Were these really judgments? These were rescue operations. These were righteous crusades against sin. Hate the sin but love the sinner. Augustine had written to that effect and many years later Mohandas Gandhi had said those exact words. People may think those words are in the Bible, but threatening Church discipline could be misunderstood—especially with sinners.

As I struggled with what I understood to be a duty of a minister regarding this disciplinary action, I spent a morning with Dr. Heppenstall on the golf course in Corona. We had a delightful time walking and talking. About half-way through the game I introduced the subject of ministry. I told him that I was growing really weary of being a spiritual detective. He stopped in the middle of the fairway and faced me with a burning question: Who has appointed you to be a spiritual detective? Where did you learn that was your work as a minister of God?

I tried to explain that I had been reading the *Testimonies*. Here I had ministry modeled for me: find the sins in the Church, preach against the sins in the Church, weed out the sins in the Church, and cleanse the Church. He smiled and continued past me down the fairway.

Finally, he stopped, turned around, and issued a hard word: You need to take another look at your understanding of ministry.

The next day I wrote a four-page single-spaced letter to another of my mentors, Dr. Alexander. He was now chair of the Church and Ministry department at the Seminary. We had occasional correspondence, but in this letter, I unloaded with some of my frustrations. My heart was spilling all over the paper. Since he had asked me to write him with challenges from the field as one on the front lines, I knew he would evaluate my words with the greatest of care and understanding. I wrote:

> As I look at my work now, and at the administration of the work, as I know it—and that is all I can do—I see little future in staying in pastoral work. I have

said this at times before when I was in a discouraged state of mind. But now for the first time in five years, I am seriously considering the options I have in a totally positive way—by that I mean, when things are going well in my church, etc. In other words, nothing has sparked me into despair. But reality is hard and brutal—and I question whether I can ever use my own potential to the heights that God expects of me. I think if I remain in the pastoral ministry much longer I will become a lazy slob.[6]

Today this letter looks to me like one of total despair, filled with contradictions despite my denials. I believed I was simply being realistic. I had suggested that I was ready for teaching, after four years in pastoral work, but I privately knew I still had some confusion to straighten out before I could be more qualified for that.

My professor sensed it all and wrote back an insightful and encouraging letter that started me on a path to resolution. Among other things he wrote:

> Methinks you need a new perspective for ministry—maybe a new look also at your doctrine of church. . . . With time on your hands, it would seem to me that your own creativity and praying could go toward some in-depth analysis of what is happening in your preaching and toward some new approaches to reach all classes of people around you, involving whatever other members of the church you can. Allow for organization and organism in terms of the church. Read, as soon as you can, Bonhoeffer's *Life Together,* and then write me of your musings.[7]

I put away the letter and drove to Pasadena. I knew that Bonhoeffer's book would be available at the Fuller Theological Seminary bookstore.

LIFE TOGETHER

A new perspective and direction in my ministry had begun. Life Together connected the dots like no other book I had ever read. The timing was good.

Dietrich Bonhoeffer was a Lutheran pastor in Germany during the Nazi regime. At the age of thirty-nine he was executed as a conspirator against Hitler, only days before the liberation of the concentration camp where he was incarcerated. I had read his book, *The Cost of Discipleship.* But as it turned out, *Life Together* was the book I needed at this point in my experience. I was involved in a new direction—one that was no longer centered in getting out of the ministry but one that was focused on understanding and accomplishing ministry.

At the height of my formulation of a battle motif philosophy of ministry I ran across a series of Jesus' stories that had been lost to me since that first Bible class in college with Professor Sage. He had called them "the parables of grace." (Luke 15).

---

6. Zackrison, *Letter to Wilber Alexander,* (1970).

7. Alexander (1921–2016), *Letter to Edwin Zackrison,* (1970).

A New Direction

Three situations: a lost sheep, a lost coin, and a lost boy. Now the notion struck me in a new way as to the work of a pastor. I sat back to listen to these scriptural insights.

A sheep had wandered off, gotten lost in its own wandering; and a shepherd was going out against all the hardships of life to find this wayward sheep. Not one of his flock went unnoticed. So, he rescued the sheep and brought it back to the sheepfold.

I was struck with the fact that this was a category of people most of us preached to—the immoral sinner—the person who is lost and enmeshed in those sins perceived by others to be most scandalous and horrible. Whenever I preached a sermon aimed at the immoral sinner I got great vibes from the congregation as they came through the door at the end of the service.

"I hope Mr. Whatshisname was listening to that sermon—he really needs what you had to say this morning, pastor!" "You really gave it to them today, pastor! Congrats!!" And it was generally said within an atmosphere of satisfaction and pious smugness.

Some people loved to hear the prostitute condemned and the robber chastised. If ever there was an "Amen!" shouted out in Church, it was in a sermon going after the immoral sinners. All the catalogs of sins found in the Bible were fair game for the preacher who spoke of and at the immoral sinners. Yet by contrast the good shepherd in this biblical passage didn't engage in this kind of work. He didn't beat up the sheep. He didn't deepen the wounds this sheep had already suffered. He simply went out into the night in a risky search to reclaim his cherished creature. The concept caused me trepidation. But it gave me a new insight. The time was ripe for fine tuning the work of a pastor. His work was not to be censure but rescue.

Jesus' second story was about a coin misplaced in the dust of the floor in the house. The operative phrase was "in the house." Could believers be misplaced and still be in the Church? What kind of sinner would that be? A moral sinner? Perhaps this was a contrast between the sins of the flesh and the sins of the mind? Outward versus inward? Adultery versus lust? Robbery versus covetousness? And the thought hit me—I had heard my mentor use this contrast but now it seemed more relevant than ever. Sermons addressing the moral sinners usually produced fewer "Amens."

Finally, Jesus spoke of a son who rebelled against his father and left home for a far country. Squandering his inheritance on those very areas that covered the immoral life, the son eventually ran out of money. And his friends went away as well. Here was a spiritual sinner. He sees the waywardness of his life, repents, returns to his father and asks forgiveness.

> In a Christian community everything depends upon whether each individual is an indispensable link in a chain. Only when even the smallest link is securely interlocked is the chain unbreakable. A community, which allows unemployed members to exist within it, will perish because of them. It will be well, therefore, if every member receives a definite task to perform for the community, that he may know in hours of doubt that he, too, is not useless

> and unusable. *Every Christian community must realize that not only do the weak need the strong, but also that the strong cannot exist without the weak. The elimination of the weak is the death of the fellowship.*[8]

Statements like this began to bring together the big picture of ministry. Church was not a club or a society. Biblically it included many of the elements of both but went far beyond either in its meaning. The basis of Church was not to be *common interests*, but rather, the basis of Church was *common parentage*. We were talking family when we talked Church. We were not talking simply about a group of people who all liked to quilt or who loved to square dance. You could get rid of friends, but you were stuck with family! That was a clue to the meaning of Church.

The essence of Church then comes from the activity of someone other than us. Any desires we must fellowship or be together for the right reasons come from outside of us. Otherwise Church would only be club or society, which are not based on common parentage. They are based on common interests. As such only the exclusive can get in.

Those who are members of Mensa International must test out at a certain IQ. Amway Diamonds are people who have accomplished a superior level of entrepreneurship based on their focused efforts that may take many years of hard work. This is the nature of clubs and societies. But it is not the nature of Church. Church has no such requirements. People of all different backgrounds, careers, interests, and strata of society can be Church.

And Bonhoeffer summed it up,

> Christianity means community through Jesus Christ and in Jesus Christ. No Christian community is more or less than this. Whether it be a brief, single encounter or the daily fellowship of years, Christian community is only this. *We belong to one another only through and in Jesus Christ.*[9]

It was gradually developing that something was more important than being the *true* Church. And that was being *truly* Church.[10]

> The church is that community called into being by the Gospel, which is God's covenant of love in Jesus Christ, and given its life through the power of God's Spirit in order to praise and serve the living God. All those who accept this calling—of whatever race, nationality, or culture—are joined together as one people commissioned by God to witness by word and deed to God's love for the world. They signify their corporate identity by their common confession of faith that Jesus is the Christ, the Son of the living God, their incorporation into the body of Christ through baptism, their thankful celebration of

---

8. Bonhoeffer, *Life Together*, 94. Emphasis supplied.

9. Ibid., 21. Emphasis supplied.

10. Crow and Duke (eds.). "The Church . . . Seeking to be Truly Church Today," *Come and See*, 325–352.

Christ's saving work and abiding presence through the Lord's supper, their common commitment to direct their lives in accord with the will of God as made known through the testimony of scripture, and their shared experience of the Holy Spirit who empowers them for ministry as disciples and ambassadors of Christ to and for the world.[11]

The lights were shining all around. We had done public evangelistic meetings, door-to-door visitation, newspaper advertising, Bible school, personal invitation to Church. What had we done to build spiritual community? Discovering that would open us all up to the evangelistic personality, the result of being *truly* Church. On the other hand, how does one go about discovering an approach that helps people to concentrate on their own spiritual growth? I was about to find out what God planned for his next chapter in my life.

THE NATURE OF CHURCH

Where Life Together *helped me was in finally giving me clues for pulling things together that I had been delineating for several years in this search for a meaningful ministerial philosophy.* It finally gave me the big picture, and once a person has the big picture clearly in mind, how to apply it becomes clearer. Several years later I would find the contrast in life experiences that would help me differentiate between Church and organization. It would take time—no question. No one just switches gears overnight.

Later I would go on a good-will trip as a member of a university symphony orchestra to eastern Europe. We gave concerts in Rumania, Russia, and Estonia. When we got to Russia we gave a concert in a music conservatory in Moscow. All of us were thrilled at the opportunity and the response we got. Our audience especially liked Gershwin's "Porgy and Bess."

After the concert we stood out in front of the conservatory performance hall and the students came up to talk to us. I noticed that many of them picked us out by the instrument we played. I had several clarinet players gather around me. And although we could not understand each other's spoken language we did understand each other's language of the clarinet. Questions ranged from "What model of Buffet clarinet do you play?" To "What size of reed do you use for playing classical symphonic music?" "Do you have a specialized barrel?" "Where did you get that ligature?" We were a *community* of clarinet players and we experienced instant enjoyment in each other's company.

In graduate school I joined a barbershop quartet and we won a talent show with the number we presented. Ever since then I have enjoyed barbershop music. In fact, I have sung in the local barbershop Christmas concerts several times. When we get

---

11. Ibid., 327.

together it's like we have known each other all our lives. We are basking in the enjoyment of sharing a love for the kind of music we sing in the barbershop *community*.

We all understand this kind of community. But Bonhoeffer pointed out very convincingly that this was not the nature of Church. He emphasized with biblical evidence that Church is not a gathering of people who share a common interest. Rather, Church is something much different. Repetition deepens impression: Church is a gathering of people who share a common parent. Church is not an organization per se in the scriptures. Church is a group of people who have responded to a call of God and become his children. And since those in Church have this connection, they are a community of people who share a common heavenly parent. So, in a real sense *church is family.* Those hymns and songs that present Christianity as "the family of God" are on to something.

Truly understood, this concept will eliminate the religious caste system so prevalent in fundamentalist organizations. Bonhoeffer's notion of the strong needing the weak, as much as the weak needing the strong, becomes understandable. I saw more clearly that my approach had been to eliminate whoever we perceived were the weak in the Church. This was a self-destructive approach to ministry.

Finally, this can be illustrated by vertical and horizontal lines. In a social organization people are united horizontally. That is, they are a society of people who associate with each other on a horizontal level. But Church does not start out on such a plane. Instead Church starts out vertically, meaning we are connected by the call of God to Jesus Christ. Church is made up horizontally of people who have responded in that vertical connection with Christ. Bonhoeffer explains,

> Christianity means community through Jesus Christ and in Jesus Christ. No Christian community is more or less than this. . . . We belong to one another only through and in Jesus Christ.[12]

This vertical dimension is the beginning; indeed, it is the first requirement in forming a sound, meaningful philosophy of ministry. How did this translate into my situation—a Christian minister struggling to understand why he was here and what God expected him to do? It meant that we needed to work on the spiritual realities of our congregation. We had spent a lot of time doing religious things. We had mainly assumed that something would happen to any person who was willing to share his faith. But what were we doing that focused on that vertical experience and the nature of the Church community that began with an adoption connection to our heavenly parent. Sermons were good, but they were not enough.

I began to see my own perspective growing, and yet I still lacked the tools to set before the people so that these ideas could bear fruit. I had learned this: God takes

---

12. Bonhoeffer, *Life Together,* 94.

you one step at a time and when you need it the next revelation will come. I might be ready for that next step.

CHAPTER TWENTY-FOUR

A Step into A New Direction

"Faith is to believe what we do not see; and the reward of this faith is to see what we believe."
— St. Augustine

THE SCIENCE OF PRAYER

ELDER JAMES WOLTER (1925–2012) *was senior pastor of the Oxnard Church.* We had met each other at The White when he was an associate pastor there. Before that he had been senior minister at a Church in Minnesota where some of my relatives attended. Now we played golf together weekly and talked about ministerial strategies since our Churches were only ten miles apart.

One day shortly after my "dental" experience at the community college, Jim and I were playing golf at the $2.00 (ministers' Monday rate) course in Ventura County. He mentioned that he was having a series of meetings in his Church led by a layman, Robert Lee Law (d. 2010), a religion graduate of Loma Linda University. These meetings, he reported, were different than any he had ever been through before. They were not the typical evangelistic meetings where a speaker went through all the Adventist doctrines. Instead they were more like a practical class or seminar in understanding how prayer works. The class met once a week for seven weeks. It was a program called "The Positive Way."

When he said program, my brain disengaged. I was done with programs and I told him so. Well, he told me he would keep me informed regarding the class. I thanked him.

For the next few weeks Jim updated me whenever I saw him. Finally, he told me that Bob Law would like to meet me and talk to me about the program. He said he had heard the Week of Prayer I had given at Loma Linda University, Riverside campus in the fall of 1970. He said he was impressed with my "sincerity and conviction." I confessed that I would like to meet Bob, but I was not interested in any more programs.

That was what Jim wanted to hear. Only the first half of my sentence registered with him. He set up an appointment at my home for us to meet Bob Law and his wife, Elsie. I was unenthusiastic, but I would give Bob a chance. I set up a tape recorder and microphone by the chair in the living room where he would be making his presentation. I would get this on tape, so I could listen to it in my pensive moments. I certainly had no intention of following through on anything he might say. My mind was made up and closed. I could not be led down another primrose path to failure.

Bob's presentation lasted for two hours. He explained everything he could about *The Positive Way* program, short of taking us through the course. It had to do with our personal Christian experience. It purported to reach out to backsliders in the Church and attempt to win them back—like the shepherd going after that lost sheep. And he gave several stories of his success.

The program was built around the science of prayer, as he called it, for personal victory with a built-in outreach component. When he finished, I asked very few questions because I had already padlocked my mind against any program long before he came. I completely missed the potential for spiritual growth that I had been looking for in my search for a meaningful philosophy of ministry. The word "program" was just too gloomy. I was being courteous to Jim, but I had no plans to buy into any new program, regardless of what it claimed. I had been burned before; I didn't care to smolder again. The German proverb said it: "He who has burned his mouth blows his soup."[1] Only I wasn't blowing any more soup.

Discouragement only came when I expected too much. And I had expected too much from the programs I had poured my heart into. I thanked the Laws and said we would think about it. I thought I had already given it enough consideration. But when they had left, there was one thought that kept gnawing at me, something that Bob had not even emphasized; the potential that this approach might hold for spiritual community building.

Bob Law had also reached out to other people in my Church. The next night our head elder, called. He asked if my wife and I would take *The Positive Way* course in Oxnard with him and his wife. He proceeded to tell me about the exciting results he had heard. As he talked, I knew he had been chatting with Bob Law, a man who never ran out of stories of personal victory! I told him I would think about it.

The next day a deacon, who was an engineer at Point Mugu, called. He asked if my wife and I would go through *The Positive Way* course in Oxnard with him and his wife. He proceeded to tell me some of the exciting results he had heard. As he talked, I knew he had been chatting with Bob Law, a man who never ran out of stories of personal victory. I told him that I would think about it. He added that I better make up my mind fast because the new round of classes would be starting the next week.

1. Peter, *Peter's Quotations: Ideas for our Time*, 174.

Robert Lee Law had one of those ingratiating personalities that made him hard to turn away. He was the personification of positive expectancy and he helped you believe that whatever he was teaching would transform your life as it had his. It was like being around Dr. Robert Schuller of the TV Church in Garden Grove—"The Hour of Power."

Because these two couples were so excited about the program, we decided to take the course over the next seven weeks. What harm could it do? It might be fun. At least we would be doing something spiritual together. And I would have witnesses to the success or failure of another *program*.

THE POSITIVE WAY COURSE AT OXNARD

I found it!—that's what people say when they discover something that alters their life for the better. Now I heard myself saying it. Three couples went through *The Positive Way* course in the Oxnard Church and there was clear evidence that here was something that dealt with basic Christian experience. The seminar took seven weeks. It was accurately a workshop in prayer. It dealt with real prayer topics and did not beat around the bush. It was not sensational. It was not particularly exhilarating. It was just authentic—real people in real time.

Robert Lee Law, author of *The Positive Way* course, was our teacher. He explained circumspectly the concepts involved and then he challenged us to try it. We were invited to apply the principles we would learn. And then we were told to bring back the results and testify to them at our next class meeting.

Every week Bob focused on the experiential aspects of prayer. We learned the *ABC's of Bible Prayer*. By the middle of the course I was becoming a believer; I was seeing very concrete results. I had heard of Elder Glenn Coon (1903–1996), an Adventist minister who preached on the science of prayer. But *The Positive Way* was a class, seven weeks in length, with a soul-winning project included—seven weeks of intense focus. I found that I could relate to an educational approach to understanding prayer.

Prayer was one of those subjects that ministers spent very little time explaining because we all took prayer for granted. Like someone had said to me, talk about prayer and what more is there to say: just go and pray. And that's what I had always done. Little had ever been said to me about actually expecting answers. God either said "Yes," or he said, "No," or he said, "Maybe." And that was clear and final. What else was there to say?

We learned in the class that our prayer life was based on certain fundamental realities. All that I had ever learned about prayer was that we should always pray *for God's will* to be done. But here we were reminded that when we knew God's will, we did not need to ask for his will to be done. Instead we were to treat expressions of God's will as specific promises.

Over 3500 promises appear in the Bible. We didn't know who had counted them, but we were taught to treat all instructions and commandments as divine promises and therefore to be counted as such. God would not ask us to obey without giving us the power to follow through. So, for example, I didn't have to pray for God to forgive me of my sins if it was his will. We already knew that it was his will to forgive not only us but me. Under what circumstances would it not be his will to forgive me? Forgiveness was a promise, guaranteed to anyone who asked. There were some conditions, but the promise was certain. So, we merely needed to experience his forgiveness.

Thinking back, I recognized that it was all contained in a text I had learned from my childhood: [9] "If we confess our sins, he is faithful and just, and will forgive our sins and cleanse us from all unrighteousness." (1 John 1:9). Forgiveness was guaranteed to those who confessed and asked. So rather than pray, "Please God, forgive me of my sin if it is your will," I could pray, "Dear God, I ask that you forgive my sins. I believe you are forgiving me of my sins because you have promised to do so in 1 John 1:9." Asking and believing were basic concepts in the science of prayer.

There was a third step. If God had promised, i.e., stated his will in a clear and straightforward way, then I could legitimately thank him for fulfilling that promise as I finished my prayer. It is done. It is finished. It is real. I know that I am forgiven—no questions asked! Astonishing in its finality. And that was an affirmation of faith in God's word.

To get us started, we were taught a specific prayer to repeat and we were given several clear biblical promises to claim over the coming week. Next, we were instructed to keep track of the answers we got whether they were peace of mind (Phil 4:7, John 14:27), help in troubles (Ps 24:19, John 16:33), patience (Heb 6:12, Rom 5:3–4), etc. We were given a sheet of paper to write them down.

The promises seemed endless and all six of us in the class went searching throughout the seven weeks for biblical promises that dealt with our daily spiritual lives. We were connected to the word from the beginning to the end of the course. Most of the promises dealt with spiritual elements—forgiveness, victory, strength—these were spiritual realities.

Were there promises for material blessings as well? That seemed like an obvious question. And our teacher, who visited us at home once a week during the seven weeks, pointed out that while there are guaranteed spiritual blessings available in the promises, this did not rule out material things. Obviously, the Bible did not list promises for certain cars, *viz.*, "Lord, please give me a new Porsche." But there were promises that had a direct bearing on the very material lives we live: "Lord, you have promised to fulfill all my needs."

[19] And my God will supply every need of yours according to his riches in glory in Christ Jesus. (Phil 4:19)

[8] Blessed are the pure in heart, for they shall see God. (Matt 5:8)

> ²⁹ And do not seek what you are to eat and what you are to drink, nor be of anxious mind. (Luke 12:29)

I may need transportation, that is not a Porsche. Even eating and drinking were needs God would fulfill. Did that mean you couldn't ask for a Porsche? No—but you had no assurance that was the car you would receive when you asked. There was no biblical promise that mentioned a Porsche. So, if that was your prayer it should be accompanied by if it is your will. In other words, there were prayers for material things that were not specifically identified as God's will, in which case we were to pray considering our commitment to him, i.e., recognize that some things are wisely left up to God. He was not a heavenly vending machine.

To deal with uncertainty, the course taught us to divide our prayers into two categories: the prayer of faith (for clear promises) and the prayer of commitment (where no clear promises were given but for what we identified to be our specific needs).

As we sought to grasp what should have been very simple principles we were required to apply rather than theorize.

> ¹⁰ When Daniel knew that the document had been signed, he went to his house where he had windows in his upper chamber open toward Jerusalem; and *he got down upon his knees three times a day* and prayed and gave thanks before his God, as he had done previously. (Dan 6:10. Emphasis supplied)

We were assigned a written prayer to pray three times a day (like Dan 6:10) during the seven-week period. If we didn't pray specifically, how would we recognize specific answers? I came to see that most of my prayers were not specific enough to make it possible for me even to identify a precise answer. This was part of the science, or an application of the material we were learning.

The first week seemed so simplistic to me that I barely fulfilled the assignment. But when we returned for the second session, the other people from our Church were the first on their feet to testify that they had been able to perceive clear answers as they had applied the principles we had learned in the first period.

I perceived that all of us were college graduates—an engineer, a musician, a nutritionist, a teacher, a physician and a minister. I determined to test it all out for the next session and my perceptions began to change. As I witnessed changes in the lives of those from my Church members, I also began to recognize specific answers to my own personal prayers and that is when I found it. I still was not sure about the effect our following these principles might have on those we prayed for, but once I began applying them, my skepticism began to vanish.

At the first meeting, we were divided into small groups, each having its own teacher. And we were asked to agree on praying for one person, one we all knew and had contact with, and this person was to be our prayer focus for the duration of the course. We were free to pray for anyone we wanted, any time we wanted, but this one person was to remain the prayer focus of all in our small group. We were to select a person who we perceived to be a backslider.

We started out with a biblical promise that called upon every one of us to use our gifts in reaching the person we were praying for. Without one's own commitment to be a vessel of grace, we were reminded, such a prayer might end up in the file folder for good but ineffectual intentions where most of my knowledge of prayer already was collecting dust.

We were to pray for God to use us to reach this person whose spiritual life we perceived was in danger. At first, this approach seemed very artificial and sometimes threatening, as well as judgmental. In my mind, I was transported back to our earlier campaign where I approached strangers with a piece of literature.

But this was different. We were only to pray that we would be brought into situations that provided an opportunity for personal contact—nothing contrived, just natural. We left that first meeting wondering how all this was going to work out. Just watch God work. Don't sweat it. Be natural. Simply recognize the situation as something God had arranged. When you run into someone you are praying for, your whole demeanor is sharpened. Eighteen times a day for the following forty-nine days our prayers would go up to God asking him to use us to bring spiritual life and direction to this person who we all knew and cared about. When we finished the course, I wondered where we were to go with this. I was about to find out.

THE POSITIVE WAY COURSE AT CAMARILLO

Our involvement with The Positive Way *course did not end when the workshop was over.* We were all so excited about it that we were keen to share what we were learning. And so, at the end of the seven-week course, we met in Camarillo to offer the class to our local congregation. Getting board approval to run the program in our Church was a minor detail because our six participants had infected the Church members with their fervor and liveliness. Indeed, people were already signing up to be in the first class in Camarillo.

Since we only had three couples, in addition to Bob Law and his wife, we had to limit the first round to eight new couples. The minute Church members heard that the class would be limited, there was a virtual run on the sign-up sheets. Priority was given to elected Church leaders simply because of the way the congregation was organized. Those who could not get in were told there would be another class starting in just seven weeks. I had never seen such positive energy in our congregation since the chartering.

Before the year was up, we had offered the course several times and by then we not only had many trained teachers, but several moderators as well. A moderator oversaw running the whole course and had under him/her around five teachers to supervise and instruct. I was pleased. People were constantly talking about the Lord's blessings because they had received specific answers to their prayers. It was like nothing I had seen. Before my eyes, I was seeing the chapters in *Life Together* enfleshed in this congregation. This class addressed the *vertical* aspect of the Christian life. Everything I had tried before, spoke mainly to the *horizontal* aspect. And that change in focus made the difference.

As members grew spiritually, they naturally looked for places to share their gratitude for the living experience that God was giving them. It was not as if no one had been committed or lacking in spirituality before this, but now there was a tangible sense of spiritual growth in the congregation. Calls for days of fasting and prayer went out from members. Seeing their prayers answered in so many ways, members longed for a prayer project that would give spiritual direction to the entire congregation as well.

One natural place to apply their new-found faith was in the construction of the new Church building. We were meeting in the First Baptist Church on Temple Street, and our Church had decided to purchase three adjacent acres that the Baptists had up for sale. It seemed like a good fit—we could share parking and we had a good relationship with the congregation.

We ordered developmental studies on the property and the whole operation became subjected to prayer. Prayer was a powerful experience where God could be observed working on our behalf. The building fund was growing at an unprecedented rate. The cost of the whole operation was a projected $300,000, and we had already raised almost a third of that in cash. I had avoided the signing of pledges because of the disasters I had observed in other churches' attempts to raise money quickly.

The Conference policy stated that as a new congregation we were expected to raise one-third of the total cost in cash. The Conference would then contribute one-third of the total cost and arrange for a loan that would cover the last third. Only then could we begin the building. But things were not working out. The studies on the land we planned to purchase from the Baptists were not encouraging. The property would require serious improvements, mainly connected to drainage problems. In fact, the more we studied it, the worse it looked and the more formidable the cost projections became.

After serious days of fasting and prayer it became clear that this was not going to work out and we reluctantly told the Baptists we could not afford to solve the projected costs associated with land improvements and would have to look for other property.

Our relationship with the Baptists suddenly went south and we found ourselves looking for another building to rent. The Methodists welcomed us back to our original arrangement. We were disappointed. I renewed my search for a new building site. We believed that God was working with us. Our new approach to prayer had prepared most everyone in the group for the fact that disappointments may come but that when one prays the prayer of commitment for God's will to be manifested, one has the assurance that God will provide in his unique way.

A Step into a New Direction

Over the next year, I examined seventeen pieces of land. I would take members of the building committee to look at some—piece after piece. One plot we particularly liked was up above the City with a full view of the Conejo Valley. A Church on that site could be seen for miles around the valley. The only objectionable feature was a giant water tower on the back of the site. But we were sure that we could erect a building that would hide this eye sore.

My family and I left for the 1970 General Conference meetings in Atlantic City, New Jersey, confident that when we got back we might purchase that property and be on our way to building our new sanctuary. But once again, our hopes were dashed. It just couldn't be arranged. Another weekend of fasting and prayer, prayers of commitment for God's will to be done and more pieces of property to examine. We claimed the promises for guidance and wisdom. and we waited.

Then it happened.

A large land company was developing hundreds of acres at the edge of the City and it had assigned some acreage of their planned community to Church plots. Once again things looked hopeful. But over the next few weeks something went awry and the development, as originally planned, fell through.

More prayer, more prayers of commitment. And I examined all the Old Testament promises to the builders of the temple. Surely some of those could be claimed for building our house unto the Lord. Meanwhile, the money was flowing in. And finally, after another weekend of prayer and fasting, the gates of heaven opened. A choice piece of property became available on Las Posas Road.

The company had reworked some of its plans. Today, over fifty years later, the Camarillo Church stands on the property that became available as a direct answer to those weekends of fasting and prayer. The plans I had inspected on architect Kirkman's desk in Auburn, Washington, in 1970, were transformed into a beautiful Church in Camarillo. Our community was united, and we rejoiced in seeing our prayers answered as they had been. The land company had even made special accommodations for us.

With the land deal pending, we turned our attention to raising the rest of the $300,000 for the overall building plan. Our architect flew down from Auburn, Washington. Within weeks he had sent a full set of plans to us and arrangements were being made for ground-breaking. How many of the dots were connected?

I had attended Auburn Academy in 1957 at my brother's invitation. I had decided to become a minister at Auburn Academy in 1958. Two of my best friends had become Bible teachers at Auburn Academy in 1969. I had been invited to give the Week of Prayer at Auburn Academy in 1970. While there I had discovered an architect in Auburn at the very time that land opened. Any connection between these dots? I couldn't avoid thinking so. I didn't share these impressions. I just watched and let things develop. But all of this was connected to prayers being offered. I felt we had all been used by God for this very task. I praised him constantly.

A NEW COMMUNITY OF BELIEVERS

My greatest satisfaction was seeing the congregation developing into a unified community of strong believers. Once more we had seen the hand of God leading us in a new direction and now we turned our minds to the purpose for which this congregation had been raised up.

Knowing that our congregation could grow to large proportions in this fast-developing City, we began to discuss where we wanted to see this Church in twenty years. The fervor of the people, virtually all who had been through this new course, focused on size and future. We were not an institutional Church; we were a community Church. This was before some of the denominational centers had moved into the nearby Thousand Oaks area. *The Voice of Prophecy, It Is Written,* and the communications center would soon come into the vicinity, but we laid our plans early enough not to be impacted by that. Our mission was Camarillo, California.

The consensus view of the membership was that we should build a Church plant that would serve 328 members. When we grew to that total we would spawn. There were some yet unworked areas like Somis and Moorpark that with time could support their own congregations. Our architect designed the plans accordingly to the wishes of the group. I marveled as I watched the enthusiasm grow with each business meeting.

My next assignment was to meet with the Conference officials to let them know of the congregation's plans. I met with the president and the executive secretary in Glendale and disclosed that we were ready to borrow the remainder of the required amount. They were caught off guard. I described briefly what had been happening. They were not up to date on our fund raising. The intense prayers of this spiritual community, the goals of the congregation came as something new to them.

They were amazed that we had raised $100,000 in just four years. But they were especially amazed when we had had no fund-raising campaign that they knew about. I broke it to them that we had avoided fund raising by taking unsigned pledges. This brought a long pause. Finally, the executive secretary asked me if I had ever thought about how much I could have raised if I had brought in a professional fund-raiser from the Conference and asked him to canvass the congregation?

I told him *yes,* I had, and so had the congregation. We had considered that, but the members had seen this approach split churches in the past and they wanted to avoid that. I told him the unsigned pledge approach had worked and had unified the congregation. He just shook his head. He could not believe it. Furthermore, the tithe had continued to climb, and the Conference offerings had never suffered. That would have caught their attention. Also, we had always gotten our ingathering goal.

Now—the time seemed right to drop the bomb. The bomb was my announcement that we wished to borrow the remainder of the funds we needed to break ground by taking out a loan with unsigned pledges. That bomb was a dud. Impossible. And I told him I couldn't come back to the congregation with a canvassing campaign because it would kill the spirit of free and joyful giving. Obviously, I was a greenhorn. I knew nothing about banking procedure. And his reply was simply—that would never work. The Pacific Union Conference would never make a loan on that basis. Out of the question! I learned that no bank or savings association or credit center would ever make a loan on that basis either.

The Conference could not budge. If we wanted to take out a loan for the remaining amount, we would have to come back with pledges signed by individual Church members committing themselves to producing the money over the next five years. Pledges, with signatures on the dotted line, not for the amount we needed, but for 120% of that amount!

That was policy. It was no great surprise. Money people don't take faith as collateral. At the Camarillo Church, we were experiencing life together. We were seeing Bonhoeffer's concept of community in action—people who had a clear understanding of community as a collection of believers who were in vertical relationship to God. This congregation was no longer simply a group of people with common interests. They were seeing their faith live and they knew how to pray and expect God's direction. They knew the difference between the prayer of faith and the prayer of commitment.

I was dealing with businessmen in the form of churchmen and they were dealing with banks. I was convinced I would get no farther. I thanked them for their time and told them I would get back to them. I imagined their conversation after I left—"He's young, he's doing a good job, but he will learn with time. . . . Can you imagine that church raised $100,000 in just four years from its founding! . . . Ed is fortunate to have such a wealthy group. . . . Amazing—but think what we could have done if they had had our fund-raiser go up there!"

The policy-centered Church had spoken. So it was our job to experience the workings of God who could speak. And it happened.

HOW THE CONGREGATION RAISED THE MONEY

I did not return home dejected. I returned home challenged. I knew that God would not abandon us now in our new direction. We had too much evidence that he was leading us. I remembered that first night when we had met together to discuss the possibility of building our own Church in Camarillo. It had been just two years before that we had seriously taken up the subject.

I had simply announced that if I was their pastor we would not be visiting anyone and asking for their money. Of course, I could be outvoted—I only had one vote and if they insisted on a fund-raising campaign where each family was evaluated and told what they could and should give, they could follow that approach—but they would have to run it. I did not come there to raise money—I came there to minister spiritually to this community of faith. I had already seen first-hand what all that emphasis on money could do to a congregation.

After that meeting, one Church member had called me aside and told me how near he had come to leaving the Camarillo Church and going back to Oxnard. He said he had come that night to see how I was going to approach the raising of the building fund. And if I had launched a visitation fund-raising campaign he would have transferred out.

I was aghast. The people were unifying with excitement about the actual thought of building their own Church in Camarillo after just two years in existence as a community of believers. The method was simple: I had handed out a 3x5 card to each family and asked them to write down what they thought they could give over the next twelve months if the Lord continued to bless them as he had during that past year. I repeated that they should not sign their name.

I had the deacons collect the cards and we added up the total in front of the congregation. The total pledged was $7,000. I wrote the total on the blackboard for all to see. And in front of them I tossed cards with the unsigned pledges on them into the trash can. It was all very ceremonious. The total was printed in the Church bulletin announcements the following Sabbath.

I told the members in the business meeting that over the next twelve months, if God continued to bless this congregation the way he had this year we would have $7,000 in the bank as the beginning of the building fund.

I insisted that they perceive these as personal pledges to God—a compact between their family and the Lord. It was not to me, not to the Conference, not to the Church. We had no record other than the total. If their family went bankrupt in the next twelve months their pledge was cancelled. If they moved away their pledge was void.

Could it work? Of course it could. These were people headed in a new direction. Six months later (not the year we had predicted), almost to the day, $7,000 had come into the building fund! Then we called another meeting.

I happily announced that all the pledges were now cancelled. And I rejoiced with them that we had reached our goal in half the time we expected. I then handed out 3x5 cards once again and called for another pledge. They wrote down their pledge without signing it and handed it in. There was no indication of who had filled out any pledge. I added up the total of the pledges, put the total on the blackboard for all to see, and again threw the cards into the waste basket in front of them.

Now I could announce that if the Lord continued to bless us all the way he had over the past year we should have, over the next twelve months, $12,000 more in the building fund. And the business meeting erupted in—a holy applause!

And so it went. With each unsigned pledge the total grew. With each goal realized we cancelled the personal pledges to God and started over until three years later we had $100,000 in the bank, drawing interest. Faith grows, and the results were there to prove it. The pressure was off, and this was community building in action. We were literally learning the meaning of that old hymn: "Standing on the Promises of God!"[2]

---

2. Carter, "Standing on the Promises, *Seventh-day Adventist Hymnal*, No. 518.

But now—the new challenge. This method of fund raising was not my idea. I had learned it from Elder Rea, my mentor. Using this same approach, he had paid off the Church I interned in. Would the Camarillo members sign a pledge? In our monthly business meeting, I told of my conversation at the Conference with leadership. I explained,

> And so, we cannot take a loan until we have $120,000 worth of *signed* pledges, but, I have pledged to you that as long as I am your pastor I will not visit you to tell you what you can or should give or what I expect you to give. Some of you could probably (and want to) give more—so why would I want to limit you to what I think you can give. That's your decision—and by the way, none of my business.[3]

I then unfolded the plan I had been working on since my visit to Glendale.

> I will only announce this approach. We will put totals in the Church bulletin each Sabbath but that's all you will hear about the building fund. This is not a political party beating on you to give. Let yourselves apply the pressure to yourselves.[4]

I laid out the possibilities. I had figured out how many categories it would take to raise that much money in five years—how many giving $1000 a month, $500 a month, $100 a month, $50 a month, etc. But these were only guidelines.

> Here is another 3x5 card. Take this card home and decide if you want to sign it or not. If you don't, throw it away. No one will visit, no one will call. When you come back on Sabbath, if you and your family decided to pledge, give the total and sign your name and drop it in the offering plate. When (or if) we get $120,000 in signed pledges I will go back to the Conference and arrange for the loan. If you want to continue the way we have been going (with unsigned pledges) don't hand it in.[5]

The member who had told me he would never sign a pledge signed it on the spot for $20,000. I told him I couldn't accept this. He asked why? I told him that he had told me that if he had to sign a pledge he would transfer back to the Oxnard Church. I didn't want him to go back to Oxnard. He slugged me—softly. It was a love slug!

THE WINDOWS OF HEAVEN OPENED

Three Sabbaths later we had a total of $120,000 in signed pledges in the offering plate and we were on our way! Could I believe it? Yes, it was simply another in a growing list of miracles at Camarillo.

3. Zackrison, "Notes from Business Meeting," (1972).
4. Ibid.
5. Ibid.

I had finally seen the power of a community united in prayer. I understood better than ever before, "life together." I had seen the unity I had hoped for. I was seeing vision of community described in the book recommended to me by Dr. A just a year before. I knew then that there were no limits to what could be accomplished when God was working with a dedicated group of disciples who viewed the promises of God as gifts to be claimed. It was invigorating.

It was a quiet evening in April 1972. My phone rang.

CHAPTER TWENTY-FIVE

Entering Educational Ministry

"My idea of education is to unsettle the minds of the young and inflame their intellects."
—Robert M. Hutchins

HE HAD TOLD ME: "HOLD OUT FOR . . ."

I took the call in the study. "If you turn this down, I'm afraid I won't be able to help you anymore!" the voice at the other end declared. Who was this? And then I recognized the voice of Dr. Edward Heppenstall, my old graduate school professor, sometime golf partner and longtime friend. I had gone to school with his children and later he had mentored me through two graduate degrees in theology at Seminary. I was happy to hear his voice and wondered what he had going on.

He got right down to business and explained his call. He let me know that Dr. Frank Knittel, president of Southern Missionary College had just called him. Dr. Knittel had informed him that the college board had just passed a request to talk to me about joining the teaching faculty of the SMC Religion Department. And then he reminded me that I had turned down five college invitations. But he had asked me to *hold out* for this one, and he hoped I hadn't changed my mind about teaching.

I sat down. I'd been waiting for this moment for two years, ever since that talk with Dr. Knittel at the General Conference convocation in Atlantic City. But I'd given up hoping. It all seemed so remote. As a religious man, I had been educated to think of delaying gratification indefinitely. I had learned that what I accomplished in this life did not count except for building a character that was becoming for the next life.

I knew that how I lived helped to decide a next life. Therefore, I had no ambition to go for what I wanted. In this way, I demonstrated my faith in God. After he heard my prayers, he would offer me what he wanted. Any other way of thinking did not demonstrate my faith in God. If I tried to obtain what I wanted, I was telling God that I lacked faith.

Dr. Heppenstall wanted me to be a college professor. He felt that he had evidence to go on—I had taken every class he offered during my years at Seminary. He believed I had the gift of teaching and that I should pursue that gift. But I had resisted. I'd received feelers from several colleges, even three completely processed invitations ("calls" as they were announced), but none of these invitations had overwhelmingly moved me.

I knew that religious men pray about these things but there didn't seem to be enough indication for me to accept them. Yet I wasn't sure what I should be looking for. I was working through my own view of ministry as Dr. H and Dr. A had suggested.

He was right. I had come to the same conclusion about "the gift." And he had told me to hold out for SMC. Somehow, my strong desire to go there might be trying the hand of God. He had followed a line of reasoning. He emphasized that there was an administration at SMC that was now putting the college on the map. I had not grown up where SMC had much credibility in academics. It had a strong spiritual reputation. Biases and reputations are not always accurate but coming from Southern California where the colleges and universities had strong academic programs had never made SMC something to admire. However, with Dr. Heppenstall's encouragement SMC was starting to have a revised reputation in my mind. He said that Dr. Knittel was strengthening the academic reputation of the school.

I knew some people who taught there that were outstanding scholars. I had known the Greek teacher, Ron Springett at Seminary and I knew he was a top-notch scholar and an outstanding teacher. I knew Smuts van Rooyen at Seminary and admired his appeal to students. I had heard that Elder Frank Holbrook was a fine theologian. But I had only known one graduate from SMC at Seminary until just recently.

THE KNITTEL "GOLDEN YEARS" OF SMC

Dr. Frank Knittel was in his first year as president of Southern Missionary College in Collegedale, Tennessee, when he called me to teach there in the spring of 1972. He had served as SMC academic dean from 1968 until his new appointment to president in 1971. We had talked briefly together at the 1970 General Conference convocation in Atlantic City about the possibility of my interest in teaching at the college.

I had gone home from that meeting and driven to my post office box in Camarillo every day for a year with a hope in the back of my mind that I might hear from Dr. Knittel. To no avail. And so, since nothing had apparently come of it, I had put the idea further on the back burner and had thrown myself into my pastoral work. During that time, I had been introduced to *The Positive Way* seminar and we had seen amazing results at Camarillo. And now the money was there to break ground for the new building.

When the phone call came out of the blue I was surprised. That's the way God works. Planning, politicking, networking—I naively did not believe in those methods of getting what I wanted. I no longer felt the need to "escape" and yet I felt pleasant over the call.

No sooner did I hang up, but the phone rang again. It was Dr. Knittel. "Ed!" He said it with finality. That was his style. One word could be a whole sentence. He told me calmly that the college board has asked him to contact me about my possible interest in coming to Southern Missionary College to teach Religion. He didn't wait for a response but kept on talking like it was a done deal.

He told me that they would fly me down to look over the college for a week and that I should not say anything before I had been there. He made it clear that I was under no obligation to accept the offer even though I came down and looked it over. But he wanted to show me everything first. He would have his secretary order the plane tickets and they would arrange a place for me to stay. It would be all on them. They wanted me to plan to talk to faculty members, students and then to him.

I had no words. I was overwhelmed. The calls I had in the past usually asked for a commitment before they showed their interest as if they were offering me the big break or doing me a favor. Suddenly it was clear to me that Dr. Knittel was hoping I would do him the favor of joining the live-wire faculty that he was building. It was a good feeling. No wonder this man was succeeding, I thought with a good feeling; he is making people feel needed, wanted, and important to his vision. So, he told me to keep checking my mailbox—the tickets would be there in a couple of days. I thanked him, and we hung up. I danced into the kitchen and almost screamed.

"Start packing!—we're moving to Tennessee!"

It felt like one of the most exciting moments in my entire life. She just looked at me. I felt the cool mist of her lack of enthusiasm. Whenever I expressed my visions for our future, she'd usually smile and sing, "Somewhere over the Rainbow." I felt she was mocking me . . . maybe. It was her way of coping with my restlessness and the threat of change. But she knew that this was something I was serious about and she showed no opposition. She seldom showed much emotion, and this was no exception. But she admired Dr. Knittel as much as I did. He had been one of her favorite professors at Andrews University where she finished her degree in English.

Pastoring had invaded our lives and was beginning to take its toll on us. My daughter Jill was becoming possessive and mildly hostile toward people who were constantly visiting our house. Recently she had stormed into the living room in the middle of my conversation with a Church elder, pointed her little three-year-old finger in his face, and said to me, "Daddy, tell that man to go home!" It was time to move. The timing was right. And now, if I chose to take this new assignment, I felt I had something to share in real time, in real place, in educating young ministers.

The next week I was on the plane to Chattanooga, Tennessee, in the heart of Dixie. The Bradford pear trees were in full bloom and the dogwoods were soon to follow. Dr. Knittel knew how to pick the time to give a call, I thought as I gazed out the window. Dr. Douglas Bennett, chair of the SMC Religion Department met me at the airport. We had graduated from Andrews University in the same Seminary class together, he with his Bachelor of Divinity degree and me with my Master of Arts degree—the class of 1964. Even though it was eight years earlier, it seemed like a couple of decades and I had not seen him since. Now we chatted about SMC as he drove me to the campus through the beautiful green countryside.

HAPPY VALLEY

Collegedale, Tennessee, was nestled in "Happy Valley," as those who lived there called it. In 1972 it was a newly incorporated City with its own officials, most of them Adventists, and its own Memorial Park, located on a high point overlooking the valley.

The little valley was self-contained. The City had its own credit union, bookstore, market, post office, gas station, hardware store, clothing store and Adventist Book Center. I couldn't help but think of this idyllic setting as a place of safety during "the time of trouble" that Adventists looked for. I was tempted to search for the tree of life amid this garden setting!

The landscape was dotted with colonial-styled buildings. On a knoll across from the college was the new Church whose architectural design was unlike anything else in Happy Valley. This was the Church my first pastoral mentor had pastored for several years, though the building was brand new and was the result of some heated controversy about how it should be designed and where it should be located. Students I met had hoped to put it in the middle of the campus to make a statement that religion was the focus of this college. That suggestion failed.

Others wanted the Church to match the look of the new college buildings being constructed on campus. But some of the opposition may have felt that it would resemble too many Baptist churches in the area. Nobody told me that, it was just my passing thought. Finally, the Church was built of orange brick with turquoise trim. No stained glass.

Curiously, the building matched nothing else on campus. The inside was painted turquoise according to the taste of the interior designer. I would discover that partly out of spite and partly out of reality, some students would refer to the new Church with its turquoise colors as the "college swimming pool."

Adjacent to the campus were the big baking company plants. Many Peterbilt diesel semi-tractors were parked in neat order along the narrow road leading to the campus, waiting for their trailers to be loaded with pastries. They stood as quiet sentinels for visitors to recognize the supreme success of the Adventists and their bakery. Here was the birthplace and home of *Little Debbie Snack Cakes.*

The baking company eventually came to be known as the largest family-owned bakery in America. Someone pointed out the half-dozen tall tanks for sugar lined up along the railroad track on the borders of the nearest plant. As we drove past this sprawling plant, I mused what Sister White had written about snacks and snacking, basically all negative. We had just covered this in Prayer Meeting, so it was still fresh in my mind.

> Parents should train the appetites of their children and should not permit the use of unwholesome foods. But in the effort to regulate the diet, we should be careful not to err in requiring children to eat that which is distasteful, or to eat more than is needed. Children have rights, they have preferences, and when these preferences are reasonable they should be respected.[1]
>
> Regularity in eating should be carefully observed. *Nothing should be eaten between meals, no confectionery, nuts, fruits, or food of any kind.* Irregularities in eating destroy the healthful tone of the digestive organs, to the detriment of health and cheerfulness. And when the children come to the table, they do not relish wholesome food; their appetites crave that which is hurtful for them.[2]
>
> I am astonished to learn that, after all the light that has been given in this place, *many of you eat between meals! You should never let a morsel pass your lips between your regular meals.* Eat what you ought, but eat it at one meal, and then wait until the next.[3]

Was this my first confrontation with "liberals" in the Adventist South, bending or ignoring her words of counsel on the health message? A whole industry, in the conservative Adventist South, based on encouraging people to discard her instructions and snack. This seemed as ironic as that warning label on a pack of cigarettes. But I soon learned that this was not a topic for conversation in Happy Valley. The Lord has blessed this bakery. Another double bind? I was still into my addiction.

To grasp the dissonance I was experiencing, one would need to understand the Adventist health message, which as I was always taught was the right arm of the Adventist work.[4] The whole medical enterprise for which the Church is best known around the world is a result of the Adventist health message. Part of that message dealt

---

1. White, *The Ministry of Healing*, 384.
2. Ibid. Emphasis supplied.
3. White, *Testimonies for the Church*, 2:374. Emphasis supplied.
4. Sister White had applied this description, "the right arm" not to the health message but to the application of it, which she termed "medical missionary work." However, in folk Adventism this was freely applied to the whole health message. See *Testimonies*, 6:229, Emphasis supplied: "*The medical missionary work is as the right arm* to the third angel's message which must be proclaimed to a fallen world; and physicians, managers, and workers in any line, in acting faithfully their part, are doing the work of the message. Thus, the sound of the truth will go forth to every nation and kindred and tongue and people. In this work the heavenly angels bear a part. They awaken spiritual joy and melody in the hearts of those who have been freed from suffering, and thanksgiving to God arises from the lips of many who have received the precious truth."

with diet and food. Sister White had cautioned against the use of refined flour and the dangers of sugar.

On one hand, we were all personally responsible for any indulgence to which we might succumb, so no one had to pig out on sweets. Evidently there was a place for cookies and cakes. On the other hand, many students worked their way through school at this bakery and I was told that it also provided generous donations to the Adventist work throughout the South. SMC even had its library built largely with bakery monies.

Looking over things I was not coming here to judge anything; I was coming to educate ministers. After all, I did not write those counsels under inspiration. It was not my responsibility that not every Adventist follows them. Why were these thoughts going through my mind?

I looked back at the breath-taking pinks and whites of the beautiful trees. The Bradford pears, so vividly in bloom were like giant white torches along the carefully manicured lawns lining the road. The valley, fresh with the soft fragrance of flowers cast against the soft blanket of bright green grass, gave a striking contrast to the beauty of the natural environment. This was a magnificent setting for an educational institution—out in the country amid nature—just as Sister White would have envisioned it with or without a pastry firm.

THE CAMPUS REPRESENTED ADVENTISM

The campus was in the final stages of a ten-year building program that had seen several of the original buildings replaced. Like so many other Adventist schools the college had been built from the perspective of the nearness of Christ's return—EC—Eschatological Correctness.

This mindset had seen no reason to build for eternity here on earth. Time was short, and so, while the buildings were substantial, they weren't built to last a hundred years and the denomination didn't have the wealth in the 1900s that it had now. By the 1950s, more than a hundred years since Christ was supposed to have returned, according to the early Adventist calculations, the campus began rotting away and a new building campaign started in the 1960s.

Now it was 1972. A new administration building, Wright Hall, located at the center of the campus, new dormitories, a new Church, a new physical education plant, a new library, a new nursing building were nearly finished.

Originally the college had been established as Graysville Academy in 1892 in Graysville, Tennessee, adjacent to Dayton, where twenty-three years later the Scopes "Monkey" trial would make headlines around the world. By then the Adventist school had become Southern Industrial School (1897) and then Southern Training School (1901), and finally Southern Junior College (1916) and had moved to its present site, some 17 miles southeast of Chattanooga. It had become Southern Missionary College in 1944, a name it retained until 1982 when it was renamed again, Southern College of Seventh-day Adventists. Finally, 104 years after its founding, SMC became Southern Adventist University, the name it has today.

I enjoyed my week as a guest at SMC, which included a buffet meal at the Bennett's, visits to the classroom of Elder Robert Francis, another friend from Seminary days, a talent show at Collegedale Academy, a Pathfinder investiture and tours of the campus. This was real Adventist living. I met the faculty and administrative officers and I ate in the cafeteria, which like all Adventist institutions served mouth-watering vegetarian cuisine.

Finally, the exciting round of visits brought me to President Knittel's palatial office in Wright Hall. Unlike other Adventist administrators in my experience, Dr. Knittel laid everything on the table without my asking: starting pay, academic rank, future graduate work at the college's expense, health insurance and retirement benefits. He put everything in writing and placed it all neatly in a folder for me to take home and study.

Finally, he turned and asked what he had forgotten. What else could he do to lure me to Southern? Taking him at his word, I ventured that since I had been out of school for seven years, if I were to accept his offer would I be able to spend the summer taking some classwork? He seemed pleased that I had asked. Where? And I told him Andrews, figuring that some graduate work there could help re-ignite my academic fervor. And he agreed. Yes, I could do that. He would supply a truck out in California for me and move my stuff to Collegedale and take whatever we needed to Michigan for the summer. This was starting to seem like an adventure. Clearly God must be in this, I thought.

All could be so smooth. Am I being rewarded for the route I have followed—study life, prayer life, family commitment, and willingness to overlook some of the painful elements of my marriage? How good this would be for my children—insulated from the world. We could grow a garden like every good Adventist was supposed to do and we would be many miles from the city—or as someone in California had half-sarcastically informed me, "seventeen miles from the nearest known sin!" Another quipster had added, "Be sure you find the spot on campus where the angels land!"

Dr. Knittel continued without taking a deep breath, asking me to go home, talk to my family and call him in three or four days with my decision. He didn't want the decision right then. I should develop my pictures and show them to my family and friends. And talk over the documents and proposals. Then call him.

He shuffled a few papers on his desk and grinned at me. His charm flowed over my head like a waterfall. Dr. Knittel did everything right. The more he talked, the greater my desire to work for him. I could have told him then and there that we were coming, but I loved the feeling of wriggle room he had given me. He clearly left me feeling that I would be doing him a service by joining his faculty.

Yes, that was why I had gone to school. That was the purpose of my commitment—to do someone a favor—ultimately God. A religious man was to follow the central injunction of the master: to minister, not be ministered to.

WAS THE TIMING RIGHT?

My thoughts tumbled around in my head as I flew back to California. I began to weigh the factors. And the realities started rolling back on my shoulders. At Camarillo we were on the verge of breaking ground for the new building, my five-year ambition. We had a momentum going. Would they be able to continue without me? I had spent practically every day of the past year either at the Ventura County planning department, or with landowners, looking at parcels of land. I had done preliminary studies on almost twenty pieces of prospective Church sites. Was this a good time to leave?

Then my little religious critic began to recite in my ear: no one is indispensable. Perhaps, but I had fought hard to get us where we were. And then, as I would hear Dr. Knittel say later, "Nobody is indispensable, but some people are irreplaceable!" We had a spiritual renewal in the Church through the help of *The Positive Way* class and because of several days of fasting and prayer we had seen the doors to a new piece of property open miraculously to us. But surely my successor could keep it going. We not only had a choice parcel of land on which to build our Church, we had the plans all drawn up. And, more importantly, we also had the spiritual drive to see us through the task.

It is true that breaking a momentum can sometimes spell disaster. Now we must move ahead and put the shovel in the ground. And I am talking about leaving? How selfish can I be? On the other hand, maybe this was a good time for a change.

Phase One: The purchase of the property—completed.

Phase Two: Drawing up the plans—completed.

Phase Three: Breaking ground and building the Church—on the verge.

All this could take years. Would SMC wait? What did God want? Did he put me here to accomplish this task? Had I finished what he sent me to do? Was it really God's will for me to go? Are these windows opening? Or doors closing? My little voice was relentless.

These were issues and struggles of a religious man. I didn't know how to determine the will of God for my life. I had read the different ideas and arguments and I even had preached on the subject. I knew there was "casting of lots" in the Hebrew scripture days though I never really understood that. There was also the "laying out the fleece." I had tried flipping coins while praying, but I always ended up feeling I was demeaning the mind God had given me.

Why did I go to school to learn about cause and effect if I was to make decisions based on the flip of a coin? All the arguments and articles I had read on discerning the will of God had boiled down to a subjective evaluation of one's life—it seemed that people ended up doing what they wanted to do anyway. But for a religious man was such an admission acceptable? If I thought it, I surely did not express it. God-talk seemed to be part and parcel of being religious.

By now the plane was landing and when I got home the questions felt heavier than ever. I was suddenly relieved that Dr. Knittel had not pushed me for a decision in Collegedale. I needed the time to be objective. My critic started up again. What if I got tangled up in heresy? I had known of people before me going into teaching only to be thrown out of the work for their heretical views. But how could that happen to me?—I studied the Bible and the prophet four hours a day, I thought while driving home from the airport.

At that point I did not understand the notion that heresy is largely in the eye of the beholder—and that perception is truth to people, often regardless of the facts. Nevertheless, the thought that I could be caught in such a horrendous betrayal of my Church gnawed at me briefly until I finally dismissed it forever.

Never. I am so conservative, so orthodox, so mainstream, so in touch with the prophet, so Adventist, I will survive. I got out of my car convinced I should accept this teaching assignment but, at the same time, unsure if God really wanted me to take it right now.

I still marvel that these very strengths such as getting up early every morning to study the prophet and the prophecies would be a major element in my future. I discovered later that many people who retaliate against heresy are not well-grounded themselves. Too often they do not study but rely on someone else, some spiritual leader or charismatic individual, i.e., their religious guru or shaman, to do their thinking for them.

I would learn this notion only as I became a personal victim much later. Studying objectively is not the benchmark of cult practice. Cults are composed of people who wait for their spokesman to speak. They are not often filled with people who think critically or creatively about what they believe. Was there such a cult leader in Happy Valley? Conscientiously weighing all these options and factors about going or staying, I finally called my Conference president.

MY VISIT WITH THE CONFERENCE PRESIDENT

"We are on the verge of building," I told him. "I want to be part of that. However, I also have believed for some time now that the Lord wants me to go to SMC as a college professor."

So, he asked me, "What will it be?"

"I want both." I answered. I had said it. Overruling God? I had spoken my mind. He hesitated and then commanded that I could not have both—And he bluntly told me: "So take the call."

I answered, "What if they will wait for a year? In that year we can have the Church up." He repeated, "Take the call or turn it down."

I persisted. I wondered if he would be willing to talk to Dr. Knittel and ask him if there was a chance that he could wait a year because I was really needed to complete this task.

He repeated abruptly, "Take the call or turn it down." He would have nothing else of it. Then he added that he didn't want a lame-duck pastor working in his Conference. With that kind of support why would I stay?

God had spoken. I took the call. But the struggle was not over. Several years later I asked Dr. Knittel about how he would have responded had my Conference president called him and presented my proposal to him. His reply was interesting. He made it clear that he wanted me on his faculty and that he would have waited for as long as it took to get me there. Just what I had expected he would say.

DIFFICULTY IN LEAVING

The experience did not help me solve the question of discerning the will of God. But I knew I was going. And shortly I came to accept that there was more to leaving than just a building program. For example, one member was facing some serious personal problems. His life seemed to be falling apart and we had grown to respect each other. So, I called him and invited him out to lunch. I told him I had a call to teach religion at SMC. He laid down his fork—and paused, looking at me.

"You're not thinking of taking that call, are you?" He said with a sad tone. I told him, "I had decided to take the call." He said he was devastated. I assured him that things were going to work out for him. I would not let him down. I would just be farther away—but as close as his phone. I reminded him that God had plans and he was valuable to his family and this Church.

It was true, but just saying it was easier than visualizing where things might be going—especially through his eyes. His would be another story, and while it was rough going for a while, he was taken by the congregation and nurtured. I knew there were others like him in the Church, but no pastor is going to stay anywhere forever—certainly not in the Adventist Church. I put those thoughts to the back of my mind, and they rolled around there.

Moving from Camarillo was not an easy move emotionally. A short time before I had accepted a call to pastor a Church in a large eastern city, and then changed my mind. I had almost taken a call to pastor another large Church in Northern California. They were both wonderful opportunities in my opinion. But both times I had been overwhelmed by the work that still needed to be done in Camarillo.

Our last Sabbath at Camarillo was nostalgic. We took pictures of the congregation to compare with the pictures we had taken on that day of organization five years before, almost to the day. We had made so many good friends and they were prayer warriors who would continue to pray for the Church, for each other and for us. My last sermon was entitled "It was in My Heart to Build a House unto the Lord," based on King David's desire to build the ancient Hebrew temple, a privilege that would go to his son Solomon.

> [1] David assembled at Jerusalem all the officials of Israel, the officials of the tribes, the officers of the divisions that served the king, the commanders of thousands, the commanders of hundreds, the stewards of all the property and cattle of the king and his sons, together with the palace officials, the mighty men, and all the seasoned warriors. [2] Then King David rose to his feet and said: "Hear me, my brethren and my people. *I had it in my heart to build a house of rest for the ark of the covenant of the Lord*, and for the footstool of our God; and I made preparations for building. [3] But God said to me, 'You may not build a house for my name, for you are a warrior and have shed blood.' (1 Chr 28:1–3. Emphasis supplied)

Two things weighed heavily on my mind: leaving people we had come to love, and not getting to finish the task of building the new Church. Of course, we would be invited back in the time to come—even to the dedication service a few years later.

MOVING TO A NEW MINISTRY

We could never have guessed what we were in for. Change often carries pain and a religious man is not exempt. But my pristine view of the Church, despite all that I had seen so far by the age of thirty, would be almost completely shattered by the time I turned forty.

We arrived in Berrien Springs, Michigan, in June 1972, just in time to enroll in three Seminary classes. The summer was an interim preparatory time to think and plan for the fall semester when I would begin my new life as a college professor. All that summer I found myself thinking about the Camarillo congregation. I thought of the building program and people facing their challenges. I wondered if the shovel was in the ground yet.

We had lived with those people for five years. We had left at a critical time. I doubt that any of them knew my own personal struggles there. Every Tuesday night I thought of the young people meeting for Pathfinders and wondered where they met now since our house was no longer available. I wondered if anyone was carrying on the evening classes. But I also thought of my future. I hated transitions. I always had. I realized how much I loved routine. But the pastoral ministry had very little to offer in that respect and I was convinced that educational work could be different.

I received letters from the members complaining that the momentum was slacking and remembered what we had learned in Seminary, "Do not give any advice to a former pastorate—do not interfere. Your day is over. They have a new pastor. Disappear."

I made the mistake of answering one of the more urgent sounding letters. The next thing I knew I had a biting letter from the Conference president instructing me to leave the Camarillo people alone! It hurt but it was my mistake. I wrote to the new pastor and apologized. That was the end of my contact with Camarillo members. Aside from some who flew to Collegedale to visit us, I had no more contact. This is a pain in the career of ministry.

The parting had not been easy. Parting had never been easy for me. Leaving for Auburn Academy with Dad standing on the railroad platform; watching Jim leave for Army basic training, and then watching him leave with his little family for mission service. I always felt anxiety at separations. When would my comfortable, predictable routine of life be established? Routine brought me peace.

Before we left Southern California, my father-in-law pulled out his maps and began to chart his plans to visit us in Tennessee. It was fun to watch him making those plans. In some way we didn't seem to be going that far away. For him my new job was an adventure and a reason he could fly his new Piper Arrow to an exciting destination in the South.

In August, Jill turned four. Mark had his first birthday party in March. Annie had plenty to do with two little children in the tight quarters of Beechwood Apartments as we endured the wicked humidity of Southwestern Michigan. I took classes from Dr. Gerhard Hasel, Dr. Hans LaRondelle, and my old college professor Dr. Walter Specht, who was now chair of the New Testament Department.

I felt more fulfilled in my excitement. Before the summer was over, I discovered that I was putting meaningful distance between Camarillo and the congregation we loved. My heart expanded. I knew now was the time for bigger things. A religious man was supposed to enjoy this contentment. I will help educate a new generation of preachers. I felt fulfilled!

For the next four years I would experience the greatest contentment and clarity of mission that I had ever enjoyed. After only one semester of teaching I knew that I had found what God wanted me to do for the rest of my life. In January 1973, when we moved into the new home we had built on Suhrie Drive, I believed that we had just built the house we would live in until the Lord returned.

I enjoyed the time in my classroom. As a pastor, no task was ever finished. As a teacher, I knew exactly what was expected of me. Each time I taught a class I revised my lectures, challenged my students to think more clearly and watched their intellectual and spiritual growth. The lives of college students were unfettered with those situations I had to deal with as a pastor. Was my thinking superficial?

I dared to believe that my college students were laying a foundation for a fruit-bearing life. My temporary place in their lives was to help them work on that foundation. And I had a good place in an Adventist educational institution in Happy Valley to help them concentrate, ponder, contemplate, think and plan—all necessary tasks in human development.

I continued my morning private prayer session each day. I pled with God to help me do meaningful ministry at SMC. I was happy because teaching was my forum. To teach and to do ministry was the combination I had watched my mentors accomplish and what I wanted to do: theology and ministry.

"Lord," I prayed early in the morning, "If it is your will, I am willing to run the Positive Way program on this campus as part of my ministry. It was developed with college students; I believe they will take to it excitedly if I can just get a chance to start it." But as the summer drew on I had no idea how to get it started. I had to prepare my classes. As usual, I felt the Black Cloud might interrupt our accomplishing God's will on this earth. Mixed blessings.

So, I would leave it all in God's hands. That decision took serious faith, but somewhere in the life of a religious man he must learn to leave God's problems with God. That's what mature religious men do—they know they are not to move ahead of God. Nevertheless, knowing what's "ahead" holds is not so easy to discern.

ASSISTANT PROFESSOR OF RELIGION

By the age of thirty I had witnessed a new dream come true. I was going to be Assistant Professor of Religion. I had almost given up hope that this would happen, burrowed into my pastorate in Camarillo and determined to make that a meaningful pastoral experience. The Lord had acted on my behalf and once he saw me contented he gave me a chance to educate pastors, to encourage young men to think through their faith as I had and come to meaningful conclusions—that being a pastor was the highest calling one could attain.

For seven years I had struggled to enjoy pastoring, to understand and develop a workable philosophy of ministry, and for the most part I had finally found meaningful direction. People to serve, a message to defend, and a pulpit to stand in and share the assurance of God's love. When I gave up hoping to get out of pastoring I had now been handed the chance to experience pastoring in a new venue—pastoral education.

So, we were in Collegedale. I could believe that here was a little valley of mostly Adventists who were conservative, Bible-believing, religious people like us. The campus was idyllic. Large expanses of bright green spread out before us. This impressed me because I was used to the brown hills and valleys of Southern California.

Unlike La Sierra College, which had beautiful lawns that needed watering from hoses, SMC lawns were naturally watered by rains that fell just when needed. I had experienced the same sort of rainfall at Auburn in Washington, but unlike the Northwest, the weather here was often warm when the rains fell, at least in the summer. You could almost watch the grass grow. The lightning was spectacular, and the thunder shook our house.

Collegedale got more rain in a week than Southern California got in a year and the summer air was clean and warm. When the rain stopped the humidity continued to the place where you felt moisture all the time. The four seasons were distinct but not as severe as Michigan. Winter was colder than California, warmer than Michigan. Summer was cooler than La Sierra, but the humidity made it feel hotter.

"Happy Valley" referred to more than just the weather. Here was an Edenic setting in which God's people were isolated from the invading cities. The stores in Collegedale were closed on Sabbath and sold no alcoholic drinks or tobacco paraphernalia. No coffee either. Coca Cola was nowhere to be seen and Dr. Pepper was only available in the vending machine at the gas station. Even the big bakery was closed on Sabbath. The only sign that Sabbath was anything but a day of rest in Happy Valley was an occasional campus patrol car cruising the area.

At sundown on Friday the local college station, WSMC-FM, converted over to sacred music and religious talks, usually from the local Vespers and Church services. The chimes played at sundown and their unique sounds wafted across the valley. Students walked around in their finest Sabbath clothes and ate in a cafeteria staffed by just a few workers who took turns serving on weekends, so all the food service staff could rest at least half the Sabbaths in a month.

This was what heaven would be like, without the patrol cars, where all would worship on the Sabbath and reach out in deed and conversation to others. When you were in Collegedale you hardly realized that there was a world out there. Here was an escape from the humdrum of the week.

The streets of Collegedale had families out for their nature walks on Sabbath. We hadn't been in Happy Valley for a month before we knew all the nature trails in the area. We knew when the azaleas bloomed and when to visit them in St. Elmo at the foot of Lookout Mountain. We found the road to the lake and the trails along its banks. We visited the waterfalls in the area. We toured the battlefields of the great American Civil War—Chickamauga and Lookout Mountain, the site of the "Battle above the Clouds"[5]—with their signs commemorating America's bloodiest war.

We read the historical Civil War signs that decorated the geography of the area and we observed with interest where the locomotive, "The General," had run out of fuel on the tracks between Ringgold and Brainerd. Peaceful now, these fields were filled with flowers, grass, woods and deer, and dotted with a few of the cannons from those historic days.

It seemed only yesterday that we had been singing that anti-war folk song "Where have all the flowers gone, long time passing. . . ." Taken from the words of a Ukrainian folk song in Mikhail Sholokhov's "And Quiet Flows the Don," the song, was introduced in 1961 by Pete Seeger and sung by such famous groups as Peter, Paul and Mary, and the Kingston Trio. The song had a haunting progression as it reached its climax: "Where have all the soldiers gone? Gone to graveyards everyone. . . . gone to

---

5. General Ulysses S. Grant would write in his memoirs: "The Battle of Lookout Mountain is one of the romances of the war. There was no such battle and no action even worthy to be called a battle on Lookout Mountain. It is all poetry." See the Internet site on "Battle Above the Clouds."

flowers everyone."[6] Though not written for the Civil War, it fit any war America had been in where she would trade her brave soldiers for flowers. Songs and plaques were raised to keep us reminded of the American sacrifices.

Moving to Collegedale was moving to another planet for us. Southern Missionary College prided itself as a conservative "School of Southern Hospitality." It jealously guarded its reputation as the straight and narrow of Adventism. It came to be known as "A School of Standards," proudly emblazoned on its official letterheads. The administration knew that this helped to attract students from all over America—even from the turf of other Adventist colleges. And while it was not considered ethical in the 1970s to recruit students outside the Southern Union Conference, the parent body of the college, no one felt compelled to refrain from talking things up wherever one went.

Every Adventist college had a reputation in those days. Legend dictated that Walla Walla College was where you went to find a spouse. Pacific Union College was where you went to get religious. La Sierra College was where you went to have fun. But Southern was allegedly the epitome of spirituality.

None of these reputations was necessarily earned or true. Most rumors aren't. And legends are usually full of holes. You could find all these things at any of these schools, but Southern enjoyed that aura of spiritual legitimacy. Academics were not necessarily considered the most important element when parents sent their children to Southern. And yet Southern was not without its scholars. It was not exaggeration that spirituality, Adventism *par excellence,* was what people often thought when they considered Southern Missionary College.

With the coming of new and more scholastically oriented administrators a new effort was made to strengthen the academic reputation of the school, without damaging its spiritual stature. Dr. Knittel wanted higher academic credentials for his teachers, especially in the Religion Department where the only doctorate held by a professor was in speech. The 1970s have often been called the *Golden Years* of SMC. It was gratifying to be a part of such an exciting enterprise.

GOD OPENS A DOOR

We lived in a college-owned house on Loblolly Lane for our first five months in Collegedale. We had a bonus of many six-legged visitors. If you got up at night and turned on the light suddenly the entire kitchen floor would become a cockroach stampede. I had never seen so many cockroaches in my life.

The previous tenant had left a dog tied up in the garage. We weren't sure if this was a gift to us, but it was not something we wanted. After several calls to the business manager we noticed one day that the dog disappeared. Her smell never left the

---

6. Smith, "Top 20 Political Songs: Where Have All the Flowers Gone," *New Statesman,* March 25, 2010.

garage. She had multiple bumps on her body—tumors we guessed. Parting with pets is seldom an easy thing for people.

My first four years at SMC were so delightful that I became a free PR agent for the college. Working for Dr. Knittel was exhilarating and challenging. He was charismatic and forward looking, a positive, critical thinker, always focusing on the big picture. He had a gift for making people feel important. Thanks largely to his vision, the college started a growth pattern that seemed never to end.

My first committee appointment dealt with the question of how we could sustain the Week of Prayer fervor in the weeks following the revival that was always generated during that week. That first semester in the fall of 1972 the faculty delivered the Week of Prayer messages and our committee was asked to follow it up with some dynamic ideas for helping the campus continue its higher spiritual plane than such in past weeks.

I really knew no one on this committee. Having never even visited the South until a quick trip two years before on our way to the East Coast, I would know only people who came from the West and so far as I could ascertain that included only one person—the dean of men, Lyle Botimer. But I had not known him when he was dean of men at La Sierra College. Lyle would be a prominent member of this committee that fall.

At the initial committee meeting I was stopped as I entered the room by an announcement that Dean Botimer was making. He was welcoming someone, he said, whose name was synonymous with baseball at La Sierra College. And then he laid it out: "The greatest baseball pitcher La Sierra every produced: Elder Ed Zackrison!" The whole committee applauded. I was stunned. I hardly knew him, and I did not believe I had any reputation like that.

But he was not done yet. Lyle then launched out on a shower of accolades for *The Positive Way* program. He said he had been dean of men at Loma Linda University, Riverside Campus. And while he was there a group of students developed a program called *The Positive Way*. He then gave his reason for bringing this up.

Our committee was for building and maintaining the spirituality of the Week of Prayer. And he suggested that he had heard that Elder Zackrison knew how to run this program. He witnessed that he had seen the spiritual energy and reform of faculty and students at La Sierra and he thought the committee should ask Elder Zackrison to run the program on our campus.

Dean Botimer insisted that *The Positive Way* was tailor-made for carrying out the purpose why our committee was appointed. I was floored. I couldn't believe this answer to my prayer. I never expected this even though I was excited that it was happening. Dean Botimer had one of those pleasing personalities that left no question that what he had to say should be followed. Now he was leading out in another round of applause. No question about it, he was into this.

I was on. I had been praying all summer for an opening to start *The Positive Way* on campus. I didn't know where to begin. I was brand new to a college campus. Usually you rely on your friends for support. I didn't have any friends here. And now Lyle Botimer, who I barely knew, had laid out a mandate before me.

I stammered about trying to find some words. Finally, I spoke.

> *The Positive Way* is a Christian Life Seminar, which I was taught to run while I pastored the Camarillo Church in Southern California. I was skeptical at first because I had lost faith in "programs." But several Church members convinced me that this may be a way of discerning the will of God and I saw things happen in their lives that I scarcely could have believed. I also saw God work in mysterious ways to open our Church building plans. This seminar was developed at La Sierra College by and with college students, but not while I was there. The main developer was a student at the college when I held the fall Week of Prayer there in 1970. This was apparently where Dean Botimer became acquainted with it.

The chair asked if I could start the program on this campus. I was struggling with my happiness at this positive answer to my prayer—that prayer of commitment of the summer. I answered him,

> I would need as many of you on this committee as possible to take the course. I need your input and leadership to make this work. It will be more powerful if you all are in from the beginning of the program. And you will understand that better as you get into the seminar.

Several of the committee members agreed to take the class and a week later we launched. Annie and I were teachers and we had two of my original group from my youth group in my internship and later members at Camarillo as teachers. One was a pre-optometry student at SMC and the other was teaching in the nursing department.

By the end of the school year over a hundred students had taken the class and they were sharing their faith in quiet and courageous ways. Students were praying for and with other students, encouraging them in their Christian walk, applying the gospel implications to their lives.

We ran the classes just as we had at Camarillo. Seven weeks, twenty students, ten teachers giving them personal attention. Two moderators led out in each class. The program started small but grew exponentially and by the end of 1976 about 2000 students had finished the course. Behind the whole operation was the support of the Knittels who were in the first class. They were my students and they both finished the course with model performance.

I was happy with the results. I believed that the Spirit was moving. The teachers of the course visited their two students each week and prayed with them. Each little group had a prayer *project*—someone who was struggling in his/her Christian walk—to pray for and ask God to use in a special way. By the beginning of the next school year we had a new course in the Religion curriculum called "Positive Way Leadership," which I taught and in which I trained moderators. It carried three semester hours of elective applied theology credit. By the end of 1973 we were running eight seminars a semester and another four in the summer. Every class filled the day we put up the sign-up sheets.

That summer I spent a week in California with Robert Law during which we revised the syllabus for a more logical development and flow.

THE MINISTRY WIDENS

Toward the end of my first year at SMC, Dr. Knittel appeared unannounced in the doorway of my office. He had come to tell me that he heard I was a "hard" teacher. I responded defensively by saying I was not an intentionally "hard" teacher. I was a serious teacher. I really did not know where this was going, but I was afraid I might be expecting too much from my students and was now going to get lectured.

He surprised me again. He wanted me to know that he considered such an evaluation to be an asset at this school. He was trying to improve the reputation of Southern in academic excellence and Religion was one area that had needed some serious attention. He was commending me for my part in that reputation. Breathing a sigh of relief, I just said, "Thank you."

Now he had another topic. He wanted to examine my workload. I had a full load of Religion classes and *The Positive Way* classes going. And he wanted to add another task. He told me he wanted me to be assistant college chaplain because he saw my role as much broader than just teaching classes. He said he was going to recommend that my chair cut my class load, so I could accomplish all that.

A moment of silence. I was not hoping for this. Finally, "Please don't," I pleaded. "I welcome the chance to work with the chaplain, but please don't cut my academic load. I have no complaints about my class load or my ministry expectations on this campus. I can do all of what you want and still teach a full academic load. This is my calling. Besides, you already need more Religion teachers. Your plan wouldn't help this department in that respect."

"Plus," I continued, "I have this philosophy of ministry that shows me that in class is where I make my contacts and outside class is where I make my applications. It is called 'theology and ministry.'"

Dr. Knittel thought for a moment. He could see that I was serious. He responded by considering seriously what I had requested. He would add that extra duty and leave the other things as they were. But he said he would check back with me later. That was the last I ever heard on the matter. I continued to teach a full load, carry *The Positive Way* program at the same rate it was growing and to serve as assistant college chaplain under the direction of the college chaplain. It was never too much. I was fulfilled.

Theology and ministry—in my understanding they had to go together. At last the religious man was seeing fruits from his labor.

HOME LIFE

At home things were never better. The children were at home with their mother. We built a new house on a choice spot in faculty row. At 4436 Suhrie Drive we were neighbors with the Gladsons. Jerry was another new member of the Religion Department. They had two daughters the same approximate ages as our two kids. We enjoyed the weather. We planted a garden and manicured the yard to our liking.

During the summer of 1973, I taught summer school. After I got out of class, I would come home, put the little family in our VW bus and drive thirty miles up to the rocky stream beds of Soddy Daisy where we would play in the water and pick out a hundred river rocks—just enough to keep our microbus from bottoming out. Then we would return and place them around the flowerbeds. About fifteen trips finished the job and we fitted them together in a self-sustaining wall around trees and plants that would enhance the beauty of our neighborhood.

We even planted a garden. The red clay soil of Southeastern Tennessee was not easy to work. However, my next-door neighbor knew all the ropes. He knew who had a tractor, so we could get a running start. We hired the tractor man to plow up six-hundred square feet of our backyard and then we purchased a used rototiller. Within the week the garden was ready to plant, and we put in seed for every vegetable we wanted—corn, radishes, peas, beans, tomatoes, watermelons and cantaloupes.

Then we went on vacation. When we returned we saw that the garden had been at work—but the race between the vegetables and the weeds had been won by the weeds. It didn't stop us—we were determined to be country folk. The whole family was out there afternoon by afternoon—cultivating, pulling weeds, watering. It was "little house on the prairie" where we were taming the land, focused on winning the war against all imposing odds.

Then one afternoon a two-foot long bright green snake came slithering out of the weeds between our feet; and that was the end of family time in the garden. From then on, the project was mine alone. I never saw a family member in that garden again—ever. And I lost the war to the weeds, the gophers and the birds.

Finally, I asked my neighbor what really grew well in Tennessee—what was hearty and how could I succeed? "Okra," was his answer. So not wanting to admit total defeat, I planted two rows of okra. Within days the okra was coming up. It grew so fast that I had to harvest it every day. I brought in box loads of okra each week. And too late I discovered I did not like okra! We tried every recipe people gave us. Nothing helped. We fried it, we boiled it, we baked it, we mixed it with tomatoes, we put it in soup. I finally went without picking it and the okra pods doubled in size and became woody.

The next summer we put the garden plot back into grass and played touch football out there. Here was a case of cognitive dissonance. Religious men, in my Adventist upbringing, grew gardens. This was what kept them in special touch with our Maker. Nature was God's book second only in authority to the Bible itself. And I understood this religious maxim from a new angle that summer in the garden. I saw the conflict between God and evil played out in that garden and God lost.

It was like a neighbor who said one day: "As I grew my garden a friend dropped by and said to me, 'Wow, you and God are doing a great job in that garden.' And my reply was, 'Yeah, you should have seen it last year when God had it all to himself!'" I concluded that perhaps the hardest part of being a religious man was with your own family. It was no problem to testify in the pulpit that you were observing the power of evil in your garden, but to tough out the fight was another story altogether.

ANOTHER KNOCK ON THE DOOR

Each year seemed more thrilling than the last until one day Dr. Knittel called me to his office and articulated that it was time for me to start working on a doctorate. He insisted that I had proven myself as a teacher and of value to the school, so it was time to continue my education.

I had been at SMC for almost three years and he wanted me to start looking for a graduate school to attend. I wrote to several universities for programs. I was teaching Christian theology, so I began looking for theology programs. Jerry Gladson was enrolled at Vanderbilt University working on a PhD in Old Testament. Ron Springett had left the year before for University of Manchester in England, working on a PhD in New Testament. Pursuing a PhD in theology seemed a balanced thing to do for the department. These were career choices for all of us.

Then I received a visitor. I answered the knock on my office door one afternoon and was delighted to find standing in my doorway, Dr. Siegfried Horn, dean of the Andrews University Theological Seminary. Dr. Horn was a world-renowned archaeologist who had almost attracted me into changing my disciplinary pursuits from theology to Old Testament back in Seminary days.

Dr. Horn was a charismatic scholar whose classes I took with eagerness. And now he was standing in my office! He had heard that I was looking for a university where I could pursue a doctorate. I said he had heard right. I was mandated to do such a thing. And then he said he wanted to tell me about his program at Andrews.

Interrupting I sought to save Dr. Horn some time, so I just told him I knew what Andrews had put together so far. I had looked at the Doctor of Ministry and it didn't meet my needs or the school's. I needed a research doctorate. The DMin was not a research degree. But Dr. Horn kept on. He confirmed that was true but beginning the following year they were launching their Doctor of Theology program with concentrations in theological studies and biblical studies. He was hoping I would seriously consider one of these programs. I told him this was new to me and that I might be interested. He left material describing it, along with an application blank. We caught up on old times, shared some small talk and then he was on his way.

If there was one point that Dr. Heppenstall had drilled into me, it concerned the practical nature of theology. In every class he had stressed the importance of applying theology in ministry, to personal lives, to the lives of those we ministered to. Theology was not to be studied for itself. It was a tool for helping people appreciate God who was pursuing them. While no one was "saved" by theology, one's life was enhanced by having as correct, sound, rational and consistent views of the meaning of scripture as possible. And one needed to do ministry concurrent with the teaching of the abstract.

Pursuing a theological degree aside from these initial guidelines had troubled me. I was a religious man and as such was concerned with seeing everything through what I perceived to be God's eyes—as closely as possible. God wanted followers. He wanted faithful adherents to truth. Why should I care about what all the theologians had written? Why should I waste my time on the chaff of the world's writers when I had truth in the prophecies and the prophet's writings?

Again, Elder Rea's words rang in my ear: He had taught me to study the Bible and the Spirit of Prophecy, so I would know I was in touch with The Truth always. These thoughts were now beginning to weigh on me as they never had before. I was to spend at least four years getting a doctorate.

To what extent would I expose my soul to the abyss of falsehood?

> As a preparation for Christian work, many think it essential to acquire an extensive knowledge of historical and theological writings. They suppose that this knowledge will be an aid to them in teaching the gospel. But their laborious study of the opinions of men tends to the enfeebling of their ministry, rather than to its strengthening. As I see libraries filled with ponderous volumes of historical and theological lore, I think, why spend money for that which is not bread?[7]

The more I read Dr. Horn's material, the more I came to believe that at Andrews I could pursue my work. Shortly I approached Dr. Knittel in his office to get his opinion. I revealed to him what I thought I was considering. He wanted to know my decision—where did I want to go for graduate work? And there was a clear excitement in his voice. I told him I would like to go to Andrews. The excitement in his voice faded. Perhaps the pause that followed was the longest one I ever received from Dr. Knittel. I only saw him speechless twice in my life, and this was the first time. But when he finally found words they were in the form of a very short sentence: "For what?" He wondered.

I told him of my visit with Dr. Horn and the news that they were starting a Doctor of Theology degree program, which looked challenging to me. It would be

---

7. White, Chapter 37, "The False and True in Education," *The Ministry of Healing*, 441.

a program where I could appeal to my denominational sources of theology while at the same time getting a helpful perspective in the fields of philosophy and theology. He asked for further confirmation—was I sure about this. I thought so, at least right now. And he shared the thought I had pondered as well—did I realize I was putting a lot of eggs in one basket—La Sierra College, SDA Theological Seminary, Andrews University—not much variety there was there?

I thought for a moment. I admitted that I supposed not. But I had no plans to work anywhere but for the Adventist Church and my commitment was to educating Adventist young people in theology and ministry regardless of what discipline they found themselves pursuing. He confessed that he had no plans to argue with that. He said he knew me and that I was the kind of teacher who didn't need a doctorate but that he thought I should have the chance to pursue one because the school owed me that opportunity. And if this was really my decision he would honor it.

He then moved to the calendar. I should start in the summer of 1975. But I would have to teach during the next school year because he had a shortage of Religion teachers since Elder Springett was away and the enrollment was skyrocketing. I could plan to move in the summer of 1976 and stay until 1979. I just answered, "fine." What an offer! What a chance!

COMPETITION AND GOSSIP

Each year teaching at SMC was more enjoyable. We were attracting intelligent and thoughtful ministerial students to our program and we were challenging them. Many of them had been Adventists all their lives—fourth and fifth generation. They came with deep roots and hearts burning for truth. New converts learned from them, listened to them, and were enriched by their presence. The Church had never been more dynamic. That should have scared me, but I did not understand the political aspect of Adventism even yet.

The department brought in speakers, each fall and spring for the ministerial retreats, who could test their thinking and planning. We were training the special forces for God. I was thrilled that I had chosen theological teaching as my lifework. To see the strength of our message by having the freedom to examine it from all angles was truly a faith-strengthening experience for me as well as my students.

Those years were not without their frictions. Jerry Gladson and I had begun teaching the same year. I didn't know that with some on the faculty that I was viewed as Dr. Knittel's choice and Jerry Gladson was Dr. Bennett's choice. This put us in competition in a way that I could not have anticipated; nor did I realize it until sometime later. The two of us were billed "the fair-haired boys" by some on the faculty. I suspect that we both felt the pressure. Jerry got classes and committee appointments that I thought I should have had and so it went.

The green-eyed monster was alive and kicking. Soon Jerry was serving on General Conference committees for biblical research chaired by his former teachers at Southern Missionary College, namely Dr. Gerhard Hasel (1935–1994) and Dr. Gordon Hyde (d. 2016). He was fast becoming known as the scholar from SMC. And he was a scholar—a very careful biblical scholar. Jerry lived directly across the street from me, so we occasionally jogged together in the mornings and learned to appreciate each other despite the jealousies on my part.

Another source of friction was *The Positive Way*. While Dr. Bennett had been through the course and was supportive of it, Jerry Gladson and Ron Springett had not. I began to hear little criticisms of the program coming through their students. But then Ron went to England so that was solved. Jerry was increasingly popular with his students and when he made a comment it was usually repeated as important whether he meant it negatively or not.

Being perceived as Dr. Knittel's choice was not without its down sides as well. Some faculty members saw me as part of the president's "in group," which set resentment in motion. One faculty member constantly badgered me about what plans the college might be pursuing, because surely, I knew—as one of "Frank's boys." I found this irritating and considered it sick. I never appreciated political cheap shots. I was not political and did not plan to become so. Furthermore, I had no "in" with the president. I found that attitude insulting and unfair.

I resented being back-handedly accused of succeeding only because the president was supporting me. I resented being placed at odds with Jerry Gladson, whom I admired and respected. And I resented resenting him. One faculty member told me in confidence how much Jerry and I were admired and how some faculty members couldn't understand why the two of us couldn't get along. I wasn't aware that we couldn't get along. To me this was pettiness I had seen elsewhere. The nameless, faceless mass was at work.

So, I walked across the street to talk with Jerry. I laid it all on the table—my jealousy, my competitive spirit, my desire to be a professional colleague as well as a friend. I opened my soul. It was a good meeting. We shared feelings and hopes. We vowed to work at working together. We recognized that we were both proactive people. We were very ambitious young theologians. I was running *The Positive Way*. Jerry was busy organizing and pastoring a new church in Hixson, Tennessee. But a competitive attitude was not healthy—it made no sense and we both vowed to avoid it.

Jerry Gladson had a reputation for being a very conservative Adventist. A brilliant student while at SMC, Jerry had been converted to Adventism as a teenager. By his own admission, he bought everything Adventist—hook, line, and sinker. He was Mr. SDA through and through. He had married Laura Hayes, the only female theology major in his graduating class. Together they had set out to do ministry. But there was no place for female ministers in the Adventist denomination, so Laura had pursued a parallel helping career.

When they came to SMC they were being influenced by Vanderbilt thought. Jerry had elected not to go to Andrews for Seminary because of the theological controversies raging at the time. But at Vanderbilt Jerry was learning the historical-critical method and Laura was pursuing a career in clinical psychology. Some in the upper echelons of administration considered both fields dangerous to the traditional Adventist message. One administrator confided, "It's just a matter of time before the Gladsons will leave the Church." I didn't believe that or understand that.

I found such speculation upsetting. With that kind of expectancy surrounding him how could he succeed? I had two things going here. I felt justified in my orthodoxy and I did not wish for a colleague to suffer from the words of gossip. On the other hand, "where there is smoke there must be fire"—didn't some wise person say that? If Jerry was criticized, wasn't something going on? Such thoughts never left the inner mind of the religious man.

The obsession with protecting The Truth never leaves. Yet upon reflection, it is shallow to think that The Truth needs protection. There is a self-preservative quality to Truth that makes it ludicrous and arrogant to consider being its protector.

With any remark that could be considered cynical, Jerry slowly became the brunt of criticism. It was subtle at first. It didn't really become grotesque for years to come, but the process of placing people on pedestals seems suspiciously akin to having secret desires of knocking them off. The more popular Jerry became, the more vulnerable he became. The same was probably true in my case, though I was oblivious to it all. As they say, "It comes with the territory."

The irony of the situation was that Jerry was inspiring students to think, not to be cynical. Yet when they became excited enough to think about their faith, they considered alternative views and then sought ways to answer those views. Such a cognitive operation was too much for people who had settled their faith. But that was what college was about.

Doctoral programs are built on the scientific method of critical thinking. In critical thinking one learns to avoid sounding dogmatic. The claims to "proof" were always open to question, in fact, in critical thinking there really is no such thing as proof. Evidence, yes. And the attempt to build faith is always an act of acquiring evidence—weight of evidence decides the issue, at least for the present.

In the end, most of these frictions were contained. They were normal behavioral and attitudinal phenomena that accompany hard working academics. Religion tends to exacerbate these attitudes, especially where true believers are concerned about spiritual purity. But they were not insurmountable problems for men who prayed together and kept their eyes on the religious goals of the college. Unfortunately, rather than confronting some of these attitudinal issues we buried them but eventually there would be a rising from that grave.

CHAPTER TWENTY-SIX

Mining the Depths of Knowledge

"Aim high! It is no harder on your gun to shoot the feathers off an eagle than to shoot the fur off a skunk."

—Troy Moore

EXCITEMENT AND SADNESS

I was accepted into the Doctor of Theology program in the spring of 1975. So, my adventure in doctoral studies began that summer when I took a room in Meier Hall, the men's residence hall at Andrews University, to work on my first language requirements—French and Hebrew.

The ThD program I was enrolled in (theological studies) required a reading knowledge of four languages—two ancient and two modern. Since there is a great deal of theological literature written in French and German, a Doctor of Theology must be prepared to tackle these modern languages. The ancient languages required were biblical languages, Hebrew and Greek, and being able to use them in research was a given. We also needed some working knowledge of Latin, but we had no exam for that in systematic theology.

During that summer I studied French in the morning and Hebrew in the afternoon. Having no family on location gave me the time to take a couple of classes in addition to the language concentrations. One of these classes, *Teaching Bible in College*, was team taught by my former dean of students (Dr. George Akers) from La Sierra College, and now dean of the School of Education. The other half of the team was my former neighbor on Knoefler Drive and Pathfinder leader who had appointed me bugler of the La Sierra Pathfinder Club (Dr. John Youngberg) when I was ten years old and now a professor in the School of Education. Being together with these former directors of my past was like an alumni homecoming.

The late afternoon gave me a chance to get in some softball games before heading to the James White Library for an evening of study. Nevertheless, that summer was not without loneliness since I was not able to see Annie and the children. And then a new level of sadness. On July 13, 1975, I received Mom's devastating phone call in the dormitory. Dad was dying, she told me. "The doctors say that if you want to see your Dad alive, you better fly here immediately."[1]

I went straight to my professors who pledged to work with me on my assignments. Some things take priority, and this was at the top of that list. I drove to Chicago and caught a plane to San Francisco. The night I arrived was the last night of Dad's life. I picked up Mom in Mountain View and we went to the hospital in San Jose. Dad and I chatted but we didn't really talk. He was in a lot of discomfort. His systems were shutting down.

HARRY ALBIN ZACKRISON (1901–1975)

Dad's hands had been restrained because he kept trying to pull out his intravenous tubes. I held his hands. He begged me to untie his hands. I comforted him and held his hands. These hands had changed my diapers and held me as a baby. These hands had written me letters when I was away at school and when I left home. These hands had expressed Dad's thoughts to me in many ways and they had created things with me—model airplanes and miniature cars and boats. These hands had taught me to play ball. These hands had built our house in La Sierra.

I had never seen Dad's hands so clean. They had always been tinted with printer's ink, no matter how hard he scrubbed them with that strong Lava hand soap. But several years of retirement had yielded clean, soft hands. These were the hands that had carried me to the doctor when I was struck down with acute arthritis as a young boy. They had caressed my cheeks when I suffered from fevers and earaches. Those hands had expressed his deep love for me even in those times when I was stubborn and belligerent, wanting to blame him for my troubles.

I held his hands there in the hospital that night and remembered when I had suffered my print shop accident back in college. I could never forget how Dad's hands would hold my broken hand. As a father I now understood the tears that welled up in his eyes as he shook his head in suffering my pain with me. Many times, he would take my healed hand and simply hold it without saying a word. I had felt his love through his hands.

My father's hands were my Father. They represented his craftsmanship as a carpenter, his professionalism as a layout artist and linotype operator, his creativity as

---

1. Phone call from my Mother, Esther Zackrison (1902–1992), July 13, 1975.

a painter, an artist and cartoonist, his careful technical skill as a fine photographer. These hands had produced fine music on the organ, the piano, the violin and the trumpet. His hands had convinced me that he could do anything. He overhauled our car with his hands. He raised large gardens with his hands. He mixed concrete and taught me how to hammer nails with those hands. I honestly didn't know of anything he couldn't do with his hands.

As I held his hands I saw how soft they were now. It was clear that life was draining from his body. His hands were almost idle. And in the next day I would watch as his lifeless hands were folded across his quiet chest for the last time. Then I realized that I would not see or hold those hands again.

I'm not sure that we ever appreciate our fathers as we should. My father was the nicest man I ever knew. He was never mean, never political and never coercive. He had the tenderest heart I have ever known. But I was too immature to tell him. I had to arrive at a lot of these appreciations after he was gone. I would give anything to have a day with Dad again. Dad's hands were always applied to the work of the Lord. If I could only hold those hands once more.

Jim flew in from Honduras the next day, but by then Dad was gone. One of the last things I remembered Dad saying to me was, "Ed, are you ever going to finish going to school?" He shouldn't have been surprised—he had taught me to love school.

The last time I had any extensive visits with Dad was in the fall of 1974. He and Mom had spent a week with us in Collegedale, attended our orchestra concert and later, for Christmas, presented me with a new Buffet R-13 professional model clarinet, which became one of my most valued possessions. They had just returned from a short visit to Sweden, a trip I had heard them hoping to take during all the years I was at home. It was the first time Dad had been back to visit his family since he came to America in the 1920s.

During his visit to Tennessee we had a chance to spend time together—he came to my classes, he showed me his pictures of Sweden and I showed him Chattanooga, Tennessee, a city in need of a lot of refurbishing at the time.

Now he was dying. Life presents one with the choice of priorities. And a dying father, the first immediate family member to present this radical change in my life, took priority. Dad died in the early morning of July 15, 1975, just a short time before Mom and I arrived at the hospital to visit him once more. He had turned 74 in June and 24 days later he died. Ironically, he died on the eighth anniversary of the chartering of my Church in Camarillo.

The funeral was held in Mountain View. Ed and Lee Jasper, close friends from our internship and Camarillo Church days, were there to comfort us. Mom flew Annie in from Tennessee for the funeral services. Elder Euel Atchley, pastor of the Mountain View Adventist Church and an old friend of the family, held the services. I was confronted with death in a new way. The way theologians deal with death in the abstract could leave the impression that death is simply another theological locus. Death in the existential reality of one's family is on a different level. Heaven took on new meaning as I viewed my father in his final resting place in Mountain View.

I had performed many funerals as a pastor. But Grandpa and Grandma were the closest relatives I had lost. And now Dad was gone. The Black Cloud was not simply a doctrine anymore. For the next few days, as we packed up Dad's things and got Mom ready to move to Phoenix where she had purchased a mobile home next door to one of her closest friends, I saw Dad walking around the apartment at night, only to shake my head and realize it was just a dream. I began to realize how deeply imbedded he was in my mind.

Dad was seventy-four years old when he died. In deep thought I came to see that he had largely shaped my model of what a religious man was. It had been a long trip for Dad. From Stockholm, Sweden to Chicago, Illinois, in America in his early 20s, Dad had pursued his hobbies and his mission in life. Hard, intense work had undoubtedly shortened his life. But that work was devoted to his religious reason for living.

When I asked him, shortly before his death, whether he had achieved the height of perfection he had always talked about, he simply said, "My life is ending. I guess God is just going to have to take me as I am. I'm in his hands." I wished I had picked up on that thought more than I had. I was too much of an ideologue. I was pursuing much of his ideology, but I had added my own unique touches. I fear that "Just as I am" is too often little more than a hymn title to a religious man.

I returned to the university with my deep sense of loss. I buried myself in my studies, and despite my sorrow, the summer soon ended. I passed both language examinations, finished my classes and returned to Collegedale for a new school year.

I would come back with my family to Michigan in the summer of 1976 for an extended stay of three years—time enough, I thought, to finish my doctorate and return once again to my enjoyable life of teaching and ministering to my students' needs.

A HOUSE IN BERRIEN SPRINGS

Just ten years after leaving Berrien Springs, Michigan, we were back for another stay. A few changes had taken place. We had two children now. No longer were we university apartment dwellers. This time we would buy a house for the three years we were scheduled to live there.

We took seriously the informal, Adventist cultural notion: *A minister only has one way to make money legitimately, and that is to buy a house and let it appreciate.* Adventist ministers were to have a "single eye"—that meant, no moonlighting. Any work on the side while drawing denominational pay was clearly an indication of a lack of commitment to the cause.

The university had changed too. Several new buildings now dotted the campus. Only one or two of my old professors were still on the active faculty and they were, for the most part, on the verge of retirement. A few of my former classmates were now on the university faculty. Some had not taken the ordination route through the pastorate, the one I had elected to take. Instead they had gone on to graduate school programs in intensive theological, biblical and historical areas. Other classmates were back, to enroll in the new doctoral programs the university was now offering. I felt I had come home.

We found a small, three-bedroom, two-story, farm-style, one-hundred-year-old house in the heart of Berrien Springs, on Main Street, just two blocks from Schrader's Market and two doors down from the local funeral home. Jill and Mark each had a room of their own upstairs adjacent to the attic. The rooms were adequate for the needs of an eight- and five-year old. A quaint stairway led directly to Mark's room and then wrapped around to form a balcony leading to Jill's room at the front of the house.

The only bathroom was downstairs and appeared to have been added on after the original house had been built. The downstairs featured a master bedroom, dining room, living room, kitchen, and a service porch on the back of the house where the washer and dryer could be placed. A bonus was the "Michigan basement"—unfinished but large enough to house the furnace and canned goods.

The little house was cute. It had a covered porch in front, an outside entrance to the master bedroom, a car port and gingerbread trim on the eaves. In front of the house were two large oak trees that provided shade. Behind the house was a small barn that would serve as my study. The main drawback was that this little barn had no heating or cooling, something that the Michigander soon finds to be both a want and a need. In addition to the study room, which occupied half of the barn, there was room for one car, a small workshop, and a loft where the kids could play.

In this barn I would think great thoughts and write doctoral treatises; that was, until the winter hit. While previous owners had insulated the little room in the barn, nothing could have prepared us for the wicked winters that would be visiting us over the next three years. During those 45 below zero (chill factor) seasons I would find myself migrating to the Michigan basement to study in front of the furnace.

The little house was a short two miles from the university, which was convenient walking or bicycle riding distance through back pathways, again depending on the weather. A Michigan summer storm could whip up in an instant and so it was advisable to listen to the weather report and always carry an umbrella. When winter came any plan to walk that far was not advisable. Those winters had not changed in our ten-year absence.

I set about to wallpaper and paint during that first summer. I worked to the background of the radio's campaign speeches and debates of Governor Jimmy Carter and President Gerald Ford running for office. In a house of that vintage I found that plumbing and electrical work were a couple of skills I had to develop.

Buying a second house involved some serious planning. First, we had to rent out our house on Suhrie Drive in Collegedale to take care of the mortgage payments. We were nervous because we had heard horror stories about what irresponsible people do to rental property. But we had never looked at our house as "rental property."

OUR HOME AND OUR RENTERS

It was our home—the place we planned to come back to in three years and live for the rest of our lives. The college business manager recommended a family to us that he said was *safe*. That meant they could be counted on to act maturely toward our cherished home. We signed them on. And then they fell through. And so, a second recommendation—and we took it trusting his judgment again.

We were told that this family would not overhaul any motorcycles in our front room. And they would have no wayward children to dismantle our rooms, two rumored denominators in rental property destruction. They had two high school age sons and we were guaranteed that they had no pets (which may have been true when they moved in). So, we could be confident that they were clean people who would be protective of our home. Once again, we accepted the word of our business manager, who was also our next-door neighbor. We could have no idea how much this family would figure into our future lives.

In the beginning our renters were simply signatures on a letter, or a check, or a voice on the phone. Our meetings were long-distance phone calls when something went wrong that we needed to fix, or questions about how some appliance worked. The father worked for the big baking firm in town. The mother was on the staff of a local evangelistic crusade team.

We loved our home. It wasn't all that we wanted it to be, but it was all we could afford at the time. The view out the kitchen window could have been taken from a country scene on an Americana jigsaw puzzle. We hoped in the future to be able to add a larger study downstairs, a family room adjacent to the kitchen, and reconfigure the present study into a guest room. We had learned from our four years in the house that a family room downstairs was not ideal for families who like to eat and socialize.

This was a house we had helped design with a local builder who came with high recommendations and a fine reputation, and we found him measuring up to both. We had children to educate and private Adventist school costs were not cheap. So, all that addition planning would have to wait. Perhaps when we sold our home in Berrien Springs we would have enough return to think about an addition.

My wife was not working outside the home and neither of us had plans for her to do so at least until the children were in school. For now this was our home—more than we had ever owned before. And it represented something of our personalities. I had built all the shelves in the downstairs study as well as the desk built-ins under the window on the front of the lower level. There was a real brick fireplace in the family room—not the molded-cement-painted-to-look-like-brick version we had had in California. I had bought books on designing children's rooms and followed the plans

I found there as I built in shelves and cupboards in the kids' rooms—hiring out the work was not a financial option.

The bright colors we chose reflected the 1970s. I could paint and wallpaper. Plumbing, carpeting, electrical work, and sheet rocking were beyond the scope of my present talents.

Friday nights were made up of family time when I bounced the kids off my legs sending them flying on to our king-sized bed. They laughed loudly. I loved those laughs. They never wanted me to quit these gymnastics and I never wanted them to stop laughing. When we moved I discovered all the bed slats had broken from these vaultings into laughter over the years. Friday night became our tradition when the whole family had Christian stories and fell asleep together in the big bed.

So, we didn't leave our little castle without some concerns about how much of it would be left intact when we returned after three years. To think of letting anyone else have this home even for a short period of time seemed unthinkable. To consider selling it was out of the question. The children would be much bigger when we returned. They would no longer be jumping on the bed. But the monthly rental check was a necessity for helping to meet the monthly mortgage payment and so we had little other choice than to rent out this most precious material commodity of ours.

ACADEMIC ROUTINE BEGINS; SHAKY FEELINGS FOLLOW

My first formal class in the fall of 1976 was from Dr. Hans LaRondelle (1929–2011). This professor was a systematic theologian (ThD) who had done his doctoral work under G. C. Berkouwer (1903–1996), the highly esteemed Dutch Reformed theologian at Free Amsterdam University in the Netherlands. Dr. LaRondelle's first words to his twelve new doctoral students were memorable: "I am here to see that you finish!"

That was encouraging. We were all tense and anxious. This was an experience none of us had faced before. But now we felt we were in good hands—Adventist hands—professors whose commitment was to provide the Church with truly Adventist Christian scholars.

By the winter of 1976 I had passed my French, Hebrew and Greek exams, which left just one language test—German—and that would be finished by January 1977. It had been a busy summer working on the house, celebrating the American Bicentennial and breaking into a heavy school routine on a higher level than I had ever been before. I took a full load of classwork for the fall quarter—three doctoral level classes.

The Doctor of Theology degree is a research degree. Each class stressed digging deeply into the subject of study. Once accepted into the program each student was expected to finish the language requirements as soon as possible. Then we were to finish our classwork over the next three years.

We were not allowed to start working on our dissertation topic or preparing for it formally until we had finished these other requirements satisfactorily and passed our forty hours of written comprehensive examinations (eight real time hours in each of five areas of theology, historical theology, philosophy, history of philosophy, and biblical studies).

When we had reached this level, having completed our classwork and passed our comprehensive exams, we could then submit a proposal for a dissertation topic, which would be studied, discussed, delimited, and considered by a large committee of about twenty professors. The idea was that we should be adequately acquainted with all areas of philosophical and theological loci before we could be considered qualified to submit anything formally.

By October I was three quarters into fulfilling requirements, but I was gradually changing my mind about what I was doing. I wanted to be an effective college professor—that was where my religion had led me.

My Greek qualifying examination was a wake-up call that made me question my future. One professor, who read my test, suggested that I should not be passed because I had not recognized a third-class Greek construction on the qualifying exam. An argument between him and my committee ensued, and he finally backed down, but when I came up for candidacy three years later he would raise the question again. I wanted no question over my head as to my scholarly qualifications. Credibility was extremely important to me. I offered to retake the exam, but my committee chair refused; I had done fine, he said.

My uncertainty in the program coalesced with my belief that I was to teach students first and subjects second. This led me to begin checking out other programs until by November I was beginning to question why I had made the decision to attend Andrews. Nevertheless, making a change now seemed impossible. We were moved in, buying a house and settled into schoolwork. The children were in their schools. I had finished many preliminary requirements and would have to start all over somewhere else. Plus, time was not on my side—I would have already squandered nearly a year of my three-year leave.

So, I called Dr. Knittel—it was what I did when I had serious professional questions. I revealed reluctantly that I was thinking I made a mistake. I was fearful of how he might respond. But he just asked me what I wanted to do to rectify it. I told him I had found a PhD program in Southern California that I could pursue. The program would give me a strong practical perspective while at the same time honoring the research in theology and biblical studies that I had already done. He could see that I was serious and had thought this through. He simply said if I went that route he would support me. No hesitation.

I wasn't really surprised at this answer. I had never felt that he was excited about my going to Andrews. He wanted me to expand my horizons—get a wider view of life. Furthermore, other programs were shorter, cheaper, and ironically carried more credibility. This was an unbeatable combination for an administrator. But he had never pressured me. He had assured me that this had to be my decision.

Andrews University, one of only two full-fledged Adventist universities at the time, was considered the finest theological education offered by the denomination. It was a General Conference institution and in the process of hiring the most capable and experienced professors in the denomination. But denominational schools are worried about home-grown talent. While they may say they have the best programs around, many gravitate to giving more credibility to those who have graduated from another university. Furthermore, I was still not convinced that the program I was in was the most helpful for what I wanted.

I wanted more classwork in ministering to young people. That would involve classes in developmental psychology and adolescent development along with general education courses that gave instruction in values development and educational psychology as well as educational philosophy. And so, with the president's approval, I made the decision during Christmas vacation of 1976 to start packing. By the middle of the vacation we were nearly packed and ready to move to California.

TRANSFERRING OUT

I climbed to the top floor of Seminary Hall to the office Dr. Gerhard Hasel, director of the ThD program, to announce my intentions. I expected that he would try to talk me out of it. But he was not in—he was overseas teaching that quarter. Next, I walked down the hall to talk with Dr. Raoul Dederen (1925–2016), my major professor and chair of my doctoral committee. I expected he too would disagree with my plans. He was out of the country and would not be back for several more weeks. So, I went down the stairs to the office of the dean of the Seminary, Dr. Thomas H. Blincoe. He wasn't in either. His secretary told me he was in another part of the country teaching an extension class. He would be back in March.

With administrators, advisors, and anyone officially connected with my program gone, I went to the registrar's office and filled out a withdrawal slip. The lady at the counter signed the paper and I was out of the program. Getting out of the program was surely easier than getting into it! I had worked for months and had to go through several committees and write several submissions and essays to get into the program. To get out took only minutes, including the trip from my house.

I was wrong about that. I just didn't know that yet. I went home, planned with SMC as to when the truck could be in Berrien Springs to pick up our stuff, and worked a little at getting the house ready for the real estate agent to show. And I waited. When the phone rang I was to learn I had not visited the right offices that morning.

REDIRECTION

Elder Lowell Bock (1923–2016) *was on the phone.* Elder Bock was the vice-chair of the Board of Trustees for Andrews University. He asked if I could come by his office at the Lake Union Conference where he served as president. He had just heard that I had withdrawn from the ThD program. Someone had heard—someone did care. Dropping out was a little more complicated than it had appeared earlier that morning. I drove to his office on Highway 31 between my house and the university.

Elder Bock appealed to me about my decision. He said the University Board had been working on this ThD for a long time and felt it was imperative to get it accredited on the first try with the Association of Theological Schools (ATS), and they felt they could not afford to have someone drop out right now. So, he had called me to his office to hear my side of the story. And he hoped that we could negotiate an understanding together so I would stay. He just wanted to know what they could do. It was a fair question and issued in a most cordial way. I couldn't remember meeting Elder Bock before, and I appreciated his visit.

I explained that I had dropped out because I felt the program was too specialized for my needs. I enjoyed being a scholar and I certainly wasn't leaving because I had to do thorough research—that I expected and was satisfied that I was getting. But I felt that my primary interest in life was teaching college and I only saw one class in my program that had to do specifically with teaching. I had already taken that class and appreciated it but felt the need for more work along that line. Then I outlined the program that was luring me.

After some thought he asked me if I could let him call Dr. Grady Smoot (1932–2018), president of the university and see if he had any suggestions that might accommodate me. That would mean I would have to wait a day before moving on my present decision. I considered this a reasonable request and told him I would do so. He thanked me, and I went back home. It was not over. Later that day I was invited to Dr. Smoot's office. The executive office was a large, magnificently furnished and decorated room with wood paneling and soft easy chairs as I recall—truly representative of what a university administrative headquarters should be.

Here I was seated before the man behind the huge desk, who was building an impressive graduate school. I was not there asking for favors, or anything special. This was his idea. I was kicking myself for not doing my research better, for not listening to advice months before. I knew now that I wanted an inter-disciplinary program, but I didn't see that Dr. Smoot's vision for the university could afford to bend for that. Nor was I asking—he was the decision-maker here. He was here to woo me back—not something I had planned or expected.

When I left Dr. Smoot's office I had agreed to postpone further plans until he could consider my concerns and let him work on the problem during the afternoon. This was a complicated day for all of us. I knew I was receiving far more administrative attention than I should have expected.

My mentor in ministry had warned me to stay out of administrators' offices. He told me that it gives the impression that I am not working. Plus, I could be perceived as a troublemaker. I was beginning to see that firsthand. But I was not seeking to make trouble. I had only been indecisive and now I knew better and hoped to rectify things before I got in any deeper.

Dr. Smoot assured me that I could expect a telephone call from him later that day. And true to his word the phone rang in my little barn study and it was the president's secretary. She immediately put him on the phone, and he told me what he had done since our visit. He told me that he had planned for me to talk to the graduate school about a possible interdisciplinary program that might rival the one I was being attracted to in Southern California. If I would go to the dean of the School of Education in the morning I might find accommodation. Before hanging up he thanked me for widening the vistas of the university.

After our conversation I had a chance to ponder what had just taken place. It was quite widely rumored that the president's desire was to turn Andrews into the Adventist Harvard of the West. Before today he had seemed remote so that I couldn't picture him as being very pliable. But I was wrong. He was very convincing that he had my best interests at heart, which, of course, was in the university's best interests as well. Did Dr. Smoot's close friend, Dr. Frank Knittel, have something to do with all this attention? I would never know.

I was delighted. I knew the dean of the School of Education. I knew that his school housed psychology, sociology, educational philosophy and methodology as well as other related areas and several doctoral programs. The last time I had spent time with this dean in his office was at La Sierra when I was called in with Jennifer for our PDA. So here I was once more in the office of Dr. George Akers!

Since leaving La Sierra College, Dr. Akers had finished his doctorate at University of Southern California, served as president of Columbia Union College in Washington, D.C., and was now Andrews' architect of the new doctoral programs in the Graduate Education Department. He spent the morning picking my brain, then laid out a program for me to consider. It was good. It had that added benefit of a distinctive Adventist flavor. Over the next three years we would relate to each other on a different basis than in the past.

That afternoon I called Dr. Knittel who told me I probably had to stay at Andrews now. I had considered their offer; I had accepted their proposal to construct a program that rivaled what I wanted in California and they had matched it.

I couldn't tell if he was disappointed or elated. But I experienced a decided sense of relief. Thinking about re-qualifying in all those areas I had worked on for the past year and a half was admittedly not a pleasant thought. Moving again was no more inviting except that we would be closer to our families in California.

So, I accepted Dr. Smoot's offer and we cancelled our plans to move. I would press on with my new program. It was still the ThD program, but it was more diversified. Instead of taking a cognate in biblical studies I would have a cognate in developmental psychology and related subjects. It was cross-disciplinary, and I would have a better grasp of my teaching skills when I finished. If I had known the future at that point I would have interpreted all this as providential.

Would my Seminary professors take to this new program? No, they wouldn't. They were not excited about my program at all. They were theologians who clung to the ancient vestiges that saw theology as the queen of the sciences. I received virtually no encouragement from my committee chair. I was so concerned about his opposition that I ultimately requested a total reorganization of my doctoral committee, which would have removed him from the committee altogether. This was not a wise move. I had already received too much administrative attention without adding this as well. The request was denied, and I was worried. It made me look manipulative, obstinate, and not only couldn't I afford that perception, I was a religious man and did not want it.

Not until after I had finished all my classwork and passed my comprehensive exams three years later did my chair call me and confess that he had finally accepted my accomplishments in the new program as credible. He was proud of me, he said. The program the school had worked out with me was made an alternative to any university student who could qualify, although to my knowledge no one ever followed in my footsteps.

A TEAM IN THE MAKING

With our daughter in school and our son in kindergarten, Annie decided that now she could seek her own academic pursuits. In consultation with Dr. Knittel regarding the needs of SMC, she came to see that her best area of pursuit would be business education rather than pursuing another degree in English.

Dr. Knittel was candid that business education was a very needy area at SMC. And while he couldn't promise anything in terms of employment at this point he thought that this would be an area where the faculty would soon need some replacement or some expansion. Business education was moving past the old shorthand mode, even past the Dictaphone. It was moving to computers. The personal computer was barely on the horizon but those in the know foresaw that an information explosion was a growing movement that must be addressed by the college.

Now we began to feel the pressures of what it was like to have both parents gone for significant periods of time. We had to stagger our times at home. I discovered that my ideology about women's rights in the marketplace was being tested in the cauldron of reality. Being home while my wife was in class, and the kids were coming home, was a new practicality even though I had thoroughly endorsed the idea and supported it, at least in my thinking. Working out the logistics now faced us.

As it turned out Annie graduated with her Master of Arts in Teaching (MAT) degree long before I finished my doctoral program. With her major in business education, we would be a new team returning to SMC. Counseling with Dr. Knittel would be turned against her as my relationship with him had been. We still didn't understand that. We were young, energetic, and idealistic. We failed to grasp that excelling in one's discipline and education meant favoritism to the more insecure around us.

We still believed that you got what you worked for and that politics (still a dirty word to me) played an insignificant role, if any at all. We still believed that what was important was that you were qualified for the job you did. We underestimated the importance of being authorized to do the job. And that was where politics often entered the picture.

What we didn't understand was that so many of the people Dr. Knittel had appointed to administrative positions were perceived by more than a few as more authorized than qualified for their positions. They were known widely as Frank's friends. Some had been good teachers or students but did not turn out to be particularly good administrators. I had no clue at the time how this would affect our future. When Dr. Knittel was confronted with this criticism, his response was, "Who should I hire—my enemies?" Of course, that wasn't the point, but it temporarily evaded the issue.

Ironically, most of these administrators would eventually turn against Dr. Knittel and force him to resign. In partnership with the new board chair, Al McClure (1931–2006), who came into office about the time we returned to Southern, these administrators would make it clear that a time for a change of president had come. Such a move would ensure their jobs but place many of us on the faculty in very vulnerable positions. We would ultimately feel the blow—mainly those who were considered teachers favored by Dr. Knittel.

The Knittel faculty would eventually be systematically dismantled for a variety of reasons. But then it would not matter that you were "Teacher of the Year" (both Jerry Gladson and Annie had been voted that by the student body), or if you had been chosen by any graduating class to be their sponsor (I served in this capacity twice). It would not matter if students signed petitions or staged protests. None of these things was considered measures of greatness or contributions to the student life and growth of the school. There were other factors to consider, most of which teachers were hardly aware.

Whether you put in class time at the school or worked overtime counseling and guiding students in their academic aspirations would make little difference. What really mattered would be the question of loyalty to the board chair. And if you supported the president when the board chair had decided it was time for him to lose his political clout in the Adventist South you were replaceable.

Local businesses would also be a consideration since these were large donors to the college. As one Conference president told me, "How you are perceived is all that matters because perceptions are reality." And I would later learn in business graduate school that once a CEO was after you, you were doomed.

Such thinking was never a part of my consideration. I was a religious man not a politician. I did not consider I was working for the Church. I was working for God and I was where God had placed me not where some churchman had put me. It was a grave miscalculation.

During my personal visit to see Elder McClure sometime later he would make another view clear to me. He would tell me of his awesome power. And he made it clear in our two-hour conversation in his Atlanta office as he fought sleeping when I talked, that when he said how it would be, it would be that way. We would learn soon. I now knew I was not working for God. I was working for politicians. It was a hard awakening.

CHAPTER TWENTY-SEVEN

A Tapestry of Subtle Shifts

"Security is the mother of danger and the grandmother of destruction."
—Thomas Fuller

PLUGGING IN THE NEW PROGRAM

MY PROGRAM WAS PROCEEDING. I took educational philosophy, educational psychology and developmental psychology classes. I found a new world of interest and excitement. I made presentations to graduate classes and marveled at what psychologists knew about the human development of values, morals, and abilities. These professors opened a world to me that I had, in my ignorance, criticized and cajoled. Having children at the developmental stages I was studying in my childhood and pre-adolescence classes was incredibly enlightening. I began to realize how myopic and shortsighted I had been.

I bought toys for my son that I would never have considered with my parochial outlook. I approached the facts of life with my nine-year-old daughter, but apparently didn't accomplish much as she wrote in a magazine article later what a poor job I had done. With few clear modern models to follow many of my attempts at parenting were plowing new ground for me. The cultural lag between learning and application would persist for a long time, but at least the possibility of understanding it had been introduced.

During these intensive three years in Michigan I thought we had good family togetherness and development despite the pressing responsibilities of graduate study. Later it would become increasingly apparent that I had missed out on three of the most precious years of my children's lives. The stress of book learning and study, goals and career focusing takes an insidious toll on people's lives. How important is it all?

I would eventually grow to resent the loss I had sustained with my children for the sake of the cause. At times I was angry with God because I believed he had placed me in this position.

MOVEMENTS IN THE DENOMINATION DURING THIS TIME

During those three years in Michigan there were other developments taking place in the denomination. They developed in increments of seeming unimportance until time would expose a tapestry of tragic elements that gradually took on connections that few of us could have foreseen.

One of these increments was the visit to Berrien Springs of an Australian Anglican theologian, Dr. Geoffrey Paxton, who had authored what turned out to be a significant book entitled, *The Shaking of Adventism*.[1] At the time I could not have been convinced that anyone from the outside could shake Adventism. Yet Adventism had a curious doctrine called "the shaking." According to this teaching of Sister White, the dross in the Church would be shaken out. Great lights would go out. I had no idea how that prophecy could be misused.

When I attended the meeting in Berrien Springs with my brother who was visiting from Southern California, at the Berrien County Youth Fair grounds pavilion, along with many from the Seminary faculty and student body, I was amused that much of what he was criticizing as lacking in Adventism had been taught for decades as standard Adventist doctrine.

The concepts of justification, sanctification, original sin, righteousness, etc., were standard emphases in both my early Seminary and later doctoral classes. The claims Dr. Paxton made seemed fabricated claiming that Adventism had never accepted these ideas. I hadn't found that claim to be fair. We believed in and freely taught justification by faith and righteousness by grace. We openly decried legalism and anything that suggested that works on our part were meritorious for our salvation was a stretch of the imagination. It did not seem that Adventists were Roman Catholic in their view of salvation as he seemed to charge—semi-Pelagian? No.

I could point to Dr. LaRondelle and Dr. Heppenstall. I could cite Dr. Desmond Ford, chair of the Theology Department at Avondale College in Australia, who had written articles in the *Ministry* for as long as I could remember, as well as on Daniel and Revelation and salvation by grace. Representative Adventist theologians to this end filled my twenty-four file drawers with *Ministry* articles. In fact, it was Dr. Ford and Dr. Heppenstall who had worked so hard to turn Robert Brinsmead around when he had attacked the Church from a perfectionism agenda. He now saw the importance of Reformation theology.

---

1. Paxton, *The Shaking of Adventism*, (1977). For a treatment of the Adventist notion of "the shaking," see White, *Last Day Events: Facing Earth's Final Crisis,* 172–182.

No longer a theological perfectionist, Brinsmead now espoused a more traditional Reformation view of justification and sanctification. That change was considered one of the great turnarounds in Adventist history of ideas. But instead of applauding these efforts, denominational leaders came to condemn them. It seemed that Brinsmead would never be listened to even if he was orthodox. Leadership would shift its views of what Adventism allegedly taught until everything looked confused. I was puzzled. It seemed little wonder that Dr. Paxton was wading through these double binds.

Official Adventism was becoming an opponent of scholarly Adventism, but the officials controlled the press. In an official capacity they presented themselves as the guardians of The Truth. Suddenly more and more scholars were feeling that they were becoming perceived as the enemy to be investigated, and a religious McCarthyism seemed to be entering the Church scene. There were many who believed that the strong supporter of this new trend was the General Conference president, Elder Robert Pierson, elected to his position in 1966 at the Detroit quadrennial convocation.

Much of the new doctrine, being passed off as official and historic Adventism had been presented at the 1974 Bible Conferences led by Dr. Gordon Hyde, secretary of the denomination's Biblical Research Institute (BRI), and former speech teacher at SMC. During my days at La Sierra College I had heard of Robert Brinsmead and his claims that we could perfect our sinful natures through the mystery of the Sanctuary Doctrine. But we were theological neophytes. We were not training to be churchmen.

Churchmen are practical. They look at the bottom line of the organization. Bible teachers are apologists for the cause. We were defenders of the faith. We knew what we believed and why we believed it. We did not involve ourselves in constructive theology. Rather we pursued the work of corrective theology regarding non-Adventists and holding the fort together regarding the Church and its beliefs. Our job was to defend purity of theological thinking.

Brinsmead was early declared an enemy of the cause. The reasons given didn't make much sense to me because I really didn't understand what he was saying. But I was more confused when he changed his view, did a virtual theological flip-flop and was still dubbed an enemy of the Church. This did not appear rational to me. Rather it seemed hypocritical. Where was the search for Truth? Why not rejoice in his reversal? I was obviously missing some political aspects of the controversy. I did not understand at that time the importance of being authorized and that this took precedence over being qualified. But then a Church official told me that Robert Brinsmead had discovered how to make "easy money." The issue was becoming clearer.

Hints of the winds of change entered one of my Seminary doctoral classes in 1977, the professor admitted that he had basically agreed with Robert Brinsmead in his perfectionist days. I raised my hand and asked how he had survived the investigation of the 1960s when Brinsmead's followers were being ferreted out of the churches and schools. He told the class that he went underground. Those who agreed with

Brinsmead often went undercover to protect themselves and their theology. At that time, he had been the chair of the theology department at an Adventist college.

This same teacher went on to present his view of perfection, the nature of Christ, and the doctrine of salvation in perfectionist terms and explained that the Adventist Church was now ready to accept this theology on a larger scale for it was the "historic" view. The "old" Brinsmead had been right on many points, he argued from an alleged historical position of Adventism. Furthermore, he said, it helped that Brinsmead had changed because now his new views would be attacked more fervently. All the perfectionists could come out of their hiding places now. I don't recall that he used the *perfectionism* idiom for his view. But that was the content.

I sensed a shared astonishment in the classroom. Those of us in the class had been schooled in Adventist colleges in America, England, Germany, Australia, and Africa. None of us knew each other well before taking this class together. While we had been educated in different parts of the world we found that we were all in basic agreement on what we had been taught as the Adventist view on these subjects and had been consistently taught the same view in these diverse areas of the world. But it was not the view our professor was claiming to teach.

While I dismissed Dr. Paxton as insignificant I was troubled by what I had encountered in this class. Here was the only graduate teacher I had had who suggested that these old Brinsmead perfectionistic ideas had any merit, and I wondered at his claim that his views were also the positions of the editorial staff of the *Adventist Review*, the general voice of the Adventist Church, as well as many General Conference officials. I began to grasp some of the rift that was developing between the educators and administrators of the denomination.

THE LEVELS OF DISSEMINATING TRUTH

The dissemination of religious truth in organized religion comes on three levels, each having its own aspects: (1) The official (administrators) level; (2) The professional (scholars) level; and (3) The folk (laymen) level. Hence expressing truth is complex. It is bound up with perceptions and interpretations and it has angles. Demonstrating it is often easier than reflecting on it. Furthermore, there is always an existing context that helps define and focus on the direction discovery of truth will take.

The Official Level is the realm of the administrative churchman—the speaker for organized religion—the person who must keep the Church operating financially and must consider the world Church. This is the realm of the religious politician. While professional scholars and influential leaders on the Folk Level may comment on the list of official beliefs of a Church, formally called the creed, the final decisions and the enforcement of this creed are in the realm of the officials—for Adventists: The General Conference in session.

The officials also hold the purse strings, which gives them almost unlimited power over the other two levels. They reside over the business of the organized Church. In an organization where officials are elected through some form of democratic process, religious politics are inescapable. The most basic study of political science reveals that politicians have one purpose that transcends all others: to get elected. This is not absent in Church politics but may increase the pressure through the religious ambiance. Nobody wants to be against God and the officials can easily slip into the mode that they are the natural representatives of God. This fact can be seen throughout Church history.

The Pope, for example, condemns artificial means of contraception for Catholic married couples. That is the official position of the Roman Catholic Church. Canon law, the official position, is interpreted and guarded by the Pope, cardinals, archbishops, and bishops. If you want to know what Catholicism teaches you must go to the traditions of the Church as preserved by the people in these offices. This is where God allegedly speaks to the Church.

For Adventists the rough equivalent would be the administrators, the Conference presidents, the Union presidents, the Division presidents and the General Conference president. These positions are formulated at the duly called official gatherings of the denomination, like the now quinquennial session, the annual councils and the Conference committees. Interestingly, no women could hold one of these important offices, reserved for ordained leaders. So as in Catholicism, ultimate authority rested in the hands of a few men.

The Scholar, the second level, includes theologians and scholars. Just as one doesn't go to the constructive Catholic theologian to hear the pronouncement of the final formulation of official Church doctrine and policy, so one doesn't look to the Adventist theologian for the final word on the Church's official teaching, except as he is handing on ("tradition") what he believes the Church teaches.

If the officials and the theologians disagree, the officials are right, and the theologians are wrong. This is a question of authorization, not necessarily qualification. Furthermore, the hierarchical infrastructure of the Church is in the officials' corner. As one minister told me, "never forget, they write the rules." "They" are the executives who keep the business solvent and operating. The scholars do exegesis on the text of the Bible, they search the historical developments of doctrine as well as the context in which it developed. They apply the scientific, philosophical methods to the process and history of religious truth, they learn the biblical languages without the help of analytical lexicons, and they apply the historical-critical method to Bible study seeking authenticity and reliability.

They study the disciplines of archaeology and geology and compare them to biblical accounts of history. They study the original languages in their contexts and go on digs in Jordan and Heshbon. They attend religious conferences of the American Academy of Religion (AAR), the Society of Biblical Literature (SBL) or the American

Society for Oriental Research (ASOR). They usually earn a research doctorate. And they give possible solutions to sticky questions—but they are not authorized to formulate binding creedal pronouncements.

The kinds of discussions that scholars indulge in often sound like foolishness to the officials. As one official frustratingly exclaimed in response to a report he had heard a young theologian present at the national convention in St. Louis in the mid-1970s, in front of the whole society—"We have just sat here and been subjected to an hour of the biggest pile of junk I have ever heard in my life!" The presentation had been taken from the theologian's graduate research project.

The scholar is largely appreciated as he/she agrees with the official and feels the pressures. Many Adventist scholars do not share freely what they really believe about Adventism's unique doctrinal positions. As a rule, scholars are outstanding wordsmiths. But sometimes, even after they have explained the situation, the layman is still confused. The vocabulary and the flow of thought are not always picked up clearly by the untrained mind. The scholar's language is filled with technical terms, each often having a technical meaning.

The Folk, is that of most laypersons—the level of folk religion.[2] This group is made up largely of Church members who listen to people preach. They may have picked up an idea at camp meeting, another one in a Church service somewhere, perhaps a statement from Sister White that hit home in some way with them that they couldn't get out of their minds. Then they synthesized their outlook and formed an opinion that became their "view." As a result, they put together their understanding of religion. Many times, I have heard Church members, even with advanced degrees in areas other than religion and theology, ask, "Don't we believe that . . . ?" And they insert some idea they have in mind but are not clear on. Here is an appeal to collective thinking, which often ironically resides in folk religion.

Folk religion is usually not very unified; in many cases not consistent much at all. Because folk religion is both dependent and independent it is often unpredictable, and sometimes the expression of emotion. It may be cultic in that it waits for a religious guru to speak simply and define its course. It may use politics. It may be dormant. It may be aggressive, or it may be passive. Folk religion is not official belief; it is not necessarily scholarly or based in the common sense of the word. Sometimes it has a semblance of scholarship, but its methodology does not always grow out of commonly accepted principles of interpretation. So, a lot of loose ends may remain after it has expressed itself.

A man once told me that prophecy was easy to understand if one considered always the natural meaning of the symbols used in Daniel and Revelation. I asked him what he meant. For example, he said, whenever a "bear" appears in Bible prophecy, it stands for "Russia." And wherever a "lion" appears it is "Great Britain." And of course, when an "eagle" appears it is the United States. He gave no consideration to the time

---

2. Outside their formal work officials and scholars also have their share of folk religion.

the prophecy was written or what the context was (or what the prophecy may have meant in 44 AD or 1450). His pseudo exegesis came from the newspaper and history books of the twentieth century not from scripture. But it was an example of folk religion. To him this was the "normal."

Another striking example of folk religion was seen in the layman who met before our Collegedale Church appointed "Committee on New Light" one spring afternoon. The elderly gentleman claimed to have new light on some chapters in the prophecies of Ezekiel and Daniel and he wanted to run his ideas past this committee hopefully to receive approval.

He explained his exegetical method as follows: Whenever we read the word "even" as applied to "years" it means literally "even years," i.e., 2, 4, 6, 8, or 1844, 1846, 1848, and so forth. In his hour-long presentation he showed us how to interpret the last day events based on this curious hermeneutic. Furthermore, he explained that when the word "even" appears in italics it is a clue from the original writer that the word *"even"* is being *emphasized*. "Writers," he suggested, "italicize words they want to emphasize."

He finished his discussion fully convinced that he had truth no biblical student had ever discovered before in the whole history of religion and interpretation—the history of the world. He then called for questions and evaluation from our committee.

Committee members pointed out two immediate problems with his hermeneutic—problems any trained professional biblical scholar would have picked up in the first few minutes of the presentation.

First, "even," in the context, was used as an appositive. That means that when you use "even" in this construction it is a way of saying "that is to say." For example, if we were to say, "This is nice, even beautiful," that would mean that "nice" and "beautiful" are to be taken as standing side by side. They are in apposition to each other. If the text says, "days, even years," it is not saying the days in the text are even years, as opposed to odd years, it is saying the days represent years in this passage or context: "days, that is to say, years."

Second, the committee pointed out something even more devastating to his "new light." The fact that the word *even* appears in italics, can also be explained. The King James Version, which is a translation from the Hebrew, Aramaic, and Greek, indicates that *a word is supplied* by the translators, by italicizing it. Italics in the KJV does not indicate emphasis. Italicized words indicate that they do not appear in the original text but are supplied to make the translation read naturally when rendered in English. So "days, *even* years" would not mean days that are "even" as opposed to "odd" years, but rather literally, days—years. The actual word "*even*" does not appear in the ancient text.

This man's theory failed on two simple counts. As logical as it seemed to him, this was a simple exercise in hermeneutical unfamiliarity. Here scholarly religion was a corrective for folk religion. And so here was a case where folk religion failed the scholarly test. It also failed the official test in that no official statement of the Church had ever been issued that could present such a view as credible.

SHOCK IN THE CHURCH

The revolution that was about to break while I was in my ThD program was not something I saw coming. I knew that Adventism periodically cleaned house. About every twenty years or more it seemed there was a theological shaking up. That I would ever be implicated or even considered in such a horrific thing was far beyond my purview. I was much too naïve and idealistic to see this possibility. I had always assumed that those attacked were guilty of the charges. "Where there is smoke, there must be fire." Surely such a rule of thumb was reliable?

Furthermore, I had assumed that Adventism was more monolithic than it was. But before I had finished my doctoral dissertation the storm was brewing. I was warned against the use of certain theological terms in my project; terms such as "forensic justification" (regarding the doctrine of salvation) and "pastoral counsel" (regarding Sister White). This was not good news to me because it was not objective or scientific. I saw it as political. And my committee members did not explain carefully what they meant. They just rationalized, "and you know why!"

While these terms had been very good descriptions in all my previous education, suddenly they had filtered into common use by folk religion and were no longer clear; in fact, they could be so distractive that some would declare them heretical. They were buzzwords that some folk religionists had picked up and considered signs of the false revival that many Adventists believed would come into the Church, before the *Parousia*.

Suddenly a jolt came from my former pastoral mentor Elder Walter Rea, who was still a pastor in Southern California. He had stumbled over a Church scandal of far-reaching financial proportions involving a member of his Church whose records had become public through a divorce. In the materials he found in the archives of the local courthouse was a document that included the names of well-known Church leaders. The list that came out of the personal connections between this member and Church leaders had to do with financial investments, allegedly using Church funds, even tithe funds.

I was not a finance person and when I saw the document I did not know the far-reaching implications it would have on the denomination politically. I had also received some shocking material regarding Sister White's alleged plagiarism, and I thought maybe this was connected. Elder Rea asked me what I thought he should do with what he was finding. But this wasn't connected to that. He had received a tip regarding the financial question and told that he might find some of that interesting material at the courthouse.

I looked over the two-page document he had sent me. It had names of leaders I was acquainted with and a corresponding column of the money they had invested, plus a rather exaggerated return on their investment. Several connections stood out. Some of the individuals had been ministers in Southern California and those names were familiar. But some of them had gone on to higher positions in the Church—local Conferences and Union Conferences, even the General Conference. And as they moved to these positions, others were added to the list in their wake. Not knowing how or wanting to evaluate this, for at this point it was just something of interest, I xeroxed off a copy of this list and passed it on to an attorney friend of mine. He too read it with interest and wondered what to make of it.

One evening I received a phone call from a Church elder who was also my partner in teaching a Sabbath School class at the Berrien Springs Church. He was calling to ask me about something he felt the board might have to deal with soon—a serious, local problem, he said. His story involved an important administrator in the local Church's employment who, he said, had been playing the state lottery and had just won a pile of money. As was routine for lotteries the news had been made public.

The elder then told me that his mother had always taught him that gambling was wrong and something a Christian should not be involved in. And this was surely true of a Church leader, didn't I think? A bad model for others in the Church. Then the punch line: isn't the lottery gambling? Was this something a Church employee should be involved in? And shouldn't the Church board meet to handle this situation?

The conversation was intense. I sensed that he was earnestly seeking my opinion. But before he could get my opinion of the situation he continued. He explained that there was a further complication. Now the suspense was building. He revealed that he had a document, which was annoying him. He shared that it was a list of names of important denominational leaders who might be involved in some questionable investments. I was hardly handling this! The suggestion was that before we moved in on our local problem we should think of the implications of this situation with these Church leaders. He asked if I thought they were gambling? And possibly with Church funds? Then he said he just wanted to call and ask me what my opinion on the matter might be.

Perhaps he knew I was the source of the document and he was masking his call behind a local crisis. I didn't want to have an opinion. I was deeply involved in doctoral research and that took all my time, thought and energy that I could muster. Plus, I smelled a political rat here somewhere. I had never faced such a question and was not sure I had an educated opinion. The lottery was new to me. I had never given any thought to the ethics involved. I had some friends who were in the stock market, but I never thought of that as gambling. The denomination was in the stock market. But what my mentor had found was not the normal stock market—it allegedly dealt with Church funds and personal involvement. Were these hedge funds—high risk with borrowed funds? And it implied a series of questionable involvements with Church funds.

Alleged was that these leaders had used these funds, even tithe, to feather their own nests. The empire had collapsed, and millions of dollars had apparently been lost. The political implications were mind-boggling. My mind was swirling. At that point I didn't even think of the allegations to the public trust or how the giving patterns of the Church might be affected if this news got out. But it was not my problem.

I had no answer to his questions. His phone call was a confusing one. But I knew who had passed on the document he was referring to. And I suspected that the move would complicate the situation. I also knew of a further complication: the employee he was talking about was physically disabled. He walked with two crutches. Charges against him could involve breaking Church policy. Even then the far-reaching ramification could be a political time-bomb. But the emotions of the congregation would be involved no matter what the Church board may do.

How the two situations may be connected was not clear to me. The natural human propensity to shelter and defend the underdog (in this case a professionally competent employee with a physical handicap) could lead to strong disunity and bitterness in the congregation.

Finally, I gave my answer, which I figured was weak. I explained that I would have to give this question some thought. This was something new to me. I knew little or nothing about lotteries and any personal feelings I may have probably couldn't be used to set precedents for the Church. I had never known anyone who won a lottery and I knew the denomination invested in the stock market. And that was that. No constructive answer there!

This situation apparently went beyond just "investing in the stock market" as would become clear shortly. I told the elder that I had given the attorney the manuscript with the names on it out of confusion. We both had a hunch that the document was going to float a long way before it disappeared.

If the board of elders ever acted on the lottery problem with the employee I never knew because I was not in attendance at any meeting that dealt with it. But a few weeks later I was shopping at a local hardware store and the person in question was the clerk who rang up my purchase.

ATTEMPTING TO FOCUS ON THE FACE OF CURRENT ISSUES

Back to my studies I went. I was determined to finish this academic project as soon as possible. What I didn't know was that all the cinder blocks of the denomination crisis had been arranged and laid. Only the mortar needed to be applied. The bricks were not all theological. In fact, some would probably say that none of the bricks were theological in the end. These political bricks were just lying in the field waiting for someone to pick them up and construct the building. There were four glaring bricks. And these had perhaps been there from the beginning of the Advent movement.

There was the question of *the nature of salvation*, and particularly how its reality was to be expressed. It took the Christian Church sixteen hundred years to deal with this brick and Adventists had largely ignored the history involved. Thinking that they were finishing the Protestant Reformation many Adventists ignored the fact that their views on salvation had a lot of Truth but lacked unity. Where Sister White had quoted the giants like Luther and Wesley, Adventists used her as their catalyst rather than going to the primary sources to see where these two views disagreed theologically. This smoldering theological issue would finally blow up like a volcano in the decades to follow.

There was the brick of *financial irresponsibility*. What I could not see when I received that list of names from the courthouse was the scandal that would arise out of it. Elder Rea would later write up the story in his book, *Pirates of Privilege*.[3] Many personnel changes would be made because of what seemed like a simple little list, but more seriously, the financial trust of the Adventist people would be shaken. Many trace the downward shift in North American Adventist liberal giving patterns to the "Davenport Scandal" as it came to be called. Coming on the heels of the Nixon betrayal of the American trust, the sociological effect was of major proportions. Many Adventists, who tended to be Republican in political orientation, were still recovering from the effects of the "Watergate Scandal." For some it had taken on the shock level of the Kennedy assassination.

A third brick was the renewed *plagiarism accusations* against Sister White, which had once more come to the front. Ever since she wrote her many volumes there had been those who charged her with plagiarism—quoting other authors without giving them due credit. She gave no credit at all except in her book *The Great Controversy*, after receiving considerable criticism. People like J. H. Kellogg and D. M. Canright, both early Adventists, had raised questions about the fact that she used sources, often direct quotations, citing no references.[4]

Amid this newly brewing firestorm, two students at Andrews University, while doing research in the Ellen G. White Estate archives on campus, stumbled across a devastating set of *Minutes* from a previously unknown (or at least unadvertised) Bible Conference held in 1919 and attended by several well-known Adventist leaders. In all my Sister White classes in high school, college, and graduate school I had never been introduced to these *Minutes*.[5]

---

3. Rea, *Pirates of Privilege*, (1984).

4. Canright, *Life of Mrs. E. G. White*, 189–206. See p. 201: "One Advent sister who had been with Mrs. White for ten years told the author personally that she had seen her copying from a book in her lap. When visitors came in she would cover the book with her apron until they had gone, then proceed with her copying. Her works show that the sister told the truth. Such work is considered dishonorable in any one. It is defined as 'literary theft.' Webster says, 'Plagiarist: A thief in literature; one who purloins another's writings and offers them to the public as his own.'"

5. The plagiarism charge in the 1970s included copying that was considerably more extensive and serious than anything ever written before by Elder Canright or anyone else. But the material found in

We could all dismiss Canright and Kellogg as heretics. But in these *Minutes*, there was a relatively long list of Adventist leaders whose credibility I had never heard questioned. In these *Minutes* we were introduced to leaders we knew from our study of denominational history, in some cases leaders who were considered a second wall of faithfulness, who were trying to anticipate a problem that could come to devastating fruition in the future.[6]

They discussed it at length, recorded their conversations, and apparently shelved the problem.[7] One can only guess that the groupthink of those present at the conference was that the general membership could not handle these concerns. As a result, Sister White's followers have always dismissed the plagiarism charge as of little consequence by calling it "borrowing,"[8] but her detractors claimed that "borrowing" implied the intention to give credit, which she seldom did.[9] Today this is called taking someone's intellectual property and the practice can destroy the credibility of an author, politician, or scholar overnight.[10]

Elder Canright wrote (in 1889),

> The rights of authorship are recognized and protected by copyright laws the world over. Any infringement of these rights, even where credit is given, is

---

the 1919 Bible Conference *Minutes* was devastating to our common understanding and those *Minutes* were recorded only four years after Sister White died.

6. J. N. Anderson asked penetrating questions in 1919 at a Bible Conference I had never heard of. "Is it well to let our people in general go on holding to the verbal inspiration of the Testimonies? When we do that, aren't we preparing for a crisis that will be very serious some day?" Couperus, ed. "The Bible Conference of 1919." *Spectrum* 10:1 (May 1979).

7. This Conference includes the observations of SDA leaders such as W. E. Howell, A. G. Daniells, C. P. Bollman, C. L. Taylor, J. N. Anderson, C. M. Sorenson, L. L. Caviness, W. W. Prescott, F. M. Wilcox, C. A. Shull, E. E. Albertsworth, W. G. Wirth, H. C. Lacey, W. H. Wakeham, C. L. Benson, T. M. French, M. E. Kern, G. B. Thompson, D. A. Parson, B. L. House, D. A. Parsons, J. W. Anderson. Anyone acquainted with the personnel of Adventist history will recognize this list as an Adventist theological hall of fame. All these leaders were contemporaries of Sister White and concerned about what the future held regarding the plagiarism charges. Some predicted that because of the assumptions the denomination had made regarding Sister White's authority in the Church, this could blow the Church wide open and destroy its credibility. The Conference left the question open and the *Minutes* were shelved in General Conference archives until they were again discovered in the 1970s in the Andrews University archives of the White Estate. This added more fuel to the controversies of that era.

8. Dr. F. D Nichol called her literary dependence on sources for her book *The Great Controversy* "literary borrowing." He justifies this on the basis that Sister White's "borrowed part was both small in amount and secondary in significance." This has become problematic in the latest research done by denominational historians. Nichol, *Ellen G. White and Her Critics*, 419.

9. Canright pointed out a charge that was more serious than just copying. He wrote, "Mrs. White . . . did more than steal her material from other authors; she sent it forth to the world as a divine revelation given to her by the Holy Spirit from God himself." Canright, *Life of Mrs. E. G. White*, 201.

10. In answering the charges Adventist writers started using the historical-critical method to justify Sister White's writing activities. This method has always been under grave criticism by Adventist scholars because it tends to destroy the traditional view of the inspiration of scripture. Ironically, articles and books appeared demonstrating that the Bible writers had plagiarized. This was met with critics' views that the Church would "bring down" the scriptures to protect Sister White.

punishable by severe penalties, and frequently by confiscation of the works involved.

> Plagiarism, or literary piracy, is the worst form of this offense. It is the appropriating of the writings of another as one's own, without quotes or credit. It is indulged in by uneducated, pedantic and unscrupulous persons, who desire to appear what they are not, or make money from the products of other minds.
>
> Mrs. White's works abound in offenses of this kind. Few Seventh-day Adventists know this. Many of the striking passages in her writings, which her followers have thought evidences of her inspiration and supernatural powers, have been found, upon investigation, to have been copied verbatim, or with but slight verbal changes, from the writings of others.[11]

We had been taught in Adventist schools that the attacks on Sister White's alleged borrowings were confined to two of her books: *Sketches from the Life of Paul* and *The Great Controversy*.[12] Dr. T. Housel Jemison (1914–1963), the author of the college textbook for Spirit of Prophecy classes required of all students in Adventist colleges when I was in college, wrote:

> It is seldom that any other work or passage is cited [from sources other than these two], although it is insinuated by critics that large portions of all her writings were the product of the minds and pens of others. Is the insinuation justified? This much is certain: *If there were works other than the two specified that would help the critic to build up his case, he would not hesitate or fail to use them.* Consequently, the problem of *the accusation of plagiarism may be regarded as limited to these books.*[13]

Nevertheless, there was an even more serious implication in the new plagiarism charge. The denomination had claimed full inspiration on the level of the biblical writers for Sister White.[14] So did this mean that the men who wrote the original thoughts that she had taken were inspired as well? And what was the denomination to do with the claim that Sister White never wrote anything she hadn't already seen in vision? Or that she never read anything before she put her thoughts in print? These questions would blow into major storms of tornado proportions in the next decade. Heads would roll and people who even allowed these topics to be discussed would be held suspect.

I continued to do my research in the safety of my library carrel hoping to graduate someday. I'm not sure that anyone was fully prepared for a forthcoming book, *The*

---

11. *Life of Mrs. E. G. White*, 192–193.

12. This was largely due to Elder Canright's examples given in Chapter 10: "A Great Plagiarist" in his book *Life of Mrs. E. G. White*, 189–206. The 1970s charges were much broader than these two examples.

13. Jemison, *A Prophet Among You*, 420. Emphases supplied.

14. In his landmark apologetic work, F. D. Nichol, long-time editor of the *Review and Herald* devotes about 20 percent of his book to the question of Sister White's "borrowings." *Ellen G. White and Her Critics*, 403–486.

White Lie, which would represent an incredible challenge even for Walter T. Rea to write based on the days I had worked as his intern.[15] Knowing him and watching him research I knew that none of his readers would be any more devastated than he was in what he was finding.

This was my mentor who had insisted on reading only Truth; and Truth was to be found in the Bible, Sister White's writings and non-fiction books. In his pain Elder Rea dedicated his book "To all those who would rather believe a bitter truth than a sweet lie."[16] I had never met or worked with anyone in the Church who could write that more honestly. And I had never met anyone in the Church who believed in and followed Sister White more fervently than Elder Rea.

Finally, there would be a general charge against the colleges—for that was where scholars would be confronted with these questions. This could be dangerous territory because professors would be answering questions of students who were not fully versed in theological matters, or who had grown up with certain folk notions that were irrelevant to the discussions.

These concerns were previewed by the leaders who attended the 1919 Bible Conference and every Bible teacher could identify with these fears and cautions. A short sample dialogue from this Conference demonstrates these concerns:

> H. C. Lacey [Professor of Theology and Biblical Languages, Washington Missionary College]: In our estimate of the spirit of prophecy, isn't its value to us more in the spiritual light it throws into our own hearts and lives than in the intellectual accuracy in historical and theological matters? Ought we not to take those writings as the voice of the Spirit of our hearts, instead of as the voice of the teacher to our heads? And *isn't the final proof of the spirit of prophecy its spiritual value rather than its historical accuracy?*
>
> A. G. Daniells [General Conference President]: Yes, I think so.
>
> J. N. Anderson [Professor of Missions and Biblical Languages, Washington Missionary College]: Would you set about to explain things as you have this morning? Would you explain that *you do not think the Testimonies are to be taken as final in the matter of historical data, etc., so as to justify a position?*
>
> A. G. Daniells: Who gives the teaching in the school on the spirit of prophecy? Is it the Bible teacher? How do you get that question before the students?
>
> C. L Taylor [Bible Professor, Emmanuel Missionary College]: Both Bible and history teachers catch it.
>
> W. H. Wakeham [Professor, Author, Battle Creek]: It comes up in every Bible class.[17]

15. Rea, *The White Lie.* (1982).
16. Ibid., 11.
17. Couperus, 38–39. Emphases supplied. When Dr. Desmond Ford made some of these same

In this charge all the bricks would coalesce to form a general center of focus throughout the denomination. To add to the confusion the charges would come from the rich and the poor, from the leadership and the less informed, from the new and old members. Some would claim that sixth generation Adventists were phony and that new converts were the wisest and most committed. Others would reverse that charge.

Freedom of speech suddenly took on new proportions. "What's the buzz? Tell me what's happening," became more than a line from the rock opera "Jesus Christ Superstar."[18] It became the first sentence of virtually every discussion going around the college circuit. Folk religion would have its day at last. The Sanctuary Doctrine came to draw ideas that had never been present before even in the Adventist theological formulations. The old accusation was resurrected that finally the *Omega apostasy* was upon us and it was centered in Adventist schools.

THE *OMEGA APOSTASY*

In 1981, a classmate of mine from academy and college, now an attorney in Central California published a book entitled, Omega, *in which he laid out a general conspiracy theory.*[19] The book was heavily laced with Sister White's quotations and the book was published by the denomination's Review and Herald Publishing Assn., and endorsed by Kenneth H. Wood, editor of the general church paper, *The Adventist Review*. Elder Wood wrote the following in his Foreword to the book:

> Occasionally a book is written in such a clear, flowing style that the reader is carried along effortlessly, as on the crest of a wave, from the first chapter to the last. And when the book deals with a subject of current interest, reading it provides maximum pleasure and benefit. The book in your hands [*Omega*] is the kind just described....
>
> But the writer has done more than demonstrate literary skill; he has come to grips with a subject that should be carefully considered by every Seventh-day Adventist. Ellen White labeled the doctrinal crisis that shook the church at the beginning of the twentieth century as the "alpha" of apostasy and predicted that in due time "omega" would follow. Perhaps no one knows exactly what she meant by using the term "omega," but Adventists would be irresponsible if they did not seek some understanding of what she had in mind. To be on guard against repeating the mistakes of history, one must learn the lessons that history teaches.[20]

---

suggestions in the 1970s he was declared a heretic and viciously attacked.
18. Webber and Rice, *Jesus Christ Superstar,* (1970).
19. Walton, *Omega,* (1981).
20. Ibid., 6–7.

Such an endorsement could be dismissed as a series of nice words if one did not experience the growing controversy in the denomination at the time. The book was purchased by administrators of some Conferences and given to every pastor in their field to read and add to his library (and hopefully warn his people of the prophecy identified there). In my experience as a pastor the only book I remember ever being distributed that way to all pastors was Sister White's book, *Counsels on Stewardship*—a book on the importance of giving money to the Church. *Omega* clearly had more of an agenda than Elder Wood's words appear to reflect.

Attorney Walton's book, in many parts of the field, had the effect of raising doubts as to the integrity of scholars in general. This constituted a rallying point and gave general ecclesiastical permission for laypersons to join in an arrogant witch hunt focused on scholars as the next few years would demonstrate.

The book *Omega* showed how to identify these people who had "infiltrated" the denomination to destroy it from the inside by giving "Nine Salient Points" (Chapter Seven). These points included: deception, divisiveness, attack on fundamental beliefs, covert attacks on the structure of the Church, special efforts to attract the youth, special attacks on Sister White's writings, a general climate of personal attack, attacks on Church standards and the claim of a reform message for the Church.[21] It was clearly an attack on scholars who were allegedly guilty of all or most of the nine points.

It is safe to say that anyone who was in the ministry, pastoral or educational, faced these points every day from the lay factor in the churches and schools. But now for a minister to write even positive observations of the organized educational work of the Church could invite accusation from self-appointed judges in the Church. When I was growing up in the Church the ordained members of the denominational clergy were held in high esteem. Adventist scholars were appreciated for their dedication to the cause of God and their determination to present to their students and the world in general the biblical credibility of the Adventist message. But there had been flaws in that wall.

Elder Andreasen had launched his all-out attack on the leadership calling Adventist leaders "liars," etc. *The Layworker* continually appeared as a monthly journal that included page after page of merciless criticism. These and other publications had the effect of giving permission to the disgruntled to complain and pine against what they saw as apostasy and heresy.

In 1960 a little book was published through the sponsorship of Elder Fordyce Detamore (1908–1980), a respected evangelist of Worldwide Bible Lectures sponsored by the Adventist Church. The booklet, *Now!* was written by Merikay McLeod, and was an imagination on the last days.[22] While it was based on Sister White's de-

---

21. Ibid., 77–86. This list looks like a table of contents from any number of copies of *Spectrum*, the journal of the Association of Adventist Forums, headquartered in Washington, D. C.

22. *Now!* was based on later chapters from Sister White's book, *The Great Controversy*. While Merikay's booklet, a term paper she had originally written for an academy Bible class, was a work

scriptions of the final moments of earth's history, it demonstrated in literary fashion the importance of not trusting Church leaders and ministers just because they were ordained to that task.

In Merikay's book, Sister White's warnings were placed in the forefront in such a way that they introduced lay suspicion of leadership. Subtle but powerful, *Omega* was of similar genre and now, with the imprimatur of the *Review* editor Kenneth Wood. One finds it hard to understand the power of a book of this nature except for its sensationalism. Its unspoken permission to legitimize a witch hunt was mind-boggling. The book was not Bible-centered, something Adventism had always claimed to be. In Walton's entire book there were only six biblical references, four of which were in the reference section at the back of the book. This was a Sister White book.

Nevertheless, the book, promoted by Adventist *leadership* nationwide, attracted and permitted the practice of discovering motives, the active ingredient in what Jesus condemned in his denunciation as "judging others."[23] And it gave permission, indeed almost called for a mandate, to suspect certain elements in the Church, namely professors in Adventist colleges, as being subversive and deceitful. This empowered some of the elements in the denomination that had slumbered until then. How certain people were finally considered guilty was not something that was clearly explained.

Omega was largely an arrangement of Sister White's statements, sometimes almost whole pages. Elder Wood's Foreword insisted that the author drew no dogmatic conclusions but rather left the decision to his readers:

> The author of this book suggests various lessons that may be learned from the "alpha" experience, but he is not dogmatic about his conclusions. He draws parallels between the "alpha" and current events within the church, but he does this primarily to stimulate thought, not to end discussion. I think the book provides a helpful perspective on current events by reminding us of the way the Lord has led us, and His teachings in our past history. It also alerts us to present and future dangers. All who read it thoughtfully and prayerfully

---

of fiction, it carried out an enfleshing of Sister White's warnings that one cannot really trust even religious leaders in the Church. The booklet launched Merikay's writing and editorial career, and its response demonstrated the proneness of Adventists to devour this type of dramatic material. The book was also adapted for theatre production as it lent itself to Adventist emphases on the last days. Probably this book found such wide acceptance because it purported to be based on the views of Sister White. Ordinarily Adventists frowned on both theatrical productions and fictional characterizations.

23. White, *Love Unlimited*, 255–256. "Christ is the only true standard of character, and he who sets himself up as a standard for others is putting himself in the place of Christ. And since the Father 'hath committed all judgment unto the Son' (John 5:22), *whoever presumes to judge the motives of others is again usurping the prerogative of the Son of God*. These would-be judges and critics are placing themselves on the side of antichrist, 'who opposeth and exalteth himself above all that is called God, or that is worshiped; so that he as God sitteth in the temple of God, showing himself that he is God.' 2 Thessalonians 2:4." Emphasis supplied.

will be better prepared to stand loyally for Christ and His truth during the coming crisis.[24]

Ironically, the book did not just stimulate thought. It encouraged attack and the author immediately went on the lecture circuit. The book became a powerful weapon to identify college Religion Departments in North America as the seats of apostasy. Especially would the pain of that attack be felt at Andrews University (Michigan), Southern Missionary College (Tennessee), and Pacific Union College (California). These were all schools that had established themselves as strongly conservative Adventist institutions.

RELIGIOUS POLITICAL CORRECTNESS

Buzz words took on new meaning. Forensic, pastoral counsel, the Sanctuary, original sin and others, were words that most of us had been raised with in our Adventist parochial education, now became dangerous terms because they could indicate what alleged heretic one might be following or even connected with. Perhaps the most iniquitous charge of all was a collective term, "new theology," a term that was freely used, usually without defining it.

New theology was not a term you could just look up in a dictionary. It had no universal technical meaning among theologians. One encyclopedia applied this term to the sermons of R. J. Campbell, a London minister and untrained as a theologian.[25] His views of God were criticized by evangelicals as being pantheistic for they expressed the immanence of God almost to the exclusion of the transcendence of God.[26] This did not seem to be related in any way to this new attack on Adventist theologians.

> In more recent times the expression 'new theology' has been associated with the ferment of ideas incoherently articulated in Bishop J. A. T. Robinson's *Honest to God* (1963), which bears obvious resemblances to Campbell's 'new theology.'[27]

The term had been used by some historians to refer to the Neo-Orthodox movement of the twentieth century. This movement was a revolt against modernism or theological liberalism in which the doctrine of original sin, among other elements was dropped.

"Original sin" had been characterized by G. K. Chesterton as "the only doctrine of Christianity which could be empirically verified, the doctrine of original sin."[28] It

---

24. *Omega*, 7.

25. Richardson, "The New Theology," in *A Dictionary of Christian Theology* (Philadelphia: The Westminster Press, 1969), 229–230.

26. Ibid., 229.

27. Ibid., 230.

28. See Hordern, *A Layman's Guide to Protestant Theology*, 106. Adventist theologian Richard Rice suggests that "sin may be the only Christian doctrine that has empirical evidence to support it."

is doubtful that the Adventist fundamentalists who utilized the term "new theology" in their attacks had reference to this movement. It is doubtful that many of them were even aware of that movement and the infiltration of that theology into college professors would not have been perceived by this group when they used the term.

There were really two ways the Adventist fundamentalists would attack "new theology." First, as the theology that Elder Andreasen demonized as his interpretation of what the book *Questions on Doctrine* was supposedly teaching. For Elder Andreasen that book represented new theology. Another way of putting it, for him it was the Omega apostasy that Sister White had predicted during the Alpha apostasy of Dr. Kellogg's day. Second and probably the more accurate of this use of the term was the perception that the Adventist fundamentalists held that Dr. Desmond Ford was an apostate and a heretic. For them new theology would be another term for Fordism, another confusing and unclear term.

At this point it is helpful to make a distinction between "Adventist fundamentalists," and "Adventist conservatives." This will be discussed and clarified later but for now the fundamentalists would not be as precise as the conservatives in their definitions. The conservatives represent a large field of carefully educated theologians who use the commonly accepted terminology of scholarship, where the fundamentalists in Adventism would be those who see truth in a more proprietary way (my doctoral committee chair would call it "parochial"), namely through Sister White. This last qualification is well represented in Attorney Walton's book *Omega*.

For these accusers "new theology" was a simplistic slogan designed to alert the Church of apostasy and heresy on the horizon. But as with most, much further clarification was not necessary. If one did not agree with a scholar or didn't understand what the scholar was saying, the easiest approach was simply to accuse him of teaching "new theology." And the condemnation resided in the accusation. Once accused he was apostate or heretical. *New theology was a slogan.*

Now the theologians in the Church could be branded with a slogan that few could define other than simply to mean the Omega apostasy. And that term was serious, even though equally ambiguous; it could be lethal to a person's professional ministerial career and immediately destructive of all he may be trying to do for the young people in his classes.

Sister White had condemned the Alpha, and she had warned of the Omega to come, which was equally worthy of the same condemnation. Even though the Omega was more suggestive of evil than substantive of reality, it had the ability to become an umbrella under which many strange views could masquerade as something meaningful.

Foreword in Zackrison, *The First Temptation*, xvii. Neo-Orthodox theologian Reinhold Niebuhr has written similar observations: "That men are 'sinful' is one of the best attested and empirically verified facts of human existence." Article on "Sin," in Halverson and Cohen, eds., *A Handbook of Christian Theology*, 350.

"The Sanctuary" came to have strange meanings as well—meanings that were never part of the original Adventist doctrine. These renditions didn't always represent either the early Adventist view or Sister White's view and therefore it was important that one defined that term as well. As a professor teaching eschatology and soteriology, I would receive questions involving these interesting insights.

It took some time to figure out what was happening, for I was not aware of having grown up in a Church where people were attacking their professors—scholars who had spent the better part of their lives being educated (usually at denominational expense) to fulfill their divine task.

To bring this to an understandable level I will cite an experience with a student in one section of my Righteousness by Faith class. A standing requirement for the class was to choose a book to read and then write a report on the book. She chose a book by Elder W. D. Frazee (1906–1996).[29] When she handed in her report she was excited, and she told me in jubilant tones that she had finally come to understand the Adventist doctrine of the Sanctuary—something she had heard about all her life but never applied herself seriously to grasping its meaning. I told her I would read her paper with great expectation.

Going through her report I read something new. The author contended that the heavenly Sanctuary is like a laundry: picture the village where you live as having only one laundry in which the work of cleaning goes on daily. Dirty clothes are your sins and the real laundry is the heavenly Sanctuary. It is in the heavenly laundry that the clothes are washed. The author submitted that this was the meaning of Eph 5:25–27.

> [25] Husbands, love your wives, as Christ loved the church and gave himself up for her, [26] that he might sanctify her, having cleansed her by the washing of water with the word, [27] that he might present the church to himself in splendor, without spot or wrinkle or any such thing, *that she might be holy* [sinlessly perfect] and without blemish. (Eph 5:25–27. Emphasis supplied)

As the story goes, you see a sign going up by the laundry one day saying that the laundry will soon be closing. Naturally, you wonder what you will do with no laundry. But in your frustration, you are relieved to see another sign go up, which tells you that classes are being held to teach you how to keep your clothes clean, so you won't need a laundry anymore. Some people won't attend the classes and thus they are never cleaned up. But the great question is: Would you attend the classes? And the correct answer is: You would if you believed the sign—unless you didn't care whether you had dirty clothes or not![30]

At this point the author unpacked his meaning.

---

29. Frazee, *Ransom and Reunion Through the Sanctuary*, 33. Elder Frazee was the founder of the self-supporting Wildwood Sanitarium (1942) in Wildwood, GA.

30. Ibid., p. 37.

> Yes, the laundry is going to close. But classes are now being held at the heavenly sanctuary. Jesus wants to teach us now how to get clean and keep clean. It can be done. It will be done. I would hate to think that our blessed Lord must stand there forever taking care of the sins that people keep sending in. There must come an end to the defiling stream if the sanctuary is ever cleansed.[31]

The implications of this view were overwhelming. What kind of spot must the Bible teacher be put on? If this was the Adventist view, then the denomination could legitimately earn the critics' judgment of legalism. This was a view foreign to the meaning of the gospel. No mention of the cross or the atonement made there. According to this view the gospel means learning to live without sin and going it alone at the end, *viz.*, coming to the place where one could live without a mediator.[32]

To try to address such a non-biblical view of the atonement would become almost a daily occurrence for those of us in the classroom. And in too many cases, if we tried to correct the students' view, which was often extreme folk religion, we could be reported as not believing in "the Sanctuary Doctrine." We could be accused of teaching the "new theology," which had a completely different meaning than the historical meaning in Christian theological heritage or of being a "Fordite."

Elder Frazee's view was new to me. It could easily be considered heretical if compared to the great historical Christian orthodox doctrines of the Church. But the problem wasn't being confronted with questions that could have come from serious, honest students. It lay in other areas where leadership conflicted with scholarship. And we were still a couple years away from that.

---

31. Ibid., 37–38.

32. For the Adventist teaching about learning to live without a mediator see the following works by Sister White: *The Great Controversy,* 425, 614; *Early Writings,* 280.

CHAPTER TWENTY-EIGHT

We've Got Problems

"The proper response to theological difficulties is more theology. We cannot
eliminate problems by ignoring them, by pretending they do not exist."

—RICHARD RICE

THE STATE OF THE RELIGION DEPARTMENT

"WE'VE GOT PROBLEMS." THE voice came from behind me as I climbed the couple dozen steps of Lynn Wood Hall, the former administration building on campus that now housed the SMC Religion Department. My arms were piled with books I was carrying into my newly refurbished office. I recognized the voice immediately.

It was Elder Robert Francis (1916–1994), a retired member of our department. Elder Francis had been a popular teacher on our staff. He had come to SMC from Shenandoah Valley Academy in Virginia where he taught Bible. His principal at Shenandoah Valley had been Elder George Akers, later my college dean of students and now my doctoral cognate academic architect at graduate school. These kinds of connections were not unusual in Adventism. We were surprised if we couldn't talk to an Adventist we hadn't known earlier and not discovered that we each knew people from our past. After all, as the song said, we were "part of the family of God."

Elder Francis and I had first met when we were students at Andrews University and each working on the Bachelor of Divinity degree. This program usually took three years after college, but Elder Francis only attended during the summers, so he had been there for several years working on it. I remembered him from stories his former students had told me—students who were then in Seminary. They all seemed to remember him as a "colorful character." I also remember seeing him in class arguing with our professors. His favorite sparring partner was Dr. Heppenstall, professor of theology and chair of the Theology and Christian Philosophy Department.

When I had visited SMC for that week considering the call I was given by Dr. Knittel and the board, I attended a couple of his classes on campus. I remembered him spending time diagramming sentences on the blackboard from Sister White's *The Great Controversy*.

Students seemed always to enjoy his classes although the word was out: If you have had a class from Elder Francis you have had all his classes. According to even his most loyal students, he tended to cover the same basic ideas in all his classes. But students remarked that they thought taking a class from Elder Francis must be like taking a class at Harvard Law School. You could not sit in his class for very long before you felt your brain stimulated and you admired him.

When Dr. Bennett, chair of the Religion Department, would invite Dr. Heppenstall to our campus for religion retreats, Elder Francis was there to share his cordiality, despite those old argument sessions in graduate school. I didn't know anyone who didn't like him even though some may not have agreed with his theology. To be popular, or at least respected, was considered a plus for any teacher on the Knittel faculty and especially in our department.

Some students liked his modified Socratic approach where he could lead a student to his conclusion through a series of formulated questions. One administrator told me, "I may not agree with Bob's theology but I'm happy that he always has a group of students gathered around him." Perhaps because of his popularity with students Elder Francis wielded a subtle control over the thinking in the SMC Religion Department. I had always been impressed with the theological unity in our department. We met the conservative, evangelical expectations of our denomination. I had never detected any serious rifts in the department.

When I joined the department, there were six members: Elder Douglas Bennett, (1925–2005) chair, with a Bachelor of Divinity degree (BD) in Old Testament and working on a PhD in speech. Elder Frank Holbrook (1927–2005) held the highest theological degree offered by the denomination at that time, a Master of Theology (MTh) from Andrews University. Elder Robert Francis (1916–1994) held a BD in theology and Elder Ronald Springett, originally from England, held the BD. in New Testament. Elder Jerry Gladson and I had joined at the same time and since then Jerry had finished an MA degree from Vanderbilt University in Old Testament. I had finished the MA in 1964 and the BD in 1966 in Theology. The BD was now called the Master of Divinity (MDiv).

That was the department in 1972: six of us—overworked, involved, happy, and unified. Contract teachers occasionally helped with lower division classes and picking teachers to fill those classes had been the only source of disagreement I could remember in our faculty. Elder Francis had raised strong objection to Elder Bennett's suggestion that our department should invite Elder Gary Patterson, pastor of the Collegedale Church, to teach a section of *Teachings of Jesus* to general freshman students.

Despite the otherwise unanimous vote and enthusiastic support of Elder Patterson by the department, Elder Francis had threatened to resign if the pastor was asked to teach a class. He was serious and firm. The pronouncement was met with complete and utter silence by the department members. I was not aware of why he would make such a threat. We waited to see if he was joking. He was not. Elder Bennett dropped the subject and moved on to other things. Elder Patterson was never asked to teach for our department. I was shocked and embarrassed. That was in 1973.

It was my first glimpse into the future. I did not think much about that incident until later when Elder Patterson became a lightning rod in the theological debate to follow years later. I apparently did not pose the same kind of threat to Elder Francis since he soon announced in staff meeting that he thought Elder Bennett should give me the Systematic Theology class he had been teaching! I appreciated that. It was this, more than anything that influenced my decision finally to pursue a doctorate in systematic theology. Teaching systematic theology was an exciting experience for me. It was very rewarding, and I pursued the importance of educating "thinking ministers."

By the time I returned from doctoral studies in the fall of 1979 the department had grown. Dr. Knittel, still president of the college, had added Drs. Lorenzo Grant (1933–2010), with a Doctor of Ministry degree (DMin) in Ethics from Howard University, Helmut Ott, with a Doctor of Education (EdD) degree in Religious Education from Andrews University, and Norman Gulley with a PhD degree in systematic theology from University of Edinburgh. Dr. Gulley was now teaching my favorite Systematic Theology class. Disappointed, I never got the class back.

By now Elder Springett had finished his PhD in New Testament from University of Manchester in England, and Elder Gladson had finished his PhD in Old Testament from Vanderbilt University. I was the only professor with an ABD ["All But Dissertation"] but I was determined to finish as quickly as possible.

Dr. Knittel had developed the SMC Religion Department from having no doctorates to having all but two. In just four years all this change had occurred. Only Frank Holbrook had no desire to go any further for a more advanced degree, and shortly afterward he accepted an invitation to join the Biblical Research Institute (BRI) in Washington, DC, as an associate director. I appreciated what I perceived was the unity of the department. We agreed on the fundamental principles of our denomination and were clearly seen as a conservative center for Adventist higher education. Our theological student enrollment was evidence of this—it was through the roof.

On this day Elder Francis would fill me in on what he thought was going awry on campus. He was not wearing his usual smile. He was clearly not in a jovial mood and I had never seen him so militant. He was serious about the campus and he was getting ready to reveal something to me—the 36-month absentee professor—that something critical was brewing. I should be made aware of it.

I sensed that he clearly viewed me as his cohort in this situation. We couldn't talk for long because we both had other appointments to meet but I was curious to hear what he was referring to. That revelation would come in due time but much later than I had expected. We were about to suffer what some would later call the Collegedale purge. Over the next five years major changes would take place and several of us, despite our training and unity would be gone.

ADVENTIST FUNDAMENTALISM VS. ADVENTIST CONSERVATISM

Aside from his friendly personality Elder Francis had two striking characteristics. He was a theological perfectionist and he was an Adventist fundamentalist.[1] For the sake of our discussion here we must look at the distinction between these two schools of thought. I am only speaking about theology, not lifestyle. And these are my distinctions—it does not mean that all Adventist theologians would agree on my definitions.

My take was that in the SMC Religion Department of six members we had five conservatives and one fundamentalist. And this will become increasingly definitive as we look at the situation that was unfolding at SMC in the 1980s. In my doctoral program at Andrews University I had only one fundamentalist instructor, Dr. C. Mervyn Maxwell (1925–1999), chair of the Seminary church history department.

These two schools of thought had functioned together for as long as the Adventist denomination had existed (since 1863). Little by little Adventists defined their belief system. At first the movement was opposed to creeds (formal statements of faith) but gradually they saw the need to identify and explain briefly their beliefs. So, a fundamental beliefs system evolved. James White, founder of the denomination, had written in 1854,

> Human creeds stand unyieldingly against the progress of light and truth. They blind the consciences of many, and stifle the voice of truth; that, were it otherwise, would cheer the hearts of the faithful and arouse the sinner to flee from coming wrath. Human creeds may have the credit of holding together

---

1. These two characteristics are usually together in this "fundamentalist" designation. While any attempt to categorize any group is never totally successful, and to some degree unavoidably subjective, Adventists enjoy identifying kinds of believers in their midst. My distinction here between conservative and fundamentalist is a way of distinguishing between two sociological groups within the Church. Other examples of categories are those of Ralph Martin and J. David Newman, whose articles appeared in *Ministry,* an Adventist periodical for the Church's ministers. In his article, "The Church in Changing Times," *Ministry* (January 4, 1990), 7–8, Martin described four kinds of Adventists: Regular Adventists, Traditional Adventists, Intellectual Adventists, and Cultural Adventists. In his article "How much Diversity Can We Stand?" *Ministry* (April 1994), 5, 26, Newman also described four kinds of Adventists under different labels: Mainstream Adventists, Evangelical Adventists, Progressive Adventists, and Historic Adventists. The labels we give here are roughly equivalent, though not altogether exact, to the following: Conservative: Regular (Martin), Evangelical (Newman); Fundamentalist: Traditional (Martin), Historic (Newman).

vast bodies of men professing Christianity; but it must be acknowledged that within their brace are all the corruptions and damning sins of the age.[2]

This view on creeds was essentially the same as the Christian Connection, a denomination from which two early Adventist leaders had hailed, James White (1821–1881) and Joseph Bates (1792–1872). Today's contemporary counterpart of the Connection, the Christian Church (Disciples of Christ), still holds this position on creeds. Nevertheless, despite their efforts to avoid identifying their doctrines in creedal form, Adventists gradually developed their own version of a creed.

In 1854 Adventist editors listed "Leading Doctrines Taught by the Review" in the masthead of the Church paper, the *Review and Herald*.[3] Here five doctrines were demarcated:

> *The Bible*, and the Bible alone, the rule of faith and duty; *The Law of God*, as taught in the Old and New Testaments, unchangeable; *The Personal Advent of Christ* and the Resurrection of the Just, before the Millennium; *The Earth restored to its Eden perfection* and glory, the final Inheritance of the Saints; *Immortality alone through Christ*, to be given to the Saints at the Resurrection.[4]

By 1874 this list had expanded and was published as "fundamental principles."[5] Since then these have developed into the fundamental beliefs, (now twenty-eight doctrines) listed in the front of official Adventist materials such as the *Church Manual* and the *Baptismal Certificate*.[6]

The common designation of the attitude toward creeds is even today preserved in the early statement, "our only creed is the Bible."[7] So the fundamental beliefs are expansions on how Adventists interpret the teachings of the Bible.

> The Bible is a perfect, and complete revelation. It is our only rule of faith and practice.[8]

> The Bible is an everlasting rock. It is our rule of faith and practice. . . . Every Christian is therefore in duty to take the Bible as a perfect rule of faith and duty.[9]

> When God's Word is studied, comprehended, and obeyed, a bright light will be reflected to the world; new truths, received and acted upon, will bind us

---

2. J. White, "Gospel Order," *Review and Herald* 5:10 (March 28, 1854), 76–77.

3. See *Review and Herald* 6:1 (August 15, 1854), 1.

4. Ibid. Emphases supplied.

5. See *Signs of the Times* 1:1 (June 4, 1874), 3. For a brief discussion of the early Adventist views of creeds see Zackrison, *The First Temptation*, 175–180.

6. See for example, *Seventh-day Adventist Church Manual*, 23–31.

7. J, White, *A Word to the Little Flock*, 13.

8. Ibid.

9. J. White, "The Gifts of the Gospel Church," *Review and Herald* 1:9 (April 21, 1851), 70.

> in strong bonds to Jesus. *The Bible, and the Bible alone, is to be our creed, the sole bond of union; all who bow to this Holy Word will be in harmony.* Our own views and ideas must not control our efforts. Man is fallible, but God's Word is infallible. Instead of wrangling with one another, let men exalt the Lord. Let us meet all opposition as did our Master, saying, "It is written." Let us lift up the banner on which is inscribed, The Bible our rule of faith and discipline.[10]

The fundamentalist designation is sometimes called traditional. The conservative is sometimes called "new theology," a term given by the fundamentalists, intended to be pejorative and viewed as heresy, apostasy and of late to refer to the Omega apostasy, as we will see in more detail later.[11]

In short, new theology in its purest sense was the term meant to refer to those Adventists who accepted the work of leading Adventist thought leaders who produced the book *Seventh-day Adventists Answer Questions on Doctrine* under the auspices of official denominational sponsorship in 1957.[12] But as a pejorative term new theology was widened in a more contemporary, broad meaning to target Dr. Desmond Ford (1929-2019), eventually declared a heretic by Adventist fundamentalists. This term was slippery with respect to its application as well as its definition.

> What is the "old theology" that is now being proclaimed as traditional or "historic" Adventism? A preliminary investigation reveals that it is perilously close, in spirit and theology, to a position taken by certain sections of the church some 20 to 30 years ago. At that time the Defense Literature Committee of the General Conference clearly repudiated positions which are now being claimed as historic Adventism. I submit that in many respects the so-called "new theology" essentially agrees with the official General Conference position of the Defense Literature Committee. A look at the facts at least throws the whole matter into perspective.[13]

I was about to get the full picture from Elder Francis of what the problems were at SMC. He was very serious about what he was planning to tell me.

---

10. White, "A Missionary Appeal," *Review and Herald* 62:49 (December 15, 1885), 770. Reprinted in *Selected Messages,* 1:416. Emphasis supplied.

11. Some Adventist fundamentalists used other terms to describe conservatives, which meant essentially the same thing: New Adventism, Jesuit Interpretation, Pagan Augustinianism, for examples. These were all terms used to cast ridicule on those in the Church who disagreed with the fundamentalists. Especially were the books of the Standish brothers laced with this terminology. See Standish (1933-2008) and Standish (1933-2018), *Adventism Vindicated,* ix, x, xi, xiv, et.al.

12. In his article "Some Historical Observations on the Present Theology 'Crisis,'" *Perspectives* 1:1 (May 1982), 18, Dr. Ronald M. Springett wrote his take on the term "new theology": "Some are now claiming that a 'new theology' permeates Adventist college Bible departments in North America. The cry is being raised which accuses this so-called new theology of forsaking the landmarks, leaving traditional Adventist positions and introducing the errors of Babylon into the church in certain quarters of the church we are being exhorted to return to the "old theology,' the traditional, or 'historic' Adventism." Dr. Springett's full article appears as Appendix III below.

13. Ibid.

THE NATURE OF ADVENTIST CONSERVATISM

Conservative Adventist theologians were professional scholars. They had accepted the theological clarity of the 1950s, primarily demonstrated in the publishing of the *Seventh-day Adventist Bible Commentary*, *Seventh-day Adventists Answer Questions on Doctrine*, and a later volume issued by the Ministerial Association of the General Conference entitled, *Seventh-day Adventists Believe . . . A Biblical Exposition of 27 Fundamental Doctrines.*[14]

All three of these publications held to plenary inspiration of scripture, a clarified view of original sin, the sinless nature of Jesus Christ as the second Adam in the incarnation and the exclusive application of the atoning sacrifice at the cross.

These are basic conservative views, and this convinced other conservative Christian scholars that Adventism was a legitimate group of Bible-believing, born-again Christians as we had always claimed we were, and not a cult. These were the points of discussion that were surfacing once more in the controversy of the Church. Conservatives do not consider Sister White to be, or use her as, a "third canon" or an inspired commentary of the Bible.

"Perfection" for the conservative held to the meaning of the *koine* (common)[15] Greek term, "maturity."[16] The conservative did not write about or speak of sinless perfection as the goal or possibility of the Christian life. All sinlessness was confined to the life and person of Jesus Christ alone. Understanding that his sinless life was applied to the believer by faith was the proper perspective of the gospel work of Christ.

Some of the practices of fundamentalist Adventists were unwritten, just acted out, such as the practice of using Sister White as an inspired commentary of the Bible. This notion could apply no intellectual brakes to keep it from sliding into viewing Sister White's writings as a third canon in addition to the Old and New Testament canons.

A comparison could be made to the Church of Jesus Christ of Latter-day Saints (Mormon) and how that church viewed its modern-day prophet, Joseph Smith. Adventists had criticized the Mormon claims that held Joseph Smith as a prophet for the last days. The Mormon belief was that the Bible was the word of God *insofar as it was translated correctly.*

This qualification required the interpretation of Joseph Smith or his inspired equivalents, to point out where the incorrect translation lay. Thus, Smith and company ended up as a final court of appeals when one sought to understand the true meaning of scripture. Theoretically if there was confusion among the elders, the writings of

---

14. *Seventh-day Adventists Believe . . . A Biblical Exposition of 27 Fundamental Doctrines* (1988). Though no single author is listed, this book was written by Drs. P. G. Damsteegt and Norman Gulley along with the editing talents of many who are listed on v-vi.

15. Summers, *Essentials of New Testament Greek*, vii, *koine* was "the Greek commonly used in the Greek-speaking world from the time of Alexander the Great to about A.D. 500." This was the Greek used in the New Testament. *Koine* distinguished this from *classical* Greek.

16. Heppenstall, "Let Us Go on To Perfection," in *Perfection: The Impossible Possibility*, 65.

Joseph Smith would clear it up. Christians have argued that regardless of any creedal statement, this essentially put Smith above the Bible in authority. And Adventists were always quick to point that out.

The Adventist fundamentalist's use of Sister White is similar to the alleged Mormon use of Joseph Smith. The fundamentalist version would look like this: The Bible is the word of God insofar *as it is interpreted correctly*. Sister White would be treated as the authoritative interpreter. One problem was that the fundamentalist had no objective norm by which to gauge when this practice should be halted (except perhaps claims and assertions). It seemed that this was a classic example of the slippery slope fallacy of logic.

In the theological views of the Adventist fundamentalist were several folk conclusions not defined by any official Church action. And while these three Adventist theological literary productions listed above are not official statements of the denomination, they do represent the clear statements of the teaching of the Church issued through denominational publishing houses and by established, recognized, and representative professors, administrators and ministers of the Church.

In Adventist fundamentalism Christ was viewed as having a sinful nature. In their zeal to press this point they were not always careful in explaining what this meant. For a conservative Adventist this would mean Jesus needed a savior. For the fundamentalist the gospel was understood as learning to follow Jesus' example producing a sinless character. The "good news" of the gospel was that this was possible, i.e., required.

For the conservative Adventist the gospel was established in the atonement completed at the cross as the salvific work of Christ alone. This did not deny the mediatorial work of Christ, it informed it. Whatever Jesus was doing in the heavenly places was not to be considered in addition to what he had already completed at the cross.

Both groups saw the law of God as set in the popular Adventist great controversy motif. The fundamentalist had Jesus overcoming sin in fallen human nature. The conservative saw the issue as human nature (as God created it) overcoming the temptation to sin.

Careful observation showed that the two views were worlds apart. Yet both views had existed from the birth of Adventism. The conservative position clearly established the need for a virgin birth doctrine and defined the issues in Eden. Jesus occupied the same legal position as Adam, not the sinful moral notion of fallen man (in need of a savior). And this was the work set up for Christ to accomplish in the incarnation. This also preserved the view of the Adam/Christ typology as set forth in St. Paul's writings of the New Testament.

> [12] Therefore as sin came into the world through one man and death through sin, and so death spread to all men because all men sinned— [13] sin indeed was in the world before the law was given, but sin is not counted where there is no law. [14] Yet death reigned from Adam to Moses, even over those whose sins

> were not like the transgression of Adam, who was a type of the one who was to come.
>
> ¹⁵ But the free gift is not like the trespass. For if many died through one man's trespass, much more have the grace of God and the free gift in the grace of that one man Jesus Christ abounded for many. ¹⁶ And the free gift is not like the effect of that one man's sin. For the judgment following one trespass brought condemnation, but the gift following many trespasses brings justification. ¹⁷ If, because of one man's trespass, death reigned through that one man, much more will those who receive the abundance of grace and the free gift of righteousness reign in life through the one man Jesus Christ.
>
> ¹⁸ Then as one man's trespass led to condemnation for all men, so one man's act of righteousness leads to acquittal and life for all men. ¹⁹ For as by one man's disobedience many were made sinners, so by one man's obedience many will be made righteous. ²⁰ Law came in, to increase the trespass; but where sin increased, grace abounded all the more, ²¹ so that, as sin reigned in death, grace also might reign through righteousness to eternal life through Jesus Christ our Lord. (Rom 5:12–21)

> ²⁰ But in fact Christ has been raised from the dead, the first fruits of those who have fallen asleep. ²¹ For as by a man came death, by a man has come also the resurrection of the dead. ²² For as in Adam all die, so also in Christ shall all be made alive. ²³ But each in his own order: Christ the first fruits, then at his coming those who belong to Christ.
>
> ²⁴ Then comes the end, when he delivers the kingdom to God the Father after destroying every rule and every authority and power. ²⁵ For he must reign until he has put all his enemies under his feet.
>
> ²⁶ The last enemy to be destroyed is death. ²⁷ "For God has put all things in subjection under his feet." But when it says, "All things are put in subjection under him," it is plain that he is excepted who put all things under him. ²⁸ When all things are subjected to him, then the Son himself will also be subjected to him who put all things under him, that God may be everything to every one. (1 Cor 15:20–28)

A conservative view of the issues surrounding the incarnation, written by a theologian at an Adventist university, appears in the Appendix 3 of my book, *The First Temptation*:[17]

> He [Christ] was *not* born with fallen man's legal status. He is the Second Adam and as such he is not subject to the covenant God made with Adam. He is subject to the eternal covenant not the Adamic covenant. Jesus was never legally in Adam as we are. In Adam all die. In Christ all are made alive. Christ was not born legally out of relationship with His father. If He was He could not but have sinned. "Christ is called the second Adam. In purity and holiness,

---

17. *The First Temptation*, 400–401. College Professor, Theology.

connected with God and beloved by God, He began where the first Adam began" (EGW, QOD, 650, italics added).[18] Yes he did take the nature of man but without its legal status of alienation. *"He was to take His position at the head of humanity by taking the* nature *but not the sinfulness of man."*[19]

So, for conservatives Jesus occupied the same legal position as Adam. This ruled out any suggestion that Jesus was a sinner, in the common understanding of the term, or that he in any way needed a savior, which would have disqualified him to be a vicarious savior. In my questionnaire for Adventist theologians as I prepared my dissertation, I included this question: "Question 8: In what way was Jesus born with a fallen sinful nature? Please explain."[20]

The respondents (all active Adventist theologians, educators and administrators) were unanimous in their concern that the very expression fallen sinful nature was easily misleading if applied to Jesus. And although it was like expressions used by Sister White it needed careful explanation, and probably should never be used at all. The scholars expressed their concern that in communicating with other Christians this description was not a helpful Christological articulation.

Another Adventist university theology professor typified the others:

> "Fallen sinful nature" is a very unfortunate term to apply to Jesus. The use of this designation to communicate with other Christians will surely end in failure. I know that Ellen White used similar terminology but there had to be a context that we are missing. We believe that Jesus was our example, but it seems to me that to use this description is to invite criticism and misunderstanding.
>
> Jesus assumed *the possibility of loss,* but he never disqualified himself as savior. To accept the nature of Adam [after the fall] would have been to place himself in need of a savior. *It must mean only* that he became capable of dying and took the risk of failure.[21]

Before the 1950s the Adventist Church had been classified by other evangelical Christians as a cult, partly because of its inadequate and confusing treatment of the dogmatic locus of the person of Jesus Christ, allegedly a treatment that did not grasp the true purpose of the atonement. But the book *Questions on Doctrine* had solved that problem by finally addressing it from a biblical standpoint.

The fundamentalists simply took the words of Sister White without first filtering them through the Bible. To do that opened her up to the judgment that she could be a false prophet. But the conservative followed a hermeneutic in harmony with the fundamental beliefs of the Adventist Church, i.e., the Bible was their *only* rule of faith and practice and the *only* authoritative source for Adventist doctrine.

18. White, *The Youth's Instructor,* (June 2, 1898).
19. White, *The Signs of the Times,* (May 29, 1901). Emphasis supplied.
20. *The First Temptation,* 399.
21. Ibid., 402–403. Emphases supplied. University professor, theology.

In short, the issue for Adventist fundamentalism regarding the gospel was whether human beings could overcome the nature Christ found himself in after 4,000 years of the effects of sin on the human race. The issue for conservatives was whether human nature could, as God created it, live in harmony with the law of God. This defined Jesus' mission as savior. The fundamentalist position was only possible if Adam's sin caused no pollution of the human nature, i.e., a Pelagian or semi-Pelagian view. The conservatives presupposed the doctrine of original sin in some form.

Dr. W. G. C. Murdoch (1902–1983), dean and professor of theology at the SDA Theological Seminary for nearly three decades, stated the conservative position clearly:

> I first of all began to teach this doctrine [original sin] in 1924 at Newbold [college in England], then in Avondale [college in Australia] and 26 years here in the seminary. My concept of the subject has broadened, but has not changed materially . . . Original sin was committed by our first parents, and has been passed on to every one of their descendants. . . . *Adventists have always taught this*, as it is implicit in our teaching of the New Birth.[22]

A main consideration was that for the fundamentalist, Sister White was the final court of appeals, whereas for the conservative the Bible was the final court of appeals. The conservative position essentially put Adventists on the level playing field with other Christians for theological discussion and understanding. Reading her as primary could hardly avoid making the Bible contradictory and confusing.

These were major differences between Adventist fundamentalism and Adventist conservatism, as seen especially in *Questions on Doctrine,* which had taken on the task of clarifying the inadequate Christological expressions of the Adventist past. Having those two lines of tradition co-existing in the SMC Religion Department presented a potential rift. But this had never developed into any open controversy that I was aware of. We didn't talk about it—the differences had never been argued or discussed. But individually we probably suspected it.

By these definitions Elder Francis was a fundamentalist and the rest of us were conservatives. Nobody forced this to become a problem. We were cooperative in our mission to educate future ministers and to help young people in general to enjoy their walk with God. Some would probably say this was a mistake to overlook the fact that these were two diametrically opposed notions.

The conservatism of the SMC Religion Department followed the established Adventist view of progressive revelation—the notion that truth is continually unfolding (or at least our understanding of it is). We had no problem with the clarifications of the 1950s. They were built into the historic, developing understanding of our Church and its thought.

Looking back on some of the developing controversy, the North American Division later put out a publication entitled *Issues: The Seventh-day Adventist Church and*

---

22. Quoted in ibid., 4. Emphasis supplied. See further, ibid., 3, 299, 305, 310.

Certain Private Ministries.[23] The real problem was clearly spelled out from an organizational standpoint in the following statement, which is also a surprisingly accurate portrayal of Adventist fundamentalism's *modus operandi*.

> The heart of the problem is their insistence that leaders, members, and ministers must agree with them or be charged with heresy and that viewpoints that differ from theirs are an evidence of apostasy in the church.[24]

After several years of working together I thought Elder Francis and I shared a mutual respect. Now I turned to see him displaying a deeply furrowed brow. But I did not immediately sense the hostility that he would later demonstrate. When I asked him what was happening, since I had been away for three years, he suggested that we were being invaded. When I asked by whom he said succinctly that *I would see.*

Our conversation had really gone nowhere now, but he tended to talk like that—sometimes he just wanted people to think. His theological perfectionism was at times unsettling, but his smile was always engaging. He knew when and where to keep quiet and rely on his infectious grin. Without a rare and occasional protest, he appeared to be one with us. But he always interpreted the prophet from perfectionistic presuppositions, something that most Adventist academics did not think was necessary.

There was a movement afoot in the Church to return to that bias, for the old Andreasen fundamentalists were coming out of the woodwork to fight their good fight again, this time spurred on by the old Brinsmead movement that had dug in at the edges and to some extent the very front of the denomination, despite the Church's rejection of it in the 1950–60s. Since no one in the SMC Religion Department was into conspiracy theories we were slow at realizing what was coming. And soon.

THE GATHERING STORM

The theological setting of the Church was firm in our eyes. Nearly everyone in our department had lived through the controversies over authority, existentialism, and epistemology at the Seminary. A number of those who had graduated with a New Testament major in the Bachelor of Divinity program had not received field appointments because of that theological battle. For many it was guilt by association. Dr. Springett was one of those graduates and he ended up working for a short time in England and then as a Bible teacher at Greater Baltimore Academy. But now that taint was behind him and he was teaching Greek, New Testament Studies and Philosophy of Religion at SMC.

---

23. These private ministries are listed in this book as Hope International, Hartland Institute, Prophecy Countdown, Steps to Life Church in Wichita, Kansas, and Rolling Hills congregation in Rolling Hills, Florida. The list could be added to, but these were apparently the most active groups in criticizing the North American Division and the General Conference at the time.

24. *Issues: The Seventh-day Adventist Church and Certain Private Ministries*, 13.

In the Church, Adventist scholars Drs. Edward Heppenstall (1901–1994), Desmond Ford (1929–2019), and Hans LaRondelle (1929–2011) had seriously appealed to Robert Brinsmead. Their approach was pastoral and theological—in Christian love they had addressed the issues he brought up. They had not followed the lead of the Defense Literature Committee, which had revolved largely around *ad hominem* arguments.[25]

In time Brinsmead, through patience and biblical appeal, would finally make a major about-face in his thinking and abandon his perfectionistic theology. This was taken by many of his devoted followers as a move to theological pollution and they became vicious in their attacks on him and those who had influenced him with Adventist historic thought. In fact, they now claimed that only they had the true historic Adventist truth and the leaders who had supported their former guru in his latest flip-flop became subject to their vitriol.

We would feel it soon, since all of us except for Dr. Gladson, who had not attended Andrews, were students of Drs. Heppenstall, Blincoe, Pease, Specht, and Alexander. These had also been my professors at La Sierra College before they moved to the Seminary. So, the fundamentalists attacked the conservatives as they gained political influence in the denomination.

Our contentment with denominational theology and mission probably allowed us to concentrate on the Adventist mission, to which we were united. And we felt no threats from anywhere. We studied our methodology in the calm setting of Happy Valley and pressed our majors to appreciate the exciting work of being pastors. We were marching to Zion!

Probably it was partly this contentment that led to our failure to recognize that in some respects the denomination was changing—a few fundamentalists who had gotten into leadership positions, mostly in denominational editorial positions, were trying to return the Church to a pre-1950s Adventism that none of us had been brought up in. This work was beginning at the top.

In an article written for the *Southern Columns,* the SMC alumni journal, Dr. Springett explained some of the concerns: "In this [article] we are more concerned with the 'old' and 'new' positions, as they are called, on the gospel (although the Sanctuary Doctrine becomes a component in a curious way as our study will show). We are concerned with these because here a teaching seems to be creeping back into the Church which administrators and teachers alike decisively rejected in the late 1950s and early 1960s."[26]

My long talks with Elder Frank Holbrook, who I considered my paternal theologian in residence, were informative and I looked to him for help in understanding not only the theology of the South but of the Southern mindset in general. We talked at

---

25. *Ad hominem* arguments attack the character of the messenger rather than the accuracy of the message.

26. Springett, "Some Historical Observations on the Present Theology 'Crisis,'" 18.

length about the Sanctuary Doctrine and how we could make it more understandable to our students, especially our theology majors who would have to face the sometimes-hostile communities where they would do their ministry.

Elder Holbrook shared his view that he saw the most helpful light in Dr. Heppenstall's treatment of the Sanctuary Doctrine in his class of the same name, and he believed that Dr. Heppenstall's theological work in that field was the most defensible that he knew of considering the biblical text. Correcting some of the older views that took little notice of the biblical context, Dr. Heppenstall had attempted to make this a biblical doctrine.

Elder Holbrook was a friend of Elder Kenneth Holland (1918–2007), editor of *These Times,* the denominational monthly evangelistic journal published at Southern Publishing Assn. in Nashville. He introduced me to Elder Holland and coached me through my first published article in that periodical.[27] After that article appeared in print Elder Holland asked for more articles and finally invited me to be an Editorial Consultant for the magazine. I was happy to accept that assignment.

For my first seven years at SMC helping to educate young men for ministry and sharing with them the excitement of the pastoral mission was a thrilling task. Going away to graduate school was just one more exciting adventure. And the thought of ever having to face controversy and attack from inside the denomination was not at all in my mind.

During my second year at SMC I had a dream in which I was unfairly treated in my ministry at the college. In the dream, when I attempted to understand what was happening, I was fired. I needed a Joseph or a Daniel to help me interpret its meaning, or perhaps it was literal? This was more than a dream. This was a nightmare.

I never shared this dream with anyone—not even my wife. It represented a personal invasion of my ministry by people I thought should have known better. It showed that when you really enjoy what you are doing, and you are conscientious about fulfilling a mission there would be people watching who would try to take you down. The devil works where he can get a foothold. I guessed I didn't need a Joseph or a Daniel. It was just a dream.

While I had never forgotten the dream, it had not occupied any significant part in my life or thinking. Only occasionally would the flashback come, and I would smile at how silly the nightmare really had been. I could only recall a couple of the facts of the dream—mainly the plot and the conclusion.

I did not apprehend fully the significance of new administrative faces at work in Washington—Church headquarters—a modified return to what they would come to claim as historic Adventism was in motion.

---

27. Zackrison, "What About the Secret Rapture?" *These Times,* May 1975, 11–13.

THE PURPOSE OF THE FUNDAMENTALISTS

The Adventist fundamentalists were calling for a public corporate repentance statement from the Church leadership for "rejecting" the 1888 message regarding righteousness by faith. They also made a call back to contemporary acceptance of that message.[28] It was originally a message delivered by two young men, a physician and a minister, and independent publishers were picking up the idea of reexamining 1888.[29] Not knowing precisely what that message was, added some confusion, which led to more discussion.

Apparently, the actual sermon notes of these men were not extant and therefore the message had to be reconstructed from notes taken by people present at the time and responses from Sister White. But that was nearly a hundred years ago. The argument insisted that Sister White had endorsed these messages, only making their alleged rejection more mysterious.[30] And from these sources the adherents concluded that this message somehow explained why Jesus hadn't returned.

The General Conference Committee had responded:

> The manuscript *1888 Re-Examined*] gives every evidence of earnest, diligent and painstaking effort; but we feel concerned over what appears to us to be a very critical attitude concerning the leadership, the ministry, and the plans of work in God's cause.
>
> All through the manuscript are aspersions and remarks which, if read by our workers and believers, would hardly make for confidence in either the leadership in God's church, or even in the church itself. The reader is left with the impression that buried in the denominational archives are documents which are being withheld from the people, documents which in your opinion should be quite freely circulated.[31]

The fact that this Conference session had taken place almost a hundred years before was even more exotic. And statements from Sister White circulated suggesting that Christ would have returned long before this if the Church had been faithful.

The Wieland and Short document was impressive, but it was deemed too negative to merit serious attention. Furthermore, the committee maintained that the leadership present at the 1888 General Conference session had, for the most part, later

---

28. The original document appealing to the General Conference to repent, entitled *1888 Re-Examined*, by Elders R. J. Wieland (1916–2011) and D. K. Short (1915–2004), had been rejected in 1951 by the GC Defense Literature Committee, and its authors had been counseled to return to their duties in Africa where both were missionaries.

29. Several documents connected to this appeal including the main document and correspondence with the General Conference were later compiled together and appeared as *A Warning and Its Reception*, (1959).

30. See Rendalen (1951–2018), "The Nature and Extent of Ellen White's Endorsement of Waggoner and Jones." Term paper, (December 1978), Andrews University.

31. Defense Literature committee, "Letter to Pastors R. J. Wieland and D. K. Short," (December 4, 1951). Reprinted in *A Warning and Its Reception*, 245.

accepted the message presented there. This is relevant because many of those harking back to the rejection of this message were part of the fundamentalist movement now in action.

Elders Wieland and Short went quietly back to Africa but copies of their document leaked out and were distributed. And in the hands of fundamentalist Adventists here was another piece of ammunition to use in the ensuing controversies. Everywhere controversy occurred there were two consistent elements of their message: the authority (or failure) of leadership and the abiding authority of Sister White. We began to see emphasis put on the fact that Adventism was responsible for delaying the Lord's return. Furthermore, it was probably connected in some way to the Omega apostasy.

Sister White had written,

> Had Adventists after the great disappointment in 1844, held fast their faith and followed on unitedly [sic] in the opening providence of God, . . . the Lord would have wrought mightily with their efforts, the work would have been completed, and *Christ would have come ere this* to receive His people to their reward.[32]

> The Lord God of heaven will not send upon the world His judgments for disobedience and transgression until He has sent His watchmen to give the warning. *He will not close up the period of probation until the message shall be more distinctly proclaimed* . . . Yet the work will be cut short in righteousness.[33]

> It is a solemn statement that I make to the church, that *not one in twenty* whose names are registered upon the church books *are prepared to close their earthly history, and would be as verily without God and without hope* in the world as the common sinner. They are professedly serving God, but they are more earnestly serving mammon.[34]

Those of us who had been schooled in the 1960s with *Questions on Doctrine* as our textbook would soon feel the full-frontal attack of those opposing our education using their derogatory term: new theology.

THE IMPORTANCE OF EXAMINING THE FAITH

To encapsulate one's work in theology in a single term without defining it better than those had who employed the slogan "new theology" usually leads to criticism and judgementalism both designed to break up the unity of the church. And "new theology" would become that rallying slogan around which fundamentalists could connect.

---

32. White, *Manuscript 4, 1883*. Emphasis supplied.

33. White, *Testimonies for the Church,* 6:19. Emphasis supplied.

34. White, *General Conference Bulletin,* (1893), 132–133. Reprinted in White, *Christian Service,* 41. Emphasis supplied.

The attacks of the old Brinsmead movement and Elder Andreasen were aimed at the book, *Questions on Doctrine*. But now the "new theology" was to be understood as the teachings of Dr. Desmond Ford. Dr. Springett pointed out:

> "Fordism" is the name given by *The Layworker* [fundamentalist journal] to the so-called "new theology" in an attempt to discredit it. Notice the anachronism in this statement, however. *Questions on Doctrine* was written long before Ford's teachings became an issue in the Church, yet the implication here is that it is full of Fordism or "new theology."[35]

From the conservative's standpoint when one is faced with doing theology, there comes a seriousness that must not be overlooked. Dr. Richard Rice, an Adventist theologian at Loma Linda University has observed,

> Haven't people lost their faith as a result of asking questions about it? . . . The solution, however, is not to avoid thinking, nor to give up as soon as we run into difficulties. The solution is to keep on thinking, to walk our way through the problems that arise. Typically, people who become disillusioned when they examine their faith have not thought enough about it.
>
> The proper response to theological difficulties is more theology. We cannot eliminate problems by ignoring them, by pretending they do not exist. Careful reflection will help us to answer many of our questions.[36]

Raising or answering questions are procedures that are necessary to producing sound thinking. But in education there is always the chance that a student here or there is not interested in thinking. For those who do not wish to think the whole educational process is criticized as raising doubts. This cannot daunt a professional teacher. His job is to continue and attempt to make the quest as exciting as possible. This does not rule out the teacher/student relationship where the teacher allows the student to ask questions in the hope of becoming informed. Nor does it rule out the "devil's advocate" invasion. Dr. Roland Loasby (1890–1974), used to put it this way, "I am here today to stir up your pure minds!"

When the cult arises there is no serious questioning, for the cult must apply only the craftiness of the cult leader. Most of that craftiness resides in accusation. Our task was to examine our faith in preparation for a field that was scattered with every kind of question and issue those students, with or without experience, would have to face. We all taught in the light of the famous maxim of Socrates, as paraphrased by Dr. Rice: "An unexamined faith can be downright dangerous."[37]

---

35. Springett, "Some Historical Observations on the Present Theology 'Crisis,'" 22.

36. Rice, *The Reign of God: An Introduction to Christian Theology from a Seventh-day Adventist Perspective*, 6.

37. Ibid.

WE'VE GOT PROBLEMS

THE REAL MEANING OF THE *OMEGA*

So exciting were our days in the classroom that some of us were caught completely off guard. We had not expected to face attacks from cult elements in our Church community. We trusted our professors and appreciated their scholarship and ministry. We were a generation of ministers who represented the contemporary Adventism that had weathered all the attacks and finally achieved the right to be heard.

Scholars of other churches did not agree with us on everything, but they respected us as Bible-loving people to a greater degree than ever before. And they recognized conservative Adventists as Christian brothers and sisters. This group was worthy of agreeing not to agree. This was a conservative posture. A fundamentalist posture would be either—"agree with me or you are apostate and going to hell."

The cult elements of Adventist fundamentalism were too glaring to share in this recognition. But it was the power of the cult that we underestimated. Southern Missionary College, Pacific Union College, and Andrews University were all considered basic conservative centers for learning ministry in the Adventist Church.

I for one had gone into the cave of academia and for the present at least did not need to spend much time on the front lines. I had handed over the reins of *The Positive Way* to two well-educated faculty members while I was away at graduate school. Both were experienced moderators in the program. We had run *The Positive Way* for four years together and watched over 2000 students complete the course. Many of these graduates had expressed to us their gratitude for the help they had received in their spiritual enrichment. I set out to teach the course in my spare time at Andrews. While at Andrews I taught Sabbath School classes on campus and later in the Berrien Springs Village Church.

In a Sabbath School class, I was teaching in Seminary Hall I ran into a doctrine that I truly thought was dead in the denomination. An older gentleman in the class dominated the time presenting an Arian view of Christ. He insisted that Christ was created, and he had not always existed. He insisted that this was the historic Adventist position and that the Church needed to return to an affirmation of this view. He felt that this enhanced God's love for his only begotten son, as an example of his love for us. I was surprised that anyone in the Church still espoused this view, but I let him talk and let the class argue with him. Of course, anyone who disagreed with him he would classify as apostate. This was apparently part of the "old theology." Later, in a visit to Southern California I ran into an evangelist who said to me, "Ed, I have discovered a new appreciation of Jesus Christ." And he proceeded to tell me he had just struck on the idea that Jesus had been God's first created being!

It was the beginning of new shock—that we had Church leaders discovering this "new light" that the Church had rejected when *The Desire of Ages* was published at the turn of the twentieth century. This man was the Conference evangelist talking.

Profile of a Religious Man

Remnants of the old traditions that had been clarified and corrected in the 1950s with the publishing of *Questions on Doctrine* were starting to stir again. But I didn't allow myself to be seriously concerned. Some of these were ancient doctrines that Christianity had rejected long before there was an Adventist—the Arian view of Christ, the view that Christ had a sinful nature, the view that righteousness was sinless perfection, the idea that the atonement was not complete at the cross. Some of these views were part of the "old theology" of Adventism but had been further defined through more careful Bible study and even in some cases with the help of Sister White.

The effort to revive some of these doctrines was the work of various Church reformers in the 1950s that the General Conference had strongly resisted as a step backward. Again Dr. Springett addressed this.

> It seems that many of these dissenting brethren are still around and see this as their hour of destiny. Fortunately, however, the files of the SMC Division of Religion are fairly complete on the old Sanctuary Awakening Fellowship literature and other publications by the old Brinsmead movement. Most of the men in our department cut their theological eyeteeth at the Seventh-day Adventist Theological Seminary opposing this kind of teaching and writing papers against it. A reading of this literature throws considerable light on the present issues.[38]

The group was apparently growing—an under torrent of people who had never accepted *Questions on Doctrine*. And, as best I could discern, they were the old Omega apostasy crowd. One of their number, who Dr. Springett and I had gone to Seminary with, dropped by our office one Friday afternoon and told us that our problem was not that we were not teaching what the Church was teaching—that we were doing, he said. Our heresy was that we were teaching what the Church was teaching. The Church was wrong according to him!

We were surprised to hear him say this because he had been chair of the Bible Department in one of the Adventist colleges. Then he continued candidly to suggest that we should each buy ourselves a printing press. He said they were not expensive. And then we could start publishing our own papers attacking the Church for its errors. He insisted that we would make more money than we were making teaching religion at Southern. This plan would create a situation for us since we had never written anything attacking the Church. But he meant that there was big (and easy) money to be had in such ventures.

It would be no surprise that as this group became more vocal they would eventually enlist the power of the Omega apostasy charge. "Omega" was as confusing a term as "new theology." Both were slogans. And it wasn't long before we would be included in the Omega designation.[39]

---

38. Springett, "Some Historical Observations on the Present Theology 'Crisis,'" 22.

39. The concept of Omega was now to become defined by Lewis Walton, the Central California

New theology is the Omega apostasy, they would claim. To make such an accusation was to indicate that the accuser knew virtually nothing about the pantheism of the Kellogg-White debate. But the attraction of these kinds of labels seemed irresistible to Adventist fundamentalists. Labels such as these were in the same category as political slogans, shortcuts to messages conveyed. Who needs to vet a presidential candidate if one can shout, "Yes, we can!" One need not think very deeply if one could rely on a slogan or a word picture that circumvented much thought.

Sloganism often characterized theological movements. Capturing the thought was the mission of those who were vowing to help us return to the pioneer truth. But returning to the pioneers sometimes entailed simply accepting slogans and we began to hear them. Conservatives also believed in "returning to the pioneers" occasionally. But they insisted that the historical context always be considered. What happened to that careful biblical study that the Church had finally devoted itself to in the 1950s that inspired not only the writing of *Questions on Doctrine* but also produced the enormous seven-volume work of the *Seventh-day Adventist Bible Commentary*?[40]

For the past forty years we had been able to rest in the assumption that the Church still believed in its notion of progressive revelation. This was the idea that as

---

attorney. His definition was virtually unlike any definition we had been given at the SDA Theological Seminary. The late Dr. Carsten Johnsen (1914–1989) spent the better part of a quarter lecturing on the *Omega* as defined by Sister White. His lectures were later published in his books, *The Mystic "Omega" of End-Time Crisis* (1981), and *Omega II*, (1982).

Dr. Johnsen was professor of philosophy and Christian ethics at Andrews University from 1968–1978. During his tenure I took doctoral level classes from him in historical and systematic theology. His academic specialty was philosophy and the history of ideas. I wrote two papers on spiritualism in his classes. (Zackrison, "A Preliminary Study of the Use of the Term 'Spiritualism' in the Writings of Ellen G. White as it Relates to the Destiny of Man," (1975). Cf. Zackrison, "Spiritualism: A Preliminary study of the Term as used in the Writings of Ellen G. White as it Relates to the Destiny of Man," (1976).

Dr. Johnsen explained the Omega apostasy on a historical and philosophical basis in the Adventist Church. First, he dealt with the Alpha apostasy of John Harvey Kellogg, and what it was exactly that Sister White was opposing in Kellogg's thought. He then demonstrated the two opposite "ditches" of spiritualism and materialism.

Spiritualism was not to be confused with spiritism, which was commonly done in Adventist eschatology. The Omega was spiritualism, which Dr. Johnsen carefully identified. He defined his philosophy as realism and explained that what attracted him to Adventism to begin with was its rock-bottom realism. His books devote a great deal of space to identifying the dangers of the Omega in the contemporary Church, i.e., the invasion of thought that spiritualizes theological and philosophical reality. This position on the Omega is consistent in the connect between Kellogg's spiritualistic pantheism and what some modern scholars have done with contemporary Adventist thought. Some of his relevant works on this subject are listed in a bibliography of his works as posted at *www.carstenjohnsen.org*.

40. This work was the product of the finest Adventist scholars the Church could produce at the time including M. L. Andreasen, Otto Christianson, Raymond F. Cottrell, LeRoy Edwin Froom, Richard Hammill, Leslie Hardinge, Edward Heppenstall, Earle Hilgert, Siegfried Horn, T. Housel Jemison, Alger Johns, Roland Loasby, Frank Marsh, Gerald Minchin, W. G. C. Murdoch, Don Neufeld, Julia Neuffer, Norval F. Pease, George McCready Price, W. E. Read, Walter F. Specht, Edwin Thiele, Daniel Walther, A. J. Wearner, Charles Weniger, Lynn Wood, Frank Yost, and others. Many of them had earned doctorates, had taught in Adventist colleges and at the SDA Theological Seminary, and several had been administrators in the Church's educational system.

time moves on the Church becomes more informed with study and grows to maturity. The Advent pioneers had subscribed to that view. The Adventist job was the call to "finish the work" of the Protestant Reformation—those areas that were left undone because of the rigid creeds Protestantism had formulated.

Apparently, our generation was not aware of all that had been fought over to produce those books. I was reminded of the foot that kicked my scholar friend when he asked why Elder Andreasen was not present at a meeting of Adventist scholars setting out to write *Questions on Doctrine*. I never did learn whose foot it was but the question that went with the kick had stuck ineradicably in my mind, "Have you not heard about the feud between Andreasen and Froom?"

Instead of isolated criticism from the edge, the fundamentalists now had insiders who had worked into important positions in the central administration of the denomination. Most of us were ignorant of this. We thought these theological issues had been settled before we came on the scene. Our job was to teach not to politicize.

There were other products of the mainline Adventist denomination we grew up in and were educated by. Dr. LeRoy Edwin Froom (1890–1974), professor of historical theology at the SDA Theological Seminary had produced seven massive volumes (7,142 pages total) of copiously footnoted and researched historical data.[41] Dr. Froom's works were impressive, and his collection of primary sources used to write them became the basic research material that spawned establishment of the Heritage Room Research Center in the James White Library at Andrews University.

Notwithstanding the erudition represented in Froom's scholarship, this movement was attempting to pull the denomination back to pre-1950 days and would call this fervent scholarship of the 1950s by that scornful term: "new theology." It sought to indicate that the Church was in compromising decline and it was time to refocus on "historic" Adventism.

To be saddled with the term "new theology" was to be labeled with suspicion that while undefinable, was intended to be lethal to one's profession. New theology became synonymous with Omega and that meant heresy and apostasy. Neither term was used as a biblical designation—they were applied to a certain parochial interpretation of Sister White's warnings. And on the downside it was licensing to hunt for the religious "witches" in the Church, especially in the educational and theological ministry. There was an automatic, irrational hysteria connected with the term new theology.

Taking away the negative intentions of the term I would think that accepting new theology as a complementary description of growth and aliveness should really be no problem. I came to accept it as an accurate and good term. New theology meant

---

41. See Froom, *The Prophetic Faith of Our Fathers: The Historical Development of Prophetic Interpretation*, 4 volumes, (1946, 1948); Froom, *The Conditionalist Faith of Our Fathers: The Conflict of the Ages Over the Nature and Destiny of Man*, 2 volumes, (1965–1966); Froom, *Movement of Destiny*, (1971).

release from the slavery of tradition and routine that represented the death of terminology and propositions that were worn out and failed to convey legitimate meaning.

In its best sense of the term "new theology" could represent the re-examination of traditions leading to the rejection of false teachings or misleading terminology in Adventism. It could mean regrouping around established and defensive Truth—straightening out areas where the "old [worn-out] theology" had failed to convey the correct understanding of what Adventists really believed and taught. After all, in *koine* Greek, which all biblical scholars were required to study and learn, "new" meant "renewed" not "different."

The "new theology" could be the progressive revelation of freshness and the renewal of the Truth of scripture. Were we also to denigrate "new" covenant and "new" life and "New" Testament and "new" birth?

In danger of accepting Adventist scholasticism that was dead, those who bought into the new theology did so by showing that Adventism was sensitive and alive. And like many terms in Christian history initially meant to depreciate and slur fellow believers, i.e., Quakers, Shakers, Dunkers, etc., the term should be taken and allowed to describe that vibrant meaning. This term should be stolen back from the fundamentalists who had relegated it to the level of a theological street walker. Obviously, my evaluation of the term "new theology" was irrelevant to the way it was being used.

STIRRING UP THE PAST AND CALLING IT HISTORIC

We had been taught that attacks were to be expected—that the Church had always been attacked from the inside as well as the outside, and our professors had presented carefully researched materials to help us as we prepared for the ministry. It probably should have been a foregone conclusion that our turn would also come, especially considering what was happening. The denomination was starting to shake and smolder, something like those volcanoes that were tired of being dormant.

A few people at the top were giving permission to violate biblical methods of dealing with doctrinal considerations. To understand some of this we need to go back in our contemporary history. A not-so-subtle move to pushback was seen at the 1974 Bible Conference, which was held on several college campuses in the English-speaking world and one of which was held on our SMC campus. During this Conference we were shrewdly introduced to a return to the old perfectionist message by two Adventist editors from Washington, D.C.

The Conference was organized by Dr. Gordon Hyde, the former chair of the SMC Speech Department and now secretary of the Biblical Research Committee (the new name for the old Defense Literature Committee) of the General Conference.

I had attended the Conference held on the SMC campus from May 13–21, 1974. Most of the presentations were about epistemological authority and hermeneutics, issues that we had been taught in Seminary were primary for the modern Church to face. And many were presented by professors we had at Seminary.

The last three reports at the Conference were devoted to the topic of righteousness by faith, and this appeared to be a disconnect. It threw us off-guard. Granted here was a legitimate concern for the Church to take up. But the last three presentations in the 1974 Bible conference took a different focus from the first dozen or so on hermeneutics and epistemology.

The first of these was presented by Dr. Hans LaRondelle, a Seminary professor with a Reformed background and who would someday become my doctoral dissertation advisor. The next two speakers were both from the editorial staff of the *Adventist Review,* the journalistic voice of the denomination, Elder Kenneth Wood (1917–2008), editor, and Dr. Herbert Douglass (1927–2014), assistant editor.

It was Dr. Douglass who presented the report that in hindsight appeared really to be the capstone of the Conference. His was also the most controversial presentation. As things settled into our understanding this presentation suggested the real purpose of the whole Conference—what some would call a curve ball because the meetings had not seemed to be going in that direction. His report had earmarks of Adventist fundamentalism—totally basing his interpretation of Sister White.

Dr. Douglass developed the notion that in Adventist eschatology we were to understand that Christ had not yet returned to earth because he was waiting for Adventists to reproduce the character of Christ in their lives, i.e., produce a sinless life.[42] This not only explained the delay of the *Parousia,* it also held the converse to be true: if we could delay the second coming of Christ we could also cause it to occur sooner—his interpretation of texts that mentioned *hastening.*[43]

This group of sinless saints would be the revelation to the universe that Satan's charge that no one could keep the law of God perfectly would be proven bogus. If we had any observers still listening to us as rational biblical Christians here they would have been shocked by what they would interpret as arrogant, parochial theology that simply would not fly biblically or have orthodox historical credibility.

Dr. Douglass built his theology primarily on a single statement from Sister White in her book, *Christ's Object Lessons*:

> Christ is seeking to reproduce Himself in the hearts of men; and He does this through those who believe in Him. The object of the Christian life is fruit-bearing—*the reproduction of Christ's character in the believer,* that it may be reproduced in others. . . .
>
> *Christ is waiting with longing desire for the manifestation of Himself in His church. When the character of Christ shall be perfectly reproduced in His people,*

---

42. Douglass, "The Unique Contribution of Adventist Eschatology, (1974).

43. Dr. Douglass would elaborate further on the question of "hasten and delay" in his booklet, *Why Jesus Waits: How the Sanctuary Doctrine Explains the Mission of the Seventh-day Adventist Church,* (1976).

then He will come to claim them as His own. It is the privilege of every Christian not only to look for but to hasten the coming of our Lord Jesus Christ (2 Peter 3:12, margin). Were all who profess His name bearing fruit to His glory how quickly the whole world would be sown with the seed of the gospel. Quickly *the last great harvest would be ripened*, and Christ would come to gather the precious grain.[44]

Dr. Douglass called his view "the harvest principle." The connection between this topic and hermeneutics that had gone before was apparently to be found in conditional prophecy, the notion that when men and women (in this case in point, Seventh-day Adventists) fail to carry out God's plans, God's prophecies are delayed. A common example of this was Jonah, a prophet of God who predicted the fall of Nineveh. Yet when Nineveh repented corporately God did not carry out the prophecy. This did not make Jonah a false prophet, nor did God's message fail, for the intent of Jonah's prediction had been immersed in the hope that repentance would be forth coming. When their sin was gone God could let the Ninevites live.

> [10] When God saw what they did, how they turned from their evil way, God repented of the evil which he had said he would do to them; and he did not do it. (Jon 3:10)

Adventists were Jonah. The world was Nineveh. So, the connection was that Adventists had failed, up to now, to carry out the task they were given in the 1844 movement and therefore God had delayed his coming. He was waiting for Adventists to carry out that task.

Dr. Douglass continued,

> Ellen White warned that Adventists must not, no matter how plausible the reasoning, blame God for the delay in the Advent.[45]

> The Biblical correlate to the principle of *conditional prophecy* is *the harvest principle*—that is, God will wait for the maturing of Christian *character in a significant number of people as the chief condition determining the time of the Advent*. Other conditions in the world will also converge in the "last days" prior to that moment when Jesus says, "It is done," and they also will be noted in this paper. It seems to the writer that all the various conditions familiar to Adventists that will converge in the end times are different developments of, and can be subsumed under *the harvest principle*, thus providing an unforced coherence in Adventist eschatology.[46]

Some listeners at the Conference had trouble with this dogmatic view. One theologian said to me, with a hint of sarcasm, that now he could see why Adventists would be

---

44. White, *Christ's Object Lessons*, 67, 69. Emphases supplied.
45. Douglass, "The Unique Contribution of Adventist Eschatology," 12.
46. Ibid. Emphases supplied.

so severely persecuted. He felt that when the world wakes up to the fact that the Adventists and their sinful living are responsible for the Civil War, two World Wars, the Korean War, Viet Nam and all the unspeakable plagues that have destroyed millions of people they can do nothing else. Especially that all the Adventists had to do was to develop a sinless character!

I was beginning to see problems. But how these would play out and what role Elder Francis and the SMC Religion Department, or even Happy Valley in general would play was not on the horizon yet. Furthermore, dwelling on such a topic could shortly cause one to blow a fuse.

There were subtle implications for a new definition of the gospel in this view. The eternal gospel was to be preached by the Adventist movement.

> [6] Then I saw another angel flying in midheaven, with an eternal gospel to proclaim to those who dwell on earth, to every nation and tribe and tongue and people; [7] and he said with a loud voice, "Fear God and give him glory, for the hour of his judgment has come; and worship him who made heaven and earth, the sea and the fountains of water." (Rev 14:6–7)

And the gospel now took on a moralistic tone in which a believer was to perfectly imitate Christ. This gospel said that we could. And so, perfectionism was no longer subtle—and with that thought those in attendance were to go home with renewed vigor.

By the time I was writing a dissertation, these things had become a controversy in the Church. But I could not be diverted from my work. So, I pondered them some more, and tried not to be distracted. I knew one thing for certain: One doesn't build a Christian theology on one statement from Sister White.

CHAPTER TWENTY-NINE

We've Become the Problem

"We do not see things as they are, we see things as we are."
—Talmudic Saying

ALL BUT DISSERTATION

I had made it through the grueling process of four language examinations, many quarter credit hours of classwork, forty real time hours of comprehensive examinations. And my dissertation proposal had been approved. Every stop on the road to finishing made the next stop look more attractive. When you get through your language exams, all you have left is the class work, I had thought. But every increment of classwork involved intense research projects that sometimes required more than a term to finish.

The next stop: get through the classwork and all you have left are the comprehensive examinations. Yet when you got to that stage, instead of having a fulfilled feeling you realized that the comps were going to require not just review of all the classwork you had taken. Now you needed six more months of reading in areas not covered in the classwork and retaining the whole historical sweep of philosophy, theology, and your cognate area (which for me was developmental psychology).

Dawn to dusk of sitting in the library or in my study at home reading, absorbing, recalling, reviewing, more note taking. No serious student is ever the same after such a grueling ordeal. If you passed the comps (and not everyone did), you thought you would be able to breathe and relax at last; and then you could exclaim excitedly that all you had left to do was to write your dissertation.

The dissertation was your contribution to original research—something no one had ever done before in quite the same way. That was the doctoral stage known as ABD—All But Dissertation. I knew several colleagues stuck at that station in their academic life. Some even gave up at that stage and informed you, I'm done, except for my dissertation! But then, suddenly, you realized how formidable that project really was.

There was no let up, and some days you wondered if it was all worth it. Your committee chair would write you cordial little notes, like—"Hurry up and finish!" So, you kept your eye on the goal; as my college dean had said, "You keep on keeping on!" Somehow that didn't sound so trite anymore.

My dissertation proposal was seventeen pages long, not including the bibliography, which was another thirty-five pages. It was approved by a committee of twenty graduate school professors. I was not present at the meeting, but my little committee (three in number) was there to defend it—they had approved it before it went to the bigger group of critics. Now it just needed the stamp of approval from the ThD faculty.

Only one professor raised questions—Dr. Maxwell (1925–1999)—the only teacher in whose class I had earned a grade lower than an A (he said I had only earned an A- in his doctoral seminar). Now he introduced two challenges: (1) Had we not all heard enough about sin (the topic I had elected to research)? And (2) The scope of the proposal covered too much time—it covered 130 years of historical, theological development.

At home, when I had announced that I was planning to write on *sin*, Annie had smiled and observed, "That's a good topic for you—the one area you are most experienced in!" I trusted she meant it as humor.

Dr. Maxwell was overruled, but he turned out to be right about the scope. It was too vast, and working with my chair, the scope of the dissertation was eventually limited to fifty years, rather than the full 130 years originally proposed. Despite (or because of) his objections, Dr. Maxwell would visit me in my James White Library carrel occasionally to see how things were going, something I appreciated. As originally approved, the title of the dissertation was: *Seventh-day Adventists and Original Sin: A Study of the Seventh-day Adventist Understanding of the Effects of Adam's Sin on His Posterity (1850–1980)*.[1] I could only hope that the original time frame was no indication of how long this project might take.

It ended up taking me five years to complete. At that point, I had covered all 130 years of research, but when I reached 1900, I had already produced 500 pages of rough draft. When I called Dr. LaRondelle he just said, "Revise your problem statement and end this thing." I did.

I returned to the SMC campus when I reached the ABD phase, and planned to continue my research in Collegedale, and perhaps spend some summers at Andrews in the James White Library (these were pre-Google days). I had had very little time after approval of my dissertation project to research in residence at Andrews because we needed to pack up, sell our house in Michigan, and move back to Tennessee.

---

1. Now published as *The First Temptation*, (2015).

INTRODUCTION TO "THE FLAWED GOD"

In the winter-spring semester of 1980, I had a student with an unusually creative theology. He and his family had lived in our house on Suhrie Drive for the three years we were in Michigan. This was his second class from me. He had taken *Righteousness by Faith* the previous semester, in the fall of 1979. He said he had enjoyed that class. Now he was enrolled in this lower level theology class, *Christian Beliefs*. Since neither class was a requirement for his major, I assumed he took the class because he liked my approach.

He felt comfortable to drop by my office after class. His mother presented me with the first volume of the revised *International Standard Bible Encyclopedia,* a very fine piece of evangelical theology (and not inexpensive). I was grateful for that gift. She explained that she had bought it for me because I had been such a good role model for her son. She went on to explain how much he had enjoyed my classes and how happy their family was to have us back in the community.

I couldn't remember having met her in person before, but I had been cashing her monthly rental checks for years. Now her son came to my office wanting to talk about a new theory he had come up with to solve the problem of theodicy, that area of theology that probes the reasons why sin is present in a righteous God's universe. I thought this was appropriate since we were studying the doctrine of God and in that unit, we covered theodicy.

He began his view that since sin is everywhere and there seems to be no way of checking it, we need to come up with a view of God that allows for a rational view of sin.

I was all ears. He said to explain this he had concluded that God is flawed. Now he had my attention. "We have a flawed God," he said. And he believed that his view explained the sin and the evil in the universe.

Theologians are taught to cut to the issue. This was not a hard cut. Philosophically, he was not thinking carefully about the implications of what he was saying. This was a faltering expression of folk religion. I didn't see much light in pursuing this kind of reasoning but as a teacher, I didn't like to brush students off. I usually employed a Socratic approach, much like how my professors had taught me.

You want to encourage students who like to explore the world of theology, if they are not dogmatic. As a professor, you are there to help them see the philosophical possibility of the theological craft. Nevertheless, I went right to the point. I asked my student if he thought that philosophically his view was tenable?

I paused to see if any light bulbs were glowing. He only looked puzzled. I could see that no answer was forthcoming. I reworded my question—is there a philosophical problem with this view? Have you thought this through? No answer. I tried again. I asked him if God is flawed would he still be God? Still no answer. Finally, I asked if non-flawed wasn't part of our overall definition of God?

The Socratic approach required a conversation, but I was getting nowhere with these questions, so I set forth an assertion. I then just laid it all out. God, by definition, cannot be flawed. If he were flawed in any way you wouldn't be talking about God. As the standard of truth, reality, genuineness, substance, form—you pick your term—God, the very use of the designation, requires no flaw, for then he would not be God. The definition of God requires the notion of unflawed.

My student either could not or would not grasp that and seemed determined to tighten his grip on his new light on the nature of God; not an unusual phenomenon with those who have set forth a personal, therefore precious, philosophical suggestion. It seemed quite clear that he now perceived himself the teacher and me his pupil. He was not there to discuss—not even to convince. He was there to pontificate. Most students were at least more perceptive.

For several days, he came back to my office after class to persuade me of the wonderful ramifications that flowed from his basic premise, a premise I found impossible to change. He finished the course with better marks than he had gotten in his previous class with me and I don't remember hearing anything more from him about his solution to the question of theodicy.

I thought nothing more about our discussions or his mother's gift for several months. I not only had a full load of students to teach along with the standard responsibilities of a college professor, i.e., committees, conventions, extra-curricular assignments, speaking engagements, but I had a dissertation to write and the pressure from the administration was mounting to finish that project.

This was college and in college a professor is required to challenge students to think. None of us in the SMC Religion Department looked at education as indoctrination. The educational enterprise has to do with examining the evidence and learning to weigh it. A college Religion class was not a baptismal class or an evangelistic series. It was not designed to be propaganda.

We would all be accused of raising doubts because doubt was at the foundation of learning. Those who made such accusations did not understand the dynamic educational process. I could safely speak for all the professors in the SMC Religion Department that we all held that a believer who had come to his/her own understanding of truth was a stronger believer than one who had only been given what was essentially a speech written out for a teleprompter. Especially in the classes for theological students it was crucial that in the short time we had a pre-ministry student, we must prepare him either for Seminary or for the field. In the Southern Union Conference not every student hired out of college was able to go on to graduate school, so we had the additional challenge of preparing him for internship. Some graduates even went directly into a Church as its new pastor.

We had clear guidelines to prepare students, during the short time we had them in class, "to be thinkers and not mere reflectors of other men's thought." Our educational philosophy had been informed by our prophet.

> Every human being, created in the image of God, is endowed with a power akin to that of the Creator—individuality, power to think and to do. The men in whom this power is developed are the men who bear responsibilities, who are leaders in enterprise, and who influence character. *It is the work of true education to develop this power to train the youth to be thinkers, and not mere reflectors of other men's thought.* Instead of confining their study to that which men have said or written, let students be directed to the sources of truth, to the vast fields opened for research in nature and revelation.[2]

This was a clear goal in the education of gospel ministers. Elsewhere she wrote along the same line.

> *All our workers must have room to exercise their own judgment and discretion.* God has given men talents which He means that they should use. *He has given them minds, and He means that they should become thinkers, and do their own thinking and planning,* rather than depend upon others to think for them.[3]

It was a delicate balance because these men would be facing strong opposition in the fields where they would work. Some religious people out there viewed Adventism as a cult and they were stubborn that our Church be treated as such. Thus apologetics[4] was an important part of preparing young ministers. That involved examining many doctrinal questions as well as creating an awareness of which questions were the important ones. The questions were often more important than the proposed answers. In our classrooms we could provide a safe house for the fledgling thinkers to develop their arguments as they learned to face some of the theological challenges they would encounter on the outside.

My entire ministry had been focused on young people—first as a youth pastor, then as a pastor, and finally as a college professor. Now I had just returned from intensive additional education in adolescence and lifespan developmental psychology as well. It would prove very useful during the very tumultuous period ahead.

THE INVASION OF THE ADVENTIST THEOLOGY SNATCHERS

On the mundane level, we needed to get started building a new addition on our home now that we had the money collected from the sale of our Michigan house. God had richly blessed us. At last we would finish this lengthy doctoral project and enjoy being back where we belonged.

---

2. White, *Education*, 17. Emphasis supplied.
3. White, *Testimonies to Ministers and Gospel Workers*, 302. Emphases supplied.
4. "In that the subject matter of religion is God, the crucial issue of religion is whether or not it possesses a knowledge of God. It is the task of Christian apologetics to show on what grounds the Christian religion possesses such a knowledge of God." Bernard Ramm, "Apologetics," in Everett F. Harrison, (ed.), *Baker's Dictionary of Theology*, 55.

As for my student, I didn't see him again. Since he was not a theology major, my interaction with him had been limited to his office visits, which he no longer made. But there were times that I wondered how he was doing with his concept of the flawed God. I saw him drive by my house a couple times, which I found odd since I lived on a cul-de-sac.

A neighbor reported that he would often park near the houses of the Grants and the Zackrisons and then either slowly drive off or park and stare at their houses.[5] The Grants lived across the street from us and next door to the Gladsons. I didn't give much thought to this behavior, but I later learned that others in the neighborhood did. I wondered if he had formed some attachment to my house where he had lived for three years. Some neighbors felt this behavior was more sinister.[6]

I did not take any of these concerns very seriously until one evening when we returned home and found him standing in the middle of our darkened garage when we opened the automatic door. That was alarming.

Later we discovered that someone had removed a TV antenna from our attic. Apparently, his family had stored the antenna there when they rented our house. I vaguely remembered seeing the antenna there when I was storing some of our goods from Michigan, but no one ever called us about it, and I couldn't remember if it was ours. But then it was gone. We had no idea when or how this had occurred. We had no knowledge of how or if he had entered our home and taken the antenna, but we didn't know who else would have done it. After the garage incident, we had all the locks in our house changed.

This disturbing behavior showed in other ways. One professor shared that the student liked to talk with him about religion, and the topics had to do with "the existence of God, the goodness of God, or lack thereof, and the validity of the scriptures."[7] And according to this teacher, I was not the only recipient of gifts from his mother given in gratitude for help with him.[8] Other than his drive-byes and the incident

---

5. "Personal Data on Major Figures in the Controversy." *SMC Faculty Document Committee Collection,* (1984), 2.

6. Ibid., 3. Apparently, we were not the only neighbors who had been stalked. Another faculty member reported that she had ordered him never to return after she had caught him parking and staring at her house. She maintained that she had a teenage daughter "with whom he was infatuated."

7. Ibid., 1.

8. Ibid., 2. Religion teachers welcome religious discussions with their students. But there was something bizarre about connected behaviors. Testimony varied. "Every time I drove into my driveway, there would be [name deleted]. He would spend hours following me about discussing topics from religion to personality problems." Another professor testified, "He would come over and talk about the same subjects, but it seemed evident that what he needed was a person to talk to and relate to. On one occasion he expressed surprise that this faculty member had regular meals with his family—something his family never did, [he] said." Another faculty member testified that he had become too literal on the Sanctuary. "[He] declared to me, 'Then you don't believe in the Sanctuary.' No amount of assurance would dissuade him. His accusations mounted from that point."

in my garage he would not surface again for several months. And this time he had a whole new agenda—no more "flawed God" theories.

The next time I would run into his speculative theology was when he launched a personal campaign against the SMC Religion Department. Now the *department* was flawed, it was filled with heretics, he would declare. What happened to his mind between our last discussion and his new theological crusade I never discovered although many reports began to circulate.

When he surfaced a few months later, he was listed as the editor of a single issue eight-page "news" paper. It was a smear sheet attacking the SMC Religion Department. My student had now become "editor." Someone had converted him to Adventist fundamentalism.[9]

This exposé was published by a printer in a little town, Ooltewah, about three miles down the road from the college. The printer used his press to go after what he saw as corruption in the Adventist Church. He started by exposing the involvement of Church officials in the Davenport Scandal.[10] As time went on he went after ordained ministers and denominational leaders with publications he called *Press Releases* and *Camp Meeting Specials*.

Basically, his papers called for the resignation of any leader he decided was not qualified for the job. He confessed that this paper was his first wandering into theological issues and he claimed that he only did so after he "stumbled across information that led him to question the theology of the Religion department of SMC."[11] Nevertheless, as far as I knew he had never met with any of us. I had never heard of him until the paper turned up on my driveway.

The table of contents on the front page of the paper (just under the plea for money to help finance this venture) showed the muckraking nature of this paper:

> SMC Students Present Testimonies of Heresy
> Tragic State of the Division in Australia
> Confusion in SMC Religion Classes
> Theologians Have Secret and Subversive Meeting in Atlanta
> SMC Policy Conflicts with Spirit of Prophecy

The contributors to this newspaper were listed as Tom Tucker, Robert McMullan,[12] Kent Millard, Florence Woolcock, David Lin and Vance Ferrell. I knew only two of these names.

---

9. Ibid., 3. One report revealed that he had met a new student at SMC, and the two had teamed up with Florence Woolcock, another Collegedale community member. But we knew nothing of this at the time. His paper would erase our naivete.

10. Hunter, "The Release," *Southern Accent,* March 18, 1982, 10.

11. Ibid.

12. The section attributed to Robert McMullan is impossible to unpack, but in his explanation of what I allegedly taught (or believed), he reveals more than anything else that his spotty attendance in class was affecting his interpretation of my lectures. Molleurus Couperus wrote: "Robert McMullan

Also included was a set of notes allegedly taken from a letter written by Elder William R. May, detailing a report of a meeting of the Adventist Laymen's Fellowship, a fundamentalist organization in Sydney, Australia. Elder May was touted as the secretary of the Southwestern Union Conference at the time. Generally, ministers in official positions as this one avoided public endorsement of Adventist fundamentalism, so I suspected that this was a pirated letter from someone's mailing list.

Elder May's alleged letter was one with a series of radical generalizations about Adventist colleges and their theology and it had now been scattered like "the leaves of autumn" to the Adventist public. The paper's editor and writers were clearly applying it to the SMC Religion Department.

In addition to these articles, there was also a rather lengthy piece contributed by an anonymous but "concerned Conference pastor." We suspected that a person who wouldn't sign his name was probably not really "concerned." Of this fraternity of writers, the first three in the above list claimed to have been students at SMC and the suggestion was left that they should be considered primary sources for the assumed whistle-blowing accounts revealed therein.

A major characteristic of the paper was its continual reference to motives, emotions, and highly subjective interpretations of the behavior of SMC teachers and administrators; in short, it was a fountain of innuendo and slander. The muckraking had begun. According to this paper Dr. Grant taught from the "apostate" magazine, *Evangelica;* Dr. Gerhard Hasel was a new leader strong in faith; Avondale College was mostly Pro-Ford; those who listen to SMC teachers do not recognize what is being taught is error; Dr. Melvin Campbell was hostile to "the Spirity [sic] of Prophecy," and so on. Here was a dark side of Adventist fundamentalism.

The most caustic writing in the paper was entitled "Open letter from a former theology student of SMC." It was submitted by a person, whose writing was filled with *ad hominem* arguments. In this letter, he attributed negative emotions to administration and faculty—they were mean, angry, explosive, unfair, and gloating. And most of these emotions were mercilessly assigned to Dr. Knittel, the president of the college.

Aside from the theological shortcomings in the scandal sheet, the attacks were so poorly organized and substantiated that anyone used to reviewing books or refereed scholarly articles would hardly know where to begin. The letter was a spraying of accusations where virtually every sentence was intended to paint as negative a view as possible while the context of the alleged professional sins was generally missing. There was no discernible positive direction to the letter. But in the process, there was

---

offered a concise summary of the faith/works issue: '*Any sound Adventist knows that a christians [sic] salvation depends on obedience to God* when he is happy to follow Christs [sic] example if he loves what Christ has done for every sinner. This is a complete reversal of what Elder Zackrison puts forward in his approach of Positive Way!'" *West Coast Forum Newsletter,* quoted in *Southern Accent,* "PUC and SMC Under Fire," March 18, 1982, 18. Emphasis supplied. To my knowledge Mr. McMullan was never a student in *The Positive Way Christian Life Seminar*.

grave convolution and untruth. And this was also true of most of the contents of the paper itself.

Despite its deceptive nature, this paper was read with interest throughout the Southern Union Conference and even at General Conference headquarters.

Omega, by Lewis Walton, was quoted as warning against authoritarian coercion. But given that this was implicitly what he himself was calling for in appealing to Church leaders to crack down on the Religion Department at SMC, the reference to Walton made no other sense than using his name as a letter of introduction to people who had embraced the book's thesis.

In general, the picture the writer painted of those hired and ordained by the denomination to teach and administer religious education to its young people was dismal. It reminded one of the 1960s when the news magazines carried weekly photographs of students taking over University of California offices—sitting on presidents' desks with smug, arrogant faces, smoking big cigars with their defiant fists held tight and waving in the air.

RELIGION PROFESSORS MEET IN ATLANTA

Before the appearance of the "news" paper, and in the wake of summer Church meetings held in Colorado, several Bible teachers from the denomination's North American colleges and universities had met informally in Atlanta in June 1981. I had just returned from an SMC Symphony Orchestra concert tour of Australia, New Zealand and Fiji, and was invited to attend this meeting the day after my return. I fought my jet lag and rode to Atlanta with Dr. Knittel and Dr. Ott on a Friday afternoon.

All who attended the Atlanta get-together did so at their own expense because of deep-felt need to discuss the present situation in the Church and how it might affect the career life of Bible teachers. Dr. Desmond Ford, visiting theology professor at Pacific Union College in Angwin, California, had been fired after the GC president had assured all of us at the meetings at Glacier View in Colorado that he would be reassigned to London, England, during a "cooling down period." When the president reneged on his promises to Dr. Ford, many Bible teachers were gripped with deep anxiety about their own futures. But while Glacier View cast a long shadow over educators, Dr. Ford was not discussed at this Atlanta meeting. This meeting was about us not theology.

There would be nothing official about this meeting in Atlanta, just a chance to fellowship and share as well as discuss some of the fearsome possibilities facing the educational wing of the denominational ministry. This same group always got together at the official Church's fall conventions, and the only additional attendees at the Atlanta get-together were a few administrators, pastors and a General Conference representative.

The organizers of this meeting wanted to discourage a perceived move towards hierarchical autocracy while reassuring Church leaders of their uncoerced support. For that reason, they felt that it would enhance the credibility of their support to convene this meeting without involving Church leaders. The fact that all participants paid their own way was a measure of their commitment to the Church and their own ministries.

Less than twenty scholars attended. I noted scholars present from Loma Linda University, Walla Walla College, Southwestern Adventist College, Southern Missionary College, Columbia Union College, Andrews University, Pacific Union College, and a couple of pastors and administrators who also had taught or were currently teaching. But a copy of the minutes would be shared with those not there and debated at the yearly theological conventions (SBL, AAR, AAOR) and at Andrews University in the fall.

Here was a credible group of Adventist scholars who all knew each other. With Dr. Ford dismissed despite promises to the contrary, all of us wondered who might be next and why. These men all had an invested interest in a well-functioning Church, having committed their lives and careers to its teaching ministry. All in attendance were veteran ministers, and their pastoral concerns were demonstrated at this informal meeting.

Scholars who could not attend sent their regards that they would join the discussion in the fall. When I arrived from Collegedale, we all exchanged small talk and I went to the restroom. After my absence of a few minutes, I was informed that I had been elected recording secretary for the Conference.

My skimpy notes from the Atlanta meeting (two sessions in all) were partly written in note hand and abbreviations, and what I had jotted down hastily, I would later fill out the details and send to the attendees. Some General Conference committees kept no minutes of meetings and because of the subterfuge that followed the Atlanta minutes, this would have been a better policy for this meeting. But these were theologians meeting together, *not politicians*. Probably no one at the Atlanta meeting gave any thought to the possibility that this meeting would be monitored and attacked as a subversive plot. The scholars in this group were used to meeting together and speaking their minds.

I kept the minutes for the two sessions I attended, and others took minutes for the other sessions. After we adjourned, I handed my notes to Dr. Lorenzo Grant, one of the organizers of the meeting. I offered to write up the final minutes for the attendees. The minutes were not important—it was the Affirmation that resulted that was significant. The group voted to send the first copy of the Affirmation to the General Conference president, and it was to be hand delivered by the GC representative present at the Atlanta meeting.

As it was reported to me when I returned the next day, on Friday night a group of the professors from the west coast were in their motel rooms discussing the proceedings of that day's meeting when one scholar suggested that to make this a memorable occasion the group ought to set forth an agreed-upon statement for Church leaders.

As they brainstormed, someone suggested calling it *The Atlanta Affirmation*.[13] Theologians often do this and have done this throughout the Christian age. Covenants, contracts, creeds, propositions and fundamentals abound in Christian history. This group was composed of theologians and historians. They would add their names to the long list of the faithful scholars who had preceded them. This was to be an *affirmation of support*.

The statement was drafted, and when I returned the next afternoon the statement had been discussed and finalized and those in attendance were invited to sign it. It was to be an affirmation. Everyone supported the statement. There were no detractors. It was not extreme or radical, simply a statement of support for Adventist leadership by educators in a time of crisis.

Returning to campus, Dr. Grant was met by a local and vocal critic on whose family's largesse the college depended. Even though she had not attended the meeting she immediately accused him of presiding over a "Fordite" meeting in Atlanta. He was taken by surprise—it was nothing of the kind. To her, this meeting smelled of "subversion." How did she know? She wasn't there. He had the copy of the incomplete minutes written in note hand and the abbreviations that I had given him to look over before I wrote up the final copy for the attendees.

Dr. Grant had not yet read the minutes, but he handed her the copy to show her that the minutes would demonstrate the purpose of this unofficial, informal get-together. He invited her to read them over and satisfy herself that this had nothing to do with subversion. He asked her to give them back after she had read the copy since this was the only notes he had. It was a terrible mistake. But once again this demonstrated the innocence of a theologian's love of the Church.

Down the line, Dr. Grant would be forced to resign his position in the Religion Department largely because of what happened next. But that tragedy would play out over the next two years. At this point in our experience at SMC we did not think in terms of friends vs. enemies. Nor did we think in terms of conservatives vs. fundamentalists. We were not paranoid—to our peril.

Hindsight would reveal that this was a time when none of us knew who our "enemies" were. In his naïve trust, Dr. Grant did not realize that before he got the notes back she would have shared them with conspiracy theorists who, like her, had not been at the meeting, but would jump at the chance to put a negative spin on it and through annotations completely distort what had been a clear statement of support that was intended to be confidential for President Wilson's eyes only.

---

13. To read "The Atlanta Affirmation," see Appendix V at the end of this book. For the response of GC President Neal Wilson (1920–2010) to the falsely annotated minutes, see Appendix VI.

How these notes got from her hand to the Ooltewah press man and Vance Ferrell's printing presses remains a mystery. And the propensity of top leaders in Washington to believe the worst about us was astounding to me. I did not live in that world. I had always trusted the ordained leadership. Ferrell's bogus version of the minutes first appeared in his own publications before it was republished in this paper. Next, Ferrell would begin publishing materials against the SMC Religion Department. Since one of his articles, filled with errors, was about me, I wrote him a letter[14] responding to the misinformation. He responded by publishing my letter.[15]

I had never heard of Vance Ferrell at the time, but Church leaders later informed me. I didn't understand that—I tried to reason with anyone who hoped to see Jesus' return. After this experience, they wouldn't have gotten the necessary refresher course in the vagaries of human nature.[16] Finally, in two unsigned partial letters on *Ministry* and *Adventist Review* letterheads, the ethically challenged publishers of this "news" paper let it be known that the GC committee was praising them for their concern and good work.

The letters published in the paper were not addressed to the editors, but rather to a certain layman in Tennessee, who had apparently sent copies of the bogus Atlanta minutes to *Ministry* and *Adventist Review* editors. Without checking with anyone involved with the meetings, he sought to inform these papers of the heretical threat in

---

14. Zackrison, "Letter to Vance Ferrell," July 24, 1982. *SMC Faculty Document Committee Collection.*

15. See Lowell Bock (1923–2016), vice-president, General Conference of Seventh-day Adventists, "Letter to Dr. Edwin Zackrison," August 3, 1982: "Dear Dr. Zackrison: I appreciate the content and tone of your reply to Vance Ferrell [in the July 24, 1982 letter]. May God help us all to serve Him faithfully in these challenging times." *SMC Faculty Document Committee Collection.* See further, Everett E. Cumbo (1925–2010), president, Illinois Conference of Seventh-day Adventists, "Letter to Edwin Zackrison," August 9, 1982: "Dear Ed: Thank you for including me in your letter to Vance Ferrell. Vance Ferrell, I think is still a member of the Adventist Church, although he is certainly anything but a supporter of Adventism. He has his own private press in the woods somewhere near Harrisburg, Illinois. I am not sure where he gets his support, but he seems to be putting out more and more critical material and circulating it far and wide. I receive several letters every month from people all over North America wondering if he is supported by the church. We have very little control over Vance. . . . Let me say how sorry I am to see this type of verbal abuse coming from anyone. There is lots of this going on in and outside the church today." *SMC Faculty Document Committee Collection.*

16. Mike Seaman, editor of the *Southern Accent,* the SMC student newspaper, wrote the following in a special edition of the student paper (March 18, 1982), 11: "Elder Ed Zackrison, Associate Professor of Religion at SMC and elected secretary of the Atlanta Affirmation meetings, gave his handwritten minutes to Dr. Grant who in turn lent the minutes to Sharon McKee, a concerned member of the Collegedale community. Soon after, a version of the minutes became public when published in *Pilgrim's Rest* [Vance Ferrell's paper].

"The published minutes have been interspersed with bracketed notes containing definitions and interpretations. Zackrison later typed official minutes and distributed these to the meetings' attendants. The official minutes differ from the publicly dispersed minutes from *Pilgrim's Rest.* Zackrison attributes this to the fact that his notes were quickly written so they could be read and typed by himself—not others who wanted to type from his notes."

the South. It was amazing where these bogus minutes were turning up when Dr. Grant had only shared them with one concerned woman in Collegedale.

As was becoming a pattern now, neither editor bothered to check the veracity of these bogus minutes with any of the scholars in attendance at Atlanta, they just took them at face value, since they no doubt confirmed their own suspicions. However, the minutes had been annotated with twisted interpretations by people who had not been in attendance but wanted to believe that this was a Fordite meeting. And then they launched into their own attacks.

The first partial letter was from *Ministry*. However, rather than being written by the editor of the journal, it was written by an associate in the GC Ministerial/Stewardship Association. Since the editor was on health leave at the time, the letter was composed by an associate. The paper had quoted only part of his letter and it was distributed liberally around the country, leaving the distinct impression that *Ministry* was a partner in the publishing enterprise of the "news" paper.

> August 19, 1981. Dear Brother: Thank you so much for your *documented* notes and papers regarding the *heresy* that has been creeping into Adventism.[17] . . . I think we already had received the minutes from the Atlanta affirmation [sic] meeting, also some interpretation of this *from Bible teachers who were sickened with what went on there.*[18]
>
> There is no doubt but that *a lasting warfare is on within Adventism regarding the theological truth of our message.*[19] Certainly we are living in the last days, and Satan is going to make every attempt to overthrow God's truth, if not one, then by another route. The kind of Evangelicalism[20] which is being promulgated will eventually destroy *the Sabbath, the state of the dead, the imminent coming of Jesus, as well as the investigative judgment, and responsible Christian living* based on *a concept of Sanctification*. It these things succeed, we might as well say that *the tithing system* could be considered legalism and the

---

17. What heresy was "creeping into Adventism" is a mystery since the Bible teachers who met in Atlanta did not deal in with doctrine, theology, or fundamental beliefs. Apparently the associate who wrote in response to the previous communication from Tennessee but without revealing what it was about. "Letter to Lee F. Greer, Jr., from W. B. Quigley" (1922–2016) August 19, 1981. Emphasis supplied. *SMC Faculty Document Committee Collection*.

18. Ibid. Emphasis supplied. The associate from the Ministerial Department had not been at the Atlanta meeting. His observation did not match what happened there. No one in attendance was "sickened with what went on there."

After accusations of subversive activities began being bandied about, SMC theology professor Norman Gulley retreated from his erstwhile enthusiastic endorsement of the Affirmation. In Atlanta he had been very vocal in expressing his disappointment with the brethren at the *Review* because one of his book manuscripts had been rejected. He was the only person during the meetings who had been reactively and proactively critical of the brethren at the *Review*. See Appendix 5, entitled, "The Atlanta Meeting."

19. This charge had nothing to do with the Atlanta meetings. No one there was discussing "our message."

20. Probably at least half of those at the Atlanta meeting would never claim the term "Evangelical."

health reform message, as you have already indicated.[21] . . . Signed, *Member of the General Conference Committee.*

The second letter, printed in the *"news" paper,* although without citing any author, was written, as we discovered later, by the editor of the *Adventist Review,* Elder Kenneth H. Wood to the same layman in Tennessee, that the associate had addressed.

> Dear Brother and Sister:
> Thank you for sending me the copy of the minutes and plans of the June 13 meeting in Atlanta. *The minutes provide clear evidence* that an organized effort is being made *to undermine the historic doctrines of the church.* Fortunately these minutes are now *in the hands of church authorities* so they will be alert to what is happening.[22]
> I appreciated your encouraging words of support for the efforts we are making to *defend the truths that God has given the Advent people.*[23]
> Your brother in Christ, Signed, *Member of the General Conference Committee.*[24]

Without knowing why or understanding what had happened, we were now walking around with a bull's eye on our backs. Life would never be the same again for any of us.

---

21. Ibid. Emphasis supplied. None of these things was discussed at this weekend retreat. The associate's rant was irrelevant to anything considered at the Atlanta meeting.

22. Elder Wood's letter was baffling to those who had attended the Atlanta meeting. A promise of support had been turned into evidence of a conspiracy to destroy the Adventist message, and apprehensions about the authoritarian leanings of Church leadership gained credibility. It couldn't have ended worse.

23. Again, this was irrelevant to the Atlanta meeting.

24. *The "news" paper,* p. 8. "Letter from Kenneth H. Wood," August 24, 1981. Emphasis supplied. *SMC Faculty Document Committee Collection.* Neither Elder Wood nor the Tennessee recipient were present at the Atlanta meetings. Nor was Elder Quigley. See below, Appendix V, "The Atlanta Affirmation," for the full text.

CHAPTER THIRTY

An Anatomy of Betrayal

> "In her zeal she would read selection after selection of her work in the assembly
> and after each reading, she would demurely say, 'The Holy Spirit gave me this poem;
> I take no credit for it of myself.' There was a widespread belief in the fellowship
> that the Holy Spirit didn't want the credit for it either."
>
> —CALVIN MILLER[1]

OPENING UP WORLD-WIDE CRITICISM OF SMC

IN 1992, THE OFFICERS of the North American Division of Seventh-day Adventists published a book entitled Issues. The book condemned groups of people who were involved in what it saw as irresponsible attacks on the Church and its institutions. Ironically, it was a good description of the kind of destructive criticism that we had suffered through ten years before.

The book described these attacks by people I call *Adventist fundamentalists*, as falling into three types: (1) Giving an exaggerated negative emphasis to conditions in the Church; (2) Seeking to undermine confidence in the ministry and denominational leadership; and (3) Bearing false witness about the Church and its leaders.[2] By the time Church leaders came to this conclusion, it was much too late to be of help to any of us. Instead we were basically left to flutter in the hostile breeze of the time. We would have welcomed the support of a book like *Issues* as we defended the Church, its teachings, and its leadership against the kind of attacks that our leaders in Washington would come to deplore in the 1990s.

---

1. Miller, *The Philippian Fragment*, (1982).
2. *Issues*, p. 15.

In the early 1980s, there was no such support available from higher ups that we could perceive. The scandal sheet that more than any other reveled in this kind of irresponsible criticism was distributed liberally all around the Southern Union Conference, even finding its way to denominational headquarters in Washington, D. C. without evoking any significant negative reaction that we were aware of.

One of the writers was reported to have been passing out the paper in front of the General Conference headquarters in Takoma Park, MD. Our homes in the Collegedale neighborhood all received the paper on our driveways. Those attending churches in the greater Chattanooga area were greeted after their worship services on Sabbath with the papers plastered on their car windshields. After Church worship service at Collegedale my two little children could be seen running around the parking lot trying to get copies of the "news" paper off the car windshields to protect their father from this venom as people filed out of the worship service on the holy Sabbath day.

My former student's editorial was entitled "Open Letter RE: SMC."[3] The letter was later printed independently of the "news" paper and sent around the world. It had even reached Thailand, where the medical director of the Bangkok Adventist Hospital wrote the SMC board chair criticizing the college for hiring such reprobate teachers, though he admitted he didn't know any of them; in fact, he didn't even know anything about the student who had written the letter.[4] He had not communicated with the administration of the college.

In his letter to the board chairman with a copy to the editor's letter, he wrote:

> It is just not fair for us to expect our good people to send their children to colleges where they are being taught material which will simply, if accepted, take them to eternal damnation.
>
> As a fellow minister of the Seventh-day Adventist Church I would earnestly pray that you will do everything in your power to see that the young people in our college in Collegedale will receive the Truth of God and not these errors which have long since been part of the fallen churches of Babylon.[5]

Why was it, I thought, that an Adventist physician half a world away, a man allegedly committed to the gospel of Jesus Christ and the Adventist Church would automatically assume that these slanderous contentions were true without having talked to any of the people involved? But he didn't quit there.

He then attacked the college and its president, Dr. Knittel.

---

3. "Open Letter RE: SMC." n.d.

4. Standish, "Letter to A. C. McClure," *Camp Meeting Special*, n.d.

5. Ibid. *SMC Faculty Document Committee Collection*. Although Dr. Standish had sent a copy of this letter to the editor he had not contacted Dr. Knittel, the president of the college, who was so prominently criticized in the letter. None of the members of the Religion faculty was contacted. The charges against Dr. Knittel were false.

> I want to say that even out here [in Thailand], thousands of miles from the United States, many of the physicians on the staff and other workers on the staff have heard very disconcerting reports about the trends in Southern Missionary College. Once this College was acknowledged as being a bulwark of Present Truth, but I must inform you that the general reputation of the College has fallen very considerably over the last few years, and this reputation has spread throughout the world field.
>
> I am afraid those who believe in the truth of God were very unimpressed when the President of the Southern Missionary College, *in defiance of the advice given by our world leader,* invited Geoffrey Paxton to the College and permitted Paxton's letter to be printed in the student paper, in which he stated that the President and he saw doctrinal matters in a very similar light. This in itself did little to enhance the reputation of the College.[6]

I had just been introduced to Dr. Russell Standish, an Australian physician who for years had been carrying on a vendetta against Dr. Desmond Ford and alleged proponents of the so-called new theology. But this would become a pattern. The letter by Dr. Standish was reprinted by the press in Ooltewah for the public to read.[7] We would also discover that the writer was a major contributor to a worldwide network of crusading Adventist fundamentalists. One of his books was advertised in the "news" paper.[8]

President Knittel answered the critical Standish letter with his take on the situation:

> I have before me your recent letter to Elder A. C. McClure and although you did not see fit to share your indictment of the college with anyone on our campus, I feel it mandatory to respond to your statement.
>
> What comes through in your letter more than anything else is your attitude that everything [the "news" paper] states is a fact, although you have not been in touch with any member of our religion department or any of our conference presidents or any of our Union office personnel or any of the General Conference personnel that have studied issues as they have related to our Seventh-day Adventist colleges and specifically Southern Missionary College.[9]

---

6. Ibid. Emphasis supplied. These accusations were false.

7. The respondent to the "news" paper had been prolific in criticizing that was like the approach of the letter. In fact, Dr. Standish (M.D.) and his brother Dr. Colin Standish (Ph.D.) had written a series of books warning about and condemning what they called the *New Adventism.* Every cult has gurus and these men functioned as gurus to Adventist fundamentalists, or cult members in the Australasian division theological battles at Avondale College. Their names would surface often. These books would later be referred to as source material for the new fundamentalist onslaught we would experience. See for example R. Standish and C. Standish, *Adventism Vindicated,* (1980). Other books by these same authors included: *Adventism Unveiled, Adventism Imperiled, Adventism Triumphant,* and *Adventism Proclaimed.* None of these books was issued from denominational publishing houses even though both men had held important positions in Adventist institutions.

8. The "news" paper, 7.

9. Knittel, "Letter to Dr. Russell Standish," October 27, 1981, 1, *SMC Faculty Document Committee*

Dr. Knittel went on to uncover untruth after untruth in the Standish letter. Then he closed with these words.

> In summary I would say that there is not the slightest suggestion in your letter that you have a sincere desire to help our college. Your letter represents assertions which you have not tested and you draw unwarranted conclusions. Frankly, your letter bristles with hostility. It would concern me if my reputation were such that many thousands of miles away from a college I should be the funnel to which anti-church garbage is sent, especially if, rather than looking at its true nature, I were to repackage it and send it on. There is not one statement in your letter which embodies the pure, the kind, the true or that which is of good report. I can only wonder at your preoccupation with the unlovely.[10]

HOME GROWN "PROFESSIONALS"

Professional printing is the product of fine craftsmanship. Adventists in North America have always been on the cutting edge of professionalism when it comes to producing quality books, impressive magazines and attractive pamphlets. Because of this, most Adventists reading the "news" paper could immediately sense the lack of professionalism, the sub-quality of layout and the amateurish writing.

The printing was so bad that one could hardly attribute this product to anyone but the proverbial crackpot or to use the evocative GC phrase from the 1950s, "the lunatic fringe" of the Church. Who could possibly take seriously anything appearing in this smear sheet? Nevertheless, the "news" paper became just the first of several subsequent attack sheets, all printed at the same press outside of Collegedale and distributed "as the leaves of autumn."

Both my parents were printers, copy editors, artists and proofreaders who worked in official Adventist publishing establishments most of their lives. I did not have to guess what they would have said if I brought this "news" paper to them to be approved for publication. What gave these papers credibility was apparently the support their writers claimed they were getting from members of Church leadership.

The editor of the "news" paper listed the "heretics" teaching at Southern Missionary College: Elder Ott, Elder Zackrison, Dr. Bennett, Dr. Grant, and Elder Springett, all ordained Seventh-day Adventist ministers.[11] He began his letter with a blanket

---

Collection.

10. Ibid., 2. The charge about Dr. Paxton was just one of the many untruths in this Standish letter. Not only had Dr. Knittel not invited Dr. Paxton to speak on campus "in defiance" of the General Conference "edicts," Standish had even misquoted Dr. Paxton's statement who had actually said, "I wish to thank your president, Dr. Frank Knittel, for treating me as a Christian brother and giving me the obvious indication that he is a servant of the truth."

11. Though not an ordained SDA minister, Dr. Melvin Campbell, former chair of the SMC

condemnation of the SMC Religion Department because it was clearly "doing things their way instead of God's way."[12]

The SMC Religion Department, he claimed, taught students "not to worry about law, judgment, punishment, or the life after."[13] None of that was true, as any of our thought-functioning students could have told him. Furthermore, he claimed that these heretics taught a "new form of righteousness by faith which downplayed the work of the indwelling Holy Spirit, limited God's changing of our character and encouraged the belief that by believing on the cross, and accepting that I am saved, is everything necessary for salvation."[14] This was heresy, he claimed.

These charges were a mix of paranoia and perfectionism. Over the years, there had been individuals with perfectionist tendencies in the Adventist Church, but perfectionism was not and never had been official Adventist doctrine. In his attack on me, the editor brought up a topic that had been of no concern to him when he took my *Righteousness by Faith* course—or when he would drop by my office after class to promote his off-beat theology. As far as I could tell, he had appreciated the class and his mother had confirmed it with her generous gift of the theological encyclopedia.

It was clear that these denunciations were not based on his experience in our classes. It seemed likely that this was a committee job. But why? And who was orchestrating this? Those were the puzzling questions. I reminded myself that every cult member has a cult leader guiding him. Cult leader, or *shaman*[15] or perhaps, a *guru*.[16] Cults have many of the same characteristics, regardless of religion.

THE CHURCH ENTERS INTO DEEPER INTRIGUE

Was someone else, someone with more credibility than this student, organizing this onslaught? How else could such a poorly designed, sadly written newsletter receive a

---

Chemistry Department and later SMC dean of students, was a member of the Department of Education who contracted freshman Bible classes for the Religion Department. He too was often cited as a faculty member who "had to go."

12. "Open Letter RE: SMC," pp. 1–2.

13. Ibid., 1.

14. Ibid.

15. In the common use of the term, a *shaman* is "a person regarded as having access to, and influence in, the world of good and evil spirits, especially among some peoples of Northern Asia and North America. Typically, such people enter a trance state during a ritual, and practice divination and healing." *Oxford Dictionary Online.*

16. *Guru* is another eastern term indicating "someone who is a teacher, guide or master of certain knowledge. In pan-Indian traditions, *guru* is someone more than a teacher, traditionally a reverential figure to the student, with the *guru* serving as a 'counselor, who helps mold values, shares experiential knowledge as much as literal knowledge, an exemplar in life, an inspirational source and who helps in the spiritual evolution of a student.' The term also refers to someone who primarily is one's spiritual guide, who helps one to discover the same potentialities that the *guru* has already realized." *Wikipedia, the* [Internet] *Free Encyclopedia.*

serious hearing? Many of us wondered if these "students" were merely stooges and stalking horses used by powerful people who wanted their involvement kept secret. The big question was the financing; who was paying for all this?

The "news" paper implied that it enjoyed the support of *Ministry* and *Adventist Review*. Could that really be possible? Were these the problems Elder Francis had foreseen and warned me about? The "news" paper claimed to be a student publication, but clearly it was not. Four of the writers, who had been students, were no longer enrolled at SMC. The other contributors had not been students in the time leading up to the "news" paper. Only one of them wrote about Southern Missionary College.

The contributors were a certain Elder May from Texas, who wrote about something taking place in Australia; then there was Florence Woolcock from New Jersey, who had been spying on the religion faculty (she will be properly introduced in the next chapter).[17] Next there was David Lin from China, whose article had nothing to do with SMC, and a contribution from an anonymous "Conference pastor," who was so concerned that he wouldn't sign his name to fifteen paragraphs of attacks and misrepresentations of a report delivered by President Knittel at the summer SMC faculty meeting.[18]

Better known was Vance Ferrell from Illinois, a professional Church critic and gossip columnist. He had now found it opportune to join the "students" who created the "news" paper.[19] As I came to understand his role better, it became apparent that this may have been a way to keep his critical press running and collecting contributions from the disgruntled.[20] What role he played in the Collegedale situation was unknown to me. A reputable journalist would have interviewed those he was quoting second and third hand.

In my opinion, a faithful Adventist would have defended the Church's educational institutions. Instead, I was beginning to see reams of material being produced on every conceivable detail of "history" in the Adventist Church that could be criticized.

---

17. "Letter to Florence Woolcock from President Frank Knittel," March 5, 1981: "The only condition under which we would give you permission to attend classes at Southern Missionary College would be that you formally enroll as a student. . . . Until then we are asking you to refrain from attending any classes at Southern Missionary College." *SMC Faculty Document Committee Collection.*

18. In fifteen paragraphs this "pastor" referred to the apostates, and subversives on the SMC Religion faculty seventeen times. To read the speech this pastor was referring to see Appendix 4 below.

19. "Atlanta the Affirmation and the Minutes," The "news" paper, 4, 5.

20. A commercial note for Vance Ferrell appears at the top of Ibid. 3: "Information you need—from Pilgrim's Rest—Information [sic] to help you prepare for the theology crisis that is enveloping us—A crisis whether we will stay with the Bible and the Spirit of Prophecy—or choose instead the thinking of learned men." None of these were issues discussed at the Atlanta meeting. Also, this was not the only commercial published in the "news" paper for Vance Ferrell and his fundamentalist criticism. None of us understood why he had moved in to straighten out SMC. We were never aware of his connection there. But then, none of us was a *politician*.

SMC BEGINS LOSING NEW CONVERTS BECAUSE OF FUNDAMENTALISTS

Ever since Sister White's dream of the Adventist ship successfully ramming the iceberg of heresy, fundamentalists in the Church had taken this as a mandate to attack what they perceived as heresies and apostasies. The context in which she used the metaphor on ramming the iceberg of heresy was the conflict with Dr. John Harvey Kellogg, who, according to her, was promoting pantheism in his book, *The Living Temple,* and she called it "the alpha of deadly heresies."

> [This heresy] is not to be met by our taking our working forces from the field to investigate doctrines and points of difference. We have no such investigation to make. In the book *Living Temple* there is presented the alpha of deadly heresies.[21] The omega will follow, and will be received by those who are not willing to heed the warning God has given.[22]

The omega to follow was left dangling, and to future generations of Adventist fundamentalists it came to indicate anything that they saw as a challenge to their own understanding of the Church's message. In the past the Church had used strong measures to stop members who, on their own initiative, had usurped the role of fighting heresy, but that was no longer the case, as far as we could see.

Some of these students who had climbed up on the barricades to fight against SMC claimed that they had been promised jobs in the Adventist Church system in return for signing up as whistleblowers. Some recent converts to Adventism claimed to have been recruited by individuals in the community, who wanted them to get "something" on their professors in the Religion Department, as they put it.

As new converts, these young men had a limited understanding of Adventist history and theology and they were vulnerable to the overtures of important people who sought to recruit them in the name of The Truth, to spy on their professors. But how could anyone guarantee them Church positions without their finishing college? Was this a clue of what was really going on? Providing positions and security meant money, a lot of money, and following the money trail wasn't much of a stretch. It may have also implied that denominational workers and organizational entities were involved.

We had never witnessed anything like this. The board member who allegedly put up the money to secure jobs for the crusading students and to get most of the professors in the Religion Department fired was theologically unsophisticated and needed help from someone with a higher theological credibility than he had to formulate a case against the department. Simple money campaigns could not do the job alone. This was cast as a righteous campaign. This must be an operation where the donor thought he was instrumental in stamping out the Omega apostasy. That would make

---

21. This book *The Living Temple* is available online.
22. White, *Selected Messages,* 1:200.

the expenditure worthwhile for it would "hasten" the *Parousia*. At this point we did not realize that one of our own was that person.

Dr. Knittel was supportive of the Religion Department. He was theologically qualified, and he knew the caliber of the faculty he had hired in the department. He was authorized by the board and his position to carry out the duties that faced him. He dealt with the students as any student personnel authority would. He brought some of them up for discipline; others could move on and they spread their vitriol wherever people would listen. As had been claimed, some were even hired by Conferences as workers, even without the required academic qualifications.[23]

There was nothing simple about what was developing. Some students were just pawns who were pushed aside once their usefulness had come to an end. Several new converts with great promise, serious and talented young men who had moved their families to Happy Valley, ended up turning their backs on the SDA Church because of what was happening. I did not follow up on all of them, but I knew of at least four who became ministers in other denominations because of this fundamentalist uprising against the Church, its administration and its faculty.

The only students who got low grades in our classes were those who did not come to class, did not take quizzes, did not turn in homework, or did not take examinations, not students who argued with us. But according to "anonymous but concerned" in the "news" paper that was not so.

> In this press release we have published several letters written by students which are critical of the apostate teaching of S.M.C. *We are sure that we could multiply these letters 100 fold if so many students would not fear reprisals in the way of lowered grades, failures to get a good recommendation and indeed in some instances even being expelled for insubordination* for protesting against apostate teaching that would destroy their faith.[24]

23. Dr. Gladson relates an experience of a freshman student who was critical of the SMC Religion Department secretly recording a session of our staff meeting with a hidden wire. Upon leaving SMC he was hired by a Conference (whose president was also critical of the SMC Religion Department) after less than one year of college. He was hired as a pastor. See Gladson, *A Theologian's Journey from Seventh-day Adventism to Mainstream Christianity*, 185-186. Other such experiences could be cited including a student who took two classes at SMC and then was hired by the General Conference to important editorial positions, after meeting before the College board to express his criticisms against the Religion Department.

24. "Response to Dr. Knittel's Faculty Colloquiem [sic] Statement Held Aug. 19, 1981," the "news" paper, 6. Emphasis supplied. Curiously such an attack on professors at the college also reflected negatively on the character of students who were pictured as willing to sacrifice their integrity to get an acceptable grade or receive a good recommendation. There is a hyperbolic element to this accusation. Did the writer mean he could find 100% of our students who lied to get through class? Or did this mean the writer could find four other students ("100 fold") who would testify in kind?

As a matter of fact, I was asked by the graduating class of 1984 to be their class sponsor. And I have student evaluations of my classes. As a college professor I did not share this low view of character attributed to SMC students. A typical student evaluation was one from a person who was in my *Studies in Revelation*: "Dear Elder Zackrison: Your systematic presentation of this class has given me a solid foundation on which to base my faith—Thanks for this excellent semester, and an impartial and

The charges were baseless, as any review of student grades would have shown, but facts were of no concern to these crusaders for "truth."

THE COLLEGE UNDER ATTACK BY FOLK RELIGION

Rumors were circulating about money. The most repeated rumor we heard was that when Grant, Zackrison, Gladson and sometimes Campbell were gone the college would receive a check for one million dollars. Or the money would be put up to encourage the college to pay for their departure. Those reported funds surely were not coming from any of these four former students writing for the "news" paper.

Elder Tom Mostert, president of the Southeastern California Conference, a classmate of mine from Andrews University, called one day to invite me to enter pastoral work in his Conference. He had met with his Conference committee and they were anxious to hire me, he said. He told me I was in trouble in the South and he told me who was behind the campaign against the SMC Religion Department and who had put up the money that the rumors had referred to.[25]

The "news" paper had spelled out the heresies of the various religion professors: Elder Zackrison did not believe in the indwelling of the Holy Spirit (not true); Elder Ott did not believe Christ is our example (not true) and he did not believe that Christ's character could be reproduced in us before the second coming (this was convoluted and needed explanation—Dr. Ott was not a perfectionist); Dr. Grant did not believe there was a Sanctuary in heaven, (not true), he taught situation ethics, (not true), and he used *Evangelica* magazine as the source for his lectures (not true). Theologically, it all came down to sinless perfectionism, a dogma they promoted, with no sense of irony, through a campaign of unethical behavior and outright lies.

The "editor" maintained that all the SMC religion teachers taught that it was impossible to keep the moral law perfectly (that was true, and that was orthodox Adventist doctrine) and he claimed that none of the teachers had been able to show him that the Sabbath was even important (not clear where that accusation came from). It was charged that Dr. Campbell had mocked Sister White in his *Philosophy of Christian Education* class, something Dr. Campbell denied doing. Finally, teachers at SMC had made it clear to the "editor" that he did not have the right to interpret quotes from Sister White—only they did (not true). Furthermore, none of the professors was said to believe in the first angel's message, (not true).[26]

---

coherent approach to a difficult book [Revelation]." *SMC Faculty Document Committee Collection.* Such an evaluation from my students was not rare.

25. When Annie shared this information with Dr. Wagner, the new president at SMC, I was suddenly no longer wanted by Elder Mostert or his Conference committee. He had been embarrassed by her sharing of this information and he denied that he had said it and he claimed that I was lying. That was not true.

26. The "news" paper, 2.

Perhaps the most commonly circulated story was that of the teacher in the SMC Religion Department who had made it clear to his classes that he was a "Ford man—and proud of it." Like so many other charges directed at the religion professors, it was based on a misrepresentation.

A physician in Happy Valley with a reputation for extremism—he had been involved with exorcism, magnetic healing, John Todd conspiracy tapes, John Birch Society literature and the off-beat cancer cure, Laetrile,[27]—not surprisingly got involved with the local vigilantes who were attacking the SMC Religion Department. He wrote to me:

> At least one teacher, *we have heard*, openly says he's a Ford man and proud of it. This is frightening, considering the position he is in to influence students, faculty, and laity. Dr. Ford is no longer an Adventist minister due to his non-Adventist beliefs. Therefore to *proudly admire*[28] his theology at an Adventist college is blatantly wrong.[29]

Dr. Grant had been asked by a student if he agreed with Dr. Ford? Dr. Grant had answered, "Dr. Ford believes in God. If you are asking, do I believe in God? Then yes, *I believe in God. I am a Ford man and proud of it.*" Only someone out to get Dr. Grant could have made anything of that.

Later Dr. Grant was said to be chewing tobacco in class. He was chewing pink bubble gum. It seemed as if the community had been gripped by hysteria. In a letter to Dr. Grant, the same physician identified the "new theology" as the theology of Robert Brinsmead and Dr. Desmond Ford.[30] Even this was imprecise since no person's theology is ever all wrong or all right. Was this referring to the old perfectionistic Brinsmead, which was condemned by the General Conference in the 1960s? or the new Protestant Reformation Brinsmead?

In closing his letter, the doctor revealed how uninformed he was with respect to the nature and purpose of theology. He wrote to Dr. Grant,

> Your comparison of being an expert in medicine and and [sic] expert in theology surprised me. There is simply no way you can compare the two. In special fields of study such as medicine, or any other profession, one can become extremely proficient through study and hard work. But, as you should know, *in the field of theology this isn't necessarily so.*

---

27. *SMC Faculty Document Committee Collection.*

28. Without the context one could only guess that this was said with proud admiration. In its context the teacher said he was simply stating a fact in the setting of the question the student had asked.

29. "Letter to Edwin Zackrison from Harold M. Cherne, MD" (1926–2016), July 27, 1981. Emphasis supplied. *SMC Faculty Document Committee Collection.*

30. "Letter to Lorenzo H. Grant, PhD [sic] from Harold M. Cherne, MD," March 9, 1981, 1. *SMC Faculty Document Committee Collection.*

> The Holy Spirit has to reveal God to us as He sees fit and as we're obedient. It is not so much the effort exerted but the willingness to receive Truth and be submissive to it that qualifies one to know God.
>
> *You may submit your life to a doctor, but I would never submit my salvation to a theologian.*[31] Wasn't it the theologians in Jesus' day that gave Him so much trouble and with whom God couldn't do very much either with or for? Wasn't it the humble but willing fishermen, the tax collectors, the prostitutes that God finally had to use? Is there a lesson here for us today? Being an expert in theology may actually be a stumbling block to salvation.[32]

This letter reflects the arrogance that proponents of folk religion often demonstrate when confronted by scholarship. Adventists do not believe in righteousness by knowledge. Theology has to do with knowledge. Since he was not a theologian this physician built up his own credibility by revealing that he had read Brinsmead's book, *Judged by the Gospel*,[33] and listened to Dr. Ford's tapes.

He also stated that he had read *Present Truth* and *Verdict* (Brinsmead periodicals) and had talked to Dr. Molleurus Couperus, "the founder of *Spectrum*." What the physician did not tell in his letter was that he had also been reading a lot of the Australian Standish brothers' works. He uses terms from them that he presents as his own. It was apparent that it was their theological agenda he was promoting.

Theology is not about feelings, which is the main appeal of folk religion, (and folk religion is rarely qualified to do precise theology). When the untrained venture into this complicated field, they often end up in a "fist fight" over pet theories and a deep conviction that those who disagree with them are enemies of decency and truth. If theology were a matter of the heart, there would probably be no place for theologians in a Church.

> Theology is thinking as carefully and comprehensively as possible about the content, basis, and significance of one's religious faith.[34]

Theology is a cognitive exercise to express faith in words. But theology is not faith. Trained theologians do not ask anyone to submit his salvation to theology for salvation. That misses the point. If medicine were guided by feeling, one would risk being suckered into every crackpot cure a "medicine man" brought to town. The same

---

31. Here the physician reveals his naïveté regarding theology as a cognitive exercise and rational discipline. He confuses religion with theology. This statement is called in critical thinking, a *non-sequitur*, a logical fallacy.

32. "Letter to Lorenzo Grant from Harold M. Cherne, MD," March 9, 1981, 2. Emphasis supplied. *SMC Faculty Document Committee Collection.* It is arguably possible that the same could be said of "folk medicine." Of course, the context does not talk about the Jewish accusers as theologians. The texts condemn them in their political perversions.

33. Brinsmead, *Judged by the Gospel: A Review of Adventism*, (1980).

34. Definition of theology is from Dr. Fritz Guy, Professor of Theology, Andrews University SDA Theological Seminary.

goes for folk religion, which is very vulnerable to crackpots, cult leaders, and fanatics because if tends to disparage objective norms of thinking about religion in favor of affective standards.[35]

The nature of these accusations should have been enough to discredit them. But there were plenty more to come. The effect this controversy was having on students was serious. Many were both troubled and confused. I looked around the campus, at faculty members who were taking sides, of new SDA students who were thoroughly dismayed. This was no longer a place that made a religious man feel at home.

THE COMMUNITY JOINS THE ATTACK

At the height of all these discussions, a layman, who was a member of the SMC board, ran into me in the parking lot of a local barbershop in Chattanooga on a Friday afternoon. He said he wanted to talk to me about the SMC Religion Department.

He began the conversation by stating that he was not comfortable with the direction the Religion Department was going. When I asked him what direction that was, he answered, "the wrong direction." And I asked him to define what he meant by "the wrong direction." His answer: "the direction it's going." End of conversation. That was *circular reasoning.* He had bought into something he had heard but he didn't know what that meant.

People would come up to me and ask about all these student reports about the Religion Department. Of course, there were no "*all* these students." At most there were three or four former students involved with the "news" paper, but we found it hard to believe that this was the work of students, especially these students. We had students who were at the top of their game. We had students who would go on to become college professors, Conference presidents and pastors of large university churches. None of the "former" students writing for the "news" paper appeared to be headed for any of those places.

Meanwhile, the editor assumed the role of protector of truth for the whole Church, closing his letter with an edict directed to his readers, "I am asking you not to go to this school, not because I don't want you to see the other side, you will, but to go here to be taught, is *like placing yourself in Satans* [sic] *hands.*"[36] And he concluded with a sulfurous quote from Sister White,

> I saw a very large company professing the name of Christ, but God did not recognize them as His. He had no pleasure in them. Satan seemed to assume a religious character and was very willing that the people should think they were christians [sic].[37] He was even anxious that they should believe in Jesus,

---

35. *Author's note:* I recommend that this would be a good time to re-read Chapter 27 ("A Tapestry of Subtle Shifts") above before proceeding any further.

36. The "news" paper. Emphasis supplied.

37. The editor added a footnote here: "as found in *Evangelica* magazine as its purpose."

His crucifixion, and His resurrection. Satan and his angels fully believe all this themselves, and tremble. But if this faith does not provoke to good works, and lead those who profess it to imitate the self-denying life of Christ, Satan is not disturbed: for they merely assume the christian [sic] name, while their hearts are still carnal, and he can use them in his service better than if they made no profession.[38]

INVASION FROM WITHIN

I wondered what had happened to my student. What had turned him into a crusading fanatic? When he was in my class, he was obsessed with the idea that God was a flawed deity, but he had not appeared militant. Now he was on a crusade.[39] I knew that these people, who now included the "editor's" parents, had not come up with this on their own. In fact, when the *Southern Accent* contacted his father for clarification after he had accused professors Grant and Zackrison of teaching heresy, he had hung up on the reporter.

> [The editor's] parents, said [his] main purpose in publishing his letter accusing the Religion Department was to warn those students who were fresh in the truth "that if they were coming here to be further grounded, they were coming to the wrong place." . . In the face of further questioning, [his father] hung up on the interviewer.[40]

We began at this time to pay attention to the fact that Elder Francis, a retired member of our department would always be surrounded by a group of students when he ate in the cafeteria. Nothing wrong with that of course, but there was something about it that made us wonder if it might have anything to do with what was going on.

I was reminded of how argumentative he had been in Seminary. Always arguing. Always keeping the class he was taking in turmoil. Always gracious. Always smiling. Always cordial. As one of my students told me, "Elder Francis once told me that Dr. Heppenstall had a mind like a steel trap. Although said admiringly, he implicitly admitted to me that he never came around to agreeing with him. I was astounded that Dr. Heppenstall always seemed to get the better of him!"

It turned out that our intuition was right. One of our own was working to bring us down. Dr. Gladson put it this way:

> All this might not have been so onerous had it not become apparent that someone on the religion faculty was strongly encouraging our critics. As Absalom undermined his own father, King David, by sympathizing with the

---

38. White, *Early Writings*, 227.
39. Reports of bizarre behavior continued to surface to add perspective to the new phenomena.
40. *Southern Accent,* March 18, 1982.

> disgruntled subjects of the realm (2 Sam. 15:1–6), Robert ("Bob") Francis, who had provoked the scene at the university church over my sermon on justification, held "court" daily in the university cafeteria. Around him gathered students, faculty, and people from the community, anyone who wanted to listen to his witty, sarcastic criticisms of the religion department.
>
> An office worker claimed Francis visited a wealthy board member almost every day to discuss the university's situation. Undoubtedly, Francis was the principal source of this board member's strong opposition to the religion department. So we had our enemies in the department as well as outside.[41]

I was puzzled. Why, I wondered, had Elder Francis reached out to me to warn me about problems in Happy Valley and counseled me on how to steer clear of them if he was trying to take us down? It seemed that his campaign against Elder Patterson had now spread to include the whole Religion Department where he had once been so popular. He had long supported the idea that Christians, with God's help, could reach a state of sinless perfection, but that still did not explain why he chose to betray his former colleagues.

---

41. Gladson, *A Theologian's Journey*, 184–185.

CHAPTER THIRTY-ONE

Background of the Collegedale Purge

"I've learned one thing—people who know the least anyways seem to know it the loudest."
—ANDY CAPP

THE COLLEGEDALE PURGE HAD BEGUN

What would later be called "the Collegedale Purge" had begun. The conflict was reaching its climax. One day I noticed that my top student had not attended my *Teachings of Jesus* class for a week. I was worried that he might be sick but then I saw him in the hall and called him in to my office. He was a diligent student—a new convert to Adventism, who had been a pastor in another denomination up until just nine months before. One of our graduates who was a pastor in his area of Georgia had run into him. Bible studies followed, and he was baptized. He had been energetic and conscientious in my class, a very clear thinker, and then he was gone. Where? Why?

"Have you been sick?" I asked him.

"No," he replied.

"What's going on? I've missed you in class, is there anything I can help you with?"

He paused, hung his head, and started sobbing. I didn't know what was up, but he was clearly conflicted. Finally, he confessed: "I stopped coming to your class because I was told you were a heretic and that your lectures were apostate. I couldn't keep coming to class because I couldn't figure out what was heretical about your teaching. No matter how hard I tried I couldn't detect any untruth. I had to believe you were too subtle for me. And it scared me. So, in my confusion I quit coming to your class."

What to say? He was being transparently honest. I was speechless.

"Can you share where you heard all this?" I asked.

He continued, "I have been attending 'secret' meetings in the community. They are held by an influential person in this city and he has supplied a voice-activated tape recorder to all who wanted one, so we can go to religion classes wearing a wire. . . . I am so mixed up. I have only been an Adventist for a few months, and I was so excited about coming here and planning to qualify to be a pastor in this denomination."

He finished by affirming that this was now off his chest and he would be back in class. He apologized that he had been so unfair. Later he wrote and sent a revealing letter to the board member he claimed was holding the meetings and supplying the equipment. And he sent me a copy.

The letter was transparent. He gave his conversion background to Adventism and how much he had looking forward to coming to school at SMC. He confessed that he had been brought into the Church by love and revealed that he wasn't seeing much love reflected right now. He quoted Jude 18 and 19 about the scoffers coming into the Church who follow ungodly desires—that they would divide the Church. He appealed personally to return to the Bible and life of Jesus. He closed by assuring that he supported Dr. Patterson and Dr. Knittel. And he supported the Religion Department that had done nothing but lead him in a closer walk with Christ.[1]

Bizarre stories poured in as time moved on. Dr. Gladson was accused of not believing in the Sabbath because two of his students had been talking together about what they had done over the previous weekend. They had been playing Frisbee at the park on Sabbath afternoon. Dr. Gladson had just come into class and was getting his notes together at the lectern. He testified later that he had not heard the conversation going on between the two students. When he was later summoned to Atlanta to meet before an investigation committee made up of Southern Union Conference officers who were checking out the stories about the apostasy in the SMC Religion Department and the alleged un-Adventist behavior of the SMC Religion faculty, he really had no idea why he was there.

They told him about the conversation he was supposed to have overheard and that it was his duty to condemn the throwing of a Frisbee on Sabbath. He was stunned. But he was told it was his duty to correct such behavior knowing they were breaking the Sabbath. Throwing a Frisbee on Sabbath was breaking the Sabbath, according to this committee. Since Dr. Gladson had not corrected these students, he had demonstrated that he did not believe in the sacredness of the Sabbath. He also admitted he hadn't overheard the conversation.

---

1. *Appendix. Zackrison/Southern College*, n.d., 28. This young man later graduated from SMC, but eventually went back to his former denomination where he had been a pastor. Another former non-SDA pastor and classmate also returned to work in his old denomination because of the behavior he had seen during this time. These two students became collateral damage of the Collegedale Purge. They had both been outstanding students. See Zackrison, "Why I Became a Seventh-day Adventist— An Interview with a former United Methodist Minister," *These Times*, Special Issue, 1981, 19–21.

Annie and I were called into the president's office on the charge that we took our children to X-rated movies.[2] How does one respond to a charge no intelligent person could possibly believe? Annie wrote to the source of the story, the board chairman, telling him that such a charge was ludicrous. First, our family didn't attend movies at all, and second, how would you get children (ages 11 and 13) into an X-rated movie?[3]

I read about myself in the *Southern Accent*: [A writer in the "news" paper] said that I had sent a Roman Catholic to spy on him, and that the Catholic brought in a priest to hold Mass for some college students in his room in the dormitory.[4]

One story was more outlandish than the last. One of the most unbelievable was a story a student shared, a story so serious that I thought it should be shared with the administration. The student came to my office to tell me that all the SMC Religion teachers were being recorded by the voice activated recorders being supplied by a wealthy layman in Collegedale. The layman was a member of the SMC board, he told me.

Not only were these recorders secretly at work in classes, but students had been making appointments with teachers to share personal problems and they were recording their conversations in their offices without the teachers' knowledge. One student even made an appointment with the SMC Religion Department to attend a staff meeting so that he could ask pointed questions, posing as a supportive student hoping to be of help to us.[5]

But a new story was more alarming. All the students attending these secret meetings had brought their cassette tapes with the "damning evidence" and the tapes had been collected and placed in a box. I told the administration that I knew this sounded extreme, but I was just sharing what a student told me. Other than his story I had no evidence that this had happened.

When the group met on campus and the box was full, the decision was made, he said, to give this box of tape recordings to a man from the General Conference, who was visiting on our campus, and was on his way back to Washington, D.C. The box was to be hand-delivered to the GC president and the fate of the whole SMC Religion Department would finally be sealed, so his story went. Based on these tapes, the college administration would finally clean things up by firing all the heretical teachers. And so, as the story went, the box of "damning tapes" was given to the GC man for transportation to D.C.

On his way to Washington with the tapes, the GC man first had to go to an appointment in Nashville. On his way to Nashville, he was killed in a tragic car crash. Upon hearing of this tragedy, according to this student, the leaders of the Collegedale

---

2. Ibid., 301. "Letter from Dr. Frank Knittel to the Zackrisons," August 3, 1982. *SMC Faculty Document Committee Collection.*

3. Ibid., 302.

4. *Southern Accent,* March 18, 1982, 8.

5. Gladson, *A Theologian's Journey,* 185–187.

cabal appointed someone to go to find the wrecked car and retrieve the box of tapes. Someone else would deliver the box to the GC president.

According to the story, the student appointed to do so found the wrecked car and did a thorough search of the vehicle for the tapes, but the box of tapes was missing. Then the charge was further enhanced: a member or members of the SMC Religion Department had allegedly caused the accident and confiscated the tapes to save their jobs.

When I had told the administrators what I had heard, I repeated that I could not verify the story in any of its details and only shared what a student had told me, thinking it might be of interest to them. I thought it sounded crazy, but if true it was a serious charge. One of the administrators then broke in and said that he could verify that this story was true. He said that the GC man had come by to talk to him before he left for D.C. He laid the box of tapes on his desk and asked what he was supposed to do with this?

He then finished the story. He said the GC man had pushed the box across his desk and said—"These are yours; you deal with them." And he left. The next thing he heard was the man had died in an automobile accident. Then I asked the administrator if he listened to the tapes? Long pause . . . Did he take the tapes? What happened to them? What was on the tapes? He said he hadn't listened to them. He admitted that he had taken them home and he threw them in his fireplace. They kept his house warm for an evening.

The stories being circulated were bizarre, but people passed them on. The excitement in Happy Valley was electric—"What's the buzz? . . . Tell me what's happening!"[6]

Anyone who had lived through the *Questions on Doctrine* controversy, the authority and existentialism controversy at the Seminary, the Brinsmead agitation, the Andreasen attack on the Church, and the alleged Omega apostasy, which all fed into the current controversies, could not help but feel that we were reliving parallel history from the last forty years.

Through all of this I had two young children in my home to teach to love the Lord, preserve my marriage, care about my credibility in the face of the untruths and distortions hurled at me daily by people claiming to love The Truth. Through it all, I wanted my children to respect the Church and its leaders.

One evening as I was tucking my daughter in bed after our stories and prayers, she began to tear up. When I asked her what was wrong, she said her teacher at school had told the class that day, they needed to pray for Jill's father. She said he no longer believed in Sister White and would probably not be saved.

Things are getting worse when they involve your children.

---

6. *Jesus Christ, Superstar.*

BACKGROUND OF THE COLLEGEDALE PURGE

VOICES FROM THE PAST SPEAK

In this setting, I was also supposed to research and write a doctoral dissertation and remain silent as one story more incredible circulated in the community at large. We couldn't predict what story would be concocted and spread next or what effect it would have. But in Happy Valley it seemed that basically any story could be believed, unless it was something positive about the Religion teachers.

I listened carefully in staff meetings, as the recording secretary of the department, to things that were developing in the Church at large. We all knew that at the end of 1979 Dr. Desmond Ford had shaken people up at a Forum meeting at Pacific Union College, where he was a visiting lecturer. Adventist Forum meetings were devoted to thorny issues related to science, history, religion and dogma where answers to existing problems were discussed in an open-ended manner. These meetings were often seen as a threat to SDA orthodoxy by Adventist leadership, because they often dealt with issues not openly discussed in official Church publications.

No matter what suggestions the scholars made, fundamentalists tended to see them as nothing more than criticism of the denomination and its leaders. Most of the meetings of the local Forum chapters stirred up little actual controversy, but the PUC Forum meeting in 1979 was a shot heard around the world because the Sanctuary Doctrine that Dr. Ford examined on that occasion was sacrosanct.

This even made the study of the Sanctuary in a college class risky. Still students were there to learn, and a college class was supposed to be a safe place to probe into difficult subject matter. To forestall being misunderstood, a professor had to insist that the students taking the class attend regularly and be serious about their studies. Plus, there was always research homework and essays connected to college class sessions.

I had always encouraged my students to bring their recorders to class and record the class sessions so they could delve into the issues as they prepared for quizzes and tests. Many had problems taking notes, and I thought that perhaps this would help their recall. All lectures were given in a specific context, and with controversial subjects this context was very important. In my classes students were required to turn in their notebook as a final assignment for the class.

Underlining this very point, President Knittel had written the following to a crusading woman from the community, who had been spasmodically (and secretly) attending classes without taking them for credit (or paying tuition for them). He wrote,

> A number of teachers have reported to me that you are attending various classes at Southern Missionary College, and we are asking you to discontinue this as a non-student does not have the prerogative of putting teachers on the spot by asking if it is permissible to attend their classes. This is especially true in religion classes in which material is presented in sequence, and people who attend irregularly and who are not forced to study for the classes tend to pick

up disconnected material. This is particularly true in the case of people who tend to be over critical.[7]

Dr. Ford had been chair of the Theology Department at Avondale College in Australia for many years before coming to PUC as a visiting professor. His temporary appointment at PUC was largely because his evangelical preaching had shaken people up in the Australasian division, his home constituency. Those who followed theological debates within the SDA Church were aware that Avondale had been the site of the original Brinsmead agitation. What was known as the old Brinsmead movement gave encouragement to the movement I have called in this book "Adventist fundamentalism."

Two decades had passed since the controversy over *Questions on Doctrine*. I figured that controversy was dead; but I was wrong. The dispute was re-emerging from the shadows where it had been hiding. I was involved in pastoral and scholarly work in Adventism during this whole period and I had not heard anything that undercut the Church's hard work in the 1950s to explain our theological positions to some of our keenest critics.

These critics did not end up agreeing with our unique Adventist positions, but they did recognize that Adventist theology, overall, was based on serious and honest biblical research, and I thought that was something to hold on to. The non-Adventist examiners did not agree with Elder Andreasen's contention that Adventists had made theological changes in their thinking. As far as they were concerned, Church representatives had merely explained the true nature of many Adventist theological positions.

What made the Sanctuary Doctrine so difficult to deal with—and hence so controversial—was that Sister White had set it forth as a pillar of Adventist faith and warned prophetically about end time attacks on this doctrine by people led by Satan. These warnings closed the field to any serious, let alone critical, study of the topic. For this reason, I couldn't find much scholarly treatment of the Sanctuary Doctrine by Adventist scholars after I left Seminary.

A long line of Adventist Bible students and scholars had paid a high price for questioning the church's Sanctuary Doctrine. The most prominent of these were O. R. L. Crosier (the original architect of the doctrine), D. M. Canright, E. J. Waggoner, A. F. Ballenger, E. Ballenger, W. W. Fletcher, L. R. Conradi, W. W. Prescott, L. E. Froom, R. D. Brinsmead, R. A. Cottrell, E. Hilgert.[8] And now the Church's orthodoxy was threatened by a well-known, loyal Australian theologian, Dr. Desmond Ford.

Dr. Ford was an Adventist theologian who held two earned PhD degrees—one in speech and rhetoric from Michigan State University and the other in New Testament from University of Manchester in England. He was a dynamic, charismatic speaker, a prolific researcher and an appreciated, careful Bible student. He had authored scholarly

---

7. "Letter from Frank Knittel to Mrs. Florence Woolcock," March 5, 1981. *SMC Faculty Document Committee Collection*.

8. For a brief history of these and other theologians in this parade of tragedies see, Ford, *Daniel 8:14, The Day of Atonement, and the Investigative Judgment*, 25–72.

books and written articles for the Adventist press, and was a firm defender of the faith. That was certainly how those of us who read his monthly articles in *Ministry* saw him.

Dr. Ford had studied under competent professors, including Drs. Edward Heppenstall and F. F. Bruce, both highly respected conservative biblical scholars. He was fearlessly honest in his attempt to demonstrate that Adventist doctrines were to be biblically accurate and defensible.

Dr. Ford was a scholar's scholar. That didn't mean every Church theologian agreed with everything he wrote. Scholars do not generally make agreement their primary concern. We had had many discussions of Dr. Ford's current work in doctoral seminars I had taken at Andrews University, and the professors were very clear when they disagreed with his views. But I didn't hear my Adventist professors classify him as a heretic or an apostate.

As a case in point I notice the argument of W. W. Prescott, a well-known Adventist theologian, writer and teacher, pointing out the inconsistent attitude regarding the inspiration of the Bible and Sister White's writings.

> Can you explain how it is that two brethren can disagree on the inspiration of the Bible, one holding to the verbal inspiration and the other opposed to it, and yet no disturbance be created in the denomination whatever. That situation is right here before us. *But if two brethren take the same attitude on the spirit of prophecy, one holding to verbal inspiration and the other discrediting it, he that does not hold to the verbal inspiration is discredited.*
>
> If a man does not believe in the verbal inspiration of the Bible, he is still in good standing; but if he says he does not believe in the verbal inspiration of the Testimonies, he is discounted right away. I think it is an unhealthful situation. It puts the spirit of prophecy above the Bible.[9]

An oft repeated off-the-cuff evaluation by some observers was that while others slept, Dr. Ford was up studying with a view to giving sound biblical credibility to Adventism's unique views. He worked hard at solving problems that Adventist scholars were aware of but could not come to a consensus on and thus tended to leave on the backburner because of their potentially explosive doctrinal content. He was one of the few Adventist scholars who courageously wrote a commentary on the book of Daniel. And it was published by an Adventist publishing house.[10]

---

9. Couperus, "The Bible Conference of 1919," *Spectrum* 10:1 (May 1979), 39. Emphasis supplied.

10. Finding a textbook for Studies in Daniel was always a stretch on the part of the instructor. Usually in my classes I used the book compiled from the *SDA Bible Commentary*, volumes 4 and 7: *A Verse-by-Verse Commentary on the Book of Daniel: A Section of Volume IV of the Seventh-day Adventist Bible Commentary*, (1955). This book had been part of the General Conference committee vote: "To request the Review and Herald Publishing Association to make available in textbook form for us in our denominational colleges *The Seventh-day Adventist Commentary* material on Daniel." Adventist textbooks on Daniel were rare. There were only two in print at the time: Ford, *Daniel*, (1978); and Maxwell, *God Cares,* 1 *The Message of Daniel for You and Your Family,* (1981). I used both textbooks for my class in Studies in Daniel.

The General Conference had long before appointed a closed committee to study the book of Daniel. This committee attempted to face the issues relating to the content and context of Daniel and resolve the conflict between those and the interpretations that were taken for granted in traditional Adventism. The scholars who were invited to serve on this committee were assured that because of the sensitivity of the subject the discussion and research would be open-ended and that no minutes would be kept.

The work of this committee was relatively unknown to anyone outside Adventist scholarly circles until the Ford controversy when the participants began to write about it. I would guess that only very few laymen even knew of the committee's existence. The committee on problems in Daniel and Revelation never reached a consensus. Now, many years later, the debate over these issues re-emerged and went public and the atmosphere within the Church became politically toxic.

WHAT IS TRUTH?

The very expression, "The Truth," had the ring of finality. Hence any tinkering or even redefining of details of especially the Sanctuary Doctrine could be interpreted as removing "a pin" from the Adventist structure that supported this doctrine, or as Sister White wrote, "solid pillars for the building."[11] She warned of the enemy bringing in "deceptions of every kind." "The enemy will bring in false theories, such as the doctrine that there is no sanctuary. This is one of the points on which there will be a departing from the faith."[12]

Yet it was undoubtedly because of the very dogmatic and uncritical presentations of that doctrine that no non-Adventist theologian or biblical scholar had ever accepted it as biblically defensible.[13] Still, these scholars accepted Adventists as legitimate

---

11. White, *Evangelism*, 224. *Evangelism* is a later compilation from Sister White's writings. This terminology is taken from her article in the *Advent Review and Sabbath Herald,* May 25, 1905, entitled, "The Work for This time: Development of the Interest at Washington," from her address of May 16, 1905.

12. Ibid.

13. See the testimony of Donald Grey Barnhouse, one of the Baptist examiners who helped write the questions for Adventist leaders to answer in *Questions on Doctrine*: "I believe that the ideas of investigative judgment and a secondary sanctuary ministry have no basis in Scripture. . . . The doctrine of investigative judgment . . . is held by no other group of Christians [than Seventh-day Adventists], and was unknown until the middle of the nineteenth century. It was promulgated at that time, in my opinion, as a means of softening the harsh blow of 'The Great Disappointment,' which 'disappointment' is portrayed so clearly by the noted Adventist historian Dr. LeRoy Froom." Barnhouse, "Foreword," to Martin, *The Truth About Seventh-day Adventism,* 7.

Martin expands this thought further (Ibid., 176): "The Adventist error is that they draw from the Scriptures interpretations which cannot be substantiated by exegesis but rest largely upon inference and deduction, drawn from theological applications of their own design."

Martin further writes: "We cannot, therefore, accept the Adventist teaching on the investigative judgment since we are convinced that it has no warrant in Scripture. We must reject what we believe to be their un-Biblical concept that the sins of believers remain in the sanctuary until the day of blotting out of sins." Ibid., 179.

Christians. The doctrine that really stuck in their craw was the investigative judgment. They saw it as undermining faith in the saving power of the sacrifice of Christ on the cross. They saw it as being built on faulty exegetical evidence, and the connections between Daniel and Leviticus were categorically rejected as cultist folk religion.

> Our Adventist brethren, in teaching this doctrine, are overlooking the fact that "the Lord knoweth them that are his" (II Tim 2:19) and it was no less an authority than the Lord Jesus Christ who declared, "I know my sheep" (John 10:14).[14]
>
> The saving grace of the entire situation is that the Adventists fortunately deny the logical conclusions to which their doctrines must lead them; i.e., a negation of the full validity of the atonement of Christ which validity they absolutely affirm, and embrace with considerable fervor—a paradoxical situation at best![15]

As a rule, these problems are only researched among scholars and are not paraded before the laity at large. When asked by the Association of Adventist Forums leaders to speak to this subject, Dr. Ford apparently believed that it would not be a problem to address objectively the problems associated with this doctrine. But this proved not to be the case. Dr. Ford was suspended from his position, and the president of the General Conference gave him six months to prepare a defense of his views. In response, Dr. Ford wrote a 425-page theological tome (with 369 more pages of appendices) entitled, *Daniel 8:14, The Day of Atonement and the Investigative Judgment*.[16]

When the Brinsmead brothers' agitation had also stirred up controversy within the Church in Australia, Dr. Ford had been called upon to deal with the aberrational nature of their theology. But this was two decades before. Central to the Brinsmeads' agitation was the nature of the Christian view of righteousness, the nature of Christ and the nature of the Sanctuary Doctrine. These three loci of theological inquiry are related but now they became a serious matter of discussion once more. And the Adventist fundamentalists of the day approached the problems from a different hermeneutical standpoint than that of traditional Adventist conservatism.

For the theologically trained biblical scholar these were difficult subjects to deal with, partly because of the myriad of denominational books and articles that had created a very fixed, and often contradictory, understanding of these doctrines among the laity of the Church.

Finally, Martin offers a pastoral observation (Ibid., 182–183): "Seventh-day Adventists, we believe, needlessly subscribe to a doctrine which neither solves their difficulties nor engenders peace of mind. Holding as they do to the doctrine of the investigative judgment, it is extremely difficult for us to understand how they can experience the joy of salvation and the knowledge of sins forgiven," 182–183.

14. Ibid., 179.

15. Ibid., 187.

16. This treatise was first available in manuscript form and then published by Euangelion Press, (1980).

Dr. Ford drew the special wrath of the SDA fundamentalist crowd by using the writings of Sister White to defend a scholarly approach to the Sanctuary Doctrine. To them he was Lucifer, but, Dr. Ford was committed to preserving the Adventist theological heritage.[17] He was an Adventist apologist.

The Brinsmeads[18] had insisted that they had the light the Church needed, and their followers made common cause with the supporters of M. L. Andreasen in America. Their views were eventually rejected by the GC committee that met to examine their work. When the Church then trained their guns on them in the early 1960s, they became living martyrs and another movement was born. The agitation could simply be described as a fight between conservatives and fundamentalists.

Adventist fundamentalists characteristically would not consider any matter settled unless they had a statement of Sister White to rely on. If not, any further discussion was considered unnecessary, and those who would not take her word as the final answer would be labeled apostates and/or heretics.

The context of the prophet's words was not always given adequate consideration. Scholars, however, had to build their arguments on scripture, not on Sister White's gift of prophecy. The Church had stated over and over from its very beginning that Sister White was not to be the basis of any Adventist doctrine.[19]

Elder A. G. Daniells, the longest serving president of the General Conference from 1901–1922, had stated the Adventist view clearly at the 1919 Bible Conference.

> I have heard ministers say that the spirit of prophecy [Sister White's writings] is the interpreter of the Bible. I heard it preached at the General Conference some years ago, when it was said that the only way we could understand the Bible was through the writings of the spirit of prophecy. . . . It is not our position, and it is not right that the spirit of prophecy is the only safe interpreter of the Bible. *That is a false doctrine, a false view.* . . . They [the early Adventists] got their knowledge of the Scriptures as they went along through the

---

17. Ford, *Daniel 8:14, The Day of Atonement and the Investigative Judgment.* Dr. Ford was particularly concerned over the Adventist use of Sister White. He wrote in his introduction (ii): "As one familiar with those writings for many years, and deeply grateful for them, it seems to the present writer that E. G. White would have been horrified had she known her writings were to be used as a basis for doctrine rather than in support of obviously biblical positions.

"She affirmed that no spiritual gift should ever be given supremacy over Scripture. While officially we have denied that we give the White writings pre-eminence, in actual practice we have been continually guilty of that very procedure. Until we repent of this, recognizing that E. G. White herself frequently corrected her own positions by Scripture (e.g. use of swine's flesh, the time to begin and end the Sabbath, the nature of the law in Galatians, the covenants, the Trinity, tithing as replacing systematic benevolence, etc.) and that her written doctrinal expressions were not original but borrowed from denominational literature, we will not make progress in Scriptural exegesis."

18. A distinction is often made between the Old Brinsmead (perfectionism) and the New Brinsmead (Reformed thought) since Robert Brinsmead later reversed his older position.

19. Couperus, "The 1919 Bible Conference," 30–31.

Scriptures themselves. . . . He [Jesus] gave this Book, and He gave men brains and thinking power to study the Bible.[20]

To complicate the local issue, the Brinsmead brothers had acquired a significant following in Australia and when they came to the United States to seek the endorsement of General Conference leaders, they were able to win more adherents. Before ever meeting with the leadership in Washington, D.C., they held meetings across the country on their way to the denominational headquarters to receive the verdict of the official Church.

Their main burden was to explain how believers could reach sinless perfection after Jesus supposedly finished his intercession for sinners in the heavenly Sanctuary prior to the second coming. They referred to themselves as the "Sanctuary Awakening Movement."

If righteousness was sinlessness produced in the believer, with the help of Christ, then it followed that the gospel was to be defined as a way of learning how to live without sinning. Fundamentalists would argue based on statements from Sister White that this was *Present Truth* (the name of the later Brinsmeads' periodical). Paradoxically, a casual survey of Adventists would probably have revealed that this was a view that many of them had grown up with. But that didn't make the view biblically supportable.

As theology teachers in the SMC Religion Department, all of us with substantial pastoral experience, we knew that our students would not be given a pass among non-Adventist peers unless they were able to demonstrate the biblical integrity of their theological positions. We did not want them to be reduced to merely addressing other Adventists in their ministry. Our task was set. We were preparing ministers who could evangelize instead of simply parroting denominational talking points. To accomplish this task a student needed to be able to think, rather than simply reflect other people's thoughts.[21]

Finally, as mentioned above, the Sanctuary Doctrine was Adventism's unique contribution to Christian theology, and the doctrine was thought to be the answer to these contentious issues. Here as well perfectionist doctrine was involved. No professional non-Adventist theologian or biblical scholar had ever accepted this Sanctuary Doctrine as biblical, particularly the investigative judgment—the notion that since 1844 God had been poring over the records of the saints to decide who would be saved and who would be lost. This was based on an interpretation of Daniel 8:14 that held that the sins of the saints were polluting the heavenly Sanctuary and that the Sanctuary therefore needed to be cleansed, a view that was rejected out of hand by those who applied accepted exegetical methods of interpretation.

Adventist fundamentalists, instead of feeling the need to study more and explain more carefully the biblical foundations of this doctrine, simply called anybody who

---

20. Daniels, Ibid. Emphasis supplied.
21. White, *Education*, 17. Cf. by the same author, *Testimonies to Ministers*, 302.

disagreed with their interpretation "apostate." It was little wonder that most Adventist theologians avoided the topic.[22]

FROM THEOLOGY TO POLITICS

Another complicating factor was the role that Church leaders came to play. Much to my surprise, Church officials took the side of three or four former students who had lodged complaints against the SMC Religion Department instead of supporting those of us who had been educated, appointed, ordained and hired to do the work of the Church.

It appeared to us that our faculty was hardly considered part of the Church proper. Instead, we would be encouraged (even pressured) to leave, to seek calls outside of Happy Valley with virtually no words of appreciation for our years of service or our ability to protect the Church against the forces undermining its theological foundations.

The Church that had paid for our education was now abandoning us. There would not be so much as a farewell party or even a cake for any of us, much less a watch! The one major defender of the SMC Religion Department was Dr. Frank Knittel, who had carefully vetted all of us and our theological positions. So, to get at the heretics in the Religion Department, the protesters now set their target on Dr. Knittel.

More scandal sheets like the "news" paper began to appear. In these papers every person accusing the Religion Department of apostasy would be described as faithful, God-fearing and believing, speaking on behalf of God's remnant Church. Every accused faculty member would be referred to as apostate, money-grabbing, deceitful, betrayer of the trust, heretic, robber of the tithe. This was the *modus operandi* of these home-grown fundamentalists long weaned off the milk of human kindness. Ironically, this was demonstrating Christian perfection.

One layman from North Carolina, whom I had never met, and to my knowledge, one who had never heard me teach or preach, sent me a post card on which he wrote the following message. [Postmarked Asheville, NC, Sept. 10, 1982]:

> To Knittles [sic] not too bright right ARM in the TREASON attempt.
> MAY YOUR RIGHT ARM SOON spend <u>FULL TIME</u> CRANKING A BROKEN DOWN "FORD" (THATS [sic] ON the WAY to A junk PILE).
> EDWIN TRAITOR ZAKRISON [sic]
> SOUTHERN MISSIONARY COLLEGE
> (KNITTLE [sic]–FORD UNIVERSITY)
> COLLEGEDALE, TENN 37315

---

22. Dr. Ford alludes to this reticence of Adventist scholars to do work on this doctrine when he writes: "Over the years it had become apparent that most of the research scholars of the church shared my discomfiture [concerning the Sanctuary Doctrine and the investigative judgment] but had concluded that little could be done." *Daniel 8:14, The Day of Atonement and the Investigative Judgment*, i.

> Vance Ferrell may have spelled your name wrong ZACKRISON but I don't spell it Pastor, Minister or even Elder. I spell it as it is TRAITOR (n. one guilty of treason, one who is false to a trust, one who betrays his country (church) (a cause or an associate)—besides you get paid to do it from sacred tithe. Ferrell didn't tell me first of your "traitor trait." NOR FELTS EITHER. You surely made a jackass of yourself by your letter mailed to him on July 24, 1982, me thinks (others too!) Keep up similar asinine, futile — [deleted] — so the true ignorance will shine forth.[23]

The same Church member had written a postcard message to Dr. Grant that was a little more amicable the year before this [postmarked July 23, 1981]. Later copies of correspondence from the same person addressed to Dr. Knittel surfaced and were distributed to the faithful. The man said that he had children at SMC, and that they were his primary source of information.

With this new information, I remembered how different my family's approach was during my student days when I came home with a complaint to Dad about a teacher or an administrator. Dad's response would be consistent and immediate: "Tomorrow morning we will go to your teacher and get this straightened out." From that point on, I was exceedingly careful that my complaints were legitimate. I had no evidence that any of this man's four children had ever been in one of my classes. I did not know any of them.

So now we were the devil and our accusers were God's warriors. Happy Valley was reminiscent of the Spanish Inquisition, minus the thumb screws and the rack. These people believed in human sinless perfection through the power of the Holy Spirit, and they were willing to destroy people to defend their doctrine. We never knew what would walk through that door on any given day.

Dr. Raymond F. Cottrell, an editor at the Review and Herald Publishing Assn., and project manager for the *SDA Bible Commentary*, would write in the early 1980s about what was happening in Happy Valley:

> Southern [Missionary College] operates as [an] agency of Southern Bible belt obscurantism. Furthermore it was (and still is) to an appreciable extent, dependent on the largesse of committed ultra-fundamentalists, who insist that the college operate on ultra-fundamentalist principles.[24]

---

23. "Letter to Edwin Zackrison from [name withheld]," September 10, 1982. *SMC Faculty Document Committee Collection*. All emphases and upper-case letters are exactly as the writer produced them on his post card.

24. Cottrell, "The 'Sanctuary Doctrine'—Asset or Liability?" A talk given at the Association of Adventist Forums meeting in San Diego, California, (2002), 6.

FOLK RELIGION RAISES ITS HEAD

When the Adventist Church decided that all its institutions of higher learning should meet accreditation board standards with respect to scholarship and advanced degrees, it predictably led to a heightened tension in academia. The tension was between religious dogma and the world of sciences in several areas such as biology, geology, physics, chemistry and biblical studies.

Graduate religion studies introduced all of us to the current theological and biblical issues. Especially inspiration was a volatile topic. Hermeneutically, Adventism had been built on the proof-text method. A good example of this approach was the Adventist classic, *Bible Readings for the Home Circle,* one of the books that had brought my family into the denomination. The method was catechistic: *question—answer—question—answer.*

College and Seminary education introduced me to a critical method of studying the Bible. Rather than taking a text from here and another from there and stringing them together in support of an Adventist doctrine we were now required to study who wrote the biblical material we were studying. Our old approach had sometimes taken texts willy-nilly from Old Testament and New Testament. The more scholarly approach asked why before ever quoting the text as proof of our position. Who wrote it and to whom was it written and what was the local situation the writing addressed?

We learned that there were no extant original manuscripts of any scriptural writings, called autographs. Instead we had a plethora of early copies with noticeable textual variants. So naturally we needed to learn how to evaluate the variant readings that had come down to us through Jewish and Christian traditions. This had not been adequately dealt with in our elementary and secondary parochial education. And since many college students had gone to Church school but were not theology or religion majors, the proof-text method was all they knew. Consequently, our approach to the Bible was often met with suspicion and outright hostility by the proponents of folk religion.

Folk religion rejects the objective approach of the scholar unless the conclusion agrees with it. Adherents find their certainties in tradition, experience and, as in the case of Adventists, Sister White's writings. We were taught to run to Sister White and to use her writings as an inspired Bible commentary although the founders of the Adventist Church and Ellen White herself had avoided, even condemned, this approach. Even though this was not the official position of the Church, actual practice made it seem like it was.

Sister White usually came away as the last word for any interpretation, the final court of appeals for Truth. Having a little library of her books was easier than going to the reference section of any other library to look up the materials needed for serious Bible study.[25] Unfortunately, many who were critical of Sister White either did not

---

25. For a succinct discussion of this use of Sister White in truth seeking and authority see

read, or read little else but her writings, although she had instructed us to see her writings as a lighted path to our primary source of Truth, i.e., the Bible.

The authors of *Questions on Doctrine* had penned the views I had always been taught in elementary, secondary, college and graduate school over the previous forty-five years.

> While Adventists hold the writings of Ellen G. White in highest esteem, yet these are not the source of our expositions. We base our teachings on the Scriptures, the only foundation of all true Christian doctrine. However, it is our belief that the Holy Spirit opened to her mind important events and called her to give certain instructions for these last days. And inasmuch as these instructions, in our understanding, are in harmony with the Word of God, which Word alone is able to make us wise unto salvation, we as a denomination accept them as inspired counsels from the Lord. But we have never equated them with Scripture as some falsely charge.[26]

> The Lord has sent His people much instruction, line upon line, precept upon precept, here a little, and there a little. Little heed is given to the Bible, and the Lord has given a lesser light to lead men and women to the greater light.[27]

Perhaps the most dangerous notion in Adventism regarding her writings was the idea that she was an inspired Bible commentary. Not only did many Church members think that this was the Adventist position, it put serious restraints on the approach of the well-meaning scholar. The Church had been wise in resisting this idea, and yet the practice lived on. For many, the Sister White corpus functioned as a third canon, i.e., an addition to the holy scriptures, with not only equal inspiration but equal authority.

After returning from graduate school in the early 1980s, I found a new concern expressed by students in my classes. For example, when I would quote Sister White for insight into the subject matter of my lecture, which I did frequently, I now had to deal with a new problem. After I quoted her, a student would inevitably raise his/her hand and ask: *Where did she copy that from?*

We were dealing with an increasingly informed student population—in many cases more informed than their parents. It was a page taken right out of the 1919 Bible Conference warnings about the cost of keeping her literary borrowing secret once people learned the truth.

After this question was asked, it often proved impossible to get through the material that I had planned to cover in my lecture. Instead of discussing the subject matter,

---

Zackrison, *The First Temptation*, 15–17.

26. *Questions on Doctrines*, 93.

27. White, "An Open Letter From Mrs. E. G. White to all Who Love the Blessed Hope," *Advent Review and Sabbath Herald,* January 20, 1903, 15. Also reprinted in White, *Colporteur Ministry*, 125; and *Questions on Doctrine*, 93.

whether exegetical or theological, the issue would then shift to the authority or literary practices of Sister White.

It did not take many of these excursions into current controversy for any of us to realize that this was not helpful. And it came to the point where it could be risky for the professor. I might be lecturing on the character of the prophet Daniel and quote from Sister White's book, *Prophets and Kings,* where she described Daniel's character. In the setting of a "news" paper environment I could now be accused of not believing in Sister White if I entertained student questions about her literary dependency—but I could also be condemned if I did not entertain that question. In either case, instead of being about the character of Daniel, the discussion now became all about Sister White. This was not the course of study we had scheduled. So, in the interest of class coherence, I became more circumspect in my use of her writings in my class lectures.

CHAPTER THIRTY-TWO

The Collegedale Purge Begins

"It is criminal to steal a purse, daring to steal a fortune, a mark of greatness to steal a crown. The blame diminishes as the guilt increases."

— Johann Friedrich von Schiller

DENOMINATION WIDE CRISIS

A LOT WAS TRANSPIRING in the Adventist Church at large in North America in the early 1980s. In the aftermath of Dr. Desmond Ford's Forum presentation at Pacific Union College on October 27, 1979, a theological firestorm broke out in the denomination and the dark smoke of inquisitorial suspicion hung like a pall over the Adventist horizon.

As if that was not enough, there were other matters tormenting the Church community, such as the controversial research by Elder Walter Rea into the literary dependency of Sister White and the discovery that Church leaders had received kickbacks for "investing" Church tithes and offerings in a real estate-based financial scheme run by an Adventist physician in California. News flashes in publications such as *Christianity Today* and *Time* magazine along with newspapers such as the *Los Angeles Times* opened these painful crises to the public.

Defenders of Church tradition and doctrine trained their weapons on perceived enemies of the Church, and ironically, they focused their attacks at the conservative colleges: particularly Andrews University, Pacific Union College and Southern Missionary College. I heard no mention of Loma Linda, La Sierra, Walla Walla, Southwestern Union, Union, Atlantic Union, Canadian Union or Columbia Union—all fully accredited North American Adventist colleges. These schools seemed immune to controversy. Talking to a professor from one of these colleges I asked him why his faculty was not under fire? He said no one could understand what they taught even if they tried!

As explained above, the SMC community was dragged into this denominational crisis when local zealots started tossing the "news" paper onto our driveways. While we were aware of the denominational crises, we did not know that we were involved until then. We would soon realize that an accusation, true or false, gains its strength from the number of people who are willing to believe it and spread it.

The "news" paper was an eye opener with respect to what it revealed about the lack of confidence in the administration of Southern Missionary College and its Board of Trustees. With that little support from the people in Happy Valley, any charge of a negative nature might seem credible. To us in the Religion Department it seemed fantastic that a paper so poorly organized and claiming to have been written by marginal former students, and falling abysmally short of Adventist publication standards, should be considered credible.

Without an Adventist Church in profound crisis, these students would not have been empowered by Church leaders to pursue their malignant work and this paper would have been looked upon as a product of incompetents. But the national Church was in turmoil. Because of this, there was a propensity on the part of the fundamentalist laity and leaders who sympathized with them to embrace wild accusations against people of Dr. Ford's cohort—the theologians of the Church—as well as the academic institutions of the Church. Legitimate authority was breaking down and extreme theological positions had become commonplace—standard, orthodox theological positions were in free fall.

In the wake of the first year after Dr. Ford's Forum presentation in California, our classrooms were filled with controversial discussions pressed on us by students concerned about the integrity of the Sanctuary Doctrine and Dr. Ford's view of justification by faith.

A significant number of students were happy that the Church was searching for a clearer definition of the gospel. Dr. Ford had raised questions to which many students wanted answers. On the main, these students were polite, mature, and courteous. They left the impression that they were clearly concerned with gospel issues. While they may not have accepted all our answers to Dr. Ford's challenges, they were polite in their disagreement.

The following year things began to change. We came under sustained attack by a hostile group of local fundamentalists. This group was rabid and not prepared to listen to our critique of those aspects of Dr. Ford's theology that we disagreed with. And since we were hearing clear presentations of the gospel message on Sabbath from our Collegedale pastor, we were unprepared for this fundamental uprising on the part of people in the community as well as some newly enrolled students.

These local zealots were underwritten by money people in Collegedale, but they also received ideological support from the *Adventist Review* in Washington. The

Review was the general organ of the Church. Editorials by Elder Wood and Dr. Douglass had, since the mid-1970s, promoted a theology that resembled that of the old Brinsmead movement of the 1960s.[1]

It was commonly thought that Dr. Douglass, in joining the *Review* staff, had influenced Elder Wood with his "harvest theology"—the version of perfectionistic theology he had introduced at the 1974 Bible Conference. This perfectionism not only contradicted what I had been taught through college and Seminary (both in the 1960s and later in my doctoral studies in the 1970s), but it was contrary to the views held by many prominent officers of the General Conference.

In 1980, Elder Wood wrote an editorial that was taken by many on Adventist college faculties as a not so veiled attack on Adventist academia. He entitled his article, "Colleges in Trouble," beginning with non-Adventist fundamentalist (Baptist) warnings regarding faith-based colleges. Pivoting from Baptist concerns that fundamentalist colleges were not living up to their claims to be truly Christian educational enterprises, Elder Wood turned his attention to Adventist colleges.

He argued that curriculum, standards and theological identity were also being compromised in Adventist schools. The SDA editor then argued that Adventist parents should be forewarned as they were in danger of losing the souls of their children in these schools.

> We confess that we are alarmed by the fact that *some of our colleges seem to be drifting away from the standards and objectives established for them by their founders.* We are alarmed by the secular climate that prevails *on some campuses.* We are alarmed by the strange winds of doctrine that blow *on some campuses.* We are alarmed by the lax moral standards that prevail *on some campuses.* We are alarmed by the feeble efforts put forth *by some administrators and faculty members* to create a spiritual climate that will prepare students for the greatest event in earth's history, the second coming of Jesus.[2]

These were explosive accusations and Elder Wood followed up the next year (1981) with a full-throated endorsement of Attorney Walton's *Omega,* the book that had leveled devastating attacks on Adventist academia.

I knew these lax standards that Elder Wood referred to could not be referring to SMC for I had never related to a school with a stricter set of Christian standards. But we recognized right away that this was a serious attack on Adventist schools. The immediate effect was to open the field for a witch-hunt. Fundamentalist zealots went to work to identify the areas of concern that had been left so general in Elder Wood's editorial and more importantly, to ferret out who in Adventist academia were responsible for betraying the old Truths.

---

1. Dr. Springett outlines this development in his article, "Some Historical Observations on the Present Theology 'Crisis,'" 18–23.

2. Wood, "Colleges in Trouble," *Adventist Review,* February 21, 1980. Emphasis supplied.

In our study of homiletics, we always impressed upon our students the importance of being mindful of the context of the biblical passages around which sermons were built. This *Review* article immediately appeared to violate that very context principle. Elder Wood's editorial focused on a letter Sister White had written in 1906 to Elder George C. Tenney, editor at the time of *Medical Missionary Magazine* as well as a teacher and chaplain at the Battle Creek Sanitarium. From 1895–1897 Elder Tenney had been coeditor with Elder Uriah Smith of the *Review and Herald*.

Sister White had written the following to Elder Tenney (as quoted by Elder Wood):

> I have been surprised and made sad to read some of your articles in the "Medical Missionary," and especially those on the Sanctuary Question. These articles show that you have been departing from the faith. You have helped in confusing the understanding of our people. *The correct understanding of the ministration in the heavenly sanctuary, is the foundation of our faith.*[3]

Apparently Elder Wood's phrase "the strange winds of doctrine," had something to do with the Sanctuary Doctrine. He had also referenced "lax moral standards" and the "feeble attempts of some administrators and faculty members" at creating a "spiritual climate" on campuses, but these concerns were pushed aside in his view, it all turned out to be about the Sanctuary issue. Sister White's letter continued:

> I must again say to our people, Keep your children away from Battle Creek. Some of our medical missionary workers are becoming leavened with infidelity. Specious heresy has been taking hold of minds, and its threads have been woven into the pattern of the figure. . . . One father writes that of his two children who were sent to Battle Creek, one is now an infidel, and the other has given up his faith in the Advent message.
>
> Those who are not walking in the light of the message, may gather up statements from my writings that happen to please them, and that agree with their human judgment, and, by separating these statements from their connection, and placing them beside human reasonings, make it appear that my writings uphold that which they condemn. I charge you not to do this work. To use my writings thus, and at the same time reject the message which I bear to correct errors, is misleading and inconsistent.[4]

The editorial was misleading because it neglected to provide the historical setting in which Sister White wrote her warning—it clearly violated the context principle. Her letter was written in 1906, five years after the Adventist Battle Creek College had moved (1901) to Berrien Springs, Michigan, renamed Emmanuel Missionary College. After the 1901 move, there was no Adventist college in Battle Creek, so if Sister White was warning Adventist parents against sending their children to college in Battle Creek, she was not referring to a denominational school.

---

3. White, *Letter T-208*, 1906. Emphasis supplied. Quoted in Ibid.
4. Ibid.

The Collegedale Purge Begins

In these references to "Battle Creek," she was not talking about any college—her warning was about Dr. John Harvey Kellogg's sanitarium where Elder Tenney was teacher and chaplain. Her warning was not against an educational institution, it was about a non-Adventist institution run by a perceived Adventist heretic. Despite this fact, the whole point of the *Review* editorial was to warn Church members against contemporary Adventist colleges. Predictably, it led to a witch hunt.

After these suggestions were in place, Elder Wood closed with his application.

> She [Sister White] urged parents to keep their children away from *the school in Battle Creek*,[5] where false teachings were being circulated.[6] Clearly parents have an obligation to know what is being taught even at Adventist schools, and to send their children only to those schools that teach *historic Adventism*[7] and will strengthen the faith of the young people who are sent there. . . .[8] Of one thing we are certain: the church as a whole will back its educators in making Seventh-day Adventist schools *truly Seventh-day Adventist*, with all that that embodies by way of doctrinal purity, idealism, and excellence.[9]

Adventist fundamentalists took this editorial as permission, if not a mandate, to purge college Religion Departments of suspected heretics. Together with Elder Wood's clear endorsement of the book *Omega,* which contained many of the same accusations and his irresponsible letter of endorsement of the activities of the local zealots in the "news" paper, the stage was set for the purge of SMC. Because of Elder Wood's generalized attack on Adventist institutions of higher learning, even those of us teaching religion in very conservative colleges such as SMC, came to be suspected of the ideological sins that Elder Wood had laid at the door of Adventist academia.

The *Review* never tried to provide any specificity when it came to Elder Wood's attack. We could only conclude that it did not intend to. It greatly complicated our

---

5. Ibid. Emphasis supplied. This is misleading. She just writes of "Battle Creek." Any implication of a school would not be an SDA school.

6. Elder Wood applies this as a warning against contemporary Adventist colleges. And since he does not identify which colleges he is referring to, we all became suspect.

7. "Historic Adventism" was a term subject to definition. Elder Wood did not unpack his meaning of the term, but it seems clear that he was using a fundamentalist definition. Adventist fundamentalists would view "historic" Adventism as perfectionistic, i.e., the "old Brinsmead view," a view that never was part of official Adventism and had been thoroughly condemned in the 1960s.

8. In his article, "Some Historical Observations on the Present Theology 'Crisis,'" Dr. Springett addressed the issue of "historic" Adventism, 23: "A careful survey of the *Review* and *Ministry* over the last 40 years, excluding very recent editions, shows that the editors and contributors in these papers over this entire period show nothing of this [perfectionistic] 'tradition.' The onus is thus clearly and firmly placed on the so-called traditionalists to explain how an entire generation of Adventist writers in the church's leading professional and lay journals know nothing of 'historic' Adventism. . . ."

9. Ibid. Emphasis supplied. Here is a suggestion of "a church within a church," a typical fundamentalist Adventist perspective. In 1994 the North American Division publication *Issues* would later condemn such views.

lives, and to our chagrin we soon discovered that there was little we could do to defend ourselves.

A BIT OF NORMALCY WAS STILL AVAILABLE IN HAPPY VALLEY

Meanwhile, I was writing a doctoral dissertation, teaching a full academic load (fifteen semester hours), and Annie and I were members of the SMC symphony orchestra. Dr. Orlo Gilbert, professor of music, and conductor of the college symphony orchestra had been a classmate of ours at La Sierra College. He and Annie had both been violin students of Professor Alfred Walters. Now Dr. Gilbert was pleased to have Annie in his orchestra. At first, I tagged along in the audience for concerts.

Later I joined the orchestra, resurrecting my clarinet skills. And I became a student of Professor Jay Craven, principal clarinet in the Chattanooga Symphony. My daughter Jill was taking violin along with many other kids in Spalding Elementary School. And my son Mark was starting out on cello (what he considered a more macho undertaking than the fiddle).

In the spring of 1981, we went to Australia, New Zealand and Fiji on a concert tour. I was invited to speak on the weekends in churches in these countries. We gave concerts at Adventist Churches, Avondale College (Australia), and Fulton College (Fiji), plus concerts in several non-Adventist venues. People would come up after my sermons and remark, "We love your accent!" That was a shocker—I thought they were the ones with accents!

In 1983 we went on a goodwill concert tour to Romania, Russia and Estonia. This was in the days of the Soviet Union, and we saw firsthand how badly many people fared under the communist regimes. My daughter Jill was in eighth grade by then and a member of the college orchestra, so the three of us were together on that tour of nineteen concerts in twenty-one days. Only my son Mark had to stay behind since he was not sufficiently proficient on his cello. Perhaps another trip in the future could include our whole family.

These were glorious days. Southern's enrollment was climbing sharply. I had classes with as many as 120 students. I enjoyed teaching and relished the added confidence that my doctoral work had given me. Dr. Bennett was concerned that we meet the theological challenges of the day and assigned new classes for us to develop. Elder Holbrook was to teach a class on *The Sanctuary*, Dr. Ott a class in *Righteousness by Faith* and Dr. Gladson took over the *Studies in Daniel* class.

I had been on leave for three years, so Dr. Bennett kept me overloaded, teaching fifteen hours a semester; and since I had done my graduate work with emphases in soteriology and eschatology, he asked me to teach sections of *Righteousness by Faith* and *Studies in Revelation* in addition to my classes in the *New Testament Gospels* and *Christian Beliefs*. I didn't mind this, but it imposed a huge workload on me since I was also researching and writing my doctoral dissertation. The practics classes—*Church*

Administration, Homiletics, and *Personal Evangelism* —were shared by three of us. Dr. Grant was assigned *Christian Ethics* and a couple sections of *Adventist History.* In staff meetings, we freely discussed the goings on in the denomination at large.

Researching and writing a doctoral dissertation requires a great amount of time, and these academic teaching loads were back breaking. I concluded that to finish this research project on time, I had to set aside four uninterrupted hours a day. But where was that time to be found?

At this point I was getting desperate: I decided that I would rise at 3:00 am and study and write until 7:00 am. Four hours at least five days a week. Surely no one would be interfering with that schedule. It took me two weeks to adjust to the new schedule—something I almost thought I couldn't do. But it did the trick. In successfully readjusting my body clock, I was on my way. This new schedule was so effective that it became my frame of study time for many years after my project was finished. I found these hours to be very productive for thinking and writing.

The order of events during this period is not crucial for this story. Fact is these events tend to run together in my memory. The period from 1979–1984 was a painful period in the history of Adventism, and we found ourselves at ground zero. Events happened very rapidly, and they brought with them a lot of personal pain. Virtually everything that happened caught us off guard. There were times when we feared daily that we might lose our jobs. And we were not just talking about jobs.

We were Christian ministers. We were talking about our calling from God. In this account, I will mention only some of the events that took place in these final days of our life in Happy Valley. Before it was over, I received a phone call from a doctor in the city. He told me that I needed to talk to a lawyer. He said he had talked to his attorney and he wanted to meet me. The doctor just wanted me to talk to him. The very suggestion put me in a state of shock. To solicit help from a lawyer was as unthinkable as seeing a psychiatrist.

A NEW INVASION OF ACADEMIA

I came out of my Studies in Revelation *class one Thursday afternoon at 4:50, heading for my office to collect what I needed to take home to join the family for supper at 5:00.* I unlocked the door to the Religion Department waiting room, which was vacant—all the professors had gone home by now. I was slightly aware that a woman I did not know was standing at the bulletin board in the hallway. When I opened the double doors to the outer office, she followed me into the waiting room.

She immediately asked if she could talk with me. I told her I was on my way home and I couldn't talk right now. If she heard any of my words she did not show it. I should have asked her to make an appointment but at that moment I did not know what her intentions were. She had only seen me walk by. I couldn't imagine she had any idea who I was.

I was wrong.

Before I could even gather my books and supplies to get home she blurted a question about what my opinion on masturbation might be. I was thirty-nine years old at the time and no one had ever asked me that question. I snap-judged that this would require more than the five minutes max I had before I needed to be home where supper was always on the table at 5:00 pm, allowing me ten minutes to get home from my class. I did not sit down. I had no time for an ethical discussion with a stranger at this time of day. I had to get home. Oblivious to my urgency, she sat down.

I had no inkling that this was to be a shot heard around the Adventist world, and that the Collegedale inquisition was about to begin. I would discover later that I was not the first professor she had cornered with this peculiar question. We had never met, but I suspected that her bluntness indicated that she had a pre-formed opinion, and that nothing good would come out of a potentially contentious discussion on what seemed to be a subject of exaggerated concern to her. She would later claim that she had been to President Knittel and all the teachers in the SMC Religion Department and other departments. I was unaware of any of this. I was packed up to go home but she was still pursuing the subject.

She continued revealing her perceptions. The chair of the SMC Psychology Department had held Prayer Meeting the night before in which he told the congregation that he agreed with Dr. James Dobson. Then she asked whether I agreed with him?

The chair was not a member of the SMC Religion Department. I had not been at the Prayer Meeting. I had no idea what Dr. Dobson had said. I didn't even know that Dr. Dobson, the well-known Christian radio physician, had been at the Collegedale Prayer Meeting—which it turned out he had not.

What had happened was that the psychology chair was in the middle of presenting a series of Dr. Dobson's movies at Prayer Meeting on various *Focus-on-the-Family* topics relative to young people. I didn't know what Dr. Dobson said in the movie or what the chair had said in the question/answer period that followed. I told her she should talk to the chair about her disagreements since he was the one who made the presentation. I dismissed myself to get home to my family.

Later I heard that, based on this five-minute chance encounter with me, this woman concluded that I had put her off because I did not believe in Sister White and that I should be fired for lying and being paid with tithe funds. She circulated the charge that I was not the only member of the SMC Religion Department who did not believe in Sister White.

She declared that she had talked to all the teachers in the Religion Department about masturbation and that none of them believed in Sister White, based on how they answered her question. I had not answered her question and that proved I was also guilty. She would enlist other voices to ask how the Church could justify paying these people from tithes to destroy the faith of our young people. She would insist on the question constantly, How can a person accept pay from the sacred tithe when he is actively attempting to raise doubts and undermine our faith?

We should all be terminated. This woman would become a columnist for the "news" paper and its in-house successor *SDA Press Release*. She would later write letters to GC personnel disclosing her version of the sins of SMC faculty members and she would spend time in Washington with leadership.

This was not the last time I would encounter people preoccupied with the subject of masturbation. One morning, as I came out of an appointment in Wright Hall, the SMC administration building, and started toward my Lynn Wood Hall office at the top of the hill, I saw one of my students sitting on the bench alongside the sidewalk. I stopped briefly to greet him.

When I asked him how things were going he came straight to the point that he was leaving SMC because of "the heresy." I didn't know what he meant so he elaborated that SMC was "full of heresy." When he told me, he had only had Elder Holbrook and me for his Religion classes, I got the message. He had received a high grade in my class. I smiled. Surely, he had found no heresy in Elder Holbrook's class. And he agreed to that.

This young man had been an Adventist for six months, he told me. Before that he had no Christian background at all. I knew that when he took my class, but I could not remember any questions or objections on his part in my class about heresy. I only remember him to be an excellent and supportive student. I asked where he would go when he left SMC. His answer was quick: "Wildwood." He had not elaborated on what "the heresy" was, but I could see that he was hoping to.

He admitted that that very morning he had been lying in bed and that his life would testify to SMC heresy. Facing the temptation to masturbate *he heard my voice*. Naturally, I wondered what I had said to him in his bed. He said that when he had taken my class I had held that the New Testament gospel taught that *no matter what we do God loves us*. He took that as permission to masturbate. My permission to do it was "heresy" and he felt that he needed to go to a school where there was no "heresy." Wildwood was that place from what he had been told.

God's love was justification to masturbate? In his mind, this way of thinking could be used to justify anything that went against the will of God and that put him over the edge. On the other hand, new believers often tend to think concretely and legalistically and see every challenge in terms of black or white. Later, I ran into another of my students who was using this same argument to justify her going dancing.

I was told later that shortly after our conversation on the bench, this young man had testified against the SMC Religion Department before the college board about "heresy" at SMC. I did not ascertain whether he had told the board the story he had shared with me. I rather doubt that, given the embarrassing nature of his complaint.

I remembered a testimony he had given in the adult Collegedale Sabbath School on his conversion to Adventism. In that talk he had told us about his out of body experiences while living for a time at a kibbutz in Israel. I wondered if this was another one; he certainly seemed to have taken leave of his indisputable intelligence.

He would later join the ranks of a handful of disgruntled former students whose accusation would be printed and circulated among the zealots in the community. Given the growing hostility of some towards SMC and its Religion Department, I was not too stunned when he was hired by the General Conference to fill, over time, a series of important positions while most of his teachers at SMC were fired.

In our graduate classes in pastoral counseling, our professors had always told us that we must learn to mask our shock at some of the things we would hear when people came to us for guidance. This student provided me with one of many opportunities to work on perfecting this skill.

A FUNDAMENTALIST CRUSADER

So, I had met Florence Woolcock, a woman who had recently moved to Collegedale from up North. She claimed that her children had been polluted by reading *Spectrum* magazine. She asserted that God had assigned her the sacred mission of cleaning up SMC—including seeing to it that *Spectrum* magazine would be kept out of the college library. Anybody who took issue with her was an agent of Satan, she proclaimed, and she promptly added them to her hit list, which the local zealots duly printed and circulated. Many of the rumors we faced were started with her.

God was allegedly calling the shots and who could argue with "God"? When one of my students labored with her she said that she was commissioned by God to do this work. In California we met people like this. Few of us took them seriously. But this was Tennessee—this was Collegedale—Happy Valley.

For the next two years, my steps were dogged by her. I never fully understood why I was targeted. I can only speculate that she saw me as especially dangerous because she thought I was a popular teacher because I always had a full classroom. She went as far as spying on me by hiding behind a cardboard room divider at the back of my classroom in the library. There she would surreptitiously take notes on my lectures apparently in the hope that I would say something incriminating. Based on what she could ostensibly hear from her listening post, she generated her own version of what I was teaching.

The classroom in question was located on the ground floor of the college library. I had specifically requested that classroom because it had a limited capacity (thirty students) and *Studies in Revelation* was one of the most popular Bible classes on campus with detailed assignments to grade. I had taught the class forty times, and it carried three semester hours of academic upper division credit. There was never a vacant seat once the class began.

One of my graduate concentrations at Andrews University had been eschatology, and *Studies in Revelation* was a class in serious technical apocalyptic interpretation for upper-division students (juniors, seniors and theology and religion majors).

My professors in eschatology had included well-known and respected Andrews University Adventist scholars: Dr. Walter Specht, chair of the New Testament Department; Dr. Gerhard Hasel, chair of the Old Testament Department, dean of the Seminary and director of the ThD program; Dr. Edward Heppenstall, chair and professor of the Theology Department; Dr. Hans LaRondelle, professor of theology and advisor of my doctoral dissertation; Dr. Roland Loasby, professor of Greek New Testament; and Dr. Robert Johnston, professor of theology and New Testament.

Mrs. Woolcock, instead of being ashamed of her underhanded tactics, proudly announced to the public that she had been hiding behind a room divider in my class to take notes on what I was teaching, without my knowing that she was there. Then she published, without ever having talked to me, the "heresy" she claimed I was teaching. From reading what she published, which she claimed to have heard, I knew she had neither done any of the class assignments nor understood what was covered in my lectures. It seemed clear that she had not come to learn anything; she apparently saw herself as God's secret agent assigned to ferret out "heresy."

Based on her skewed understanding of my classroom presentations, she launched an all-out attack on me. Later, when I asked her specifically why she had not written anything about the one lecture that she had actually attended (a student was absent one day and she came in and sat in his seat uninvited), she said she hadn't been listening to me because she was thinking about what she was going to say to me after class let out.[10] Ironically, my lecture that day had been on the Adventist understanding of the judgment.

Sneaking secretly around trying to get information to hang a professor was not only subversive, it was unethical.[11] In my twelve years of teaching at SMC, none of us in the department had ever had to face anything like this. Our students were honest and intensely interested in the subject matter of this class and the other classes I taught.

---

10. "Wagner-Woolcock Discussion," *Appendix, Zackrison/Southern College* (November 7, 1983), 90: "F[lorence] W[oolcock]: What he was talking about I don't know because I was concentrating on when the class was over what I was going to say on this."

11. Ibid. "F. W.: The reason I was in the library listening was because I wanted to get a blessing. Our house was in the midst of being built, we didn't have any heat in the house. I spend a lot of time because I love reading Ellen White's writings, I love the *Review,* and I love our message and I always spend a good part of my day in the Ellen G. White room to keep warm because we didn't have any heat in our house. And I said to Mrs. Doherty [employee in the Heritage Room], do you think it would be all right, I always wanted to attend religion classes, because I was not raised in the Adventist message and I never had the opportunity, and *of course I didn't have the money because if I had the money I would have been attending* or I would have had heat in my house and *so she very kindly bent the rules* a little and said, 'well you can sit in there and listen in on the class.' And this is where I heard the doubts being presented and one of them was at the end of the class period after you were done talking about Rea and how devastating his book was going to be upon our people when it came out." Emphases supplied.

For the most part, the questions they raised indicated that they were grappling with the subject matter, and I had always done my best to answer their questions honestly.

Next, Mrs. Woolcock took it upon herself to print up warning notices. She stood in the hallway outside my classroom with her stack of fliers, handing them out to my students as they filed in and out of my class. She stood at the door when they entered and met them with more material when they left. Students sent me pictures they had taken of her standing at the crosswalk to chapel handing out her fliers.

I was puzzled that the administration did nothing. In business, a supervisor need only yell, "Security!" and the harasser would be removed from the premises. But that was not the case here. She walked freely around campus and stood at the crosswalks as students proceeded to the chapel, handing out her broadsides attacking me for teaching "heresy" in my classes.

I would learn later that the administration had told her to desist but that she had refused to comply. In April 1981, Dr. Knittel had written to her,

> Your constant activity in and around our classrooms has been nothing but a point of disturbance. *I am asking you to stay out of our classroom buildings and our library as long as you feel you must pass out your own material.* You have been a disturbance here and *you have made many statements to people which are absolutely false.* At this point you seem to generate problems on our campus and I am asking you to stop passing out your material immediately. *I do not wish to resort to a legal order, but I will do so* if I discover that in the future you are in any of our campus buildings passing material around or agitating in any way.[12]

She wrote for the "news" paper and later *The SDA Press Release*. She also wrote long letters to the General Conference and the *Adventist Review* that were copied and spread around the community. Incredibly, she received letters back from leaders at the General Conference endorsing her witch hunt and these letters of support were printed in the local scandal sheets for all to see.

Elder Kenneth H. Wood, the editor of the *Adventist Review*, responded to her letters encouragingly. In one of them he wrote,

> Recently I spent considerable time studying God's relation to His people anciently. I was impressed with how He continued to be patient with them even when they were in the rankest apostasy.... Many things are not right, but God is still in His heaven. In His own time He will carry forward His purposes. In the meantime we must be loyal and do our best to turn things around. I sense a good deal of frustration in your letters. *You have reason for frustration,* but take heart as you realize that the Lord has "seven thousand in Israel who have not bowed the knee to Baal."... *Do what you can as an individual to stand for*

---

12. "Letter to Mrs. Florence Woolcock from Dr. Frank Knittel," April 24, 1981. Emphases supplied. *SMC Faculty Document Committee Collection.*

the truth and encourage others, but do not let the enemy push you into doing things that will discredit the cause which we all love.[13]

She repeated that Elder Zackrison did not believe in Sister White and should be fired for accepting the sacred tithe since he was teaching the new theology. She continued that I was teaching Dr. Ford's version of the doctrine of the pre-advent judgment. So now I was a Fordite. Her charges were taken up by Vance Ferrell (a veteran of the old perfectionist Brinsmead movement).[14] He publicized twenty-six "heresies" that I allegedly taught.

Perhaps out of fear that the SMC charges would die a natural death, Vance Ferrell reproduced the "news" paper in his periodic papers a year after it had been originally distributed. I appealed to him in a letter of July 24, 1982, to cease and desist—that this was not helping the Church with its struggles. I sent him my phone number, so he could call me since he had never followed Matthew 18 and Christ's method for settling such disputes, yet he insisted on keeping these issues alive.

Instead of calling me he printed more material of a muckraking nature for the public to read. He claimed that what he had printed in his material was between my students and me. Why he was publishing this was therefore left unclear. From then on, he would quote her, and she would quote him, both echoing each other's paranoia. Repeatedly, she charged that everything I lectured on was aimed at raising doubts about the Truths of Adventism.

He alleged that if this ever ended up in a court battle that students would be coming from all over the world to testify against me. Most of his publication was irrelevant to what I had written in my letter and tended to meander all around on various subjects and charges.[15]

Eventually, she would charge me with being an undercover Catholic Jesuit who had infiltrated the Adventist educational system. In a two-hour interview arranged by Dr. Wagner in his office on November 7, 1983, she repeatedly called me "a liar."[16]

What made her accusations so lethal and so credible to the local zealots was the encouragement she received by established leaders at the General Conference, especially Elder Wood. He wrote to her,

> For a number of years I have been following the work of Vance Ferrell and his Pilgrim's Rest program. *Everything that I have read thus far indicates that*

---

13. "Letter from Elder Kenneth H. Wood to Mrs. Florence Woolcock," January 18, 1982, 1. Emphases supplied. *SMC Faculty Document Committee Collection.*

14. Springett, "Historical Observations," 23.

15. These behaviors were not unusual among Adventist fundamentalists.

16. "Wagner-Woolcock Discussion," *Appendix, Zackrison/Southern College* (November 7, 1983), 90, 93, 95, 97, 106, 107, 118. These were the direct hits, but the overall interview carried the general charge that I was a liar—motivation? To keep my job.

> *Brother Ferrell is telling the truth and is a strong defender of the true Adventist faith.*[17]

But she wanted more than general support. She wanted Elder Wood to embrace a particular conspiracy theory concocted by a conman by the name of Alberto Rivera (1935–1997), who claimed to have been a key player in an alleged Jesuit master plan to subvert Protestant churches by having their operatives infiltrate the leadership of these churches.

Alberto Rivera's claims were featured in two comic books published by Jack Chick (1924–2016) Publications, and since his enumeration of churches infiltrated by Jesuit priests started alphabetically with Adventists, a self-appointed Adventist evangelist Mike Clute met with Rivera and after running a series of names past Clute left with a tape and the names of four Jesuits masquerading as Adventists: Desmond Ford, Walter Rea, Samuele Bacchiocchi (1938–2008) and Roland Hegstad (1926–2018).

These "revelations" set the zealots on fire, and Mrs. Woolcock pled with Elder Wood to accept them. But this proved one bridge too far. Elder Wood was no friend of ours, but he was not about to concede the possibility that his colleagues were Jesuit plants. When he took issue with her on this point, his usefulness to her was over. She wrote back,

> I differ with you about the Jesuits having infiltrated the church. . . . Alberto claims that the SDA church is more infiltrated than any other protestant denomination. And that the Colleges is [sic] where most of them are. . . . After I read these comic books . . . it has the ring of accuracy. There are too many facts presented to charge it all to falsehoods. . . . Our colleges have turned into being tools of Satan to turn our young people away from truth. . . . Of course we hope teachers will change, and we love them; but they know this message better than the young people they are deceiving.[18]

A reader could sense her frustration building as the letter progressed:

> Perhaps things are so bad with these doubters and Jesuits in the G.C. that you feel helpless to do anything, but with God *all* things are possible. If each one of us individually, will be willing to sacrifice, personal feelings, reputation, jobs, money, and even life itself. And if enough people can come to this place, then

---

17. "Letter from Elder Kenneth H. Wood to Mrs. Florence Woolcock," January 18, 1982, Emphasis supplied. *SMC Faculty Document Committee Collection.* Contrast this view with that of other SDA officials in footnote 15 in Chapter 29 above. See also Aage Rendalen, "The Social Cost of Conspiracy Theories," *Adventist Today,* March 2017.

18. "Letter from Mrs. Florence Woolcock to Elder Kenneth H. Wood," January 18, 1982, 1. "Dear Elder Wood, I thank you for your letter which encouraged me a little and discouraged me even more. Do you *really* think that the new theology which questions the year-day principle, the investigative judgment and not being able (through Christ) to overcome sin is a *slightly* different view from historic Adventism? I don't really think you meant that did you? Or did you? And by the way, I don't think 'historic Adventism' is just a viewpoint but God's message to His people and the world." *SMC Faculty Document Committee Collection.*

God can work. But if we are all going to hang back and let the devil say we can't do anything, then where is our faith in Him [sic]. It is mere talk. You speak of patience. How patient do we need to get [sic]. Untill [sic] the devil takes over the whole denomination?[19]

Toward the middle of her letter she began naming names,

> And what about Duncan Eva [sic]. I understand he was counsellor to Neal Wilson. I hear he stands on the side of the new theology.... Mrs. Gladson told my neighbor, who has gone to her for psychological help that Ellen G. White is a fraud! Dr. Knittle [sic] is a liar from the word go. He has lied to me and about me. He is the King of the Apostates, and unless he is gotten out of SMC, you may as well turn the school over, with most of the teachers to the Fordites.... Gary Patterson and Al McClure are new theology.... Gary Patterson called the members at Ooltewah church blasphemers because they dared to question their minister on some of his teachings of new theology.... I should pay tithe (God's money) to pay the apostate teachers to spread apostasy and pay General Conference, Union men (McClure), conference men (Gary Patterson), to do *nothing* about it.[20]

Again, she appealed to Alberto's comic books,

> Alberto has been raised up by God to let us know why some of these things are happening and how *important* it is to insist that teachers be told that they *must* leave our colleges if they are found to be teaching error. At this point preservation of the teaching of the *message God has given us to proclaim is of utmost importance,* even at the price of unifying with Jesuits and false brethren who are determined to lead our message away from what God has given us to proclaim.[21]

Mrs. Woolcock closed her long letter with perhaps the most devastating threat that any Adventist could make to an administrator: redirecting the tithe.

> If I sound a little fristrated [sic].... I do have a right to be. Somebody isn't doing their [sic] job and I don't believe it is God—that's not doing His. Somebody isn't listening, and I know it isn't God that's not. *Half of my tithe is going to* [the editor of the "news" paper], to help him become a true minister of the remnant church. *The other half is going to Vance Ferrell,* who is trying to do something, about this situation. And that's where it will continue to go untill

---

19. Ibid., 2. "I want no unity with false teaching and false doctrines.... My church has *no right* to use my tithe to support their teachings of doubt to my children. I love them, and I am outraged that such things are allowed to go on, while leaders act as if all is well."

20. Ibid., 2, 4.

21. Ibid., 3.

[sic] somebody in the leadership decides to do something positive about this deplorable situation.[22]

STUDENT TESTIMONY

Several students from my Studies in Revelation class came to me after reading the "news" paper. They wanted to know in what class I had taught all this "heresy" because they had never heard any of this from me. I told them simply, "in the class you just took from me." They couldn't believe it.

Because of these claims, students, who knew none of this was true, started passing around petitions to counter the charges. To my knowledge, none of the petitions were ever taken seriously by anyone in authority. That was troubling since the only person standing between us and the zealots was our college president Dr. Knittel. And when he was pressured to resign in the spring of 1983, we knew that it was just a matter of time before we would face the same fate.

Our careers and our ministry were on the line.

---

22. Ibid., 4–5. Emphasis supplied.

CHAPTER THIRTY-THREE

Crisis at the College

"Politicians are the same all over. They promise to build a bridge where there is no river."
—NIKITA KHRUSHCHEV

CUMBERLAND HEIGHTS

IN JUNE 1982, I received an invitation from a pastor I did not know, to speak to his congregation in middle Tennessee. The Cumberland Heights Church had a reputation for being "solidly Adventist," and I was told it had many retired Adventist workers in the congregation. The pastor asked if I would teach the youth Sabbath School class, speak for the Worship Service in the main sanctuary, and then hold an open question and answer period in the afternoon in the Fellowship Hall, as many in his Church had heard disturbing rumors about Southern Missionary College and read the scandal sheets that had been circulating.

He felt it would be wise to have someone from the college talk to the people and answer their questions. Since my name had been circulated widely, he had called me. I happily obliged, and the date was set for July 10, 1982. I preached a sermon on Luke 15, entitled, "A Concerned God." For the afternoon meeting the hall was full. Tape recorders and ghetto blasters lined the front row, and the forest of microphones on the pulpit resembled a press conference at the local law enforcement office as the Chief of Police was about to give an update on a criminal case.

I began the meeting by smiling and telling the group I was happy that this was being taped and they should know that I was also taping it, at which point I held up my micro recorder. "I know you will be careful to quote me correctly if you share what went on here today!" A chuckle rippled through the audience.

The floor was open for questions. I made it clear that they could just stand and ask their question, or they could write it out. I would answer every question that came to me in either form. If there were duplicates, I would answer both since I knew that repetition is often necessary for people to grasp new information. The meeting began around 3:00 pm and I estimated that there were probably about 150 people present. The meeting would go for more than two hours.

Following opening prayer, the first questioner couched an accusation in the form of a question about the book *Omega*. He wanted to know why the SMC Religion Department had "stopped Attorney Lewis Walton from visiting the SMC campus" to lecture on the so-called Omega apostasy. I explained that the SMC Religion Department was neither asked nor given the opportunity to decide whether Lewis Walton could speak on our campus. He had been invited by the local chapter of the Adventist Forums.

I also explained that the SMC Religion Department had its own lecture series, but because of the controversial nature of the Adventist Forums, the department had passed a policy stating that it only invited speakers who were denominational employees. For that reason, our department would not have had the freedom to invite Attorney Walton as he was not employed by the Church.

The SMC Religion Department was therefore not involved in any way in lining up Attorney Walton as a speaker. His vocal organizers had allegedly requested that he be permitted to use the Collegedale Church pulpit but Elder Gordon Bietz, the pastor, already had the pulpit scheduled. Since the Forum people were told that this was the only weekend the attorney would be available, they sought another venue. It was my understanding that he had spoken at another Church in the area. We had been alerted to this by our administration. A group of Walton's supporters had engineered all of this without going through official denominational channels. Even though we had nothing to do with his visit, the Religion Department was accused of being guilty of censuring.

The second question came from the same questioner. It also dealt with the book *Omega*. "Are you wrongly opposed to the [book] *Omega?*" But by the time I finished answering the first question this one had been rephrased by the questioner: "Why do 'the papers' so strongly oppose Walton?" His tone was not friendly.

I asked what papers he was referring to and he answered the *SMC Southern Accent*, the *PUC Campus Chronicle*, *Spectrum*, and the *Southern Columns*, the alumni journal for SMC. I couldn't speak for these papers, but I had read a review of the book in our *Southern Accent*, so I answered, "I can only speak for the *Southern Accent*." I held up the paper, which I had brought with me. "Here is a book review on *Omega* in this paper . . . it is the most positive report on the book that I've read."[1]

At this point the pastor interjected that he wished that "certain people" in the audience would not monopolize the question time so that others could pose their

---

1. Gentry, "*Omega*: A Book Review." *Southern Accent* (March 18, 1982), 20–21.

questions. Next question: "I've got a regular file on you and *you are not exactly my fan.*"[2] This was a poorly worded cheap shot, but I knew what he was trying to say.

"Why are students not permitted tape recorders in theology classes?" I told him I could only speak for my classes. "I encourage all my students to record my lectures—I always have. The practice is good for reviewing for a test. I also record my lectures."[3] He sat down, noticeably disappointed.

That was followed by a question regarding why only students could sit in on our classes. I didn't recall anyone being kept from visiting classes if proper arrangements had been made, if there was a vacant seat available. I could have added that *these were college classes that students had paid for,* not open forums for the community, but I didn't.

NO HOLDS BARRED

Some of the questions got more personal. The next questioner asked: "Why did you help Walter Rea write *The White Lie?*"[4] I had heard a rumor that Elder Rea had suggested this when he spoke at Covenant College, a Presbyterian school on Lookout Mountain near Chattanooga. I hadn't been at the lecture, and some of those who had been there couldn't remember hearing him make that statement. At any rate, I answered that "I had no hand in writing his book."[5]

I asked the questioner if he had been at Elder Rea's Covenant College lecture. He said "no." I told him I hadn't been there either and that anything I could say would be hearsay. I told them about the assignment I had received from Dr. Robert Olson (1920–2013), secretary of the Ellen G. White Estate in Washington. He had told me that Elder Rea was planning to publish a book on his findings regarding Sister White's alleged plagiarizing. Dr. Olson had called to ask me if I would be willing to serve on a committee in Washington looking into this. I had accepted the assignment.

The first and only assignment I was given as a member of this committee was to visit Elder Rea in California and get what information I could about his rumored book. The White Estate's hope was that, if possible, I might talk him out of publishing it. I requested that Dr. Springett go with me since he had a doctorate in literary criticism, which could come in handy. Dr. Olson agreed, and the two of us flew to Southern

---

2. "Transcript of the Cumberland Heights Discussion," *Appendix, Zackrison/Southern* (July 10, 1982), 38.

3. Ibid.

4. Ibid., 39–40.

5. I later received word from a former student, who had heard the rumor, who said he was on the platform and had introduced Elder Rea at the Covenant College lecture. He related to me, "I can't remember that he even mentioned you. If he had said that you had had anything to do with that book, I for sure would have remembered it." It was another story fabricated by people preaching sinless perfection.

California at denominational expense. We stayed with my mother in Glendale for a week at her expense and made several visits to Elder Rea at his home in Arcadia.

I described to the Church members my internship under Elder Rea in 1967 and I pointed out that no one had taught me more about taking Sister White seriously than he had. I told them that he had put me on a study plan of reading Sister White's writings and taking notes for several hours each day, a plan I was still following. I explained that Elder Rea had allowed Dr. Springett and me to read his manuscript in its prepublication form except for the last chapter, which he said he hadn't finished yet. I also explained to my audience that I was sure I had been appointed to this committee because of those eight months in 1966–1967 when I had interned under Elder Rea and we were friends. The White Estate obviously thought that they could use the help of somebody who was on friendly terms with him.

After two or three visits with Elder Rea, Dr. Springett and I finally negotiated *an agreement with him not to publish his book.* He agreed on condition that Elder Neal Wilson would meet his requests. Dr. Jerry Wiley, his attorney and the vice-dean of the School of Law at University of Southern California, met with us and drew up the terms of the agreement. Dr. Wiley would call Elder Wilson, General Conference president, with the agreement. If Elder Wilson accepted the conditions, *Elder Rea would agree not to publish his book.*

After some deliberation, Elder Wilson rejected the agreement. No more discussion—he stubbornly would not hear of any agreement. I was surprised. We had accomplished the very thing we had been sent to California to do, only to have it squashed by the "First Minister" of the Church. Elder Rea's reply was predictable and simple: "Fine! Then we go to press! . . . And we sign the movie contract as well." I could only shake my head in disbelief.

The book was eventually published as *The White Lie*.[6] We did not hear more about the made-for-TV movie that a major film studio in Southern California had been negotiating with Elder Rea. The film was rumored to be the story of how Elder Rea, a hard-core supporter of Ellen White's prophetic gift, had to reframe his faith when he uncovered the shocking facts about her plagiarism. We left California wondering why we had been sent there to begin with.

When we got back home to Collegedale, Dr. Knittel called the White Estate and took Dr. Springett and me off the committee. False rumors about our "collusion" with Elder Rea were already swirling around, and it was anybody's guess what the toxic rumor mill in Happy Valley was going to make of these mendacious stories.

Dr. Knittel did not know what the repercussions might be. He explained to the White Estate that I was already teaching a full load of classes and researching and writing a doctoral dissertation. I did not have time to devote to another committee assignment for the General Conference. That was the extent of our involvement with

---

6. Rea, *The White Lie*, (1982).

Elder Rea and his new book, "So, in answer to your question," I told my inquisitor at Cumberland Heights, "No, I did not help Elder Rea write his book."

After my lengthy explanation, I asked him, "Now, brother, does that help to change your perception at all?"[7] And he simply answered, "Not really." As far as he was concerned, it was case closed, and truth was not a necessary factor. His face showed genuine disappointment at my explanation. It appeared that he wanted to believe the worst, and my story would make it impossible for him to do so. I simply said, "I see; perhaps it does some of the rest of you."

Facts were clearly confusing those who wanted to believe the worst. I have often thought back on that day and the look of disappointment on that man's face. I found it difficult to understand the appalling negativity of these ardent critics, especially since they belonged to my own faith community.

The meeting lasted for over two hours. When I got back to campus, I had the tapes transcribed to a manuscript, which came to twenty-five single-spaced typewritten pages. The questions had followed a predictable line. I was amazed at some of the inquiries and how passionately people seemed to want to believe the most negative rumors they had heard or read. They were apparently looking for fulfillment of prophecy.

My understanding of the Church as the family of God was being challenged. I saw this as just a small-scale version of what was going on all over the Southern Union Conference. A vicious fundamentalist uprising fanned by lies, conspiracy theories and influential families with money was spreading across the land.[8]

THE ADVENTIST CATECHISTIC SESSION

For the record, here are some of the questions I was asked in that afternoon meeting at the Cumberland Heights Church. Here are some of my answers (in the order the questions were asked):

---

7. *Appendix, Zackrison/Southern College,* 40.

8. For perspective see Rendalen, "The Cost of Conspiracy Theories." *Adventism Today,* March 6, 2017: "After leaving church employment and the Seventh-day Adventist church, I spent 1981–1982 in Collegedale, where my in-laws lived. I saw firsthand how the social fabric of the community was ripped apart by a group of Torquemada wannabees pushing the Jesuit conspiracy theory. They won the support of key people in the community who had enough money to blackmail the college and the local conference to do their bidding. Incongruously, these vigilantes found supporters in high places, such as Kenneth Wood, editor of the *Review,* and the president of the Southern Union Al McClure. Kenneth Wood, in a letter to the flakiest of the Collegedale vigilantes, written on Jan 18, 1982, encouraged her and the other heresy hunters who were patrolling the community with theological pitchforks to keep up the good work but he drew the line at her Alberto-based charge that the church was shot through with Jesuits. In frustration, she wrote back to Wood: 'Perhaps things are so bad with these doubters and Jesuits in the GC that you feel helpless to do anything, but with God *all* things are possible.' It certainly was possible to get rid of the college president and destroy the religion department by getting rid of its most popular and creative professors and replace them with a retired authoritarian bureaucrat and compliant traditionalists vying for a seat on the infamous EGW chair of theology endowed by the very people who had led the crusade against the college."

Question: "Have you ever taken theology classes under Ford?"
Answer: "No."[9]

Question: "What did you think of the Ringgold meetings where students testified that several teachers were teaching new theology?"
Answer: "I don't know. I was not there."[10]

Question: "Do you at SMC make the students read *The White Lie?*"
Answer: "No."[11]

Question: "My daughter works in the student aid at Andrews [University] and she sees how crooked things are going on in the church."
Answer: "I'm not aware."[12]

Question: "Do you agree with the fact that the Adventist church runs casinos in Las Vegas?"
Answer: "I was not aware of that."[13]

Question: "What do you think of Andrews University giving money through the neo-science department to the Mafia to deduct from income tax and then they get it back again as a donation?"
Answer: "I had not heard of this."[14]

Question: "Do you believe, or does the Religion Department believe, that Christ began his second and final phase of ministry that we call the investigative judgment?'"
Answer: "No issue."[15]

Question: "Do you agree with Ford that Sister White was just a pastoral authority? Would you explain the 'new theology?' I've heard that some of the faculty members defend Dr. Ford, is that true?
Answer: "'New theology' is never defined, and Dr. Ford is not the subject of our lectures."[16]

Question: "Did one professor ask his students to sign a statement in support of Des Ford?"
Answer: "No."[17]

Question: "Has the Church been fair to Dr. Ford?"

---

9. Ibid., 41.
10. Ibid., 42.
11. Ibid., 43–44.
12. Ibid., 43.
13. Ibid.
14. Ibid., 43–44.
15. Ibid., 44.
16. Ibid., 46–45.
17. Ibid., 46–47.

Answer: "A matter of opinion. Probably not."[18]

Question: "Is it possible to live without sin?'"
Answer: "Only in Christ."[19]

Question: Are the Heritage Singers allowed on the SMC campus?
Answer: I don't know.[20]

Question: Are there any pastors in the Collegedale area who go along with Ford?
Answer: Not aware.[21]

Question: Why is Southern Missionary College dropping its name?
Answer: Board decision.[22]

Question: After we are baptized should we sin anymore?
Answer: No. But we do.[23]

Question: Can we achieve perfection in this world before Christ comes?
Answer: Only in Christ.[24]

Question: Is it true that Dr. Knittel does not believe in the blueprint?
Answer: Yes. He said in a chapel talk that there is no "blueprint." This is just a figure of speech. A blueprint shows every detail even down to the kind of nails to be used. Sister White did not do this. She gave principles for Adventists to apply. That is not a blueprint.[25]

Question: Did Dr. Knittel say that *Messages to Young People* should never have been written?
Answer: He made a statement in his Sabbath School class. He said the book should never have been issued in the form that it has been. The book is a compilation, not a book organized by Sister White. Many people agreed with him. This was his opinion. He said in passing that the tone of the book is more negative than he believed Sister White would have been had she written it as published. Many young people agree with this.[26]

Question: Do you blame Sister White for the divisions in the church?
Answer: No.[27]

Question: Do you pass out Ford tapes in your class?

18. Ibid., 47.
19. Ibid., 47–48.
20. Ibid., 49.
21. Ibid., 49–50.
22. Ibid., 50.
23. Ibid., 50–51.
24. Ibid.
25. Ibid., 51–52.
26. Ibid., 52.
27. Ibid., 53.

> Answer: No.[28]
>
> Question: I notice you didn't quote Mrs. White in your sermon.
> Answer: I sometimes do but she asked us not to. I try not to. The basis of our doctrine as Adventists is the Bible not Sister White.[29]

The big question was yet to come. I changed my tape recorder a few times. Fortunately, I had brought several tapes. By now, I had noticed that most of the questions had been lifted from Vance Ferrell's materials or the "news" paper. I was amazed at how widely the circulation of these papers had been and how readily people believed their scurrilous propaganda. I had grown up in an Adventist society where these kinds of materials carried no credibility. But Happy Valley was unique. This was the buckle of the Adventist Bible belt.

I was beginning to understand better the conversation with a classmate from Seminary who told Dr. Springett and me that we could make a lot more money than the Church was paying us if we just bought our own offset press and began cranking our publications that questioned the integrity of the official Church—a career path that he himself had chosen to follow.

> Question: Do you believe in the indwelling of the Spirit?
> Answer: Yes.

Not all theological questions can be easily answered by a yes or a no. But this was the question I was expecting because it had been raised in the "news" paper—something I had supposedly said in my *Righteousness by Faith* class. I had spoken in response to a recent outburst of hysteria about indwelling demons and exorcism that had been visited upon Collegedale.

CHRIST IN YOU

The topic in my class had been, "Christ in You." As a Christian, what do the scriptural writers mean by the expression "Christ in you?"

> [9] But you are not in the flesh, you are *in the Spirit,* if in fact the *Spirit of God dwells in you.* [10] Any one who does not have the Spirit of Christ does not belong to him. But if *Christ is in you,* although your bodies are dead because of sin, your spirits are alive because of righteousness." (Rom 8:9–10. Emphases supplied)

While the issue was a standard part of the class, there was a local context, which made this question highly relevant—and controversial. When the local scandal sheet, the "news" paper, accused me of not believing in the "indwelling of the Spirit," it did not

---

28. Ibid., 53–54.
29. Ibid., 54.

mention the local context, and thus its readers were told that I was a rank heretic, denying a scriptural teaching.

Our Collegedale community was at the time still recovering from a serious outbreak of religious fanaticism. For the better part of a year (1980), Happy Valley had encountered a new religious phenomenon. In his report to the College Board, President Knittel had described it as follows,

> Within the past few months there has arisen a little group in our community who have become involved with exorcism—the casting out of demons from various individuals who are troubled with a variety of ailments, both physical and mental. There was no real public dimension to this until a couple of months ago when through a marathon session involved one full night and parts of another day and night, the group allegedly cast out more than seventy demons from one of our employees in our computer department. Each of these demons was named after one of the causes of allergies, such as "cookie" (because of the sugar involved).[30]

In non-Adventist fundamentalist churches (usually Pentecostal), this "ministry" was often called spiritual warfare. But on American soil such phenomena had not been seen in Adventism since the earliest days of its history, and after a few years the new denomination had strongly opposed charismatic phenomena and classified them as fanaticism.

The Collegedale demon craze started when seminars were held around the area by SDA laymen from Michigan who were stressing that the "latter rain"[31] was going to involve the casting out of demons. In fact, the advocates suggested that this might be the missing purification process that would prepare the Church for the *Parousia*. Once more, the idea that God required people to reach sinless perfection before the second coming of Christ was generating aberrant theology and controversy. The speakers at these seminars promised how to produce the sinless perfection needed for translation that the Adventist fundamentalists were looking for.

Sister White wrote of the latter rain of the Spirit. The event would only occur as our minds were stayed on Christ.[32] The effect would be to cleanse hearts of all selfishness.[33] To receive this latter rain, one must work diligently for Christ[34] because the indolent would never receive it.[35] At one point it had been predicted to fall in 1908.[36]

---

30. President Frank Knittel, "Report to College Board," *SMC Faculty Document Committee Collection* (March 10, 1980), 1.

31. In Adventism the latter rain is an illustration from the Jewish agricultural year applied to a revival involving the "outpouring of the Holy Spirit" just prior to the *Parousia*.

32. White, *Selected Messages*, 3:204.

33. White, *In Heavenly Places*, 348; White, *Maranatha: The Lord is Coming*, 95.

34. White, *Last Day Events*, 193.

35. White, *In Heavenly Places*, 338.

36. White, *Selected Messages*, 3:83.

Some on the SMC faculty and staff (though none from the Religion Department) were for a time engaged in this new phenomenon. Individual members of the Religion Department took a firm stand against it. It became personal to me in that one of our moderators in *The Positive Way*, and a member of the SMC English Department faculty, became deeply engaged in the practice.

She came to see me and testified that she was spending whole weekends in what she called this "wonderful spiritual warfare ministry." She would come back to school on Monday mornings exhausted but energized. She had found a practical way, she said, to apply the claiming of promises as taught in *The Positive Way Christian Life Seminar.*

Not only were individuals filled with these evil spirits, we were told, but houses, mobile homes and college classrooms were infested as well, so the story went. We heard of exorcisms being performed on a classroom before the students could enter and on a student in the college trailer court. Students in the dormitories were beginning to practice it on roommates and friends.

Some of those who received these spiritual interventions were rumored to have had histories of mental illness. An exorcism session could last for thirteen to fourteen hours, according to those active in this ministry. Our *Positive Way* moderator had ordered demons to come out of their hosts, and they would obey reluctantly, revealing their names as they exited.[37] Some were very resistant; hence some sessions were drawn out over many hours. I did not ask for a demonstration, so I never saw or participated in the phenomenon. But there were definite theological implications to such practice.

The demons that were cast out had names: "Coca Cola," "snack cakes" and "chocolate" along with many and varied allergies. In her own case, this faculty member told her class that she had been filled with an evil spirit named "Dr. Pepper." She told of how for years she would sneak down to the gas station on campus at the noon hour where the vending machine dispensed Dr. Pepper. With no one witnessing, she had drunk that forbidden caffeinated brew. Only recently did she become aware that she was nourishing an active demon in her body by that very name, "Dr. Pepper."

She was excited as she testified how the demon "Dr. Pepper" had been cast out of her through these exorcism methods and how that had helped to convince her that this ministry was valid and finally something she was being called to lead out in. This miracle was the clincher for her.[38] In the Sabbath School a new resident to Happy

---

37. President Frank Knittel, "Presentation to College Board," *SMC Faculty Document Committee Collection.* (March 10, 1980), 1: "We began to hear rumors that one of our teaching staff members was very much involved with the entire matter of demon possession. There was the story of one occasion a demon was cast out of a classroom before class could begin. There came to be a discussion among the students because allegedly class time was taken up with discussion of demon possession. One girl came to our campus chaplain in fear because, as she related it, it had been suggested to her that if a demon were cast out of her, she could be cured of asthma. One student stopped in the hall and with vehemence declared that he had a class from the teacher involved and that he did not want to hear any more about demon possession in his class and he expected me to put a stop to it."

38. Ibid. "All of these incidents arose rather quickly within a very short period of time, together

Valley, who was a staff member at the college, told of his recent move into the community. He and his family were riddled with allergies (not unusual in the deep South). But not until he was shown by one engaged in this ministry did he and his wife and kids experience relief from these allergies. The allergies, he said, were literal demons. When they were cast out, relief finally came to his home. Each came out of his body announcing its name. Even his eighteen-month-old baby had been exorcised.[39]

President Knittel's report to the college board continued,

> I ultimately wrote our employee a letter stating that his job with us was not on the line, but that if it became necessary to repeat the performance, we surely would review his case, because it would be very damaging to the school to employ anyone who periodically became possessed with demons. I had hoped the matter would cease there, but unfortunately it did not.[40]

At first this phenomenon was confusing. Demons could be a figure of speech, but in his report to the Sabbath School, this staff member insisted that these were *literal* demons. They were actual, bodily demons that came out of him and his family by name in the exorcist session.[41] He repeated several times that these were literal devils that had taken up residence in his body.

All of this called into question the efficacy of Christian conversion, which traditionally promised freedom from demon possession, or demon "harassment" as those in this "ministry" called it. A Christian who continually struggled with bodily demons was hardly a picture of Christian freedom and deliverance. And this immediacy with the demonic had frightening theological implications. Not until these exorcisms had been performed had any relief come to this staff member's home, he said.

---

with one involving student discipline. One of our young dormitory residents came to us after we decided to give him a chance for a new start after he was in trouble on one of our other campuses for homosexuality. To our sorrow, he continued in his homosexual pattern here, and at the close of the first semester we told him it would be necessary for him to leave. Our teacher involved with exorcism became much interested in the matter and spent a great deal of time with the boy and ultimately cast the demon homosexuality out of him, according to his report. He then presented himself to our dean of students and stated he was now cleansed and wanted to be reinstated. Within the week, however, he rather badly frightened another student with his behavior and there was some discussion about strangling the other student, and of course we did not change our position regarding the homosexual students' relationship to the school.

"At this point, I felt it mandatory to have some formal recognition to the entire situation, so I wrote a letter to the teacher stating that we could not tolerate a plan whereby students in difficulty could run to be exorcised in order to avoid being dropped from school. The letter indicated that if the teacher were to develop the reputation of being the last resort of every student in social or academic difficulty, the resulting outcome would be damaging to both the teacher and the school."

39. Ibid.

40. Ibid.

41. As a rule, these participants were instructed not to call it "exorcism" because that was Roman Catholic terminology and referred to a specific Catholic ritual followed by the priests, which was not used locally by those engaged in spiritual warfare.

I attended the early Sabbath worship service at a neighborhood Adventist Church during an exorcism seminar and heard the visiting preacher suggest that in this ministry we had the answer to the sins in the Church. He told the congregation that before Christ comes again, the Church will be purified, and a sinless group of people would emerge. This group would prove that the law of God could be kept and finally Christ would return and claim his own. By casting the demons out of our brothers and sisters we could hasten the coming of our Lord!

This movement came to play a significant role in the attack that would later be launched against the college and the Religion professors. Many involved in the movement would be foremost in the attack on the Religion Department because we did not get on board and join it. What initially worried us about this movement were the logical expectations to be found in its aberrant theology.

FILLED WITH THE DEVIL VS. FILLED WITH THE SPIRIT

From the point of view of folk religion, the mixture of perfectionism, fundamentalism, and old Brinsmeadism was attractive to some in Happy Valley. The theological implications were staggering, to say nothing of the Christian walk. "Spiritual Warfare" had always been classified as fanaticism by Adventists and thus was never incorporated into Church culture.

From a biblical standpoint, this theology amounted to an attack on personal responsibility. For example, if you were filled with demons, any sin you committed would be the demon committing the sin in you. To overcome drinking Dr. Pepper, for example, you had to cast out the demon called "Dr. Pepper" before the sin was overcome. To overcome any sin, you had to get rid of the demon that was doing the sinning.

Logically then, the opposite also had to be true, i.e., if you were truly filled with the Holy Ghost, you would be living a sinless life since the Holy Spirit was bodily "in you." All the sinless actions were being performed by the Spirit in you. When did human responsibility enter the picture? Such theology had no place in Adventism. Still, here was the answer, the preacher suggested in that early Sabbath sermon, to the question of how "the final generation" was finally to achieve sinless perfection!

This view was appealing to those who held to the so-called "harvest principle" of the Adventist fundamentalists. Reaching this coveted state of sinless perfection, in their thinking, would clear the way for the *Parousia*. As I evaluated what was happening, it struck me that none of this could be found in mainline Adventist theology. This was an immediacy of the divine bordering on mysticism. And there was clearly a pantheistic element in this. Could this be a manifestation of Ellen White's warning about the Omega of all apostasies?

Bombarded with questions from students and community members, those of us in the Religion Department distanced ourselves from this "ministry." I shut down *The Positive Way* program on campus out of concern that it had been used to promote it.

Despite all the good that had been accomplished through this class over the previous ten years, I could see that the program could be twisted and given a very unfortunate spin. Our own moderator had seriously compromised our entire approach. *The Positive Way* did not support the idea that all sins were the direct result of *literal* demons occupying a Christian.

Critics of *The Positive Way* program had sometimes charged that we were turning God into a celestial vending machine. But now I was confronted with a moderator doing just that and suggesting that this was the secret to attaining sinless perfection. It left me little choice, I had to shut it down. *The Positive Way* class promoted an active prayer life focused on recognizing gifts Christ had won on our behalf and taking seriously God's promises in the Bible. It was never promoted as a road to sinlessness or a redefinition of the biblical gospel.

I spent time with our moderator, but to no avail. The word about the exorcism program at Southern had spread and as I spent the summer of 1982 doing research at James White Library at Andrews in Michigan I was asked to give a report to the doctoral brown-bag luncheon that met on Thursdays at noon. The talk was recorded (unknown to me) even though I had been assured that no recording would be done. And somebody sent a copy of the recording back to our moderator, who then took me to task. I still could not see where any of this would finally lead.

The administration worked patiently with her, but she was finally told that in her position as a faculty member she could not carry on this ministry at the college.[42] She rejected all efforts by the administration to stop what she was doing. By now, she was in high demand, she said, spending weekends casting out the demons from people all around Happy Valley, services she performed at no cost. This encouraged her to believe that she was doing God's work.

The college administration finally decided that it had no choice. She was fired together with the other staff member. It apparently came to a head when she had cast out "the demon of lithium" from a student who had been diagnosed with bipolar disorder. This drug had been prescribed by a physician. The administration argued that the college could not risk the legal implications that could result from such action. Added to that was the fact that she was promoting a theology at odds with the Adventist Church.

Dr. Knittel's opposition to this movement was used by his enemies to finally remove him as president, although, as we shall see, they did not stop there. In the

---

42. Ibid., 2. "I [Dr. Knittel] finally called our teacher in for a conference, and Dr. Hanson [the college academic dean] and I spoke with her together. There was no denial of the substance of the rumors, and there was rather a defense of the total situation. I finally told this teacher that our college was not the arena in which this rather new development in our church could be enacted and that our college students were not appropriate subjects and that our college teachers could not appropriately be the enactors. I told her that her continued stay with us would necessitate her removal from the rites of exorcism."

Index to Sister White's writings[43] many references to "demons" could be found. Those involved in this ministry insisted that these descriptions were to be taken *literally*. For example, there was the "demon of evil and cruelty" strengthened by the "demon power of alcohol,"[44] the "demon of greed,"[45] the "demon of jealousy,"[46] the "demon of strife,"[47] the "demon of unkindness,"[48] to name a few.

If these were valid perceptions, the list could be almost endless. In each case, one was to read these as references to actual, personal demons that needed to be cast out. I was not aware that anyone in the Adventist Church had ever held such an outlandish view of these statements before these spiritual warriors showed up.

In stretches of twelve to thirteen hours of exorcist activity, sometimes fifty to sixty demons were driven out of a person's home and life. One student came to my office to tell me excitedly that he now understood for the first time in his life what "true ministry" meant. He said he was now casting out the demons of his roommates and others in the dorm where he resided. They all had demons living in them, he said!

One report told of a Collegedale resident who was tied up to a tree in the forest with copper wires to aid in the exorcism. Another report told of a Collegedale physician, who later would attack the Religion Department, was practicing "animal magnetism." I didn't know what kind of pseudo-science he was dabbling in, but it did not seem surprising that later he would support the fundamentalists at war with the theology professors and the administrators who defended us.

To some local exorcists, we were either filled with the Holy Spirit or possessed by the devil. In logic, this kind of argument is called "the fallacy of false dilemma," i.e., a wrong-headed either/or argument.[49]

---

43. *The Comprehensive Index to the Writings of Ellen G. White*, 1:787–788.

44. White, *Temperance*, 39. "Those who sell intoxicating liquor to their fellow men . . . receive the earnings of the drunkard, and give him no equivalent for his money. Instead of this, they give him that which maddens him, which makes him act the fool, and turns him into *a demon of evil and cruelty*." Emphasis supplied.

45. White, 92. "Judas, . . . surrendered his soul to *the demon of greed* . . ." Emphasis supplied.

46. Whte, *Patriarchs and Prophets*, 650. Speaking of King Saul, she wrote that "*the demon of jealousy* entered the heart of the king." Emphasis supplied.

47. White, *The Adventist Home*, 106. "If the law of God is obeyed, *the demon of strife* will be kept out of the family, and no separation of interests will take place, no alienation of affection will be permitted." Emphasis supplied.

48. White, *The Sanctified Life*, 16. "Some who profess to be servants of Christ have so long cherished *the demon of unkindness* that they seem to love the unhallowed element and to take pleasure in speaking words that displease and irritate." Emphasis supplied.

49. Chaffee, *Thinking Critically,* Sixth Edition, 457. "The fallacy of the false dilemma—also known as the either/or fallacy or the black-or-white fallacy—occurs when we are asked to choose between two extreme alternatives without being able to consider additional options." Chaffee gives examples: "She loves me; she loves me not;" "If you're not part of the solution, then you're part of the problem;" "If you know about BMW, you either own one or you want to." And Adventists in this "ministry" could add a new one, "You are either filled with the Spirit or filled with demons."

The question of "Christ in you," a biblical expression, came up in my *Righteousness by Faith* class.

> [10] But if Christ is in you, although your bodies are dead because of sin, your spirits are alive because of righteousness. [11] If the Spirit of him who raised Jesus from the dead dwells in you, he who raised Christ Jesus from the dead will give life to your mortal bodies also through his Spirit which dwells in you. (Rom 8:10–11)

I suggested that because of its subjectivity, we should be suspicious of any view that stressed a mystical immediacy with the divine. Adventists had fought long, hard battles with this in history. I explained to my class that having "Christ in you," or "the indwelling of the Holy Spirit," means that the principles of Christ guide our lives. I pointed the class to the explanation in Sister White's instruction.

> No repentance is genuine that does not work reformation. The righteousness of Christ is not a cloak to cover unconfessed and unforsaken sin; *it is a principle of life* that transforms the character and controls the conduct. Holiness is wholeness for God; it is the entire surrender of the heart and life to the *indwelling of the principles of heaven*.[50]

The law of God is written in the heart. This is a metaphor for accepting the instructions of Christ whole-heartedly. Only one student had ever objected to this notion in all the many times I had taught the class. For over half an hour he argued for a literal Christ bodily inhabiting in the manner that demons did. When I finally saw that I was not getting through to him, I moved on since the class was getting restless. This student subsequently became a writer for the "news" paper, and he made it a point to tell people that I did not believe in "the indwelling of the Spirit."

Here is how I dealt with the question of the indwelling of Christ at the Cumberland Heights Church meeting, verbatim from the transcript:[51]

> Zackrison: Have you heard of *The Positive Way* program?
> Questioner: No.
> Zackrison: It's a seminar in Christian living that we have run for ten years at SMC. The first assignment that every student [taking the class] is given is to pray three times a day for the indwelling of the Holy Spirit. It is a conundrum how anybody could conclude after ten years of my teaching that class on campus that I didn't believe in the indwelling of the Spirit!
>
> In my teaching of salvation, I am principles oriented. I didn't want an emotional answer, or glossolalia, or Pentecostalism, or that sort of thing. Much of that can't be tested and the Bible says, "Beloved, do not believe every spirit, but test the spirits to see whether they are of God; for many false prophets have

---

50. White, *The Desire of Ages*, 555–556. Emphases supplied. For a brief discussion of this issue see, Zackrison, *The First Temptation*, 340–344.

51. *Appendix, Zackrison/Southern College*, 57.

gone out into the world." (1 John 4:1). But test them how? By the word, by the testimony, by the Law and so on; by something substantial, something real. By the objective principles lived out in the life of the believer.

I finally suggested that "Christ in you," from the practical sense, means that through the "indwelling of the Holy Spirit," and by his power, the principles of Christ are being applied and followed in your life. It is always by your choice. This preserves your responsibility.

Toward the end of the meeting, every question from the audience revealed a preoccupation with sinless perfectionism. Can we live without sin? Can we keep the Sabbath perfectly?

THE CLOSE OF THE MEETING

As the meeting wound to a close, a man, who I did not know, stood up about halfway back in the auditorium, and asked for the floor. The pastor recognized him, and the man spoke. He shared that he enjoyed the meeting we had had. He had heard the stories about the SMC Religion Department and my part. Every bad thing he had heard about us he had passed on without checking anything out.

He had never met me or heard me speak. He had never read anything I had written. Obviously, he had never attended a class I taught. But after hearing me talk and answer questions the congregation would bring up, he realized how wrong he had been and asked my forgiveness. From now on he said he would be praying for me and hoped that God would reverse any negative affect he might have had.

It was moving. I believed the Spirit was working in this meeting. Here was an example of the very thing I had been talking about—the principles of Christ being applied under the influence of the Holy Spirit. The audience responded graciously to his public confession. I could hear them uttering "Amen" and other verbal assurances.

When I left the auditorium, a group of older men, who I took to be retired ministers, had gathered in the foyer. They all had their hands out and their smiles on as I walked through them. Most of them hugged me. All said they appreciated the meeting and they said that they would be praying for me.

On my way home that afternoon I thought of this man who acted the Christian behavior that Jesus had taught. I thought, we can talk about whether sinless perfection is the answer to the problems in the Church and the world; we can theorize about whether anyone must attain to such a state. What bothered me was that there was such a discrepancy between the theology of perfection and the behavior of those who promoted it. It seemed as if the more certain people were in their perfectionist convictions, the less perfect their behavior became.

PONDERING THESE THINGS

As I left the congregation, I thought about a story Dr. Walter F. Specht, my major professor in college, had told in his Philosophy of Religion class. A woman approached the well-known English theologian and preacher Charles Spurgeon after hearing one of his sermons. When she got his attention, she said, "I thought you would be happy to know, pastor, that I have not sinned for two years now." He shook her hand and replied quietly, "Well sister, you must be mighty proud of that!" And she replied, "Indeed I am!"

As humans, we have many blind spots. It is a symptom of the human condition. Every religious movement has its built-in cult elements, and Adventism is no exception. These are mostly people who crave certainty but have a hard time determining what is theologically correct and must wait for someone else to tell them what to believe. We were seeing a lot of this.

As professors, we could not lean on anyone. We had to do a good job every time we entered the pulpit or stood behind the lectern in the classroom, often at the risk of being misunderstood. The kind of activism we were seeing was breaking up the unity of the Church and spreading confusion about the mission of the Church.

Through my entire ministry I had encouraged people, when they saw what they considered to be sins or shortcomings in their "brethren," to follow the procedure Jesus outlined in his teachings.

> [15] "If your brother sins against you, go and tell him his fault, *between you and him alone*. If he listens to you, you have gained your brother. [16] But if he does not listen, *take one or two others along with you*, that every word may be confirmed by the evidence of two or three witnesses. [17] If he refuses to listen to them, *tell it to the church*; and if he refuses to listen even to the church, let him be to you as a Gentile and a tax collector.
>
> [18] "Truly, I say to you, whatever you bind on earth shall be bound in heaven, and whatever you loose on earth shall be loosed in heaven. [19] Again I say to you, if two of you agree on earth about anything they ask, it will be done for them by my Father in heaven. [20] For where two or three are gathered in my name, there am I in the midst of them." (Matt 18:15–20. Emphasis supplied)

If we are offended, we are to talk to the offender in private. If that does not resolve our disagreements, we are to take someone with us and sit down with the other party. If that still doesn't get the results we want, we are then told to take it to the Church and accept its evaluation. All these steps were to be followed to the letter. In our case, they had hardly been followed at all.

Overlooked was the fact that all of us had been repeatedly tested and tried in the cauldron of the Church's preparatory process to qualify us for the college classroom. When we were attacked, we asked for a meeting with our teachers, administrators and with those who had hired us as well as our educated peers. None of this was ever granted to us during this difficult time.

In the case of the SMC Religion Department, no one except Dr. Frank Knittel had followed that instruction. When we asked for a hearing before the General Conference, it was forcefully denied. The same was true in the Southern Union Conference and the SDA Theological Seminary where we had all been educated. No one who was qualified to judge our theology was ever allowed to do so.

A benefit to following Matthew 18 was the blessing that often led to and followed reconciliation. If every time we were offended, we would get up the courage to visit with the offender in person, we might reevaluate our own understanding of the issue. Usually those who are offended but do not talk with the offender, resort to talking about the offender—that is called gossip. The time had come for people who felt so free to gossip—stop and consider what this was doing to the Church community.

Over and over during that afternoon at Cumberland Heights, the people gave evidence that this admonition of our Lord had seldom if ever been followed. Individuals claiming to be committed Christians who followed the Bible had simply ignored this simple instruction. This was to be an example of what "perfect people" do—they obey the Lord.

Often, Adventists sought justification from Sister White. Some made their living by tearing apart the Church community with their scurrilous publications, and under the guise of standing up for truth, they had justified their refusal to follow Jesus' teaching by claiming to protect the Church and The Truth. But truth protects itself. It does not need protection.

During the week that followed the meeting I received a letter from the pastor. He thanked me for the work I had done on Sabbath and expressed that the congregation had appreciated the question/answer period especially and were willing to take my answers at face value until hard evidence might prove to the contrary.[52] I thought about the letter. This was how Adventist fundamentalism worked: Forgiveness seldom went beyond momentary suspension of disbelief, always conditional and ready to be retracted at a moment's notice.

It seemed to me that the pastor had at least come part way. But after that day with them I was still on trial—who knew? I might have been lying. Who had put such people in charge of my ministry? I wondered. It was tragic to see the beloved Church being poisoned by this kind of toxic Phariseeism. To Adventist fundamentalists, wrath came first, and forgiveness was never final. For them Christ never actually buried our sins "into the depths of the sea," even though that's what the promise said. They just went into cold storage. Suspicion ruled.

> [19] He will again have compassion upon us, he will treat our iniquities under foot. *Thou wilt cast all our sins into the depths of the sea.* (Mic 7:19. Emphasis supplied)

---

52. "Letter to Edwin Zackrison," July 12, 1982. Emphasis supplied. *SMC Faculty Document Committee Collection.*

I thought of how reluctant my parents had always been about criticizing the brethren—how uncritical they had been in the face of puzzling events that involved duly appointed Church leadership. I saw that my parents were Christians even though their sociology may have been Adventism. Following the simple procedure of Jesus could keep the Church from splitting apart. I came to appreciate their perspective. I saw that the Church could be headed for a serious awakening. And I saw once more the patience of God at work in the affairs of humanity.

As I drove, I focused on the blessing God had given me that afternoon. Someone had had the courage to stand up and speak on behalf of my ministry at Southern Missionary College. I viewed this day at Cumberland Heights as a gift granted me by the Holy Spirit, even if temporary. There are gifts we receive as we seek to do God's will, and I had not questioned that though such dramatic gifts may be few and far between, my place was to cherish them and hold them as indications of the Lord's love for me as his disciple. I was content to accept that the playing field had, to some degree, been leveled at least for one day.

One of the men in the audience, who happened to be the owner of the biggest ghetto blaster at the front of the auditorium, was an old Norwegian. He apparently did not agree with anything I had said. He was noticeably unhappy with all my answers and resistant to any attempt to change his settled perceptions. The pastor mentioned that his only comments about the meeting had been that "Elder Zackrison is a tough old Norwegian!" That was all the compliment he was able to muster, but I took it as his best effort to find meaning in that afternoon session.

It was sad seeing so many people preferring fantastic tales to the clear truth, but I left with a little spring in my step.

CHAPTER THIRTY-FOUR

The Wind Down

"When you come to a fork in the road—take it."
—Yogi Berra

A NEW ADMINISTRATION

WITH THE ENFORCED SABBATICAL *of Dr. Frank Knittel in the spring of 1983, we knew our fate was sealed—now it was just a matter of time and tactic.* All the denominational politicians had fallen in line against us, without, to my knowledge, having ever sat in on any of our classes. The new college president, Dr. John Wagner, was hired to carry out the board chair's wishes to clean out the Religion Department. We all suspected that this was the real job he had been hired to do.

We felt completely betrayed. The board had appointed us scapegoats for a denominational malaise that we had had no part in creating. Dr. Wagner was brought in to take care of the bloodletting that the board members were too squeamish to take care of. I guess they did not wish to sully their names by accepting responsibility for such tactics.

While Dr. Wagner tried to put on a warm front for us, it was clear that his mandate was to discover some tactic that would eventually get us thrown out of our ministry at SMC—although the integrity of our ministry was never questioned. This was all about hierarchical authority and the right of political Church leadership to deal with an organizational problem any way they wished. I was once more reminded of Elder McClure's ominous warning to me that he had "unbelievable power," and that whatever he said would happen, *would happen.*

The rumors of who the designated scapegoats were always came down to three teachers: Lorenzo Grant, Jerry Gladson and Edwin Zackrison. Reasons were never given, but the names were usually uttered together. The three of us were all tenured full professors, but that gave us no sense of security since that meant little to any board of a religious college.

Getting rid of Bible teachers had never been a difficult task for the denomination. The only thing that might complicate the task was a conscientious and ethically minded administrator like Dr. Knittel and the type of a supportive board chair as we had had in Elder H. H. Schmidt (1910–2010). But Dr. Knittel was on leave, with no plans to return, and Elder Schmidt had recently retired.

President Wagner was an honest, conscientious leader, who saw his job as college president in spiritual terms and he would soon come to hate the situation in which the board had put him and eventually he, too, would fall victim to politically motivated retribution. But he lacked the force of character and understanding of the situation that Dr. Knittel had had. He was a man of personal integrity and mission, who was deeply conflicted about betraying the Religion Department. It appeared to be tearing him up emotionally. But he had a job to do.

This was an administrator who called his college faculty "a youth ministry team." And through inner campus mail he supplied every faculty member with a Sister White statement each week. I posted every one of them on the bulletin board above my desk in my office.

While some faculty members lampooned him as a new Pollyanna and chuckled whenever the phrase "youth ministry team" appeared in his directives, I appreciated this mission perspective because my view was that while we were on this faculty for academic reasons, we also had a spiritual task to fill—to minister to the souls of our students. And that required truth in all areas of theology and ministry.

I could not discern when Dr. Wagner realized the seriousness of what was happening to us in Happy Valley. Years later he would talk humbly to me about the grief this assignment had caused him. When it was all over, I could not blame him for the pain he inflicted on us as well as himself. He could see the situation from our perspective, but for whatever the reasons, he did not have the courage to change things in our favor. Undoubtedly, the die was cast when he accepted the job. And by the time he repented and apologized my life had been destroyed.

Throughout my academic career, I knew deans of students who faced these kinds of pressures for speaking on behalf of students. Those who were known for being honest and fair usually did not stay long in their positions. Some were branded as "pro-students," and ironically, that reputation would come to dog them. It was one of those professional double standards that set one up to fail. A dean was hired to serve the interests of the students while being expected to settle any dispute in favor of the administration.

Several deans I knew, persons of integrity and tenure, were drawn into the authoritarian gears of Adventist academia for such reasons. A few such people included

Dr. George Akers, Dr. Kenneth Blanton, Elder Lyle Botimer, Dr. Melvin Campbell, Elder David Osborne, Dr. Florence Stuckey, and Dr. Nelson Thomas.

We had seen Dr. Knittel destroyed by politics and leaders either joining forces with heresy-hunting vigilantes or lacking the will to stand up to them. Dr. Knittel's demise had been hastened by some of the very people he had brought into the administration—people some faculty members had felt very uneasy about from the beginning. And true to expectations these people now turned on him.

After Dr. Knittel was gone, none of us wanted to see the same thing happen to Dr. Wagner. But in political systems some things seem unavoidable. Trying to understand politicians was hard for those committed to ministry. And we had no political power. The Russian premier and occasional philosopher, Nikita Khrushchev, once wrote, "Politicians are the same all over. They promise to build a bridge where there is no river."[1] When politics masquerades as religion, double standards multiply; injustice and subsequent pain are common outcomes to those who refuse to play. History was replete with such demonstrations. On the other hand, it is the presence of spiritual, conscientious people mixed into those systems that keeps any semblance of ethics and justice alive.

Religious men and women have an aura about them that gives ethics and spirituality a chance to survive and thrive within Church structures often dominated by ethically challenged leaders seduced by ambition. Unfortunately, it takes time and painful personal experience to open the eyes of many believers to this reality, and our students, most of them still at the dawn of adulthood, did not always understand what was happening before their very eyes.

A NEW POLITICAL TACTIC

When Dr. Wagner took the reins as president of Southern Missionary College (SMC), by then renamed Southern College of Seventh-day Adventists (SCSDA), he inherited a Religion Department that was overstaffed. In addition to Dr. Bennett, the chair, the Religion Department employed Dr. Gladson, Dr. Gulley, Dr. Grant, Dr. Springett, and me. In addition, we had two new professors, who had been hired without input from the department—Dr. Jack Blanco, another systematic theologian, called from a pastorate in Southeastern California Conference and Dr. Gordon Hyde, another speech teacher called out of retirement.

We now had three systematic theologians in a Religion Department that offered only one course in the discipline, a class that I had taught until I went to graduate school. Now Dr. Gulley taught my class.[2] It made no sense to some of us: three full

---

1. Goodman, *The Forbes Book of Business Quotations*, 664.

2. Usually when a college administration sends one of its professors off to graduate school at the total expense of the college, the professor is asked whether he wants his old academic load back when he returns. I was never contacted or asked. I came back with a doctorate in the area I had been

professors with doctorates in systematic theology. This was apparently what Dr. Hyde meant when he called us "overqualified." It didn't take much insight to realize that this overstaffing had nothing to do with meeting academic needs and that it had everything to do with politics.

We were never given an explanation why these teachers had been added to the department at a time when the college announced the need to cut back on religion teachers. At a time when two teachers needed to be dropped two more were added. Dr. Hyde had been called out of retirement to join our department, and at the same time we were informed that Dr. Bennett would no longer be department chair. Dr. Hyde would take over that position. So now we had two full professors of homiletics (preaching) since both Drs. Hyde and Bennett had doctorates in speech (the department offered one class in preaching).

If those of us in the department had been consulted, Dr. Hyde would probably not have been on our short list. His reputation among Adventist scholars was that of cunning politician rather than qualified scholar. But the decision to hire him was announced by autocratic fiat, and as far as we could see, this was how the college would handle appointments to the Religion Department from now on.

Our opinions meant nothing to the politicians who were now running things. It was widely believed that this autocratic way of handling new hires was driven by the chair of the board in collusion with the main financial underwriter of the college, a long-time supporter of the local heresy-hunting vigilantes, theologically directed by a retired Bible teacher.

Dr. Bennett quit talking to me, and I heard through the back door that he blamed me for the machinations that had led to his removal from department chair. To me this was laughable, and I doubted that the story I had heard was true. I couldn't believe he was blaming me for his misfortune. But despite that, I went to his house to get these feelings talked out (according to the procedure outlined in Matthew 18). We had known each other for twenty years and we had worked together for twelve. I hated to give up on our friendship over a misunderstanding.

When I asked him about that rumor, he was initially mute. He finally admitted reluctantly that he did feel that I was responsible for his fall from grace. He was a private person and would rather carry a grudge than face it head on. His late wife would have called it Southern behavior.

As we talked, he did not attempt to hide his bitterness. He told me that what I had heard was true: he blamed me. I was one of Frank's boys and he said that I had used that influence to unseat him. He was hostile toward Dr. Knittel. He was not willing to reconcile with me.

A year later, he would be one of only four who would testify against me in my grievance process. The three others were Dr. Hyde along with Professor David Smith,

---

teaching, i.e., systematic theology, but was never asked to teach the class again. Instead I was loaded down with a whole slate of freshman classes.

an English teacher, who thirty-two years later would become president of the college, and Dr. Norman Gulley from the Religion Department. I had made many visits to Dr. Gulley, praying with and encouraging him daily through his dark depression caused by the hate mail he was receiving from Church members around the world reacting to an excellent *Sabbath School Quarterly* he had recently written on the nature of Christ.

I was startled when I was informed that these were my accusers. Dr. Hyde I perceived was capable of anything, Professor Smith I did not know, Dr. Gulley I had befriended, Dr. Bennett had falsely accused me, but as old friends, I had attributed that to momentary despair and not hard-edged resentment.

Thirty-two faculty members signed up to speak on my behalf at the grievance hearing. I was told that I was embarrassing the president and that I should call off the grievance process. I said I would do that if the false charges against me were dropped. If not, I requested a lawyer to be present for a settlement. All of that was denied.

The administration had succeeded in splitting our department. Intrigue now took the place of good faith. Neither my department chair, college administrators nor board members talked to me about any of this—it was left to me to resolve the situation, which I was not given the power to do. Our unified department was a thing of the past.

We would discover eventually that the two new teachers had been hired with the assurance that Dr. Grant and I would be fired before they assumed their positions.[3] But upon examining the charges brought against us, Dr. Wagner could see that the assaults on the Religion Department had basically no theological substance; the accused were not Fordites, liberals, fundamentalists, heretics or apostates, just mainline Adventists.

Since he could not fire us for teaching orthodox Adventist doctrine, some other strategy needed to be devised. As charges were fine-tuned, our sin would eventually be identified as defending ourselves against a hierarchy of leaders who, by definition, were always right and who ruled with the authority of God. We had been designated as scapegoats and we were expected to disappear into the desert for the good of the people.

Still, however much of a role autocracy plays behind the scenes, it would be discredited if used as an argument. Instead, the argument against us was couched in terms of staffing: We were now overstaffed so two religion teachers must be let go. But how could two teachers who had been at the college for a significant amount of time (8–12 years) be thrown out? "Last in, first out," right? Wrong.

That principle was now tossed out the window in favor a new principle tailor-made for the two new teachers; they were older and had worked for the Church

---

3. For a significant and amazingly accurate account of this story see "Glad Tidings from Southern College," *Adventist Currents,* February 1984, 9–10, 28. See further Cook and Jennings, "Report on Southern College," *Spectrum,* 13:2, 12–18; and "PUC and SMC Under Fire for Error," *West Coast Forum Newsletter,* 2:1, January 1982.

longer. Suddenly our seniority at Southern College was of no consequence. Much as the Adventist Church had maligned the Roman Catholic Church over the years, its leadership had always been enamored with the power that lay in the Catholic Church's hierarchical structure. Its clergy was expected to obey the orders of their superiors. In Adventism, one of the mercies granted by Catholicism to errant clergy was missing. While Catholic clergy would be reassigned, Adventist ministers and teachers often found no meaningful position within the Church after being embroiled in controversy, even when innocent of charges.

PROFESSOR SUBJECTED TO PREJUDICE

Because of the attacks directed at us ("once accused, obviously guilty"), we were damaged goods, some more than others. The fact it was all based on slander, with no basis in truth, was irrelevant. The important fact was that we had come under attack. Accusation implied guilt. As in Stalinist Russia, to be accused was to be guilty of the offense.

We were not the only ones who wondered why the college administration and the Southern Union president wanted to get rid of us. Many people spoke out on our behalf and they wrote us when we were finally gone to express their condolences. But Dr. Wagner continually asserted to all who enquired of him that *if all the facts were known*, they would be satisfied that he had done the right thing in pressuring us to leave. I asked him many times to tell me what all these incriminating facts were and to tell me what the board had been told. He refused to do so. We were as doomed as the musicians on the *Titanic*.

With Dr. Grant's fall from grace, there was something else in play—something no one spoke about publicly: *a long-standing undercurrent of racial resentment.* The stories of racism and its many varied manifestations in the Adventist Church in the American South were common. When I joined the Religion Department in 1972, I was told that SMC was the last private college in the South to be integrated.

One college under-administrator liked to say, "I'm not prejudiced, I think everybody should own one." If an interracial couple was appearing to form, the administrators were to get on the phone and alert the parents. A GC officer told me as we played horseshoes during a break at the Glacier View Conference in 1980, "You guys at Southern [Missionary College] have the right idea—you keep the standards high and the colored enrollment low." I didn't question him as to what he meant; I got the point. I also knew of the administration's efforts to recruit black students. An influential board member with deep pockets was reported to have referred to the African American president of the North American Division as "that [N word] in Washington."

For the most part these attitudes festered below the surface and only occasionally did they bubble over. For the most part they were part of the "Old South." To those of us raised in the West, these were shocking accounts. I was told by many Southerners that this was equally offensive to them. Usually the ugliness was couched in humor, but there was no missing the animus behind the words.

The official who celebrated our low enrollment of African American students was right when it came to the numbers. Black enrollment at SMC was low, and to some of us this was frustrating because its implied prejudice and an inhospitable environment for African American students. The standard explanation for these low numbers was our proximity to Oakwood College in Huntsville, Alabama, 105 miles west of Collegedale. Oakwood was a General Conference sponsored Adventist college for black students, who attended there for several reasons not connected with SMC; largely, many said, to learn and preserve American black culture.

When I left for doctoral studies, the African American enrollment at SMC was estimated at under fifty out of the college's approximate enrollment of a thousand students.

Shortly before my departure to graduate school in 1976, Dr. Knittel called the Religion faculty together and explained that he had arranged for a budget for another professor in the Religion Department. He asked us to talk among ourselves and decide who we would like to join our department. Only one stipulation: he must be an African American. He went on to explain that we wanted to attract more black students and the logical place to start, he felt, was to add a black Religion professor.

He pointed out that the only black staff member was currently working in the cafeteria as a cook. We met and discussed names. Finally, the name Elder Lorenzo Grant surfaced. Elder Grant was youth director of the Columbia Union Conference in Washington, D.C. Elder Francis asked, "Is this that guy in that movie?" Other than seeing him in "that movie," no one in the department knew him. Yes, he had played the lead role in "So Many Voices," a film about worldly communication, directed and produced by Elder Jan Doward of the General Conference youth department. "Then he's our man!" Elder Francis exclaimed. And with that the discussion was over. Elder Francis had just pronounced Dr. Grant as "our man!"

Dr. Knittel checked out his ministerial record and his educational background and he was on campus just before I moved with my family to Berrien Springs. To everyone's excitement, we discovered that he was in the process of finishing a doctorate from Howard University in Ethics. He became our first professor of Christian Ethics.

Elder Grant was instantly popular with both faculty and students on campus. He was scholarly, humorous, creative, personable and thought-provoking. He had a crystal-clear understanding of what higher education was. He had grown up in St. Louis and graduated from Columbia Union College and Andrews University.

He was polite—a necessary character trait for anyone in the Religion Department but especially for a black professor in a basically white college with a confusing history with reference to race relations. An outstanding speaker, he soon had a weekly Sabbath morning radio program on WSMC-FM. The fact that he reminded everyone of Bill Cosby did not hurt his image.

Yet with some in the community there was criticism, with weakly camouflaged racial undertones. We ignored those "feelings" as something unchristian and archaic, something not becoming of genuine Adventism. But now, seven years later, the fact that he was always listed as the first one who "had to go," caused some to wonder at the real motives of those pushing to get rid of him.

I was not a Southerner. I paid careful attention to the forms of prejudice around me. I noticed that racism was something people whispered about, hoping not to be branded as prejudiced. I invited Dr. Grant to lecture in my New Testament Gospels class when we studied Jesus' treatment of Gentiles. I wanted him to address what looked like Jesus indulging in Jewish xenophobia. His lectures were revealing as he spoke from experience.

The nation had gone through the tumultuous 1960s only a decade or so ago, which had featured strong resistance to the civil rights movement. But that resistance was not only in the South—it was an all-American adjustment to the fact that no citizen could or should be excluded from the guarantees and rights of the U.S. Constitution and Declaration of Independence, no matter how much some people disliked it.

For Christians, this should have been an easy call, but too many Christians led their communities in fiery opposition to desegregation and the call for full civil rights for African Americans. Although few people spoke openly about it, it was clear that some Adventists in Happy Valley shared these attitudes.

Most residents were initially polite and courteous toward the Grant family. But it is fair to say that for some, Dr. Grant was a trophy, or something of a mascot. Dr. Knittel had hoped to see him as the first black teacher of more to come, but some influential people of Collegedale seemed to view him as little more than a token black.

A white college with a black theologian did not hurt the reputation of either the Religion Department or Southern College in general, at least outside the South. A staunch Seventh-day Adventist, Dr. Grant was straight forward and orthodox in his ministry. He was a brilliant Adventist conservative. Yet some of those who felt that a colored man needed to know his place were offended. Knowing one's place was not just something traditionalists expected of women tempted by feminism; it had for three centuries been the deference that Southern whites demanded of African Americans.

To some Southerners there was still a line they were uncomfortable seeing crossed by African Americans. These lines were not spelled out as such, but the lines were nevertheless real. Many still felt more comfortable with blacks in subordinate roles that trivialized their abilities than in positions of equality and prominence. These racially defined lines were possibly holdovers from the plantation era. The Adventist administration in the Southeast is segregated to this day, with white and black Conferences.

Despite Dr. Grant's courteous manners, he was—from what I heard—resented by members of the local dynasties for being insufficiently deferential, especially to their leading ladies. They accepted grudgingly the idea of civil rights and legal equality for African Americans but with the mental reservation that white people were still more equal than blacks and that equality was not a thing to be flaunted. The times "they were a-changing," but these local aristocrats, their commitment to Christianity notwithstanding, acted as if the civil rights movement had only taken place in the history books. Cultural change takes time.

In his office Dr. Grant had hung a large portrait of Dr. Martin Luther King, Jr., the Baptist civil rights leader from Atlanta. When a white co-ed came into his office one day and asked sarcastically, "Why do you have a picture of *him* hanging on your wall?" Dr. Grant paused, and then replied quietly and courteously, "Because if it weren't for him, I would be picking cotton today!"

Of course, no one dared to be too overt about making use of "the race card"—knowing that might set off a social powder keg. Still, as time went on, it was clear that elements of the unreconstructed South had it in for Dr. Grant. But obviously any animosity could not come in racial wrappings. The next best thing was theological wrappings. Dr. Grant had to be classified as a heretic and apostate.

As we neared the end of our stay at SMC, I was called to Wright Hall, the SMC administration building, and told, "Ed, you need to pull away from Lorenzo. 'They' are out to get him, and it looks like they will win. I don't want to lose you when we lose him." The warning was intended to protect me. But personally, I took the warning as devastating and offensive. Hoping that this was not racial slur, I went immediately to talk to Dr. Grant who lived directly across the street from me on Suhrie Drive.

THE SPLINTERING OF THE RELIGION DEPARTMENT

Dr. Grant and I talked theology for an hour. It was not an inquisition. We just didn't know each other very well yet. I asked no pointed questions, I just dialogued with him. During that hour I got to appreciate him. After that hour I knew that none of the issues he faced were theological. I remembered when Dr. Grant had referred to the GC brethren, all of whom he knew intimately from working with them at Washington, D.C., headquarters of the Church, as "these cats have a clear purpose." And I remembered the surprising and angry response of Elder Francis—this was clearly an issue of a black man stepping out of "his place." Respected leaders were not to be referred to as "cats," especially not by a black man. It was my perception at the time.

After talking to Dr. Grant, I realized we were soulmates. He was clearly a scholar, a deeply committed minister, a man of firm principle and a person who cared about students and their Christian walk. He had an aura of caring about him. This I later would see as he ministered to his students.

I did not know how cruel the future would become for both of us, but I knew that if he was going to be fired because he was black, I would be honored to stand by his side and defend him or go with him *for that reason*. But it seemed to me that race could not be used against Dr. Grant, which meant that he must be eliminated on trumped up charges. In a denomination in crisis, the obvious way to get rid of a theology professor would be a contrived charge of subversion, with a theological burr.

We began to get reports from the field that men in our department were speaking on the Southern Union Church circuit. On Sabbath mornings they were telling congregations that they had come to clean up the Religion Department. The members were to be patient—soon all would be solved. These reports were incredibly painful to me. It was clear that this was no longer about the counterfeit charges brought against us by local vigilantes. Had our theology been an issue, we would all have been questioned, interrogated and vetted. We could have handled that, but against the raw power of the Church hierarchy, we were doomed to lose. The history of Christianity showed that. The Pope would always win over Hus . . . Wycliffe . . . Luther . . . Calvin . . . Zwingli . . . whoever happened to be in his crosshairs.

Any attempt to defend ourselves, or the college, or each other, gave us the reputation of being uncooperative and disloyal in the eyes of the powers that ruled. We would find out that there were scorekeepers in the chair's world and there were spies throughout the organization keeping an eye not only on us but all ministers who might step out of line and attend meetings of a perceived "heretical" nature.

The Southern Union Conference was beginning to resemble a police precinct. Informants would attend unauthorized meetings of a theological nature with a view to reporting on ministers who attended. Except for the spies from the office any other attendee was viewed as subversive. Apparently, professors were not qualified to check out what was going on in the Church. But that didn't matter. It was the bodily presence of a minister that was offensive. None of this coincided with anything I had been taught. In my world professors were the most qualified to evaluate what was going on.

On the college campus, our chair was the chief intelligence officer. When I was warned about him by personnel at headquarters in Washington, D.C., I did not know how to relate to it, so I brushed it aside. But as time went on, I began to see what these people had meant. When pastors would contact the Religion Department to have me speak in their churches on Sabbath, they would be told I was not available or I was out of town. This was seldom true.

When I heard about this from the pastors who had asked for me, I confronted the administration about it. Instead of giving me an explanation, I was accused of having made up these stories. In my defense, I submitted the pastors' letters to Dr. Wagner, who seemed ignorant of the fact that the Religion Department was trying to isolate me. I concluded from this that someone other than Dr. Wagner was orchestrating this. No acknowledgements or apologies ever followed.

From the moment he took over the Religion Department, Dr. Hyde had kept a tab on everybody—this was his reputation we had heard about over the years. No matter what I did creatively to fulfill my duties at the college, he interpreted as negatively as possible. He would seize on little things and carefully document them (a paper trail) to create a personnel file bulky enough to support charges of incompetence or insubordination. I concluded that the last thing Dr. Hyde wanted from any of us was something creative and fresh, attuned to doing contemporary youth ministry.

One day at quitting time, he called me into his office when I was rushing on my way to a Sabbath School planning committee meeting at a local restaurant called by the campus chaplain. He said my committee could wait. Out of the blue he asked if there were professors at the Seminary who should not be teaching there?

I wondered where that question had come from. I responded that I did not grade my university professors. I appreciated all the teachers I had had there. He looked disappointed. I further explained that the only professor I had ever heard much negative about was Dr. Gerhard Hasel. Several students thought he shouldn't be there, but I didn't agree with them. I appreciated his classes and his advice. We were good friends. We taught a Sabbath School class together at the Village Church in Berrien Springs where we also served together on the Church board.

THE NEW LIFE SABBATH SCHOOL

When Dr. Hyde stopped me, I had been on my way to a planning session to brainstorm a new college Sabbath School. Because of his interference, I missed the meeting completely. He kept me in his office for two hours, and when I left, I was sure his real agenda may have been to stop me from going to my meeting.

I had been asked by the Collegedale Church board and the SCSDA campus ministry committee to chair, organize and run a new Sabbath School on campus. I had been involved with Sabbath Schools on campus ever since joining the faculty more than ten years earlier. Missing this meeting put off the launching of the new Sabbath School by several weeks.

I had recently taken a class at Fuller Theological Seminary in Southern California from Dr. Peter Wagner (1930–2016) and Rev. Rick Warren on "How to Plant a Church." It had been a very inspiring and instructive class. As I recall, several other Adventist pastors were in the class as well.

The professors' major concern in that class was targeting and reaching people who did not go to Church at all, logically called "the unchurched." My brother Jim, who was educational secretary for the Southern California Conference and a doctoral student at Fuller, also took the class. I suspected that there were a lot of people in Happy Valley who were "unSabbath Schooled," as I called them. So, I was anxious to share and apply the principles and methods I had learned at Fuller to a new Sabbath School aimed at students and faculty who did not attend Sabbath School. What were we doing to reach them? When I finally had a chance to share my plan with the committee a couple of weeks later, the members excitedly bought into the idea.

Many Adventists, especially the more scholarly types, thought of Sabbath School as the interactive nerve center of the Church, certainly the educational center. I thought that with the principles and procedures I had learned at Fuller, we could be successful in reaching those who appeared unreachable. We decided to call it "New Life: A Sabbath School for the unSabbath Schooled." Our target and mission were carefully composed.

I recruited Dr. Springett and Dr. Campbell, both very creative professors, and they were just as excited about the prospect as I was. We eventually added Dr. Gladson and Dr. Grant to the group of organizers and presenters. We put up some low-key notices around campus, inviting anyone who did not make it a habit to attend Sabbath School to meet with us in the choir room of the new music building for an informal get-together. We wanted to hear from them why they didn't attend Sabbath School.

To our surprise, fifty people showed up on that Sabbath morning, and we handed out questionnaires. The Fuller class had focused on addressing "the felt needs" of the unchurched. So, we tried to perceive the felt needs of these unSabbath Schooled students and faculty. Based on the input we received, we set out for a start at the beginning of the new year of 1984.

From the first meeting, New Life Sabbath School had a full room of people. Not surprisingly, some of the locals were less than thrilled. I had made 4x8 foot felt banners and hung them around the room where the class met. The banners reflected the topics we had studied each Sabbath during the quarter. Each Sabbath we would add the Sabbath School lesson title for the day. The banners also featured standard Christian symbols but the conspiratorially minded leader of the local vigilantes, I was told later, was immediately suspicious that there were *Jesuit symbols* on those banners. And why was there a cross on one of the banners? Obviously, something was very wrong.

The very week after we launched, Dr. Springett and I each received a letter from Dr. Hyde accusing us of unfairly criticizing the other Sabbath Schools on campus, something we had no right to do. Of course, we had done no such thing, but at this stage of the game, a mere accusation created facts on the ground, as far as the administration was concerned. And every complaint added accusatory paper to our personnel files. We were not competing with any other Sabbath Schools. We were reaching out to a specific target group—students and faculty who seldom if ever attended Sabbath School. There were a lot more people who responded than we had initially expected, but we had stated that this was a Sabbath School for the unSabbath Schooled.

By the end of January 1984, we were attracting over 100 students and faculty members each week to New Life. A few weeks after we started up, a faculty member, unbeknownst to us, wrote the following letter to each member of the College board.

> My wife and I have been going to this SS since the first week in January. This is the freshest idea involving worship to come to this campus since we came here in 1968. I find myself now wishing that the week would pass more quickly so that we can again enjoy the pleasures of this group. The past six or seven Sabbaths there have been 130+ people there. The room is filled to overflowing with students, faculty and off campus visitors and I have heard remarks that some of these kids have not been to SS for years! This Sabbath School is a

very positive influence on this campus, something we need so much more of! I wish you could all visit the "New Life" Sabbath School when these men [Jerry and Ed] are presenting the lesson. Their ability to bring out students' participation is better and more enjoyable than any class or SS I have ever attended![4]

Much of our success came from paying attention to the *felt needs* that our respondents had expressed in the questionnaires we had passed out. We included all the traditional elements of Sabbath School, but we put them in contemporary forms.

We placed symbolic elements throughout the room of the Sabbath School. We had a living plant to symbolize *life*. Dr. Campbell believed that eating encouraged *dialogue*, so we had a table with fruit and crackers and those in attendance were encouraged to bring food to put on the table and then stand around and socialize together. The Almond Joy became the official candy bar for it represented the *joy of meeting together* with new life in the Sabbath School together. Everyone was supplied with a *name tag* with only attendees first name on it.

We began writing *interactive responsive readings* and teaching them in the meeting.[5] We presented a *missionary talk* every week but used actual missionaries and enlarged the mission spirit to include what students could do. We organized community *projects* for students to fulfill. Dr. Gilbert invited members of the SMC symphony *orchestra* to provide the accompaniment for song service and hymn singing. One of our goals was to get as much participation as possible.

The leaders met each week in an open session, inviting anyone who wanted to participate in the planning for the next Sabbath meeting and to discuss what was happening and how things could be improved. We emphasized that we are all created in the image of God and that includes *thinking and creativity.*

Remarkably our main critics were our department chair, who had never attended our class and the indefatigable heresy hunter, Mrs. Woolcock, who focused on what she could decipher from the banners or other unique elements of the service. Dr. Hyde's stated concern that we threatened the existing Sabbath Schools in the Collegedale Church was not entirely irrational, although unfounded. But we never quite understood why our success should turn his lips pale with anger. He never indicated any desire that we succeed in our effort to reach people on the margins of the Church.

---

4. Davis (d. 2007), Director of SMC Libraries. "Letter to the Board of Trustees," *Appendix, Zackrison/Southern College* (May 16, 1984), 276–277. In private conversation, Charles Davis testified to me that before New Life Sabbath School, he and his wife had not been to Sabbath School for years.

5. Eventually some of these would be published. See Campbell and Zackrison, *Interactive Readings for Christian Worship* (2003); and Campbell and Zackrison, *Readers Theatre for Christian Worship: Biblical Stories of Courage and Faith,* (2003). See also Zackrison, "Worship Renewal Among the Contemporary Churches: Adventist Churches," in Webber, (ed.) *The Complete Library of Christian Worship*, (1993), 3:3–7. And Campbell and Zackrison, "Responsive Readings and Scripture Readings," *Worship Leader* (July/August 1994), 19–26, 35. All these publications were based on our work in the New Life Sabbath School.

The previously mentioned letter that he wrote to Dr. Springett and me still qualifies as one of the most confusing communications I have ever received from a Church leader in my thirty-five years in the SDA ministry. It represented serious lack of understanding of the facts. He wrote:

> As ordained ministers of the Seventh-day Adventist Church, with some years of pastoral experience, you are well informed as to church polity. This raises a question as to the tone, nature and purpose of the announcements that were posted over the campus last week. It also raises a question as to the relationship which both the notices and the meeting would have to the appointed and elected leadership of the Collegedale Church, and the various branches of its Sabbath School.[6]

We had been elected to leadership positions by the Collegedale Church, and we had been asked by the Church board to lead out in this new venture. It was Dr. Hyde who was uninformed. But our personnel files continued their ominous growth, and perhaps that was the real intent behind the reprimand.

The day after his letter arrived, I received another letter from the campus ministry office covering our efforts at establishing the new Sabbath School. It included the following thoughts:

> From the questionnaires you gave me, it looks like you have put a lot of thought into the development of this new Sabbath School. If you would pass the information which you gathered from the questionnaires on to me when you are done with it, I'm sure that I could use the input.... Thank you for your willingness to work with Campus Ministry in reaching more students on this Campus for our Lord. I'm looking forward to supporting you in this program next semester.[7]

Apparently, our chair felt frustrated that he had not been able to discover anything about us that justified the wrath of the local vigilantes, so he asked each of us to write up some sort of personal confession/apology that owned up to mistakes we might have made. He asked us to think of something that would satisfy them. He felt that such letters would carry weight with the constituency and show us to be humble. What he was hoping for was something no doubt more culpable paper for our personal files. This was right up my alley. I never hid from mistakes I had made, and I was more than happy to cooperate.

He asked to carefully show where we had made mistakes and explain how we were guilty. He asked us to explain what we had done or would do to turn matters around.

---

6. "Letter to Edwin Zackrison and Ronald M. Springett from Gordon M. Hyde." *Appendix, Zackrison/Southern College* (December 13, 1983), 133. Note: We had both been "appointed and elected" by the Collegedale Church board.

7. "Letter to Edwin Zackrison from Leslie A. Mathewson, SCSDA chaplain's office." *Appendix, Zackrison/Southern College* (December 14, 1983), 134.

We were to "throw a bone" to our accusers. It seemed to me to be a cruel ploy. But such tactics tend to work with a religious man. The call to confess *mea culpa* ("through my fault") was an old Roman Catholic tactic—used to control the clergy. As far as I know I was the only one in the Religion Department who complied with his request. In time, Dr. Hyde would use my "confession" against me, as evidence that I should be fired. My place within the department was now at the bottom of the standings.

Our chair was a clerical hit man, and it was clear why he had been sent to join our faculty. My colleague in Washington, D.C. who had warned me against him, had said not to turn my back on him. He insisted that this was someone who was "deep in dirty church politics." But religious men have a hard time crediting such negative assessments to their superiors, and when they do, it is often too late.

I did not know at the time that Dr. Hyde had told the administration that if I were not fired, he would resign.[8]

THINGS FALLING APART

Annie and I were both on the college faculty. She was a member of the Business Department. She was chosen by the student body in 1983–1984 as Teacher of the Year. I was asked by the senior class of 1984 to be faculty sponsor of their class. This was the second time at SMC that I had been given that honor. My student evaluations were incredibly supportive. But 160 statements of carefully written evaluations from students who had seen me work in class for full semesters couldn't offset the "news" paper and its false, incendiary charges still being pressed by certain board members whose financial support the college could not do without.

The word on the street said that money had been raised to facilitate our termination. As mentioned previously, the president of the Southeastern California Conference told me in plain words, which board member he had heard was bankrolling our termination. A professor at the Seminary had already shared that same information with me so this revelation was not new.

We began to hear that Dr. Wagner was spreading the word that I was hoping to leave the faculty. But I had no other job offer and I refused to concede anything to lying vigilantes and morally challenged superiors who had it in for me for no good reason. I also realized that my chances of finding another job within the denomination would be slim given the slander that I had been exposed to, slander that my superiors

---

8. Telephone conversation: Dr. Ronald M. Springett and Professor Ellen Gilbert." *Appendix, Zackrison/Southern College* (May 16, 1984), 322: "Gordon [Hyde] was promised by Al McClure if he took his present job [as the new chair of the Religion Department] that Ed Zackrison and Lorenzo Grant would be removed. Since this wasn't done and even though circumstances have changed, Gordon demanded that the releasing of these two men still be done. . . . Ron also said that he saw board members before the Monday (May 14 [1984]) Board meeting. They said, 'Gordon [Hyde] would resign if Ed was not released [fired].'"

had chosen to validate. It would take a truly courageous Church leader to hire me with such a dark cloud hanging over me.

I had never actively sought any position in the denomination in my professional life. I was a religious man—God had his plans for my life and would take care of me. I didn't have to blow my own horn. If God wanted me to leave the college, I might not understand why but he would provide the ways and means to follow him out of Happy Valley, if that was his will. Yet I did not believe that he would resort to conniving with liars to do so. I had a simple faith; I believed God would deliver me from evil, no matter how well-financed opponents were.

Dr. Wagner would come to my office to talk—no summoning to his administrative suite in Wright Hall. I appreciated this except that now he was putting me under intense pressure to get me to say I would leave if I got any job somewhere else. I was increasingly convinced that he was carrying out orders.

When I half-heartedly agreed that I might be persuaded to leave if the right offer came along (a tenured full-professorship in another Adventist college or university—God would not have dragged me through nine years of a grueling ThD education to see me sidelined into some other line of work), *he interpreted that as my promise* to leave without any offer.

I said, "the right offer," he heard "promise to leave by the end of the school year." He was frantic to have something final to present to the board member determined to get me fired and he was not going to let such nuances get in his way. I had no question that God had given me the spiritual gift of teaching and I saw it as my Christian duty not to renounce that gift.

Dr. Wagner's compromise with professional ethics would become even more egregious when the same board member who was implicitly coercing the college by the unspoken threat of withholding critical financial support rewarded him by hiring his wife to write his biography. When Annie confronted him with this conflict of interest he became unglued. Things were now seriously intensifying. The president's version of our private conversation was that I had agreed to leave, and when I contested that, I was accused of being rebellious. The fact that I had not been offered any other job did not make any difference.

During this time, I attended the Conference area meeting in the Collegedale Church, hosted and chaired by Dr. Gary Patterson, president of the Georgia-Cumberland Conference. I was shocked when the board member who had reduced Dr. Wagner to his errand boy stood up in the meeting and publicly challenged Dr. Patterson in front of the 300 or so people present. He insisted that he and his family would no longer give their tithes and offerings to the Conference as long as he, Dr. Patterson, was president there. That was his speech. I had never heard anything like this! I have never heard anything like that since. I was in shock!

I could not believe what I was hearing. He was openly demanding publicly that the Conference bow to his will and fire it's duly elected president, without any stated reason other than his say-so. I concluded that the Church was falling apart.

Never in my forty years as an Adventist and my twenty years as an Adventist minister at the time had I ever witnessed a member try to intimidate financially an entire Conference into abandoning all semblance of democracy to get rid of a leader who could not be manipulated. And in front of 300 witnesses!

Given the fact that his family was one of the richest SDA families in the U.S., his tithe and offerings had to be substantial. When Dr. Patterson received an invitation to be president of another Conference, this same person did his best to smear his reputation and keep him from getting that job, but that attempt also failed.

Even in God's work, money presents a temptation to the politically elite. The pressure on Dr. Patterson had to be nearly unbearable. I was taken back to that day when Elder Francis had made the threat against him in our departmental meeting. I began to connect the dots. The characters in the overall plot were emerging from the shadows. Little was hidden any more. By now it seemed clear who was bankrolling the purge of the Religion Department and who the "theological" brain behind this initiative was.

I remembered how years ago, Elder Francis had worked to keep Elder Patterson out of the classroom. Elder Francis belonged to the older generation of autocratic theologians and leaders who had a hard time coming to terms with modernity. But now it seemed he had recruited someone with wealth to resume his campaign against Elder Patterson. When we learned that Elder Francis was in constant contact with his equally autocratic, but much richer, alter ego on the board, it came as no big surprise.[9]

My faith began to falter. I finally inquired at another college what the chances were of getting a teaching job there. It was too late. I was not hirable. All the Religion Department at that college had been my friends and classmates either in college or graduate school, but not one was willing to recommend that I be hired. I also realized I was far too conservative for that faculty.

The academic dean from another SDA college said he would love to hire me in his Religion Department, but he didn't dare. None in the system was willing to stick out the neck. My name was Mudd. I took a step back to contemplate my options. God had called me to SMC and if he wanted me to leave, he would provide a way out. Nothing was opening, I dared to hope that that might mean things would finally blow over. It was a hopeful dream.

Around this time, I learned of Dr. Hyde's threat to resign if I were not fired. Of course, that could save me—he could resign—he had come out of retirement, why

---

9. Gladson, *A Theologian's Journey*, 185: "An office worker claimed Francis visited a wealthy board member almost every day to discuss the university's situation. Undoubtedly, Francis was the principal source of this board member's strong opposition to the religion department. So, we had our enemies in the department as well as outside."

couldn't he just go back in? At this point my faith hit bottom.[10] I had never felt so betrayed in my life. My faith was tried as never before. I continued my morning prayers for wisdom and deliverance.

Moving is hard on families. My kids had their friends from years at Spalding Elementary School and Collegedale Academy. They were heavily invested in their music. We were settled in a house we had built to retire in. But what we wanted carried no weight with anyone making decisions for us. I had never seen the machine from this angle before.

In religious organizations leadership decides it's time for you to go—then leadership will insist that this is the Lord's will. Religious leaders will almost always push responsibility for dubious and wrong-headed decisions onto God. Church leaders always speak highly of God's will, since—amazingly—he always sides with them.

It leaves you little room for appeal when God has decided against you. In fact, as Dr. Wagner would argue, my unwillingness to see his effort to get rid of me as God's will was proof of my insubordination. As a religious man, I was ultimately called to obey God. I was called to share in ministry. But now, as a Church worker, I was required to obey mandates of committees as though they were the voice of God.

My attitude, it was asserted, was evidence of my insubordination. Yet Dr. Wagner and his administration did not own the college. Neither did the person who had put up the war chest to get rid of us. To me, this was a clear violation of trust and abuse of power and from my study of history, that was the story of organized religion. But this is not religious history. This is political history. And that was why some of the professors in the SCSDA Religion Department had ended up with targets on their back.[11] My spiritual comfort was in believing that it was not God who had it in for me.

---

10. *Appendix, Zackrison/Southern College* (May 16, 1984), 322.

11. "Glad Tidings from Southern College," *Adventist Currents,* February 1984, 9: "In the autumn of 1982, McClure—without consulting Southern College administration—informed the newly appointed Hyde that he would soon become religion division chairman and that two religion teachers would be gone by the time he assumed the chairmanship in January 1983. Deeply hurt, department chairman Bennett stepped down, knowing that the union president would have it no other way."

CHAPTER THIRTY-FIVE

Resolution

"We have no right to ask when sorrow comes, 'Why did this happen to me?' unless we ask the same question for every joy that comes our way."
—Philip S. Bernstein

THE CHARGE OF INSUBORDINATION

Eventually I received an unsolicited nibble. I was told this nibble could turn into "an official call." But the fit was not right. When I declined for what I thought was in the interest of my family and the will of God I was officially charged with insubordination for not accepting it.

Now the administration concluded that there were reasons for my dismissal, though they did not share those reasons with me. I had no ultimate say in my future. There was no "come, let us reason together." It was sheer obedience that was expected and required. And that tries the soul of a religious man.

The argument was that I had disobeyed God by not complying with the mandate of the executive administrative committee. Or so they said. This was not God speaking and I knew it. And so, the standoff continued. In my professional history I had turned down no less than fifteen calls—never had I ever been accused of insubordination. And Annie asked the committee members point blank, "Have any of you received a call you turned down? And were you ever charged with insubordination?"

This was all part of a cruel ploy.

RESOLUTION

TO WHOM DOES GOD SPEAK?

Prior to this latest feeler, all suggestions of possible jobs were just vague intimations about jobs invented and funded by those who had raised the infamous war chest to get rid of us. None of them existed. The clear message was: "Just get out of town." "We really don't care where you go or what you do—just leave!" But nobody charged him with subverting the way of the Lord who had called me to SMC. These were people who believed in sinlessness and that this was the way heaven would be run.

According to one rumor, there was an opening in the Lake Union Conference to run an outreach ministry on secular university campuses. None of these campuses had such a position—I would be creating it. But it was all just rumor. For a religious man God does not work that way. I had been sent by the college board to earn a Doctor of Theology degree; I had done just that. It had taken me nine years of hard work. Now I was supposed to deny that God had anything to do with it? They had told me that *God sent me*. Now God had other plans based on false stories. *I should take a job for which I had no training or interest.*

Dr. Grant would eventually take one of these offers and find out exactly what I had suspected. It was created by prejudiced monied people simply to get him out of Happy Valley. Someone had just put up the funds to get him out of SMC. And we had already seen the plan, *Either you do as I say or I will not give you the money.* And Dr. Grant buckled under the pressure. He just could not take this abuse anymore. I did not blame him.

These offers were always presented as being from God. Hence, turning one down was interpreted accordingly. They were nothing but inquiries geared to "feel me out" about leaving. "Why are you fighting God?" I was asked. But I was not fighting God. I didn't follow a lying God.

God had called me to teach in the Religion Department at this college and I had done nothing but faithfully carry out that assignment for twelve years. I had obtained the proper qualifications to accomplish that. Any meaningful new offer would have to be within that setting. And nothing was forthcoming. But here it did not look like God was calling the shots. The family with the money did. They were now playing with the future of three families, mine, Dr. Gladson's and Dr. Grant's. To say that it was deeply upsetting to all of us is a gross understatement.

The other theologian who had been hired to replace me on the faculty, told me that if I moved back to Berrien Springs I could soon be teaching at the Seminary. Pure speculation. It carried no credibility with me. I didn't think that it was true or official—just an attempt on his part to nudge me out of Collegedale to justify his presence on the Religion faculty. But what was I to expect? I had gotten my PhD from an Adventist university, his was from a worldly university.

I had no desire to teach at the Seminary, he had no say in the matter, and if I had any interest it was now clear that possibility was closed forever. I knew how the system worked and right now it was working against my sacred call to the ministry. If the Seminary wanted me, the Andrews board would have called me. This man was not on that board and I concluded that he was just making all this up.

As for doing secular campus ministry, I lacked both training and inclination for such work. I had just spent nine years of hard work to obtain a ThD to teach theology in an Adventist college or university and that was what I intended to do. I also had a family to think of—did they have any desire to go back to the deep freeze of Southwestern Michigan? Did they have a desire to sacrifice their father to another five years of graduate study?

Then Elder Everett Cumbo, president of the Illinois Conference in Brookfield, (the city where my parents were living when I was born in 1941) called, asking to talk with me about a possible position in his Conference. This was the rumored campus outreach job I had heard about. I would operate on the campus of University of Illinois, Chicago Circle, where I would pursue secular campus ministry. I said that we could talk about it, knowing I would not be interested if there were no teaching job connected.

I was told I would really be challenged by this offer—and that I would receive a call if I gave any encouragement. I am sure that this offer had been made in the knowledge that I had at one time expressed an interest in someday living back in Chicago. But at this point in my life, that thought was as deep as my momentary desire to become a dentist. Nothing in Chicago could have appealed to me that wasn't college teaching or possibly publishing work.

The pressure to accept the Brookfield possibility (and that was all it was) was so intense that Annie and I packed up the kids and drove to Chicago to check things out. We got as far as Louisville, Kentucky, where our brand-new Plymouth K car blew a head gasket. We left the car in Louisville to be repaired and took a rental car for the rest of the trip. Was God trying to tell us something? A religious man does not miss a hint like this.

Before arriving in Chicago, we were confronted with one of the worst snowstorms of the year and as we walked around various places trying to keep our balance on snow and ice, we were not warming up to the thought of moving there. But weather was only one concern.

Hinsdale, the nearest school for the kids, had only a ten-grade school and no violin program. Our daughter would have to go away to boarding school and by doing so she would lose years of violin studies at which she had excelled. Our cost of housing would double. Annie would have no job. In short, our expenses would soar, and our income would plummet. It was not a good fit, we all agreed. And our wonderful house would be gone.

I responded to Dr. Wagner that we couldn't accept this call because I did not believe that it came from God. He was not happy with that decision. He made it clear that he thought I had agreed to leave, and this was a chance to do so. I told him it was not what I felt called to do. It was a job offer without a teaching component. Teaching was my calling.

I had always taught my children that when a person gives you a message there are two aspects to it. First, there is *what they say*. Second, there is *what they mean*. I subjected Dr. Wagner's message to this norm. He looked at me and said, "You need to take this." And I looked at him and heard what me meant, "I need you to take this."

Dr. Wagner was mouthing the directions of the executive committee of the college board. They had had a "season of prayer," he said, and the Lord had *impressed* upon each of them that this was his will. I had to accept this call—God had told them that. Turning this down would be slapping God in the face! But he still meant, "I need you to take this call." I knew it wasn't for me or my ministry or my family. It was for his job. This was what he had been hired to do.

I responded honestly, "My family and I have also had a 'season of prayer' and God couldn't have been clearer in telling us not to take this call." End of conversation.

Finally, the committee abandoned the God-talk and just threatened me, "If you don't accept this call, you will be terminated." Money was speaking—not God. Why didn't they just tell me that to begin with? This was a business decision. It had nothing to do with God. They planned to fire me from the beginning. Why bring God into it? To me this was a mockery of prayer. Were they using God as an alibi for their unethical behavior? As that board member with money had told me in the parking lot, "I don't like the direction the Religion Department is going." What direction? "The wrong direction."

And so, it was finally on the table. This was a matter of obeying them, not God.

"No," I said, "Not true. I am not insubordinate. I am obeying God."

We had been falsely accused, we had been refused qualified examination, and now we were to be thrown out because someone with a lot of money and little or no understanding of theology had bought into a crazy conspiracy theory and wanted to get rid of us. I saw no evidence of God at work here—at all.

It might have been different had I received a call to teach at Loma Linda University, or Walla Walla College, or Pacific Union College. That, to me, would have made sense. I had the right qualifications for that sort of position. I was not prepared to handle a mystical voice said to be that of God and emanating from a closed committee that had not even kept minutes of such a voice.

I was being told that God had spoken to the committee but not to my family. I believed in prayer. I had taught prayer seminars for the past fifteen years on a grand scale. I had witnessed careful answers which I believed were from God. I always had clear direction when I prayed, and I knew that this was not the genuine article. God was giving me the direction I had prayed for with my family.

Frustration expresses itself in different ways. Annie looked at me one day and in her uncommon exasperation, she said, "I am so mad I would like to go out and order a big pork sandwich; but this Church has even made it impossible to do that!" Not only was she not a pork eater, She was a strict vegetarian. But it was the best laugh we had had in weeks.

LEAVE THE CHURCH?

At this very time an interesting situation did open that was tempting. A friend of mine from La Sierra days was an editor and national representative at an Evangelical publishing house near Chicago. This institution specialized in college-level Evangelical materials—books, pamphlets, Bible study, etc. She called one afternoon to see if I might be interested in book work. She had heard of my troubles at SMC and submitted my name as one qualified to take her place as she was moving to another publisher.

She told me their board would be meeting the next day and asked if I might be interested in joining the firm? It was in the Chicago area, but it was not connected to the SDA Church. It was very clear that there were some people in the Church who did not want me at SMC. This decision would mean leaving Adventist work for good. I was open to the Lord's leading and I told her that I would check with my employer since I owed the college a pile of money ($70,000) for my doctoral education.

While this job also meant moving close to Chicago, at least we would no longer have to deal with what was now a toxic atmosphere of Collegedale toward us, and the uncertainty of an outreach ministry that might not materialize and for which I had no training or interest.

So I called the business manager and told him of the offer. "Well," he said, "Remember that the college has $70,000 invested in your doctoral education so if you leave here, you will have to pay us back." My contract with the college was clear: I had to work for the school until the debt was paid off. Here was the ultimate double bind: If I left I would have to pay back the debt in hard cash. If I stayed I would be fired and ruined for denominational work forever. Not great alternatives. Where was God's hand in this decision?

I responded to the business manager, "I will be glad to stay to amortize that debt. Thanks." For a moment I thought that I might be saved by my monetary obligation to the school. There was certainly no way I could come up with $70,000 to buy my freedom. It was of course just an illusion. That was just pocket change to those telling us God's will.

I called my friend and told her the news. She said their board had accepted her recommendation to hire me and I would be hearing from them the next day. When they called, I reluctantly told them that I could not accept their attractive offer. They were very understanding, and it was a relief to be able to turn down a job offer without recrimination! They didn't accuse me of insubordination.

It is not often that a religious man is as confused as I was at that point, especially since I felt very strongly that we were following the Lord's will. He wanted us at to stay at the college. To add insult, when I finally left the faculty, the administration dismissed my educational debt ($70,000) by simply asserting that it was just "a paper figure!"[1] Pocket change!

THE STORM TAKES ITS TOLL

I had to turn down a serious chance to work with a reputable and well-known Christian publisher and a future in Christian publishing work. It was the only other work apart from teaching that I had always felt called to—and all for nothing, as it would turn out. We were caught up in a maelstrom of Church politics that was causing no end of dissonance for my family and me, as well as for my students who continually called to offer solace. God seemed no longer to oversee this Church.

It was not over yet.

As the storm clouds continued to gather, I received correspondence from Dr. Heppenstall, retired and living in Carmel, California. He said my relatives had contacted him and he had been checking around to see if I was salable after all that was going on in Happy Valley. The campaign to get rid of me was constantly gathering momentum although no coherent reason was forthcoming. What seemed well-defined was that Southern Union president, Elder McClure, was now supporting those who wanted me off the Religion faculty. He had told me two years prior to this that he had "awesome power," and it was clear that he was not going to be restrained by something as trivial as a good reason.

Dr. Heppenstall had been told that theology was not the issue. Now it was my attitude that was given as the reason. And it was true; I was not moved by the political use of prayer.

The current student evaluations had come in. Of the 170 evaluations for the semester few of my students could find anything to say negatively. The statements came from students in all my classes. Some were theology majors many were general students. But the spirit of the messages was captured in the following typical responses:

> [Elder Zackrison is the] best teacher I have had, not only in my four years of college, but in all my 16 years of formal education. I wish some other teachers could learn the teaching techniques he employs—truly teaching, instead of just filling heads with facts to "spit back" on a test. He truly moves his students to think—to grasp concepts, to experience life, to really enjoy learning, for it becomes an enjoyable experience in his class.[2]

> Dear Elder Zackrison, Hi! Well I have honestly tried my best at writing this exegetical outline. I have worked on it for five days for a total of approximately 17 hours. I feel drained and unsatisfied—but also happy to be finished, and

---

1. Ibid., 28: "Wagner responded by saying that the $70,000 for Zackrison's education was a 'paper figure.'"
2. "Teacher Effectiveness Evaluation, 1984." *Appendix, Zackrison/Southern College*, 163.

definitely brighter concerning the deep truths of Daniel. I want to really understand this book of Daniel. I read the chapter at least twenty times—each time becoming more involved and aware of the deep insight of God's word.

I have asked myself why do I spend so much time—why does it take me so long—why do I struggle with my Bible study? I pray continually, I feel my Christian experience—for witnessing and teaching—and I feel I must strive for perfection. You have a way of motivating my drive—but it is the subject that really motivates me. [The book of] Daniel is a very controversial issue in our church, the prophetic truths have been a mystery—yet the truths are becoming clearer to many for the end is drawing closer. I'm seeking a new deeper spiritual, experience and a closer walk with Christ and I grow by communicating with our Father in prayer and Bible study.

I appreciate your *time*—your guidance and your insight. You are my "favorite" Theology professor. I'm glad you give us the opportunity to find our own answers and conclusions, through independent study. Now—I must learn how to do a good job with my assignments without spending hours and hours on a task that should only involve a few.[3]

There was no evidence that these positive evaluations carried any weight at all with the Church politicians. From what was in print from Ooltewah and sent to me from the board I would have to conclude that all 170 students were dishonest. They were lying, or they were trying to get a recommendation for a job, or they were ready to testify against me in court. Of course, this was far more difficult to accept since all 170 evaluations were anonymous. To my knowledge no official ever referenced them in support of any of us in the department.

Because of my relatives' request, Dr. Heppenstall had visited with Elder Tom Mostert, president of Southeastern California Conference and a former classmate of mine in the Master of Arts program, class of 1964, at Andrews University. He had also visited with Elder Ralph Watts, Jr., president of the Southern California Conference. He had talked with them about their possibly calling me to pastor in their Conferences. I did not know Elder Watts, and I had not talked with Elder Mostert since I marched with him twenty years before, other than a phone call.

Filling me in on what he had found, Dr. Heppenstall wrote the following regarding his visit with Elder Mostert:

> He said that the issue was not a theological one as far as giving you a call to work in his conference; that no one individual from SMC's Bible Department influenced him or his board. Evidently the reports came from *quite a large number of sources* which resulted *in a careful investigation of all the facts*.[4]

3. Ibid., 163–164.

4. Ibid. "Letter to Edwin Zackrison from Edward Heppenstall." (March 15, 1984), 247. Emphasis supplied. While this was Dr. Heppenstall's honest report to me, I knew he was just sharing the spin that the politician had put on it. It was not true that Elder Mostert had gotten the word from "quite a large number of sources"—the so-called nameless, faceless masses we had never been allowed to

RESOLUTION

As Annie and I talked it over, it was clear that this claim of "large number" could not be true. No one had carefully investigated all the facts or sat down with us. This was one of those statements issued by a very accomplished Church politician in the same category as "everybody knows such and such." I found this approach insulting, cruel, and false. Dr. Heppenstall admitted that the Conference presidents he had contacted (two altogether) had told him "they couldn't take a chance" on me. He wanted to know what I had done that was so serious. He didn't know—I didn't either. And all he could get was something nebulous about my "attitude."

Elder Mostert wrote nothing to me. Elder Watts, the other Conference president (whom I had never met) wrote an apologetic letter that said, straight out, "At this time we are not prepared to extend a call to you."[5] No reason was given.

Elder Mostert had earlier called me and informed me that he had a position for me on the staff of the Loma Linda University Church; that Dr. Louis Venden, pastor of the Church, had visited him and asked specifically for me to join him as his associate minister. Why this offer was rescinded no one ever shared with me. We talked for probably ten minutes. The gist of his conversation I later shared with Dr. Heppenstall:

> To the statements concerning "my having a place to go if I got fired." Yes, I made a statement like that to Tom Mostert. I specifically called him in December, two months after he had contacted me to tell me that he would not give me a call at that point (*unless I wanted it at that point*) since "*some on this campus might be of a mind to strong-arm me into taking it.*" I told him then that I was not sure I wished to pastor a church at that time; that I would work that through since it was a thought I had not processed.
>
> When I called him two months later (December, 1983) I asked him if the offer was still open. He said yes. And at that time I told him that I was checking as to what my options were since it seemed that my support here [at SCSDA] was drying up, what with the new retrenchment approach of the administration. . . .[6]

I had already talked to Dr. Heppenstall about the latest approach of the board chairman. Since he could not get any of us on heretical charges, he was resorting to retrenchment as the reason two or three professors in the SCSDA Religion Department

---

face at SMC. Several months later when I was living back in Southern California, the principal of La Sierra Academy called me about teaching Bible at La Sierra Academy, a position that would turn into department chair the following year. Less than an hour later I was informed that no call could go through to me for that position. And still later, I was told by personnel in the Conference office that Elder Mostert had forbidden anyone to give me a call—I was not "hirable." But when he went out of town my "friends" in the office gave me the call and I would teach there for the next ten years. Even politicians have blinders. I had grown up in La Sierra. I was on home turf. When I finally entered the classroom at LSA, I had a class where two-thirds of my students were children of my classmates from LSA in the 1950s.

5. Ibid. "Letter to Edwin Zackrison from Ralph Watts, Jr." (March 19, 1984), 255.

6. Ibid. "Letter to Dr. Heppenstall from Edwin Zackrison." *Appendix, Zackrison/Southern College* (March 19, 1984), 253. Emphases supplied.

"had to go." Yet he was the one responsible for our being overstaffed. Perhaps this was the "attitude" I was now being charged with.

No one mentioned the fact that Dr. Knittel had informed the college board five years before that education experts were predicting that college enrollments would be dropping and that college administrations had to begin planning for that. Instead of heeding this warning, SCSDA had overstaffed its Religion Department, on orders from Atlanta headquarters.

But now the Religion Department was being blamed for the dropping enrollment[7]—all because of wild-eyed accusations with no basis in reality—even though our enrollment was still very high.

My letter to Dr. Heppenstall continued:

> I did not suggest to Tom [Mostert] that pastoring would be my last choice if I could not find anything else. Neither did I suggest that it would simply be a place to get a job in his Conference should I get fired. My suggestion was of an entirely different nature: I do not want to accept a pastorate until I am totally convinced that is what the Lord is calling me to do. I have told you the same thing. I came to Southern College with no question but that God wanted me to teach here. I do not think it is fair to Him, to my family, or to the Conference, or to the people in the church to take a pastorate on any other basis. If that is an unchristian or an anti-administrative attitude then they should drop me.[8]

By the end of 1983, we in the SCSDA Religion Department found ourselves in the precarious position of a Jonah; to save the school, it had been determined that we needed to be thrown overboard.

ORDERS FROM ATLANTA HEADQUARTERS

As far as we knew, these machinations were being orchestrated from the office of the Southern College board chairman in Atlanta, who met briefly only once with our department. He never wrote to us or called us to encourage us individually either as employees or ministers. In short, he made it clear that he was not going to show any public support for us.

When finally, the Religion Department had asked President Knittel to talk to him about possibly placing a statement of support in the Union paper, *The Southern Tidings*, Elder McClure refused, citing an incident in Stone Mountain, GA, involving Dr. Grant and me.

That summer I had been at the James White Library at Andrews University doing research for my dissertation when I ran into Elder Smuts van Rooyen, an Andrews

---

7. Hunter, "Felts and the Release." *Southern Accent,* (March 18, 1982), 10.

8. "Letter to Dr. Heppenstall from Edwin Zackrison." *Appendix, Zackrison/Southern College.* (March 19, 1984), 253.

University theology professor, at an afternoon softball game on campus. We sat together in the bleachers watching his son play and talked about what was going on in the Church at large. He told me that he had been offered a job on the pastoral staff of the Loma Linda University Church. This sounded like a good offer. So, we engaged in friendly conversation.

Elder van Rooyen, a classmate from Seminary days and a graduate and former theology professor at Southern Missionary College, told me that he was seriously weighing his options. He said his position at Andrews was becoming tenuous and he was looking for offers. He had two, he said. Two offers? He was very concerned about where the Church was headed.

But two offers? Yes. The one to Loma Linda, which I already knew about, and the other one to join Dr. Desmond Ford in his gospel ministry in the planning stages in Auburn, California—Good News Unlimited (GNU). It was clear to me that his love for preaching the gospel was attracting him to GNU, and I did not know a more powerful preacher in the Church than Elder van Rooyen. He had recently held a very successful Week of Prayer on our campus at SMC.

When Elder van Rooyen told me, he was considering joining Dr. Ford in his ministry in California, I was ambivalent. I thought doing so would be a poke in the eye of the General Conference president, one of the most accomplished bureaucratic infighters in Adventist history. He further told me he would let me know his decision as soon as he made it.

Elder Smuts van Rooyen was a religious man. He told me he would be speaking at the Stone Mountain SDA Church in a couple of weeks and might still be wrestling with the decision at that time. I told him I would look forward to hearing his decision and that I knew God would guide him. Though I didn't say anything, secretly I was hoping that he would take the position at the LLU Church.

The next week, Dr. Knittel called our department together and announced that Elder van Rooyen would be speaking at the Stone Mountain SDA Church the following Sabbath. He said that he trusted that we would not go down there "waving flags for Smuts." I took this as a warning and decided not to visit him despite my commitment to him. I would contact him some other way.

Coming out of Church on that Sabbath, I ran into Dr. Grant who asked if I would like to ride with him to Stone Mountain to see Smuts. I took this to be a divine directive and felt compelled to go to encourage Elder van Rooyen. I agreed to go with him. We would obey Dr. Knittel's instruction not to "wave any flags," but the way it worked out, we might as well have. It turned into a suicide mission.

We arrived in Stone Mountain, GA, about halfway through Elder van Rooyen's talk in the afternoon since we got lost trying to find the Church. During the break we went to talk with him about his decision—would he be going to Loma Linda? He still had not made up his mind. We spent five minutes with him expressing our hopes. The meeting was called back to order and we disappeared out a back door of the Church and went home. We had accomplished our mission, which was to encourage him to go to Loma Linda.

Elder van Rooyen was one of the most effective communicators of the gospel in the Adventist Church. Losing him would be a tragic loss for the Church. By the following Monday all hell had broken loose. A nameless spy had seen us enter the Stone Mountain SDA Church, talk to Smuts during the break and this supposedly shocking news starting up with outright lies was then passed on to Elder McClure who pounced on it.

"Grant and Zackrison paraded up the center aisle of the Church to make sure everyone in the place would see them," the spy reported, according to Elder McClure. So, we were accused of disobeying Dr. Knittel's orders not to "wave the flags for Smuts." We were insubordinate. We were uncontrollable. Another nail had been pounded into our coffins.

On Tuesday, Dr. Grant and I were ordered to report to a meeting in a Seminar room at the Atlanta International Airport before Elder McClure, board chairman, Dr. Gary Patterson, Conference president, Dr. Larry Hanson, academic dean, Dr. Frank Knittel, college president, and Dr. Douglas Bennett, Religion Department chair. Dr. Knittel, for one, had been flown in from his vacation in the West just for this meeting.

For a couple of hours, we were grilled on anything that could be concocted against us. Now they thought they had hard evidence to blame on us. The overreaction was absurd. Charges against us rolled out of their mouths: (1) We were the reason the college was losing student enrollment. (2) We had written articles for *Evangelica*. (3) We had gone to "wave flags for Smuts" at Stone Mountain in direct defiance of Dr. Knittel's order. (4) We were the subjects of the "news" paper. (5) Perceptions were reality and (6) We had placed the college in the hands of the devil on that previous Sabbath by showing up at that meeting at the Adventist Church.

The most twisted spin was placed on the events of that Sabbath. I reminded them of the reality that Elder Smuts van Rooyen, whom they now demonized, had recently held an incredible Week of Prayer at Southern Missionary College. But for some reason that was irrelevant. The fact that we cared about his soul was immaterial. The fact that he was a close friend of ours for the past twenty years was not important. Where was their concern for Elder van Rooyen, a minister of the gospel and a highly regarded Church theologian? And how could these men justify sitting there in judgment on our motives based on the flimsy "evidence" presented there?

Dr. Patterson reminded us that "perceptions are reality." We knew what he said, but what did he mean? That facts are unimportant? He had read that somewhere. It was a political concept. I didn't care. Facts were my concern. This group obviously didn't care about that. We were reliving the Spanish Inquisition. I told my story, why I had gone to talk with Smuts. It made no impact at all. As far as I could perceive, no one in this group demonstrated one whit of caring about Elder van Rooyen. As for us, the testimony of an unidentified spy, someone who had never talked to us, had nailed us. Reaching out to this mighty worker was aiding and abetting a friend of Desmond Ford, the designated enemy of all things Adventist and grand wizard of heresy. I could not express the depth of my disappointment.

The kangaroo court that met that day in Atlanta declared us guilty on all counts, whatever they were; we were never told. The case was closed. I would learn later that Elder van Rooyen already had a target on his back and eventually, because he ended up joining Good News Unlimited, I was told, he would be de-ordained—a procedure I had never heard of before. Ordination was the Church's way of recognizing a person's divine call to the ministry. Now God had withdrawn his calling?—at the behest of people who had never impressed anybody with their spiritual qualities?

Both Dr. Grant and I agreed that the session would have been even worse had it not been for the presence of Dr. Knittel and Dr. Patterson, who did their best to bring moderation and perspective to the meeting, but it was resounding that the two of them were also under considerable pressure from the most extreme elements in the room. But they were the closest to support we had. Both would eventually pay for that. When paranoia and money rule, theology makes no real difference. Church politicians, all too often, are like their secular counterparts, driven by ambition and more than willing to abandon principle where there is a monetary incentive to do so, or there is fear of losing the next election.

THINGS HEATING UP TO A TERMINATIVE DECISION

Dr. Grant finally gave up and took one of those manufactured calls that turned out to be nothing but a sham to get him off the faculty. But given that the unofficial firing of Dr. Grant could be seen as having been driven by racial animus, the Southern Union president encouraged representatives of the African American community to demand that it be balanced out by getting rid of a white professor as well: Zackrison.

On May 16, 1984, Dr. Grant issued the following affidavit:

> This is to affirm that on May 14, 1984, on the occasion of the Southern College board meeting held in Wright Hall of that campus, that the following conversation took place in the corridor just outside Conference Room A.
>
> At about 10:00 a.m., following a presentation I had made to the board, as I left the conference, I was approached by one of the board members who had left the meeting simultaneously by another exit. The gentleman, a [black] conference president, was very solicitous and spoke with the obvious intention of comforting and encouraging me that 'justice' would be done at this meeting. This is the pith of that conversation:
>
> Conference President: "That [Grant's address to the board] was a fine job. We were really sweating that you might try to defend those other guys. . . . A lot of these guys are saying, 'Now that Grant is gone, everything is OK. We don't

need to do any more housecleaning.' *But we're not going to let them just get rid of the black. Some of us think we need to be fair and get the white guys too. And the chief is all for it too."*

Grant: "You mean Al [McClure] is for it?"

Conference President: "Yeah, man. McClure is supporting us."

Grant: "Well, lots of luck."

[Signed] Lorenzo H. Grant, May 16, 1984.[9]

At first no one apparently realized what a huge mistake it was for the board to justify my firing on racial grounds. It was obvious to the board members that they would have to find some other reason than race to get rid of a black teacher, but they fell into the trap of thinking that the law did not protect white people the way it did black people.

The rumor spread quickly that the board members were taking out insurance policies to protect themselves on the chance that I would sue. I never said I would sue—I never threatened to sue. I never planned to sue. But I had been supplied with a lawyer by the Collegedale Adventist community. On my own, I couldn't afford to sue—on denominational payroll you could not hire a lawyer even if you wanted to. Plus, I did not want to sue. I loved the Church and I loved the gospel. I loved my children and I wanted them to be Adventists. But on the other hand, this was a kind of Adventism I had not seen before. All the lawsuit fears were in the heads of the board members.

Teachers were not allowed to retain lawyers under threat of losing our jobs, unlike the board members, who had a retinue of lawyers. Under the Pierson administration, the denomination had taken the position that any member who sued the Church would be disfellowshipped and fired. A leading lawyer for the General Conference told me that he had brought this up—how difficult a position he was put in when the GC had passed this new ruling—especially since the GC was in the process of suing several members. What's good for the goose should be good for the gander, he had told Elder Pierson.

Now the board had entered a reverse racial discrimination mode. And suddenly the whole issue was openly racial. All along I had suspected the issues were racial. I was not surprised. We were headed for a head pop.

My suspicion that the crusade against Dr. Grant had, in important ways, been racially motivated, began to look more plausible. Why else would a leading member of the black Adventist community be encouraged to propose that I be fired to atone for getting rid of the black Dr. Grant? A board member called to tell me that if I should decide to go to court, he would supply me with all his notes and minutes from the meeting, so I could present my case fairly. I answered that I had no interest in pursuing court action. I just wanted to preserve my ministry.

9. Ibid., 321. Emphasis supplied.

Resolution

MORE MISLEADING ACCUSATIONS

The report immediately went out from headquarters that I had sued the college, another lie. At a Biblical Research Institute meeting in Loma Linda a vice-president of the General Conference announced that I had sued the Church and that I would never work for the denomination again. I had never met this official; I had only seen his picture in the *Review*. He was black.

After he made this stunning announcement, one of my professors from Andrews University stood up in front of the group and told the official to his face that what he had just said was a lie. But in the Adventist hierarchy, authority tends to trump truth and, in a pinch, groundless rumors and bald lies are much too often seen as a convenient substitute and a symbol of loyalty. Consequently, the official story was that I had sued the Church. Annie responded, "They say we don't believe in the investigative judgment. Boy, are they wrong about that! We *demand* an investigative judgment!"

I was a religious man who desired only to pursue the ministry God had called me to. A court case would undoubtedly be tied up in legal procedures for the next ten years. And in the process, my ministry would be destroyed. Amazingly, before the controversy was over, Elder McClure would declare that he had "no evidence of any heresy being taught by the Southern College Religion Department." He even made that statement before a faculty meeting on campus. Our confusion was fully developed.

So, what was the issue? It came down to two unspoken charges: by drawing the wrath of extreme right-wing vigilantes (fundamentalists), we had exposed the college to negative publicity and by defending ourselves, we had made it difficult for the denomination to get rid of us.

By saying anything in our own defense, we were now guilty of insubordination. We were being sacrificed in the hope that it would restore unity to the Church and funding for the college, and to add insult to injury, we were expected to accept with a smile the vilification of our characters and the destruction of our careers.

The president of the Southern Union, Elder McClure, threw his lot in with the reactionary mob baying for our blood and was handsomely rewarded with the denominational "Medal of Leadership" for his successful effort to purge integrity from the SMC Religion faculty and as another token of gratitude on the part of Church leaders, he was promoted to the General Conference vice-presidency.

Where was God in any of this? Only a religious man would even be naïve enough to care to ask that question.

CHAPTER THIRTY-SIX

The Final Pleas for Support

"He jests at scars that never felt a wound."
—WILLIAM SHAKESPEARE

SEEKING SUPPORT

EFFORTS TO GET THE *president of the General Conference, to give us a hearing proved futile.* He told us not to come to Washington to meet with him because he would not under any circumstance support us. Dr. Knittel had arranged for the large college van to drive the whole department to Washington to discuss things with the president. His response was that he would not meet with us. He would not hear us or listen to us. Why? Because if he did we would go back and say that he supported us, and he didn't support us. And *we would then feel free to teach anything we wanted to teach.*

His mind had been made up for a long time. When someone sent him the spurious minutes from the Atlanta meetings edited and distributed by Vance Ferrell we were told by a colleague present that he held up the bogus Ferrell document in front of GC workers and proclaimed that he would investigate that. According to this source he vowed that everyone whose name appeared on the list would be thrown out of the Church. *He said he would get every one of them.*

When I sent him a copy of the actual minutes of the meeting, he never acknowledged that he had received them even though he had recognized and presented the phony notes publicly as credible in front of many witnesses. Critics claimed that he lacked qualities we should expect to find in a spiritual leader of the denomination. All over the world he was the subject of attack as one who had brought untold damage upon the Church. It was a widespread opinion that he ruled the Church like the CEO of a corporation and the only things that seemed to be sacred to him were organizational unity and numerical growth. These were powerful elements of critique.

Initially, when the SMC Religion faculty came under attack, we were urged to write for denominational periodicals. Get your names out there so people will know you, we were ordered. Three of us wrote for a new periodical, *Evangelica*, which was edited and published at Andrews University by ThD students. Their editorial staff asked our department to submit articles for the new journal. Professors from other Adventist colleges were also enlisted to write, which they did. At least one of the editors had been a theology graduate student of ours at SMC.[1]

After the firing of Dr. Ford, the editorial staff of *Evangelica* openly sided with his Reformation approach to theology, and by the time our articles appeared, the journal was charged with Fordism. Anyone writing for the magazine was therefore charged with a theological crime, regardless of what article he may have written.

The three of us who had articles coming out in the journal contacted the editors of *Evangelica* and asked them not to print our articles because of growing pressure, but they said they had already gone to press. By then the editors themselves were under attack as well. No one ever remarked about the content of our articles, which we had spent time on. We were only reprimanded on where our articles had appeared. One would think we had written for *Playboy* to judge from the reaction.

Dr. Gladson and I were both on the masthead as editorial consultants at *These Times*, the monthly evangelistic journal published by Southern Publishing Assn., our denominational publishing house in Nashville. We wrote for that journal as well.[2] I submitted an article to *Ministry*, published in 1983, regarding how pastors might deal with theological disagreements in their congregations.[3] I became a general editor for the General Conference periodical, *Collegiate Quarterly*, and enlisted faculty members and students at SMC to write for it, quarter after quarter.[4]

---

1. See Zackrison, "Justification in the New Testament," *Evangelica*, (April 1981). My article was based on a paragraph from *Questions on Doctrine*, (p. 408) and expanded on in a lecture by Dr. Raoul Dederen at Seminary from his class in Roman Catholic Theology where he showed the difference between the Roman Catholic and Protestant biblical views on salvation.

2. Here are a few of the articles I wrote and had published in *These Times* during this time: "What About the Secret Rapture?" (May 1975), 11–13; "Fight the Good Fight of Faith," (January 1980), 23–26; "The Rapture," (April 1980), 31–33; "How to Live in Anticipation of the End-Time," (April 1980), 48–50; "Why I Became a Seventh-day Adventist," (May 1981), 19–21; "Does Hell Burn Forever?" (March 1982), 24–25.

3. Zackrison, "When Christians Differ," *Ministry*, (August 1983), 19–21.

4. Here are a few of the articles I wrote and had published in the *Collegiate Quarterly* during this time (in addition to the editing): "The Foundation Resource," (June, 1981), 86; "Glory for Me," (April, 1982), 53; "Grace Under Fire," (December, 1983), 41; "Hiding the Word," (December, 1983), 79; "Some Wisdom for Daily Living," (December, 1983), 97; "God's Camelot," (December, 1983), 107. In addition to these articles see "Confrontation," *Colloquium: The Teacher's Presentation-Ready Experimental Quarterly* (Berrien Springs: Andrews University Department of Religious Education), (July 30, 1983), 15–31; "When Legalism Finally Drops Away," *College People*, (May 1983), 36–37; "The Shockability Factor," *College People*, (July 1985), 9–12.

Dr. Grant, Dr. Campbell, and I held workshops and youth rallies around the Southern Union Conference. And I presented Weeks of Prayer at several Adventist academies. All this was in addition to teaching a full load and researching and writing a doctoral dissertation.

Little Creek Academy, a self-supporting secondary school in Knoxville, had requested several times my coming there for their Week of Prayer. I had in the past spoken for several of their Vespers programs on Friday nights. I had turned down the Week of Prayer requests because I had too much work at the college.

With this new directive to get out there, I finally called the Little Creek Academy principal and told him I would hold their Week of Prayer if they still wanted me. He said the school board had met and withdrawn the invitation because of trouble at the college. I understood. We usually got the message that the nameless, faceless masses were at work. We were never told who these people were.

Later he called me back and apologized; he said he had gone back to his board and asked them to reconsider. Reluctantly they had consented. Under those circumstances, I was not anxious to go but agreed to the assignment anyway. When I got up to speak that first night, I think all the school board members were in the audience. I spoke for thirteen Worship services, Chapel periods, and the Sabbath Church Worship service.

After I finished the week and returned to the college, I got one of the most complimentary letters I had ever received in my ministry, from the board members encouraging me and telling me how much they had appreciated my talks—a letter of commendation and apology.

During this time, the Religion Department met together to consider a proposal for a Religion Department alumni journal, and I was elected to edit the proposed quarterly journal. Dr. Gladson, Dr. Springett, and I put together a 24-page mock-up with articles and alumni news along with a heritage section of Adventist history.

We named the journal *Perspectives*. The first issue was proposed to be published in May 1982, and we received the galley proofs from the College Press in March 1982. Dr. Knittel took the pilot copy paste-up of the magazine to show Elder McClure before it went to press. He wouldn't even look at it. It was time for him to exercise his awesome power. There would be no journal coming out of the Religion Department, he declared!

So, another avenue was closed to us. This was becoming the norm. The orders coming from Atlanta were so inconsistent that I knew that doing nothing was lethal and doing anything was also lethal.

FINISHING DOCTORAL STUDIES

Through all this tumultuous life, I was still researching and writing my doctoral dissertation. Every morning from 3:00–7:00 I could put away my concerns and work on my project. It had now been four years since my proposal had been approved. In the summer of 1982, after several summers in the James White Library away from the family, I had finally finished my research.

I found escape in the research, but I was under a lot of pressure to finish up. Dr. Knittel called me to his office several times to check on my progress. He reminded me regularly that I needed to get this done. He was getting questions from the board about where I was in my progress.

Dr. C. Mervyn Maxwell, still chair of the Church History Department at Seminary, stopped by my research carrel in the James White Library several times and on one visit, he remarked, with genuine regard in his voice, how fortunate I was. I was getting to do something he had never even had a chance to do—reading all this source material from beginning to end!

I appreciated his words. He saw me sitting at the library tables by the hour reading the *Review and Herald, Signs of the Times, Youth's Instructor,* books and articles. From 1850 to 1980—I turned every page in these Adventist journals and books. Not only did I find material about original sin in Adventist sources, I also came across intriguing material that gave me ideas for future articles or books on Adventist history.

Finally, in the summer of 1982, I closed the last page of the primary sources. I was now writing about the last decade of Adventist history and I was beginning to prepare for the oral examinations in which I would defend my research project, which at times had looked like it wouldn't be finished. I had been hoping to take the oral examination in March 1983, but it ended up not being scheduled until January 1984.

Once my dissertation was written, I had planned a family trip to Walt Disney World in Orlando, Florida, to reward the kids for what I had come to call their impatient patience. By now we were keyboarding the final draft. Annie was a professional and had brought home a new word processing machine from her lab at the college. The world had still not been introduced to an uncomplicated personal computer. The Apple McIntosh was still a few months away from the market.

Annie was working on my Bibliography—a major project of fifty-two pages listing primary and secondary references. The dedicated word processor was still awkward to use. Pagination was especially difficult. So, she said, "bring me your final chapter and we will be on our way to Orlando!"

I sat down at the word processor to try my hand at something completely new to me. I carefully formulated the final arguments: "Chapter VI: Epilogue: Conclusions and Observations." I had dealt with the biblical materials, the historical developments, the setting of the Adventist development of thought and the theological implications of my findings.

Writing the conclusion did not take long—sixteen pages of observations and insight from a very interesting research project. Finally, after a couple of hours of carefully divesting my brain of five years of discovery, I had sixteen pages done. And like an evening anchor on network television I signed off—it was done! My closing statement was pastoral in its content: "Christian theology must attempt to fulfill the Master's wish: 'that they may be one.'" (John 17:11).[5]

When you transition from a typewriter to a word processing computer there is a procedure that you must always follow but at first was unfamiliar to me. Before you even print your material, *you are to save it.* But the important thing to do at this juncture was to get to Orlando and I just punched the print key. The screen went black.

I never discovered where those sixteen pages went—into the ether of electronics. I never saw them again. Annie entered the room and said, "We're all packed and ready to go—are you finished?" Yes, I was finished. The pith of the dissertation had vanished—pith that to this very day I still consider my finest writing. We never found it. No Orlando until I rewrote those sixteen pages. She asked how many pages I had lost—Sixteen. She calmly insisted that I would need to re-write those sixteen pages before we could leave on our family trip. Meanwhile she would finish the Bibliography with exactly a sixteen-page gap before it.

Even though the material was fresh in my mind I do not have a photographic memory and re-writing was a strenuous task. It was the one-too-many job for the day.

We headed for Orlando, stopping to drop off the final draft at the post office destined for Dr. LaRondelle in Berrien Springs.

To some extent, researching and writing this thesis had kept me sane through the emotionally grueling period we had gone through in Happy Valley. Now, as I rode the Disney rides with my son, the work was in the hands of my doctoral committee, and all I could do was wait for whatever re-writes they might require. For a few days at least, the pressure was off. And that was welcome by my family (and me). The entire family breathed a huge sigh of relief.

---

5. Zackrison, *Seventh-day Adventists and Original Sin: A Study of the Early Development of the Seventh-day Adventist Understanding of the Effect of Adam's Sin on His Posterity.* Andrews University Doctoral Dissertation, 1984, 416. See also *The First Temptation,* 361.

CHAPTER THIRTY-SEVEN

Settlement

"You have not converted a man because you have silenced him."
—John Morley

THE DISSERTATION DEFENSE

Our end was near. Any further fight now would be futile. Dr. Grant was gone. Dr. Knittel was gone. We were beyond the writing on the wall. The only mystery left now was *how* it would end. We were resigned to our fate. But I still had the task of defending my dissertation hanging over me. I was saddened that what should have been one of the most exciting moments in my life was taking place under such a dark cloud. I was struggling not to give in to bitterness. It was all so unfair.

My defense was set for the winter of 1984. I drove alone to Berrien Springs, rehearsing as I drove. My committee had scheduled two hours for the oral examination in which I was to give a short overview on my project and then answer any questions that the six-man committee chose to ask me. The defense was an open session and many of my former students from SMC, who were now Seminarians, were in attendance in Seminary Hall. "You kept us on the lid; we wanted to see you on the lid!" one of my former students quipped with honest humor. Undoubtedly, he spoke for a number of those gathered in the peanut gallery.

Dr. Roger Nicole, the Andrew Mutch chair of theology at Gordon-Conwell Theological Seminary, whose main campus is in South Hamilton, Massachusetts, just north of Boston, was my external examiner. Gordon-Conwell is a neo-evangelical Seminary founded by Billy Graham and others in the neo-evangelical movement.

Dr. Nicole examined me over the historical section of my dissertation. His main criticism was that I did not set forth as strong an apology for St. Augustine as he would have liked. He did not question my knowledge of Augustine, but as an Augustinian he had hoped I would make a stronger case in his favor than I had. After all, it was generally accepted that St. Augustine was the father of the doctrine.

This mild objection was countered by other members on the committee. They defended me and explained that they would not have shown any more affinity for Augustine than I had. For half an hour the argument between the committee members and Dr. Nicole continued as I watched the clock tick by. I was not unhappy about that. While the setting and the subjects were different, I mused during the arguing how St. Paul may have felt in his ordeal before the Sanhedrin. It all seemed familiar to me!

> [30] But on the morrow, desiring to know the real reason why the Jews accused him, he unbound him, and commanded the chief priests and all the council to meet, and he brought Paul down and set him before them. (Acts 22:30)

> [1] And Paul, looking intently at the council, said, "Brethren, I have lived before God in all good conscience up to this day." [2] And the high priest Ananias commanded those who stood by him to strike him on the mouth. [3] Then Paul said to him, "God shall strike you, you whitewashed wall! Are you sitting to judge me according to the law, and yet contrary to the law you order me to be struck?" [4] Those who stood by said, "Would you revile God's high priest?" [5] And Paul said, "I did not know, brethren, that he was the high priest; for it is written, 'You shall not speak evil of a ruler of your people.'"
>
> [6] But when Paul perceived that one part were Sadducees and the other Pharisees, he cried out in the council, "Brethren, I am a Pharisee, a son of Pharisees; with respect to the hope and the resurrection of the dead I am on trial." [7] And when he had said this, a dissension arose between the Pharisees and the Sadducees; and the assembly was divided. [8] For the Sadducees say that there is no resurrection, nor angel, nor spirit; but the Pharisees acknowledge them all.
>
> [9] Then a great clamor arose; and some of the scribes of the Pharisees' party stood up and contended, "We find nothing wrong in this man. What if a spirit or an angel spoke to him?" [10] And when the dissension became violent, the tribune, afraid that Paul would be torn in pieces by them, commanded the soldiers to go down and take him by force from among them and bring him into the barracks.
>
> [11] The following night the Lord stood by him and said, "Take courage, for as you have testified about me at Jerusalem, so you must bear witness also at Rome." (Acts 23:1–11)

My defense did not become violent, but the disagreements among the parties did resemble the passage of time in the Council.

During the reception, after the committee had approved my dissertation and was now gathered to eat cake and drink punch, Dr. Nicole came over to me and showed me four books that he thought I would enjoy glancing through—all in French and German and strongly Augustinian. I was interested. He was so courteous and gracious that I was impressed. A gentleman scholar!

He had not questioned me at all on the Adventist section of the dissertation—simply saying that after my historical section he had no more questions. He admitted that he was not well-informed on the theological developments in the Adventist tradition. Here was a man whose letters included a ThD from Gordon-Conwell and a PhD from Harvard University. He was a historical pattern of the neo-evangelical movement.

I was saddened to hear twenty-six years later that he had passed away. He had been a professor of theology at Gordon-Conwell for forty-one years. These books that he brought to show me were rare books from his personal library of 26,000 volumes.

The defense resulted in very few revisions as my committee had worked long and hard with me before going into that final meeting. Nevertheless, my next few weeks were given over to final polishing. My graduation was scheduled for the spring of 1984. My family was there along with the Blantons and their kids. My nephew David graduated with his BA at the same session, so two Zackrisons marched on that triumphant day!

Having finished my Doctor of Theology, which had more requirements than any other degree at Andrews at the time, the administration gave all the ThD candidates the choice of having our degrees granted "Doctor of Theology" or "Doctor of Philosophy." After some thought I decided to take the PhD because it had a broader appeal and was probably better known. I didn't know what the future might hold once the war in Collegedale was over.

In Happy Valley, the faculty was informed about the event in the public relations sheet for employees of Southern College:

> Ed Zackrison successfully defended his doctoral dissertation entitled, "Seventh-day Adventist Understanding of the Effect of Adam's Sin on His Posterity." The 40 people who attended the oral defense, most of them former students of Ed's, were invited to a reception at which Dr. G. F. Hasel presented Dr. Edwin Zackrison. After the reception Ed's former students treated him to pizza.[1]

Dr. Gary Patterson was present at the graduation and after the ceremony he told me, that he had sat there popping his buttons in pride for me as my professors boasted of my achievements. At the same time, he thought about what was going on at Southern where people were trying to crucify me. Here was irony! But his theory that "perception is reality" was proving correct.

I appreciated his thoughts. We both lived in a world of double binds. As I have gone through all the correspondence I wrote and received during this time, I have relived a lot of experiences I had forgotten. Reading my diaries of those days helped

---

1. Cherie Smith, ed. *Southern Communique,* January 27, 1984, 1.

me to understand my own psyche as I struggled to deal with integrating that experience with my faith.

In a letter I wrote to my former mentor, Dr. Frank Knittel, who was by then chair of the English Department at Loma Linda University, thoughts from the fox hole were filling my mind:

> The security of your friendship means more to us every day. What has been a number of years of the greatest peace and bliss we have ever experienced here at Southern College has now turned into a progressive hell. I now recognize all that you shielded us from. And the more I feel the biting and cutting of those in Wright Hall the more I respect you and the more I understand why you had to get out when you did.
>
> I remember once on graduation weekend (1981) your telling me that what I needed most of all was faith. You proceeded to answer my hopeless response that if I could not express faith in God perhaps I could express faith in your faith in me. And that carried me through. My faith in God is stronger now as I have learned to live with non-supportiveness from those in power. But you are irreplaceable in learning to have faith in myself. The faith you expressed in me is unearned but is so soothing for my scars.
>
> Last night was very rough. The children were sobbing late into the night. They are feeling the anxiety of the situation more than ever. We have talked about it too much and we have not shielded them as we [probably] should. We don't know how. We think we see cracks in the wall and then someone mortars them up again. We are just about to resolve some issue and then somebody attacks from the rear. There are times this past week that I have come very close to simply walking out of the situation but [Annie] is always high when I am low and vice versa and somehow we carry each other through. But we're not sure what we are doing to our children.
>
> John Wagner called yesterday and thanked me for a letter I had written trying to clear up the misunderstanding between Tom [Mostert], he, and me. Then he proceeded to tell me that he hadn't figured out why God called him here to do what he was doing. I didn't have the heart to level with him since he wouldn't listen anyway—that God has had little to do with it—either his coming or what he is doing.
>
> We are at the end of the rope. Gerald Colvin[2] was in town looking for a Bible teacher yesterday and says he wants to call me but doesn't dare.
>
> The hardest thing for me this morning is the sudden realization that after nine years of telling my son I will play with him when my dissertation is finished I am out of a career, and still don't have any time for him. That poor boy is almost a total stranger to me and all for the "Lord's work." He begs me to play with him and now I am preoccupied with my own pity and troubles.

---

2. Colvin (1939–2013) had been chair of the Psychology department at Southern. Now he was academic dean at Southwestern Adventist College in Keene, Texas.

This has hit me harder than anything yet. I am crushing him. I guess I really can take all the attacks on me better than ever; but him? And then I sit in my study and look at it all—3000 books and for what?[3]

LETTING GO AND LETTING GOD

After the graduation weekend at SMC, I discovered that I had not been assigned any classes for the summer of 1984, so we decided to take a long-needed vacation up the East Coast. We really didn't know what the immediate future held for us. But we didn't think we would make it through the summer. We were resigned since our protectors were all gone.

In addition to Dr. Grant and Dr. Knittel, we kept hearing that "Zackrison and Gladson were next" for the chopping block. I cannot fully describe the inner turmoil we went through from day to day (although the letter above shows some of that frustration). The drive from Charleston, South Carolina up the coast to Boston should have been relaxing, but I was struggling. There were no phones to take although we occasionally made a check-in call with a couple of faculty members who might have some current news for us.

Our reputations had been so badly damaged by what had gone on for four years that we wondered how we would ever recover. Here is where the religious man finally faces reality and just says let's go. A popular saying among Christians has often been "Let Go and Let God." These words appeared as sermon titles, book titles, quotations from historical figures and bumper stickers.

Elizabeth Peale Allen, daughter of Dr. Norman Vincent Peale, wrote what she understood the saying meant:

> We need to let go of our own will. We must claim as our own the incredibly hard prayer that Jesus prayed: "Father, if you are willing, take this cup from me; yet not my will, but Yours be done" (Luke 22:42). We need to let go and let God do what God wills. This submission will lead to peace and joy, even when the way is difficult. "Father, I place my life in Your hands!" (Luke 23:46).[4]

Those are just words until you experience the helplessness that comes with that territory. All of this had occurred at the hands of other Adventists. God does not reveal his methods. The lyrics of the old hymn by William Cowper (1774), told the story in verse.

> God moves in a mysterious way His wonders to perform;
>   He plants His footsteps in the sea and rides upon the storm.

---

3. Zackrison, "Letter to Frank Knittel," January 28, 1984, 1–2.

4. Allen, "Learn to Let Go and Let God." *Guidepost Magazine,* Sept. 24, 2012. Internet site: https://www.guideposts.org/faith-in-daily-life/learn-to-let-go-and-let-god.

> Deep in unfathomable mines of never failing skill
> > He treasures up His bright designs and works His sov'reign will.
>
> Ye fearful saints, fresh courage take; the clouds ye so much dread
> > Are big with mercy and shall break in blessings on your head.
> Judge not the Lord by feeble sense, but trust Him for His grace;
> > Behind a frowning providence he hides a smiling face.
>
> His purposes will ripen fast, unfolding every hour;
> > The bud may have a bitter taste, but sweet will be the flow'r.
> Blind unbelief is sure to err and scan His work in vain;
> > God is His own interpreter, and He will make it plain.[5]

Karl Marx was wrong when he proclaimed that religion was the opiate of the masses, although I understand the context of his assertion. For a religious man, God is the one who keeps us alert and alive. The religious man does not resign himself to an agnosticism that leads to unbelief in God. He just waits, hanging on that hard prayer of Jesus.

The events that led up to the end, were swift. Dr. Knittel had resigned (gone on sabbatical) in 1983 and left that summer. I waved as he and his wife drove into the dusk. Dr. Grant had taken a contrived call to Maryland. No one really questioned that I was next, and no deliverance was on the horizon. In the end, a theologian is no match for an administrator. The story of Luther and the Pope, in the short term, always ended the same way no matter how many times I heard or read the story.

The last few months in Happy Valley were hard, but many of my students were champions of support. They wrote letters to the board members. People gave me paper after paper, letter after letter, until I had a collection of over a thousand pages that laid out in detail the Collegedale story.[6] Supporters compiled a 500-page collection of primary sources, copied them off on legal-sized paper and sent the compilation to every member of the college board to inform them of the setting and background of all that had taken place.[7] There was no indication that the compilation had any effect on any board member. When I reminded Dr. Wagner of the compilation several years later, he told me he didn't remember it.

Looking back, I think we completely misjudged what was happening. Facts were not meaningful to those baying for our blood. While an academic considers facts semi-sacred, some administrators seem to disregard information that will get in the way of accomplishing what they see as their job. Professors face rooms full of questioning students every day. They do not involve themselves in politics or the wielding of authority, and they are doomed to lose in a contest with raw administrative

---

5. Cowper, "God Moves in a Mysterious Way." *The Seventh-day Adventist Hymnal*, 107.

6. My collection of documents became known as the *Appendix Zackrison Southern College* and was in two volumes of 500 pages each.

7. This collection became known as *Faculty Document Committee Collection*.

power. For us it was not the Pope and Luther, it was Wilson and Ford that changed the playing field.

When Dr. Ford was fired, the atmosphere changed. This was not because all theologians in the Church agreed with him, but because the excitement of research and thinking had been dealt a death blow. After I spoke at the Church pastored by one of my former students who had been at the top of his class both at SMC and at Seminary, he shared over lunch that the ministry was nothing like I said it would be. He admitted that I was so excited in my classes about ministry that he caught my enthusiasm. But he sadly told me that there was no excitement in the ministry anymore.

His testimony broke my heart. I knew he spoke from his personal experience. Now every minister was viewed through the prism of the Omega conspiracy theory. He later left the ministry and the Adventist Church, went to law school and became a successful attorney. He joined another denomination. He was one of the brightest students I had at SMC.

"Bright" described many of my students. Some went back and took law. Others went back and took medicine, clinical psychology, marriage and family therapy, hospital chaplaincy and education. They cared deeply for people, but they ultimately did not feel welcome in the Adventist pastorate because they refused to become mere reflectors of other people's thoughts—the very thing that their education had been designed to avoid. Many simply left to protect their integrity. My heart continued to break with every new departure. But the fundamentalists rejoiced.

When Dr. Knittel was forced to resign, several colleagues on the faculty quit in protest. Some students refused to have anything more to do with the Adventist system. Sadly, I could multiply these experiences, and I am sure there are more students who followed the same course. These were some bright, exciting students. Some have stayed in touch. One became a national representative for a large electronics firm. Another, one of the ablest editors Adventism had, walked out and has spent his years as a public high school teacher. He is master of several foreign languages—speaks and writes them fluently.

Sadly, too many Adventist fundamentalists welcomed this. It meant the end was near. The shaking had begun. They seemed to rejoice at each new disaster. In retrospect, I think most reasonable Adventists today would agree that the triumph of Adventist fundamentalism in the 1980s has exacted a dreadful toll on the Church. But at the time, forces of obscurantism were triumphant. In Happy Valley some of these extremists made life miserable for others. To them, if a local Church grew, it was blamed on satanic forces generating a false revival. If a Church congregation had not grown, it showed that the minister hadn't been doing his job. Catch 22!

At the beginning of every new term, I had always supplied my students with a two-page handout of Sister White's quotations on learning that had been compiled by

Dr. Alexander, my theology mentor in college.[8] These were instructions on how to teach Bible and religion to college students. They formed my philosophy of education.

I vowed to each student in my classes that this would be my instructional philosophy in that class. Teaching them to think, evaluate, search and engage themselves in the exciting task of thinking through their faith would be the pathway to their success as an intelligent pastor. Too often I observed that those who learned these methods, the best were often attacked the hardest.

SALEM, MASSACHUSETTS

It all appears quite ironic now. It was long ago. On our trip up the East Coast to places we had never visited before, we finally arrived in Salem, Massachusetts—an interesting town that was a center of witch hunts in early American history. We found a motel, and, in the morning, we visited the witch hunt museums. In one of them a theatre group reenacted one of the trials and showed the devastating results of that era's fake news—the resultant deaths of a few female "witches." For some reason, I was familiar with such stories even though I had never read much about Salem.

That night in the motel, I made a phone call to Collegedale. I was told we needed to get home as fast as possible; a court date had been set for our trial. Witch come home! The administration was anxious to get this done before school started in the fall and we were already in the month of July.

We checked out and drove straight through to Tennessee. Once home, we were informed that our trial would begin in a week. We had no one to represent us but we must be ready. Of course, it was not a trial with lawyers present. We could not have a lawyer. We must defend ourselves; but the board had already issued the plans to terminate me. No action would be taken against my wife since she was not in the Religion Department. But I was to go. She could stay on the faculty; the case would be against me.

We prayed. We talked with the lawyer the community had hired to defend us anonymously. Somehow, I could not shake Salem from my mind. Citizens had been hanged because of the false charges. This time, nobody's life was at stake, but the parallels were haunting. Yet pursuing that was not helpful. We needed to figure out a strategy. We got on the phone and lined up over thirty people who offered to testify for me. Some were gone for the summer, but they would fly in for the trial.

THE COLLEGEDALE [SALEM] WITCH TRIAL

The night before the trial, the chair of the committee that was going to examine me called. This was in violation of college policy, which said that the chair could have no

---

8. See Appendix I below.

contact with the defendant. But as long as I had him on the phone, I told him I would like to have a lawyer present. He said absolutely not. I asked him why. He said that would violate college policy. I told him then we would not go to trial.

When I had given a report to the board[9] in which I explained why we needed to reconsider the whole board policy of retrenchment, I recited the contributions I had made to the college over the past twelve years and I appealed to the board to solve the Religion Department problem some other way than having heads roll.

When I finished the report, I invited questions. The only question I got was whether I had talked to a lawyer. The nameless, faceless mass was at work again. Were we being followed wherever we went? But before I could answer the question, Dr. Patterson jumped to his feet and said before the board that he hoped I had seen a lawyer—the board had seen several lawyers. The discussion ended but nothing changed.

So, I told the chair, while we were on the phone—I would not attend the trial if I couldn't have a lawyer there to help me. That was out of the question—they had already flown people in to testify. We hung up.

Later that evening I got a second call. This time the chair was asking me to cancel the meeting because the president had only found four people to testify against me and two of them were on the verge of backing out. English teacher David Smith had dropped out confessing that he didn't even know me. Dr. Gulley came by my house apologizing profusely that he had been strong-armed into testifying against me. He was on the verge of tears. He said he had not been told that I would be present to hear his testimony against me. So, he had also backed out. Now the president was down to two witnesses, both with histories of attacking me.

I asked if the charges would be dropped? If so I would gladly stay and teach in the fall. I suggested that I had never had any desire to leave this job I not only loved but believed God had called me to. The chair just responded—we couldn't do that. Period. Another double bind. We couldn't have a meeting where the president of the college would be embarrassed. I couldn't have a lawyer. We needed to have the meeting but no lawyer. I was confused again. I asked the chair if he knew that he was not supposed to be talking to me? That he was breaking college policy? And then I simply asked, where do I report that? The phone went dead.

I don't know how long before the phone rang again. But when it did the voice told me I could have a lawyer. The witnesses would be eliminated so Dr. Wagner wouldn't be embarrassed. No one hid behind the prayer arguments anymore. It was clear to me that the pressure was on them. Did they care if I may be embarrassed? My embarrassment was apparently immaterial.

I called the lawyer. I had not hired him. I had only talked to him at the request of community members. The community had hired him over my protests. But we had been giving him material to evaluate our situation.

---

9. See Appendix 8 below.

THE END

At 9:00 am at Collegedale Academy we met in a seminar room. Surprise! The college had a lawyer present. My lawyer laid down a 1,000-page collection of materials documenting the past four years of harassment—it included correspondence, phone call transcripts, class notes, hundreds of letters, newspaper articles, diary entries, student petitions and testimonies and faculty petitions.

The college lawyer blanched. He turned to Dr. Wagner and said, "You never told me about this!" Nobody said anything, but all sat in stunned silence. Finally, the college lawyer invited the community lawyer representing me to join him in a classroom down the hall—just the two of them.

CHAPTER THIRTY-EIGHT

Closure

> "Someone once told me to cheer up, things could be worse.
> So, I cheered up, and sure enough, things got worse."
> —Harry A. Zackrison

THE FINAL MOVEMENTS WERE RAPID

The meeting in the seminar room at the academy took less than half an hour. Apparently opposing lawyers can work fast together when one is confronted with a thousand pages of revealing evidence. When they finally emerged, they delivered the verdict. My wife would receive the standard year's salary. I would receive two year's salary. All our moving expenses would be paid as long as we moved anywhere within the contiguous United States. The college would guarantee purchase of our house. My doctoral debt of $70,000 would be cancelled—it was just a paper figure.[1] The school would absorb the cost of my doctoral regalia. And our denominational employment records would not be altered.

There were some deadlines. We would have twelve days to get out of Dodge. The rationale was that we were to be gone by the time the new school year started. This was of great importance to Dr. Wagner and his financial sponsor. No guilt was to be attributed to either party. That was routine. I blamed them, they blamed me, but none of that was official! Mouths closed.

The president immediately divulged all these details to the faculty because of the rumors that circulated that I had gotten millions of dollars to leave, presumably for fear that we would sue the college for reverse discrimination.[2] In order to counter

---

1. See Footnote 1, Chapter 35 above.
2. We neither sued the college nor threatened to sue the college. This rumor of our alleged litigation

this rumor, he read the confidential agreement to the faculty (as my mentor had told me, they write the rules).

Since we had no place to go, we did what people do—we went back to what had once been home. We flew out of Atlanta for Los Angeles and from there we headed to Riverside where Dr. and Mrs. Knittel put us up for a couple of days. The Knittels had contacted real estate agents so the next morning we had a slate of houses to tour.

Since I had grown up in La Sierra, I wanted to live there. We were currently homeless wanderers separated from the friends we had been forced to leave behind in Collegedale. We were also jobless. At the end of our day of house hunting, we put in a bid on a four-bedroom, two-and-a-half-bath house with a swimming pool on Peacock Lane. I began to feel my love for California returning. I had been gone for twelve years but I was still a Californian.

Peacock Lane had been developed while I was a student at La Sierra Academy in the 1950s. It was upscale compared with Knoefler Drive where Dad had built our house in the 1940s. Our bid on the house was low but it was accepted, and we hopped back on a plane and flew to Collegedale the next day. So far, we were well within the dictated twelve-day limit.

SHAKING THE DUST OFF OUR FEET

Our home on Suhrie Drive was teaming with faculty members and students as we packed furiously on Sunday morning. A picture etched in my mind's eye is from my home study—that of one of my brilliant students. As I came into the study, I saw him standing straight, holding in his hand and staring at my name plate that had been on my office door in the Religion Department for twelve years. The sadness on his face was memorable. He was shaking his head in disbelief and disappointment.

When the truck arrived, we had several college students and colleagues to help us load it. In our grief, we indulged in a symbolic act of rebellion by drinking the devil's own brew, Coca Cola and Dr. Pepper, whenever we sat down in our screen porch to take a break. Life was not right.

When the new school year started and the college faculty returned from their vacations, some couldn't believe we were gone. What happened during the next school year we only heard about from friends with whom we had taught for the past twelve years. In my files, I saved no less than two reams of these letters of support and commiseration.

On our way to the airport to fly to California, we had put our kids on an Amtrak train to New Orleans, where they would be met by their grandparents, who were at the General Conference convocation making a presentation. The last thing I remember was seeing both Jill and Mark gesturing to us as the train pulled out—they were saying

---

was all fabrication, but it spread fast around the Adventist circuit.

"good-bye" by imitating swimming—their message was clear: *Please find a house with a swimming pool!*

We were happy to comply. For a while, we knew, they would be strangers in a strange land, but with a pool in the backyard and a landscape bathed in sun and brightened by mountains, they could hardly get a better introduction to their new life.

BROODING ABOUT THE FUTURE

When we arrived, we attended the La Sierra Collegiate Church and there we ran into a member of the School of Religion, a friend from our internship days. He had been the Bible teacher at the academy when I was youth pastor. Now he was a professor at Loma Linda University, Riverside campus. He greeted us warmly and then asked what we were planning to do. Annie volunteered that we had come home and were hoping that perhaps there might be a place for us on the faculty someday.

His only comment was, "Don't plan on it." I remember the pain that coursed through my back as I heard that simple, insensitive remark. I was too hurt to be disappointed. I just absorbed it. But as with most emotional jolts we absorb, the brain retains them. It was not his fault. He had no idea what we had faced and from what we were hoping to recover.

The first week after our move to La Sierra, we were invited to ride with friends and colleagues to a Joan Baez concert at the Universal Studios Amphitheater in Hollywood. A university faculty member had chartered a bus, and this was a chance for fellowship with several old friends. A box of soft drinks was being pushed up and down the aisle in the bus and we were all invited to help ourselves to whatever drinks we wanted during the trip. The box was filled with cans of Ginger Ale, Seven-Up, Coca Cola, Pepsi Cola and Dr. Pepper.

I surprised myself by the sudden attack of paranoia I succumbed to. Having just come from Southern College where caffeinated drinks not long ago had been thought of as names of demons, I was thinking that maybe this was a trap to test us. It pained me to realize how much damage Collegedale had inflicted on me. I looked around for cameras.

THE ROAD TO RECOVERY

It seemed that at every turn I was plagued by the question of what kind of future we might have. My mind had become so twisted by living under surveillance for the last five years that I did not know if I could correct the downward course my mind had primed me for. I tried to relax but I didn't expect ever again to be invited to speak in an Adventist Church. Then I got a call from a former SMC student of mine, now a pastor in the Conference. I had officiated at his wedding in Tennessee when he was pastor there. He asked if I would speak at his Church.

In my conversation with this pastor, I learned that he was enrolled at Claremont Graduate School. When we met at a restaurant in the city for lunch, he told me that he believed he was so much like me that he could predict what was going to happen to him if he stayed in the Adventist ministry. And he wanted me to know that he was retraining to leave the pastorate to become a hospital chaplain. He expressed his disappointment in what had happened to me and others he respected, particularly Dr. Grant. Another of our best students preparing for the worst.

A couple of weeks later, another pastor called. He welcomed me back to Southern California and asked if I would be the weekend speaker for his Church's retreat—three talks. Another couple of weeks went by and the principal of an academy in Orange County called. Would I be their Week of Prayer speaker?

Then the pastor of the Collegiate Church called and asked if I would serve on the Church Worship committee. And of course, he wanted two sets (28 in all) of banners to hang in the Church. And so it went. Would I give a month of general Sabbath School lesson studies in the sanctuary of the Loma Linda University church? "Please remember, it will be telecast."

As exciting as this all was, these appointments were not easy. I was so paranoid I hardly understood myself. Living under surveillance of spies and Church politicians had taken a toll. I couldn't force the thought out of my sick mind that any day now the nameless, faceless mass would strike again.

Occasionally I was daring to hope that the Lord was opening a new window of ministry for me. Calls began to come from ministers around the country, many former students of mine, asking me to pray and counsel with them as they tried to deal with the new political pressures they were feeling in the SDA ministry. How do you minister to a Church with hidden spies and vigilantes looking to nail you for some ideological crime? How do you deal with the Omega conspiracy mindset?

Getting our ministerial prerogatives straight was a very difficult task in this changing society. I remember the vivid point that a visiting speaker had made in a chapel talk at the university when he began his sermon with the words, "most of you don't give a shit about the homeless people in this country." Now that he had our attention, he added that we were more offended that he had used the word "shit" in the pulpit than that the homeless people needed help. Ministry is a notion that threatens and challenges the religious man.

While at least two of my ministerial colleagues were setting up retreat centers for Adventist ministers to deal with these things, I felt no compulsion to open any new organization. I was just thinking about my own future. Would I stay in the Church? Would I stay in the teaching profession? But somehow Southern California, "home" as we had called it, was presenting a different perspective that in time would help me reach a degree of emotional equilibrium.

I now understood more fully what both Dr. Heppenstall and Dr. Alexander had meant. They had told me I needed to reconsider my view of Church and ministry. I had done just that.

LAYING SOME DEFINITE PLANS

Considering my options, I wondered about making changes of direction. I was convinced that the educational ministry that I was involved in was probably a thing of the past. Several friends who had suffered a similar fate had opted for Marriage and Family Therapy (MFT), Law, Medicine or Clinical Psychology programs.

I made a trip to Loma Linda University and talked to the MFT faculty. They assured me that they would accept me into their program, but they were not excited about my planning to attend LLU. They counseled me to go to another school, like University of Southern California. When I finished, they urged me to let them know and at that point they could consider hiring me to teach in their program at LLU. No promises, of course.

My uncle, Dr. Louis P. Thorpe, had taught for many years in the Psychology Department at USC but he was long gone. The only USC faculty member I knew was Dr. Jerry Wiley, who was then vice-dean of the USC School of Law. He had been head elder at the Church I interned in when he took me out to lunch attempting to talk me into accepting the position of senior pastor after Elder Rea left. That was several years ago now and well before the Collegedale purge. Now I asked Dr. Wiley if he knew anyone on the faculty of the graduate MFT program at USC. He said he did—he was a good friend of the chair of that program.

Dr. Wiley arranged a luncheon between himself, the MFT chair and me. We had a delightful lunch and conversation. But the chair told me his department only accepted two people a year into the MFT program and they had been chosen in June; this was September. However, he said, in the light of what I had been through, and the fact that one of their two had just dropped out of the program, he would suggest that I be allowed to enter the program in January 1985. They had never done that—accepted a new student between semesters—but he would pursue it.

A month later he confirmed that I had been accepted and I could begin my program at USC in January! I quietly enrolled. I would drive the sixty miles to Los Angeles once a week beginning in January. I had two years of salary but no paid tuition. And I knew how fast the time would fly.

A GLIMPSE OF SUNSHINE FROM FLAT TOP ROCK

Up at the end of Peacock Lane there is a path that leads over the mountain. One can climb a couple hundred steps and enjoy a view of the City of Norco. Today there is a beautiful golf course in that area but in 1984 there were just the boulders and brown sage bushes. But the hike was exhilarating.

To relieve some stress, I explored the mountain—it was very much like Rattlesnake Hill at the end of Knoefler Drive where my neighbors and I had spent so many summers camping, hiking and building forts. As I came down the hill, I noticed that off to the right was a huge boulder that was flat on the top. We had grown up with rocks like that on Sunshine Mountain. I climbed up and sat down. Somehow, the pain of separation and grief was less when I was on top of the highest rock on the highest level of the mountain. I relaxed, on my back, and stared up at the sky.

Where are you God? Why am I here? I thought life was complete and delightful in Happy Valley but that was years ago now. And I was lying on a flat rock, which my kids and I named "Flat Top Rock." I had no answers. I just let my brain go into neutral. If I closed my eyes, I could think that at forty-two years of age my life was not completely over. I had never taught a day in my life with my doctorate after nine years of grueling preparation. These were fleeting thoughts.

I don't know how long I laid there. It was pleasant in the September afternoon sun. One of the assets of La Sierra was being at the mouth of the Santa Ana canyon where there was a breeze that started up every day around 3:00 pm. However hot the weather got we always knew that a gentle wind would cool us off each day.

Finally, I got up. I had probably slumbered a little, prayed and meditated on Flat Top Rock. But it was time to go home—maybe take a swim, arrange my study, pick some fruit from the little orchard of citrus trees around the pool. There was plenty to be relaxed about, but I had lost the ability to relax. So, I stiffly descended the hill.

When I walked up to the front door, I heard my name being called. I was wanted on the phone. It was Dr. Wendel Tucker. I didn't know him, but I knew he was principal of La Sierra Academy. And he got right to his point. He told me he had lost his Bible teacher and heard that I was in the area. He wanted to know if there was any chance that I could teach a couple of senior Bible classes for him on a substitute basis?

Too fast. I was not finding this pleasant. He was right. I didn't know him. He was wrong in thinking that I had any interest in teaching high school seniors. And he apparently didn't know that I had two years to get completely retrained for a different career. I told him thank you and I was flattered that he had called but no, I could not teach for him. I revealed that I was enrolled at USC and I needed to make use of my time very carefully because I had no job and I had two years to get re-educated.

He was thinking silently. Then he asked if I would at least come down to the academy and meet him and see where I used to go to school? I had no excuse why not. So, I told him I could be down there in an hour. It wouldn't hurt to meet him. And that was that.

When I stepped into the classroom, I no longer cared if these were elementary or high school or graduate students—I knew instinctively that a classroom was where I belonged and wanted to be. I walked around the Bible classroom—the room where

I had taken two years of high school Bible in the 1950s. The desks had been replaced. The blackboards were now whiteboards. No chalk—magic markers now. Everything else was pretty much the same.

This would only be a temporary job and I would only teach two classes. But it did not appeal to me and it would be a waste of my precious retraining time. So, I had to tell him once more, "no." Thanks for the invitation but I couldn't do that. I was one of the lucky ones—I had gone straight from pastoring to college teaching. I had bypassed academy teaching. I clinched it by confessing that I didn't have a secondary teaching credential. I couldn't do this. I had taken a doctoral cognate (minor) in adolescent behavior, but that didn't meet federal requirements for secondary educators. I wasn't certified. I couldn't do this.

Behind all this brave talk, I knew I wanted a college classroom and not a counseling office. But he wasn't offering me that. So, I turned him down. I went home thinking about the classroom. And as I walked into my study on Peacock Lane, Dr. Tucker was on the phone again.

He had a new line of attraction. He would like me to teach full time until the end of the school year. That would be two sections of senior Bible, one section of junior Bible, and two sections of sophomore Bible. Five classes with an hour break somewhere in there each day. This man had been working. My pause kept him talking.

He went off on another attack: *This was something I owed this school—this was my school.* It was clear that he didn't understand that I had left this school after my sophomore year because my brother thought I wasn't going to be accepted for my junior year. I didn't say anything, but I was thinking: *No, I don't owe this school anything!*

More silence. But then he switched to the most provocative thought yet. I have never discovered why he set the words in this point of our conversation. But he then said that he had been told that *if he hired me he would come to regret it.* And he asked me what I thought about that. My reply was equally insensitive. *I told him that was his risk, not mine.* I insisted that nobody was asking him to take that risk. I was not going to argue with him about anything—especially about getting a job I really had no interest in.

It was time for another confused response. I thought about what he had said and through my puzzlement and confusion I heard myself say that if he hired me full time for the next semester I would consider it. And I reminded him that I could only work four days a week because one day I would have to be at USC. A religious man does those things—he doesn't act precipitously.

FRIENDS IN UNEXPECTED PLACES

In the afternoon breeze I returned to Flat Top Rock. I laid down on my back and looked up to see if I could see God. "What is going on?" I said out loud. A risk? Be serious. Why would an administrator who really wanted me to work for him call me a risk? But that was the nameless, faceless mass speaking—even in California I was being followed. And I thanked God for the opportunity at USC. That's where he wanted me right now.

I felt comfortable. I slumbered again on *Flat Top Rock*. The rock was warm from the September sun. I was in the quiet of the hills where I felt relaxed and safe. This had been a long day. This had been a taxing, stressful summer.

Finally, I climbed down and returned home. The phone was ringing again. It was Dr. Tucker again. He surprised me by telling me that he had jumped the gun. By that he meant that as we talked earlier he had not checked any of this out with the Conference power force. And as he tried to get it cleared he had been told he could not hire me. No reasons—just that *I was not hirable.*

Now it came home: This was Tom Mostert's Conference. He had already made it crystal clear that I was not welcome there. The Conference office was one block from the academy. Why had I even considered that I would be having a chance in this Conference? I had already been shut out from jobs I wasn't even interested in to begin with.

For a third time, I climbed up to *Flat Top Rock*. This time I took Jill and Mark with me. I needed their support since the afternoon was starting to resemble life back in Happy Valley. In a pensive moment they assured me that if I were offered that job they needed me to know that *they wanted me to take it.* I never told them how those words stayed in my mind.

I reminded them that I would be their teacher. I pushed it. Would they be embarrassed having a parent on the faculty? I reminded Jill that she knew what it felt like to be watched all the time. Imagine how Dr. Tucker's children felt when their father was attacked and criticized. Would they really be comfortable in the same situation?

How could they know? They were in the identity-forming period of their lives and the best thing that could happen would be for their father to be nowhere around. But I didn't say any of that. I just thanked them for their kind and honest words.

We talked for half an hour and lay on our backs looking up to see if we could see God. I didn't see him. Finally, it was time to go home for supper. The phone was ringing. It was a friend I had known for many years.

"Apparently, you know a few people in this neighborhood," he said.

"Yes, I grew up here. I was four years old when we moved to La Sierra."

"Well, a bunch of us got together and have been calling Dr. Tucker to let him know that if he doesn't hire you we will pull our kids and send them to Loma Linda. I think he will be calling you back soon."

He did call back.

It had taken three trips to *Flat Top Rock* to talk to God about a job I didn't even want. But when you pray and ask for guidance, you must deal with the results. I approached Annie. "You're a credentialed high school teacher," I said. "Are you willing to help me deal with situations I might not be prepared for?"

It would be ten years before I learned what had happened on that day at the Conference office, the angry back and forth and how the decision to hire or not to hire me went down. Dr. Tucker never informed me, and I never asked; when I finally found out, the information came from people much farther up the administrative ladder.

LIFE HAS FEW CLOUDLESS DAYS

In his 1957 childhood memoir, My Mother's Castle, *French writer and movie maker Marcel Pagnol tells the story of his enchanted childhood summers in the mountains of Provence at the beginning of the twentieth century.* In the epilogue to the book, he brings the reader up to date on what happened to his family and friends that played such a prominent role in the tales of his childhood.

His best friend Lili died in the northern woods during World War I. His brother Paul, who became one of the last shepherds of Provence, died in his 30s and his beloved mother passed away when he was fifteen. His father, a public-school teacher, never remarried, and the two of them could never bring themselves to speak about her because of the enormous grief that her memory was wrapped up in.

At the end of this litany of misfortune that befell him at the close of such a glorious childhood, Pagnol added these unforgettable words:

> Telle est la vie des hommes. Quelques joies, très vite effacées par d'inoubliables chagrins. Il n'est pas nécessaire de le dire aux enfants.[3]

I wish that Pagnol's words had not resonated so much with my life's experience. I wish with Job that after having dedicated my life to serving God and my fellow human beings to the best of my ability, I would have been able to go through life without attracting as much pain and suffering as I have. A religious man knows that there is no satisfying answer to be had to the problem of suffering beyond trusting God. That is easier said than done.

For ten years after moving back to California, life was good. I taught at La Sierra Academy and took great pleasure in teaching Bible, directing and producing musical theatre, which required orchestras that provided my kids with opportunities to continue playing their instruments and preserve their musical investment from Happy Valley. I ran Christian drama groups and we regularly went on tour, even to Australia and Europe.

But once again, things went awry. My marriage, which had never been very successful or satisfying, finally ended. At first, the Adventist community accepted it as one of all too many misfortunes to be visited upon couples of long standing, but when angry accusations turned into toxic rumors of infidelity, the cost in bad publicity to the academy, the university, where I now was a tenured professor of theology and ministry, finally exceeded their willingness to stand by me and I was once more *persona non grata* in my own Church. Finally, I offered to resign.

---

3. Translation: *That is how life is. A few joys that are quickly replaced by unforgettable sorrows. There is no need to tell the children about that.*

What pained me the most was that these rumors were now being fanned by some in my own family. I had been able to survive Collegedale because of my family; when it turned on me, it was more than I could bear.

One day I was alerted to the fact that somebody pretending to be me had left a brazenly false confession of my alleged marital misdeeds in the commentary section of *Spectrum Magazine's* online blog. It was the cruelest blow yet. But I knew I didn't have to go far to find the person(s) responsible. As if this was not enough, my son Mark ended up dying under tragic circumstances. Grief and anger nearly destroyed me.

Where was God in all this? Where was his caring Church? I made a 4x8-foot banner and hung it in my living room. I called it "My Church." There were probably a dozen names on it cut carefully out of brightly colored felt. They were my Church of God. I finally understood that seeking the "true church" was a fool's errand. The challenge of the Bible is to *be,* not to *find,* the true church: *to be truly church.*

Thanks to my interdisciplinary doctorate I was able to get teaching professorships at several colleges and universities. It did not save me from pain, but it delivered me from despair.

Despite the temptation to walk away from my faith, I came to realize that a religious man does not "throw the baby out with the bathwater." Believing in a Church with walls can bring security, but as one of my friends told me, "When you have security, you don't really live." I had to repeat that many times to understand what he meant. I think I am beginning to understand that.

"When you have security, you don't really live." By that standard, I have lived a very full life so far.

Appendixes

APPENDIX 1

"The Educational Philosophy Used in This Course," *Handout for all of Edwin Zackrison's Academy and College Classes*. Compiled by Wilber Alexander, PhD, Professor of Applied Theology, SDA Theological Seminary.

APPENDIX 2

"The Collegedale Story," by Dr. Frank Knittel, President, Southern College of Seventh-day Adventists.

APPENDIX 3

"Some Historical Observations on the Present Theology 'Crisis,'" by Dr. Ronald M. Springett, Associate Professor of Religion, Southern College of Seventh-day Adventists.

APPENDIX 4

"Remarks at SMC Faculty Colloquium," by Dr. Frank Knittel, President, Southern College of Seventh-day Adventists.

APPENDIX 5

"The Atlanta Affirmation," by SDA Educators, Administrators and Pastors.

APPENDIX 6

"A Response to the Atlanta Affirmation," by Elder Neal Wilson, President, General Conference of Seventh-day Adventists.

APPENDIX 7

"Support Letter," by Dr. Edward Heppenstall, Former Chair, Department of Theology and Christian Philosophy, Andrews University Theological Seminary.

APPENDIX 8

"Remarks Before the Southern College Board of Trustees," by Dr. Edwin Zackrison, Professor of Religion, Southern College of Seventh-day Adventists.

APPENDIX 9

"The Image Problem," by Elder Edwin Zackrison, Associate Professor of Religion, Southern College of Seventh-day Adventists.

APPENDIX 1

The Educational Philosophy Behind the Methods Used in This Course[1]

"Faithful teachers should be placed in charge of the Bible classes, teachers who will strive to make the students understand their lessons, not by explaining everything to them, but by requiring them to explain clearly every passage they read. Let these teachers remember that little good is accomplished by skimming over the surface of the word. Thoughtful investigation and earnest, taxing study are necessary to an understanding of this word." *Counsels to Parents, Teachers, and Students*, p. 483.

"It is a law of the mind that it gradually adapts itself to the subjects upon which it is trained to dwell. If occupied with commonplace matters only, it will become dwarfed and enfeebled. If never required to grapple with difficult problems, it will after a time almost lose the power of growth. As an educating power the Bible is without a rival. In the word of God, the mind finds subject for the deepest thought, the loftiest aspiration. The Bible is the most instructive history that men possess. It came fresh from the fountain of eternal truth, and a divine hand has preserved its purity through all the ages. It lights up the far-distant past, where human research seeks vainly to penetrate. In God's word we behold the power that laid the foundation of the earth and that stretched out the heavens. Here only can we find a history of our race unsullied by human prejudice or human pride. Here are recorded the struggles, the defeats and the victories of the greatest men this world has ever known. Here the great problems of duty and destiny are unfolded. The curtain that separates the visible from the invisible world is lifted, and we behold the conflict of the opposing forces of good and evil, from the first entrance of sin to the final triumph of righteousness and truth; and all is but a revelation of the character

---

1. *Handout for all of Dr. Edwin Zackrison's Academy and College Classes, Southern Missionary College, La Sierra Academy, Loma Linda University Riverside Campus, La Sierra University.* This handout was the first item studied on the first day of every class the author taught at the institutions listed above. It was originally compiled by Dr. Wilber Alexander, Professor of Applied Theology at Andrews University SDA Theological Seminary. All statements are direct quotations from Sister White's writings.

of God. In the reverent contemplation of the truths presented in His word the mind of the student is brought into communion with the infinite mind. Such a study will not only refine and ennoble the character, but it cannot fail to expand and invigorate the mental powers." *Patriarchs and Prophets*, pp. 596–599.

"This is the way in which the schools of the prophets were conducted. Time was given in the class for a faithful study of the thoughts presented. Hearts were warmed and the voice of praise and thanksgiving was heard. The sacred gospel was humanized, as in the teachings of Christ. Much was accomplished for both teachers and students. Time was given for each one to partake of the heavenly repast,—to study the truths presented, and then to add that which he had received from God." *Counsels to Parents, Teachers, and Students*, pp. 436–437.

"When the right spirit is cherished by teachers and students, they will have special grace from God, enough for each, enough for all, enough continually and forever. As the teacher learns from the divine Teacher, the Bible becomes a lesson book such as God designed it to be, giving clear conceptions to those who strive to grasp its grand and glorious truths. As the students search for truth as for hidden treasure, their minds are enriched with the highest of all knowledge. There is shed into the mind a flood of light on the problem of human life. They see how it is possible for men and women to be sanctified through a belief of the truth as it is in Jesus." *Counsels to Parents, Teachers, and Students*, pp. 437.

"It is the student's privilege to have clear and accurate ideas of the truth of the world that he may be prepared to present these truths to other minds. He should be rooted and grounded in the faith. Students should be led to think for themselves, to see the force of truth for themselves, and to speak every word from a heart full of love and tenderness. Urge upon their minds the vital truths of the Bible. Let them repeat these truths in their own language, that you may be sure that they clearly comprehend them. Be sure that every point is fastened upon the mind. This may be a slow process, but it is of ten times more value than rushing over important subjects without giving them due consideration. It is not enough that the student believes the truth for himself. He must be drawn out to state the truth clearly in his own words, that it may be evident that he sees the force of the lesson and makes its application." *Counsels to Parents, Teachers, and Students*, p. 434.

"In all your teaching never forget that the greatest lesson to be taught and to be learned is the lesson of copartnership with Christ in the work of salvation. The education to be secured by searching the Scriptures is an experimental knowledge of the plan of salvation. Such an education will restore the image of God in the soul. It will strengthen and fortify the mind against temptation, and fit the learner to become a worker with Christ in His mission of mercy to the world. It will make him a member of the heavenly family, prepare him to share the inheritance of the saints in light." *Counsels to Parents, Teachers, and Students,* pp. 434–435.

"The teacher of truth can impart effectively only that which he himself knows by experience. Christ taught the truth because He was the truth. His own thought, His character, His life experience, were embodied in His teaching. So with His servants: those who teach the word must make it their own by personal experience. They must know what it is to have Christ made unto them wisdom and righteousness and sanctification and redemption. Every minister of Christ and every teacher should be able to say with the beloved John, 'The life was manifested, and we have seen it, and bear witness, and show unto you that eternal life, which was with the Father, and was manifested unto us.'" 1 John 1:2. *Counsels to Parents, Teachers, and Students,* p. 435.

APPENDIX 2

The Collegedale Story

BY DR. FRANK KNITTEL
President, Southern College of Seventh-day Adventists

MY FIRST INKLING THAT *our religion department was under serious attack came after my return from the South Pacific tour of the Southern Symphony Orchestra in June 1981.* The Zackrisons and the Reiners[1] and the Gilberts and Mrs. Marie Krall were on this trip, and I do not recall a single conversation with any of these people about prevailing controversy involving the religion department.

I did not know there was not a good feeling on the part of Mr. Reiner[2] as far as the Zackrisons were concerned because he had consistently opposed the addition of their home which they had requested after their return from Dr. Zackrison's study leave to Andrews. After their appeal to the Administrative Council had been turned down, Ron Barrow[3] asked for permission to build an addition to his house. This was also denied. I conveyed to both families the decision of the committee and indicated the matter was closed. Zackrisons and Barrows accepted this.

The Administrative Council had voted a monetary ceiling on house values for both new and remodeled homes, and the Zackrison and Barrow requests did not meet that action. However, it was pointed out to me that the action of the Council was not a legal one since the contracts which the Green Meadows [college housing district] dwellers had originally received from the college stipulated that any changes affecting Green Meadows housing matters had to be approved by all current Green Meadows home owners. Therefore the matter of home valuation was referred to a newly formed Green Meadows committee, which subsequently recommended a policy change—one that would allow both the Barrows and the Zackrisons to make home additions in accordance with their earlier requests.

1. *Author's note*: While the story about Mr. Reiner's interchange with the Zackrisons is true, he and his wife were not on the Australian trip.
2. Mr. Reiner was SCSDA business manager.
3. Mr. Barrow was also a part of the SCSDA administration.

In later months the accusation was made that I had somehow negotiated as a special deal the arrangements for the Zackrisons and the Barrows both to make their additions, but this assertion is flatly a falsehood, as a matter of fact, my word to the Zackrisons had been a final one, and I told them we would not be discussing it further. *After that,* Mr. Reiner was the person who suggested to the Zackrisons that perhaps the matter could still be negotiated, and he suggested to them the possibility of re-opening their request. This was a total surprise to me.

None of this reflects the theological accusations made later, but it does explain at least part of the reason for the hostility which Mr. Reiner has felt for years toward the Zackrisons.

EARLY THEOLOGICAL ACCUSATIONS

During the summer of 1981 I became aware of the accusations of Mrs. Florence Woolcock relative to the religion department, and specifically Dr. Zackrison. Her accusations, public denunciations in meetings, private denunciations to individuals, and printed material criticizing the religion teachers and very specifically Dr. Zackrison are a matter of record and need not be repeated here. The publications of John Felts are also a matter of record and excerpts need not be listed in this paper.

Immediately following the accusations of Mrs. Woolcock and John Felts both Sharon and Ellsworth McKee were in communication with me and stated what Woolcock and Felts had already charged. The McKee charges were vague, and when I asked Ellsworth for specific examples of misteaching by Zackrison or others, he stated he did not know enough about theology to discuss them. This admission was very startling in view of the fact that accusations of a serious nature had been made. Ellsworth did suggest he bring Bob Francis with him so that Francis could explain the issues. I declined to get clarification from Francis about charges presented by Ellsworth especially when the charges were no more or less than that which both Woolcock and Felts had made. At no time did anyone present to me any *specific* charges of impropriety of teaching of the men in the religion department.

LATER CHARGES

Shortly after the Felts and Woolcock material first appeared, I received the first comments from non-Collegedale people of an accusatory nature regarding our religion department. Various people were accused of various things, *but not one single accusation was made that had not appeared in Felt's publications or in Vance Ferrell's publications.* As a matter of fact, at no time since this problem began in 1981 have I ever heard an accusation against Ed Zackrison that was not a clone of something in the Adventist underground press, namely *The SDA Press Release, The Adventist Layworker, Collegedale Tidings,* and various printed materials of Florence Woolcock and Vance Ferrell.

Appendix 2

THE HEARING COMMITTEE

Elder A. McClure decided that a hearing committee was needed to deal with the problem of the accusations against the religion department. This committee was formed, and McClure was the chairman. Since one of the most vocal critics of the religion teachers was a Steve DeLong, he was invited to come to a committee meeting. He brought along another student, one who had already left Southern for Wildwood, if I remember correctly.

Steve made accusations against me, Gary Patterson, Zackrison, Ott, Gladson, and Grant. He declared he had tapes which supported his accusations. When he was asked to play the tapes, he did play some of them, but they in no way substantiated his accusations against anyone. He then stated that his primary evidence was on "another tape," but he refused to play that for the group.

DeLong had stated to several people on the committee prior to the meeting that he had earlier asked me to arrange for him to meet with the hearing committee, but that I had refused his request. When I asked him in front of the committee if he indeed had ever asked me to arrange such a meeting, he reluctantly admitted he had never asked me for a meeting with the hearing committee. I then asked him if he had told people the lie that I had denied him an opportunity to meet with the hearing committee, and he reluctantly admitted that he had told people such a lie. I then asked him point blank, "Then you do admit lying to those people?" He rather quietly replied that he had lied. I then turned to the committee in DeLong's presence and stated that I did not see how on earth we could put any confidence in any statement of DeLong in view of the fact that in regards to the issue at hand he was already a confessed prevaricator.[4]

Following the hearing committee, but while all members were still in the room, I stated very emphatically to Elder McClure that I wanted to set the date right then for another meeting—one when the teachers accused by DeLong and his friend could speak to the accusations made against them. Elder McClure declined to set up another meeting, and although in subsequent weeks I twice asked him to set up such a meeting, he declined to do so. The teachers involved were very much deprived their rights of due process in a refusal to let them speak to the charges made. Several days later it was reported to me that Ellsworth McKee had made the statement that DeLong had represented "proof" of the guilt of the theology teachers in teaching "heresy," but I never checked this out. I saw no point in doing so, since it was already apparent that Ellsworth and his wife and parents took Steve DeLong's accusations at face value. Still later a conference officer from Ohio stated that Steve DeLong had been hired as a minister by the Ohio Conference and that the McKees were paying his salary.

From all that transpired in connection with the hearing committee, I came to have the very distinct opinion that McClure and Whitehead and Roll were interested in hearing only the accusations against the religion teachers and had no interest in

---

4. The DeLong story is related in Dr. Gladson's book, *A Theologian's Journey*, pp. 185–186.

hearing any kind of defense provided by the teachers. By the time I left Southern College, it was plainly a fact that whenever an accusation against Zackrison was made to McClure, he took it as a very serious problem; but whenever I tried in any way to present another side of the issue, he had no interest in hearing anything but the charges.

REACTION OF THE BOARD CHAIRMAN TO RELIGION TEACHERS

Immediately after Ron Springett published his article in the Southern Columns [SMC Alumni Journal] about perfectionism,[5] *Elder McClure stated to me, "Springett and Ott and Gladson have got to go!"* When I asked the reasons for this declaration, the answer was, "Their credibility is gone." Further probing on my part yielded Elder McClure's opinion that the three men he mentioned had broached topics privately and publicly which had raised questions "among students" and "in the field," and thus their credibility was gone. My position was that a general assertion such as that could not be the cause for dismissal but that we should consider specific charges which could be verified. McClure admitted he had no such information.

In the spring or early summer of 1982 (I am not sure of the exact date—it could be verified by checking records of plane trips) I attended a hospital board meeting at Madison, Tennessee. Elders McClure and Whitehead and I rode on the same plane that evening from Nashville to Chattanooga, where I disembarked while they continued to Atlanta. The three of us had a three-seat row together on the right side of the plane facing the front. During this flight our conversation turned to the religion department. Elder McClure told me that my failure to get rid of men in the religion department was affecting my "credibility" as well as that of the men in the department.

Whitehead stated emphatically, "We have to do something." McClure then stated that we would never solve the problem until we had moved someone out of the department in order to "prove" to the "field" that we were "doing something." When I suggested that Dr. Lorenzo Grant had indicated he had asked for a leave of absence and that perhaps if he were granted the leave there might be some relief from the critics, McClure's response was that we could never get by with the departure of Grant only—the black field would never understand—and that if Grant went, we would have to let a white person go as well. I asked how a choice would be made in selecting the "white" person who would have to leave. Whitehead's quick response was, "You make the decision any way you see it, and we will support it!" My final response was "You mean we should just go 'Eeny meeny miny mo . . .?'" The response was a shrug, and with that the matter was dropped.

Sometime later but not at the time of this flight, McClure observed to me that "Zackrison, Grant, and Gladson have got to be moved." When I suggested that

---

5. See Appendix 3 below.

he had already fingered Ott and Springett earlier, his response was that they all caused problems.

It came to be very clear that no one in the religion department had the clear confidence of the Union officers who were also officers of the college board. By the summer of 1982, it was very obvious to me that someone from the religion department would have to be fired in order to appease the board chairman, even though that chairman repeatedly assured me that he had no specific evidence which could be presented as cause.

RELATIONSHIPS WITHIN THE DEPARTMENT OF RELIGION

During the time that I was dean at Southern College, there was very little comment made to me about the chairman of the religion department by his departmental colleagues. Occasionally a complaint would come from the field that our religion majors were not being screened very well before being recommended as ministerial graduates. My constant reply was that we would continue to do our best to assure all conferences of quality graduates but that our larger problem was that conferences persisted in hiring most of their graduates *before* checking with our department, and thus the college could not do much by way of quality control. In cases when a recommendation was sought *after* promise of employment, it was almost invariably the case that the student was later told by conference personnel about any negative statement from the department, and ill feelings often resulted.

By the latter part of the 1970's there came to be a rather steady dribble of complaints from the ministerial secretaries of the conferences. The rather common opinion of these complaints was that when the ministerial directors came to the campus for student evaluations with the department, the department as a whole did not seem to have a common position. There was a feeling that prior to the ministerial-religion department meeting, the religion department men should get together and agree on their presentations to the ministerial directors. Occasionally a suggestion would come that we need to have new leadership in the department. I spoke with Doug Bennett [Religion department chair] about the entire process under question, and he reviewed the total procedure with me and expressed eagerness to serve the conferences in the best manner possible.

During this same time there came to be clear knowledge that there was rather serious dissatisfaction among at least some of the religion teachers with the leadership of the department. During the last several years I was at Southern, most of the religion teachers expressed to me and/or the academic dean their wish for a change in leadership or for more effective leadership.

On separate occasions both Dr. Gully and his wife came to see me about the confusion in the department, and both stated their very plain position that the department would never be on an even keel and provide a satisfactory working situation unless there were a change in leadership. Mrs. Gulley was earnest in her expression that her husband's near-breakdown—and subsequent reduced load for many months—was the result of poor departmental working conditions, most of which resulted from indecision of where the department was going professionally because of ineffective leadership. Dr. Gulley's position paralleled that of his wife.

On separate occasions Springett and Ott and Grant and Gladson all indicated their feelings, and these duplicated those of Gulley. When Zackrison returned from his Andrews study leave [1979] and had been on campus for a year, his position was that he did not care who was the chairman as long as the job would be done effectively. He did not then feel any more than anyone else in the department that departmental matters were proceeding in an organized fashion. His position was similar to that of Grant—if they had a complaint, they were unafraid to voice it to the chairman, and when departmental meetings were convened, they spoke their convictions. Without question their forthrightness caused the chairman uneasiness. What the chairman did not know was that some members of his department who professed great loyalty to him in his office were very critical of the chairman when they visited with either the dean or the president.

In the spring of 1982 Dr. Bennett came to my office relative to what he felt was a very clear degeneration of attitude and morale in the religion department. He finally stated that he was not "married" to the job of chairman and that if I thought it would be advisable for him to step down as chairman, he would be glad to do so—in fact, if I thought it advisable for him to seek a position on another campus, he would do so. I told him very clearly that it was not necessary—in fact would be a mistake—for him to feel he needed to leave. I urged upon him that he had a positive contribution to make to the college and the department. But I did finally say that my opinion was that it probably was in the best interests of the department and the college to have a change in chairmanship. I believe my words were almost exactly these: "Doug, in view of all the turmoil we face with all this, and in view of some of the hostility you face in the department and some of the agony you have undergone and doubtless will face, I would have to say that it doubtless would be in the best interests of the department and the college to have a change in chairmanship. I would like to be free to proceed on such a basis. The best way to handle this would be to have a note from you stating what you have told me here."

Such a statement never came, although the very next day after talking with Doug I was at a Florida Hospital board meeting and told Elder McClure what had transpired.

In summary of this, others in the department complained far more critically about departmental leadership than Zackrison, and at no time did he ever make a point of having a conversation with me on the topic of the necessity of getting rid of Doug. Others in the department did so.

APPENDIX 2

THE ATLANTA MEETING

During the month of the South Pacific tour of the college orchestra a meeting was set up in Atlanta for representatives from the religion departments of Adventist colleges to discuss their present and their future. I never had a definitive discussion with anyone relative to the selection process of representatives, but I have been told that those teachers who seemed to be under considerable fire at colleges were the primary invitees.[6] I think a number of college presidents were invited—in fact, one college president later told me he had planned to attend but at the last minute he had a conflict of appointments.

I was very reluctant to go since the meeting came the very day after my arrival home from the orchestra tour, and I needed to get my office work caught up. As I looked at the program I noted that Smuts Van Rooyen was listed as the worship speaker for Friday morning. Since he had been dropped from Andrews during my absence from the country, I was apprehensive about his attendance at any meeting of Adventist religion teachers. I was informed, however that because of his Andrews standing he had been advised to cancel his Atlanta appointment.

To my mild surprise in Atlanta I noted that the spirit of the men was very positive, even when discussing some rather sensitive issues, especially those relating to what some of the men perceived as deliberate attempts to keep theology teachers out of print in Adventist journals. The only person in the group to be quite vehemently antagonistic to the church press was Dr. Gulley, who was very desirous of putting into the record a very strong protest directed primarily against the *Adventist Review*. The other men felt such a position would be counterproductive, and the rest of the meeting was not marked by further recrimination. I attended the meeting only on Friday, but both Dr. Veltman and Dr. Provonsha [1920–2004] later informed me the rest of the meeting over the week-end was earnest but very unmarred by hostility.

Dr. Zackrison's name has been frequently attached to the Atlanta meeting, but he had no part in its arrangements and had no prior knowledge of its purpose. Any criticism of him for his attendance is shallow indeed.

ABORTING ATTEMPTS TO CLEAR NAME

In an attempt to help the department of religion in its crisis, I met with the religion faculty on several occasions. I also called for a meeting of conference presidents and the faculty, and we had one such meeting on the Southern College campus. While the meeting was cordial, I did not feel it really got very far because it was only a preliminary meeting and the topic needed many hours of intense discussion. Moreover, I had already become aware that while participants from off-campus were cordial,

---

6. My understanding was that all college teachers in North America were invited but very few could afford paying their own expenses to attend.

when they returned to their own offices they persisted in repeating the charges against Zackrison and others which appeared in the hostile periodicals.

Zackrison asked for permission to help get started a departmental magazine which would be the vehicle for getting information before the field about the various theological positions of the teachers. He spent a great deal of time with this project and attempted to include the conference presidents as consulting editors. At the last the chairman of the board put a stop to the project because he said the material was too inflammatory because it dealt with current issues. Later, this was used as a criticism of Zackrison.

Such criticism was unfounded. It is foolish to publish anything that is supposed to help settle issues if there is no reference to the issues. The articles which were proposed all dealt with church doctrines and the position of the religion department regarding them. I often wondered if some people were afraid that Zackrison and others would so ably defend themselves that no more accusations could be levelled. I thought then and still believe that refusal to publish this departmental magazine certainly deprived the teachers—especially Zackrison—of a significant opportunity to set their record straight before the field. It had been planned that the magazine would be sent to every minister in the Union and to all board members of all the conferences as well as the college board.

ZACKRISON AND DUE PROCESS

In August of 1982 I was informed by an officer of the General Conference that Elder McClure had made plans to call a college board meeting immediately in order to fire me, Zackrison, and Grant. This General Conference officer informed me that he had told McClure that such a plan was highly irregular. Subsequently, the plans were aborted. This was my first knowledge that Zackrison was in such disfavor with the Southern College board officers that they would even think of firing him in total disregard of due process. When I spoke with McClure and Whitehead about this, I could see plainly they had no idea of the contents of the Southern College *Working Policy*. It has subsequently been of no surprise to me that the Southern College Board recently voted to dismiss Zackrison, though some now aver that no such intent was ever in the mind of the board—only the intent to intend to dismiss.

WHY ZACKRISON?

This is a riddle I cannot answer except to surmise that Dr. Zackrison has been the most open man in the department of religion. He has never tried to hide behind a façade of "the brethren," "the church," or "the college." When issues arise, he deals with them openly and candidly. If he has uncertainties, he does not present a bluff of being unquestionably right. He has openly admitted theological gaps in the theology of the

Seventh-day Adventist church, and he has been very ready to explain his own personal process of personal, professional, and spiritual maturity. Some have declared this process of maturation to be spiritual anarchy, but they happen to be people who do not understand that the pursuit of a personal perception of truth forces one into constant evaluation and change. If one's ideas do not change, there is no mental growth.

APPENDIX 3

Some Historical Observations on the Present Theology "Crisis"[1]

BY DR. RONALD M. SPRINGETT
Associate Professor of Religion, Southern College of Seventh-day Adventists

SOME ARE NOW CLAIMING that a "new theology" permeates Adventist College Bible departments in North America. The cry is being raised which accuses this so-called new theology of forsaking the landmarks, leaving traditional Adventist positions and introducing the errors of Babylon into the church. In certain quarters of the church we are being exhorted to return to the "old theology," the traditional or "historic" Adventism.

But what is the "old theology" that is now being proclaimed as traditional or "historic" Adventism? A preliminary investigation reveals that it is perilously close, in spirit and theology, to a position taken by certain sections of the church some 20 to 30 years ago. At that time the Defense Literature Committee of the General Conference clearly repudiated positions which are now being claimed as historic Adventism. I submit that in many respects the so-called "new theology" essentially agrees with the official General Conference position of the Defense Literature Committee. A look at the facts at least throws the whole matter into perspective.

CURRENT ISSUES

A partial explanation of this situation involves the history of offshoot activities, as well as recent developments. It is not news to most people by now that certain theological

---

1. The writer of this article, Ronald M. Springett, Ph.D., Associate Professor of Religion, taught Greek and Philosophy of Religion at SMC for many years. This article had appeared in the college's alumni journal in the spring of 1982. When the Religion Department attempted to reprint it in its projected departmental journal, *Perspectives,* in May 1982, pp. 18–23, Elder Al McClure, SMC board chairman, stepped in and would not allow it, ordering it pulled. The whole paper was pulled and never allowed to appear. Reprinted here by permission of the author.

issues are at the center of lively discussion in the church. These issues are referred to by numerous clichés in different circles. For convenience sake we may describe these as an old and new view of the sanctuary, and an old and new view of the gospel. Both of these issues are complicated by the recent challenges to the writings of Ellen G. White and her role in the church. The facts are that elements of both the old and the new views of the sanctuary have existed side by side in the church for decades.[2] However, at Glacier View in 1980, Dr. Desmond Ford gave a new twist to some of the traditional positions. The church was unable to accept (Ford's) views in their entirety as there presented, but sufficient questions were raised on some points to warrant the formation of a Daniel and Revelation Committee, which has already been appointed and is now beginning to work.

In this paper we are more concerned with the "old" and "new" positions, as they are called, on the gospel (although the Sanctuary doctrine becomes a component in a curious way, as our study will show). We are concerned with these because *here a teaching seems to be creeping back into the church which administrators and teachers alike decisively rejected in the late 1950s and early 1960s.*

Indeed, our observation is that the so-called old view of the gospel, which is being promoted zealously in some quarters now, smacks very heavily of a legalistic type perfectionism[3] which has appeared from time to time in the history of the church. A brief historical sketch may help to illustrate.

HISTORY OF SDA PERFECTIONISM

Perfectionism refers to the notion that perfection is a state of total sinlessness attainable in this life. It should not be confused with character development or Biblical perfection.

A type of perfectionism was first encountered in our midst in the fanatical exhibitions which cropped up between 1843 and 1909.[4] At this time certain people considered themselves to be as innately perfect (sinless) as Christ was. They "urged upon people human tests and manufactured crosses, which Christ had not given them to bear."[5] These early perfectionists looked down on those who were not yet perfect (sinless); they claimed to heal the sick and perform other miracles.[6] Their meetings often consisted of physical demonstrations of Spirit possession with much noise and commotion. In 1900 one group (led by a Conference president no less) espoused the

---

2. B. Haloviak, "Pioneers, Pantheists and Progressives," General Conference of Seventh-day Adventists. Typescript, Glacier View Papers, 1980.

3. Where "perfectionism" is used in Dr. Springett's article this is referring to "sinless" perfectionism. There is a biblical view of "perfection" which Christ provides. Sinless perfectionism teaches that we can achieve sinlessness before the *Parousia*. Achieving that state, according to that view, is the meaning of the "good news" of the gospel.

4. *Selected Messages,* Book 2, pp. 25–30.

5. Ibid. p. 27.

6. Ibid.

"doctrine of Holy Flesh." Jesus, in His struggle in the Garden of Gethsemane, it was thought, had actually in that experience attained "holy flesh." The adherents of this doctrine claimed that "those who follow the Saviour must also acquire the same state of physical sinlessness as an essential preparation for translation."[7]

Ellen White, in her counsels to this "holy flesh" group, discouraged the physical and emotional displays and forbade the noise and confusion at such meetings. But she also got to the heart of the theological problem involved and uttered one of her clearest statements concerning the biblical gospel (in relation to Christian perfection) that can be found anywhere in her writings.

> The Scriptures teach us to seek for sanctification to God of body, soul, and spirit. In this work we are to be laborers together with God. Much may be done to restore the moral image of God in man, to improve the physical, mental and moral capabilities. Great changes can be made in the physical system by obeying the laws of God and bringing into the body nothing that defiles. And while we cannot claim perfection of the flesh, we may have Christian perfection of the soul. *Through the sacrifice made in our behalf,* sins may be perfectly forgiven. Our dependence is not in what man can do, it is in what God can do for man through Christ. When we surrender ourselves wholly to God, and fully believe, *the blood of Christ cleanses from sin.* The conscience can be freed from condemnation. *Through faith in His blood,* all may be made perfect in Christ. Thank God that we are not dealing with impossibilities. We may claim sanctification. We may enjoy the favor of God. *We are not to be anxious about what Christ and God think of us, but about what God thinks of Christ, our Substitute.* Ye are accepted in the Beloved. The Lord shows to the repenting, believing one, that Christ accepts the surrender of the soul, to be molded and fashioned after His own likeness.[8]

Thus, Ellen White boldly asserted the claims of the Christian gospel in the face of early perfectionism. This whole statement needs to be taken seriously. It should not be read in a sense that would negate sanctification. *It is clear from other quotations from E. G. White that anyone who does not wholeheartedly strive for the development of character and the eradication of sin from the life, has already departed from the faith.*[9]

The modern counterparts of these perfectionists have abandoned the appearance, though not the essence, of the early doctrine. They rarely, if ever, teach now that *physical* perfection is possible. They do teach, however, that *moral* or *soul* perfection is possible by some *special* experience, i.e., works, or by some special in-filling of the Holy Spirit, or a combination of these, and that this is *in addition* to the sacrifice of

---

7. Ibid. p. 31.

8. Ibid. pp. 32, 33. (Emphasis supplied). See also *Selected Messages,* Book 1, p. 367; *Testimonies for the Church,* Vol. 5, p. 744, and *Review and Herald,* Sept. 3, 1901.

9. *Testimonies for the Church,* Vol. 2, p. 549; *Selected Messages,* Book 1, pp. 380, 381; *Ministry of Healing,* p. 452; *Christ's Object Lessons,* p. 356; *Steps to Christ,* pp. 57–58.

Christ, which, in itself, was not enough to save us.[10] This is crucial to understand that this is opposed to the soul perfection that E. G. White taught which was clearly based in the perfect forgiveness of the sins of those who remain in Christ.

It is true that perfectionism of one kind or another had persisted in our ranks among fringe elements of the church since these early days. However, in the past, the attempts of its adherents to thrust it into the mainstream of the church have been decisively and repeatedly repulsed by the administrators, editors, and teachers within the church. Consequently, contrary to the statements of these adherents, it has never been either the official or the historic view of the mainstream Seventh-day Adventist church, as a perusal of all official statements of SDA fundamental beliefs through the years will show.

THE "AWAKENING" MOVEMENT

A classic example of the re-appearance of this phenomenon of perfectionism in relatively recent times may serve to clarify the point. Perfectionism found a champion in the late 1950s and early 1960s in a young Australian farmer who was born on September 9, 1933 and baptized into the church in October 1953. This young man was Robert Daniel Brinsmead. Brinsmead connected soul perfection with the Adventist Sanctuary concept. His teachings can be summarized thus: (1) Man has two divisions to his mind; the known or conscious level, and the unknown or subconscious level; (2) Justification removed known (conscious) sins and represented Christ's daily work in the Sanctuary; (3) Sanctification represented the removal of subconscious sins or *latent* evil, that which renders us as it did Adam in a state of sin, thus perfecting the soul. Or, as he put it:

> If the saints are to be perfected before Jesus comes, then they must be freed of this state of sin before Jesus comes. . . . Therefore, the cleansing of the sanctuary must embrace the elimination of hereditary and cultivated sinfulness from the unconscious mind.[11]

Brinsmead rightly saw that absolute perfection before God involved not merely the forsaking of sins, but the eradication of SIN, i.e., the sinful nature of man. Here was how it worked, however:

> The daily service dealt with specific sins—the light which shines forth from the most holy place is to lead us to the experience where we will fully repent or not just this and that sin, as such, but of the very principle of sin.[12]

---

10. H. Douglass, *The End* (Mountain View: Pacific Press, 1979), p. 136.
11. R. D. Brinsmead, *Man Born to be King,* pp. 94–95.
12. Idem. *Sanctuary Syllabus,* 2, p. 56.

The notion that the two apartments of the Sanctuary deal with, i.e., were symbolic of, two parts of divisions of the human mind was a clear departure from official Adventist teaching on the Sanctuary (although G. C. Tenney and J. H. Kellogg were suggesting something of this nature). Brinsmead needed this doctrine, however, to teach innate moral soul perfection (the twin brother of innate immortality of the soul) *before* the second coming of Christ—as he wrote:

> Each believer is the sanctuary of the living God, a candidate for this cleansing of the sanctuary.[13]

> The blotting out of the record of sin takes place in the minds of the worshipers (Heb. 10:1–3) . . . as well as in the record books of heaven.[14]

Whether Brinsmead intended to have a following or not is a debatable point; the facts of history show, however, that he and his following soon took on the appearance of an offshoot movement. A regular paper entitled *Present Truth* was published in which the typical claims of those with "new light" were set forth. Among these claims were usually found numerous charges that the church's administrators, teachers, and scholars were in error, that perfectionism was the traditional teaching of fundamental Adventism.

Brinsmead's perfectionist movement was called the "Awakening," his following, the "Sanctuary Awakening Fellowship." It claimed to be the true message of 1888 in its unadulterated pure form—truly a revival message.[15] In his very first manuscript, written in 1957, Brinsmead claimed that papal Babylon "the king of the North" was entering into "the glorious and holy mountain," i.e., the SDA church.[16]

This accusation that the church was drifting toward papal Babylon was reiterated by Brinsmead on numerous occasions.

> Around the globe God's elect will mourn for what is transpiring before our very eyes. Having embraced a little Protestant theology in a limited area of doctrine, and finding it stimulating to be called "Christians" by the churches around them, some now take a determined swing away from the peculiar "confines" of Adventism to embark on a reckless abandonment of the faith.[17]

---

13. Idem. Tract, "The Open Door," p. 2.
14. Idem. *A Doctrinal Analysis of "The History and Teachings of Robert Brinsmead,"* p. 32.
15. Idem. *Gems of Truth.* News Bulletin Special Issue, Sept., 1967. See also Idem. *What was the 1888 Message?*
16. Idem. *The Vision by the Hiddekel,* p. 100.
17. Idem. *The Australian Division Committee's Report Reviewed,* p. 24.

APPENDIX 3

THE ROLE OF "QUESTIONS ON DOCTRINE"

These and many other charges by Brinsmead were aimed primarily at the book Seventh-day Adventists Answer Questions on Doctrine, *a book put out in answer to a series of questions composed for Adventist leaders by interested editors of the evangelical Eternity magazine, Donald Barnhouse and Walter Martin.* The scholars and administrators responsible for this book, he charged, had compromised denominational doctrines in 1956 with the publication of the book.

> Men who have stood professedly as leaders of the Third Angel's Message have unobtrusively carried the corpse of the final atonement out the back door of the church to the graveyard of our pioneers' theological "misconceptions;" and with it has gone the heart of the third angel's message.[18]

The General Conference Defense Literature Committee answered the charges as follows:

> The only changes accruing from the meeting in 1956 with Drs. Barnhouse, Martin, and others were that certain men who had for years accused the Seventh-day Adventist church of certain unchristian teachings were convinced that they had been misinformed. Among the things of which they accused the Seventh-day Adventist church were (1) being legalistic and trusting in obedience to the law for salvation, (2) not believing in the atonement on the cross as the basis of Christian faith and hope, (3) believing that Satan, the scapegoat, had some part in the salvation of man, (4) not understanding the meaning of righteousness by faith, etc. THESE MEN WERE NOT CONVINCED that Seventh-day Adventists really believed in a divine and sinless Christ who died for the sins of the world, and they understood as never before the Seventh-day Adventist position concerning the investigative judgment and related doctrines. There is, of course, nothing wrong in trying to convince our opponents of what we as Seventh-day Adventists believe in regard to these things. Only critics of the church could want to prolong these old misunderstandings.[19]

A hearing was arranged in Washington for Brinsmead at which time the committee reported:

> The committee could not accept Brinsmead's deductions on instantaneous sinless perfection, forgiveness of sin, righteousness by faith before and since 1844, the nature of Christ, and some points in his sequence of last-day events allegedly based on Ellen G. White statements.[20]

---

18. Idem. *The Third Angel's Message*, pp. 10–11.

19. *An Answer to an Unworthy Attack on the Church* (General Conference of Seventh-day Adventists: Defense Literature Committee, 1968), p. 2.

20. *The History and Teaching of Robert Brinsmead* (General Conference of Seventh-day Adventists: Defense Literature Committee, 1962), p. 13.

Brinsmead answered this document with a pamphlet listing 15 objections to the doctrinal errors of the "officers," i.e., the administrators of the General Conference. His seventh objection contained eight points supposedly compromised in the book *Questions on Doctrine*. Some major points were (1) The nature of Christ; (2) The remnant; (3) Babylon; (4) The third angel's message; (5) The final atonement.[21] This hearing committee for John and Robert Brinsmead met in March, 1961. Its members were Elders Lowe (Chairman), Cottrell, Neufeld, Olsen, and Roenfelt. Following the hearing, Elder W. R. Beach drafted a letter to the Brinsmead brothers setting forth the findings of the special committee. Brinsmead printed the letter in its entirety, along with his answers to its 16 objections to his teaching. Concerning the atonement on the cross, Elder Beach states in the letter:

> The brethren cannot accept your claim that the atonement on the cross was insufficient to purge the soul completely from sin. You consider a further atonement necessary if men of this generation are to become eligible for the kingdom.[22]

Brinsmead constantly hammered at the positions taken in the book *Questions on Doctrine*. In his view, the book was a pernicious sellout to Babylonian Protestantism. Here, in his thinking the scholars and administrators of the church had compromised its unique message. And he was not alone in these accusations. M. L. Andreasen, whose credentials were also lifted by the brethren, attacked both the book and *Ministry* magazine as heretical.[23] The Defense Literature Committee of the General Conference, which framed the answer to Brinsmead's accusations about the book, was aware of the fact that some did not agree with the position of the majority of the brethren and recognized this fact:

> We know of no major doctrinal error in the book *Questions on Doctrine*. Most of the few criticisms which have been leveled against it are concerned with changes in emphasis, incomplete coverage, or semantics. A few have impetuously taken extreme views on the divine-human nature of Christ. No book ever written could avoid all criticisms, but any careful student who reads all of *Questions on Doctrine* dispassionately, including the appendixes, remembering that it was limited in scope to certain questions submitted by non-Adventists, will not find in it surrender of any of our fundamental doctrinal positions. That it does not adequately present the views of certain individuals does not prove the charge of compromise.[24]

---

21. R. D. Brinsmead, *A Doctrinal Analysis*, pp. 13–16.
22. Idem., *Errors of the Brinsmead Teachings,* a Copy of a Special Committee Report of the General Conference of Seventh-day Adventists, p. 7.
23. M. L. Andreasen, *Letters to the Churches*, Series A, No. 2, pp. 9–14.
24. *An Answer to an Unworthy Attack on the Church*, p. 2.

Appendix 3

"NEW LIGHT" ON RIGHTEOUSNESS BY FAITH

According to the Sanctuary Awakening Fellowship (SAF) Newsletter, *June 15, 1966, p. 4, the latter rain fell in 1888 with the preaching of Jones and Waggoner—at least these were the first showers.* They make note of the fact that Ellen White considered the message of Righteousness by Faith the beginning of the Loud Cry. She also stated that, if they had been accepted by God's professed people, the work could have been finished and Christ would have returned. The SAF *Newsletter* interpreted this to mean that in four or five years Christ would have come. However, the Laodicean church did not accept the perfectionist interpretation of righteousness by faith (which SAF *Newsletter* people believed was the 1888 message) and Christ had not come in four or five years, so the church must have rejected the truth and accepted a Babylonian interpretation of righteousness by faith, viz., *that* is why Christ has not yet come. This is followed by the SAF *Newsletter* understanding of righteousness by faith as preached in 1888, which we quote:

> It was the message of "justification by faith." Elder George I. Butler was the President of the General Conference. In a little book of his, written four years earlier, he declares that he had always believed in justification by faith. Yet he rejected the message in 1888. The explanation of this seeming contradiction is that there are two versions of the doctrine of justification by faith. The former rain version, preached by Peter upon the Day of Pentecost, still continues into this modern day. It was the former rain version which Elder Butler, in common with Protestants generally, had always believed. But it was the distinctively Seventh-day Adventist latter rain version which was first presented by Elders Jones and Waggoner at Minneapolis in 1888. As the literal rain in Palestine ripens and perfects the grain for harvest, so the spiritual latter rain is required to perfect the characters of God's remnant people, and seal them to stand sinless without a Mediator during the time of trouble, while still clothed in sinful mortal flesh.
>
> Therefore, Jones and Waggoner preached a much more complete righteousness by faith than had ever been known on earth before—(except by Enoch).[25]

The article continues by quoting Luke 14:16–24, the parable of those invited to the supper who made excuses not to attend. Three excuses are given in the text. Thus only three calls are recorded. According to SAF *Newsletter*, these three calls to the feast in Luke 14:16–24 represent the three invitations extended to the Seventh-day Adventist church. The first was that of Jones and Waggoner in 1888. The second was the message of the two delegates from Africa, Elders Wieland and Short, whom the General Conference tried to silence in 1950, according to this SAF *Newsletter* article the truth

---

25. "1888 and the Latter Rain," *Sanctuary Awakening Fellowship Newsletter,* Vol. VI, No. 6, June 15, 1966, p. 4. This article is initialed (E.P.).

could not be silenced, so the Lord raised up Elder Hudson of Baker, Oregon, to circulate the "document" and the church disfellowshiped him for his pains. The third call to the Adventist church was that of Robert D. Brinsmead and others, for which he was cast out of the synagogue. The article concludes with this paragraph:

> It is very important to bear in mind that Jones and Waggoner in 1888, Wieland and Short in 1950, and Brinsmead since about 1960, have all presented exactly the same LATTER RAIN message. Although there is an increasing maturity of expression with each new presentation, there is no change in vital content. The Lord has raised up Brother Robert Brinsmead to hold aloft the same torch of truth today that Elder Jones bore in 1888.[26]

These statements are extremely interesting to say the least and a discussion of them would be beyond the purpose of this article. It may be noticed, however, that according to the first quotation, the distinctive Adventist view of righteousness by faith is not that which was preached by Peter at Pentecost. That is a Babylonian view held by Butler and other Protestants. *In fact none of the Apostles, not even Jesus it seems, was aware of the distinctive "Adventist" view.* Even the Old Testament prophets were ignorant of it. Enoch it seems may have known about it. Generally, it was unheard of until the SAF *Newsletter* group and their predecessors discovered it in the pioneers and in their interpretations of Ellen White. Thus the Adventists' distinctive concept of righteousness by faith, according to this article, bypasses the entire New Testament and most of the Old Testament and finds its basis in a brief Old Testament reference to Enoch. This basic outline was, of course, "backed up" by numerous quotes from the pioneers, Ellen White, and scripture, by Brinsmead and others, in practice.

CHURCH REJECTED "NEW" VIEWS

The church reaction to this doctrine is history; it was a resounding NO! Those who persisted in the doctrine were disfellowshipped; others went underground. Desmond Ford and Edward Heppenstall, however, worked with Brinsmead and finally convinced him that he was in error. The fact that he has gone off on another tangent is no reflection on them.

The SAF *Newsletter* dated August 25, 1965, outlined what this group taught was the denominational deviation from the divine plan. The Sanctuary Awakening Fellowship characterized themselves as super-loyal Adventists trying to get the church back to the "blueprint." Here it is stated in an article called "Let Us Keep the Issues Simple and Clear," that the majority of the church, including the officers of the General Conference, are asleep and complacent in the face of grave danger, basically theological in nature. Instead of telling the members the "truth" about the SAF *Newsletter* version of "righteousness by faith," the General Conference had formed a committee

26. Ibid.

to disfellowship the very people who were trying to warn the church. Thus the General Conference was responsible for burying the errors of Neo-Adventism as the SAF *Newsletter* describes it. Back in those days the views opposed by the SAF *Newsletter* were also called *"new Theology"* or *"new Concept."*[27]

The Brinsmead, or SAF *Newsletter* group, felt that the church had deviated theologically on three basic issues. First of all on the nature of Christ, which inevitably led to the second deviation from the fundamental "Adventist view" of perfection. This in turn it was claimed led to a deviation from the "Adventist view" of the Sanctuary. The SAF *Newsletter* was a regular source of Brinsmead theology and was published every three weeks at Summit, California, and edited by G. Harvey Rue, M.D.[28]

UNDERGROUND MOVEMENT

The church's refusal to countenance the SAF doctrines drove the movement underground as a dissenting but silent group in the church. This silence was not one of acquiescence but a festering silence. The underground movement included numerous ministers, who lost their credentials, as well as laymen, and not a few people in "high places" who lent support and sympathy to the group and expressed their dissent to the church's views and publications.

It seems that many of these dissenting brethren are still around and see this as their hour of destiny. Fortunately, however, the files at the SMC Division of Religion are fairly complete on the old Sanctuary Awakening Fellowship literature and other publications by the old Brinsmead movement. Most of the men in our department cut their theological eyeteeth at the Seventh-day Adventist Theological Seminary opposing this find of teaching and writing papers against it. A reading of this literature throws considerable light on the present issues.

Few people are aware, for example, that G. Harvey Rue was the editor of Brinsmead's SAF *Newsletter* for approximately ten years. More people are aware that George Harvey Rue is the editor of an unofficial paper circulating in certain sections of the church. This paper, *The Layworker,* contains the same incessant criticism of the church and its administrators, as well as a downgrading of the denominational schools as did the old SAF *Newsletter.* The summer 1981 issue, for example, contains criticism of denominational publishing policy (p. 5), the Adventist medical work (p. 6), and the theology of our administrators and teachers (p. 20), from which we quote:

> While I basically approve the effort to root out "Fordism," yet few of our leaders are clear on their own theology; especially the 2300 days, and the Sanctuary, or even the reliability of EGW's inspiration as the agent bearing the

---

27. B. C. Letter, "New Concept," *Sanctuary Awakening Fellowship Newsletter,* Vol. 3, No. 4, Feb.15, 1963, p. 2.

28. "Let Us Keep the Issues Simple and Clear." *Sanctuary Awakening Fellowship Newsletter.* Vol. 5, No. 8, Aug. 25, 1965, pp. 1, 2. No author listed.

Testimony of Jesus. If these leaders are going to judge men like Ford, their first step should be a clear-cut repudiation of all the theology taught in *"Questions on Doctrine"!* Remove the "beam in their own eye" Fordism is all through the church, especially leadership.

"Fordism" is the name given by *The Layworker* to the so-called "new theology" in an attempt to discredit it. Notice the anachronism in this statement, however. *Questions on Doctrine* was written long before Ford's teachings became an issue in the church, yet the implication here is that it is full of Fordism or "new theology."

If that quotation sounds familiar against the limited historical background provided in this paper, a reading of the perfectionist literature of the old Brinsmead movement would supply many points of contact between his perfectionist teaching and the doctrines now being foisted upon the church from certain quarters. Much more enlightening is the material from the Defense Literature Committee of the General Conference which combats the extreme views on sanctification and perfection taken by Brinsmead.

A reading of *The Layworker* soon brings the conviction that it earnestly desires a revival of this era or something like it. Even the tapes listed on the back page of *The Layworker* evoke memories of the old Brinsmead movement—such names as William Grotheer [1920–2009], Robert Wieland[29] (of Wieland and Short fame). New names appear, too. A series of tapes called the "Bangkok series" refers to the tapes of the Standish brothers. Their scathing attacks on the scholars and institutions of the church are highly prized and eagerly digested by the continuers of the old Brinsmead tradition, whether in the form of tapes, unofficial mimeographed sheets, or their new unofficial book, *Adventism Vindicated.* Another name appearing is Leroy Moore, whose tapes and unofficial book, *The Theology Crisis,* are considered grist for the theological mills of the perfectionists.[30]

Yet another person coming into print in recent months who appears to be reviving the old SAF message is Vance Ferrell. Ferrell was an old Brinsmead follower and appeared regularly in the pages of the SAF *Newsletter* back in the 1960s.[31] Vance Ferrell now publishes under the name of the "Pilgrim's Rest" organization. His theology

---

29. Wieland and Short requested that the editors of the SAF *Newsletter* not advertise their book (*1888 Re-Examined*) in their material. See their letter in the Defense Literature Committee's, "Some Current Errors in Brinsmead Teachings." (Washington: General Conference, 1963), pp. 43–44.

30. Compare these books with: *Some Current Errors in Brinsmead Teachings* (General Conference of Seventh-day Adventists: Defense Literature Committee, October 1963). Also, *The Brinsmead Agitation, Its Background, Attitudes, and Some of Its Teachings* (General Conference of Seventh-day Adventists: Biblical Research Committee, 1969), pp. 51ff. Neither of the books (Standish or Moore) was official and they do not represent the positions of the church, nor are they published by denominational presses. R. R. Standish and C. D. Standish, *Adventism Vindicated* (Paradise: Historical Truth Publications, 1980), A. L. Moore, *The Theology Crisis, A Study in Righteousness by Faith)* (Corpus Christi: Life Seminars, 1980).

31. See SAF *Newsletters,* Vol. 6, No. 6, June 15, 1966, pp. 1, 3; Vol. 5, No. 7, Aug. 10, 1965, pp. 1–2; Vol. 3, No. 4, Feb. 15, 1963, pp. 1–2, etc.

was recently published in a local flier[32] and labeled "traditional Adventist theology." A comparison of this theology with the old SAF theology shows that Ferrell's views are substantially in agreement with the old SAF positions. Ferrell's publications are quite in line with SAF thinking. The church has "gone to the dogs" in his view. Our schools are full of heresy and the institutions and administrators are not much better. Some of the views he expresses now seem to be lifted right out of his articles in the old SAF *Newsletter* literature.

We are surprised to note that even a very recent book from denominational presses contain implied criticism of present denominational schools by drawing false contrasts between them and Battle Creek College. The historical inaccuracies of this book amount to a serious misrepresentation of the situation.[33] Although this and other books avoid or tone down direct criticism of church officials, they still contain a serious implied criticism, not only of scholars and schools, but automatically, of the Union and Conference men also, since they allow what these books see as heresy and decadent Adventism to continue unabated. Furthermore, although such books reek with a perfectionist theology, which the old Brinsmead folk are justly proud of, they claim, as do the Brinsmead perfectionists, that this is historic Adventism. One can scarcely be accused of arbitrary judgment, therefore, if one identifies the present manifestation of perfectionism with the old Brinsmead faction.

"HISTORIC" ADVENTISM?

Now, is this teaching really the "historic" position of Adventism? We think not. A careful survey of the *Review* and *Ministry* over the last 40 years, excluding very recent editions, shows that the editors and contributors to these papers over this entire period know nothing of this "tradition." The onus is thus clearly and firmly placed on the so-called traditionalists to explain how an entire generation of Adventist writers in the church's leading professional and lay journals knows nothing of "historic" Adventism. A reading of this literature will show, on the contrary, that a long list of scholars, teachers, preachers, administrators, and other denominational workers preach and teach contrary to the type of perfectionism that is now being proclaimed as "historic" Adventism.[34] Now, if the so-called traditionalists are correct, the church was sadly mistaken when it admonished Brinsmead to cease teaching perfectionism and related doctrines. A gross error was committed, also when M. L. Andreasen's views were rejected, and he was disciplined. And, ever since then the entire deluded church—lock,

---

32. V. Ferrell, "They're Teaching Error in Our Schools," *SDA Press Release,* Vol. 1, No. 5, p. 4. Ferrell advertised his literature in *The Layworker,* July 10, 1980, p. 16.

33. L. R. Walton, *Omega* (Washington: Review and Herald Publishing Association, 1981). For delineation of the inaccuracies of *Omega* (both theological and historical), see reviews by Robert M. Johnston and Walter Utt, in *Spectrum,* Vol. 12, No. 2, Dec. 1981, pp. 53–62, and Douglas Hackleman, in LLU *La Sierra Criterion.* Vol. 53, No. 8, Jan. 29, 1982, pp. 6–8.

34. We are in the process of completing this listing at the moment.

stock and barrel—has been teaching and preaching the most pernicious new theology. For the church to countenance these charges is tantamount to self-destruction. The thousands of people baptized since the mid-fifties, according to this charge, have been terribly misled and, for over thirty years, the blind having been leading blind, our schools the foremost among them. We are asked to believe that the mainstream Adventist church is Babylon and only a few lonely outposts now officially connected to the church can claim to be the remnant, the preservers of "true" Adventism.

Thus it seems that what is being proclaimed as "old theology" or "historic Adventism" is anything but that. I'm afraid that, if we do not study this unfortunate historical episode from the 1950s and 1960s more carefully as it relates to the present situation, we may be destined to repeat that history.

APPENDIX 4

Remarks at the SMC Faculty Colloquium[1]

BY DR. FRANK KNITTEL
President, Southern College of Seventh-day Adventists

CHRISTIAN CRITICISM

I don't know where to begin with a problem as complex and as far reaching and as easily misunderstood as that which has faced our entire school during the last several months—the summer months most specifically and directly. What I am saying to you this hour is taken directly from a manuscript and will become a formal part of the minutes of the proceedings of this occasion. I want to minimize the risk of being further quoted out of context, and I also want all of you to be able to refer to my comments at your will and leisure.

I think it important at the first to establish some premises regarding the nature of criticism—and the first premise is that criticism can be very productive of good, that it can foster excellence of performance and helpful self-evaluation. Without positive criticism of others and analytical self-study of a severely critical nature there generally is no human progress. But we must first examine some guidelines. They abound aplenty in both the Scriptures and the Spirit of Prophecy, but they can be condensed to a few basic principles. In making this summary for us all this afternoon, I shall be speaking about positive, constructive, Christian criticism that is designed to help God's work, not debase it.

---

1. In the end of the summer of 1981, just prior to the beginning of a new school year, the breaking point for the SMC Religion Department was beginning. At the Faculty Retreat (August 16, 1981), Dr. Knittel, SMC president, directed his remarks about what was going on to the faculty as a whole. This is the manuscript of his remarks at that faculty meeting in Ooltewah, Tennessee. The headings are supplied.

Remarks at the SMC Faculty Colloquium

CRITICISM OF SOUTHERN MISSIONARY COLLEGE

If we sense a problem which we feel needs a remedy, it is first our responsibility to speak first and directly to the people about whom the problem resides—not neighbors, friends, colleagues, local church leaders, or conference or union conference officers, unless, of course, they are the specific subjects of our concern.

Second, it is our duty to speak specifically with reference to specific events, statements, and other contributing factors. I once knew a secondary administrator whose favorite pastime was that of calling in his teachers and informing them they were not quite up to par professionally, but whose chief compliant was a general "There are a lot of little things that have added up." Somehow those little things never got entered into the ledger, and the faculty was in a constant turmoil about their standing.

Third, our criticism is not to be shared with our own children or with students at our schools—that is part of the inspired injunction that we are not to go public with our criticism.

Fourth, whatever we do or say should be done first of all with the intent of rescuing a brother or sister from harm, spiritual or otherwise, but especially spiritual. Our goal should be first that of helping him or her whom we feel is in error to come closer to Jesus Christ.

My final postulate is that in many, many cases the raising or the repeating of a question is to damn, even without accusing anyone of anything.

THE NEED FOR CREDIBLE SUPPORT OF THIS COLLEGE

With all of this, I want it clearly understood that when it comes to a college such as ours, the interests, concerns, and genuine well-being of those who look to us as their college are very vital to us. We must have the support, prayers, and counsel of our constituents beyond the board and faculty.

In the church of God on this earth we need each other. I never visit a church without asking the pastor and the head elder and others about their reaction to our campus. Through the years the response has been a uniformly positive one—very positive, in fact. And I know it is disappointing to some people to hear that our ministry in the field and our local church leaders with not many exceptions still have a very positive attitude about SMC and are very resentful of the charges being hurled about.

Most regrettably during the past few months while some very serious accusations have been made, almost none of the accusers have bothered to speak directly with those being attacked. Many reasons have been cited—too timid, don't want to be a troublemaker, am not educated enough to talk *with* professors, that person is not educated enough to talk about them. As for reprisals, if some people use that method of revenge, so be it, but they do not have the prerogative of suggesting that others work that way. And finally, if people do not communicate with those they accuse of having problems because they do not want to get involved, then why are they involved?

Through all of the commotion of this summer, I have really refrained from turning to discouragement or great histrionic public outbursts. I have visited worker's meetings and have been most cordially received. This is not because I have felt our accusers have in general had positive motives. Our loudest voices have come from the following ranks of people: (1) a known forger (2) a person whose main claim to fame is that for the last year his last child lived at home the father was so hostile to the child that he never uttered one single word to her (3) a person whose own family is humiliated by the parent antics and whose spouse and children have written this parent off (4) a person whose life up to this point has been so unscrupulous, ill-tempered and irreligious and even immoral that a member of that family finally came to me in order to encourage me by giving the facts of the character of this person.

With these people we probably will never have any influence to the good, and for our own good we must leave them to their own devices. For others we will need to tell our story as we never have done before. But more of that later.

HOW THE CURRENT CRITICISM OF SOUTHERN BEGAN

My statement is neither a defense nor an offense, but rather is a critical and analytical evaluation of circumstances and events. It is not my purpose to bog down into a morass of personal invective or accusations for directly in contrast with our accuser I will express none of this. I cannot make my statement, however, without making references to certain happenings that have included specific individuals, and yet even with this I will refrain from making any value judgments regarding the character or motives of other people. God has not asked me to do this, even though some events have rather clearly suggested very specific motives. Probably a chronological view of all of this is in order at this point.

I first became aware of the attacks upon our religion department in a very unusual manner. About a year ago our church showed some Dobson films for prayer meeting and one of the last films included the topic of masturbation. Dr. Dobson has a rather calm, dispassionate view regarding the subject and his main thesis is that the attitude of parents in the fact of this issue should simply be that of trying to direct the thinking of their children away from sexual fantasies to thinking that is more profitable and challenging. His approach certainly is that if parents discover their young people are involved with masturbation, the attitude of the parents should not be one of damnation and hell fire; and they should not try to give children the impression that they are on the verge of committing the unpardonable sin.

The church pastoral staff asked Dr. Gerald Colvin to give a statement following the film, and Gerald Colvin's very well-worded position was that parents have the responsibility of helping children guide their thoughts into activities more meaningful and profitable than masturbation and that the proper approach was that of getting something profitable into the mind rather than simply laying the guilt burden upon young people and thinking that this guilt complex would solve the problem. I knew nothing of the meeting or of Dr. Colvin's part in it until I received a twenty-two-page letter on masturbation from a lady in the community.

Coming out of the cold the letter somewhat mystified me, but the lady followed the letter with an appointment to see me. In this appointment she very seriously chided me because of the Dobson film had been shown in the first place, although I assured her that the college had nothing to do with that. She did state that the college had a great deal to do with employing Dr. Colvin and that the statements were totally out of harmony with the writings of Ellen White and the position of the church regarding the topic.

Obviously, had I dismissed Dr. Colvin at once, I would have saved our school a tremendous amount of trouble!! I told her I was unaware that our church in any way had a formed position regarding the subject and also suggested that through the years our church had steered very clear of making a formal response to Ellen White's statements relative to what she referred to as self-abuse. I further observed that Mrs. White's comments at this point were something of an enigma to the leadership of our church because there's no scientific or other empirical evidence demonstrating that many or most or all the people who ever masturbated became feeble-minded, were dwarfed physically, were plagued with serious organic diseases, or were blind.

THE INSPIRATION OF ELLEN WHITE AT STAKE

I pointed out to the lady in our conference that my own evaluation was that Ellen White was talking about people who had turned themselves totally loose to sexual abuse, that she often referred to the habit of sexual abuse, but this was not the sort of thing that either Dr. Dobson apparently talked about in the film or that Dr. Colvin had discussed in his follow-up. As patiently as I could I suggested that this was an area of Ellen White's writings somewhat baffling to the Seventh-day Adventist church and that perhaps at some time our church might make a formal response to this issue, because it is one that is being currently tossed about so freely as evidence that Ellen White was giving only personal points of view when talking about self-abuse sexually and was not writing under the direct inspiration of God.

It was rather surprising to me when the response came immediately that there was no point in talking with me any further because it was very obvious that I did not believe in the Spirit of Prophecy. This statement was even more puzzling in view of the fact that before our student body and before scores of churches throughout the United States and in many camp meeting talks and week of prayer talks I have stated very openly and avowedly that I believe wholeheartedly in the inspiration of the writings of Ellen White. I have admitted quite openly, too, that some of our use of the writings of Ellen White as individuals and sometimes even as writers or administrators has been less than desirable; but when we declare that the medieval church made poor use of the Scriptures, we are certainly not declaring that the Scriptures of the middle ages were not inspired.

Before my accuser left my office, I did attempt to clarify my position by stating that at a recent Fall Council one of the main topics of discussion was the question of whether or not women should be ordained as ministers in the Seventh-day Adventist Church. I stated that those of us in attendance at Fall Council remembered very vividly that people giving speeches or a pro-opinion nature sometimes used the identical quotations from writings of Ellen White to support their points of view although their points of view were completely opposite each other. Somehow if two different but responsibly thinking church leaders can take a quotation and make it say two things diametrically opposed, something is wrong; but this does not make the statement uninspired.

THE RELIGION DEPARTMENT AND THE SPIRIT OF PROPHECY

The lady in my office was totally unimpressed with any statement that I could make regarding my belief in Ellen White and subsequent to the visit in my office she visited members of the religion department to discuss masturbation and inspiration. Their response was essentially the same as that of Dr. Colvin and me, and subsequently all of us as a group were dismissed as being unbelievers in the writings of Ellen White.

From this point on there was nothing any religion teacher could do or say to change that opinion. Obviously, also, if the religion department did not believe in Ellen White, that meant the religion department also subscribed to all of Dr. Ford's theses because of his rather pronounced view relative to the Spirit of Prophecy. By the time most of this preliminary activity was well underway the first semester came to a close, and I was still unaware that our religion department was yet to face the real fire.

During the second semester the lady who had unilaterally denounced our religion department took her campaign to the halls of our campus. For some strange reason I was not aware of this until well into the second semester. She stood in the halls, and as students came out of the classes told them openly and with a great show of piety that they were being taught heresy. She further told them that the teachers did not believe in the Spirit of Prophecy and she further made it a practice to wander in and out of classes at will and from these classes spread stories of alleged occurrences that defy cataloging or description.

DR. KNITTEL AND THE SPIRIT OF PROPHECY

It was the same disregard for actuality that caused this same lady to print in the newest Seventh-day Adventist publication in Collegedale the statement that in chapel I told the student body there was no temple in heaven. I had the manuscript of this talk before me and a tape of it besides and the allegation is totally completely false. The accuser knows this, but willfully persists in perpetuating a lie. Furthermore, it is also a flat, open untruth that I told her or our student body that *Adventist Home, Child Guidance* and other books which she mentioned in the same article should never have been printed. Some three years ago in a Sabbath School class I made the statement—from which I do not back away now—that I often wished the *Messages to Young People* had not been compiled. I even think I gave a personal opinion that the compilation should not have been published.

My experience at using *Messages to Young People* has not been a good one, but my feeling about a compilation has absolutely nothing to do with whether or not the writer of the original statements from which the compilations are made was inspired. I have often said that I am uneasy with some of our compilations because it is very difficult to take single excerpted quotations or paragraphs and put them together in a volume without violating context. Also, there is likewise the danger that too many wallops which are packed into a single book can become a battering ram rather than a guide. Eating too much meat substitute food in too great a quantity and in too highly a concentrated form can have just as an injurious effect upon our body—though perhaps not the same effect—as eating meat.

DISCERNING THE PLACE OF ELLEN WHITE AS THE LESSER LIGHT

A small group of students attached themselves to this principal accuser. The first one who came to see me stated his primary contention that the teachers in the religion department did not consider Ellen White equal to the Scriptures. When I asked him how to evaluate Ellen White's own statement that she was the lesser light, he said categorically that she never said such a thing.

When I told him he could find the statement in *Colporteur Ministry,* page 124, his comment was that someone had probably added this. He came into my office and left my office with the very avowed contention that any teacher who taught that the writings of Ellen White were in any way subordinate to or authoritatively derived from the Scriptures or who felt that her writings were not completely parallel to the Scriptures and equal to them in every way—I say any teacher who did not teach this was both a non-believer in the writings of Ellen White and a heretic as well as a follower of Desmond Ford.

The second student of this group who came to see me had a concern about perfection as it was not taught in the Bible class. His position was that it was impossible for him to sin, that teacher was a heretic. I tried to explain to him the historical setting of this and how Ellen and James White had fought this untruth all through their ministry because it led to a holy flesh concept, but it was to no avail.

Appendix 4

The discussion kept coming around to his own personal concern which simply was that if he believed the way he thought he was taught in our religion classes, then it would be all right for him to masturbate when in reality he knew that he should not be doing so; and if he could somehow come into a state of life making it impossible for him to sin, then he would no longer be able to participate in his sexual fantasies. He declared that our religion department had not taught him to accomplish this goal of perfection.

The next person who waited upon me in my office is a retired adult who had a primary burden involving sodomy. By that time, I was really beginning to wonder where these people were all coming from. His contention at first was that one of our prospective teachers in a previous school had advocated oral sex. Questioning, however, did not produce the fact that what had happened was that the teacher had really stated that the Bible took no position on the topic. His accuser however declared that oral sex and sodomy were the same, and there of course are quite a number of texts denouncing sodomy.

The teacher, of course, did not consider the two as being the same and I have yet to discover a Biblical expositor who does. As a matter of fact, when you look up the word "sodomy" in *Encyclopedia Britannica* the only comment is "see homosexuality." Obviously, this secular encyclopedia does not consider sodomy and oral sex in the same vein. Our *SDA Bible Commentary* in no way identified sodomy with oral sex. The teacher being accused certainly believes the same as our church commentary. Homosexuality cannot possibly be condoned by the Scriptures. This includes sodomy. The topic of oral sex is not discussed in the Scriptures as a specific activity.

The third conference I had with a young married couple, although the young man did essentially none of the speaking. His wife declared that she had been taught heresy in her religion classes and she had notes to prove this. I asked her to bring the notes to me and asked her to be very specific, but I received no response to this. In all of this I should point out that the total number of people who have called me or come into my office or written to me stating accusations—I repeat the total number—does not exceed 15 or 20. This does not include three appointments which I have made specifically with people that I have asked for an appointment because I understood they had questions, though I would assuredly not put them into the rank of accusers. I declare to you absolutely as a fact that in every single instance of a phone call or a conference when people have leveled charges against religion teachers or others on our staff, I have asked people to supply me in writing with a statement which gives specific information involving specific people.

To this moment I have yet to receive such a statement. The charges invariably are vague, but they are just as direct. I have been accused by some of covering up the heretical misdeeds of teachers in our religion department [and] I am forced to ask the question, "Cover up what? How is it possible to cover up a generality? How is it possible to cover up an accusation which has not been given substance in verbal or written form?"

WHAT THE RELIGION DEPARTMENT TEACHES AND WHAT IT DOES NOT TEACH

I will pose before you the three generalities that have come my way. The first is that our religion department does not teach a proper theology in the area of perfection. Once that generalization has been made, however, the punch line never materializes. Let me explain what our religion department does *not* teach. Our religion department does *not* teach that at the eve of the second coming and at the time of the second coming only those people who have actively aligned themselves as members of the Seventh-day Adventist Church are perfect enough to merit eternal life.

We cannot allow our religion department to teach this because it is not a doctrine of our church. Moreover, our religion department does not teach that for some chronological period before the second coming of Christ those who will have eternal life have come to the place that they no longer have control over their will as to whether or not they will sin. Our religion department teaches that mankind—even those who inherit eternal life—will always be free moral agents and that those who have chosen God as their pattern will eternally represent that pattern while those who have chosen Satan will go down in destruction with him.

The Bible does not give an answer to a very possible facet of the matter of perfection. But the Bible does teach that belief in Jesus Christ must be accompanied by faith in Him as a Redeemer and that this combination will produce attitudes and the desire for a lifestyle which will result in personal reform if necessary. This reform will ultimately give to us individually a life which our Lord can sanctify and set apart as holy both in this life and also in the life to come.

Our religion department does not teach that the Seventh-day Adventist Church membership per se must carry the guilt for the Spanish American War, World War I, World War II, the Korean War, the Vietnamese War, the holocaust in Europe and all of the uncountable and unspeakable atrocities of the last seventy or eighty years. There are some who support such a philosophy, but our church as a communal institution has not done so. Yet, there are those who declare that if the individual members of the Seventh-day Adventist Church had been perfect enough in 1900 the Seventh-day Adventist Church alone would have thus forced the Lord to come.

If indeed the Seventh-day Adventist Church as a corporate body bears the guilt that the second coming has not yet taken place, is it any wonder that in the last days entire nations should seek to blot us out? If we have been preaching for a hundred years that we as a church have delayed the coming of the Lord, then would it not be the most logical thing in the world to totally obliterate this church that has been the real impediment to the plan of salvation? My friends, the Spirit of Prophecy and the

Bible are very clear in telling us that the reason for the tremendous animosity against the true believers of God in the last days is because those people are working with God to accomplish something on this earth, and they are not fighting *against* God who want to get something done but can't because we Seventh-day Adventists are thwarting His plans.

I know that many of you are aware that the perfectionists' concepts promulgated by the Brinsmead brothers and especially Robert Brinsmead in the sixties and were not resisted and repudiated by our Seventh-day Adventist Church leadership are now making very serious inroads in the Seventh-day Adventist Church. Unfortunately, some material which has come from our own presses verge in this direction, together with other material not printed by our publishing houses, but widely distributed among our people through the medium of our Book and Bible houses. I say this in no way as any kind of a condemnation or even criticism of our presses or bookstores. I am simply stating a fact. The recent book entitled, *Adventism Vindicated,* is a striking parallel of the Brinsmead material of the 1960's. All our religion teachers received their theological training under those very same people commissioned by the Seventh-day Adventist Church to repudiate the Brinsmead concept of perfection; and until our church takes a different posture relative to this theology, our teachers will continue to teach that which has been the philosophy of our church.

THE CHARGE OF ANTI-ELLEN WHITE INSPIRATION

A second charge has been that our teachers do not believe in the divine inspiration of the writings of Ellen White. Here again perhaps it would be well to identify what we teach and what we do *not* teach on this campus. First, we make no claims for Ellen White beyond what she, herself, claimed. *We do, however, accept her claims.* Second, we teach on this campus that the writings of Ellen White are not additional canon of the Scriptures and we support her own position that she is a lesser light. There are many ways in which this can be interpreted. The E. G. White Estate uses the analogy of two light bulbs—one a 100-watt light and one a 60-watt light. The 100-watt bulb gives more light than the 60-watt bulb, yet both derive their light from exactly the same source—even the same socket if you please. My own personal philosophy is that the writings of Ellen White were given to our specific church at a specific time for a rather restricted purpose. While the Scriptures in general are designed to accommodate the needs of all the world, it has not been the purpose of God to use the Spirit of Prophecy as a general religious witnessing tool, but rather that the Spirit of Prophecy should be used to help guide our specific church. Since the writings of Ellen White declare that their purpose is to direct people to the Bible and since Ellen White, herself, wrote that her writings must bear the test of Scriptures, which if properly used we would not have needed the modern Spirit of Prophecy, I say because of all this I have no trouble in accepting Ellen White's own testimony that her writings are the lesser light. Our religion department teaches all of this.

I would hope that all of us including the people in our religion department would teach our young people that they must be so firmly grounded in the Scriptural Word of God that they could be an effective witness to the world without the writings of Ellen White to support their witnessing concepts. Ellen White, herself, declared that her writings may be used to prove theological points when proselyting or evangelizing outside of our church. People must be brought into a knowledge of the modern Spirit of Prophecy as they are convicted to the Third Angel's messages, but it is not a good practice to try to persuade people of Scriptural truths because Ellen White supports those truths.

THE CHARGE OF FORDISM

A third point of contention is that the religion department and I, and who knows who else on this campus, individually and collectively are supporters of Ford. For reasons that I will not go into publicly but will be glad to explain privately there is no way that I could personally attach credibility to Dr. Ford's theological premises. He is brilliant and erudite, but I have not for the last thirteen years been able to consider him my religious or spiritual mentor. Still, he and I share many beliefs in common. Those who know what the Seventh-day Adventist Church believes and who know what Dr. Ford believes recognize immediately that there is a great body of material which Dr. Ford believes that is basic theology of the Seventh-day Adventist Church.

The fact that he and I share these common beliefs does not make me a Ford follower. The Pope and I share many common theological beliefs, but this does not make me a papist or a Catholic and it does not make the Pope a Seventh-day Adventist. Unfortunately, we are living in an age of cultism—that is, people seem to feel that everyone must either be a follower of or a denouncer of someone else.

The question has been asked me a few times in the recent past, "Why don't you stand up in public and denounce Ford?" My reply is also a question, "Has the Lord given me this mandate? Can we not be satisfied with discussing theological issues without attaching someone's name to the issues?" A critic of the school asked me a few weeks ago why the members of our religion department did not write a paper in which they denounced Ford and declared their allegiance to Ellen White. What a foolish question. Our allegiance in spiritual matters is to God and God only. Why must we seek to transfer that allegiance to a person? Is it logical to confine ourselves to being Paul followers or Isaiah followers?

Our religion department quite voluntarily and on its own prepared a paper which was recently published in the *Southern Tidings*. In this paper they did not denounce anybody and have received a few comments that obviously the religion department must support Ford because in this document they did not denounce him. I neither expect nor wish our religion teachers to stand before their classes denouncing people. The position paper of the Glacier View conference expresses very adequately an answer to issues to which Dr. Ford raised. Our department subscribes to that statement and as long as our church supports that consensus statement—and I expect it to continue doing so—our religion department will continue to teach the philosophy of that consensus paper. The same holds true of the statement of fundamental beliefs adopted by the General Conference in 1980.

THE *EVANGELICA* EPISODE

Finally, I think it only fair to all of us, including the members of the religion department, to identify some situation and happenings that have added fuel to the fire. I admit, and members of the religion department admit that some significant tactical errors have been made regarding *Evangelica*. This appeared innocuous enough when it came on the horizon as an idea something more than a year ago.

At that time the group of students at Andrews University and others that were interested in some type of periodical free from denominational control expressed their interest in having a magazine which would provide an open forum in which church leaders and church scholars could write on topics and interest from opposite points of view. Certainly, some of those involved with the periodical had not given indication to us here at least that a great hazard existed.

From the very start the hope was voiced that Smuts van Rooyen could be the sponsor of this publication, and at that time Elder van Rooyen was not in the problem he subsequently faced at Andrews University. He was rather fresh from an extremely successful camp meeting appointment here and there was no hint of any kind of change of posture. It was almost a year ago that several of the men in our department were asked to submit articles for this new magazine. At this point I will state very freely that going into print with a new magazine without having first a facial conference with the editors is very risky, especially in the area of theology.

The appeal made to our men was that they would help give the magazine credibility and also help set a proper tone. There is no question that a wrong tone came to be very obvious with the very first edition. I think everyone hoped that this might change. It did not; and subsequent issues gave decreasing promise of anything better. The *Evangelica* newsletter—which is a separate publication—is nothing more than a rag. The men in our department asked to have their articles returned, but this privilege was denied them. I made phone calls myself and frankly came away from that experience feeling I had not been told the truth by some of the editors.

A supply of *Evangelica* magazine was sent to each of the religion departments in our colleges and on some of the campuses, including ours, the magazine was made available to those who wanted it. This was a mistake. It also was not wise to direct the reading attention of students to the magazine, especially of the general posture and tone of the publication.

Having anything to do with *Evangelica* in any way shape or form from the very start has been bad news and I freely admit this. I have never taken any other posture. I have taken the position that in no way is it to be a departmental item or is it to be made available to our students through any process involving any agency of this school and it is not to be used as an assignment either required or optional on this campus.

I should point out that for those of you who have not read the articles submitted by three of our teachers, I do not criticize the articles. Had they appeared in other publications, they would stand on their own positive merits. Even our most ardent accusers have not criticized the content of the articles.

EVANGELICA VS. *SPECTRUM*

I feel compelled to say something here that perhaps I should not, but it has become a real burden with me. In terms of general posture of theology or whatever there is little or no difference between *Evangelica* and *Spectrum* when we consider the entire history of the latter. *Spectrum* has the official endorsement of the Seventh-day Adventist Church and some of the very people who were present at the meeting when this endorsement was given and who voted in favor of this endorsement had been some of the most outspoken critics of the members of our theology department because of their articles in *Evangelica*.

Ladies and Gentlemen, I am sorry, but I don't buy that. There is not yet an article which has appeared in *Evangelica* which does not have its counterpart at some time in *Spectrum* both in tone and in its posture as far as the Seventh-day Adventist church is concerned.

My saying this, however does not commend *Evangelica* nor does it condemn *Spectrum*. I simply state this to demonstrate that people are swayed by an emotion of the hour and somehow feel free to say most anything they want to because they can hide in the sanctity of the knowledge that that which they are criticizing is an unauthorized and hence an unorthodox publication. None of this, however, changes the fact that it was not wise for any of our people to be involved with *Evangelica* in the first place.

AN ATLANTA MEETING OF SCHOLARS

A second factor was a meeting held in Atlanta the first week in June by members of the theology departments of most of our North American colleges. Much has been made of the very clear fact that this was an "unauthorized meeting" meaning that the meeting was not arranged through or in consultation with any formal General Conference Committee, although a General Conference representative was there. Meetings of this sort have been held in the past by all types of employees—including many groups of educators—but the timing of this meeting together with a general attitude of distrust within our church gave all sorts of unfavorable connotations to the meeting.

People on the various campuses were invited who had been particularly singled out in their own respective areas for criticism. If anyone here thinks that the experience of our religion department is unique in North America, that person is sadly misinformed. While it is probably true that there has been more discussion relative to the SMC situation than any of our colleges, the fact is still true that the other religion departments have also faced a spring and summer of very agonizing duress. The Atlanta meeting was arranged during the time our orchestra was abroad and I had no knowledge of it until the day of the meeting.

I subsequently learned that it had been originally planned to have the meeting in the Chattanooga area, but that Mr. Brinsmead heard of the gathering and decided to shift the location of one of his meetings to Chattanooga to coincide with that of our teachers. Because of this the teachers shifted their meeting to one of the hotels adjunct to the Atlanta airport. I think they were wise in doing so.

A person from each of the campuses represented acted as a spokesman and a liaison person for that campus, and Dr. Grant was that person from SMC. He was also the chairman for the first day of this two-day meeting. Although I had just barely arrived on campus from the Australian trip, I agreed to the invitation to accompany our group, being totally ignorant of what the meeting was all about but having some interest in what several of our men were attending. I drove down with one of our other teachers and returned to the campus that evening. I did not return for the Sabbath meetings.

It has been charged that this gathering was a group of Ford supporters. Friends, I can plainly tell you this was not so. There were teachers from our various colleges and also a representative from the General Conference. Ford and his theology were not an item for the agenda. As a matter of fact, it had first been planned that Smuts van Rooyen would give the devotional the first meeting, but after he came into his problem with Andrews University, the group cancelled him out. I think this, together with the move to Atlanta, should be ample indication that the group did not want to be identified with either a Brinsmead movement or a Ford movement. They wanted to be identified totally on their own.

Several people have suggested to me that the roster of names contains key Ford supporters and yet not one of those individuals has been able to identify one single person that falls into that category. Friends, somehow I must make it plain to you that because of circumstances of a rather highly emotional personal and professional cast over the last thirteen or fourteen years, *Dr. Ford does not enjoy much support in the academic community* and again I will be glad to discuss with you individually if you so desire.

As a means of historical record one of our teachers kept a running account of all of the various ideas discussed at this meeting. One of our other teachers received an inquiry by someone who was concerned that this meeting had been some sort of a subversive gathering. In order to allay these suspicions, this teacher simply gathered up the handwritten notes which had been made along with his letter of response. He did not even keep a copy for himself. He had no idea that these would be typed up and then distributed literally all over the United States. I have a copy on my desk and will be glad to show it anybody who so desires.

THEOLOGIANS, THE CHURCH AND PUBLICATIONS

There are two or three things that bother some people. One is a suggestion that the religion teachers keep count of the articles they submit to the *Review and Herald* and *Ministry* magazine in order to ascertain how much of the material is actually used. A bit of background to this would be enlightening. Our college teachers throughout North America have long complained because they had what they felt was considerable difficulty in having their articles published in either the *Review and Herald* or the *Ministry.*

On the other hand, they have been told quite often that these periodicals do publish material which is sent to them. They want to know where they stand with this. Certainly neither the *Review* nor the *Ministry* magazine can turn itself into a forum for departmental publications. I can think of nothing drearier than to have the *Review* filled up each week with articles from theologians. Theologians tend to have a penchant for clothing the murky with the obscure, and too frequently get their jollies by pretending to understand the writings of each other.

I, personally, think one of the most desirable conferences could be that between our church theologians and the authors of our church publications so that there can come to be a common understanding of that which is desired by editors and readers and that which is a burden for theologians. We have never really had this sort of conference in our church. Subsequently, there has developed a situation of mutual distrust and this simply adds fuel to the first of near paranoia of distrust that now afflicts our church. Without question our church scholars would like some kind of a church magazine that affords scholars some give and take as far as theological issues are concerned and the *Review* is probably not that vehicle. I recognize that to some people the thought of give and take in theology is tremendously frightening.

Somehow a lot of people have the idea that within the Seventh-day Adventist Church there has never been any theological back and forth. I wish all our church members could be observers at our Fall Councils where there is more back and forth than we sometimes wish.

If you think for a moment that all theological issues are cut and dried as far as our church is concerned, you really are suffering under a delusion. I consider the matter of tithe paying very definitely part of the theology of our church, but I can assure you that there are all sorts of concepts abroad in our church relative to what the tithe actually constitutes and what it should be used for; and don't ever suggest to some people that the question of the ordination of women is not a theological issue; because to a host of people it very much is just that.

THE ATLANTA AFFIRMATION DOCUMENT

Righteousness by faith is a very distinct theological study within our church and anyone even casually acquainted with the 1888 General Conference and the subsequent ramifications can understand that there was a real theological issue about which there was a great deal of back and forth.

Some one dozen points were codified by the group in Atlanta and were sent out by them far and wide as a statement of what they formally voted, although many other things were discussed. The item pertaining to the church publications has been considered by some to be a hostile posture, but the group is very positive in its assurance that this was not designed to be a point of intimidation and was not designed as a confrontation issue. Perhaps I should throw in here parenthetically that almost immediately after this meeting a number of people in attendance were notified that their material—some of it rather lengthy—would soon be incorporated in subsequent issues of the *Review and Herald.*

One person called me and asked if I had a copy of the subversive secret twelve statements issued by this group and was truly disappointed to discover that this had been sent out by this group everywhere and was neither secret nor subversive. No one is sorry that the recording of the proceedings have been sent out, for there was nothing that should be hidden from anybody. I should point out that at one place in this document a statement is made that perhaps the Seventh-day Adventist Church ought to be able to make it alone without Ellen White. This statement is not a statement of the group—rather it is a statement of some who responded to Fred Veltman after Fred submitted his initial report on the Walter Rea matter. This observation simply came from someone to Fred Veltman before he got to the meeting and did not represent anyone there; and Fred did not identify this person by name.

THE PHENOMENON OF SMUTS VAN ROOYEN

I said I would not get into personalities here and really prefer not to do so. I do mention, however, very sketchily some things pertaining to Smuts van Rooyen.[2] There is no

---

2. Elder Smuts van Rooyen was a classmate from Andrews University in the 1960s of most members of the SMC Religion department. He had been an SMC faculty member and took an invitation to the School of Religion at Loma Linda University, Riverside campus, in 1972. After teaching there for a time, Elder van Rooyen joined the Andrews University Religion department and was a candidate for the ThD degree in the Seminary. He was well-known as a very effective Week of Prayer speaker and a touring leader of the AU gymnastic team. He was a particularly good friend of Dr. Grant and Elder Zackrison who were the two professors who briefly attended his meeting in the Stone Mountain

person on this campus more sorry about his circumstances than I am. When he was here he was a dear friend and I well remember sitting in my office with Elder Cummings some years ago calling Smuts in Africa asking him if he would be willing to come to the Collegedale church as our pastor. I had hoped that sometime down the line he could rejoin us as a staff member. Unfortunately, at the present time that does not seem to be in the cards. I would like to say, however, that I do believe that if more people would have been more aware of what was transpiring in Smuts' thinking, it might have been possible for a group of his theological friends to save him from the position in which he now finds himself. In no way do I wish to imply that I fault the administrators or teachers at Andrews University.

In the fairly recent past people there very earnestly sought to save Smuts for the Seventh-day Adventist Church, but to no avail. I will say about this what I have said about students many a time. There is scarcely if ever a person who goes astray on our campuses but who could have been pulled back by the right person at the right time. I somehow feel we don't have enough awareness for this among our colleagues for each other. Unfortunately, the general lack of emotional support in academia for Dr. Ford lost Smuts a great deal of personal support which may have altered his life. My fear is that he will be used and dropped—and then what?

Unfortunately, Smuts' plight caused us a further problem here. Sometime back during a meeting with our religion division I mentioned that Smuts had been invited by the Atlanta Forum to be a weekend speaker and suggested that although I would not tell our faculty members they could not go to his meeting, it would certainly be unwise for members of the religion department to show up in view of the other difficulties besetting us.

Two of our theology teachers attended the meeting, rather naively hoping that their presence would largely be unnoticed. Quite predictably the opposite was true, and our Union president and other Union officers received complaints including some from our own staff members here. These staff members have never bothered to talk to our men. Sad day!! Five years ago, this would have made no difference. Right now, in the attitudinal environment which surrounds us this trip to Atlanta signified to a group of people both defiance of administrative wish and support for Ford. You see, when we look for issues, we can pull them up like weeds. We have an eyeball-to-eyeball meeting about all of this which effectively shortened a little family outing of mine from three days to twelve hours, but the meeting was worthwhile; and those of us representing the college and the board and our Union staff came away from the meeting quite assured that our teachers had not acted defiantly, but perhaps given the hostile climate, unwisely.

The men who attended the meeting were quite candid in stating that although after I reminded them of my counsel to avoid the Atlanta Forum meeting, they had decided rather spontaneously to attend and neither one of them at that juncture

---

Seventh-day Adventist Church near Atlanta.

recalled my counsel. I checked with another person in the division before ever talking with these men, and he told me very openly that upon my reminding him of it he remembered my earlier counsel but for the life of him had forgotten it and had even considered attending the meetings in Atlanta himself, but was prevented from doing so by family matters. I can assure you he was very grateful for those family matters.

SUMMATION

In closing I would like to say that I have never known of a group of people who are going to be more on the spot in or out of the classroom than will be the members of our religion department this coming year. Everything they say will be weighed unmercifully by those who are curious and by those who are amused. It may disappoint some people to know that I support the men in our religion department. When clear empirical evidence demonstrates that people do not wish to teach or live in harmony with the standards of the Seventh-day Adventist Church, I then have no alternative to but seek their separation from this college if they are employed by it. But to take such a position to the basis of conjecture or wish or hostility is pure folly and I will not do it.

Until circumstances change I will continue to support all you teachers the same way. I well remember a few years ago when our English departments were roundly assailed and damned. The grossest speech I ever heard made by any professional man was made by a professional educator as he mercilessly attacked the entire spectrum of English teaching in our Seventh-day Adventist colleges in North America. It was at a meeting which was held in the primary room of the Pioneer Memorial Church at Andrews University and it was attended by most of the English teachers, all the college presidents, and an array of General Conference personnel. There was scarcely anything of which our teachers were not accused. It has been only four or five years ago that our science teachers were under real fire and there was a real movement for a loyalty oath by these teachers.

I frankly am not sure that the Seventh-day Adventist Church is emotionally and attitudinally prepared for higher education and the hazards it poses if threats to our church organization and unity such as posed by Walter Rea and Desmond Ford are constantly going to result in attacks upon our educational institutions. Then I wonder if we really should be in the business of higher education or if we should simply content ourselves with elementary and secondary church schools. From the day of its founding our church seminary has been the focus of attack by a critical mass of Seventh-day Adventists and only those people associated with Loma Linda University know the agony of being totally suspect by throngs of people. I think there is a place for us, and probably we need to do a better job of identifying that place. This is going to be the topic of most of our faculty meetings this coming year.

In addition to this, we are taking other positive steps. We are sending a roster of campus speakers to our pastors in a hundred-mile radius as well as to those in the larger metropolitan areas of our union. We want our people out in these churches for weekends, for Sabbath services, for retreats, for seminars, and for whatever else may come our way by means of service.

Also, the members of the religion division and I will be frequent guests at workers' meetings through this union for the indefinite future. We will both tell the message of the school and become acquainted with the ministers. If necessary, we will take off our wigs and shoes and show we do not have horns and hooves. We will get a lot more coverage in the *Tidings* than in the past. I agree with our speaker of yesterday who said SMC is a premier college of our church. We are not going to lose that vitality.

And as I write these lines, I really get very heated up and angry that any ill-informed or any mischief-making people should try to defame our school and faculty as some have attempted in the recent past.

I am not a war hero of the navy, but I can tell you with all my heart in the words of one of our early navy heroes, I have just begun to fight.

APPENDIX 5

The Atlanta Affirmation[1]

BECAUSE OF OUR SHARED commitment to the building up of the church and to the preservation of its unity, we have come together to explore ways in which our ministry may contribute to these ends. As a result of our prayer and worship as a group, and of our frank discussions with one another, we together affirm:

1. That we are confident in the providential origin and distinctive message and mission of the Seventh-day Adventist Church.

2. That we take seriously our call to the ministry of the Seventh-day Adventist Church and that we intend to be faithful to that call.

Because careful theological study led to the founding of our movement, and has always been considered the means to advance in our knowledge of truth, we further affirm:

3. That the task of theological inquiry is linked inseparably to our vision and way of life, and that we are irrevocably committed to the responsible fulfillment of that task.

4. That the atmosphere of openness, curiosity, trust and love for one another necessary for fulfilling the task must be preserved.

5. That advances in the knowledge of truth occur, as has been the case from our movement's beginnings, when a variety of gifts and viewpoints come to expression.

---

1. *SDA Educators, Administrators and Pastors*. On June 12 and 13, 1981, a group of seventeen teachers from seven different Seventh-day Adventist colleges and universities met in Atlanta, Georgia. The meeting, which had no connection with any organization, was funded by individual church members who were deeply concerned over recent developments in the church. The participants, whose names appear below, discussed the current divisiveness within the church and sought ways of increasing mutual confidence among its various groups. There was a strong feeling that cooperation between the teaching and administrative ministries was especially important currently. This was a statement of those who attended in expressing their support. Appendix 6 shows GC president Neal Wilson's reaction.

6. That we are bound in solidarity with one another and with our colleagues in the teaching ministry and are committed to support one another in our efforts to be honest, creative and redemptive through scholarly investigation.

7. That we are committed to work with church administrators in their efforts to unify the church through theological dialogue, Bible study, fellowship and prayer.

In the light of these affirmations we call attention to, and express our concern over, the following points:

1. That the dismissal or withdrawal under pressure of certain teachers and pastors from denominational employ has given rise to grave concern among many members of our church.

2. That loyalty to the church is now often measured with reference to certain personalities or publications rather than to Scripture.

3. That well-meaning attempts to respond creatively to theological questions now confronting Adventism have been interpreted in some circles as jeopardizing the integrity of the church and its message.

4. That the credibility, and therefore effectiveness, of seminary and certain other religion faculties—made up of the very persons prepared to serve the church theologically—are now being eroded.

5. That the treatment of recent theological controversy in the *Adventist Review* and *Ministry* has not always reflected the variety of viewpoints that exist in the church, and that this one-sidedness has fostered an attitude of suspicion and a sense of impotence among a substantial number of our members.

6. That both critics and defenders of currently dominant expressions of Adventist doctrine have stated their views in a manner tending to divide rather than to heal.

7. That energies which should go into the building up of the church are now being wasted in dealing with the consequences of the present climate of distrust and alienation.

8. That frustrations associated with developments we are noting have engendered hurt, dismay, and cynicism among our students, our colleagues in other academic disciplines, and the general membership of the church.

On the basis of the foregoing, we recommend:

1. That teachers, pastors, administrators, and other church members attempt now to stop the polarizing process that threatens our unity and future as a movement by cooling rhetoric, easing tensions and enhancing mutual trust within our community.

2. That they take frequently opportunity to express confidence in the truthfulness of the Adventist message.

3. That they continue, in light of the present situation and in faithfulness to our Lord, to learn about, examine, and renew the heritage God has given to us all.

Signed,

Dalton Baldwin	Jack Provonsha
Ted Chamberlin	Richard Rice
Douglas Clark	Charles Scriven
Jon Dybdahl	Charles Teel
Larry Geraty	Fred Veltman
Jerry Gladson	Edwin Zackrison
Lorenzo Grant	Robert Zamora
Norman Gulley	Adrian Zytkoskee

APPENDIX 6

A Response to the Atlanta Affirmation[1]

BY ELDER NEAL WILSON
President, General Conference of Seventh-day Adventists

Nothing that I have read or heard justifies this kind of a meeting, which purported to speak for the scholarly community, and was intended to influence the leadership of the church and to say something very significant to the church in general. Numerous scholars and theologians have made it very clear to me that this meeting did not speak for them. I think you will discover, Lorenzo, that if you expect any major segment of our people to be included and to listen, you will need to approach things through the organizational structure of this church. In my judgment, this is one of the great safeguards God has provided, and it is comforting to discover that the vast majority of our people worldwide do not pay much attention to isolated voices here and there.

In your letter you indicate, "A number of us did feel a bit frustrated that you were apparently unable to respond to the volume of mail you must have been receiving." Very frankly, Lorenzo, I did not intend to respond to the letter which I got from several of you, because in reading it over several times, a reply seemed both unnecessary and unwise. The answers to several of the questions you raised in that letter were self-evident. Furthermore, there was an element of arrogance and accusation which did not encourage me to respond.

You also indicate in your letter that situations were developing that seemed to threaten the church in general. Frankly, Lorenzo, while I see pockets of unrest and confusion and uncertainty, I do not find any general worldwide threat to the unity and harmony of this church. Certainly we know that we will face difficult times and that we will experience a time of shaking. At the same time, there are so many assurances

---

1. Neal C. Wilson, "Letter to Dr. Lorenzo Grant," Washington, D.C., November 25, 1981. This letter is a response of Elder Wilson to the Atlanta Affirmation. Dr. Grant was the chair of the Atlanta meeting. The letter indicates how differently politicians and scholars interpret situations.

in God's messages to this church that help me to know that we are destined to move forward together in strength and to accomplish His mission.

Please be assured, Lorenzo, that I hold nothing against the men listed on the document. I am unable to explain what you did, but I am willing to accept that your motives were positive and I have no interest at all to retaliate.[2] I just hope that all of us learn something out of these experiences that will help us to do better on another occasion.

Naturally, I was interested in the two letters which you enclosed, especially the one which you wrote to Dr. Mervyn Maxwell. It seemed that you labored so diligently to defend what you had done, and in the process actually raised more questions than you answered. It also seems to me that some of your comments and words, such as "paranoia," "pirated minutes," "I must wonder at the depth of your integrity," "this kind of egocentricity," "shameful," etc., were really an overkill and could have been more tactfully and judiciously stated.

You made quite a point, Lorenzo, of the 200 years of denominational services represented by those who met at the meeting, and also the average age, and it is precisely because of this that I would have expected a better and different approach to the concerns which you had! You indicated in your letter, "Not one of us has ever been called into question on matters of theology or personal integrity." I would agree with you, Lorenzo, on the matter of personal integrity, but I would have you know that while individuals themselves may not have been called into question, the theology of several of you has been seriously questioned at various times.

You asked the question, "Who dares question our *right* to assemble?" I certainly agree with you that it is our choice. We can each exercise certain inalienable "rights," but I think we must also be prepared for the results and consequences of our actions. It is not always a matter of what is right. As the Lord indicates to us, it is far more important to ask ourselves whether it is producing and wise and redemptive, and whether it shows pastoral sensitivity, and is going to be for the upbuilding of the church and the bringing about of harmony and unity. As Paul admonishes, there are many things which are in themselves right and lawful, but they are not expedient. As a minister and a leader there are many things I refrain from doing because I know they will have no positive results in the lives of others or in fulfilling God's commission for His church.

I was disappointed in what I consider to be a lack of judgment on the part of those who should have known better.

---

2. This conflicted with reports we were getting from Washington, D.C. In fact, one of the signers of the Atlanta Affirmation document was present at a meeting at headquarters when Elder Wilson proclaimed that he would get everyone who had signed this document. He would personally see to it that they were fired.

APPENDIX 7

Edward Heppenstall Support Letter[1]

BY EDWARD HEPPENSTALL
Former Chair, Department of Theology and Christian Philosophy,
SDA Theological Seminary

142 San Remo Rd.
Carmel, CA 93923

Feb. 12, 1984

Dear Tom,

I am taking the privilege of addressing you this way, since you were one of my students some time ago. Last week I had planned to see and talk with you relative to Edwin and [Annie] Zackrison. Dr. and Mrs. ——, [Annie's] parents, called to tell me that the Administration of Southern [Missionary] College had reversed their decision and planned not to fire anyone. Hence I cancelled my appointment with you. Later I phoned the Zackrisons. [Annie] told me that this report was not quite like that. The College Administration still wants them out and to accept the first call they get; but the protest from faculty, students, other church workers had been so strong, that the college faced a serious loss of both faculty and students if they went through with it. Because of all this, I need to write you further.

I was told that Lou Venden had planned to make Ed associate pastor with him at Loma Linda, but that criticism of Ed sent to you from one member[2] back there had resulted in the committee's action to avoid introducing a "controversial figure" in your conference. At least that is how it came to me.

---

1. Edward Heppenstall, "Letter to Tom Mostert [President of Southeastern California Conference], February 12, 1984. *Appendix, Zackrison/Southern College,* p. 214–215.

2. Elder Mostert's earlier report of a "large number of sources" was now reduced to "one [unidentified] member." This was clearly more accurate.

Appendix 7

I am quite well acquainted with all this criticism against certain faculty members and the former president of the college. At various times in past years I was invited to speak at weekend and graduation services at Southern [Missionary] College. Even then I came across and read this radical lying yellow journalism.

These days, the church is plagued by name calling and unbridled hostile judgments against those with whom they do not agree, particularly by the perfectionists.

I personally have received so much libelous attacks by such men as ——, a minister utterly without integrity and compassion. I have seriously considered suing him on advice from my lawyer. All this kind of thing would not be so bad, if so many who read these lies did not believe them, without even trying to find out if it is true. I am appalled to learn the Administration of Southern [Missionary] College and members of the board accepted these falsities and have proceeded to discredit and destroy these two dedicated Christian teachers. This kind of malicious hostility in the church is worse now and more prevalent than at any other time I can think of in the last fifty years.

Ed Zackrison was pastor, builder of the new church at Camarillo, Southern California Conference. They were both admired and loved by the church members. Pastors do not come any better either in speaking, administration and the winning of souls. Both Ed and [Annie] are hard responsible workers, always on the job.

To learn of those who do the devil's work seeking their destruction is incredible to me, especially under the pretense of defending the faith. No one should listen to these castigations that seek to put the lives and the ministry of these two young people in jeopardy, to say nothing of their wonderful children. They are emotionally mature and morally impeccable. The Adventist church cannot afford to lose people of this quality.

Tom, I urge you not to believe the criticism made against them. May I recommend that you see them for yourself and draw your own conclusion? Dr. Frank Knittel, former president of Southern [Missionary] College, now the head of the English department at LLU University, La Sierra Campus, can give you all the facts. Please give Ed and [Annie] the opportunity to answer for themselves. Let us do justice to these intelligent loving Christians, both born into this faith and wholly committed to it.

I understand that they are to stay on teaching until the end of the school year. I do not know how much longer they will continue to teach there. They are just lame ducks. I am convinced that a sincere honest effort to know and understand them, will keep them in this faith and in the service of the Adventist church.

With warm Christian greetings and prayers for the triumph of truth and righteousness, I am

Sincerely yours in Christ,
Edward Heppenstall

APPENDIX 8

Remarks Before the Southern College Board of Trustees[1]

BY DR. EDWIN ZACKRISON
Professor of Religion, Southern College of Seventh-day Adventists

PRESIDENT WAGNER, CHAIRMAN MCCLURE, and Members of the Board. I want to thank you for the opportunity you have given me to address the Board today. Only as first-hand information is given to you can you make intelligent decisions about the future of this college. I commend you for your willingness to dialogue and for your spirit of open communication.

GRATITUDE FOR PAST SUPPORT

I can only thank you for your support during these past twelve years that I have been privileged to teach at Southern College. Because of your commitment and generosity, I have enjoyed professional and personal growth. You have financed my graduate education at Andrews University. You have trusted me with your young people. This is an awesome responsibility which I have taken very seriously. The happiest day of my life was when I unexpectedly received a call to teach at Southern Missionary College, and this happiness has grown daily as I have discovered the joy of using the gift that the Lord has given me—College teaching—leading third and fourth generation Adventist young people to a revitalized experience with Jesus Christ.

Today, however, we are considering the perceived overstaffing situation in the Division of Religion. In a period of declining enrollment, can the College really justify

---

1. This presentation was made by the present writer before the SCSDA College board in May 1984. While at the conclusion I invited any questions Board members might have, the only question was, "Is it true that you have talked to a lawyer?"

seven full-time teachers? Are these problems and perceptions that make these cuts necessary? First, let me give you the good news about the Division.

I believe we have the finest Religion staff of any of our Adventist Colleges. Every member of the division holds an advanced degree, and a diversity of specialty areas is represented: Old Testament, New Testament, Systematic Theology, Biblical Languages, and Homiletics. Each man has a life-time of commitment to the Seventh-day Adventist Church and a wealth of pastoral, education, and teaching experience. Our students consistently place at the top of their classes on the entrance examinations at the Seminary.

Without question, our department places more men in the field than any other Adventist College. Our graduates are serving with distinction in pastoral, teaching and administrative positions both here in north America and overseas.

Under the previous leadership of Dr. Douglas Bennett and the current leadership of Dr. Gordon Hyde, we now have sufficient manpower to become highly involved in student spiritual activities. The administration has repeatedly urged us to perform outreach ministry since our role involves not simply academic excellence, but we function also as a "youth ministry team." Finally, we have the staff that makes such a dream a reality.

When I joined the staff here in 1972 the enrollment was approximately what it is now, and we had a staff of five. Our classes were often over 100 students. It was not unusual to have 250 students per semester per teacher. I still meet students who claim to have taken classes from me in those days and I could swear I have never seen them before. In those days we pled for a broader administrative perception that would allow us to have seven teachers to do more with the mainstream of student life. At last we have a realistic student-teacher ratio. Even with seven teachers our Division racks up a respectable profit for the school. But it would be a plus for our school, I think, to demonstrate this way that religion is indeed a priority item at Southern College.

Our smaller classes have led to better rapport with the students, to more time for individual counseling, to more time for preaching appointments and personal study, to better classroom preparation, and to greater involvement in general campus ministry. For example, two of us are engaged in diligent efforts to win back Collegedale students, faculty and community who have quit going to Sabbath School, and with somewhat amazing success. Several of us are actively engaged in making major contributions to the General Conference research programs and to the Review and Herald Publishing projects which entail a doctrinal volume of the Commentary Series. Dr. Hyde has been instrumental in securing word processors for our department, further facilitating our work and leaving us more time for the important aspects of ministry. His concern for student-faculty socials, his implementation of a lecture series and a film series, and his diligent efforts at student placement has strengthened our department.

Remarks Before the Southern College Board of Trustees

A SAMPLE OF STUDENT OPINION

Let me share with you a few comments that will indicate how our students feel about the education they have been receiving in our classes:

From a current business student: Dr. Zackrison, I've really enjoyed Christian Beliefs. It has whetted my appetite for digging into the Bible. I've grown spiritually from being in your class.

From a current theology major: Thank you so much for the inspiration you have passed on to me in Christian Theology and Pastoral Ministry. It has been a great boost to my courage in facing the unknown in the ministry and theology. I really thank God for you earnest sharing of your experiences in ministry.

From a current nursing student: I wish to express my gratitude for your friendship, your organized and systematic method of teaching, and your inspiring words of wisdom. You have been a special significant person who has encouraged my spiritual insight and growth. Praise God and thank you!

From parents of a current student from Atlanta: As parents, Doctor Zackrison, we have, of course, loved our daughter and attempted to give the direction which we felt appropriate. But, we also know the value of dedicated, Christian educators and the influence they can have. This is especially true when a student places special trust and confidence in and feels a special respect for a particular faculty member. We feel we must express in writing our thankfulness to you for the important positive contribution you have made, are making and will continue to make in her education, character and spiritual development. It is such a sense of relief and confidence for parents to know their child is seeking mature, Christian advice and instruction.

From a graduate student at University of Louisville: Thank you for your belief in the search for truth guided by the Holy Spirit and for your dedication to sharing inspired truth with your students. Your whole department has my undivided support.

From a medical student at the University of Maryland: I am not ashamed of my education. I have learned to think for myself and that in a balanced way from professors who love the Lord, the Bible and the Seventh-day Adventist church and their students. If I had to do it all over again, I am sure that I would travel the same road to SMC again, it has been very worthwhile.

From a Bible worker: Many times I remember my days at SMC and I can't help but praise the Lord for such a great opportunity. That's why I'm writing.

From a young mother in Tennessee: I would like to express my appreciation for your Christian example as a fellow servant for our Lord Jesus. Thank you for always being honest presenting the truth of the Gospel to us. My sincere gratitude for our friendship as I've grown and matured as a new follower in the faith of Christ.

From a pastor in Kentucky: Elder Zackrison, I've always wanted to express to you my gratitude for all you've done for me as a friend and as a teacher. As a friend, I really appreciate the time you spent with me as we sat in your office and talked. That really meant a lot to me. As a teacher, I appreciate so much and respect you for your solid biblical approach to the subjects covered; for your open-minded approach and helping us to never be afraid of truth; and to always trust God to lead and guide in our lives.

From a pastor in Virginia: I must thank God for bringing me to SMC . . . I thank Him that I was able to take classes under you and receive a strong undergirding for my ministry. I must thank you for instilling those precious qualities of a caring church.

CURRENT ISSUES AT SOUTHERN COLLEGE

This small sample from my recent correspondence files could probably be duplicated by all my colleagues in the Division of Religion and underscores the fact that our students are proud of Southern College and the quality of education they received in the Division of Religion. Our students are satisfied customers.

Why then have we scheduled a special Board Meeting to discuss cutting back teachers in the Division of Religion? Let me explore some possible explanations:

1. *Charges of heresy.* It is no secret that our Division of Religion has suffered from severe criticism of theological teachings. These charges have been published and republished, enlarged and embellished until they have been accepted as fact in some quarters. There is little point in dwelling on these charges since both our previous president, Dr. Frank Knittel, and our present president, Dr. John Wagner, have published statements denying the heresy accusations. Elder McClure, in a faculty meeting of August 1982 also declared that "there is no evidence of heresy." Just last year the General Conference sent an accrediting body to our campus and interviewed scores of people. Their conclusion which they published in their committee report of March 1983 stated: "Based on a number of interviews with students and faculty, the committee did not find any evidence that any religion teacher has taught heresy in the classroom or has supported any unorthodox teachings or practices in their private conversations."

   Even though the charges of heresy are false, I would like to state this morning that some of my responses to these attacks have been less than gracious. I have been angry, defensive and hurt. My witness under suffering has not always been Christ like. For this I apologize, particularly to any of you here who may have been hurt by my words as I have talked directly to you.

An insight to my commitment to the Seventh-day Adventist Church, I would like to present my background as a third-generation Seventh-day Adventist. My parents and grandparents were Adventist workers. My entire education (Grade 1 through a Doctor of Philosophy degree) has been in Adventist schools, for my entire life goal has been to serve this church.

During the past three years as rumors reached me about alleged uncertainties in the minds of some regarding my theological positions, I have invited my chairmen, Dr. Bennett and Dr. Hyde, my presidents, Dr. Knittel and Dr. Wagner, my board chairman, Elder McClure, and some of your Board Members, to attend my classes, either announced or unannounced, or even to send tape recorders into my classes. To date no administrator or Board Member has accepted this invitation. I would like to broaden the invitation to include each person in this room today. I would be delighted for you to come to my classes anytime. See for yourself the sometimes cynical, sometimes sophisticated, sometimes hostile, sometimes pointed questions our young people are asking. Witness the challenge we face to making our doctrines and the love of Jesus Christ relevant to today's youth.

2. *Credibility Loss.* Some may say, however, that even though there may not be heresy in the Department, still the field "perceives" that there is heresy. They further may claim that the attacks, the rumors, the "newspapers," have damaged our effectiveness beyond repair. My answer to this suggestion is always, "With whom have we lost our effectiveness?" I have found that with my constituency, that is, my students, I have not lost effectiveness.

My student evaluations are available for any of you to view. The opposite is more likely true. As our students have seen the unjust attacks and distortions of information printed and circulated to the point of threatening our careers, they have become even more sympathetic and softened to the claims of the Gospel. Not all of us have the same ministry style. My students for instance are very social—I try to participate in the mainstream of student life—student organizations and extracurricular activities. This gives me exposure not only to students in class but also provides opportunities for a life-witness to them where they are. In this ministry style we have little time for the field. Therefore, we are heavily dependent on administrators and ministers to keep up our credibility with the field, so we can do campus ministry. This takes mutual trust.

Part of the credibility problem stems from the era of distrust we are experiencing in the church today. We theologians are generally held in suspicion since the days of Glacier View. You administrators are also viewed the suspicion since the Davenport fiasco. Some of you in this room have felt the pain, along with us, of having your names, your correspondence, your actions, printed and misrepresented in the right-wing journals. You have experienced hostility from laity in your executive committees and your constituency meetings as a result. This is then no time to begin suspecting each other, to talk about cutting out those whose credibility has suffered. We need to reaffirm our commitment to support each other and to redouble our efforts to earn the trust of our constituencies so that once again the leaders of our church be it administrator or theologian, can enjoy confidence from the laity.

I also believe some specific things can help us with our credibility, such as invitations to each of us to speak at your camp meetings, workers meetings and youth rallies. By the same token, I plan to invite you administrators into my classroom so that you can share with our ministerial students the heavy burdens of administration. I believe articles in the *Southern Columns, Southern Tidings* and *Unlock Your Potential,* which clearly reaffirm our belief in our doctrines would be helpful to the field. I believe our Department could offer continuing education courses for your ministers and teachers. I would like more dialogue and interchange with the Conference administrators so that our friendships could lead to greater trust and support of each other.

3. *Personal Differences.* A third reason some may give for cuts in the Division is that there has been disharmony, lack of morale, and lack of team spirit in the Division of Religion. Yes, we have had anxieties and conflicts. After three years of attacks and uncertainties, we have all become raw and tender.

   Let me explain the situation by use of an analogy. We are in a ship that has headed into a heavy storm. Our view is apprehensive and anxious knowing that the lifeboat cannot hold us all. Already we have seen three of our cohorts lost at sea (Elder Peeke, Dr. Ott, and Dr. Grant). We have had a change in captains. John Wagner is now at the helm. We have a new first mate, Gordon Hyde. We have not known these men long enough to understand or trust them fully. Now the news comes that there is a leak in the ship. The order is given to head for the lifeboat. There is an unwritten code for the priority by which life is to be saved; however this code is forgotten as each man scrambles to secure a position in the boat. The only way to save oneself is to push someone else out of the boat. Those who are already weak are stunned by the coldness of the water and the lack of assistance from their mates.

   I think this analogy can explain the interpersonal relationships we have experienced in our Department this year. Since Dr. Wagner's letter to the Board in November explaining the likelihood of two men losing their jobs, we have all been preoccupied with the question, "Lord, is it I?" We have all reacted to this threat in different ways—withdrawal, discouragement, suspicion, secretiveness, unkind words, isolation. I have already taken steps to reverse my response to this situation. I have repented where necessary; I will continue to do so.

If you, the Board, will give our new captain, John Wagner, the authority to raise the lifeboat, to pull each of us from the water, I predict that each one of us will unite to help in repairing the ship so that it can safely take our precious passengers to shore. Once the uncertainties of retrenchment are over, our minor differences in viewpoint, in style of ministry and in personality will dissolve and we can get on with the business of working together for our young people. Each man, with his unique talents, is needed to accomplish the task. Not only is this important for the men in the Division of Religion; it is important for our president. We have a faculty who is eager to trust him, to follow him, to unite behind him. Any precipitous cuts in our Department would violate that trust. Allow him to be the man of integrity and compassion that he wishes to be.

4. *Financial exigency.* The final reason that we may cite for retrenchment in the Division of Religion is financial exigency. With declining enrollment, it seems necessary to cut staff to balance the budget. Yes, the financial picture is important, but let us talk about perceptions. Will it appear to be financial exigence to cut men in the Religion Division while adding administrative offices from outside the college? Will it appear to be financial exigence to cut men with continuous contracts, necessitating a financial settlement, and outstanding educational debts while retaining men on one-year contracts?

Will the savings of one or two salaries be worth the cost of more heartache, more polarization, more "bad press," more discouraged students and church members? For no matter how the cuts are made, there will be grief. Those of us who have been here for long periods of time have built up loyalties among students, which must not be underestimated. If those of us who have been under attack are released, I can assure you that the pseudo-Adventist presses will be running tomorrow morning proclaiming their victory. The Adventist Layman's Council will send out a signal to the church that they, not the Board nor the administration of Southern, are running our college. Likewise, the new men in the Department who have been active in speaking and promoting the image of the Department must not be terminated, for to terminate them would be to alienate another segment of our church.

If indeed we are somewhat overstaffed, we are qualified to assist the college in many other areas. We have men with training in areas of speech, education, communication. We can assist with recruiting, counseling, cross-discipline teaching, speaking and writing. But most of all we can continue what we have started this year in improving the spiritual tone of the campus.

It is time, then, to stop the bickering. It is time to quit talking about splits coming in the church. It is time to quit talking about past problems. It is time to stop the pain and the uncertainty. If I have been a part of the credibility problem at Southern, I want to be a part of the healing process. If I could tell you all the doors which have closed to my leaving here, you would understand why I feel, without question, that the Lord still has a work for me to do at Southern College.

Several years ago, I developed a wart on the end of my finger. It was unsightly, but it could be treated. A short time later I was involved in an accident that cut off the end of my finger. That solved the problem of the wart, but it left me with only half a finger. I think now I would prefer the wart and treat it than to have the unsightly stump of a finger I was left with. I had no choice in my accident. Today, however, we have a choice. Amputation may remove a wound, but it also impairs the functioning of the body.

IS CHRIST DIVIDED?

Our situation at Southern reminds me of Paul's problem in the early church. There was in-fighting, low morale, charges and countercharges. In exasperation he declares in 1 Corinthians 1: "Now this I say, that every one of you saith, I am of Paul; and I of Apollos; and I of Cephas; and I of Christ. Is Christ divided?" May I expand the text a bit: "Now some of you are saying, I am of John Wagner, I am of Frank Knittel; and I of Gordon Hyde and I of Doug Bennett, and I of Desmond Ford, and I of Vance Farrell. Is Christ divided?"

We need to put all of this behind us. We need to say with Paul, "For I am determined not to know anything among you, save Jesus Christ, and him crucified."

Elder McClure, Dr. Wagner, members of the Board, I renew my pledge myself to this task before you this morning. Things have already begun to turn around on this campus, but we must all join hands together and make our collective witness and commitment to Jesus Christ and unity in him. Experientially this is done by pulling together, not by pulling apart. Pulling together will speak louder than anything else—more than any doctrinal manifesto or Board action. The balm of the Holy Spirit is able to make changes in people's perceptions without the aid of administrative action.

In fact, there are times when administrative action can interfere with the very work the Spirit is already in the process of accomplishing. Pulling together now will have a drawing power for this college like nothing else. The Lord has great things for Southern College; we are on the mend. But continued progress will be accomplished only as we all: administrators, faculty members, and Board Members, make our daily motto that of Paul's: "But this one thing I do, forgetting those things which are behind, and reaching forth unto those things which are before. I press toward the mark."

I assure you that this is my commitment to Southern College, and I would invite each board member to join me in it.

Thank you.[1]

---

1. *Author's Note*: When I finished making this presentation I invited questions. The first question was: "Is it true that you have you talked to a lawyer?" To this another board member interjected, "I hope he has been, the board has a whole collection of lawyers." That ended the discussion. But it indicated that at least to the questioning board member my whole presentation was a waste of time. The presentation had no effect that I ever discerned. At this meeting the Board members voted to terminate me. I was reminded of the words of Robert Warner, my academy music teacher when I commended him on the wonderful effect he had on my life. He simply said, "Ed, nobody cares."

APPENDIX 9

The Image Problem[2]

BY DR. EDWIN ZACKRISON
Associate Professor of Religion, Southern College of Seventh-day Adventists

MATTHEW 9:10–13. *[10] AND as he sat at table in the house, behold, many tax collectors and sinners came and sat down with Jesus and his disciples.* [11]And when the Pharisees saw this, they said, to his disciples, "Why does your teacher eat with tax collectors and sinners?" [12] But when he heard it, he said, "Those who are well have no need of a physician, but those who are sick. [13] Go and learn what this means, 'I desire mercy, and not sacrifice.' For I came not to call the righteous, but sinners."

Because of this philosophy Jesus had an image problem.

An image problem is a credibility gap. Somehow people have come to think ill of you. Sometimes we bring this on ourselves—like the preacher who is 200 pounds overweight who gives a lecture on self-control and temperance at a stop-smoking clinic—he has a credibility gap—an image problem. But not all image problems are necessarily earned in that way. Often, they are simply misconceptions.

JESUS HAD AN IMAGE PROBLEM

I suppose it wouldn't be too hard to analyze why Jesus had an image problem. However, to do so would immediately throw you into the company of such men as Judas, and Jesus' brothers—none of whom have ever gone on to become known as great saints in the Christian church, although one of Jesus' brothers was later converted. However, just a small peek at some of the physical evidence may not hurt us.

Having a PR department made up largely of tax collectors and prostitutes probably didn't help Jesus' image problem, unless you see his mission from the standpoint

---

2. This presentation was made by the present writer for Vespers at the beginning of the school year in 1984.

of attracting tax collectors and prostitutes to him for changing their lives. But, of course, good Pharisees would not take such a perspective.

Refusing to follow the accepted norms or traditions of the church didn't help his image problem either. Jesus and his disciples walked through fields on the Sabbath in direct violation of accepted Jewish behavior. Jesus undoubtedly would have helped a shepherd rescue a lamb on Sabbath (in harmony with Jewish law), but when he attempted to rescue a lamb of God on the Sabbath he was severely derided and declared an apostate.

Rejecting the offer to announce his aspirations to the physical throne of David did not enhance his image either. Politics were the Jewish leader's bag. Politicians have one over-riding goal in life—one motivation that supplants all others—one desire that takes second place to no other: *to get elected*.

Image problems hurt the politicians because such problems interfere with elections. Jesus was obviously a bit naïve or a poorly trained politician—the people he associated with, the things he said (even in public), and the things he did—poor taste, utter defiance of leadership. Surely all these things contributed to the image problem he suffered from all his life on earth.

I suppose it didn't help that he had not come up through the Sadducee ranks either. His whole image problem seems to have begun when he was born too early in wedlock—after all, anyone can count.

To finish off things, he died the lowest form of criminal execution available at the time—in exchange for the lowest criminal Barabbas—who was let free to dramatize the leadership's true attitude toward him.

HOW DOES THE HOLY SPIRIT TURN THINGS AROUND?

Have you ever thought about the drawbacks with which the Holy Spirit had to work to turn things around? Have you ever stood in awe at how he did it?

When people complained that Jesus had a following that was less than socially adequate, the Spirit taught that this was his mission—to reach the dregs of society.

While the leaders were extolling the traditions and historical positions of the synagogue and the temple, the Spirit revealed that Jesus cared more for the things of God and that human traditions had become more important to the Jews than divine truth.

While the politicians scurried to avoid anyone thinking they were part of the Christian following, the Spirit was revealing that Christ's mission was to serve, not lead.

While the enemies of Christ did their best to hold up his alleged illegitimate birth, the Spirit was revealing that the reason Jesus had no human father was because he had a divine father.

And when human beings put Jesus on the cross to show the universe what man supposedly thought of him, the Holy Spirit revealed that what may appear as apostasy to man could be righteousness to God.

Appendix 9

Jesus had an image problem. And it all began with his human relationship.

IMAGE PROBLEMS

Let's look at "image" problems for a few minutes. The topic is very relevant because Christians have always suffered from image problems. Jesus warned—a servant is no greater than his master—if they persecuted him they will persecute his followers.

Because of misunderstanding the early Christians suffered from image problems. The Romans blamed Christians for burning down Rome. One of the reasons for this was because Christians were considered a secret society—therefore when Rome burned it must have been their secret plotting.

Christians were understood by all to be cannibals—it had come from good, credible sources, the Roman populace said. Even their teacher had said, "To be my disciple you must eat my flesh and drink my blood."[3] Since the teacher was dead, the Romans surmised that the Christians took children, wrapped them in bread dough and baked them in ovens for their rituals. Jesus had told his followers—in order to love me you must hate your parents[4]—what greater proof did anyone need that these Christians were anti-social, against the family, destroyers of society.

The early Christians had an image problem. Spies suggested that Christians were not only apostates but atheists—they did not believe there was a God. When they worshiped—there was no God there—who were they worshipping? They refused to worship Caesar. They had no images. Obviously, they were atheists—all you had to do was put two and two together.

Having grown up an Adventist I have come gradually to recognize that Adventists have an image problem. I first saw Canright's book while a student at the seminary. The brochure was a piece of anti-SDA literature. So, I sent for the book *Seventh-day Adventism Renounced,* along with another book advertised in the brochure, *Forty Bible-Supported Reasons Why You Should Not Be a Seventh-day Adventist.*

As I read these two books I recognized some preposterous claims about Adventists. As time went on I canvassed and discovered that not everyone thought those books were so preposterous—they read them and believed them. They were all over the field where I was colporteuring—I was glad I had read them and was prepared to answer the charges found there.

The area I canvassed not only held a challenge for an Adventist, but a Bible salesman had just covered the same territory and sold thousands of dollars' worth of Bibles, then offed with the money and delivered no Bibles. So, I found out that religious book salesmen also had an image problem and I inherited their image problem.

Some have said that perceptions are realities. I guess I have to agree that it is possible to see it that way—but while that is a catchy-concept, I think it is a bit Madison

---

3. John 6:53.
4. Luke 14:26.

Avenue-ish—it is the kind of saying that a Public Relations firm would use in advertising its services—because if perceptions were actually realities then, of course, all Bible salesmen in Merced, California, are crooks—because that was the perception. All Adventists are preposterous and hold monstrous beliefs—as those books said. And Jesus is the apostate the Jews of his day, particularly the leadership, accused him of and perceived him to be.

I'd like to suggest that rather than looking at perceptions as realities and lamenting that—we ought rather to fasten our thinking on the notion that perceptions can be changed.

CHANGING PERCEPTIONS

As a child I ran with the neighborhood kids. And an old crotchety man moved in to the neighborhood behind my house. The first thing he did was fence in his yard, so we couldn't pick his peaches. Next, he walled up one of his windows. Next, he would yell at one of the black kids in the neighborhood who had scaled his fence—he ran him off and told him to stay out of his orchard. Stories literally flew around the block about him. He was prejudiced, he was mean—he walled up the window because that was where he put his torture chamber.

At night we saw things coming out of his fireplace. In the daytime we heard strange noises. We re-routed our steps so as not to be tempted by his peaches. We froze with fright when we happened to see him looking out through his window.

One day I was bored. I was hitting stones with a baseball bat. It was the bottom of the ninth inning—tie game, the White Sox were up with two outs and Minnie Minoso was coming to bat and did I let that rock fly—the White Sox hadn't won a pennant since 1919 and I would change that. And they won that game—my home run cleared the fence—and when I heard the crash I came out of my fantasy to realize I had just sent the ball—not into the center lane of the Dan Ryan Freeway but rather the kitchen window of Frankenstein.

My heart stopped beating. My brain waves were flat—I know that because no signals were getting through to my feet. When I saw his face appear in the hole I knew my major league career was over.

He called me. Because I have always been by nature very obedient and because nothing else but alterosuggestion could work to get me to move I slowly paced my way to where he was standing. On the way I saw his butcher knife gleaming in the sunlight. I heard the machines start up. That man had an image problem.

He said, "Eddie, you broke my window" (very perceptive man). "We are going to fix it. I want you to come into my house." That was it! I obeyed. Dead at 13 years of age.

I made it through the door. I watched for ghouls, black cats, trap doors—nothing. He handed me a broom—probably his wife's transportation. "Clean up the mess," he said, "I'll get the car." The car? "Yes, we're going to the hardware store."

We got the window. He talked me back to reality. He was a nice guy—part of the strategy—no, really, he was a nice guy.

He was old—but nice. From that day on I never went by his house when he was home but that he talked to me—clear through college we were friends. I'm sure he's dead now. But what a change—images can be changed. Perceptions can be changed.

The Holy Spirit is the agent who works on this world to change misconceptions about God. But for us faith is a necessary element.

Because there is a Holy Spirit who actively works to vindicate God to the world, perceptions are being changed all the time. Look at Paul and how his perceptions changed. Look at the disciples and see how their perceptions were changed. Look at Nicodemus and Joseph, both members of the Sanhedrin, had their perceptions changed.

DOING GOD'S WORK INVOLVES AN IMAGE PROBLEM

It should come as no surprise to us that any attempt to do God's work will be accompanied by an image problem. And now I speak specifically of the higher educational work of our church.

I recently talked with a young person who said this school isn't much like he expected. "Well, I had heard it was apostate and I haven't found it to be that at all." I said, "be careful, don't be too sure that there aren't some apostates around. Stay close to Jesus."

Later I talked with another young person. She remarked that "this school isn't much like I thought it would be." I wondered what she had expected. "Well, I had heard it was spiritual and I find a lot of the world here." I said, "be careful, don't be too sure that there aren't some Christians around here. Stay close to Jesus."

I was once told, before accepting the call to teach at Southern Missionary College twelve years ago—"Don't go to that place to teach—it is a terrible place." Why? "It's racist, it's anti-intellectual, it's like a big plantation with a few masters who rule it." They painted a gruesome picture of you people.

Somebody else heard about my call to come here and called me up and said "you have to go there—it is the most wonderful place in the world.

Some time back a man told me that Southern Missionary College was the only place he would send his daughter or son, if he had a daughter or son. And just to make conversation I asked him why? "Why?" He said, "That's the best school we have." "Why do you say that?" "Well," he said, "because you keep the standards high down there and the black enrollment low."

I have thought about that many times since our conversation. That answer is a double bind for a Christian. If we deliberately keep the black enrollment low that we can't be a school that has very high standards.

I share these perceptions with you for a number of reasons.

Who knows what you have heard about Southern College of Seventh-day Adventists? But whatever it was—it was just an opinion.

If you heard bad reports about Southern College of Seventh-day Adventists, you must remember that we are in good company—for Jesus also had an image problem.

If someone told you this was heaven on earth—please don't believe him—you're in for an awfully rude awakening. You will find here what you set out to find because we are little different than any other generation that has lived—very little different from the generation that ended up crucifying Christ—that is one of the messages of the Gospel: people who thought they were righteous woke up to the fact of their own deep, radical corruption.

HOW STANDARDS CHANGE

You see there is a difference between living by standards and living by principles that are personified in Jesus Christ. Standards change but we don't always change with them—we become identified with our standards and then get emotionally attached and think anyone who doesn't live by our standards is somehow an apostate or something worse. Then we become judgmental and unloving and sometimes just downright gross in our attitudes toward them.

When I joined the faculty here the big buzz was over hair length. I was appointed to a "hair committee" and we discussed for hours whether a boy's hair should touch the top of his ear. One committee member suggested that it be allowed to go to the middle of his ear lobe—which was a really liberal position—then we engaged in a long discussion about how some boys have longer ear lobes than others and that might not be fair to all.

For several years, the wearing of a beard was considered practically anti-social and the Faculty Senate and the faculty in general argued and debated the beard. Then everybody got tired of the argument and today there are even some of our ministers who wear a beard like James White, Abraham Lincoln, William Spicer, and even our Lord.

Standards and rules change. But they are surely necessary to the running of any closely associated society as he have in a boarding school.

Perhaps we would covet the title for our school, rather than the hopes that we could be known as "The School of Standards" (which by the way has struck several other North American SDA colleges as a bit pretentious—whether we recognize it or not; as though we were the only ones with any standards). Perhaps rather we would like to be known as a School of Principles—a place with a real image problem. You see, any place that holds by the personified principles of Jesus Christ will have an image problem, because there is a principle involved: "The disciple is not above his teacher." "The servant is not above his master."[5]

---

5. Matthew 10:24.

If indeed we have an image problem because we are indeed the school where love for sinners can be found—where people can come to start again; where young men and women can find patient and long-suffering teachers; where Freshmen can find understanding deans and upperclassmen; where righteousness is lived rather than just talked; where there is an inordinate collection of young people who desire an atmosphere where the Lord can work; where people will accept you even though you are different—even though you are white, or have a Spanish accent, or Scandinavian; where you cannot only get a pervasive education—religious sayings along the walks, religious statements over the teacher's doors, prayers before class, but you can also get a respectable academic training that will open options for you in practically every legitimate walk of life; if these are the things that are causing our image problem—what else is new?

Probably nobody who ever lived had a greater image problem than Jesus—simply because no one ever loved greater than Jesus.

THE MIND OF CHRIST

Have the mind in you that was in Christ Jesus. He emptied himself to become "God with us."

> Like your landlord becoming your tenant.
> Like your managing director up before you for an interview.
> Like Beethoven lining up for a ticket to his own concert.
> Like a principal having to sit in the corner.
> Like a good architect living in a slum built by a rival.
> Like Picasso painting by numbers.
> God lived among us.

He learned obedience through suffering, He learned by suffering from an image problem. Why should it be any different with us? Suffering from an image problem can be turned by the Holy Spirit into the greatest blessing if the reason for the image problem is right.

One evening my phone rang. My name is so and so. Hello, I don't know you. I know you don't. I'm calling you because you are an apostate—I read it in the papers. I'm not an apostate—those papers were not true—they exaggerate—I have an image problem. Don't tell me that—I wouldn't have called you. I called you because you were an apostate and I am on the verge of apostasy—only you would understand me. And so, the Holy Spirit brought good out of pain. We talked for an hour until neither of us were apostates.

SUMMATION

For some of you—this is your first vespers at College. You have come with your own image problem to a college with an image problem—to a faculty with an image problem, to an administration with an image problem.

We welcome you. And once we all recognize that there are no beings in all God's universe that has such an image problem as does the human race, we can work on things that matter.

Perhaps then we can minister to each other's image problem—perhaps then we can understand the deeper meanings to Jesus' response to the Pharisees who condemned him for caring about people.

"It is not the healthy who need a doctor, but the sick. Go and learn what that text means, 'I require mercy, not sacrifice.' I did not come to invite virtuous people, but sinners."[6]

At that point you know the mission of this school and why the Holy Spirit led you here.

---

6. Matthew 9:13.

Bibliography

Allen, Elizabeth Peale. "Learn to Let Go and Let God." *Guidepost.* Internet.
Andreasen, Millian Lauritz. "Introductory Speech by M. L. Andreasen." Glendale, CA: Typescript.
———. *Letters to the Churches.* Conway: Gems of Truth, n.d.
———. *The Sanctuary Service.* Washington: Review and Herald, 1937.
Appendix: Zackrison/Southern College, Legal Brief, 1984.
Auburn Adventist Academy Student Handbook. Auburn, WN: Auburn Adventist Academy, 1978–1979.
Auburn Academy Catalogue. Auburn, WN: Auburn Academy, 1957.
Barnhouse, Donald Grey. "Are Seventh-day Adventists Christian? A New Look at Seventh-day Adventism." *Eternity,* September 1956.
Bayly, Joseph. *The Gospel Blimp.* Grand Rapids: Zondervan, 1960.
Bonhoeffer, Dietrich. *Ethics.* New York: Macmillan, 1975.
———. *Life Together.* San Francisco: Harper & Row, 1954.
Bourdeau, A. C., and Dr. John Harvey Kellogg. *Interview at Dr. J. H. Kellogg's House.* Battle Creek, 1907.
Campbell, Melvin, and Edwin Zackrison. *Interactive Readings for Christian Worship.* New York: iUniverse, 2003.
———. *Readers Theatre for Christian Worship: Biblical Stories of Courage and Faith.* New York: iUniverse, 2003.
———. "Responsive Readings and Scripture Readings." *Worship Leader,* July/August 1994.
Canright, Dudley M. *Life of E. G. White.* Cincinnati: Standard, 1919.
———. *Seventh-day Adventism Renounced.* Nashville: B. C. Goodpasture, 1948.
Chaffee, John. *Thinking Critically.* 6th ed. Boston: Houghton Mifflin, 2000.
Christian, Lewis Harrison. *Sons of the North.* Mountain View: Pacific, 1943.
Clark, Jerome. *1844: Religious Movements.* 3 vols. Nashville: Southern, 1968.
Cook, Joan Marie, and Marie Jennings. "Report on Southern College." *Spectrum* 13.2 (1982).
Cottrell, Raymond F. "The 'Sanctuary Doctrine'—Asset or Liability?" San Diego: AAF, 2002.
Couperus, Molleurus, ed. "The Bible Conference of 1919." *Spectrum* 10:1 (1979).
Crow, Paul A., and James O. Duke, eds. "The Church . . . Seeking to be Truly Church Today." In *Come and See.* Denver: General Assembly, Christian Church (Disciples of Christ), 1997.
Cullmann, Oscar. *Immortality of the Soul or Resurrection of the Dead? The Witness of the New Testament.* London: Epworth, 1958.
Douglass, Herbert E. "The Unique Contribution of Adventist Eschatology." Washington: General Conference of SDA, 1974.

———. *Why Jesus Waits.* Washington: Review and Herald, 1976.
Duewel, W. Michael. *Earth: Theatre of the Universe.* Portland: Rose City, 1974.
Duvall, Evelyn Millis. *Facts of Life and Love for Teen-Agers.* New York: Popular Library, 1956.
Ellen G. White Estate. *Comprehensive Index to the Writings of Ellen G. White.* 3 vols. Mountain View: Pacific, 1962.
Ford, Desmond. *Daniel.* Nashville: Southern, 1978.
———. *Daniel 8:14; The Day of Atonement, and the Investigative Judgment.* Casselberry, FL: Euangelion, 1980.
Frazee, W. D. *Ransom and Reunion Through the Sanctuary.* Nashville: Southern, 1977.
Froom, LeRoy Edwin. *The Conditionalist Faith of Our Fathers: The Conflict of the Ages Over the Nature and Destiny of Man.* 2 vols. Washington: Review and Herald, 1971.
———. *The Prophetic Faith of Our Fathers.* 4 vols. Washington: Review and Herald, 1946, 1948.
General Conference of SDA. *Church Manual.* Washington: General Conference, 1959, 1990.
———. *Guidelines toward a Seventh-day Adventist Philosophy of Music.* Washington: General Conference, 1972.
Gentry, Patti. "Omega: A Book Review." *Southern Accent*, March 18, 1982.
Gladson, Jerry. *A Theologian's Journey from Seventh-day Adventism to Mainstream Christianity.* Glendale, AZ: Life Assurance Ministries, 2000.
———. *Out of Adventism: A Theologian's Journey.* Eugene, OR: Wipf & Stock, 2017.
"Glad Tidings from Southern College." *Adventist Currents*, February 1984.
Goodman, Ted, ed. *The Forbes Book of Business Quotations.* New York: Black Dog and Leventhal, 1997.
Habada, Patricia A., and Rebecca Frost Brillhart, eds. *The Welcome Table: Setting a Place for Ordained Women.* Langley Park: TEAM, 1995.
Halverson, Martin, and Arthur A. Cohen, eds. *A Handbook of Christian Theology.* Cleveland: World, 1958.
Harrison, Everett I., ed. *Baker's Dictionary of Theology.* Grand Rapids: Baker, 1960.
Haynes, Carlyle B. *Our Times and Their Meaning.* Nashville: Southern, 1929.
Heppenstall, Edward. "Let Us Go on To Perfection." In *Perfection: The Impossible Possibility.* Nashville: Southern, 1975.
Hordern, William E. *A Layman's Guide to Protestant Theology,* Revised and Expanded Edition. New York: Macmillan, 1968.
Jehovah's Witnesses. *From Paradise Lost to Paradise Regained.* Brooklyn: Watchtower, 1958.
Jemison, T. H. *Facing Life: Guidance for Christian Youth.* Mountain View: Pacific, 1958.
———. *A Prophet Among You.* Mountain View: Pacific, 1955.
Johnsen, Carsten. *The Mystic "Omega" of End-Time Crisis.* Sisteron, France: The Untold Story Publishers, Center of Christian Realism, 1981.
———. *Omega II.* Yucaipa: US Business Specialties, 1982.
Kellogg, John Harvey. *The Living Temple.* Internet.
Lewis, C. S. *The Chronicles of Narnia.* 7 vols. San Francisco: Harper Collins, 1950.
———. *Mere Christianity.* San Francisco: Harper Collins, 1952.
———. *Perelandra.* San Francisco: Harper Collins, 1943.
———. *Screwtape Letters.* New York: Harper Collins, 2001.
Maxwell, C. Mervyn. *God Cares, Vol. 1: The Message of Daniel for You and Your Family.* Boise: Pacific, 1981.

———. "Ready for His Appearing." In *Perfection: The Impossible Possibility*. Nashville: Southern, 1975.
Martin, Ralph. "The Church in Changing Times." *Ministry,* January 1990.
Martin, Walter R. *The Truth About Seventh-day Adventism*. Grand Rapids: Zondervan, 1960.
McLeod, Merikay. *Betrayal*. Loma Linda: Mars Hill, 1985.
———. *Now!* World Wide Bible Lectures, n.d.
Milton, John. *Paradise Lost*. 1667.
———. *Paradise Regained*. 1671.
Ministerial Association of General Conference of SDA. *Doctrinal Discussions: A Compilation of Articles Originally Appearing in* The Ministry, *June 1960–July 1961, in Answer to Walter R. Martin's Book* The Truth About Seventh-day Adventism. Washington: Review and Herald, 1961.
Newman, J. David. "How Much Diversity Can We Stand?" *Ministry*, April 1994.
Nichol, Francis D. *Ellen G. White and Her Critics*. Takoma Park: Review and Herald, 1951.
Niebuhr, H. Richard. *Christ and Culture*. New York: Harper Colophon Books, 1951.
North American Division of SDA. *Issues: The Seventh-day Adventist Church and Certain Private Ministries*. Washington: North American Division Officers, 1992.
Numbers, Ronald L. *Prophetess of Health: A Study of Ellen White*. New York: Harper and Row, 1976.
Olsen, M. Ellsworth. *A History of the Origin and Progress of Seventh-day Adventists*. 2d ed. Takoma Park: Review and Herald, 1926.
Paxton, Geoffrey. *The Shaking of Adventism*. Wilmington: Zenith, 1977.
Peck, Robert F., and Robert J. Havighurst. *The Psychology of Character Development*. New York: Wiley, 1960.
Peter, Laurence J. *Peter's Quotations: Ideas for our Time*. New York: Bantam, 1980.
Price, George McCready. "Letter to M. L. Andreasen." Typescript, 1959.
Quebedeaux, Richard. *The Young Evangelicals: Revolution in Orthodoxy*. New York: Harper & Row, 1974.
Ramm, Bernard. "Apologetics." In *Baker's Dictionary of Theology*, edited by Everett F. Harrison. Grand Rapids: Baker, 1960.
Randall, Charles. "The Burbank Case: Do Seventh-day Adventists really have a Representative Church Government?" *Adventist Perspective*, 2000.
Rea, Walter T. *Pirates of Privilege*. Turlock: M&R, 1984.
———. *The White Lie*. Turlock: M&R, 1982.
Read, W. E. "The Investigative, or Pre-Advent, Judgment: Does This Teaching Have Any Biblical Basis?" *Doctrinal Discussions*.
Rendalen, Aage. "The Jesuit Hall of Fame and the Social Cost of Conspiracy Theories." Typescript. January 2017.
Rice, Richard. *The Reign of God: An Introduction to Christian Theology from a Seventh-day Adventist Perspective*. Berrien Springs: Andrews University Press, 1985.
———. "The Relevance of the Investigative Judgment." *Spectrum* 14.1 (1983) 32–38.
Richardson, Alan. *A Dictionary of Christian Theology*. Philadelphia: Westminster, 1969.
Schwarz, Richard W. *John Harvey Kellogg, Father of the Health Food Industry*. Berrien Springs: Andrews University Press, 1970.
———. *John Harvey Kellogg, M.D.* Nashville: Southern, 1970.
———. *Light Bearers to the Remnant: Denominational History Textbook for Seventh-day Adventist College Classes*. Mountain View: Pacific, 1979.

BIBLIOGRAPHY

Schwarz, Richard W., and Floyd Greenleaf. *Light Bearers: A History of the Seventh-day Adventist Church.* Nampa: Pacific, 2000.

Seventh-day Adventists Answer Questions on Doctrine: An Explanation of Certain Major Aspects of Seventh-day Adventist Belief. Washington: Review and Herald, 1957.

Seventh-day Adventists Believe . . . A Biblical Exposition of 27 Fundamental Doctrines. Washington: Ministerial Association General Conference of SDA, 1988.

SDA Bible Commentary. 7 vols. Washington: Review and Herald, 1955.

SMC Faculty Document Committee Collection, 1984.

Spalding, Arthur Whitefield. *Origin and History of Seventh-day Adventists.* 4 vols. Washington: Review and Herald, 1961.

Springett, Ronald M. "Some Historical Observations on the Present Theology 'Crisis.'" *Perspectives,* May 1982.

Standish, Russell R., and Colin D. Standish. *Adventism Vindicated.* Paradise: Historic Truth, 1980.

Stonehouse, Ned B. *J. Gresham Machen: A Biographical Memoir.* Edinburgh: The Banner of Truth Trust, 1987.

Summers, Ray. *Essentials of New Testament Greek.* Nashville: Broadman, 1950.

Unruh, T. E. "The Seventh-day Adventist Evangelical Conferences of 1955–1956." *The Adventist Heritage* 4.3 (1977).

Vandeman, George E. *Planet in Rebellion.* Nashville: Southern, 1960.

Walton, Lewis. *Omega.* Washington: Review and Herald, 1981.

White, Ellen G. *Acts of the Apostles.* Mountain View: Pacific, 1911.

———. *The Adventist Home.* Nashville: Southern, 1952.

———. *Christian Service.* Washington: General Conference, 1947.

———. "Christ Our Hope," *Review and Herald,* December 20, 1898.

———. *Christ's Object Lessons.* Washington: Review and Herald, 1900.

———. *Colporteur Ministry.* Mountain View: Pacific, 1953.

———. *Counsels on Health.* Mountain View: Pacific, 1951.

———. *Counsels on Stewardship.* Takoma Park: Review and Herald, 1940.

———. *Counsels to Parents, Teachers, and Students.* Mountain View: Pacific, 1913.

———. *Counsels to Writers and Editors.* Nashville: Southern, 1946.

———. *The Desire of Ages.* Mountain View: Pacific, 1940.

———. *Early Writings.* Washington: Review and Herald, 1882.

———. *Education.* Mountain View: Pacific, 1903.

———. *Evangelism.* Washington: Review and Herald, 1946.

———. *Fundamentals of Christian Education.* Nashville: Southern, 1923.

———. *General Conference Bulletin,* 1893.

———. *Gospel Workers.* Washington: Review and Herald, 1915.

———. *The Great Controversy Between Christ and Satan.* Mountain View: Pacific, 1950.

———. *In Heavenly Places.* Washington: Review and Herald, 1967.

———. *Last Day Events: Facing Earth's Final Crisis. Facing Earth's Final Crisis.* Nampa: Pacific, 1992.

———. *Love Unlimited.* Mountain View: Pacific, 1958.

———. *Maranatha: The Lord is Coming.* Washington: Review and Herald, 1976.

———. *Messages to Young People.* Nashville: Southern, 1930.

———. *The Ministry of Healing.* Mountain View: Pacific, 1909.

———. *My Life Today.* Washington: Review and Herald, 1952.

———. *The Sanctified Life.* Washington: Review and Herald, 1937.

———. *Selected Messages.* 3 vols. Washington: Review and Herald, 1958.

———. *Sons and Daughters of God.* Washington: Review and Herald, 1955.

———. *The Story of Patriarchs and Prophets.* Mountain View: Pacific, 1913.

———. *Temperance.* Mountain View: Pacific, 1949.

———. *Testimonies for the Church.* 9 vols. Mountain View: Pacific, 1948.

———. *Testimonies to Ministers and Gospel Workers.* Mountain View: Pacific, 1923.

———. *Thoughts from the Mount of Blessing.* Mountain View: Pacific, 1956.

White, James, ed. *A Solemn Appeal Relative to Solitary Vice, and the Abuses and Excesses of the Marriage Relation.* Battle Creek: Steam Press of the Seventh-day Adventist, 1870.

Wieland, R. J., and D. K. Short. "1888 Reexamined." In *A Warning and Its Reception.* Baker: Hudson, 1959.

Wittschiebe, Charles E. *God Invented Sex.* Nashville: Southern, 1974.

Zackrison, Edwin. "A Preliminary Study of the Use of the Term 'Spiritualism' in the Writings of Ellen G. White as it Relates to the Destiny of Man." Typescript. Term Paper. Course: Studies in Doctrine of Man," Andrews University, July 1975.

———. "Class Pastor's Response to 'The Courage to Care.'" Typescript. June 7, 1963.

———. "Confrontation." *Colloquium: The Teacher's Presentation-Ready Experimental Quarterly.* Berrien Springs: Andrews University Department of Religious Education. July 30, 1983.

———. "Does Hell Burn Forever?" *These Times*, March 1982.

———. "Edward Heppenstall: Influence as a Teacher." Typescript. Paper read at Anaheim Convention, Andrews Society of Religious Studies, 1989.

———. "The Foundation Research." *Collegiate Quarterly*, June 1981.

———. "Fight the Good Fight of Faith." *These Times*, January 1980.

———. *The First Temptation: Seventh-day Adventists and Original Sin.* Bloomington: iUniverse, 2015.

———. "Glory for Me." *Collegiate Quarterly*, April 1982.

———. "God's Camelot." *Collegiate Quarterly*, December 1983.

———. "Grace Under Fire." *Collegiate Quarterly*, December 1983.

———. "How to Live in Anticipation of the End-Time." *These Times*, April 1980.

———. "Hiding the Word." *Collegiate Quarterly*, December 1983.

———. "Inclusive Redemption." In *The Welcome Table*, 155–78. 1995.

———. *In the Loins of Adam.* New York: iUniverse, 2004.

———. "Justification in the New Testament." *Evangelica*, April 1981.

———. "The Rapture." *These Times*, April 1980.

———. *Seventh-day Adventists and Original Sin: A Study of the Early Development of the Seventh-day Adventist Understanding of the Effect of Adam's Sin on His Posterity.* Berrien Springs: Andrews University Doctoral Dissertation, January 1984.

———. "The Shockability Factor." *College People*, July 1985.

———. "Some Wisdom for Daily Living." *Collegiate Quarterly*, December 1983.

———. "Spiritualism: A Preliminary Study of the Term as Used in the Writings of Ellen G. White as it Relates to the Destiny of Man." Typescript. 1976.

———. "Transcript of the Cumberland Heights Discussion," *Appendix: Zackrison/Southern College.* Legal Brief. July 10, 1982.

———. "What About the Secret Rapture:" *These Times*, May 1975.

———. "When Christians Differ." *Ministry*, August 1983.

———. "When Legalism Finally Drops Away." *College People*, July 1985.

———. "Why I Became a Seventh-day Adventist—An Interview with a former United Methodist Minister." *These Times*, Special Issue, 1981.

———. "Worship Renewal Among the Contemporary Churches: Adventist Churches." In *The Complete Library of Christian Worship*, edited by Robert E. Webber, vol. 3. Nashville: Star Song, 1993.

www.ingramcontent.com/pod-product-compliance
Lightning Source LLC
Chambersburg PA
CBHW080528300426
44111CB00017B/2642